Colonized Bodies, Worlds Transformed

Bioarchaeological Interpretations of the Human Past:
Local, Regional, and Global Perspectives

UNIVERSITY PRESS OF FLORIDA

Florida A&M University, Tallahassee
Florida Atlantic University, Boca Raton
Florida Gulf Coast University, Ft. Myers
Florida International University, Miami
Florida State University, Tallahassee
New College of Florida, Sarasota
University of Central Florida, Orlando
University of Florida, Gainesville
University of North Florida, Jacksonville
University of South Florida, Tampa
University of West Florida, Pensacola

Colonized Bodies, Worlds Transformed

Toward a Global Bioarchaeology of Contact and Colonialism

Edited by Melissa S. Murphy
and Haagen D. Klaus

Foreword by Clark Spencer Larsen

University Press of Florida
Gainesville · Tallahassee · Tampa · Boca Raton
Pensacola · Orlando · Miami · Jacksonville · Ft. Myers · Sarasota

First cloth printing, 2017
First paperback printing, 2021

26 25 24 23 22 21   6 5 4 3 2 1

Library of Congress Cataloging-in-Publication Data
Names: Murphy, Melissa Scott, editor. | Klaus, Haagen D., editor. | Larsen,
  Clark Spencer, author of foreword.
Title: Colonized bodies, worlds transformed : toward a global bioarchaeology
  of contact and colonialism / edited by Melissa S. Murphy and Haagen D.
  Klaus ; Foreword by Clark Spencer Larsen.
Description: Gainesville : University Press of Florida, 2017. | Includes
  bibliographical references and index.
Identifiers: LCCN 2016035937 | ISBN 9780813060750 (cloth) | ISBN 9780813068626 (pbk.)
Subjects: LCSH: Human remains (Archaeology)—United States. | Archaeology and
  history—United States. | Ethnoarchaeology—United States. | Human remains
  (Archaeology) | Archaeology and history. | Ethnoarchaeology. | Social
  archaeology.
Classification: LCC CC79.5.H85 C65 2017 | DDC 930.1—dc23
LC record available at https://lccn.loc.gov/2016035937

The University Press of Florida is the scholarly publishing agency for the State University System of Florida, comprising Florida A&M University, Florida Atlantic University, Florida Gulf Coast University, Florida International University, Florida State University, New College of Florida, University of Central Florida, University of Florida, University of North Florida, University of South Florida, and University of West Florida.

University Press of Florida
2046 NE Waldo Road
Suite 2100
Gainesville, FL 32609
http://upress.ufl.edu

Contents

Figures

Tables

Foreword

For much of the last five or so million years of our evolution, humans have migrated, colonizing territory already occupied by other humans. Not until the later Holocene do we have the depth and breadth of the archaeological and historical record, providing the essential context for documenting and interpreting the remarkable picture of outcomes of contact and colonization. Melissa S. Murphy and Haagen D. Klaus's book makes clear that an essential record for developing a broader picture of the processes, patterns, and outcomes of contact and colonization is provided by the study of human remains.

Bioarchaeology, although originating in descriptive approaches to the study of bones and teeth, views human remains as representing once-living people as if they were alive today. Specifically, it views the remains of past people in relation to lifeway reconstruction, population and demographic history, and the influence of political, economic, and social forces of the earlier societies they represent. This approach to the study of ancient remains is well illustrated in the 14 chapters presented in this book. Starting with the excellent overview of the state-of-the-art of the bioarchaeology of colonization and contact, the reader is provided with disciplinary context for the case studies to follow. Murphy and Klaus have a singular purpose in delving "deeper into the study of contact and colonialism through new and synthetic bioarchaeological research of colonial encounters, culture contact, and colonialism from diverse areas of the world." In my view, the book succeeds by addressing leading questions of interest to the growing community of scholars interested in the dynamics—cultural, social, and biological—and outcomes when one society collides with another: Why did contact and colonialism result in such different outcomes around the world? How were the colonizers affected by the encounters? How did behaviors and identities of both colonizers and colonized change?

These questions and the broad focus of the book offer new research avenues, new geographic foci, and fresh insights into contact and colonialism.

Indeed, the reader will be impressed with just how far the field has come since the early 1980s, and especially since Henry Dobyns's role in defining the field as largely demographic, focusing on European-introduced epidemic diseases, widespread death, rapid population decline, and ultimately the disappearance of native peoples. Simply put, the study of contact and colonization is no longer limited to the catastrophic "guns, germs, and steel" narrative. Rather, as Christopher Stojanowski succinctly states in his concluding chapter, the field has expanded, providing a new "database of the colonial experience" and showing the local, regional, and global footprint of contact and colonialism. The contributors to the book emphasize that although of course the field needs to continue its focus and strength on biology viewed in historical context, it must also broaden its scope by building bridges that capture the human experience involving the linkages between biology, culture, and society (e.g., processes involving social transformation and the role of structural violence).

The central 12 chapters of the book present new findings on regions and populations not previously published (e.g., the Samuel George Morton African collection; South Africa) or address new topics in regions with considerable bioarchaeological depth (e.g., Spanish Florida, Nubia, Belize). The picture of contact and colonization is one of exploiter and exploited, but the line between the two is blurred in some key respects. Earlier research emphasized complete advantage to the exploiter and complete disadvantage to the exploited. In Spanish Florida, for example, the late prehistoric Mississippian social and political hierarchies provided the built-in economic framework by which the elite channeled surplus food (especially maize) and labor to the Spanish authorities. In this arrangement, both natives and Spaniards benefited—the hereditary native elite maintained their status and access to wealth, and the Spanish presence was supported by having the regional resources in order to sustain a presence in the region (Thomas 2013). It is true, however, that while this system was economically beneficial to both native elites and Spanish authorities, the human skeletal record representing the former shows long-term health declines and labor exploitation (e.g., various essays in Larsen 2001), the development of new social relationships within communities (Stojanowski 2013), and variable outcomes from community to community (Hutchinson 2006).

The pages that follow build on what has been previously learned via past bioarchaeological research, reemphasizing the complexities of the contact and colonialism experience. Certainly, there are common features when viewed globally, but the details at the local and regional levels allow us to build the larger temporal and spatial perspective that anthropological science provides. This book joins the rich and expanding bioarchaeological literature on the study of what conditions were like in the dynamic circumstances for multiple settings and time periods around the world.

Clark Spencer Larsen
Series Editor

REFERENCES CITED

Hutchinson, D. L.
2006   *Tatham Mound and the Bioarchaeology of European Contact: Disease and De-population in Central Gulf Coast Florida*. University Press of Florida, Gainesville.
Larsen, C. S. (editor)
2001   *Bioarchaeology of Spanish Florida: The Impact of Colonialism*. University Press of Florida, Gainesville.
Stojanowski, C. M.
2013   *Mission Cemeteries, Mission Peoples: Historical and Evolutionary Dimensions of Intracemetery Bioarchaeology in Spanish Florida*. University Press of Florida, Gainesville.
Thomas, D. H.
2013   War and Peace on the Franciscan Frontier. In *From La Florida to La California: The Genesis and Realization of Franciscan Evangelization in the Spanish Borderlands*, edited by T. J. Johnson and G. Melville, pp. 105–130. Academy of American Franciscan History, Berkeley.

1

Transcending Conquest

Bioarchaeological Perspectives on Conquest and Culture Contact for the Twenty-First Century

MELISSA S. MURPHY AND HAAGEN D. KLAUS

Contact, as once defined by Dobyns (1983), was seen only as the straightforward process of Native American acquisition of European pathogens. We now understand culture contact to be a much more complex and nuanced phenomenon, and one not just restricted to the Columbian exchange. For millennia, human societies have been colonizing new territories, encountering peoples different from themselves, and becoming entangled in long-term biological and cultural transformations as a consequence. These phenomena represent some of the key local, regional, and global adaptive transitions of humankind in a process of both biological and cultural transformation. Contact between the Eastern and Western Hemispheres beginning in A.D. 1492 was perhaps the largest and most transformative of its kind, as it brought together human populations that had previously been unconnected; our species would never be the same (Crosby 1972; Wolf 1982). Perhaps only the transition from foraging to farming had greater impact on overall configurations of culture, relationships with the environment, and economy. European contact and its aftermath was, after all, unsurpassed in its global scale, degree of violence, and speed. In less than four hundred years, the biological structure of virtually every human population was transformed in myriad and intricate ways.

Still, conquest and colonialism in the recent human past are not well understood scientifically. They have long been shrouded by incomplete histories written mostly by the victors and filled with deterministic suppositions and simplistic stereotypes regarding Native American biocultural inferiority and passive demographic collapse. Since the 1990s, bioarchaeological studies have progressively revealed that conquest and its aftermath embodied some of the most complex biocultural morasses of known history. Yet past work has only begun to scratch the surface of contact, conquest, and colonialism, which are all processes that bioarchaeology is uniquely suited to explore.

The purpose of this volume is to delve deeper into the study of contact and colonialism through new and synthetic bioarchaeological research of colonial encounters, culture contact, and colonialism from diverse areas of the world while also integrating new theoretical perspectives from historical archaeology. We seek to promote a next generation of contact and colonialism studies in bioarchaeology, attending to new questions that have emerged from previous pioneering research (e.g., Baker and Kealhofer, eds. 1996; Larsen and Milner 1994; Verano and Ubelaker 1992): How did colonialism unfold among regions and peoples not yet well studied (i.e., populations from Argentina, Peru, Africa)? Why did contact and colonialism produce such varied biocultural outcomes? How were the colonizers—so often assumed to be the monolithic drivers of colonial outcomes and impervious to the process they initiated—also affected and transformed by these events? How did native peoples adjust and adapt to the myriad challenges of their colonial worlds? What were the biocultural effects of conquest and colonialism on people long understudied by bioarchaeologists, such as Africans or mestizos? Beyond the effects of demographic decline, how did new behaviors, identities, and power structures transform population genetic structures or human phenotypes? How can mortuary archaeology contribute to the bioarchaeological study of conquest and contact? What can elements of social and archaeological theory—such as the concepts of "third spaces," dialectical negotiations, and archaeologies of transitions, embodiment, materiality, agency, and structural violence—contribute to the understanding of contact and colonialism?

Many scholars and the lay public understand that European conquest and colonization of indigenous populations were some of the key "establishing events of the modern world" (Mann 2011:6–7), but colonialism was practiced in various forms for nearly five thousand years before the European "Age of Discovery" and was considerably variegated from the colonial product with which most are familiar. For example, McIlvaine et al.'s (2014) study of biological distance in the first millennium B.C. Greek world suggested that the colonizers, their founding populations, and the local populations with which they interacted were relatively phenotypically indistinguishable. Extensive gene flow, trade, geography, and shared regional

ancestry led to outcomes in which the common assumption of a dichoto-
mous relationship between the colonizer and the colonized is shown to
be untenably simplistic. Additionally, a growing number of studies have
shown that native experiences were remarkably varied and that indigenous
groups endured the effects of colonialism that shaped the consequences of
colonial encounters, native-native encounters, and modern human biology.
Another perspective on colonialism far removed from the Western tradition involves the remarkable human odyssey of the expansion into Oceania. There, the colonizers encountered no previous human inhabitants but
often faced resource-poor and hostile island environments that generated a
great deal of biological stress (e.g., Buckley et al. 2014), particularly among
the first generations of colonists as they established a foothold in the vast
Pacific Ocean.

This volume begins a wider exploration regarding the experiences of the
colonized and colonizers, as well the interregional and intraregional experiences of colonial encounters and entanglements (Cusick 1998; Gosden
2004; Lightfoot 1995; Lyons and Papadopoulos 2002). Rather than focusing
on one hemisphere or one region, we invited participants from a few different areas of the Old and New Worlds—such that the volume makes the
first steps toward a global representation in its vision and comparison of
colonial encounters, contact, and colonialism.

Biological Dimensions of Contact and Colonialism

Traditionally, historians, demographers, and epidemiologists envisioned
that contact and colonialism chiefly involved a biological phenomenon
involving inevitable indigenous acquisition of European diseases and
cataclysmic depopulation (Crosby 1972; Dobyns 1966, 1983; Ramenofsky
1987; Zubrow 1990). In essence, the New World was cast as a disease-free
paradise wrecked by foreign pathogens (Sale 1990; and see Merbs 1992).
However, a trio of pioneering edited volumes, partially inspired by the Columbian Quincentennial (Baker and Kealhofer 1996; Larsen and Milner
1994; Verano and Ubelaker 1992), led the field in new investigations of European conquest in the Americas. While again heavily focused on issues
involving biology and health, these volumes blazed fresh empirical trails
that provided novel and provocative perspectives. They continue to serve as
exemplars for any researcher interested in the bioarchaeology of colonialism or culture contact in general, but they still represent only a fraction of
the work conducted on the subjects. Furthermore, despite progress in other

geographic regions, much of the current picture of postcontact population biology remains skewed toward North America when there is literally an entire world filled with colonial experiences.

The biological impact of European contact on indigenous peoples in the Americas has embodied several interrelated debates (Ubelaker 1992; Verano 1992). While all researchers share in the consensus that demographic decline was precipitous, numerical estimates can differ by an order of magnitude (e.g., 1.8 million people versus 18 million people for North America) (Cook 1998; Crosby 1992; Dobyns 1983; Henige 1998; Mann 2002). In addition, scholars debate the varied timing, geographical extent, and type(s) of epidemics or pandemics that were endured by native peoples (Cook 1998; Dobyns 1983; Henige 1998; Ramenofsky et al. 2003; Ubelaker 1992, 2000).

Syntheses of ethnohistorical documents, archaeological evidence, and osteological analyses are capable of scientifically testing the current understanding of the legacies of the biocultural impacts of Europeans in the Americas. Archaeological study of the consequences of European contact has advanced to include the reconstruction of settlement data for paleodemographic reconstructions (Freter 1997; Paine 1997; Ubelaker 1992; Vradenburg et al. 1997) and the evidence of atypical mortuary patterns such as mass burials, high proportions of cremations, unique spatial treatment, and native participation in European religious rituals that seem to replace of indigenous customs such as with funerary rites (Cohen et al. 1997; Hutchinson and Mitchem 2001; Kealhofer 1996; Larsen 1990; Tiesler and Zabala 2010).

One of the most important findings from the first generation of bioarchaeological contact studies was that even the broadest consequences of contact and colonization could no longer be assumed as uniform or monolithic. In fact, what has emerged from these studies (e.g., Larsen 1994) is a vision of the inherent variability of contact consequences in the Western Hemisphere. The timing, mode, and tempo of postcontact changes varied immensely due to complex interrelationships between precontact patterns of health and disease, ecology, population density, sociopolitical complexity, and the relationships between the colonizers and the colonized. That is, while certain trends are clear, these biocultural phenomena were so complex that any attempt to consider a single predictive theory seems a misguided effort.

Methodologically, multidimensional or holistic inquiries that synthesize multiple lines of biological, archaeological, and historic evidence are necessary in order to begin to appreciate the underlying variables that affected the biological responses of indigenous communities to contact (Baker and Kealhofer, eds. 1996; Milner 1996). Also, the nature and intensity of early European contact in these communities varied over time and included trade, conflict, missionization, colonization, and enslavement (Baker and Kealhofer 1996; Dobyns 1992; Preston 2002; Radding 2000; Ramenofsky et al. 2003) or a combination thereof—all factors that must be considered in bioarchaeological investigations of health, disease, and demography. The majority of acute infectious diseases do not affect the skeleton, thereby confounding most attempts to understand the nature, timing, and type of high-mortality epidemics believed to be responsible for much (but not all) of documented native depopulation and declining health (Aufderheide 1992; Larsen and Milner 1994).

POSTCONTACT (MOSTLY WESTERN HEMISPHERE) SOCIETIES: PORTRAITS OF COLONIAL DIVERSITY

Studies of human remains from the postcontact Americas offer a microcosm of the diversity and dynamism of contact and colonialism. The northeastern region of North America was a nexus of French, Dutch, and British entrepreneurial-minded colonialism. Baker's (1994) examination of human remains opened some of the first windows on native life in what would become Massachusetts. She describes a late impact of epidemic disease in the seventeenth century, setting the stage for the survivors undergoing forced political transformations and aggregation in villages. In the wake of these events, demographic structures appear to have become imbalanced. To the northwest, Pfeiffer and Fairgrieve (1994) indicate that Old World diseases, when introduced in 1634, decimated Iroquoian peoples. Their comparative studies of pre- and postcontact Iroquoian remains derived from ossuaries unite multiple lines of skeletal evidence spanning infection, anemia, and oral health data to suggest that Iroquois health was already on the decline and that when contact was initiated, the trend for increasing biological stress was only amplified.

Much of the southeastern and southwestern regions of the future United States fell under the domain of the Spanish. The Spanish followed a highly structured approach to colonization involving three related aims: first, to extract wealth from the natural and human resources of an occupied area; second, to establish a military presence to block territorial access to other competing colonial powers; and third, to convert the indigenous people into taxable Catholics (Walker 2001). Skeletal evidence indicates that initial encounters such as the De Soto *entrada* resulted in violent confrontation

(Hutchinson and Norr 1994) as well as far more complicated, dynamic, and often negative outcomes for native populations under Spanish rule. One early and short-lived setting was Tatham Mound on the central Gulf Coast of Florida (Hutchinson 2006). There, negative health changes arose quickly during the Early Contact period, marked by a rise in dental caries frequency and alveolar infection, a doubling of enamel hypoplasia frequency, and hematogenous osteomyelitis and treponemal infection. Traumatic injuries included those from metal weapons, demonstrating possible violent interactions with the Spanish.

The most comprehensive and multidisciplinary collection of studies regarding the bioarchaeology of contact and colonialism emerges from the mission period of the southeast coast of the United States in the Georgia Bight (Larsen 2001; Larsen et al. 2001, 2002). Among other key findings, Larsen and his colleagues uncovered postcontact upsurges of morbidity among the Guale Indian population that included declining female fertility likely tied to increased biological stress, reductions in childhood growth velocity, poor-quality diets, reduction in enamel defect prevalence especially in the Late Contact period (perhaps owing to increased acute forms of stress), and a dramatic postcontact increase in osteoarthritis prevalence likely related to labor extraction. Changes in inherited tooth size reflected major changes in social organization, social identity, and radically altered systems of mate exchange among the Guale (Stojanowski 2005a, 2010, 2013), in contrast to the Apalachee of northern and central Florida, who maintained larger populations and avoided aggregation, resettlement, and extinction (Stojanowski 2005b). Ultimately, the Spanish mission system was destroyed by war with the British in the early eighteenth century that led to dispersal and disintegration of the Guale peoples.

In the Central Plains, Reinhard et al. (1994) found a markedly different experience and history among the Ponca and Omaha Native Americans from 1780 to 1820. There, the survivors of epidemics and their descendants capitalized on the fur trade to emerge as a political and economic force. On the one hand, diet may have actually improved during the postcontact period; the introduction of firearms and horses increased hunting efficiency and access to protein, and iron implements contributed to more effective foraging and cultivation. On the other hand, osteoarthritis was more pronounced among Omaha and Ponca women, suggesting more intense levels of habitual labor. Patterns of lead isotopes in their bones indicated trade in lead objects, and use of lead-based cosmetic pigments led to bioabsorbtion; despite whatever gains were made, female health suffered particularly.

Spanish incursions into the Pueblo southwest borderlands were not as successful as in other areas, and the region's economic potential disappointed the Spanish (Stodder 1994, 1996). Postcontact demographic declines spread northward along trade networks from Mexico, worsened by epidemics, warfare, migration, population aggregation in missions, and famine. Skeletal data from postcontact Hawikku, San Cristobal, and Pecos indicate the prevalence of infectious disease, porotic hyperostosis, enamel defects, and traumatic injury (particularly cranial fractures resulting from violence between Puebloan, non-Puebloan, and Spaniard peoples).

California was a latecomer to the contact phenomenon, becoming a node of European colonialism beginning in 1782. Analysis of Chumash Indian remains of the mission period by Walker and Johnson (1994) indicates that major dietary changes unfolded for mission inhabitants, who consumed primarily terrestrial (C_3 pathway) foods that contrasted with their marine-centric late-precontact diet. Femoral midshaft dimensions are smaller postcontact, possibly reflecting a decrease in mechanical loading consistent with increased sedentism. Mission records also hold a key point: while smallpox had multiple opportunities to be introduced into the Chumash population (with the first case reported in 1844), there was no single, massive wave of epidemic disease, *contra* earlier hypotheses of uniform epidemic waves (i.e., Dobyns 1983) sweeping through the Americas in the 1600s (see Walker and Johnson 1994:118).

The Pacific Northwest also experienced relatively late and even more distinct outcomes; these were the last native North Americans to experience contact during the mid- to late nineteenth century. Cybulski's (1994) examination of nearly six hundred historic skeletons, written records, and modern health data reveals depopulation and increased postcontact mortality and the presence of tuberculosis. Carious lesion prevalence is remarkably low (between 0.3 and 0.8 percent) compared to other postcontact groups, but by the twentieth century, dental caries frequencies skyrocketed as high as 49 percent as non-native foods rich in carbohydrates and refined sugars were adopted.

While the postcontact health of the subordinated native peoples has been a primary focus of bioarchaeological investigation in North America, a smaller, parallel body of scholarship has been also developing regarding the health of the colonizers and their descendants. They, too, appear to have suffered from unique forms of morbidity; clearly, the postcontact world was a challenging place for nearly anyone to live in. Among the early-seventeenth-century voyages of so-called exploration, Samuel de Champlain describes members of his crew anguishing from *mal de tere*, which is consistent with severe scurvy; analysis of 35 skeletons from Champlain's crew buried on St. Croix Island appear to have been affected by long-term vitamin C deficiency, with their suffering compounded by futile surgical interventions aimed at curing the disease (Crist and Sorg 2014).

King and Ubelaker's (1996) study of an early Colonial farmstead cemetery at Patuxent Point, Maryland, along with Craig and Larsen (1993) and Larsen, Craig, et al.'s (1995) study of homesteaders in Illinois, offer examples of European health on the frontier. The patterning of metabolic stress and activity pattern markers, as well as poor oral health, suggest extremely difficult lives (Larsen 2002:222). From the skeletons of historic American soldiers can be inferred similar high-morbidity experiences that "turned relatively healthy young men into physical wrecks, unless they perished in combat first" (Sledzik and Sandberg 2002:185). As continuous westward expansion increased, so did opportunities for admixture. European cranial morphologies in historic Native American cemeteries (Gill and Gilbert 1990) are thought to be signs of limited Euro-American gene flow with Native Americans on the Great Plains.

Several bioarchaeological studies of Africans in the Americas also provide a tentative glimpse of the well-being of enslaved Africans and their descendants. These peoples occupy a unique position in regards to the other groups that have been discussed up to this point (i.e., colonizers and the colonized), failing to fit neatly into either category. Forcibly removed, transported, and marginalized, Africans shared some similarities with indigenous groups (high mortality, elevated disease burdens and workloads), but they were neither colonizers nor indigenous. Skeletal remains of enslaved Africans in Barbados (Corruccini et al. 1982, 1985; Corruccini, Handler, et al. 1987; Handler et al. 1986; Handler and Lange 1978; Jacobi et al. 1992), Colonial Campeche (Tiesler et al. 2010), South Carolina (Rathbun and Steckel 2002), and the south-central United States (Davidson et al. 2002) reveal correlates of a consistent high-morbidity lifestyle, including high mortality, low life expectancy, high prevalence of enamel defects, poor oral health, strenuous physical labor, elevated infection, inadequate nutrition, lead poisoning, and congenital syphilis.

Less overall research has been conducted in Central America, and most of these studies have focused on the Maya. Skeletal data suggest that Maya population health had been deteriorating since the early history of their civilization (Storey et al. 2002), and contact helped set the stage for further biological instability in the postcontact era. One early center to become established in New Spain was Campeche, Mexico, and this urban setting served as a complex and negotiated multiethnic interface between the Maya, Europeans, and Africans (Tiesler et al. 2010). The skeletons of those buried in the Campeche churchyard brought to light a mosaic of biocultural complexity, including very high prevalence of porotic hyperostosis and lesions produced by chronic infections (Rodríguez 2010), with the oral health of mestizos and natives suffering particularly (Cucina 2010).

A synthesis of stable isotope, oral health, porotic hyperostosis, and enamel defect data at Lamanai, Belize, indicated that the postcontact transition did not relate to a significant dietary shift for the Maya there, perhaps due to environmental constraints; the traditional maize diet at Lamanai, which was complemented by some terrestrial and marine food sources, could not change, as there simply were few alternatives in terms of dietary resources. An increase in other skeletal stress markers at Lamanai likely emerged from other causes, such as intensifying trade and interaction with the colonizers in northern Yucatán.

Cohen et al. (1994, 1997) describe life and death at the Tipu *visita* mission in west-central Belize. Episodic childhood metabolic stress was apparently endemic, with up to 90 percent of canines exhibiting hypoplastic defects at Tipu, yet other forms of disease and stress markers were far more rare, suggesting a healthier postcontact community that was able to buffer against the strains of the postcontact world (also Harvey et al., this volume; Jacobi 1997, 2000). Extensive study of the Tipu Maya metric and nonmetric dental traits indicates that the people buried there were exclusively Maya and that they seemed to demonstrate a greater degree of reproductive isolation in this relatively remote location.

In the South American Andes, scholars have long relied on incomplete and biased ethnohistoric sources to characterize contact and its enduring aftermath (Pillsbury 2008) while bioarchaeological studies are few in number. Ubelaker (1994; also Ubelaker and Newson 2002) has assembled a biohistory of the northern Andes of Ecuador, which, like other areas of the Andes, shows a general trend of decreasing health during the pre-Hispanic era. Ubelaker and Newson (2002) find that frequencies of periostitis, traumatic injury, and various oral pathological conditions increased in prevalence by the Late Historic period in their investigation of human remains from two churches in Ecuador and these results fit the broader hemispheric pattern.

At the site of Puruchuco-Huaquerones on the outskirts of modern Lima, Murphy et al. (2010, 2011) describe remarkable violence directed toward a number of native peoples including low velocity gunshot wounds (and the earliest evidence of such projectile injuries in the Americas) possibly associated with the Siege of Lima in 1536. Other evidence from this site may indicate the young were drawn into violent conflict during the early Colonial conjuncture (Gaither 2012; Gaither and Murphy 2012) and the upheavals that accompanied it.

On the north coast of Peru, Klaus and coworkers identified major increases of morbidity and new forms of disease when compared to late pre-Hispanic health patterns in the town of Mórrope (Klaus et al. 2009; Klaus and Ortner 2014; Klaus and Tam 2009a, 2009b, 2010). There, skeletal evidence indicates declines in female fertility, increased prevalence of nonspecific infection, anemia, growth faltering, surging osteoarthritis prevalence, and worsening oral health. Biological transformation did not stop there, and the people of Mórrope also appear to have experienced sociopolitically driven changes to their gene pool involving increased gene flow mostly with other local native communities (Klaus 2013). However, Mórrope was just one community, and an initial regional perspective has begun to demonstrate that these health outcomes were far from universal, even within the same valley (see Klaus and Alvarez-Calderón, this volume).

Some of the last regions of the world to be affected by European contact were the Pacific islands of Polynesia. Pietrusewsky and Douglas (1994) assessed postcontact changes among native Hawaiians. Some biological patterns, such as oral health, appeared to have changed little. Postcontact declines in dental wear correspond to a softer diet or lessened reliance of the dentition as tools. Yet, distinct increases in childhood stress are inferred from the patterning of enamel hypoplasias. Postcontact prevalence of degenerative joint disease is also elevated to indicate a greater intensity of habitual labor.

Prior to contact, indigenous peoples of Easter Island (Rapa Nui) numbered some nine thousand inhabitants and were engaged in endemic warfare related to conditions of environmental degradation and sparse resources. Approximately fifty years after first contact, Spanish, English, and French ships began to stop more frequently on the island. Historic accounts describe violent conflict, trafficking of indigenous women in exchange for European goods, the introduction and spread of sexually transmitted diseases, and the kidnapping of fourteen hundred islanders during 1862 and 1863 by Peruvian and Spanish slavers. Osteological analysis of human remains from Easter Island by Owsley et al. (1994) correlates with historically documented population stress, and includes cranial fractures, shotgun wounds, and treponemal disease. In the end, European contact resulted in the near complete extermination of the population and effective destruction of indigenous culture (Owsley et al. 1994:175).

UNRESOLVED ISSUES, NEW QUESTIONS, AND NEW INTERPRETATIONS

The preceding overview outlines a wide range of biological transformations resulting from the collision between the Old and the New World. Many of these often involved particularistic and unique patterns of declines in health and offer multiple examples that independently refute unitarian hypotheses of contact. However, these studies, which represent the first generation of the bioarchaeology of contact, are just the beginning of a broader and timely bioarchaeological focus on the interactions between and the fates of cultures in contact.

Issues raised by Baker and Kealhofer (1996:4–6) still resonate: What other biological factors, besides epidemic diseases, promoted population declines, and to what degree might disease and depopulation actually have been decoupled phenomena? To what extent were pathogens interchanged and modified between colonizers and the colonized? Under what conditions did native populations demographically rebound? Given that many, if not most, colonized populations were not pushed into immediate extinction, how did people compensate, adapt, and transform under disjunctive and often very stressful conditions? How can emergent and newly developed methods, such as biogeochemistry, ancient DNA analysis (including NextGen sequencing techniques), and proteomics deepen current understandings, especially in light of the fact that evolutionary biology unites all of bioarchaeology and paleopathology (Zuckerman et al. 2012)?

Another issue that comes to light is that many past bioarchaeological studies of postcontact peoples is that they were perhaps overly focused on the concept of measuring "health." In other words, a good deal of earlier work hinged upon comparing the frequencies of pathological lesions in one sample of skeletons versus another (such as with the kinds of comparisons that can be drawn between precontact versus postcontact assemblages), and one group is deemed "less healthy" or "more stressed" than the other. As part of our field's earlier descriptive origins, such comparison is certainly a starting point, if not still one of the most fundamental ways to assess the biological effects of contact and colonialism. However, it should not be the exclusive raison d'être for this kind of work. If the focus of a particular research agenda involves changes in biological stress, we can and should strive to employ more sophisticated tools from paleoepidemiology to transcend the potentially problematic use of crude prevalence (or frequency data) (Klaus 2014). Even the concept of "health" in bioarchaeology appears to require some productive rethinking (Temple and Goodman 2014).

Further, as we understand that the biological changes stemming from contact went well beyond changes in diet or the prevalence of skeletal lesions (e.g., Stojanowski 2010, 2013), it seems necessary to begin broadening the scope of the bioarchaeology of colonialism. Further expansion of phenotypic approaches to biological interaction patterns and microevolution (e.g., Stojanowski 2005a, 2005b; McIlvaine et al. 2014) will no doubt be productive. Such foci allow for bridges to be built between human biology and culture involving the integration of empirical data with social theory (i.e., ethnogenesis, social perception, and even possibly behavioral reflections of certain levels of group consciousness [Stojanowski 2005b]). Additional topics are as of yet virtually unstudied, such as potential postcontact microevolutionary changes in ontogeny and growth (beyond stature), the effects of early life stress on later mortality, and even more cutting-edge work in epigenetics (such as the possibility of sequencing ancient methylation patterns associated with stress response genes [Kinnally 2014]).

The opening of this chapter acknowledges that contact, conquest, and colonialism were a global phenomenon; it is clear that past work has involved a strong geographical focus (if not an unintended bias) toward North America, and this is another starting point. How can expanded focus on Central and South America enrich the broader reconstruction of postcontact biological diversity and variation? Further, conquest and colonialism did not play out only in the Western Hemisphere, and the superordinate powers were not exclusively European. Thus, the bioarchaeology of contact must expand its vision toward settings further afield in Africa, Asia, Australia, and beyond. Native Americans were but one group of stakeholders interacting with many other peoples and forces in the postcontact world. What about consequences and costs for the colonizers? What about the experiences of the peoples forced into slavery and pulled into the postcontact world against their will? What about the middlemen and groups at the periphery of contact zones affected by the distant ripples of change and transformation?

One field of study that has been left out of the discussion of the bioarchaeology of colonialism is the African diaspora. Although this is starting to change, much of the scholarship on the clash of the Old and New Worlds in the sixteenth century is positioned around encounters between

Europeans and Indians, to the exclusion and erasure of free and enslaved Africans and their descendants in the construction of the colonial past (Bennett 2009; Bryant et al. 2012; Weik 2004). American historical archaeologists have long noticed that "you cannot fully understand the European colonial experience in the Americas without understanding that of the African" (Singleton 1999:1). This elision reverberates with social and political implications over how and for whom the past is studied and written and over issues of representation, power, and inequality in the present day (Wilkie 2004). African diasporic bioarchaeology in North America has experienced explosive growth in the past twenty-five years (Angel et al. 1987; Blakey 2001; Blakey and Rankin-Hill 2009; Corruccini, Jacobi, et al. 1987; de la Cova 2011; Hutchinson 1987; Mackey and Blakey 2004; Martin et al. 1987; Owsley et al. 1987; Rankin-Hill 1997; Rathbun 1987; Rose and Rathbun 1987), but other regions of the Americas or Africa have not seen the same growth and consequent incorporation of research from African diasporic bioarchaeology (but see Price et al. 2012; Renschler 2007; Schroeder et al. 2009, 2013; Shuler 2011; Shuler and Schroeder 2013; Tiesler et al. 2010). However, the broader issues are not limited to locating free and enslaved Africans and their descendants via the bioarchaeology of colonialism, but also about developing both scientific and humanized ways of understanding how this key group of people were transformed by the colonial experience and its aftermath.

While a focus on the biological aspects of postcontact societies is critical, by itself, such efforts are anthropologically insufficient. Contact led equally to a culturally transformative phenomenon and is an exemplar of a biocultural phenomenon. As noted by Stojanowski (2010, 2013), Klaus (2013), and others, alterations in the social fabric can and do lead to measureable behavioral transformations of human beings that translate into biological realms. Along these lines, the bioarchaeology of contact stands to gain much interpretive depth from parallel developments in social bioarchaeology, funerary archaeology, and historical archaeology—and from these perspectives more questions arise.

The archaeology of colonialism and colonial encounters has flourished recently with attendant work in a variety of contexts and subject areas. Specifically, a recent surge of archaeological work has extended the definition and study of colonial encounters to include prehistoric cases of colonialism on a global scale (Alcock et al. 2001; Cusick 1998; Gosden 2004; Lyons and Papadopoulos 2002; Schreiber 1987, 1992, 2005; Stein 2005). This work highlights the arbitrary nature of the history-prehistory divide and brings into high relief the *processes* of indigenous transitions, continuities, and changes under colonialism (Oland et al. 2012 and references therein; Lightfoot and Martinez 1995; Lightfoot et al. 1998; Naum 2010; Silliman 2005, 2009; Vitelli 2011). Perhaps since the history-prehistory divide is perceived as vast, bioarchaeologists have been slow to incorporate these insights and challenges into the bioarchaeological investigation of contact, colonialism, and culture contact (for an exception see Tung 2012).

The Body in Life: Colonized Bodies, Transformed Peoples

By the nature of their subject matter, bioarchaeologists are uniquely situated to study the effects of colonialism on those individuals—and the bodies—who experienced colonial rule. "Colonialism is inherently a corporeal enterprise" (Boddy 2011: 119), and in this volume the contributors highlight how bodies were affected by the "heroic, event-oriented" colonial encounters, such as violence, disease, forced migration, and settlement, as well as day-to-day activities and tacit "bodiliness" of the colonial experience: those activities that sought to "normalize" and "civilize" the daily lives of the colonial subjects (Boddy 2011:119; Murphy 2012). We emphasize that although we describe with the broadest of brush strokes some of the possible experiences, we also recognize and hope to emphasize again that there was considerable variability in how the colonial enterprise was enacted, enforced, and experienced and that the body itself can hold a compelling record of these facts.

Violence under the mantle of colonialism took many forms, from tangible reminders of power and domination such as scars, whip marks, and the removal of body parts to material reminders of lethality involving the corpses of those who were dispatched during violent encounters. The arrival and invasion of the Europeans brought increasing levels of violence, including outright battles between native peoples and the Spanish, but also raids and increasing levels of internecine conflict between indigenous peoples. Interpersonal violence such as lashings and beatings by colonial authorities were also common. Structural violence is often overlooked in bioarchaeological investigations of European conquest and colonialism (for an exception see Klaus 2012), but its effects and legacy should not be underestimated (Farmer et al. 2006; Galtung 1969). Deeply embedded in the colonial and postcolonial world, some indigenous and enslaved communities may have experienced and endured reduced mortality, increased morbidity, and lifelong suffering as consequences of hierarchical social structures. Similarly, the Mongols used warfare and violence to terrorize, plunder, and sometimes conquer peoples in China, Central Asia, Iran, and Eastern Europe (Barfield 2001).

Native peoples were frequently forced into planned towns or missions that followed European ideals, with a central plaza, a church, and a cemetery arranged on a grid. For example, in colonial Peru these *reducciones* were meant not only to keep track of people for census and tax purposes but also to Christianize and "civilize" them, affecting all aspects of daily life. These resettlements also likely altered familial residence patterns and domestic spaces, allowing only nuclear families to live in the same dwelling, rather than the entire extended family (Cummins 2002). Dependent upon the colonial power in question (Dutch, French, English, or Spanish), efforts to convert indigenous peoples to Christianity and to situate the church as the ritual center of the community may have been central to these forced settlements. We wonder how colonial entanglements between members of similar cultural milieus or between different European groups altered residential patterns or familial patterns or enforced means of civilizing the colonized subjects.

Slavery, forced labor, and economic intensification separately and in conjunction with each other profoundly altered the lives and bodies of native peoples. Patterns of osteoarthritis or cross-sectional geometry in various postcontact groups, such as the Guale of Spanish Florida, Omaha and Ponca peoples of the Plains, and Muchik Indians of Peru's north coast serve as good examples of how bodies were employed as productive agents in the postcontact settings. In particular, the Guale and Muchik were used as laborers in an ever-intensifying economic system in part expressly designed to extract their labor—to the point that various joint systems were often pathologically altered or destroyed (Klaus et al. 2009; Larsen, Ruff, et al. 1995). On the Plains, habitual horseback riding for men promoted unique articular modifications to the hips and lower limbs (Reinhard et al. 1994).

In some colonial contexts, traditional systems remained in place (e.g., *mit'a* in Andean South America) and were then supplemented by the right to use labor of indigenous peoples within a specific geographic region (e.g., *encomienda*), as well as workshops organized to produce European goods and other commodities. Although many indigenous peoples likely suffered under these conditions (Klaus et al. 2009), some indigenous elites may have colluded with the colonizers to advance their own interests (Ramírez 1996).

Labor was often profoundly linked to the production of new and exotic food items and the intensification of the production of traditional foods

(Crosby 1972; Dietler 2007; Earle 2012; Mintz 1985; Pilcher 2006; Sharma 2012). In the Americas, this Columbian exchange irretrievably altered global food systems at the production, distribution, and consumption levels (Crosby 1972; Dietler 2007; Earle 2012; Mintz 1985). Despite food's intimate connection with the formation and expression of identity, many colonized peoples consumed new and exotic foods introduced during colonialism, and other colonized peoples rejected the foods and attempted to consume their traditional diets (Dietler 2007). Whether or not colonial subjects embraced these new foods likely varied by gender, race, ethnicity, and class (among other variables), but the consumption patterns may reveal important information about the nature of contact and colonialism (Dietler 2007:222; Sharma 2012). Foods formerly considered exotic and perhaps identified as a marker of status later transitioned to commonly consumed items present in the diets of most colonial subjects (Earle 2012; Mintz 1985; Sharma 2012). Consumption of European foods in the Americas, especially wheat and wine, were important means of civilizing and indoctrinating native peoples and reducing their "indigenousness" (Earle 2012:343, 348). Dietary transitions from traditional foods to newly introduced foods left profound legacies on health and destroyed or dramatically altered subsistence with results observable by bioarchaeologists.

In the colonial context, dress, body, and self are seen as one—with dress communicating the self and social identities (Loren 2003). Dress and the body were key aspects in the colonial discourse—inappropriate dress was politically and sexually charged (Loren 2003). Colonial authorities attempted to regulate and control what types of clothing, dress, and adornment were appropriate. Under Inca colonial rule, it is estimated that nearly a third of all subject communities were completely moved and resettled in places far from their homelands and were required to wear their traditional dress and speak their native tongue (D'Altroy 2015:374).

In its extreme form, the colonial enterprise completely changed all aspects of life. European authorities attempted to impose their customs on their indigenous subjects, forcing them to modify or abandon their own traditional practices, including such practices as habits of dress, work, bodily comportment, speech, adornment, cleanliness and domestic order, foods they deemed edible and how they were consumed, how they expressed their sexuality, how they gave birth, fell sick, were healed, or how they died (Boddy 2011:119). We offer that other guises of colonialism, such as the entanglements between Iron Age Britons and the Roman Empire or between Nubia and New Kingdom Egypt, did not produce such stark changes. This leads to questions regarding how all of these different case studies compare and contrast with one another. Although we will emphasize the experience of those colonized, the colonizers themselves also felt the impact of these encounters, but in vastly different ways (Gosden 2004; Rothschild 2008).

BODIES IN DEATH: POSTCONTACT MORTUARY ARCHAEOLOGY

The way people construct and practice corporality in life extends to their experiences and rituals of death. Some of the most direct avenues in this direction can be understood through the study of dead bodies themselves in the postcontact world. How did the living interact with their dead? Was their interaction with the corpse short-lived or protracted? How did the living position the dead, arrange their arms and hands, and dress them? What kinds of social messages did they intentionally or unintentionally embed in these acts? Indeed, archaeothanatological approaches as advocated by Duday (2006, 2009) and employed in postcontact settings by Tiesler and Zabala (2010) and Klaus and Tam (2015) have significant potential in answering these questions.

Integration of mortuary archaeology with bioarchaeology can broaden our vision of cultural constructions of the body in contact situations. The mortuary archaeology of the postcontact Americas is less developed than studies of skeletal biology. Much of what has emerged is relatively descriptive (Cohen et al. 1997; Hill 1996; Jacobi 2000; Kealhoffer 1996; Larsen 2001), usually emphasizing variations in burial pit size and shape, positioning of the corpse, and grave goods.

Transformations of burial patterns in Spanish Florida (Larsen 1982) and the Tipu mission (Cohen et al. 1997) effectively illustrate apparent ideological change (i.e., authentic shifts in religion-related belief and practice). Baker (1994) demonstrated that precontact burial rituals persisted at seventeenth-century Narragansett sites in hybrid configurations with Christian rites. Similarly, Hutchinson's (2006) work at Tatham Mound suggests that mortuary space there was a cyclically dynamic, socially negotiated domain as objects of European manufacture were interwoven into indigenous burial patterns in a way that suggests their use as prestige goods, especially with indigenous women. Wrobel (2012) argues that burial patterns in historic Chau Hiix, Belize, embodied syncretism and expressions of resistance. At Puruchuco-Huaquerones in Peru, Murphy et al. (2011) examined evidence that control of dead bodies represented a hotly contested and conflictive social and ritual domain between the Spanish and local Andeans, while Klaus (2013) and Klaus and Tam (2009a) considered the process of hybridization of local and Spanish mortuary customs as a reflection of ethnogenesis.

Mortuary archaeology is a natural avenue to further contextualize and theorize postcontact bodies. Issues such as postcontact agency, ethnic identity, ethnogenesis, ritual resistance, and the symbolic construction of the burial as a representation of real or desired social situations are key areas of future exploration. The relationship between health status, social status, and mortuary ritual also remains largely untapped.

ORGANIZATION OF THIS VOLUME

This volume brings together 12 investigations that incorporate many of the previously discussed approaches, concepts, and themes to demonstrate variations of the profoundly transformative effects of contact, colonial encounters, and colonialism; it represents a starting point for the second generation of bioarchaeological contact studies. This collection includes encounters that were not limited to the European conquest of the Americas (after Stein 2005). And while many contributors focus on the time span after the fifteenth century and draw on additional contextual lines of evidence from historical and ethnohistorical sources, several contributors showcase data sets of colonial encounters and entanglements prior to this century and from "shared or partially shared cultural milieus" (Gosden 2004:26–31). All of the chapters in this volume address a facet or several facets of contact, colonial encounters, and colonialism, and they are united by their emphases on several pertinent topics. First, each of the contributions explores the biocultural impacts of conquest using novel combinations of multiple and independent lines of evidence that integrate paleodemography, skeletal biological stress, disease, nutrition, genetic structure, and myriad archaeological contexts that advance bioarchaeological methods and theory. Various authors also integrate discussions of the nature of "indigeneity," ethnogenesis, microevolution, population histories, and culturally generated phenotypes in relation to identity and the formation of hybrid and novel identities such as native, colonizer, and mestizo. Several chapters present nuanced interpretations of the transformations of mortuary practices after culture contact and colonialism.

We organized the contributions into three themes: life, death, and mortuary practices; frontiers, colonial entanglements, and diversity; and the body and identity under colonialism. The chapters in the first section share in their incorporation of the effects of colonialism on mortuary practices alongside their investigations of its effects on skeletal health and disease, diet and population movements, traumatic injuries, and degenerative joint disease, among other osseous traces of life and death on the human skeleton. In Chapter 2, Melissa S. Murphy, Maria Fernanda Boza, and Catherine Gaither highlight the study of mortuary practices after conquest and colonialism—Inca and Spanish—and how bioarchaeologists might integrate mortuary data with data on morbidity and mortality in the interpretation of the effects of colonialism. They describe early postcontact burials from the cemetery of 57AS03 at the site of Puruchuco-Huaquerones and explore why a subsample of these funerary contexts were interred in an atypical fashion, departing from the traditional Late Horizon/Inca burial pattern. Many of the individuals buried atypically had perimortem injuries; however, they did not possess distinctly higher frequencies of nonspecific indicators of stress or signs of infectious diseases (porotic hyperostosis, cribra orbitalia, periosteal reactions, abnormal bone loss) than those individuals who were interred in traditional mortuary fashion.

In Chapter 3, Michele R. Buzon and Stuart Tyson Smith depart from some of the other chapters in that they examine the relationship between indigenous groups and "more local" foreign powers that are not European but peoples from ancient Egypt and Nubia in the Third Cataract of the Nile. They bring together mortuary analysis, strontium isotope indicators of geographic origins, biological affinities, skeletal evidence of traumatic injuries and activity patterns, and evidence of nutritional deficiencies and infectious disease from human remains that date before, during, and after the New Kingdom Egyptian occupation of Upper Nubia at the sites of Tombos and Kerma. They note that culture contact and colonial entanglements can be long-term, spanning many millennia, and that the Quincentennial/first contact models, while valuable, are insufficient to examine the transitions in social, political, and economic relations in these colonial contexts. Using the earlier burials from Kerma as the baseline, Buzon and Smith present a nuanced picture of cultural identity at Tombos during and after Egyptian rule, with evidence for the assertion and subsequent revival of Nubian identity, as well as hybridity and continuity of the Egyptian burial practices that predominated during the colonial period. These data are supported by the ^{87}Sr/^{86}Sr values and craniometric data from Tombos with evidence for local Nubians and the offspring of Egyptian immigrants. Their paleopathological analyses show a decline in physical activity and labor and violence, as well as a slight, but not entirely statistically significant, decline in skeletal indicators of nutritional deficiency under Egyptian colonial rule; these are interesting and slightly unexpected patterns, particularly since the expectation is that colonial subjects were passive and powerless recipients of colonial rule.

In Chapter 4, Haagen D. Klaus and Rosabella Alvarez-Calderón begin to assemble the first regional picture of the consequences of contact and colonialism in Peru's north coast. With multiple lines of evidence from mortuary archaeology, skeletal markers of health, and diet, Klaus and Alvarez-Calderón compare previous work in the Lambayeque town of Mórrope with burials excavated from the ruins of another colonial site at Eten (ca. 1530s–1750s). They find that the Muchik population of Eten was not only significantly less biologically stressed than their neighbors in Mórrope but also that they did not develop hybrid mortuary rituals and appear rather Christianized. This chapter also touches on variable interplays between health, social change, cultural resistance against colonialism, treatment of the dead, and the diversity of indigenous ethnogenesis in a single Peruvian river valley.

In Chapter 5, Lauren A. Winkler, Clark Spencer Larsen, Victor D. Thompson, Paul W. Sciulli, Dale L. Hutchinson, David Hurst Thomas, Elliot H. Blair, and Matthew C. Sanger investigate the relationship between social status and well-being among the Guale from St. Catherines Island in Spanish Florida (A.D. 1607–1680). Specifically, they examine stress through dental caries, linear enamel hypoplasias, tooth size, and long bone length. Their analysis of mortuary data identifies postcontact social status variation on the basis of funerary offerings and proximity to the altar, and they integrate ethnohistorical evidence to enrich their interpretations. While the authors do not find any direct relationship between stress markers and mortuary offerings, there were spatial relationships between well-being and proximity to (or distance) from the altar. Although the study of colonialism in Spanish Florida has a long history, this work at St. Catherines Island represents new directions involving the spatial dimensions of mortuary and skeletal data on an intracemetery level. The authors conclude with discussions about their findings within the context of Spanish colonialism in Spanish Florida and the implications for bioarchaeology of colonialism.

All of the authors in the second section of the text employ different perspectives of frontiers and borders and colonial entanglements in studying their collections of human remains, finding that there is considerable diversity in how different groups adapted, responded, lived, and died under colonialism. In Chapter 6, Amanda R. Harvey, Marie Elaine Danforth, and Mark N. Cohen examine health among the Tipu Maya of postcontact Belize through the prism of Naum's (2010) concept of frontiers created under colonialism. The authors embrace a multi-method approach where diverse lines of independent but complementary data are assembled to characterize the health of the 588 Tipu Maya during the sixteenth and seventeenth centuries. Their analysis integrates data from ethnohistory, mortuary patterns, paleodemography, multiple expressions of subadult health (i.e., macro- and micro-enamel defects, anemia, Harris Lines), adult health (i.e., specific and nonspecific skeletal infection), traumatic injury, and cortical bone maintenance. Hypothesizing that the Tipu population living in the tumultuous Yucatán would demonstrate particularly high rates of skeletal pathological conditions (particularly violent trauma), Harvey and her colleagues observed quite the opposite. They argue that the frontier nature of Tipu was itself a contested hybrid space—a kind of borderland, or "third space." Living in this liminal zone between the different political spheres likely allowed Tipuans to create a distinct identity and social experience that, compared to other postcontact Maya communities, shielded them from greater degrees of biological stress and morbidity.

Chapter 7 is an important contribution, as the bioarchaeology of contact and colonialism has long been underdeveloped in last region of South America to be colonized. Here, Ricardo Guichón, Romina Casali, Pamela García Laborde, Melisa A. Salerno, and Rocío Guichón open windows on the contact experience in Tierra del Fuego in southern Argentina. These authors explore colonialism to the very end of the archaeological record at the Salesian mission of La Candelaria, which was founded in 1897 and abandoned in the 1940s. Drawing from diverse documentary sources, Guichón and his colleagues construct a remarkably contextualized case study and a guiding theoretical framework involving "double colonialism." Diversity in mortuary practices at La Candelaria indicates that peoples buried there possessed distinct social identities (i.e., clergy, settlers, and Selk'nam natives). Paleopathological study of the human remains indicated mission residents experienced a notable degree of biological stress in the forms of porotic hyperostosis, cribra orbitalia, dental enamel hypoplasia, nonspecific periosteal reactions, worsened oral health, and a high prevalence of skeletal tuberculosis, all emerging as functions of socioeconomic reality created by the mission setting.

In Chapter 8, Megan A. Perry's research in Jordan spans the divide between investigations of the imperialism and colonialism in the Old World versus the New World, and between prehistory versus history. Perry probes the effects of the early Byzantine Empire on health and quality of life at the sites of Faynan and Aila in Jordan. With textual, material, and archaeological data, she notes that life under imperial rule in these regions was not as drastically different as life under imperial rule by the Europeans, since the Nabataeans had established social and political structures that were influenced by Greco-Roman ones. However, she is able to establish that as influence of Byzantine imperial rule waxed and waned, lives and health of the imperial subjects at Faynan and Aila similarly wavered. She explores quality of life and health through the exploration of dental enamel hypoplasias, periostitis, porotic hyperostosis/cribra orbitalia, as well as strontium ratios, which may act as proxies for either population movement or for dietary diversity.

In Chapter 9, Kristina Killgrove presents new and emerging bioarchaeological perspective on life in Rome during the middle of the Imperial period (first–third centuries A.D.). She challenges the core/periphery models for understanding migration, diet, and disease and questions whether life in urban Rome and the greater metropolitan area was relatively good, with access to abundant resources and sociopolitical capital, or whether life in the core of the Roman world was a "pathopolis" marked by rampant infectious disease, poor sanitation, and low-quality food resources. She compares archaeological and historical narratives with previously published bioarchaeological data and her own work at two cemeteries, Casal Bertone and Castellaccio Europarco, to broaden baseline understandings of physiological stress. She finds that people from the two sites experienced similar levels of biological stress and lower frequencies of porotic hyperostosis and dental enamel hypoplasias than the other samples in the comparison. There is considerable diversity in the levels of biological stress, however, and much remains to be unearthed in order to fully understand the etiology of this diversity. Killgrove explores the different explanations for why certain groups, some of them lower-class groups, had higher frequencies of physiological stress, and cites lead exposure, poor sanitation, and lack of access to clean water and high-quality food sources to explain these patterns. This contribution is among a handful of pioneering bioarchaeological investigations of Imperial Rome that challenge previous dichotomizing views of life in Rome. Most critically, she integrates the important component of class to the different effects of life under imperial rule, something that Deagan

(2003) invited scholars to investigate in the Americas but which clearly has salience for other colonial contexts.

Identity and the body, as it is inscribed, modified, measured, and examined, are the jumping-off points for the third section, as all of the contributors take up different and sometimes multiple dimensions of identity from the skeleton and its archaeological context. In Chapter 10, Vera Tiesler and Pilar Zabala synthesize documentary evidence and osteological data to reveal a humanized history of the varied patterns of cultural resilience, adaptation, and elimination of head-shaping practices in Mesoamerica and the Andes. Throughout many regions of the pre-Hispanic Americas, a wide diversity of indigenous body-modification practices combined artificial cranial deformation and other practices of identity, status, and gender. Perceived by the Spanish as a non-Western and "uncivilized" practice that was an affront to the new order in corporeal and theological terms, artificial cranial deformation was aggressively targeted for extirpation. Tiesler and Zabala's analysis indicated that head shaping was a vital practice of body modification that was assaulted and sometimes transformed in creative and unexpected ways in the various Iberian strongholds of Hispanic America while it was progressively eliminated in more peripheral settings.

In Chapter 11, Marie Elaine Danforth, Danielle N. Cook, J. Lynn Funkhouser, Barbara T. Hester, and Heather Guzik report on demography, diet, mitochondrial DNA, and patterns of biological stress in a sample of human remains from the Moran site in Mississippi, which was likely part of New Biloxi, a settlement established under the French colonial regime. This study is noteworthy, because at the time of this writing, skeletal remains have been identified at only six French colonial sites in the United States. These authors test whether the historically documented policies implemented under the *Code noir* were actually practiced and enforced at the settlement, effectively segregating the European settlers, the enslaved Africans and their descendants, and the Native Americans. The authors were surprised by the large number of young males of predominantly European ancestry that they encountered at the site. Stable isotope data indicated that their diets were dominated by C_3-based plants (probably wheat), and only one individual had a C_4-based diet (maize). Although the human remains were small statured and few possessed high levels of enamel defects, Danforth and her colleagues found fairly low levels of physiological stress. They conclude that either the burials from Moran were not a part of New Biloxi, and did not suffer to the degree that the settlers of New Biloxi reportedly suffered, or that there was strict enforcement of segregation, with the remains of other groups interred elsewhere, and that the conditions were not as poor for the Moran group as historical documents about New Biloxi have led scholars to believe.

In Chapter 12, Isabelle Ribot, Alan G. Morris, and Emily S. Renschler compare two case studies of Africans in order to investigate identity, origin, and population affinity of diasporic populations. In the first case study, from Cobern Street in Cape Town, South Africa, the authors integrate stable isotope data and burial data with craniometric variation. In the second case, craniometric data are studied in a sample of Africans from the Samuel G. Morton Collection derived from a group of enslaved people brought to colonial Cuba. In the Cobern Street setting they find evidence of both first- and second-generation immigrants or imported slaves from sub-Saharan Africa, as well as the possible presence of people of Asian descent (either slaves or immigrants). In contrast with the Cobern Street case study, Ribot and her colleagues find high levels of diversity represented in the Morton sample, with some individuals from a single origin within Central, West, or East Africa, some individuals exhibiting multiple possible African origins, and finally, some other individuals exhibiting complex patterns of heterogeneity that may reflect origins and admixture from Asia, Europe, or Mesoamerica.

In Chapter 13, Alejandra Ortiz, Melissa S. Murphy, Jason Toohey, and Catherine Gaither assemble diverse lines of evidence—namely, biodistance data, mortuary patterns, ethnobotanical and zooarchaeological data, dress, and adornment—from Magdalena de Cao Viejo during the colonial period. They seek to understand the construction, manipulation, and negotiation of identity at this *reducción*, and although their sample is small, they find that the Magdaleneros were biometrically and morphologically most similar to Spanish comparative samples, rather than pre-Hispanic samples from the Central Andes. They contrast these observations with archaeological data and argue for evidence of material and cultural hybridity as well as the continuity of local beliefs and practices.

Finally, in Chapter 14, Christopher M. Stojanowski assumes the monumental responsibility of integrating the chapters with the themes of the volume to propose some critical visions and prospects for a postcolonial bioarchaeology and for bioarchaeologists in general. He calls on practitioners to engage with higher-level questions and a broader theoretical framework that represents a bold and ambitious agenda for future bioarchaeological investigations.

CONCLUSIONS

The contributions to this volume represent work concerning a wide range of the biocultural impacts of colonialism, and they underscore the tremendous variability in how people fought, coped, survived, thrived, or perished during colonialism. This collection highlights the variability of the biocultural impacts of colonialism to emphasize that it was not just "guns, germs, and steel" and that colonialism was not a moment in time, but a protracted and protean process with complex legacies.

Building upon previous work, this volume presents new results from regions previously understudied or unknown and integrates new developments in theory, particularly from historical archaeology. From the outset, we attempted to expand the scope of the bioarchaeology of contact and colonialism to the maximum extent possible toward the goal of building toward not just hemispheric, but multivocal and global perspectives on these issues. Yet, this book takes only some of the first steps in pursuit of this larger goal; it is by no means exhaustive or authoritative. The topics broached here are only a fraction of those that could be considered a part of a truly global bioarchaeology of contact, conquest, and colonialism. Much remains to be explored about the variability of colonial entanglements in Asia, Africa, and Australia, and especially when under the yoke of colonialism *before* European expansion into the Americas. To these ends, we hope the volume sparks new conversations and dialogue among scholars around the globe to consider some of themes that unite the chapters. Ultimately, future research will no doubt reveal still unknown histories and experiences concealed by the passage of time, and advance yet further scientific and humanistic understandings of this key adaptive transition of the human species.

ACKNOWLEDGMENTS

The editors would like to thank Meredith Babb at University Press of Florida for her patience and counsel. We would also like to acknowledge the contributors for their commitment and participation. Finally, we thank Ken Nystrom and the anonymous reviewers for their constructive criticism and guidance.

REFERENCES CITED

Alcock, S. E., T. D'Altroy, K. D. Morrison, and C. M. Sinopoli (editors)
2001   Empires: Perspectives from Archaeology and History. Cambridge University Press, Cambridge.

Angel, J. L, J. O. Kelley, M. Parring, and S. Pinter
1987   Life Stresses of the Free Black Community as Represented by the First African Baptist Church, Philadelphia, 1823–1841. American Journal of Physical Anthropology 74:213–229.

Aufderheide, A.
1992   Summary on Disease before and after Contact. In Disease and Demography in the Americas, edited by J. W. Verano and D. H. Ubelaker, pp. 165–166. Smithsonian Institution Press, Washington, D.C.

Baker, B. J.
1994   Pilgrim's Progress and Praying Indians: The Biocultural Consequences of Contact in Southern New England. In In the Wake of Contact: Biological Responses to Conquest, edited by C. S. Larsen and G. R. Milner, pp. 35–45. Wiley-Liss, New York.

Baker, B. J., and L. Kealhofer
1996   Assessing the Impact of European Contact on Aboriginal Populations. In Bioarchaeology of Native American Adaptation in the Spanish Borderlands, edited by B. J. Baker and L. Kealhofer, pp. 1–13. University Press of Florida, Gainesville.

Baker, B. J., and L. Kealhofer (editors)
1996   Bioarchaeology of Native American Adaptation in the Spanish Borderlands. University Press of Florida, Gainesville.

Barfield, T. J.
2001   The Shadow Empires: Imperial State Formation along the Chinese-Nomad Frontier. In Empires: Perspectives from Archaeology and History, edited by S. E. Alcock, T. D'Altroy, K. D. Morrison, and C. M. Sinopoli, pp. 10–41. Cambridge University Press, Cambridge.

Bennett, H. L.
2009   Colonial Blackness. A History of Afro-Mexico. Indiana University Press, Bloomington.

Blakey, M. L.
2001   Bioarchaeology of the African Diaspora in the Americas: Its Origins and Scope. Annual Reviews in Anthropology 30:387–422.

Blakey, M. L. and L. M. Rankin-Hill (editors)
2009   The New York African Burial Ground: Unearthing the African Presence in Colonial New York, Volume 1: Skeletal Biology of the New York African Burial Ground. Howard University Press, Washington, D.C.

Boddy, J.
2011   Colonialism. Bodies under Colonialism. In A Companion to the Anthropology of the Body and Embodiment, edited by F. E. Mascia-Lees, pp. 119–136. Wiley-Blackwell, Malden, Massachusetts.

Bryant, S. K., B. Vinson II, and R. O'Toole

2012   Introduction. In *Africans to Spanish America: Expanding the Diaspora*, edited by S. K. Bryant, B. Vinson III, and R. O'Toole, pp.1–26. University of Illinois Press, Urbana-Champaign.

Buckley, H. R., R. Kinaston, S. E. Hlacrow, A. Foster, M. Spriggs, and S. Bedford

2014   Scurvy in a Tropical Paradise? Evaluating the Possibility of Infant and Adult Vitamin C Deficiency in the Lapita Skeletal Sample of Teouma, Vanuatu, Pacific Islands. *International Journal of Paleopathology* 5:72–85.

Cohen, M. N., K. O'Connor, M. Danforth, K. Jacobi, and C. Armstrong

1994   Health and Death at Tipu. In *In the Wake of Contact: Biological Responses to Conquest*, edited by C. S. Larsen and G. R. Milner, pp. 121–133. Wiley-Liss, New York.

1997   Archaeology and Osteology of the Tipu Site. In *Bones of the Maya: Studies of Ancient Skeletons*, edited by S. L. Whittington and D. M. Reed, pp. 78–86. Smithsonian Institution Press, Washington, D.C.

Cook, N. D.

1998   *Born to Die: Disease and New World Conquest, 1492–1650*. Cambridge University Press, Cambridge.

Corruccini, R. S., J. S. Handler, R. J. Mutaw, and F. W. Lange

1982   Osteology of a Slave Burial Population from Barbados, West Indies. *American Journal of Physical Anthropology* 59:443–459.

1987   Implications of Tooth Root Hypercementosis in a Barbados Slave Skeletal Collection. *American Journal of Physical Anthropology* 74:179–184.

Corruccini, R. S., K. P. Jacobi, and J. S. Handler

1985   Distribution of Enamel Hypoplasias in an Early Caribbean Slave Population. *American Journal of Physical Anthropology* 66:158.

Corruccini, R. S., K. P. Jacobi, J. S. Handler, and A. C. Aufderheide

1987   Implications of Tooth Root Hypercementosis in a Barbados Slave Skeletal Collection. *American Journal of Physical Anthropology* 74:179–184.

Craig, J., and C. S. Larsen

1993   *Archaeological and Osteological Investigations at the Cross Cemetery, Sangamon County, Illinois*. Contract report prepared for the Roosevelt National Life Insurance Company. Hanson Engineers Incorporated. Springfield.

Crist, T. A., and M. H. Sorg

2014   Adult Scurvy in New France: Samuel de Champlain's "Mal de la terre" at Saint Croix Island, 1604–1605. In *Advances in the Paleopathology of Scurvy: Physiological, Diagnostic, and Biocultural Perspectives*. Special Issue, edited by J. J. Crandall and H. D. Klaus. *International Journal of Paleopathology* 5:95–105.

Crosby, A. W.

1972   *The Columbian Exchange: Biological and Cultural Consequences of 1492*. Greenwood Press, Westport.

1992   Summary on Population Size before and after Contact. In *Disease and Demography in the Americas*, edited by J. W. Verano and D. H. Ubelaker, pp. 277–278. Smithsonian Institution Press, Washington, D.C.

Cucina, A.
2010   Social Inequality in the Early Spanish Colony: Oral Pathologies and Dental
            Enamel Hypoplasia in the Skeletal Sample from Campeche. In *Natives, Eu-
            ropeans, and Africans in Colonial Campeche: History and Archaeology,* edited
            by V. Tiesler, P. Zabala, A. Cucina, pp. 11–129. University Press of Florida,
            Gainesville.

Cummins, T.
2002   Forms of Andean Colonial Towns, Free Will, and Marriage. In *The Archae-
            ology of Colonialism,* edited by C. L. Lyons and J. K. Papadopoulous, pp.
            199–240. Getty Research Foundation, Los Angeles.

Cusick, J.
1998   *Studies in Culture Contact: Interaction, Culture Change, and Archaeology.*
            Center for Archaeological Investigations, Southern Illinois University, Car-
            bondale.

Cybulski, J. S.
1994   Culture Change, Demographic History, and Health and Disease on the
            Northwest Coast. In *In the Wake of Contact: Biological Responses to Con-
            quest,* edited by C. S. Larsen and G. R. Milner, pp. 121–133. Wiley-Liss, New
            York.

D'Altroy, T. D.
2015   *The Incas.* 2nd ed. Wiley-Liss, New York.

Davidson, J. M., J. C. Rose, M. P. Gutmann, M. R. Haines, and K. Condon
2002   The Quality of African-American Life in the Old Southwest near the Turn
            of the Twentieth Century. In *The Backbone of History: Health and Nutrition
            in the Western Hemisphere,* edited by R. Steckel and J. Rose, pp. 226–277.
            Cambridge University Press, Cambridge.

Deagan, K.
2003   Colonial Origins and Colonial Transformations in Spanish America. *Histori-
            cal Archaeology* 37(4):3–13.

de la Cova, C.
2011   Race, Health, and Disease in 19th-Century-Born Males. *American Journal of
            Physical Anthropology* 144:526–537.

Dietler, M.
2007   Culinary Encouners: Food, Identity, and Colonialism. In *The Archaeology of
            Food and Identity,* edited by K. Twiss, pp. 218–241. Center for Archaeological
            Investigations, Occasional Paper No. 34, Carbondale.

Dobyns, H. F.
1966   Estimating Aboriginal Populations: An Appraisal of Techniques with a New
            Hemispheric Estimate. *Current Anthropology* 7:396–449.
1983   *Their Numbers Become Thinned: Native American Population Dynamics in
            Eastern North America.* University of Tennessee Press, Knoxville.
1992   Native American Trade Centers as Contagious Disease Foci. In *Disease and
            Demography in the Americas,* edited by J. W. Verano and D. Ubelaker, pp.
            215–222. Smithsonian Institution Press, Washington, D.C.

Duday, H.

2006   L'archéothantologie ou l'archéologie de la mort (Archaeothanatology or the Archaeology of Death). In *Social Archaeology of Funerary Remains*, edited by R. Gowland and C. Knüsel, pp. 30–56. Oxbow, Oxford.

2009   *The Archaeology of the Dead: Lectures in Archaeothantology*. Translated by A. M. Cipriani and J. Pearce. Oxbow, Oxford.

Earle, R.

2012   The Columbian Exchange. In *The Oxford Handbook of Food History*, edited by J. Pilcher, pp. 341–357. Oxford University Press, Oxford.

Farmer, P., B. Nizeye, S. Stulac, and S. Ksehavjee

2006   Structural Violence and Clinical Medicine. *PLOS Medicine* 3:1686–1691.

Freter, A. C.

1997   The Question of Time: The Impact of Chronology on Copan Prehistoric Settlement Demography. In *Integrating Archaeological Demography*, edited by R. Paien, pp. 21–42. Center for Archaeological Investigations, Occasional Paper No. 24, Carbondale, Illinois.

Gaither, C.

2012   Cultural Conflict and the Impact on Non-Adults at Puruchuco-Huaquerones in Peru: The Case for Refinement of Methods Used to Analyze Violence against Children in the Archaeological Record. *International Journal of Paleopathology* 2:69–77.

Gaither, C., and M. S. Murphy

2012   Consequences of Conquest? The Analysis and Interpretation of Subadult Trauma at Puruchuco-Huaquerones, Peru. *Journal of Archaeological Science* 39:467–468.

Galtung, J.

1969   Violence, Peace and Peace Research. *Journal of Peace Research* 6:167–191.

Gill, G. W., and B. M. Gilbert

1990   Race Identification from the Midfacial Skeleton: American Blacks and Whites. In *Skeletal Attribution of Race*, edited by G. W. Gill and S. Rhine, pp. 47–51. University of New Mexico Maxwell Museum of Anthropology, Albuquerque.

Gosden, C.

2004   *Archaeology and Colonialism*. Cambridge University Press, Cambridge.

Handler, J. S., A. Aufderheide, and R. S. Corruccini

1986   Lead Contact and Poisoning in Barbados Slaves: Historical, Chemical, and Bioanthropology Evidence. *Social Science and History* 10:399–425.

Handler, J. S., and F. W. Lange

1978   *Plantation Slavery in Barbados*. Harvard University Press, Cambridge.

Henige, D.

1998   *Numbers from Nowhere: The American Indian Contact Population Debate*. University of Oklahoma Press, Norman.

Hill, C. M.

1996   Protohistoric Aborigines in West-Central Alabama: Probable Correlations to Early European Contact. In *Bioarchaeology of Native American Adaptation in the Spanish Borderlands*, edited by B. J. Baker and L. Kealhoffer, pp. 17–37. University Press of Florida, Gainesville.

Hutchinson, D. L.
2006   *Tatham Mound and the Bioarchaeology of European Contact: Disease and Depopulation in Central Gulf Coast Florida*. University Press of Florida, Gainesville.

Hutchinson, D. L., and J. M. Mitchem
2001   Correlates of Contact: Epidemic Disease in Archaeological Context. *Historical Archaeology* 35:58–72.

Hutchinson, D. L., and L. Norr
1994   Late Prehistoric and Early Historic Diet in Gulf Coast Florida. In *In the Wake of Contact: Biological Responses to Conquest*, edited by C. S. Larsen and G. R. Milner, pp. 9–20. Wiley-Liss, New York.

Hutchinson, J.
1987   The Age-Sex Structure of the Slave Population in Harris County, Texas: 1850–1860. *American Journal of Physical Anthropology* 74:231–238.

Jacobi, K. P.
1997   Dental Genetic Structuring of a Colonial Maya Cemetery, Tipu, Belize. In *Bones of the Maya: Studies of Ancient Skeletons*, edited by S. Whittington and D. M. Reed, pp. 138–153. Smithsonian Institution Press, Washington, D.C.
2000   *Last Rights for the Tipu Maya: Genetic Structuring in a Colonial Cemetery*. University of Alabama Press, Tuscaloosa.

Jacobi, K., D. C. Cook, R. S. Corriccini, and J. S. Handler
1992   Congenital Syphilis in the Past: Slaves at Newton Plantation, Barbados, West Indies. *American Journal of Physical Anthropology* 89:145–158.

Kealhofer, L.
1996   The Evidence for Demographic Collapse in California. In *Bioarchaeology of Native American Adaptation in the Spanish Borderlands*, edited by B. J. Baker and L. Kealhofer, pp. 56–92. University Press of Florida, Gainesville.

King, J. A., and D. H. Ubelaker
1996   *Living and Dying on the 17th Century Patuxent Frontier*. Maryland Historic Trust Press, Crownsville.

Kinnally, E. L.
2014   Epigenetic Plasticity Following Early Stress Predicts Long-Term Health Outcomes in Rhesus Macaques. *American Journal of Physical Anthropology* 155:192–199.

Klaus, H. D.
2012   The Bioarchaeology of Structural Violence: Theoretical Model and Case Study. In *The Bioarchaeology of Violence*, edited by D. L. Martin, R. P. Harrod, and V. R. Pérez, pp. 29–62. University Press of Florida, Gainesville.
2013   Hybrid Cultures . . . and Hybrid Peoples: Bioarchaeology of Genetic Change, Religious Architecture, and Burial Ritual in the Colonial Andes. In *Hybrid Material Culture: The Archaeology of Syncretism and Ethnogenesis*, edited by J. Card, pp. 207–238. Center for Archaeological Investigations, Southern Illinois University, Carbondale.

2014   Frontiers in the Bioarchaeology of Stress and Disease: Cross-Disciplinary
              Perspectives from Pathophysiology, Human Biology, and Epidemiology.
              American Journal of Physical Anthropology 155:294–308.

Klaus, H. D., C. S. Larsen, and M. E. Tam
2009   Economic Intensification and Degenerative Joint Disease: Life and Labor on
              the Postcontact North Coast of Peru. *American Journal of Physical Anthro-
              pology* 139:204–221.

Klaus, H. D., and D. J. Ortner
2014   Treponemal Infection in Peru's Early Colonial Period: A Case of Complex
              Lesion Patterning and Unusual Funerary Treatment. *International Journal of
              Paleopathology* 4:25–36.

Klaus, H. D., and M. E. Tam
2009a   Surviving Contact: Biological Transformation, Burial, and Ethnogenesis in
              the Colonial Lambayeque Valley, North Coast of Peru. In *Bioarchaeology
              and Identity in the Americas,* edited by K. Knudson and C. Stojanowski, pp.
              136–154. University Press of Florida, Gainesville.

2009b   Contact in the Andes: Bioarchaeology of Systemic Stress in Colonial Mór-
              rope, Peru. *American Journal of Physical Anthropology* 138:356–368.

2015   *Requiem Aeternam?* Archaeothanatology of Mortuary Ritual in Colonial
              Mórrope, North Coast of Peru. In *Living with the Dead in the Andes,* edited
              by I. Shimada and J. L. Fitzsimmons, pp. 267–303. University of Arizona
              Press, Tucson.

Larsen, C. S.
1994   In the Wake of Columbus: Native Population Biology in the Postcontact
              Americas. *Yearbook of Physical Anthropology* 37:109–154.

2001   Bioarchaeology of Spanish Florida. In *Bioarchaeology of Spanish Florida: The
              Impact of Colonialism* edited by C. S. Larsen, pp. 22–51. University Press of
              Florida, Gainesville.

2002   *Skeletons in Our Closet: Revealing Our Past through Bioarchaeology.* Prince-
              ton University Press, Princeton.

Larsen, C. S. (editor)
1990   *The Archaeology of Mission Santa Catalina de Guale:2. Biocultural Interpreta-
              tions of a Population in Transition.* Anthropological Papers of the American
              Museum of Natural History No. 68. American Museum of Natural History,
              New York.

2001   *Bioarchaeology of Spanish Florida: The Impact of Colonialism.* University
              Press of Florida, Gainesville.

Larsen, C. S., J. Craig, L. E. Sering, M. E. Schoeninger, K. F. Russell, D. L. Hutchinson, and
              M. A. Williamson
1995   Cross Homestead: Life and Death on the Midwest Frontier. In *Bodies of Evi-
              dence: Reconstructing History through Skeletal Analysis,* edited by A. Grauer,
              pp. 139–159. Wiley-Liss, New York.

Larsen, C. S., A. Crosby, M. C. Griffin, D. L. Hutchinson, C. B. Ruff, K. F. Russell, M. J.
              Schoeninger, L. E. Sering, S. W. Simpson, J. L. Takás, and M. F. Teaford
2002   A Biohistory of the Georgia Bight: The Agricultural Transition and the Im-

pact of European Contact. In *The Backbone of History: Health and Nutrition in the Western Hemisphere*, edited by R. Steckel and J. Rose, pp. 406–439. Cambridge University Press, Cambridge.

Larsen, C. S., M. C. Griffin, D. L. Hutchinson, V. E. Noble, L. Norr, R. Pastor, C. B. Ruff, K. F. Russell, M. J. Schoeninger, M. Schultz, S. Simpson, and M. F. Teaford
2001   Frontiers of Contact Bioarchaeology of Spanish Florida. *Journal of World Prehistory* 15:69–123.

Larsen, C. S., and Milner, G. R. (editors)
1994   *In the Wake of Contact: Biological Responses to Conquest*. Wiley-Liss, New York.

Larsen, C. S., C. B. Ruff, and R. L. Kelly
1995   Structural Analysis of the Stillwater Postcranial Human Remains: Behavioral Implications of Articular Joint Pathology and Long Bone Diaphysial Morphology. In *Bioarchaeology of the Stillwater Marsh: Prehistoric Human Adaptation in the Western Great Basin*, edited by C. S. Larsen and R. L. Kelly, pp. 107–133, Anthropological Papers No. 77, American Museum of Natural History, New York.

Lightfoot, K.
1995   Culture Contact Studies: Redefining the Relationship between Prehistoric and Historical Archaeology. *American Antiquity* 60(2):199–217.

Lightfoot, K., and A. Martinez
1995   Frontiers and Boundaries in Archaeological Perspective. *Annual Review in Anthropology* 24:471–492.

Lightfoot, K., A. Martinez, and A. Schiff
1998   Daily Practice and Material Culture in Pluralistic Social Settings: An Archaeological Study of Culture Change and Persistence from Fort Ross, California. *American Antiquity* 63(2):199–222.

Loren, D. D.
2003   Refashioning a Body Politic in Colonial Louisiana. *Cambridge Archaeological Journal* 13(2):231–237.

Lyons, C. L., and J. K. Papadopoulos (editors)
2002   *The Archaeology of Colonialism*. The Getty Research Institute, Los Angeles.

Mackey, M. A., and M. L. Blakey
2004. The New York African Burial Ground Project: Past Biases, Current Dilemmas, and Future Research Opportunities. *Historical Archaeology* 38:10–17.

Mann, C.
2002   *1491: New Revelations of the Americas before Columbus*. Knopf, New York.
2011   *1493: The New World Columbus Created*. Knopf, New York.

Martin, D. L., A. L. Magennis, and J. C. Rose
1987   Cortical Bone Maintenance in an Historic Afro-American Cemetery Sample from Cedar Grove, Arkansas. *American Journal of Physical Anthropology* 74:255–264.

McIlvaine, B. K., L. A. Schepartz, and C. S. Larsen
2014   Evidence for Long-Term Migration on the Balkan Peninsula Using Dental and Cranial Nonmetric Data: Early Interaction between Corinth (Greece)

and Its Colony at Apollonia (Albania). *American Journal of Physical Anthropology* 153:236–248.

Merbs, C. F.
1992   A New World of Infectious Disease. *Yearbook of Physical Anthropology* 35:3–42.

Milner, G. R.
1996   Prospects and Problems in Contact-Era Research. *In Bioarchaeology of Native American Adaptation in the Spanish Borderlands*, edited by B. J. Baker and L. Kealhoffer, pp. 198–208. Gainesville: University Press of Florida.

Mintz, S.
1985   *Sweetness and Power: The Place of Sugar in Modern History*. Penguin, New York.

Murphy, M. S.
2012   Colonized Bodies, Colonizing Bodies: The Bioarchaeology of Contact and Colonialism in the Central Andes. Invited keynote address at the 31st Annual Northeast Conference on Andean Archaeology and Ethnohistory, Boston University, 19–20 October.

Murphy, M. S., C. Gaither, E. Goycochea, J. W. Verano, and G. Cock
2010   Violence and Weapon-Related Trauma at Puruchuco-Huaquerones, Peru. *Americam Journal of Physical Anthropology* 142:636–649.

Murphy, M. S., E. Goycohea, and G. Cock
2011   Resistance, Persistence, and Accommodation at Puruchuco-Huaquerones, Peru. In *Enduring Conquests: Rethinking the Archaeology of Resistance to Spanish Colonialism in the Americas,* edited by M. Liebmann and M. S. Murphy, pp. 57–76. School for Advanced Research Press, Santa Fe.

Naum, M.
2010   Re-emerging Frontiers: Postcolonial Theory and Historical Archaeology of the Borderlands. *Journal of Archaeological Method and Theory* 17:101–131.

Oland, M., S. Hart, and L. Frink (editors)
2012   *Decolonizing Indigenous Histories. Exploring Prehistoric/Colonial Transitions in Archaeology*. University of Arizona Press, Tucson.

Owsley, D. W., G. W. Gill, and S. D. Ousley
1994   Biological Effects of European Conquest on Easter Island. In *In the Wake of Contact: Biological Responses to Conquest,* edited by C. S. Larsen and G. R. Milner, pp. 161–177. Wiley-Liss, New York.

Owsley, D. W., C. E. Orser, and R. W. Mann
1987   Demography and Pathology of an Urban Slave Population from New Orleans. *American Journal of Physical Anthropology* 74:185–197.

Paine, R.
1997   The Need for a Multidisciplinary Approach to Prehistoric Demography. In *Integrating Archaeological Demography: Multidisciplinary Approaches to Prehistoric Population*, edited by R. Paine, pp. 1–20. Center for Archaeological Investigations, Southern Illinois University, Carbondale.

Pfeiffer, S., and S. I. Fairgrieve
1994   Evidence from Ossuaries: The Effect of Contact on the Health of Iroquoians.

In *In the Wake of Contact: Biological Responses to Conquest*, edited by C. S. Larsen and G. R. Milner, pp. 47–61. Wiley-Liss, New York.

Pietruseweski, M., and M. T. Douglas

1994   An Osteological Assessment of Health and Disease in Precontact and Historic (1778) Hawai'i. In *In the Wake of Contact: Biological Responses to Conquest*, edited by C. S. Larsen and G. R. Milner, pp. 179–196. Wiley-Liss, New York.

Pilcher, J.

2006   *Food in World History.* Routledge, New York.

Pillsbury, J. (editor)

2008   *Guide to Documentary Sources for Andean Studies, 1530–1900.* 3 vols. University of Texas Press, Austin.

Preston, W.

2002   Portents of Plague from California's Protohistoric Period. *Ethnohistory* 49:69–121.

Price, T. D., J. H. Burton, A. Cucina, P. Zabala, R. Frei, R. H. Tykot, and V. Tiesler

2012   Isotopic Studies of Human Skeletal Remains from a Sixteenth to Seventeeth Century AD Churchyard in Campeche, Mexico: Diet, Place of Origin and Age. *Current Anthropology* 53:396–433.

Radding, C.

2000   Conquest, Chronicles, and Cultural Encounters: The Spanish Borderlands of North America. *Ethnohistory* 47:767–775.

Ramenofsky, A. F.

1987   *Vectors of Death: The Archaeology of European Contact.* University of New Mexico Press, Albuquerque.

Ramenofsky, A. F., A. Wilbur, and A. Stone

2003   Native American Disease History: Past, Present, and Future Directions. *World Archaeology* 35:241–257

Ramírez, S. E.

1996   *The World Upside Down: Cross-Cultural Contact and Conflict in Sixteenth-Century Peru.* Stanford University Press, Stanford.

Rankin-Hill, L. M.

1997   *A Biohistory of 19th-Century Afro-Americans: The Burial Remains of a Philadelphia Cemetery.* Bergin & Garvey, Westport.

Rathbun, T. A.

1987   Health and Disease at a South Carolina Plantation: 1840–1870. *American Journal of Physical Anthropology* 74:239–253.

Rathbun, T. A., and R. H. Steckel

2002   The Health of Slaves and Free Blacks in the East. In *The Backbone of History: Health and Nutrition in the Western Hemisphere*, edited by R. Steckel and J. Rose, pp. 208–225. Cambridge University Press, Cambridge.

Reinhard, K. J., L. Tieszen, K. L. Sandness, L. M. Beiningen, E. Miller, A. M. Ghazi, C. E. Miewald, and S. V. Barnum

1994   Trade, Contact, and Female Health in Northeast Nebraska. In *In the Wake of Contact: Biological Responses to Conquest*, edited by C. S. Larsen and G. R. Milner, pp. 63–74. Wiley-Liss, New York.

Renschler, E. S.
2007   An Osteobiography of an African Diasporic Skeletal Sample: Integrating
            Skeletal and Historical Information. Unpublished PhD dissertation, Depart-
            ment of Anthropology, University of Pennsylvania, Philadelphia.
Rodríguez, M.
2010   Living Conditions, Mortality, and Social Organization in Campeche during
            the Sixteenth and Seventeenth Centuries. In *Natives, Europeans, and Afri-
            cans in Colonial Campeche: History and Archaeology,* edited by V. Tiesler, P.
            Zabala, and A. Cucina, pp. 95–110. University Press of Florida, Gainesville.
Rose, J. C., and T. A. Rathbun
1987   Preface. *American Journal of Physical Anthropology* 74:177.
Rothschild, N. A.
2008   Colonised Bodies, Personal and Social. In *Past Bodies: Body-Centered Re-
            search in Archaeology,* edited by L. Borić and J. Robb, 135–144. Oxbow, Ox-
            ford, U.K.
Sale, K.
1990   *The Conquest of Paradise: Christopher Columbus and the Columbian Legacy.*
            Knopf, New York.
Schreiber, K.
1987   Conquest and Consolidation: A Comparison of the Wari and Inca Occupa-
            tions of a Highland Peruvian Valley. *American Antiquity* 52:266–284.
1992   *Wari Imperialism in Middle Horizon Peru.* Museum of Anthropology, Uni-
            versity of Michigan, Ann Arbor.
2005   Imperial Agendas and Local Agency: Wari Colonial Strategies. In *The Ar-
            chaeology of Colonial Encounters,* edited by G. Stein, pp. 237–263. School for
            Advanced Research Press, Santa Fe.
Schroeder, H., J. A. Evans, T. O'Connell, K. A. Shuler, and R. E. M. Hedges
2009   Trans-Atlantic Slavery: Isotopic Evidence for Forced Migration to Barbados.
            American Journal of Physical Anthropology 139:547–557.
Schroeder, H., K. A. Shuler, and S. Chenery
2013   Childhood Lead Exposure in an Enslaved African Community in Barbados:
            Implications for Birthplace and Health Status. *American Journal of Physical
            Anthropology* 150:203–209.
Sharma, J.
2012   Food and Empire. In *The Oxford Handbook of Food History,* edited by J.
            Pilcher, pp. 241–257. Oxford University Press, Oxford.
Shuler, K. A.
2011   Life and Death on a Barbadian Sugar Plantation: Historic and Bioarchaeo-
            logical Views of Infection and Mortality at Newton Plantation. *International
            Journal of Osteoarchaeology* 21:66–81.
Shuler, K. A., and H. Schroeder
2013   Evaluating Alcohol Related Birth Defects in the Past: Skeletal and Biochemi-
            cal Evidence from a Colonial Rum Producing Community in Barbados,
            West Indies. *International Journal of Paleopathology* 3:235–242.

Silliman, S.
2005   Culture Contact or Colonialism? Challenges in the Archaeology of Native
            North America. *American Antiquity* 70(1):55–74.
2009   Change and Continuity, Practice and Memory: Native American Persistence
            in Colonial New England. *American Antiquity* 74(2):211–230.

Singleton, T.
1999   Introduction. In *"I, Too, Am America": Archaeological Studies of African-
            American Life*, edited by T. Singleton, pp. 1–17. University Press of Virginia,
            Charlottesville.

Sledzik, P. S., and L. G. Sandberg
2002   The Effects of Nineteenth-Century Military Service on Health. In *The Back-
            bone of History: Health and Nutrition in the Western Hemisphere*, edited by R.
            Steckel and J. C. Rose, pp. 185–207. Cambridge University Press, Cambridge.

Stein, G. J. (editor)
2005   *The Archaeology of Colonial Encounters: Comparative Perspectives.* School for
            Advanced Research Press, Santa Fe.

Stodder, A. L.
1994   Bioarchaeological Investigations of Protohistoric Pueblo Health and De-
            mography. In *In the Wake of Contact: Biological Responses to Conquest*, edited
            by C. S. Larsen and G. R. Milner, pp. 97–107. Wiley-Liss, New York.
1996   Paleoepidemiology of Eastern and Western Pueblo Communities in Proto-
            historic and Early Historic New Mexico. In *Bioarchaeology of Native Ameri-
            can Adaptation in the Spanish Borderlands*, edited by B. J. Baker and L. Keal-
            hofer, pp. 149–176. University Press of Florida, Gainesville.

Stojanowski, C. M.
2005a   Spanish Colonial Effects on Native American Mating Structures and Genetic
            Variability in Northern and Central Florida: Evidence from Apalachee and
            Western Timucua. *American Journal of Physical Anthropology* 128:273–286.
2005b   *Biocultural Histories in La Florida: A Bioarchaeological Perspective.* Univer-
            sity of Alabama Press, Tuscaloosa.
2010   *Bioarchaeology of Ethnogenesis in the Colonial Southeast.* University Press of
            Florida, Gainesville.
2013   *Mission Cemeteries, Mission Peoples: Historical and Evolutionary Dimen-
            sions of Intracemetery Bioarchaeoloyg in Spanish Florida.* University Press of
            Florida, Gainesville.

Storey, R., M. M. Lourdes, and V. Smith
2002   Social Disruption and the Maya Civilization of Mesoamerica: A Study of
            Health and Economy of the Last Thousand Years. In *The Backbone of History:
            Health and Nutrition in the Western Hemisphere*, edited by R. Steckel and J.
            C. Rose, pp. 283–306. Cambridge University Press, Cambridge.

Temple, D. H., and A. H. Goodman
2014   Bioarcheology Has a "Health" Problem: Conceptualizing "Stress" and
            "Health" in Bioarchaeological Research. *American Journal of Physical An-
            thropology* 155:186–191.

Tiesler V., and P. Zabala
2010   Dying in the Colonies: Death, Burial, and Mortuary Patterning in Campeche's Main Plaza. In *Natives, Europeans, and Africans in Colonial Campeche: History and Archaeology,* edited by V. Tiesler, P. Zabala, and A. Cucina, pp. 70–94. University Press of Florida, Gainesville.

Tiesler, V., P. Zabala, and A. Cucina (editors)
2010   *Natives, Europeans, and Africans in Colonial Campeche: History and Archaeology.* University Press of Florida, Gainesville.

Tung, T.
2012   *Violence, Ritual, and the Wari Empire. A Social Bioarchaeology of Imperialism in the Ancient Andes.* University Press of Florida, Gainesville.

Ubelaker, D. H.
1992   North American Indian Population Size. In *Disease and Demography in the Americas,* edited by J. W. Verano and D. H. Ubelaker, pp. 169–176. Smithsonian Institution Press, Washington, D.C.

1994   The Biological Impact of European Contact in Ecuador. In *In the Wake of Contact: Biological Responses to Conquest,* edited by C. S. Larsen and G. R. Milner, pp. 147–160. Wiley-Liss, New York.

2000   Patterns of Disease in Early North American Populations. In *A Population History of North America,* edited by M. R. Haines and R. H. Steckel, pp. 51–57. Cambridge University Press, Cambridge.

Ubelaker D. H., and L. A. Newson
2002   Patterns of Health and Nutrition in Prehistoric and Historic Ecuador. In *The Backbone of History: Health and Nutrition in the Western Hemisphere,* edited by R. Steckel and J. Rose, pp. 343–375. Cambridge University Press, Cambridge.

Verano, J. W.
1992   Prehistoric Disease and Demography in the Andes. In: *Disease and Demography in the Americas,* edited by J. W. Verano and D. H. Ubelaker, pp. 15–24. Smithsonian Institution Press, Washington, D.C.

Verano, J. W., and D. H. Ubelaker (editors)
1992   *Disease and Demography in the Americas.* Smithsonian Institution Press, Washington, D.C.

Vitelli, G.
2011   Change and Continuity, Practice and Memory: A Response to Stephen Silliman. *American Antiquity* 76:177.

Vradenburg, J., R. Benfer, and L. Sattenspiel
1997   Evaluating Archaeological Hypotheses of Population Growth and Decline on the Central Coast of Peru. In *Integrating Archaeological Demography: Multidisciplinary Approaches to Prehistoric Populations,* edited by R. Paine, pp. 150–172. Center for Archaeological Investigations, Southern Illinois University, Carbondale.

Walker, P. L.
2001   A Spanish Borderlands Perspective on La Florida Bioarchaeology. In *Bioarchaeology of Spanish Florida: The Impact of Colonialism,* edited by C. S. Larsen, pp. 247–307. University Press of Florida, Gainesville.

Walker, P. L., and J. R. Johnson
1994   The Decline of the Chumash Indian Population. In *In the Wake of Contact: Biological Responses to Conquest* edited by C. S. Larsen and G. R. Milner, pp. 109–120. Wiley-Liss, New York.

Walker, P. L., P. Lambert, and M. J. DeNiro
1991   The Effects of European Contact on the Health of Alta California Indians. In *Columbian Consequences. Volume 1: Archaeological and Historical Perspectives on the Spanish Borderlands West*, edited by D. H. Thomas, pp. 349–364. Smithsonian Institution Press, Washington, D.C.

Weik, T.
2004   Archaeology of the African Diaspora in Latin America. *Historical Archaeology* 38:32–49.

Wilkie, L.
2004   Considering the Future of African American Archaeology. *Historical Archaeology* 38(1):109–123.

Wolf, E. R.
1982   *Europe and the People without History*. University of California Press, Berkeley.

Wrobel, G. D.
2012   Mortuary Evidence for Maya Political Resistance and Religious Syncretism in Colonial Belize. In *The Bioarchaeology of Individuals*, edited by A. L. Stoddard and A. M. Palkovich, pp. 68–82. University Press of Florida, Gainesville.

Zubrow, E.
1990   The Depopulation of Native America. *Antiquity* 64:754–765.

Zuckerman, M. K., B. L. Turner, and G. J. Armelagos
2012   Evolutionary Thought in Paleopathology and the Rise of the Biocultural Approach. In *A Companion to Paleopathology*, edited by A. Grauer, pp. 34–47. Blackwell, New Chichester, U.K.

I

Life, Death, and Mortuary
Practices after Contact
and Colonialism

2

Exhuming Differences and Continuities after Colonialism at Puruchuco-Huaquerones, Peru

MELISSA S. MURPHY, MARIA FERNANDA BOZA,
AND CATHERINE GAITHER

In the popular imagination and in common perceptions of Spanish conquest of the Inca Empire, two images endure. In the first, a small band of Spaniards atop horses and armed with guns and steel conquered native peoples—an outcome that was swift and inevitable. Andeans either died at the hands of the Spaniards, as victims of warfare, execution, torture, and structural and symbolic violence, or they perished by the epidemic diseases introduced by the Spaniards and European animals, and native populations were decimated. The second image is that of the "Noble Savage" who either resisted Spanish colonial rule outright but died defending the cause, or who passively succumbed to conquest but then survived and persisted, carrying on components of an idealized pre-Hispanic past.

Neither of these images accurately encapsulates the full complexity of the process of Spanish colonialism of the Inca Empire, whether from the early moments of contact, through the implementation of the forced resettlements and Toledan reforms (*reducciones*), to the moment of independence from colonial rule or its enduring legacy in the modern world. Nor do they account for the variability in the implementation of Spanish colonial rule and the decades it took for the Spaniards to fully control their native subjects, or the prehistory of sociopolitical complexity, imperialism, and colonialism that preceded the arrival of the Spaniards.

Historians, anthropologists, and archaeologists alike have noted how existing practices and material objects are often recalibrated and recombined into new forms within colonial contexts, and how colonial entanglements were inherently variable (Dietler 2010; Estenssoro 2001; Griffiths

2006; Hodges 2005; Lightfoot 2005; Loren 2008; MacCormack 1991; Prince 2002; Ramos 2010; Rupertone 2001; Silliman 2009; Vitelli 2009). Comaroff and Comaroff (van Dommelen 2006:111, quoting Comaroff and Comaroff 2001:113) describe this state as the "in-betweenness" of indigenous and colonial activities and processes. White (1991) termed this variability and fluidity "the middle ground" in his treatment of the relationship between Europeans and the Algonquins in the Great Lakes region. White and other scholars depart from the straightforward characterization of conquest and assimilation and cultural persistence by emphasizing the many facets of indigenous and European relations after conquest and invasion and including accommodation and mutual understanding (White 1991).

While much scholarly emphasis has been placed on the archaeology of European colonialism, there has been little theorizing of pre- and non-European forms of colonialism, particularly in bioarchaeology (but see, for exceptions, Dietler 2010; Gosden 2004; Lyons and Popadopoulos 2002; Rothschild 2008; Stein 2005; and Tung 2012). But Native Andean peoples experienced colonialism—either as colonizers or as subjects—for centuries before the arrival of the Spanish in the sixteenth century.[1] How did these different forms of colonialism affect the lives and deaths of people in the Central Andes? During the Middle Horizon (A.D. 600–1000), Wari authority was ascendant and coalesced into an empire that ruled much of the central highlands (Isbell and McEwan 1991; Rowe 1956; Schreiber 1992, 2005). While the exact relationship between the Wari Empire and the polities on the central coast is unknown, evidence of Wari presence has been identified at Pachacamac, as well as Huaca Pucllana and several other central coast sites (Kaulicke 2001; Roach 2010). The period between the Wari and Inca Empires, the Late Intermediate Period (A.D. 1000–1470), showed tremendous variability in sociopolitical organization, but no single expansionist state dominated until the Inca expansion began (Conlee et al. 2004).

The Incas exercised different strategies in the growth and expansion of their empire, ranging from militaristic exploits, indirect rule with alliance building, direct rule, and forced resettlement, to name a few (Alconini 2005; Covey 2000; D'Altroy 2002:248–262; Dillehay 1977, 1979; Malpass 1993; Malpass and Alconini 2010; Meddens and Schreiber 2010; Menzel 1959; Morris 1998; Morris and Thompson 1985; Pärssinen 2003; Sandweiss 1992; Schreiber 1987). By the time Pizarro and the Spaniards established their capital in Lima in A.D. 1535, the people on the central coast of Peru had experienced both Wari imperial influence and indirect Inca rule.

The relationship between the Inca Empire and central coast polities is fairly well documented, and has been characterized as peaceful and co-operative with little disruption of the preexisting social order (Cobo 1964 [1653]; Eeckhout 2004; Rostworowski 1975; Wallace 1998). The central coast was controlled by at least four different polities, but the Ychsma is the only one identified both archaeologically and ethnohistorically and the group that likely controlled the Lurín and Rímac valleys (Conlee et al. 2004; Haun and Cock 2010; Rostworowski 1978). The Ychsma polity was divided into a dozen or so minor polities, with eight located in the Rímac valley and centralized around the famed oracle site of Pachacamac (Conlee et al. 2004; Haun and Cock 2010; Shimada 1991; Rostworowski 1978). Of the Ychsma minor polities, the Lati controlled the region of Puruchuco-Huaquerones, the area of study, during the Late Intermediate Period. Ethnohistorians indicate that the communities residing in the Rímac and Lurín valleys on the central coast of Peru were peacefully incorporated into the Inca Empire around A.D. 1470 through the co-option of preexisting sociopolitical structures (Cobo 1964 [1653]:2:299–302; Rostworowski 1975; Rostworowski 2002:174). Growing bioarchaeological research bolsters this view (Bethard 2013; Haun and Cock 2010; Williams and Murphy 2013). Still, few central coast polities and valleys have been investigated and many questions remain, particularly those concerning regional and diachronic variability.

Established in 1535, the Spanish capital of Lima and its hinterlands were bustling, with an urban core that contained Spanish men, indigenous peoples from Central America, enslaved and free Africans, and local Andean peoples of all social strata and *castas* residing there (Lockhart 1968, 1991; Massey 1992; Powers 1995; van Deusen 2010). The Spanish colonial experience on the central coast was likely extremely variable, depending upon one's social position and familial relationships. Several local lords and elites from the central coast prospered under Spanish rule, some even swearing their fealty to Francisco Pizarro or other Spanish masters (Rostworowski 2002; Spalding 1999; van Deusen 2010:251–253). Violence was particularly rampant, and the city residents witnessed part of the Inca uprising and the siege of Lima during this time (D'Altroy 2002; Del Busto Duthurburu 1978; Guamán Poma de Ayala 1980 [1615]; van Deusen 2010; Vega 1980).

In this chapter, we follow previous scholars who have shown that the body acts as the "basic nexus of colonialism" (Dietler 2010:13; Ballantyne and Burton 2005; Comaroff 1985; Stoler 2002; Stoller 1994; Young 1995). In the introduction of this volume (Murphy and Klaus) and in many of the chapters (e.g., Tiesler and Zabala, Harvey et al., and Winkler et al.), the authors detail the various ways the body is implicated in and itself manifests colonialism. From the material traces of violence in traumatic injuries to the embodiment of social inequality through the osseous evidence of infectious disease and physiological stress, we focus on how bodies of the dead from Puruchuco-Huaquerones may provide information about the different colonial entanglements experienced by people on the central coast of Peru during the Inca Empire and during the early Conquest Period.[2] Specifically, we attempt to access how the biological colonized body incorporated the material and social lived worlds and how the mortuary treatment of the dead body may reflect dramatically changing material and social worlds under colonialism, both Inca and Spanish (Klaus and Alvarez-Calderón, this volume; Krieger 2005:352; Murphy and Boza 2016; Murphy et al. 2010; Rothschild 2008).

ARCHAEOLOGICAL CONTEXT

The site of Puruchuco-Huaquerones is located in the middle portion of the south side of the Rímac valley on the central coast, just outside the city center of modern-day Lima (Figure 2.1). The archaeological zone is composed of three architectural compounds (Palace of Puruchuco, the Pyramids with Ramps of Huaquerones, and the Annex) and several cemeteries. Two of the cemeteries, Huaquerones and 57AS03, have been excavated. Built at the end of the Late Intermediate Period (A.D. 1000–1450), the Palace first served as the seat of the local Ychsma ruler (Tabío 1965; Villacorta Ostolaza 2001, 2004), and likely later housed the Inca functionary (Jiménez Borja 1988; Villacorta Ostolaza 2001, 2004). Most of the burials from the cemeteries of Huaquerones and 57AS03 are Ychsma and date to the end of the Late Intermediate Period, the Late Horizon, and shortly after Spanish conquest (ca. A.D. 1475–1540) (Cock and Goycochea 2004).

The large sample of burials from Huaquerones and 57AS03 (n = approximately 1,286) has allowed scholars to establish a baseline pattern for Ychsma/Late Horizon mortuary treatment within these cemeteries (Cock 1999, 2001, 2002, 2006; Cock and Goycochea 2004; Haun and Cock 2010). Individuals were interred in a seated and flexed position, and oriented to the northeast (Figure 2.2) (Cock and Goycochea 2004; Murphy et al. 2010). Individuals were wrapped in several layers of textiles, and the bundles were given their bulk with raw cotton, plant materials, or a combination of different organic materials as fill (Cock and Goycochea 2004; Haun and Cock 2010; Murphy et al. 2011). In some cases, the principal individual, almost always an adult, was interred with one or more subadults (Biers

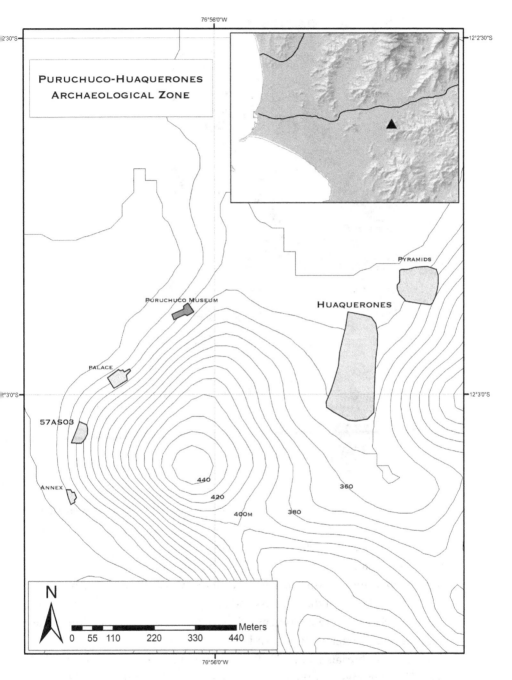

Figure 2.1. Map of the location of Puruchuco-Huaquerones on the central coast of Peru (*inset*) and the relationship between the cemeteries of Huaquerones and 57AS03 within the archaeological zone of Puruchuco-Huaquerones (map by Jason Toohey).

Figure 2.2. A typical Late Horizon burial from Puruchuco-Huaquerones (photo by Melissa S. Murphy).

2003; Cock and Goycochea 2004; Murphy et al. 2010). The Late Horizon burials presented a wide variety and great number of associated mortuary offerings; *Spondylus* shells, metal artifacts, weaving implements and baskets, staffs, maize and beans, coca, coca bags, and *calero* gourds, musical instruments, and ceramic vessels were all recovered. Researchers have interpreted variation in the richness and complexity of some of these burials and their elaborate preparation as evidence for social differentiation in the Huaquerones cemetery (Cock and Goycochea 2004; Murphy 2004). The Late Horizon burials from 57AS03 share the normative funerary pattern with Huaquerones, but the deceased were placed in smaller bundles, and most of the bundles contained only one individual. The two cemeteries appear to differ in the type, quantity, and quality of mortuary offerings, but these analyses are ongoing and more detailed results are forthcoming.

A subset of burials from 57AS03 departs from the pattern described above and was classified as atypical. These individuals did not conform to the northeast orientation, nor were they placed in a seated and flexed position. Instead, they were found in supine and prone positions, semiflexed, or in a combination of positions (Murphy et al. 2010, 2011). The orientation and burial position were inconsistent and showed no overall pattern, except nonconformity. Usually, these atypical individuals were wrapped in one or two textiles with few or no offerings, and then placed in shallow graves at the peripheries and superficial layers of 57AS03 (Murphy et al. 2010, 2011). They do not represent one mass grave, but individual interments, and some of them were intrusive into the Late Horizon burials. The investigators, Cock and Goycochea, have hypothesized that these burials represent early Contact Period burials, distinct from the Late Horizon pattern, but also prior to the implementation of Christian burial rites (Murphy et al. 2010, 2011). A small group of burials ($n = 13$) could not be classified because there was insufficient information or context to determine mortuary treatment. Future archival and laboratory work may clarify the classification of some of these individuals, but here these burials are referred to as unknown.

Methods

The remains of 389 individuals, 208 from Huaquerones and 181 from 57AS03, were visually examined to estimate age-at-death and sex and for evidence of pathological conditions associated with physiological and systemic stress, disease, and traumatic injuries (Table 2.1). We use these data to test whether or not the communities interred at the cemeteries of Puruchuco-Huaquerones experienced Spanish conquest as expected in the first of the two tropes introduced at the beginning of this chapter, with increased levels of violence, physical stress, and disease in the early years of the Conquest Period in comparison to during the Inca occupation of the central coast of Peru. First, we hypothesize that the effects of physiological stress and disease will be greater and the levels of violence will be higher and more severe at the Late Horizon/early Conquest Period cemetery of 57AS03. Second, lethal violence, specifically perimortem injuries, will be more common among the atypical burials from 57AS03.

The sex and age-at-death estimation and the recording of all conditions followed published standards (Buikstra and Ubelaker 1994; Goodman and Martin 2002). Here we examine the presence and frequency of enamel hypoplasias, porotic hyperostosis, cribra orbitalia, periosteal reactions, and

Table 2.1. Sample composition of Huaquerones and 57AS03

	Adults ≥ 15 years	Subadults < 15 years	Males	Females	Ind	TOTAL
Huaquerones ALL	138	70	72	58	8	208
57AS03 ALL	108	73	59	46	3	181
TOTAL (combined)	246	143	131	104	11	389

abnormal bone loss/lytic lesions. Tooth enamel is sensitive to physiological perturbations from disease and/or nutritional deficiencies, and an enamel abnormality develops in the area of ameloblastic activity that is a permanent record of physiological perturbation during subadult growth and development (Goodman and Rose 1991; Hillson 1996; Neville et al. 2002). All tooth types were examined for evidence of enamel hypoplasia, and the frequency of hypoplasias per tooth was recorded. The location, severity, and state of healing of cribra orbitalia and porotic hyperostosis lesions were described and scored according to standard protocols (Buikstra and Ubelaker 1994; Ortner 2003; Stuart-Macadam 1985). Because radiographs were not taken for the current study, it is not possible to conclusively determine whether the identified lesions were caused by marrow hypertrophy (i.e., anemia). Therefore, porotic hyperostosis and cribra orbitalia were treated as types of metabolic diseases rather than as exclusive evidence for anemia (Ortner 2003; Walker et al. 2009).

Only individuals with at least 50 percent of their postcranial skeleton preserved (i.e., at least 6 of 12 long bones) were included in the statistical analysis of periosteal reactions and lytic lesions. We examined the frequency and distribution of pathological conditions by individuals. If the periosteal reactions or lytic lesions were present on more than one skeletal element, then we noted it as an individual with multiple indicators and interpreted this as possible evidence of a systemic infection, disorder, or evidence for an infectious disease (after Goodman and Martin 2002:34; Ortner 2003).

An estimate of female fertility was calculated by the D_{30+}/D_{5+} ratio, which is the inverse of the proportion of skeletal individuals older than 30 years (D_{30+}) over the number of individuals older than 5 years (D_{5+}) (Buikstra et al. 1986; Klaus 2008; Klaus and Tam 2009; Larsen et al. 2002). Here it is assumed that lower rates of female fertility may reflect increased physical demands and activity and increased physiological stress on females. Studies of female energetics indicate that such stress will compromise a

Table 2.2. Mortuary treatment of adults from 57AS03 (individuals ≥ 15 years of age)

	Adults	Males	Females	Indeterminate
57AS03 ALL	108	59	46	3
Late Horizon	38	17	19	2
Atypical burials	57	32	25	0
Unknown	13	10	2	1

woman's ability to become pregnant and carry the fetus to full term (Bogin 2001; Ellison 1994; Ellison and O'Rourke 2000). These measures were then compared to published statistics on female fertility from pre-Hispanic and Colonial sites in the Central Andes.

In the analysis of trauma, individuals were examined macroscopically and evidence of traumatic injuries was recorded by the skeletal element, by the location of the injury on the skeletal element, and by any additional complications of the injury (Buikstra and Ubelaker 1994; Lovell 2008). The shape, location, and size of injuries were also recorded. While it is difficult to differentiate perimortem injuries from postmortem damage on archaeological assemblages of human skeletal remains, conservative attempts were made to establish the timing of the injuries based on osseous evidence and burial context (Berryman and Haun 1996; Berryman and Symes 1998; Sauer 1998; White et al. 2011) (for a detailed elaboration of the methods of trauma analysis, see Murphy et al. 2010 and Murphy et al. 2014). Previous research demonstrated a high frequency of perimortem injuries in the burials from 57AS03 (Murphy et al. 2010), but these analyses did not report antemortem injuries or analyze prevalence using odds ratios by age categories.

We analyzed the frequency of the above conditions by sex, by cemetery (Huaquerones and 57AS03), and by burial type (atypical versus Late Horizon burials at 57AS03). Burials from 57AS03 were classified as Late Horizon, atypical, or unknown based on baseline data from previous work at the site of Puruchuco-Huaquerones (Table 2.2). Variables considered include burial orientation, burial position of deceased individual, bundle preparation, presence or absence of mortuary offerings, and placement within the cemetery. Age estimates were used to classify individuals into the odds ratio age categories (Table 2.3). The prevalence of the conditions was then analyzed using odds ratios and Fisher's exact tests (Klaus 2014; Klaus and Tam 2009; Waldron 1994).

Table 2.3. Age classes used in this study

Age classes	Summary age ranges (years)
1	0–4.9
2	5.0–14.9
3	15.0–24.9
4	25.0–34.9
5	35.0–44.9
6	45.0+

Note: After Klaus 2008, 2014; Klaus and Tam 2009.

RESULTS: HUAQUERONES VERSUS 57AS03

Here we present the comparative results for the cemeteries of Huaquerones and 57AS03. In the following, we detail the results and their implications in understanding subadult and adult systemic stress between the two cemeteries, as well as the early effects of Spanish conquest on those individuals with perimortem injuries from 57AS03. The prevalence for all of the pathological conditions examined, except one, is higher among the Huaquerones burials than among the burials from 57AS03, indicating a decrease through time in these conditions (Table 2.4). However, among those conditions with a higher prevalence at Huaquerones, only the differences in frequency of porotic hyperostosis, cribra orbitalia, lytic lesions, and antemortem fractures are statistically significant (Fisher's exact, $p \leq 0.05$). The one pathological condition examined that shows a higher prevalence at 57AS03 is the prevalence of perimortem fractures.

SYSTEMIC STRESS AND DISEASE

There is an overall decline in the prevalence of the childhood conditions examined between the Huaquerones and 57AS03 cemeteries. Enamel hypoplasias were 1.3 times more likely to occur in the Huaquerones cemetery than in 57AS03 (Table 2.4). The prevalence was higher at Huaquerones across all of the age groups examined, except for the adults between 25.0 and 44.9 years of age. The prevalence of porotic hyperostosis and cribra orbitalia were also higher among the Late Intermediate Period/Late Horizon burials from Huaquerones than the Late Horizon/early Conquest Period burials from 57AS03; this was seen across all age groups, and the overall differences were statistically significant (Fisher's exact, $p \leq 0.05$). Males outnumber females in the frequency of enamel hypoplasias, porotic

Table 2.4. Odds ratio results comparing Huaquerones and 57AS03

Pathological condition	OR1	OR2	OR3	OR4	OR5	OR6	ÔR all	Interpretation
Enamel hypoplasias	1.339	~	1.905	1.714	0.398	1.200	1.402	More prevalent at Huaquerones
Porotic hyperostosis	**3.691**	~	2.946	**8.667**	**10.784**	~	**4.227**	More prevalent at Huaquerones, differences are significant
Cribra orbitalia	1.11	**11.000**	1.795	2.743	2.613	3.333	**1.662**	More prevalent at Huaquerones, differences are significant
Periosteal reactions	1.587	3.542	1.531	**4.343**	1.029	0.409	1.527	More prevalent at Huaquerones
Abnormal bone loss	~	5.429	0.905	2.132	1.660	~	**3.170**	More prevalent at Huaquerones, differences are significant
Antemortem fractures	0.267	~	0.473	2.438	**2.478**	~	1.403	More prevalent at Huaquerones
Perimortem fractures	~	~	0.441	0.494	**0.226**	~	**0.439**	More prevalent at 57AS03, differences are significant

Note: Values in bold represent statistically significant differences (Fisher's exact, $p \leq 0.05$); values greater than 1.01 represent a higher prevalence in Huaquerones, and values less than 0.99 represent a higher prevalence in 57AS03; ~ indicates that the odds ratio could not be calculated because one of the cells has zero cases.

hyperostosis, and cribra orbitalia at Huaquerones and 57AS03, but none of these differences are statistically significant.

The prevalence of periosteal reactions decreased through time, and these reactions were 1.5 times more likely among the Huaquerones burials than among the burials from 57AS03, but the differences were not statistically significant. However, periosteal reactions were 2.4 times more likely among individuals older than 45 years from 57AS03. Lytic lesions were 3.2 times more likely at Huaquerones, and these differences were statistically significant (Fisher's exact, $p \leq 0.05$). Males outnumber females in the frequency of periosteal reactions and cases of abnormal bone loss at both cemeteries, but these differences are not statistically significant (Fisher's exact, $p \geq 0.05$). Fertility (D_{30+}/D_{5+}) increases slightly during the Late Horizon/Conquest Period burials from 57AS03 (Table 2.5), but the D_{30+}/D_{5+} ratios are

Table 2.5. Comparison of D_{30+}/D_{5+} ratios

Site/Period (study author)	D_{30+}/D_{5+} ratio
Huaquerones, Late Intermediate Period/Late Horizon (this study)	0.5306
57AS03, Late Horizon/Conquest Period (this study)	0.4462
Magdalena de Cao Viejo, Colonial Period (Gaither and Murphy 2017)	0.4000
Lambayeque late pre-Hispanic (Klaus and Tam 2009)	0.4397
Lambayeque postcontact, Morrope (Klaus and Tam 2009)	0.6028
Lambayeque postcontact, Eten (Klaus and Alvarez-Calderón, this volume)	0.4030

comparable to the ratios reported from pre-Hispanic Lambayeque samples and Middle/Late Colonial Lambayeque samples (Klaus and Tam 2009:363). The fertility ratio is not nearly as low as reported for the combined post-contact Lambayeque sample (Klaus and Tam 2009:363), suggesting that the communities from Puruchuco-Huaquerones did not experience negative drops in the rates of female fertility during the Late Horizon and early Conquest Period.

Thirteen individuals (seven adults and six subadults) from 57AS03 possess bilateral lesions (either lytic or periosteal) or have multiple skeletal elements affected by lytic, proliferative, or both types of activity, perhaps indicating affliction with a systemic infection or a specific disease. Eleven individuals from Huaquerones (eight adults and three subadults) possess bilateral lesions or have multiple skeletal elements affected with periosteal reactions or lytic activity. Both cemeteries contained only one individual who possessed both lytic lesions and periosteal reactions on multiple skeletal elements. Although individuals from 57AS03 were 1.4 times more likely to possess multiple lesions or multiple skeletal elements affected, the higher frequency of individuals with multiple lesions at 57AS03 is not statistically significant (Fisher's exact, $p \geq 0.05$).

Four subadults from 57AS03 have a pattern and distribution of lesions that are consistent with a differential diagnosis of scurvy. These individuals show extensive distribution of abnormal porosity on the cranium and post-cranial skeleton, such as the greater wings of the sphenoid bone, the maxillary palate, the mandible, the root of the zygomatic bones on the temporal bone, as well as in areas of muscle attachments on both scapulae. The long bones of a fifth individual are abnormally shaped, which may be consistent with a nutritional deficiency.

VIOLENCE AND TRAUMATIC INJURIES

Previous research indicated that the frequency of perimortem fractures was higher at 57AS03 (Murphy et al. 2010), but this research did not compare the prevalence using odds ratio analysis, nor did the previous research report on the frequency of antemortem fractures. These analyses were performed for the present study, and they support the previous research. Perimortem fractures are proportionally 2.3 times more likely at 57AS03 than at Huaquerones, and these are statistically significant (Table 2.2). The prevalence of perimortem fractures is higher at 57AS03 across all of the odds ratio age categories analyzed. In contrast, antemortem fractures are 1.4 times more likely to occur among the burials from Huaquerones, but these differences are not statistically significant (Fisher's exact, $p \geq 0.05$). Children and young adults from 57AS03 are more likely to have antemortem fractures, and adults from Huaquerones were more likely to have antemortem fractures (Table 2.2).

RESULTS WITHIN 57AS03: LATE HORIZON AND ATYPICAL BURIALS

A secondary objective of this study was to explore if physiological stress, traumatic injuries, or disease experiences were somehow related to atypical mortuary treatment of the adults at the cemetery of 57AS03 by comparing the prevalence of these different paleopathological conditions by mortuary treatment (Tables 2.5, 2.6). The atypical burials from 57AS03 show higher prevalence of enamel hypoplasias and porotic hyperostosis, but cribra orbitalia has a higher prevalence among the Huaquerones burials (Table 2.6). However, none of these differences were statistically significant. Periosteal reactions are 1.3 times more likely to occur among the burials from Huaquerones than those from 57AS03 (Table 2.6). Lytic lesions are 3.1 times more likely to occur among the burials from 57AS03. Neither of these differences in frequencies was statistically significant (Fisher's exact, $p \leq 0.05$)

Seven adults from 57AS03 possess multiple periosteal reactions or lytic lesions (and in one case, an individual displayed a combination of lesion types), and six of these burials are interred atypically. In one atypical burial, a partially disturbed multiple burial contained the incomplete skeletons of an adult male, an adult female, and an adolescent. The adult female exhibited a combination of extensive bone formation and bone loss on nearly her entire cranium (Figure 2.3). This individual has extensive proliferative and lytic osseous activity on her cranium with both active and remodeled activity; three main foci of osseous activity were identified, predominantly

Table 2.6. Odds ratio results, comparing prevalence of pathological conditions between the Late Horizon and atypical burials (adults ≥ 15 years of age)

	OR3	OR4	OR5	OR6	ÔR all	Interpretation
Enamel hypoplasias	0.167	0.909	1.333	0.500	0.997	Higher prevalence among atypical burials
PH	~	0.875	0.364	~	0.250	Higher prevalence among atypical burials
CO	24.000	2.000	0.476	~	1.844	Higher prevalence among Late Horizon burials
Periosteal reactions	~	3.500	0.525	~	0.750	Higher prevalence among atypical burials
Abnormal bone loss	~	~	0.773	~	3.118	Higher prevalence among Late Horizon burials
Antemortem fractures	1.667	2.750	1.440	3.333	2.056	Higher prevalence among Late Horizon burials
Perimortem fractures	0.583	0.629	0.191	~	**0.287**	Higher prevalence among atypical burials, differences are statistically significant

Note: Values in bold represent statistically significant differences (Fisher's exact, $p \leq 0.05$); values greater than 1.01 represent a higher prevalence in the Late Horizon burials and values less than 0.99 represent a higher prevalence in the atypical burials; ~ indicates that the odds ratio could not be calculated because one of the cells had zero cases.

on her left and right parietal and occipital bones. The inner and outer tables of bone were affected, and the rims of the lesions are smooth and rounded with areas of stellate-like striations in the osseous reactions. While some of the lesions possess a gummatous appearance, the large destructive lesions on the left and right parietal bones are distinct from the gummatous lesions typical of treponemal disease (Ortner 2003:193); but treponematosis cannot be ruled out. If these lesions are consistent with osteomyelitis, then it is likely that they are traumatic in nature, caused either by blunt force injury, an open wound, or trepanation (Ortner 2003:193). No other lesions were detected on this individual, and neither of the other two individuals in the burial exhibited any pathological conditions. Although this particular female was buried atypically and displays extensive osseous activity affecting the cranium, it is difficult to ascertain whether or not it was her disease state that led to an atypical mortuary treatment. And while the number of individuals with multiple lesions or periosteal reactions are mostly atypical burials, the prevalence of the other pathological conditions were not statistically significant and show no patterning indicative of a relationship between mortuary treatment and pathological condition.

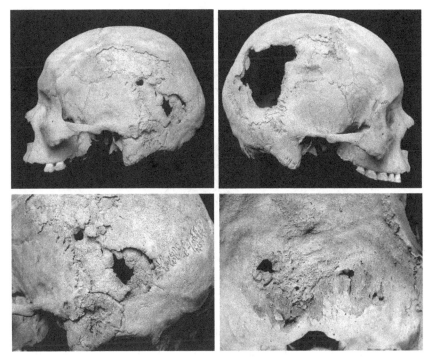

Figure 2.3. Cranium of an adult female with extensive proliferation and resorption of bone on the left and right parietal bones and occipital bone (photo by Melissa S. Murphy).

Antemortem fractures are 2.1 times more likely in the Huaquerones burials, and the prevalence is higher among all of the age categories examined; however, none of these differences are statistically significant. Only perimortem fractures show both a higher prevalence among the atypical burials (3.5 times more likely) and a statistically significant difference (Table 2.6). This increase in perimortem injuries among these atypical burials suggests that lethal injuries and violence spiked during the early Conquest Period.

Discussion and Conclusion

Our results partially reject the first hypothesis. We did not find that the overall prevalence of disease and the effects of physiological stress are higher among the Late Horizon/early Contact Period burials from 57AS03. However, we did find that the levels of violence and lethal perimortem trauma were significantly higher at 57AS03. The childhood conditions that are more prevalent at Huaquerones (porotic hyperostosis, cribra orbitalia, and enamel hypoplasias) may indicate that life under Inca rule disrupted homeostasis for most of the people from this community and caused some physiological stress. However, Huaquerones people likely fared better than some of their pre-Hispanic counterparts (Williams and Murphy 2013). Many of the cases of porotic hyperostosis and cribra orbitalia were mostly healed or with barely discernible porosity, so they do not represent severe manifestations of these childhood conditions (Williams and Murphy 2013). However, subadults from 57AS03 may have experienced higher levels of physiological stress than their adult counterparts, given the higher likelihood of porotic hyperostosis and cribra orbitalia in these younger age categories (Table 2.3). The four possible cases of scurvy and the additional possible case of vitamin or nutritional deficiency from 57AS03 bolsters an interpretation that children were exposed to greater degrees of physiological stress and exposure to pathogens at 57AS03 than at Huaquerones, even though the overall prevalence rates of these conditions for adults and subadults were higher at Huaquerones.

Adults likely recovered from the physiological stress or never developed severe expressions of the conditions in the first place. The stable isotope data from Huaquerones shows that the diet incorporated a variety of plant and animal foods and it provided sufficient protein, vitamins, and other nutrients (Williams 2005; Williams and Murphy 2013), which may have aided in the response to any episodes of stress. Currently, no data yet exist on the stable isotope analysis of diet from 57AS03, so further in-depth comparisons await these data.

There is a higher prevalence of enamel hypoplasias at Huaquerones for most of the age categories, except OR5 (35.0–44.9 years), which is 2.5 times more likely in the burials from 57AS03. This result is in contrast to the overall pattern in the prevalence for enamel hypoplasias between the two cemeteries, so it may represent the introduction of sample bias for that particular category; or for an unknown reason these middle-aged adults from 57AS03 experienced a brief period of physiological stress that was not detected or recorded by other osteological indicators of childhood stress. A closer examination of the number of defects per individuals and the average number of enamel hypoplasias between age categories and samples may help explain this anomaly.

The prevalence of periosteal reactions and destructive lytic lesions decreases through time at the cemeteries, so it appears that the adults from 57AS03 may have either experienced fewer episodes of stress or were better buffered or more capable to recover from these periods of stress. Adults from 57AS03 may also have been exposed to fewer infectious diseases or illnesses that cause lytic lesions in the skeleton. Female fertility is also higher in 57AS03, indicating that females may have been exposed to less demanding physical activities or less physiological stress during the early Late Horizon/early Conquest Period.

The most dramatic result is the spike in the prevalence of perimortem injuries among the atypical burials from 57AS03. This is consistent with the second part of first hypothesis, as well as the entire second hypothesis. These results are not particularly surprising given the previous research; however, these analyses are more nuanced and detailed in that all age categories were exposed to higher levels of lethal violence. The higher prevalence of antemortem injuries at Huaquerones may also reflect greater physical demands or more intense types of activity during life under Inca rule, which may also have affected female fertility in the Huaquerones community, since it is slightly depressed relative to 57AS03 and the pre-Hispanic Lambayeque samples.

The atypical burials from 57AS03 show a higher prevalence of enamel hypoplasias, porotic hyperostosis, and periosteal reactions than the Late Horizon burials from 57AS03, but, unlike the prevalence of perimortem fractures, none of these differences in prevalence were statistically significant. The atypical mortuary treatment at 57AS03 coincided with the occurrence of lethal perimortem injuries and not with higher levels of infectious disease, nor with the exposure to higher physical demands or greater amounts of physiological stress.

This work helps to highlight how the human body itself acts as a nexus of colonialism by comparing the experiences of people from the central coast of Peru during Inca rule and early Spanish conquest. We hypothesized that physiological stress, disease, and violence would all be more prevalent at 57AS03 than at Huaquerones and we found only partial support for this hypothesis. Physiological stress and disease were more prevalent at Huaquerones, but lethal violence was more prevalent at 57AS03.

During the Colonial Period, the Spanish authorities forced Native Andeans into planned towns (see Klaus and Alvarez-Calderón and Ortiz et al., this volume). However, forced resettlement was also a strategy employed by the Incas to more effectively distribute people for resource exploitation, to control production of resources by a specialized community, to undermine sociopolitical resistance of the conquered group, and as a means to incorporate a new group (D'Altroy 1992; Pärssinen 2003; Rowe 1982).

Existing bioarchaeological evidence indicates that communities interred at the cemetery of Huaquerones were fairly homogeneous and predominantly local to the central coast with little evidence of the wholesale resettlement practices commonly employed by the Incas in some regions of the Inca Empire (Bethard 2013; Haun and Cock 2010). While the communities at Puruchuco-Huaquerones likely did not suffer from forced settlement, the Inca control of the Rímac valley may have caused slightly more physiological stress and disease within the community from Huaquerones in comparison to life during the early Conquest Period. Violence dramatically increased during the early Conquest Period and the people interred at 57AS03 suffered from increasing levels of violence and warfare, either Spanish-indigenous violence or indigenous versus indigenous violence. It is possible that this community survived the wave of earliest epidemic diseases that swept Andean South American only to succumb to the rampant violence of the time. Because it was the earliest years of the Conquest Period, the transition to strict colonial rule was only beginning.

Aberrant mortuary patterns have provided indirect information about disease epidemics in protohistoric or early contact communities (Hill 1996; Hutchinson and Mitchem 2001; Kealhofer 1996). Mass burials, a high proportion of cremations, skewed age or sex profiles, and burials in specific mortuary features can also result from social disruption, high rates of mortality, warfare, sacrifice, and natural diseases—in the absence of colonialism and none of these are mutually exclusive (DeWitte 2010; Hutchinson and Mitchem 2001; Kacki et al. 2011; Margerison and Knüsel 2002). The atypical burials from 57AS03 do not demonstrate higher degrees of morbidity from physiological stress or disease, but we conclude that these individuals were likely interred as they were because of the violence and chaos that occurred during the early Conquest Period because of the higher prevalence of perimortem injuries. While the protracted Andean mortuary rites were likely abandoned, the expedient treatment of the atypical burials in the community's cemetery likely maintained the sacred religious and cosmological geography, specifically the connection between the community, its ancestors, and nature and between the deceased and his or her kin (DeLeonardis and Lau 2004; Doyle 1988; Ramos 2010:10; Salomon 1995).

Life in the Inca provinces may have been more difficult than life in the core during the Inca occupation of the central coast, at least for this community. It should be noted that chronology is a thorny problem in differentiating the Late Intermediate Period from the Late Horizon on the central coast (Conlee et al. 2004; Dulanto 2008; Guerrero 1998; Haun and Cock 2010), and the Late Horizon is extremely short (less than 65 years), so there may be some overlap in the lives and deaths of these communities during the Late Intermediate Period and Late Horizon. Given the proximity of this region to all of the goods, people, and services coming into Peru under Spanish colonial rule, some central coast communities may have prospered, while others, such as the one at 57AS03, perished due to increasing levels of violence.

People experienced colonial rule differently, a point made by Tung (2012) when she theorized about the biocultural effects of Wari imperial rule on the imperial subjects and that is apparent in other imperial encounters covered in this volume (Killgrove; Buzon and Smith; Perry). The human remains from Huaquerones and 57AS03 represent only one minor polity, the Lati polity, of twelve in the Rímac and Lurín, so it may be that other communities fared differently than the people from Puruchuco-Huaquerones. There is a dearth of information about life during the Middle Horizon and Late Intermediate Period on the central coast of Peru, so it is not entirely clear how people may have experienced the rise, influence, and collapse of the Wari Empire and its aftermath. Furthermore, additional work is needed to compare the effects of Inca colonialism in other Inca provinces and more work is needed from the Inca capital in Cuzco (but see Andrushko 2007). What was life and death like in these regions, or for those regions that resisted and fought Inca rule, such as the Cañari or Chachapoyas? Were their long-term effects of this resistance and was opposition detrimental to these communities? Killgrove (this volume) and Perry (this volume) describe how life under imperial rule did not directly translate into highest quality of life or superior diets and these studies underscore the variability of life under different forms of imperial rule and from different locales within these empires (core versus provinces).

Chapters in this volume have demonstrated how Spanish colonialism and its effects varied by region: Klaus and Alvarez-Calderón show dramatic intra-valley differences in experiences under Spanish colonial rule between Eten and Mórrope, and Ortiz et al. have found that the people from Magdalena de Cao Viejo in the Chicama valley may have fared better than those from Eten and Mórrope in the Lambayeque region, just a few valleys to the north of the Chicama. Environmental and ecological variables likely contributed to this variability, but local policies may also have played a role. Colonialism is a process that was fluid and ever-changing; the temporal context is critical for in-depth analysis of its effects and people, such as those people interred at 57AS03, experienced the Conquest Period vastly differently than the Colonial Period.

ACKNOWLEDGMENTS

The authors are grateful to the reviewers for their feedback and reviews and in particular we recognize Ken Nystrom for his constructive criticism. Bryn Mawr College, the University of Wyoming, the National Science Foundation (grant #0618192) and the Wenner-Gren Foundation for Anthropological Research (#6791) supported this research. MSM would also like to acknowledge the students and colleagues who participated in her lab seasons during 2006 and 2007 from Bryn Mawr and Haverford Colleges, San Marcos, and PUCP: Maria Fernanda Boza, Julie Burrill, Britta Volz, Jennifer Suarez, Alexandra Fenton, Jessica Wurtz, Mellisa Lund, and Alejandra Ortiz.

NOTES

1. Here we follow Dietler's definition of colonialism as "the projects and practices of control marshaled in interactions between societies linked in asymmetrical relations of power and the processes of social and cultural transformation resulting from those practices" (2010:18).

2. For Peru, Quilter designated the Conquest Period as A.D. 1532–1570 and the start of the Colonial Period at approximately A.D. 1570 (Quilter 2017), a convention we apply here.

REFERENCES CITED

Alconini, S.
2005   The Dynamics of Military and Cultural Frontiers on the Southeastern Edge of the Inka Empire. In *Untaming the Frontier*, edited by B. J. Parker and L. Rodseth, pp. 115–146. University of Arizona Press, Tucson.
Andrushko, V.
2007   *The Bioarchaeology of Inca Imperialism in the Heartland: An Analysis of Prehistoric Burials from the Cuzco Region of Peru.* Ph.D. dissertation, Department of Anthropology, University of California, Santa Barbara. University Microfilms, Ann Arbor.
Ballantyne, T., and A. Burton (editors)
2005   *Bodies in Contact: Rethinking Colonial Encounters in World History.* Duke University Press, Durham.

Berryman, H., and S. Haun
1996   Applying Forensic Techniques to Interpret Cranial Fracture Patterns in an
            Archaeological Specimen. *International Journal of Osteoarchaeology* 6:2–9.
Berryman, H., and S. Symes
1998   Recognizing Gunshot and Blunt Cranial Trauma through Fracture Inter-
            pretation. In *Forensic Osteology*, edited by K. Reichs, pp. 333–352. Charles
            Thomas, Springfield.
Bethard, J. D.
2013   *The Bioarchaeology of Inka Resettlement Practices: Insight from Biological Dis-
            tance Analysis.* PhD dissertation, Department of Anthropology, University
            of Tennessee, TRACE: Tennessee Research and Creative Exchange, Nash-
            ville.
Biers, T.
2003   A Bioarchaeological Analysis of the Falsita Type Mummy Bundle from an
            Inca Period Cemetery Lima, Peru. Unpublished Master's thesis, Department
            of Anthropology, San Diego State University, San Diego.
Bogin, B.
2001   *The Growth of Humanity.* Wiley-Liss, New York.
Buikstra, J. E., L. W. Konigsberg, and J. Bullinton
1986   Fertility and the Development of Agriculture in the Prehistoric Midwest.
            American Antiquity 51:528–546.
Buikstra, J. E., and D. H. Ubelaker (editors)
1994   *Standards for Data Collection from Human Skeletal Remains.* Arkansas Ar-
            chaeological Survey, Fayetteville.
Cobo, B.
1964 [1653] *Historia del nuevo mundo I.* Biblioteca de Autores Españoles, Madrid.
Cock, G. A.
1999   *Estudio de evaluación arqueológica del area ocupada por el asentamiento
            humano Túpac Amaru, en el sitio arqueológica de Huaquerones-Puruchuco,
            distrito de Ate-Vitarte, prov. y dpto. de Lima.* Informe Final. Copies available
            from R.N.A.: A-9401. Instituto Nacional de Cultura, Lima, Perú.
2001   *Recuperación de contextos funerarios del Periodo Inca y ampliación de in-
            vestigaciones en el cementerio de Huaquerones-Puruchuco, dentro de la zona
            arqueológica de Huaquerones-Puruchuco, distrito de Ate-Vitarte, prov. y dpto.
            de Lima.* Instituto Nacional de Cultura, Lima, Perú.
2002   Inca Rescue. *National Geographic* 201:78–89.
2006   *Proyecto de recuperación de contextos funerarios en el cementerio 57AS03.
            Zona arqueologica Huaquerones-Puruchuco distrito de Ate-Vitarte, prov. y
            dpto. de Lima.* Report on file. Instituto Nacional de Cultura, Lima, Perú.
Cock, G. A., and C. E. Goycochea
2004   Puruchuco y el cementerio Inca de la quebrada de Huaquerones. In *Puru-
            chuco y la sociedad de Lima: Un homenaje a Arturo Jiménez Borja,* edited by
            Luis F. Villacorta Ostolaza, Luis Vetter Parodi and C. Ausejo Castillo, pp.
            179–197. Concytec, Lima.

Comaroff, J.
1985   *Body of Power, Spirit of Resistance: The Culture and History of a South African People.* University of Chicago Press, Chicago.

Comaroff, J., and J. Comaroff
2001   Revelations upon Revelations. *Interventions: International Journal of Postcolonial Studies* 3(1):100–126.

Conlee, C. A., J. Dulanto, C. J. Mackey, and C. Stanish
2004   Late Prehispanic Sociopolitical Complexity. In *Andean Archaeology*, edited by H. Silverman, pp. 209–236. Blackwell, Oxford.

Covey, R. A.
2000   Inka Administration of the Far South Coast of Peru. *Latin American Antiquity* 11:119–138.

D'Altroy, T.
1992   *Provincial Power in the Inka Empire.* Smithsonian Institution Press, Washington, D.C.
2002   *The Incas.* Blackwell, Malden.

Del Busto Duthurburu, J. A.
1978   *Historia general del Peru: Descubrimiento y conquista.* Libreria Studium, Lima.

DeLeonardis, L., and G. Lau
2004   Life, Death, and Ancestors. In *Andean Archaeology*, edited by H. Silverman, pp. 77–115. Blackwell, Oxford.

DeWitte, S. N.
2010   Age Patterns of Mortality during the Black Death in London, A.D. 1349–1350. *Journal of Archaeological Science* 37:3394–3400.

Dietler, M.
2010   *Archaeologies of Colonialism: Consumption, Entanglement, and Violence in Ancient Mediterranean France.* University of California Press, Berkeley.

Dillehay, T.
1977   Tawantinsuyu Integration of the Chillón Valley, Peru: A Case of Inca Geo-Political Mastery. *Journal of Field Archaeology* 4:397–405.
1979   Pre-Hispanic Resource Sharing in the Central Andes. *Science* 204:24–31.

Doyle, M. E.
1988   *The Ancestor Cult and Burial Ritual in Seventeenth and Eighteenth Century Central Peru.* Ph.D. dissertation, Department of Anthropology, University of California, Los Angeles. University Microfilms, Ann Arbor.

Dulanto, J. A.
2008   Between Horizons: Diverse Configurations of Society and Power in the Late Pre-Hispanic Central Andes. In *The Handbook of South American Archaeology*, edited by H. Silverman and W. H. Isbell, pp. 761–782. Springer, New York.

Eeckhout, P.
2004   Pachacamac y el proyecto Ychsma, 1999–2003. *Bulletin del'Institut Français d'Études Andines* 33:403–423.

Ellison, P. T.
1994   Advances in Human Reproductive Ecology. *Annual Review of Anthropology* 23:255–275.

Ellison, P. T., and M. T. O'Rourke
2000   Population Growth and Fertility Regulation. In *Human Biology: An Evolutionary and Biocultural Perspective*, edited by S. Stinson, B. Bogin, R. Huss-Ashmore, and D. O'Rourke, pp. 553–586. Wiley-Liss, New York.

Estenssoro, J. C.
2001   El simio de Dios: Los indígenas y la iglesia frente a la evangelización del Perú, XVI–XVII. *Bulletin Institute Francais Études Andines* 30(3):455–474.

Gaither, C. M., and M. S. Murphy
2017   Changing Times: A Bioarchaeological Glimpse of Life and Death in a *Reducción* on the North Coast of Peru. In *Magdalena de Cao Viejo*, edited by J. Quilter. Peabody Museum Press, Harvard University, Cambridge.

Goodman, A. H., and D. Martin
2002   Reconstructing Health Profiles from Skeletal Remains. In *The Backbone of History*, edited by R. H. Steckel and J. C. Rose, pp. 11–60. Cambridge University Press, Cambridge.

Goodman, A. H., and J. C. Rose
1991   Dental Enamel Hypoplasias as Indicators of Nutritional Status. In *Advances in Dental Anthropology*, edited by M. A. Kelley and C. S. Larsen, pp. 279–293. Wiley-Liss, New York.

Gosden, C.
2004   *Archaeology and Colonialism: Culture Contact from 5000 to the Present.* Cambridge University Press, Cambridge.

Griffiths, N.
2006   *Sacred Dialogues: Christianity and Native Religions in the Colonial Americas, 1492–1700.* LuLu Enterprises, Great Britain.

Guamán Poma de Ayala, F.
1980 [1613]   *Nueva corónica y buen gobierno.* Transcribed by F. Pease. Biblioteca Ayacucho, Caracas.

Guerrero, D.
1998   Prehistoria. In *Historia del Distrito de la Molina*, edited by Luis Tord, pp. 63–106. Municipalidad de La Molina, Lima.

Haun, S., and G. A. Cock
2010   A Bioarchaeological Approach to Search for Mitmaqkuna. In *Distant Provinces in the Inca Empire: Toward a Deeper Understanding of Inka Imperialism*, edited by M. Malpass and S. Alconini, pp. 193–220. University of Iowa Press, Iowa City.

Hill, M. C.
1996   Protohistoric Aborigines in West-Central Alabama: Probable Correlations to Early European Contact. In *Bioarchaeology of Native American Adaptation in the Spanish Borderlands*, edited by B. J. Baker and L. Kealhofer, pp. 17–37. University Press of Florida, Gainesville.

Hillson, S.
1996   *Dental Anthropology*. Cambridge University Press, Cambridge.

Hodges, C.
2005   Faith and Practice at an Early-Eighteenth-Century Wampanoag Burial Ground: The Waldo Farm Site in Dartmouth, Massachusetts. *Historical Archaeology* 39(4):73–94.

Hutchinson, D. L., and J. M. Mitchem
2001   Correlates of Contact: Epidemic Disease in Archaeological Context. *Historical Archaeology* 35(2):58–72.

Isbell, W. H., and G. F. McEwan (editors)
1991   *Huari Administrative Structure: Prehistoric Monumental Architecture and State Government*. Dumbarton Oaks, Washington, D.C.

Jiménez Borja, A.
1988   *Puruchuco*. Biblioteca Nacional Del Perú, Lima.

Kacki, S., L. Rahalison, M. Rajerison, E. Ferroglio, and R. Bianucci
2011   Black Death in the Rural Cemetery of Saint-Laurent-de-la-Cabreriesse Aude-Languedoc, Southern France, 14th Century: Immunological Evidence. *Journal of Archaeological Science* 38:581–587.

Kaulicke, P.
2001   La sombra de Pachacamac: Huari en la costa central. In *Huari y Tiahuanaku: Modelos vs. evidencias*, edited by P. Kaulicke and W. Isbell, *Boletin de Arqueologia PUCP* 4:313–358. Pontificia Universidad Catolica del Peru, Lima.

Kealhofer, L.
1996   The Evidence for Demographic Collapse in California. In *Bioarchaeology of Native American Adaptation in the Spanish Borderlands*, edited by B. H. Baker and L. Kealhofer, pp. 56–92. University Press of Florida, Gainesville.

Klaus, H. D.
2008   *Out of Light Came Darkness: Bioarchaeology of Mortuary Titual, Health, and Ethnogenesis in the Lambayeque Valley Complex, North Coast of Peru (AD 900–1750)*. Ph.D. dissertation, Department of Anthropology, Ohio State University, Columbus.

2014   Frontiers in the Bioarchaeology of Stress and Disease: Cross-Disciplinary Perspectives from Pathophysiology, Human Biology, and Epidemiology. *American Journal of Physical Anthropology* 155(2):294–308.

Klaus, H. D., and M. E. Tam
2009   Contact in the Andes: Bioarchaeology of Systemic Stress in Colonial Mórrope, Peru. *American Journal of Physical Anthropology* 138:356–368.

Krieger, N.
2005   Embodiment: A Conceptual Glossary for Epidemiology. *Journal of Epidemiology and Community Health* 59:350–355.

Larsen, C. S., A. W. Crosby, M. C. Griffin, D. L. Hutchinson, C. B. Ruff, K. F. Russell, M. J. Schoeninger, E. Sering, S. W. Simpson, J. L. Takas, and M. L. Teaford
2002   A Biohistory of the Georgia Bight: The Agricultural Transition and the Impact of European Contact. In *The Backbone of History: Health and Nutri-*

tion in the Western Hemisphere, edited by R. H. Steckel and J. C. Rose, pp. 406–439. Cambridge University Press, Cambridge.

Lightfoot, K. G.

2005   *Indians, Missionaries, and Merchants: The Legacy of Colonial Encounters on the California Frontiers*. University of California Press, Berkeley.

Lockhart, J.

1968   *Spanish Peru, 1532–1560: A Colonial Society*. University of Wisconsin Press, Madison.

1991   Trunk Lines and Feeder Lines. In *Transatlantic Encounters: Europeans and Andeans in the Sixteenth Century*, edited by K. Andrien and R. Adorno, pp. 90–120. University of California Press, Berkeley.

Loren, D. D.

2008   *In Contact: Bodies and Spaces in the Sixteenth- and Seventeeth-Century Eastern Woodlands*. Altamira, New York.

Lovell, N. C.

2008   Analysis and Interpretation of Skeletal Trauma. In *Biological Anthropology of the Human Skeleton*, edited by M. A. Katzenberg and S. R. Saunders, pp. 341–386. 2nd ed. New York, Wiley-Liss.

Lyons, C. L., and J. K. Papadopoulos

2002   *The Archaeology of Colonialism*. Getty Research Institute, Los Angeles.

MacCormack, S.

1991   *Religion in the Andes: Vision and Imagination in Early Colonial Peru*. Princeton University Press, Princeton.

Malpass, M. (editor)

1993   *Provincial Inca: Archaeological and Ethnohistorical Assessment of the Impact of the Inca State*. University of Iowa Press, Iowa City.

Malpass, M., and S. Alconini (editors)

2010   *Distant Provinces in the Inca Empire: Toward a Deeper Understanding of Inka Imperialism*. University of Iowa Press, Iowa City.

Margerison, B. J., and C. J. Knüsel

2002   Paleodemographic Comparison of a Catastrophic and an Attritional Death Assemblage. *American Journal of Physical Anthropology* 119:134–148.

Massey, D.

1992   Politics and Space/Time. *New Left Review* 196:65–84.

Meddens, F. M., and K. Schreiber

2010   Inca Strategies of Control: A Comparison of the Inca Occupations of Soras and Andamarca Lucanas. *Ñawpa Pacha* 30:127–166.

Menzel, D.

1959   The Inca Occupation of the South Coast of Peru. *Southwestern Journal of Anthropology* 15:125–142.

Morris, C.

1998   Inka Strategies of Incorporation and Governance. In *Archaic States*, edited by G. Feinman and J. Marcus, pp. 293–309. School for Advanced Research Press, Santa Fe.

Morris, C., and D. Thompson
1985   *Huánuco Pampa: An Inca City and Its Hinterland*. Thames and Hudson, London

Murphy, M. S.
2004   From Bare Bones to Mummified: Understanding Health and Disease in an Inca Community. Unpublished PhD dissertation, Department of Anthropology, University of Pennsylvania.

Murphy, M. S., and M. F. Boza
2016   Convertiendo a los vivos, disputando a los muertos: Evangelización, identidad y los ancestros. In *Definiendo el derrotero: Posibilidades y perspectivas para una arqueología histórica en el Perú*, edited by R. Alvarez-Calderón, Z. Chase, A. Traslaviña, N. Van Valkenburgh, and B. Weaver. Fondo Editorial PUCP, Lima.

Murphy, M. S., C. M. Gaither, E. Goycochea, J. W. Verano, and G. A. Cock
2010   Violence and Weapon-Related Trauma at Puruchuco-Huaquerones, Peru. *American Journal of Physical Anthropology* 142:636–650.

Murphy, M. S., E. Goycochea, and G. A. Cock
2011   Persistence, Resistance and Accommodation at Puruchuco-Huaquerones, Peru. In *Enduring Conquests: Rethinking the Archaeology of Resistance to Spanish Colonialism in the Americas*, edited by M. Liebmann and M. S. Murphy, pp. 57–76. School for Advanced Research Press, Santa Fe.

Murphy, M. S., B. Spatola, and R. Weathermon
2014   Allies Today, Enemies Tomorrow: A Comparative Analysis of Perimortem Injuries along the Biomechanical Continuum. In *Bioarchaeological and Forensic Case Studies of Violence: How Violent Death Is Interpreted from Skeletal Remains*, edited by D. Martin and C. Anderson, pp. 261–288. Cambridge University Press, Cambridge.

Neville, B. W., D. D. Damm, C. M. Allen, and J. E. Bouquot
2002   *Oral and Maxillofacial Pathology*. 2nd ed. W. B. Saunders, Philadelphia.

Ortner, D.
2003   *Identification of Pathological Conditions in Human Skeletal Remains*. Academic Press, Amsterdam.

Pärssinen, M.
2003   *Tawantinsuyu: El estado Inca y su organización política*. Instituto Francés de Estudios Andinos, Lima.

Powers, K. V.
1995   *Andean Journeys: Migration, Ethnogenesis, and the State in Colonial Quito*. University of New Mexico Press, Albuquerque.

Prince, P.
2002   Cultural Coherency and Resistance in Historic-Period Northwest-Coast Mortuary Practices at Kimsquit. *Historical Archaeology* 36(4):50–64.

Quilter, J. (editor)
2017   *Magdalena de Cao: An Early Colonial Town on the North Coast of Peru*. Peabody Museum Press, Harvard University, Cambridge.

Ramos, G.
2010   *Death and Conversion in the Andes: Lima and Cuzco, 1532–1670.* University of Notre Dame Press, Notre Dame.

Roach, J.
2010   Mummy Bundles, Child Sacrifices Found on Pyramid. National Geographic News. Electronic document, http://news.nationalgeographic.com/news/2010/10/photogalleries/101025-mummies-wari-peru-lima-pyramid-science-pictures, accessed May 20, 2014.

Rostworowski, M.
1975   Pescadores, artesanos y mercaderes costeños en el Perú prehispánico. *Revista del Museo Nacional* 41: 311–349.

1978   *Señorío indigenas de Lima y Canta.* Instituto de Estudios Peruanos, Lima.

2002   *Pachacamac: Obras completas II.* Instituto de Estudios Peruanos, Lima.

Rothschild, N. A.
2008   Colonised Bodies, Personal and Social. In *Past Bodies: Body-Centered Research in Archaeology,* edited by B. Borić and J. Robb, pp. 135–144. Oxbow Books, Oxford.

Rowe, J. H.
1956   Archaeological Explorations in Southern Peru, 1954–1955. *American Antiquity* 22:135–150.

1982   Inca Policies and Institutions Relating to the Cultural Unification of the Empire. In *The Inca and Aztec States, 1400–1800: Anthropology and History,* edited by G. A. Collier, R. I. Rosaldo, and J. D. Wirth, pp. 93–118. Academic Press, New York.

Rupertone, P. E.
2001   *Grave Undertakings: Roger Williams and the Narragansett Indians.* Smithsonian Institution Press, Washington, D.C.

Salomon, F.
1995   "The Beautiful Grandparents": Andean Ancestor Shrines and Mortuary Ritual as Seen through Colonial Records. In *Tombs for the Living,* edited by T. Dillehay, pp. 315–353. Dumbarton Oaks, Washington, D.C.

Sandweiss, D.
1992   *The Archaeology of the Chincha Fishermen: Specialization and Status in Inka Peru.* Bulletin of the Carnegie Museum of National History, Pittsburgh.

Sauer, N.
1998   The Timing of Injuries and Manner of Death: Distinguishing among Antemortem, Perimortem, and Postmortem Trauma. In *Forensic Osteology,* edited by K. Reichs, pp. 321–332. Charles Thomas, Springfield, Illinois.

Schreiber, K.
1987   Conquest and Consolidation: A Comparison of the Wari and Inca Occupations of a Highland Peruvian Valley. *American Antiquity* 52:266–284.

1992   *Wari Imperialism in Middle Horizon Peru.* Museum of Anthropology, University of Michigan, Ann Arbor.

2005   Imperial Agendas and Local Agency. In *The Archaeology of Colonial Encounters: Comparative Perspectives,* edited by Gil Stein, pp. 237–262. School of American Research Press, Santa Fe.

Shimada, I.
1991   *Pachacamac Archaeology: Retrospect and Prospect. Pachacamac: A Reprint of the 1903 Edition by Max Uhle.* University Museum Monograph 62. University Museum of Archaeology and Anthropology, University of Pennsylvania, Philadelphia.

Silliman, S.
2009   Change and Continuity, Practice and Memory: Native American Persistence in Colonial New England. *American* Antiquity 74(2):211–230.

Spalding, K.
1999   The Crises and Transformations of Invaded Societies: Andean Area (1500–1580). In *The Cambridge History of the Native Peoples of the Americas,* edited by F. Salomon and S. B. Schwartz, pp. 904–972. Cambridge University Press, Cambridge.

Stein, G. (editor)
2005   *The Archaeology of Colonial Encounters: Comparative Perspectives.* School of American Research Press, Santa Fe.

Stoler, A. L.
2002   *Carnal Knowledge and Imperial Power: Race and the Intimate in Colonial Rule.* University of California Press, Berkeley.

Stoller, P.
1994   Embodying Colonial Memories. *American Anthropologist* 96(3):634–649.

Stuart-Macadam, P.
1985   Porotic Hyperostosis: Representative of a Childhood Condition. *American Journal of Physical Anthropology* 66(4):391–398.

Tabío, E.
1965   Una tumba tardía de Puruchuco, Lima. In *Excavaciones en la costa central del Perú, 1955–1958,* edited by E. Tabío, pp. 91–101. Academia de Ciencias de Cuba, Departamento de Antropologia, Havana.

Tung, T.
2012   *Violence, Ritual, and the Wari Empire: A Social Bioarchaeology of Imperialism in the Ancient Andes.* University Press of Florida, Gainesville.

van Deusen, N. E.
2010   Diasporas, Bondage, and Intimacy in Lima, 1535 to 1555. *Colonial Latin American Review* 19(2):247–277.

van Dommelen, P.
2006   Colonial Matters: Material Cultural and Postcolonial Theory in Colonial Situations. In *Handbook of Material Culture,* edited by C. Tilley, W. Keane, S. Kuchler, M. Rowlands, and P. Spyer, pp. 104–124. Sage, London.

Vega, J. J.
1980   *Incas contra Españoles.* Pacific Press, Lima.

Villacorta Ostolaza, L. F.
2001   Arquitectura monumental, forma, función y poder: Los asentamientos del valle medio bajo del Rímac. Unpublished Master's thesis, Pontificia Universidad Católica del Perú, Lima.

2004   Los palacios en la costa central durante los periodos tardios: De Pachacamac al Inca. *Bulletin de l'Institut Français d'Études Andines* 33:539–570.

Vitelli, G.

2009   *Equilibrium, Well-being, and Exchange: The Basis of Algonquian Mortuary Practice in Seventeenth Century Southern New England.* PhD dissertation, Department of Archaeology, University of Reading, Reading, England.

Waldron, T.

1994   *Counting the Dead: The Epidemiology of Skeletal Populations.* Wiley, Chichester, U.K.

Walker, P. L., R. R. Bathhurst, R. Richman, T. Gjerdrum, and V. A. Andrushko

2009   The Causes of Porotic Hyperostosis and Cribra Orbitalia: A Reappraisal of the Iron-Deficiency-Anemia Hypothesis. *American Journal of Physical Anthropology* 139:109–125.

Wallace, D. T.

1998   The Inca Compound at La Centinela, Chincha. *Andean Past* 5:9–33.

White, R.

1991   *The Middle Ground: Indians, Empires and Republics in the Great Lakes Region, 1650–1815.* Cambridge University Press, Cambridge.

White, T. D., M. T. Black, and P. Folkens

2011   *Human Osteology.* 3rd ed. Academic Press, New York.

Williams, J. S.

2005   *Investigating Diet and Dietary Change Using the Stable Isotopes of Carbon and Nitrogen in Mummified Tissues from Puruchuco-Huaquerones, Peru.* Ph.D. dissertation, Department of Anthropology. University of Calgary, Calgary.

Williams, J. S., and M. S. Murphy

2013   Living and Dying as Subjects of the Inca Empire: Diet and Health at Puruchuco-Huaquerones, Peru. *Journal of Anthropological Archaeology* 32:165–179.

Young, R.

1995   *Colonial Desire: Hybridity in Theory, Culture and Race.* Routledge, New York.

3

New Kingdom Egyptian Colonialism in Nubia at the Third Cataract

A Diachronic Examination of Sociopolitical Transition (1750–650 B.C.)

MICHELE R. BUZON AND STUART TYSON SMITH

Much of the research on colonialism in the past has focused on the interaction between European colonizers and the native peoples of the New World, in part because of the burst of scholarly activity that marked the Columbus Quincentenary. These studies contributed significantly to our understanding of the circumstances and results of contact between these groups, including several important bioarchaeological studies (e.g., Verano and Ubelaker 1992). However, despite the substantial research, the paradigm of first contact between Europeans and North American natives has only limited usefulness for the examinations of long-term contact situations, especially in other regions and time periods (Hill 1998). Fundamental differences exist between the Quincentennial model and circumstances between familiar local polities, and this necessitates alternative views of culture contact (Smith 1998). For instance, colonial interactions can be found in groups with histories of political, economic, and social relations that spanned many centuries or millennia. Additionally, the catastrophe of introduced disease and the development of capitalism and the modern world system are lacking in many of these alternative examples (Smith 1998).

In the New World, not all colonial studies involve European powers. Considerable excellent research has broadened our understanding of the colonial relationship between indigenous groups and more local foreign powers such as the Aztec, Inca, Wari, Zapotec, and Maya (i.e., Covey et al. 2013, King 2012; Murphy et al., this volume; Oland 2012; Rodríguez-Alegría

2012; Schreiber 2005; Wernke 2012). In the Old World, alternatives to the first contact model include, among others, the Roman Empire, involving a situation in which the Romans and the people they conquered had been already familiar with each other's similarities in material culture, technology, social organization, religion, and ritual (Gardner 2007; Wells 1998). An additional example, which is the focus of this chapter, is the relationship between ancient Egypt and Nubia in the Nile Valley, where the conquerors and conquered were familiar with each other and where political tactics by each side varied over the many centuries of interaction.

Despite the differences in the European/New World model, some of the recent theoretical frameworks in this area are valuable in approaching research (see Winkler et al., this volume). As Stein (2005) noted, each colonial situation is unique. As a result, the relationship is dependent on the colonizer, host, colony, precontact situation, goals and methods of the colonizer, and the reaction of the colonized (see alternative contact situation in Danforth et al., this volume). Models of cultural entanglement emphasize the impact of the intertwining on the colonial power and indigenous groups, taking into account agency on both sides, despite the unequal relationship (Dietler 1998, 2010; Hall 1993; Perry, this volume; Smith 2013; Stahl 2002; Thomas 1991; Tiesler and Zabala, this volume). Hart et al. (2012) suggest that it is important to examine the processes of transition—how events and relations have been shaped by indigenous agency. Such "decolonized archaeology of transitions" views indigenous histories as continuous rather than focusing on the colonial encounter as a defining moment (Silliman 2005). Rubertone (2012) also emphasizes the need to examine groups before, during, and after the colonial relationship, as archaeological materials can provide evidence of lived experiences and long-term processes that are unattainable in written texts. Lightfoot (2012) highlights the constant interchange during the course of long-term colonial entanglements that can result in transformations of foreigners and indigenous peoples into a broader heterogeneous population. Material culture, practices, and the people themselves become intertwined through an active process of intercultural consumption and interaction (Buzon 2006a; Dietler 2010; Smith 2013).

Through an integrated bioarchaeological approach (Buzon 2012), this study combines archaeological data from skeletal remains and material culture in a carefully contextualized analysis of patterns and residues that can shed light on lived experiences and practices (Smith 2013). Specifically, the present research examines burials from Upper Nubia at the Third Cataract of the Nile River that were interred before, during, and after the New Kingdom Egyptian (1500–1050 B.C.) colonial occupation of Upper Nubia (Figure 3.1). Via the analysis of mortuary practices, strontium isotope indications of geographic origins, biological affinities, skeletal evidence of traumatic injuries and activity patterns, and indicators of nutritional deficiency and infectious disease, we create a diachronic picture of life for Nubians and Egyptians in this area as they experienced various transitions in their social, political, and economic relations over the course of a millennium.

HISTORICAL BACKGROUND OF INTERACTION BETWEEN NUBIA AND EGYPT

Nubia consists of the southern third of Egypt (which today is inundated by the reservoir of the Aswan High Dam) and northern Sudan, stretching from the First to Sixth Cataracts of the Nile. The granite cataracts created a navigational obstacle that also marked key cultural boundaries and political borders both between Egypt and Nubia, and within Nubia itself (Figure 3.1). Relations between Egypt, Lower (northern) Nubia, and Upper (southern) Nubia varied over time, shifting between Egyptian and Nubian dominance (Adams 1977; Edwards 2004; Morkot 1987; O'Connor 1993; Smith 1995, 2003; Török 1997; Trigger 1976). Nubia possessed many resources desired by Egypt, including gold in the Eastern Desert and Nile Valley and numerous items to the south, including ebony, panther skins, ivory, monkeys, giraffes, wood, cattle, dates, and palm nuts (Smith 1998; Zibelius-Chen 1983).

Evidence for contact between these groups in the Nile Valley begins with the Nubian A-Group, a stratified complex chiefdom located in Lower Nubia, interacting with Egyptians in the Predynastic era (ca. 3500 B.C.) through the trade of luxury and staple goods. The A-Group consciously borrowed some Egyptian motifs while maintaining a very distinct culture of their own. The collapse of the A-Group was likely precipitated by punitive Egyptian campaigns (ca. 2900 B.C.) in the Early Dynastic and Old Kingdom Periods. After a hiatus (ca. 2400 B.C.), Lower Nubia was reoccupied by people referred to as the C-Group, who traded mercenaries and other workers in exchange for goods with Egypt. In Upper Nubia, the increasingly complex and centralized Kerma culture engaged in a thriving trade with Egypt. In response to Kerma's surging strength, Egypt commenced its first considerable imperial expansion by building a chain of fortresses from its border south to the Second Cataract, securing Lower Nubia during the

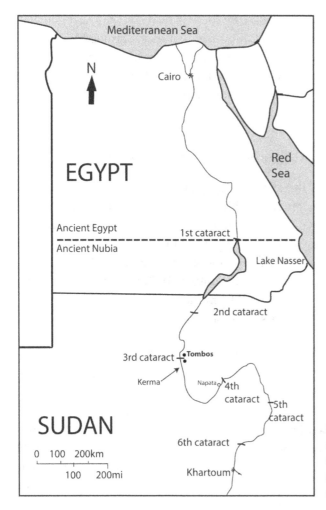

Figure 3.1. Location of Tombos and sites mentioned in the study (map by Michele R. Buzon).

Middle Kingdom Period (ca. 2040–1650 B.C.) (Edwards 2004; O'Connor 1993; Smith 1998, 2003, 2013).

However, by 1680 B.C., Nubians centered at Kerma expanded their control into Lower Nubia, where C-Group and Egyptian expatriates ultimately recognized Kerma as the ruling power. This intense Kerman threat was eventually defeated by Egypt by approximately 1500 B.C. The New Kingdom pharaohs reconquered Lower Nubia and invaded Upper Nubia. North of the Third Cataract, colonial towns were established, ending at Tombos, just 10 km from the former capital at Kerma. Lower Nubian elites were co-opted and drawn into the Egyptian cultural sphere. Local Upper Nubians rulers were allowed more autonomy in a more hegemonic imperial system

(Morkot 2001, 2013; Smith 2003). By roughly 1070 B.C., the Egyptian New Kingdom Empire collapsed. Within a few centuries, a strong Nubian ruler emerged at Napata near the Fourth Cataract. Soon after, circa 728 B.C., the Napatans had conquered Egypt, ruling as the Twenty-Fifth Dynasty of Egypt for a century (Edwards 2004; O'Connor 1993; Morkot 2013; Smith 1998, 2003, 2013).

BIOARCHAEOLOGY IN UPPER NUBIA AT THE THIRD CATARACT

This study examines the effects of Egyptian colonial activities in Nubia, specifically in the region of the Third Cataract of the Nile. This area was an important strategic boundary between Egypt's direct and hegemonic imperial strategies, as Tombos is the southernmost colonial establishment. Egyptians served in governmental positions in these colonial towns in Nubia (Kemp 1978; Morkot 2001, 2013; Smith 2003; Török 1995); presumably, these administrators brought with them support staff members such as officers, scribes, and civil workers, in addition to lower-class settlers who worked as farmers, hunters, crafts specialists, and servants (Adams 1984; Hayes 1973; Kemp 1978; Trigger 1976). Families of Nubian origin who had settled in Egypt during earlier times may also have been present in the New Kingdom colonial towns in Nubia (Säve-Söderbergh and Troy 1991).

Excavations at Tombos by the authors through the University of California, Santa Barbara (2000–present), and Purdue University (2010–present) are currently ongoing. The New Kingdom component discussed in this study was primarily excavated in 2000 and 2002; several Egyptian-style mudbrick chamber and pit tombs, which appear middle-class in nature, were excavated in addition to a large Egyptian-style pyramid, the burial place of Siamun, Scribe-Reckoner of the Gold of Kush, a third-level Egyptian administrator (Smith 2003). The use of the cemetery at Tombos began in the mid-Eighteenth Dynasty, circa 1400 B.C. Human skeletal remains excavated at Tombos are curated at Purdue University. Approximately one hundred discrete individuals and intact crania that date to the New Kingdom Period are included in this study, primarily from the middle-class area.

As stated above, a long-term diachronic approach is best in order understand the transition that occurred as a result of colonial relationships. Burials dating prior to the New Kingdom Egyptian occupation of Nubia are not present at Tombos, though in the coming years our ongoing project will be investigating a nearby Nubian cemetery at Akkad, located just across the river from Tombos. As a baseline for the Third Cataract region before Egyptian occupation, this study uses human skeletal remains that were excavated at Kerma, located just south of Tombos at the Third Cataract. As the capital of a powerful state in Upper Nubia, Kerma was a large urban center occupied for approximately one thousand years (2500–1500 B.C.) (Bonnet 1990) with extensive agricultural and pastoral production. Burials excavated by Reisner (1923) date to the Kerma Classic Period (ca. 1750–1550 B.C.) and are housed at the Duckworth Laboratory at the University of Cambridge. Approximately three hundred individuals were available for study. The Tombos cemetery was used continually from the colonial New Kingdom Period through the Napatan Period (Smith 2007; Smith and Buzon 2014), allowing for examination of the postcolonial period. Approximately fifty intact individuals or crania dating the Third Intermediate and Napatan Periods (ca. 1070–650 B.C.) excavated in 2010 and 2011 are examined here.

INDICATIONS OF IDENTITY AT THE THIRD CATARACT

CULTURAL IDENTITY

We examine the cultural dynamics of the colonial period in this region through evidence for intercultural interaction and cultural entanglements. Older acculturation models seen in Quincentennial studies that emphasize the dominant European culture transforming a passive Native American culture have been reevaluated, as discussed above. Similarly, Egyptological ideas that emphasized the use of ancient Egyptian material culture and emulation of Egyptian practices by Nubians as representing a natural acculturation toward a more sophisticated and therefore inherently appealing Egyptian culture (David 1988; Emery 1965; Grimal 1992) have also been challenged (Morkot 1995; Smith 1997, 1998; Török 1997; Yellen 1995). Instead of focusing on a dominant core and passive periphery, our approach takes a bottom-up agent-centered perspective to examine the intertwining of the historical trajectories of Egypt and the Nubian Kerma culture by tracing cultural threads and taking into consideration the process of adoption, adaptation, rejection, or indifference in intercultural borrowing (Dietler 2010; Silliman 2009).

Before the New Kingdom Egyptian colonial period in Nubia, Kerma burial practices were quite distinct from those of their Egyptian neighbors. Burial practices at Kerma include a flexed body position with head to the east facing north, placed on his or her side upon a bed and/or cow's skin. The body was buried under a tumulus, or a circular mound often decorated with stones with some built up using masonry (Bonnet 1990; Edwards 2004; Geus 1991). In contrast, contemporary Egyptian burials follow rituals based on Egyptian theological ideas. Burials were extended with heads to the west and placed in coffins with rectilinear tomb chapels and pyramids for the elite. Specialized grave goods, such as *ushabti* figurines and canopic jars, were included to aid the deceased in the afterlife (Ikram and Dodson 1998; Smith 1992). Egyptian and Nubian pottery styles were also quite dissimilar, with most Egyptian pottery being mass-produced on a slow wheel while Nubian pottery was handmade with elaborate decoration (Gratien 1978; Lacovara 1987). Starting with the Nubian elite, and later the rest of the population, archaeological evidence and Egyptian texts document the use of Egyptian cultural features by Nubians (O'Connor 1993).

At Tombos, the large pyramid tomb of the New Kingdom administrator Siamun and his mother, Weren, reflects contemporary elite burial traditions in Egypt, and is especially typical of tombs found at the Egyptian capital at Thebes with its T-shaped chapel design, east-west alignment, decoration of funerary cones, and clay cones stamped with the name and title of the deceased (Smith 2003; cf. Kampp-Seyfried 2003; Ryan 1988). The middle-class pit and underground mudbrick chamber tombs also follow Egyptian funerary architectural styles with typical communal tombs. Grave goods such as decorated coffins, statuary, and amulets provide evidence for Egyptian funerary beliefs (cf. Grajetzki 2010). The majority of individuals for which burial position could be assessed (ancient looting caused disturbance and commingling) display an Egyptian extended position. However, within this largely culturally Egyptian cemetery, we found four burials of women using Nubian practices. Their bodies were flexed, oriented with head to the east. These burials were found in the communal tombs with Egyptian-style individuals lying above and around them (Figure 3.2). One of these burials included a Kerma-style pot. Nubian pottery was also found in association with Siamun's pyramid. Given that Egyptian burials were public events, we interpret these Nubian burials as individual assertions of Nubian cultural identity within this Egyptian colonial community (Smith 2013) as an indication of the interaction and likely intermarriage between Egyptians and Nubians during the colonial occupation (Buzon 2006a; Smith 2003).

The postcolonial use of the Tombos cemetery reveals cultural entanglements and hybridity in burial practices, including both a strong Nubian

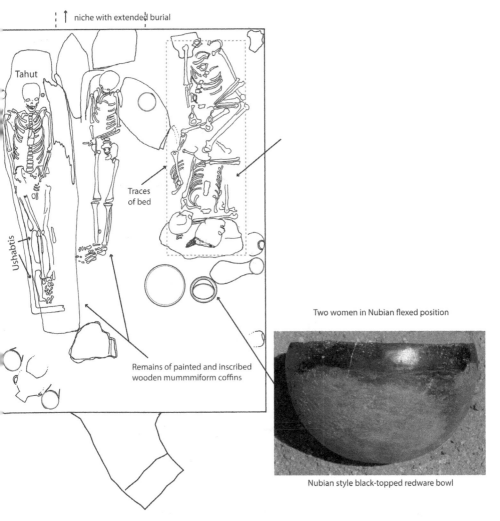

niche with extended burial

Tahut

Ushabtis

Traces
of bed

Two women in Nubian flexed position

Remains of painted and inscribed
wooden mummmiform coffins

Nubian style black-topped redware bowl

Figure 3.2. Egyptian- and Nubian-style burials in New Kingdom Unit 7 at Tombos
(created by Stuart Tyson Smith).

revival and continuity of entrenched Egyptian colonial features. Some
Egyptian-style pyramid tombs continued to be used in the subsequent
Third Intermediate and Napatan Periods in addition to new Egyptian-style
chamber and pyramid tombs. During this postcolonial period, there is also
a new separate zone of Nubian-style tumulus grave features that extend
through the Napatan Period. Within the tumuli, all but two burials were
in the Egyptian extended style with head to the west; however, they were
placed Nubian-style on a bed (Figure 3.3). One woman was found in a

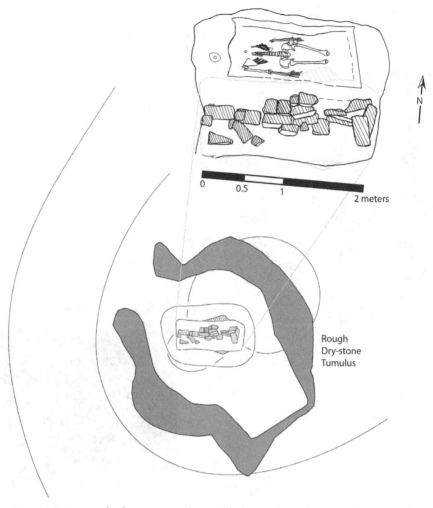

Figure 3.3. Egyptian body position within a Nubian tumulus grave in Third Intermediate Period Unit 3 at Tombos (created by Stuart Tyson Smith).

flexed position on a bed, and one child was extended but with the head to the east. Within the pyramid and chamber tombs, a Napatan burial demonstrated both Egyptian and Nubian features with an extended burial in a coffin placed on a bed with a group of tall red polished beakers using Egyptian technology—but shaped and decorated in Nubian ceramic traditions (in this case, a black-topped design echoing a popular motif from Kerma). Imported copper alloy bowls with running bulls in the Iron Age Levantine "international style" and an elaborate openwork box with a motif referencing the cow-goddess Hathor reflect the Nubian preference for and long-standing religious emphasis on cattle (Smith 2006, 2013). This postcolonial component reflects a multicultural mosaic of Egyptian and Nubian cultural features in their burial practices (Smith and Buzon 2014; for other examples, see, in this volume, Guichón et al., Harvey et al., Klaus and Alvarez-Calderón, and Tiesler and Zabala).

GEOGRAPHIC IDENTITY

With the known use of Egyptian cultural features by Nubians in burial practices, determining the biocultural composition of the Tombos colonial population is challenging. Were the four women who were buried using Nubian practices the only Nubians buried in the cemetery, or did some local Nubians choose to be buried using Egyptian practices? As an alternative means of identifying immigrants and locals in the Tombos sample, strontium isotope ($^{87}Sr/^{86}Sr$) analysis was employed (Buzon and Simonetti 2013; Buzon et al. 2007). Strontium isotope analysis is based on the phenomenon that the strontium present in food and water ingested by people reflects the geological age and bedrock composition of the region from which they originate (Faure 1986). While additional baseline data for strontium isotope signatures in the Nile Valley region are still needed, Buzon and Simonetti (2013) indicate that it may be possible to identify the presence of Egyptian immigrants in Nubian sites at the Third Cataract (Figure 3.4).

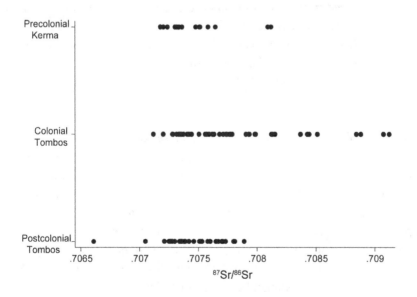

Figure 3.4. Strontium isotope values at Kerma and Tombos.

Egyptian sites have higher median $^{87}Sr/^{86}Sr$ values (0.70777) than Nubian sites (0.70757); median $^{87}Sr/^{86}Sr$ values decrease from north to south from Memphis, Egypt, to Kerma, Nubia (Buzon and Simonetti 2013).

Fifteen individuals from Kerma were analyzed for strontium isotope ratios (Buzon and Simonetti 2013). The Kerma samples have a fairly restricted range from $^{87}Sr/^{86}Sr$ = 0.70718–0.70764, with one outlier at $^{87}Sr/^{86}Sr$ = 0.70809 (mean = 0.70748, median = 0.70736). New Kingdom colonial Tombos samples do not follow this same pattern. Colonial samples range from 0.70712–0.70912. The Tombos $^{87}Sr/^{86}Sr$ local range was determined to be 0.70710–0.70783. Of the 53 colonial Tombos samples, 18 (34 percent) were above this local range, indicating that they could be immigrant Egyptians, given their higher $^{87}Sr/^{86}Sr$ values (Buzon and Simonetti 2013); all of the individuals with higher $^{87}Sr/^{86}Sr$ values were buried using Egyptian practices. While the group of individuals sampled for this analysis is only a small proportion of the total individuals buried at Tombos during the colonial period, this study suggests that a significant number of local Nubians and the offspring of Egyptian immigrants born at Tombos are included in the cemetery population. This finding supports the idea that local Nubians were buried at Tombos using Egyptian practices along with some local Nubians who adhered to their native rituals. In contrast, the postcolonial sample at Tombos shows a more restricted $^{87}Sr/^{86}Sr$ range (0.70661–0.70789) that is more similar to Kerma, indicating that Egyptian immigration to Tombos ceased in the postcolonial period. Two individuals have $^{87}Sr/^{86}Sr$ values that are below the established local range; $^{87}Sr/^{86}Sr$ data for sites upstream from Tombos are scarce, though preliminary work suggests these lower values could be similar to Fourth Cataract region were Napata was located (Buzon and Simonetti 2013).

BIOLOGICAL IDENTITY

As a complementary method to the analyses of cultural entanglements evidenced by burial practices and geographic indications of locale, the biological affinities of the Tombos colonial sample have also been evaluated (Buzon 2004, 2006a). Using cranial measurements on intact crania, the Tombos sample was compared with other contemporary skeletal samples from Nile Valley sites in order to investigate the composition of the burial population. As a reference, cranial measurements were analyzed in groups of Egyptian burials from Egyptian sites (Memphis, Qurneh, Abydos, Sheikh Ali) and Nubian burials from Nubian sites (C-Group, Kerma) using principal components analysis and logistic regression (descriptions

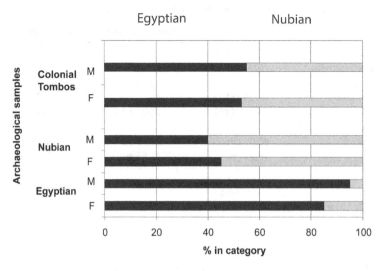

Figure 3.5. Logistic regression of cranial remains from Tombos and comparative Egyptian and Nubian samples.

of the summary data and samples can be found in Buzon 2006a). Egyptians were found to be a more distinct, homogeneous group who were classified correctly much more frequently than the Nubians, who were a more heterogeneous group with approximately half classified as Egyptian and half as Nubian (Buzon 2006a). While the process of differentiating Egyptian and Nubian crania is less than straightforward, these results suggest that the Tombos sample could be compared with the other Egyptian groups in order to determine if there is a large local Nubian component included (Figure 3.5).

The analysis of the Tombos colonial sample indicates that approximately half could be classified as Egyptian. This finding indicates that the colonial town included a substantial number of Nubians in addition to immigrant Egyptians. An alternative interpretation could be that Tombos is composed primarily of Nubians, as the classification is similar to what is seen in Nubian (C-Group and Kerma) samples (Buzon 2004, 2006a). However, given the context of the Tombos cemetery with its strict adherence to Egyptian burial practices in the structure of Siamun's pyramid and other tombs, as well as textual information regarding colonists in Nubia, it seems more likely that both Egyptian immigrant colonists and local Nubians were buried at Tombos (Buzon 2006a; Smith 2003). While the craniometric analysis of the Third Intermediate Period and Napatan Period individuals is

Table 3.1. Paleopathological analyses in Third Cataract adults

	Precolonial Kerma	Colonial Tombos	Postcolonial Tombos
Cranial injuries	21/187 (11%)	1/72 (1%)	
Ulna parry fractures	14/23 (61%)	1/7 (14%)	
Enamel hypoplasia	14/66 (21%)	12/52 (23%)	5/32 (16%)
Cribra orbitalia	39/293 (13%)	3/69 (4%)[a,b]	8/42 (19%)
Osteoperiostitis	47/107 (45%)	6/31 (19%)	6/24 (25%)
Maximum femur length			
Female	43.05 cm	41.93 cm[b]	44.14 cm
Male	46.35 cm	43.82 cm[a]	45.59 cm

Note: Data from Buzon 2006a, 2014.
[a]Statistically lower than precolonial Kerma
[b]Statistically lower than postcolonial Tombos

ongoing, a study examining dental nonmetric traits in the sample reveals similarities between the postcolonial Tombos sample and other Egyptian and Nubian groups; the postcolonial Tombos population is likely the descendants of the mixed Egyptian-Nubian community that began in the colonial period (Schrader et al. 2014; see also Ribot et al., this volume).

PALEOPATHOLOGICAL ANALYSES

Within the context of the data presented above regarding various indicators of identity and entanglement between Egyptians and Nubians at Tombos, the goal of paleopathological analyses of these samples is to provide a glimpse of how the daily lives of the Third Cataract inhabitants were affected by these sociopolitical changes. How does a culturally and biologically mixed group of Egyptian and Nubians in the colonial Tombos community compare to the precolonial local Nubians at Kerma? Did the descendants of colonial Tombos in the postcolonial sample experience similar conditions? This section will diachronically consider activity patterns, traumatic injuries, nutrition, and infection within the precolonial (Buzon 2006b), colonial (Buzon 2006b), and postcolonial (Buzon 2014) Third Cataract samples. Due to the paucity of juveniles in all samples, only adults are examined here (see Table 3.1).

EVIDENCE OF HABITUAL PHYSICAL ACTIVITY

One of the Egyptian Empire's chief imperial goals was access to trade goods. High-value bulk trade goods made up a significant part of the ancient trade, including wine, olive oil, wood, resins, and textiles. Additionally, metals were extremely important for Egypt. For example, the Nubian gold obtained for the Temple of Amun at Thebes could support 9,000–17,000 workers for a year; this was a small fraction of the total amount of gold shipped to Egypt (Smith 1995). Siamun's titles suggest an involvement in assembling the annual tribute payment from the conquered territory, especially gold (Morkot 2013; Smith 2003). The acquisition of goods and demand for tribute have the potential to transform the political economy affecting community structure, patterns of production, and organization of labor, which may alter everyday activities of the host polity population (Brumfiel 1991; D'Altroy and Hastorf 2001; Lightfoot et al. 1998; Silliman 2001). While Trigger (1976) argued that Egyptian expansion had a negative effect on Nubian labor, others (Morkot 2001; O'Connor 1993; Török 1995) have proposed that local activities were relatively uninterrupted and interactions were positive. How were the everyday lives of people at the Third Cataract altered by these sociopolitical transitions? Possible changes over time are examined via entheseal remodeling and osteoarthritis, markers of strenuous physical activity.

The skeletal sample from Kerma shows the highest mean entheseal marker scores out of numerous skeletal samples in Nubia. In addition, osteoarthritis levels are high compared to other regional groups (Schrader 2012). The evidence for arduous physical labor in the Kerma samples is likely accounted for by the agro-pastoral economy in the fertile floodplain, which would have required intensive agriculture and animal husbandry (Adams 1977; Morkot 2001). In contrast, colonial Tombos consistently had very low mean entheseal marker scores (Schrader 2012), similar to what was found in a colonial cemetery in Lower Nubia (Scandinavian Joint Expedition to Nubia Pharaonic sample) (Schrader 2013; see also Klaus and Alvarez-Calderón, this volume). Osteoarthritis levels were also found to be very low in colonial Tombos (Schrader 2012). The data indicate that the colonial Tombos sample engaged in limited levels of intense habitual physical activity. These individuals were likely members of the middle to upper socioeconomic class who served as bureaucrats, professionals, and tradespeople (Schrader 2012). In the postcolonial Tombos sample, entheseal remodeling and osteoarthritis scores are higher in comparison with the colonial sample, indicating more-strenuous long-term activities in the group. After the collapse of the Egyptian Empire, the flow of resources may have decreased, necessitating an increase in agricultural labor to support the population. The extraction of granite from nearby quarries in the cataract area (Harrell 1999) may have provided an additional source of income (Schrader 2013).

INTERPERSONAL VIOLENCE AND TRAUMATIC INJURIES

Previous research investigating violent injuries during conquest and warfare (e.g., Klaus 2012; Larsen and Milner 1994; Martin and Frayer 1997; Murphy et al. 2010) has found wide variation in the evidence for interpersonal violence during the colonial process. What role did violent conflict play in the Egyptian occupation of Nubia? Cranial injuries and parry fractures are used here as measures of violent conflict (Angel 1974; Lambert 1997; Wood-Jones 1910).

Precolonial Kerma reveals a high rate of violent injuries: 11 percent (21/187) of individuals had cranial injuries, and 61 percent (14/23) of ulna fractures could be classified as parry fractures (Judd 2004). While the Kerma sample predates the New Kingdom colonial occupation, the sample dates to a period of intense Egyptian-Nubian interaction during the late Middle Kingdom and Second Intermediate Periods. The levels of injuries reflect Egypt's aggressive military campaigns in Nubia (Buzon and Richman 2007; Judd 2004). The colonial Tombos sample portrays a different story for the New Kingdom Period. When compared with Kerma, the colonial Tombos rates are significantly lower: 1 percent (1/72) of crania was injured, and one of seven (14 percent) ulna injuries could be considered a parry fracture. It is clear that the Egyptians altered their colonial strategies during the New Kingdom with the increased use of diplomacy and inclusions of Nubians into the administration, resulting in a more peaceful coexistence (Buzon and Richman 2007). While the analysis of traumatic injuries in the postcolonial Tombos sample is ongoing, preliminary research indicates that the level of injuries remains similarly low, which corresponds with the suggestion that postcolonial Tombos remained prominent within the larger Nubian polity (Buzon 2014; Smith 2006).

EVIDENCE OF NUTRITIONAL DEFICIENCY AND INFECTION

The nonspecific indicators of nutritional deficiency and infection used here include enamel hypoplasia (continuous linear horizontal groove or pits on anterior teeth), cribra orbitalia (coalescing foramina on orbital roof), and osteoperiostitis (osseous plaques of bone with demarcated margins or irregular elevations). Maximum femur length is also presented as a way to evaluate stunted growth during childhood (Buikstra and Ubelaker 1994; Steckel et al. 2002).

At the Third Cataract of the Nile, the landscape of the region changes significantly from what appears to the north. Kerma is located in an area that is considered the most fertile and productive in Nubia. A broad flood-plain allows for significant cultivation with Nile paleochannels that permitted basin irrigation and high agricultural yields (Adams 1977; Welsby 2001; see also Klaus et al., this volume). As an urban center with extensive production, Kerma also traded heavily with Egypt, importing Mediterranean commodities as well as other goods (Bonnet and Valbelle 2006). Thus, the Kerma population likely had considerable access to nutritional resources; however, frequent movement of individuals and goods along the Nile may have allowed for a higher exposure to infectious disease (as also suggested by Perry, this volume, and Killgrove, this volume). The Kerma sample (Buzon 2006b) shows low to moderate rates of these three pathological conditions in both males and females—enamel hypoplasias are found in 21 percent (14/66), cribra orbitalia is found in 13 percent (39/293), and osteoperiostitis is found in 45 percent (47/104). The vast majority of cribra orbitalia and osteoperiostitis cases were healed. Female maximum femur length is 43.05 cm, and male maximum femur length is 46.35 cm (Table 3.1).

Located just 10 km to the north of Kerma, colonial Tombos likely also had excellent agricultural resources. In addition, the incorporation of this colonial town into the Egyptian trade network may have offered supplemental goods (Buzon 2006b). In the Tombos colonial sample, enamel hypoplasia is found in 23 percent (12/52), cribra orbitalia in 4 percent (3/69), and osteoperiostitis in 19 percent (6/31). Female maximum femur length is 41.93 cm, and male maximum femur length is 43.82 cm. Cribra orbitalia and osteoperiostitis lesions all showed evidence of healing. Many of these frequencies are similar to Kerma with only two revealing statistical differences: colonial Tombos has a significantly lower rate of cribra orbitalia, and the male maximum femur length is significant shorter in the Tombos colonial sample (Table 3.1).

Although it has been suggested that the Upper Nubian region was abandoned after the fall of the New Kingdom (Shinnie 1996; Trigger 1976), the Tombos cemetery refutes this idea, showing continued use through the Napatan Period (Buzon 2014; Smith and Buzon 2014). The postcolonial Tombos sample (Table 3.1) displays a rate of 16 percent (5/32) for enamel hypoplasia, 19 percent (8/42) for cribra orbitalia, and 25 percent (6/24) for osteoperiostitis (all healed). The female maximum femur length is 44.14 cm and the male maximum femur length is 45.59 cm (Table 3.1). Again, these frequencies are similar to the precolonial and colonial samples. However, the rate of cribra orbitalia is significantly higher in the postcolonial sample when it is compared with colonial sample, and the postcolonial female maximum femur length is significantly higher than the colonial female length.

Overall, the rates of these conditions are very similar through time at the Third Cataract (Buzon 2006b, 2014; found also by Perry, this volume, and Killgrove, this volume). There is a significantly lower rate of cribra orbitalia in the colonial Tombos sample in comparison to both the precolonial and postcolonial samples. However, the lack of juvenile individuals in these samples meaningfully hampers the interpretation of these data. Based on very small sample sizes, it has been proposed that the high active cribra orbitalia rate in the colonial Tombos juveniles along with the low adult rate indicates that children were not surviving bouts of ill health (Buzon 2006b). Thus, the higher rates of healed cribra orbitalia in the adults could indicate that the precolonial and postcolonial groups may have been better able to recover from these childhood stressors (Buzon 2014; Murphy et al., this volume). The shorter maximum femur length in colonial Tombos (males shorter than precolonial and females shorter than postcolonial) may also provide support, since adult long bone length is strongly influenced by the environment (Tanner 1978). However, the genetic component should also be considered. The colonial Tombos sample includes immigrant Egyptians, who were likely shorter than the Nubians. The postcolonial sample may include larger numbers of Nubians, since the flow of Egyptian immigrants to Nubia ceased after the New Kingdom (Buzon 2014; Buzon and Simonetti 2013; Gibbon and Buzon 2016).

Egyptian-Nubian Interaction at the Third Cataract

The consequences of contact between the Egyptian Empire and Nubians at the Third Cataract of the Nile River are firmly situated within the centuries of interaction between these groups. The previous trade relations and military movements between Egypt and Nubia resulted in outcomes that differ significantly from circumstances of first contact. While the expressions of cultural identity and daily lives of the Nubians in this region may have been altered, physical devastation and destruction of local culture is *not* evident (see also Harvey et al., this volume). Nubians selectively incorporated aspects of Egyptian culture into their expressions and intermarried, resulting in a new entangled biocultural identity (see, in this volume,

Harvey et al., Tiesler and Zabala, and Ribot et al.) in the aftermath of the Egyptian Empire, which ultimately contributed to their success in ruling Egypt in the Napatan Period. The mixed Egyptian-Nubian community at the Third Cataract was successfully and relatively peacefully incorporated into the Egyptian system as reflected in the low levels of physical activities and evidence for infection and nutritional issues. Continuing as an important political center, Tombos may have shifted some activities through the transition from Egyptian to Nubian rule, but it continued to thrive as a community.

ACKNOWLEDGMENTS

Support for excavations at Tombos and analyses was provided by the National Science Foundation (BCS 0917815/0917824, 0313247), the National Geographic Society, the Schiff-Georgini Foundation, University of California Santa Barbara Academic Senate and Institute for Social, Behavioral and Economic Research, American Philosophical Society of Physical Anthropologists, Killam Trust, Institute for Bioarchaeology, Purdue Alumni Foundation and College of Liberals Arts, and donations from James and Louise Bradbury, Nancy Delgado, Francis and Jim Cahill, Jan Bacchi, and Connie Swanson Travel.

We thank the people of Tombos and the National Corporation for Antiquities and Museums in Sudan for their support and assistance during our field seasons, especially Hassan Hussein Idris, Salah Mohammed Ahmed, Abdelrahman Ali Mohamed, and Al-Hassan Ahmed Mohamed. Ali Osman M. Salih (University of Khartoum) and David Edwards (University of Leicester) generously shared the University of Khartoum concession. We are grateful to our Nubian archaeology colleagues and the Acropole Hotel for their assistance and encouragement.

REFERENCES CITED

Adams, W. Y.
1977   *Nubia: Corridor to Africa.* Princeton University Press, Princeton.
1984   The First Colonial Empire: Egypt in Nubia 3200–1200 BC. *Comparative Studies in Sociology and History* 26:36–71.
Angel, J. L.
1974   Patterns of Fractures from Neolithic to Modern Times. *Anthropologiai Kozlemenyek* 18:571–588.

Bonnet, C.

1990   *Kerma Royaume de Nubie: L'antiquité africaine au temps des Pharaons.* Mission archéologique de l'Université de Genève au Soudan, Genève.

Bonnet, C., and D. Valbelle

2006   *The Nubian Pharaohs: Black Kings on the Nile.* American University in Cairo Press, New York.

Brumfiel, E. M.

1991   Tribute and Commerce in Imperial Cities: The Case of Xaltocan, Mexico. In *Early State Economics,* edited by H. Claessen and P. van de Velde, pp. 177–198. Transaction, New Brunswick, N.J.

Buikstra, J., and D. Ubelaker (editors)

1994   *Standards for Data Collection from Human Skeletal Remains.* Arkansas Archaeological Survey Research Series No. 44, Fayetteville.

Buzon, M. R.

2004   A Bioarchaeological Perspective on State Formation in the Nile Valley. Unpublished Ph.D. dissertation, Department of Anthropology, University of California, Santa Barbara.

2006a   Biological and Ethnic Identity in New Kingdom Nubia: A Case Study from Tombos. *Current Anthropology* 47:683–695.

2006b   Health of the Non-elites at Tombos: Nutritional and Disease Stress in New Kingdom Nubia. *American Journal of Physical Anthropology* 130:26–37.

2012   The Bioarchaeological Approach to Paleopathology. In *A Companion to Paleopathology,* edited by A. L. Grauer, pp. 58–75. Wiley-Blackwell, New York.

2014   Tombos during the Napatan Period (~750–660 BC): Exploring the Consequences of Sociopolitical Transitions in Ancient Nubia. *International Journal of Paleopathology* 7:1–7.

Buzon, M. R., and R. Richman

2007   Traumatic Injuries and Imperialism: The Effects of Egyptian Colonial Strategies at Tombos in Upper Nubia. *American Journal of Physical Anthropology* 133:783–791.

Buzon, M. R., and A. Simonetti

2013   Strontium Isotope (^{87}Sr/^{86}Sr) Variability in the Nile Valley: Identifying Residential Mobility during Ancient Egyptian and Nubian Sociopolitical Changes in the New Kingdom and Napatan Periods. *American Journal of Physical Anthropology* 151:1–9.

Buzon, M. R., A. Simonetti, and A. Creaser

2007   Migration in the Nile Valley during the New Kingdom Period: A Preliminary Strontium Isotope Study. *Journal of Archaeological Science* 34:1391–1401.

Covey, R. A., B. S. Bauer, V. Bélisle, and L. Tsesmeli

2013   Regional Perspectives on Wari State Influence in Cusco, Peru (c. AD 600–1000). *Journal of Anthropological Archaeology* 32(4):538–552.

D'Altroy, T. N., and C. A. Hastorf

2001   *Empire and Domestic Economy.* Plenum, New York.

David, A. R.

1988   *Ancient Egypt.* Phaidon, Oxford.

Dietler, M.
1998   Consumption, Agency, and Cultural Entanglement: Theoretical Implications
            of a Mediterranean Colonial Encounter. In *Studies in Culture Contact: Inter-
            action, Culture Change and Archaeology*, edited by J. G. Cusick, pp. 288–315.
            Southern Illinois University Press, Carbondale.
2010   *Archaeologies of Colonialism: Consumption, Entanglement, and Violence in
            Ancient Mediterranean France*. University of California Press, Berkeley.

Edwards, D. N.
2004   *The Nubian Past: An Archaeology of the Sudan*. Routledge, London.

Emery, W. B.
1965   *Egypt in Nubia*. Hutchinson, London.

Faure, G.
1986   *Principles of Isotope Geology*. Wiley-Liss, New York.

Gardner, A.
2007   *An Archaeology of Identity: Soldiers and Society in Late Roman Britain*. Left
            Coast Press, Walnut Creek, California.

Geus, F.
1991   Burial Customs in the Upper Main Nile: An Overview. In *Egypt and Africa*,
            edited by W. V. Davies, pp. 57–83. British Museum Press, London.

Gibbon, V., and M. R. Buzon
2016   Morphometric Assessment of the Appendicular Skeleton in the New King-
            dom and Napatan Components from Tombos in Upper Nubia. *International
            Journal of Osteoarchaeology* 26:324–336.

Grajetzki, W.
2010   Class and Society: Position and Possessions. In *Egyptian Archaeology*, edited
            by W. Wendrich, pp. 180–199. Wiley-Blackwell, Oxford.

Gratien, B.
1978   *Les cultures Kerma: Essai de classification*. Publications de l'Université de
            Lille Villeneuve-d'Ascq.

Grimal, N.
1992   *A History of Ancient Egypt*. Blackwell, Oxford.

Hall, M.
1993   The Archaeology of Colonial Settlement in Southern Africa. *Annual Review
            of Anthropology* 22:177–200.

Harrell, J.
1999   The Tumbos Quarry at the Third Nile Cataract, Northern Sudan. In *Recent
            Research in Kushite History and Archaeology: Proceedings of the 8th Interna-
            tional Conference of Meroitic Studies*, edited by Derek A. Welsby, pp. 239–
            250. British Museum Press, London.

Hart, S. M., M. Oland, and L. Frink
2012   Finding Transitions: Global Pathways to Decolonizing Indigenous Histories
            in Archaeology. In *Decolonizing Indigenous Histories: Exploring Prehistoric/
            Colonial Transitions in Archaeology*, edited by M. Oland, S. M. Hart, and L.
            Frink, pp. 1–15. University of Arizona Press, Tucson.

Hayes, W. C.
1973   Chapter IX—Egypt: Internal Affairs from Tuthmosis I to the Death of
              Amenophis III. In *Cambridge Ancient History, Volume 2, Part 1: The Middle
              East and the Aegean Region, C. 1800–1380 BC,* edited by I. E. S. Edwards, C.
              J. Gadd, N. G. L. Hammond, and E. Sollberger. 3rd ed. Cambridge University
              Press, Cambridge.

Hill, J. D.
1998   Violent Encounters: Ethnogenesis and Ethnocide in Long-Term Contact
              Situations. In *Studies in Culture Contact: Interaction, Culture Change and
              Archaeology,* edited by J. G. Cusick, pp. 146–171. Southern Illinois University
              Press, Carbondale.

Ikram, S., and A. Dodson
1998   *The Mummy in Ancient Egypt: Equipping the Dead for Eternity.* Thames &
              Hudson, New York.

Judd, M.
2004   Trauma in the City of Kerma: Ancient versus Modern Injury Patterns. *International Journal of Osteoarchaeology* 14(1):34–51.

Kampp-Seyfried, F.
2003   The Theban Necropolis: An Overview of Topography and Tomb Development from the Middle Kingdom to the Ramesside Period. In *The Theban
              Necropolis: Past, Present and Future,* edited by N. Strudwick and J. H. Taylor,
              pp. 2–10. British Museum Press, Cambridge.

Kemp, B. J.
1978   Imperialism and Empire in New Kingdom Egypt (c. 1575–1087 B.C.). In *Imperialism in the Ancient World,* edited by P. D. A. Garnsey and C. R. Whittaker. Cambridge University Press, Cambridge.

King, S. M.
2012   Hidden Transcripts, Contested Landscapes, and Long-Term Indigenous History in Oaxaca, Mexico. In *Decolonizing Indigenous Histories: Exploring Prehistoric/Colonial Transitions in Archaeology,* edited by M. Oland, S. M. Hart,
              and L. Frink, pp. 230–263. University of Arizona Press, Tucson.

Klaus, H. D.
2012   Bioarchaeology of Structural Violence: Theoretical Model and Case Study.
              In *The Bioarchaeology of Violence,* edited by D. Martin, R. P. Harrod, and V.
              R. Perez, pp. 29–62. University Press of Florida, Gainesville.

Lacovara, P.
1987   The Internal Chronology of Kerma. *Beiträge zur Sudanforschung* 2:51–74.

Lambert, P. M.
1997   Patterns of Violence in Prehistoric Hunter-Gather Societies of Coastal
              Southern California. In *Troubled Times: Violence and Warfare in the Past,*
              edited by D. L. Martin and D. W. Frayer, pp. 77–110. Gordon and Breach,
              Amsterdam.

Larsen, C. S., and G. R. Milner (editors)
1994   *In the Wake of Contact: Biological Responses to Conquest.* Wiley-Liss, New
              York.

Lightfoot, K. G.
2012   Lost in Transition: A Retrospective. In *Decolonizing Indigenous Histories: Exploring Prehistoric/Colonial Transitions in Archaeology*, edited by M. Oland, S. M. Hart, and L. Frink, pp. 282–298. University of Arizona Press, Tucson.

Lightfoot, K. G., A. Martinez, and A. M. Schiff
1998   Daily Practice and Material Culture in Pluralistic Social Settings: An Archaeological Study of Culture Change and Persistence from Fort Ross, California. *American Antiquity* 63(2):199–222.

Martin, D. L., and D. W. Frayer (editors)
1997   *Troubled Times: Violence and Warfare in the Past*. Gordon and Breach, Amsterdam.

Morkot, R.
1987   Studies in New Kingdom Nubia 1: Politics, Economies and Ideology: Egyptian Imperialism in Nubia. *Wepwawet* (3):29–49.
1995   The Foundations of the Kushite State. *Cahier de Recherches de l'Institut de Papyrologie et d'Égyptologie de Lille* 17:229–242.
2001   Egypt and Nubia. In *Empires: Perspectives from Archaeology and History*, edited by S. E. Alcock, T. N. D'Altroy, K. Morrison, and C. M. Sinopoli, pp. 227–251. Cambridge University Press, Cambridge.
2013   From Conquered to Conqueror: The Organization of Nubia in the New Kingdom and the Kushite Administration of Egypt. In *Ancient Egyptian Administration*, edited by J. C. Moreno García, pp. 911–964. Brill, Leiden.

Murphy, M. S., C. Gaither, E. Goycochea, J. Verano, and G. Cock
2010   Violence and Weapon-Related Trauma at Puruchuco-Huaquerones, Peru. *American Journal of Physical Anthropology* 142:636–650.

O'Connor, D.
1993   *Ancient Nubia: Egypt's Rival in Africa*. The University Museum, University of Philadelphia, Philadelphia.

Oland, M.
2012   Lost among the Colonial Maya: Engaging Indigenous Maya History at Progresso Lagoon, Belize. In *Decolonizing Indigenous Histories: Exploring Prehistoric/Colonial Transitions in Archaeology*, edited by M. Oland, S. M. Hart, and L. Frink, pp. 178–200. University of Arizona Press, Tucson.

Reisner, G. A.
1923   *Excavations at Kerma. Parts I–III*. Harvard African Studies 5. Peabody Museum of Harvard University, Cambridge.

Rodríguez-Alegría, E.
2012   The Discovery and Decolonization of Xaltocan, Mexico. In *Decolonizing Indigenous Histories: Exploring Prehistoric/Colonial Transitions in Archaeology*, edited by M. Oland, S. M. Hart, and L. Frink, pp. 45–65. University of Arizona Press, Tucson.

Rubertone, P.
2012   Archaeologies of Colonialism in Unexpected Times and Unexpected Places. In *Decolonizing Indigenous Histories: Exploring Prehistoric/Colonial Tran-*

sitions in Archaeology, edited by M. Oland, S. M. Hart, and L. Frink, pp. 267–281. University of Arizona Press, Tucson.

Ryan, D. P.
1988   The Archaeological Analysis of Inscribed Egyptian Funerary Cones. *Varia Egyptiaca* 4:165–170.

Säve-Söderbergh, T., and L. Troy
1991   *New Kingdom Pharaonic Sites: The Finds and Sites*. Almqvist and Wiksell Tryckeri, Uppsala, Sweden.

Schrader, S. A.
2012   Activity Patterns in New Kingdom Nubia: An Examination of Entheseal Remodeling and Osteoarthritis at Tombos. *American Journal of Physical Anthropology* 149(1):60–70.

2013   Bioarchaeology of the Everyday: Analysis of Activity Patterns and Diet in the Nile Valley. Unpublished PhD dissertation, Department of Anthropology, Purdue University, West Lafayette, Indiana.

Schrader, S. A., M. R. Buzon, and J. D. Irish
2014   Illuminating the Nubian "Dark Age": A Bioarchaeological Analysis of Dental Non-metric Traits during the Napatan Period. *HOMO—Journal of Comparative Human Biology* 65:267–280.

Schreiber, K. J.
2005   Imperial Agendas and Local Agency: Wari Colonial Strategies. In *The Archaeology of Colonial Encounters*, edited by G. J. Stein, pp. 237–262. School of American Research Press, Santa Fe.

Shinnie, P. L.
1996   *Ancient Nubia*. Paul Kegan International, London.

Silliman, S. W.
2001   Theoretical Perspectives on Labor and Colonialism: Reconsidering the California Missions. *Journal of Anthropological Archaeology* 29:379–407.

2005   Culture Contact or Colonialism? Challenges in the Archaeology of Native North America. *American Antiquity* 70:55–74.

2009   Change and Continuity, Practice and Memory: Native American Persistence in Colonial New England. *American Antiquity* 74:211–230.

Smith, S. T.
1992   Intact Theban Tombs and the New Kingdom Burial Assemblage. *Mitteilungen Des Deutschen Archäologischen Instituts Kairo* 48:193–231.

1995   *Askut in Nubia: The Economics and Ideology of Egyptian Imperialism in the Second Millennium BC*. Kegan Paul, London.

1997   Ancient Egyptian Imperialism: Ideological Vision or Economic Exploitation. Reply to Critics of Askut in Nubia. *Cambridge Archaeological Journal* 7:301–307.

1998   Nubia and Egypt: Interaction, Acculturation, and Secondary State Formation from the Third to First Millenium B.C. In *Studies in Culture Contact: Interaction, Culture Change and Archaeology*, edited by J. G. Cusick, pp. 256–287. Southern Illinois University Press, Carbondale.

2003   *Wretched Kush: Ethnic Identities and Boundaries in Egypt's Nubian Empire.* Routledge, London.

2006   A New Napatan Cemetery at Tombos. *Cahier de Recherches de l'Institut de Papyrologie et d'Égyptologie de Lille* 26:1–6.

2007   Kirwan Memorial Lecture. Death at Tombos: Pyramids. *Sudan and Nubia* 11:2–14.

2013   Revenge of the Kushites: Assimilation and Resistance in Egypt's New Kingdom Empire and Nubian Ascendancy over Egypt. In *Empires and Complexity: On the Crossroads of Archaeology*, edited by G. Areshian, pp. 84–107. Cotsen Instutite of Archaeology at UCLA, Los Angeles.

Smith, S. T., and M. R. Buzon

2014   Identity, Commemoration and Remembrance in Colonial Encounters: Burials at Tombos during the Egyptian New Kingdom Empire and Its Aftermath. In *Remembering and Commemorating the Dead: Recent Contributions in Bioarchaeology and Mortuary Analysis from the Ancient Near East*, edited by B. Porter and A. Boutin, pp. 187–217. University Press of Colorado, Boulder.

Stahl, A. B.

2002   Colonial Entanglements and the Practices of Taste: An Alternative to Logocentric Approaches. *American Anthropologist* 104:827–845.

Steckel, R. H, P. W Sciulli, and J. C. Rose

2002   A Health Index from Skeletal Remains. In *The Backbone of History: Health and Nutrition in the Western Hemisphere*, edited by R. H. Steckel and J. C. Rose, pp. 61–93. Cambridge University Press, Cambridge.

Stein, G. J.

2005   Introduction: The Comparative Archaeology of Colonial Encounters. In *The Archaeology of Colonial Encounters*, edited by G. J. Stein, pp. 3–31. School of American Research Press, Santa Fe.

Tanner, J. M.

1978   *Fetus in Man: Physical Growth from Conception to Maturity.* Harvard University Press, Cambridge.

Thomas, N.

1991   *Entangled Objects: Exchange, Material Culture, and Colonialism in the Pacific.* Harvard University Press, Cambridge.

Török, L.

1995   The Emergence of the Kingdom of Kush and Her Myth of State in the First Millennium BC. *Cahier de Recherches de l'Institut de Papyrologie et d'Égyptologie de Lille* 17:243–263.

1997   *The Kingdom of Kush: Handbook of the Napatan-Meroitic Civilization.* Handbuch der Orientalistik 31. Brill, Leiden.

Trigger, B. G.

1976   *Nubia under the Pharaohs.* Westview Press, Boulder, Colorado.

Verano, J. W., and D. H. Ubelaker (editors)

1992   *Health and Disease in the Southwest before and after Spanish Contact.* Smithsonian Institution Press, Washington, D.C.

Wells, P. S.
1998   Culture Contact, Identity, and Change in the European Provinces of the Ro-
            man Empire. In *Studies in Culture Contact: Interaction, Culture Change and
            Archaeology*, edited by J. G. Cusick, pp. 316–334. Southern Illinois University
            Press, Carbondale.

Welsby, D. A.
2001   *Life on the Desert Edge: Seven Thousand Years of Settlement in the Northern
            Dongola Reach, Sudan*. 2 vols. BAR International Series 980. Archaeopress,
            Oxford.

Wernke, S. A.
2012   Andean Households in Transition: The Politics of Domestic Space at an Early
            Colonial Doctrina in the Peruvian Highlands. In *Decolonizing Indigenous
            Histories: Exploring Prehistoric/Colonial Transitions in Archaeology*, edited by
            M. Oland, S. M. Hart, and L. Frink, pp. 201–229. University of Arizona Press,
            Tucson.

Wood-Jones, F.
1910   Fractured Bones and Dislocations. In *The Archaeology of Nubia Report for
            1907–08, Volume II: Report on the Human Remains*, edited by G. Elliot-Smith
            and F. Wood-Jones, pp. 293–342. National Printing Department, Cairo.

Yellen, J. W.
1995   Egyptian Religion and the Formation of the Napatan State. *Cahier de Recher-
            ches de l'Institut de Papyrologie et d'Égyptologie de Lille* 17:243–263.

Zibelius-Chen, C.
1983   *Die ägyptische Expansion nach Nubien: Eine Darlegung der Grundfaktoren*. L.
            Reichert, Wiesbaden.

4

Escaping Conquest?

A First Look at Regional Cultural and Biological Variation in Postcontact Eten, Peru

HAAGEN D. KLAUS AND ROSABELLA ALVAREZ-CALDERÓN

On September 28, 1532, Francisco Pizarro and his band of mercenaries took their first steps into the Lambayeque region of what is now northern Peru. They were but passing through this coastal territory, making their way to Cajamarca where a historic confrontation with the Inka emperor Atahualpa awaited. Pizarro's route on October 4 probably took him within sight of a small, ethnically Muchik coastal fishing village called Ätim before arriving in Zaña the following day (Mendoza 1985:178–179). To the Muchik people of Ätim, the passage of these strange foreigners must have been as peculiar as it was transient. Yet, a little more than 13 months later, the Inka empire would fall and permanent European colonization of Andean South America would commence. Ätim eventually became known as Eten, and its people could scarcely have anticipated the transformations that would follow in the years and decades to come.

In this chapter we attempt to characterize the colonial experience of the people who lived and died over two centuries in Eten. As part of the long-term efforts to characterize the colonial experience on the north coast of Peru, Eten was the second large historic site excavated by the Lambayeque Valley Biohistory Project from 2009 to 2011. Our previous work at the ruins of the contemporaneous Lambayeque town of Mórrope uncovered a wide range of negative biocultural transformations among the native Muchik population. In this chapter we seek to evaluate if the negative changes that unfolded in Mórrope equally affected other native communities in the Lambayeque region. We compare archaeological, ecological, skeletal biological, and funerary pattern data between Eten and Mórrope. Instead of supporting a uniformitarian notion of postcontact outcomes in the Lambayeque region, this work points to a previously unknown range of locally and dynamic effects of Spanish conquest in this region of Peru's north coast.

New Frontiers in the Archaeology and Bioarchaeology of Conquest in Peru

Despite emergence of a social archaeology paradigm (Benavides 2001) and calls for historic Andean archaeology (Schaedel 1992), the archaeology of postcontact Peru has long been understudied (Cummins 2002). Peruvian archaeology has almost exclusively focused on pre-Hispanic cultures (Shimada and Vega-Centeno 2011), while postcontact studies were largely considered to be in the realm of historians. Their analyses of invaluable (but often incomplete and biased) higher-level administrational and ecclesiastical sources revealed remarkable transformations, conflicts, and challenges in colonial Peru (Pillsbury 2008). Recently, a growing number of Peruvian and North American scholars have at long last initiated archaeological studies of historic Peru. These initial studies portray forms of culture change, conflict, accommodation, and ideology never even hinted at in written historical sources. For example, Wernke's (2011, 2013) pathbreaking research at Malata (Colca valley) documented material and mortuary evidence of an intricate and dynamic web of dialectical tensions between the missionaries and local peoples and *not* ethnocidal erasure of indigenous culture, as local historical documents depict. Such tensions resulted in a mutually constitutive process that produced new hybrid Euro-Andean social and religious fields during the early days of the colonial encounter in Malata.

On the north coast of Peru, excavation of Magdalena de Cao (El Brujo complex) in the Chicama valley by Quilter (2007, 2011) has revealed the operation, organization, and internal dynamism of a coastal colonial settlement. The work at Cao compellingly points to creation of hybrid rituals in colonial households and in funerary rituals, possibly expressing indigenous identity or resistance (Quilter 2011; Murphy et al., this volume). Hybrid fields also permeated local textile production at Magdalena de Cao, as Brezine (2013) demonstrated combinations of European and indigenous materials, technology, and embellishment related to native re-creation of community identity in a time of social disruption. In the Cuzco region, Chatfield's (2013) archaeometric studies of technical attributes of ceramic production shed light on previously unknown and complex technological interchanges. Guichón et al. (this volume) demonstrate the final stages of the European colonization of South America, illustrating the remarkable variation in timing, tempo, and final stages of the broader colonial program in southern Argentina into the early twentieth century.

Human skeletal remains have now been studied at several colonial Peruvian sites (Klaus 2008; Klaus and Tam 2009a, 2015; Murphy et al. 2011; Ortiz et al., this volume). These works varyingly integrated both skeletal and mortuary pattern data from historic settings, productively bridging two highly complementary, but often unevenly integrated, sources of information (and see Goldstein 2006, Gowland and Knüsel 2006, and Knüsel 2010 for various perspectives on the historical lack of broader mortuary archaeology-bioarchaeology syntheses). There are many fundamental questions that confront historic Andean archaeology and bioarchaeology. First, the nature of postcontact biological variation in the Central Andes remains virtually undefined. With the exception of Ubelaker's long-term and regional bioarchaeology program, which included Colonial period skeletons from Ecuador in the Northern Andes (Ubelaker 1994; Ubelaker and Newson 2002; Ubelaker and Ripley 1999), local, regional, and hemispheric-level understandings of contact consequences remain incomplete in South America. Second, work by Klaus (2008), Murphy et al. (2011; this volume), Ortiz et al. (this volume), and Guichón et al. (this volume) provides bioarchaeological snapshots—while this is clearly of value in their descriptions of specific times and places, the necessary wider diachronic and synchronic perspectives have yet to come into focus. We do not yet know if contact outcomes in the Central Andes varied by region and time or tended to be isomorphic. This question, on various scales, can also be found cross-cutting all the chapters of this book.

More broadly, many earlier bioarchaeological studies of contact-era skeletons were not frequently interlaced with archaeological reconstructions of historic societies. Postcontact bioarchaeology can integrate Palkovich's (1996) context-embedded approach and Buikstra's (1977) holistic research design to incorporate funerary data, ceramic analysis, settlement pattern data, or iconography, for example. Some of the pioneering studies of postcontact cemeteries in the Western Hemisphere reflected a descriptive and processual paradigm, emphasizing the quantification and description of types and variation in use of grave goods and positioning of the deceased (i.e., Baker 1994; Cohen et al. 1994, 1997; Larsen and Thomas 1982; but also see Jacobi 2000). More recently, theoretically inclined interpretations of postcontact burial rituals that incorporate consideration of group identity, ethnogenesis, hybridity, and resistance have begun to encompass various perspectives (Klaus 2013; Klaus and Tam 2009b, 2015; Murphy et al. 2011; Stojanowski 2010, 2013; Tiesler et al. 2010; Winkler et al., this volume). Taphonomic approaches to burial have demonstrated significant promise to further understandings of postcontact cultures (Klaus and Tam 2015; Murphy et al. 2011; Tiesler and Zabala 2010) and are specifically concerned with the ritualized treatment and conception of dead bodies (Fitzsimmons and Shimada 2011). Moreover, very little is known about the archaeology of postcontact Andean burial. Death and burial was a major fulcrum of cultural conflict in colonial Peru (Klaus and Tam 2015; Murphy et al. 2011; Ramos 2010), and taphonomic approaches are ideally suited to explore the ideological contestation of death and burial in the historic Andes.

Biocultural Contexts

THE POSTCONTACT LAMBAYEQUE VALLEY COMPLEX

The Lambayeque Valley Complex, consisting of the Motupe, La Leche, Lambayeque, Reque, and Zaña River valleys, was the largest hydrologically integrated valley system in the New World (Figure 4.1). Of the entire Peruvian coast, Lambayeque contained the greatest amount of arable land and about a third of the total population in the late pre-Hispanic era (Kosok 1965). The area was a center of influential pre-Hispanic cultures and of key developments beginning in the Late Formative era, with increasing technological, sociopolitical, and economic complexity marking the trajectory from the Cupisnique (1500–650 B.C.), Gallinazo (or Virú; 200 B.C.–ca. A.D. 100), Moche (A.D. 100–750/800), and Sicán (A.D. 900–1375) cultures (Alva and Donnan 1993; Alva Meneses 2012; Millaire and Morlion 2009; Shimada 1990, 1994, 1995, 2000, 2014). Lambayeque was also home to a distinctive Muchik ethnic group that crystallized during the Moche era. These peoples maintained a vibrant cultural substratum under the surface of all later archaeological cultures (Klaus 2014a).

It did not take the Spaniards long to perceive the relatively sunny and warm climate, potential for seaports, and expanses of arable land on the north coast of Peru. Lambayeque became a key center of agricultural production, but anthropological understandings of colonial Lambayeque are relatively poorly developed. Unlike other regions of the Andes, Lambayeque lacked a chronicler, and much of what has been learned to date is derived from meticulous study of historic documents (e.g., Ramírez 1996).

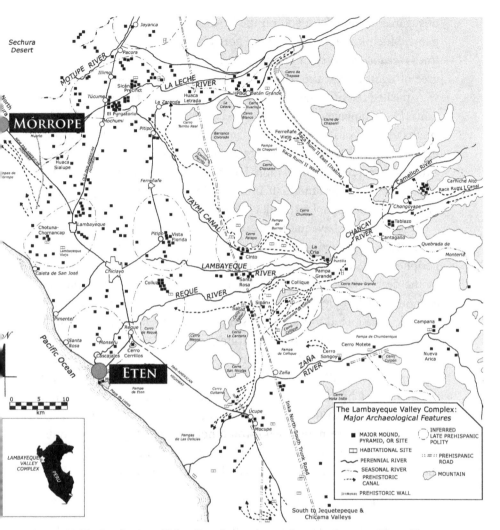

Figure 4.1. The Lambayeque Valley Complex on the northern north coast of Peru. The ruins of the colonial settlement of Eten are on the southern bank of the Reque river, just 400 meters off the coastline (map by Haagen D. Klaus).

The picture that emerges indicates that the disruption during the first years following conquest was minimal but that by the 1590s, nothing less than a socioeconomic rupture had occurred (Ramírez 1996).

As in other regions of the New World, the basic Spanish agenda was to extract the maximum amount of natural resources, manipulate native labor, and convert the people into taxpaying Christians. In Lambayeque, the valley was converted into colossal haciendas focused on production of sugarcane and alfalfa and on the herding of cattle and swine. Pre-Hispanic Muchik communities were forcibly resettled into newly created towns (*reducciones*) of unprecedented density to facilitate the greatest degree of control over the native population. In many cases, communities were pushed out of sustainable territories and resettled into marginal locations. One Lambayeque *reducción* was placed in "sickly terrain," and the deaths of most of its native inhabitants reportedly preceded its abandonment (Ramírez 1996:31). While aggregate north coast census data point to a nearly 93 percent depopulation, Lambayeque populations stabilized and began to rebound around 1630, only after losing approximately 40 percent of its indigenous peoples (Cook 1981:143–144).

In colonial Lambayeque, local ecology was degraded through monocrop agriculture, overgrazing, destruction of desert forests, and, in the valley peripheries, damage to irrigation canals that allowed land to be reclaimed by the desert. Local pre-Hispanic political systems that promoted socioeconomic reciprocity and collective well-being were disassembled. The Muchik were forced to the lowest strata of a new economy that exhibited proto-capitalist characteristics emerging from feudalistic roots. The local population was resituated into a structural poverty trap, and escape was engineered to be as difficult as possible (Klaus 2012). Less is known about the nature of the Church, but oral histories from Túcume indicate that inquisition-derived terror tactics were used to achieve conversion, and included burning alive those natives who would not convert atop the pyramids of Túcume. Such oral histories are concordant with archaeological finds atop the monumental platform mounds at that site (Heyerdahl et al. 1995).

THE COLONIAL EXPERIENCE IN MÓRROPE

The first bioarchaeological study of the postcontact north coast began with excavation of the Chapel of San Pedro de Mórrope. Mórrope is located on the northwest perimeter of the Lambayeque Valley Complex on the transitional edge between a *monte* desert scrub microenvironment and the hyper-arid Sechura desert. Occupation of the immediate area goes back at least to the Late Moche era (A.D. 550–750/800) and is still inhabited by people of Muchik descent. A local abundance of clays led to a community-level craft specialization using pre-Hispanic *paleteada* ceramic production technology (Cleland and Shimada 1998) that also still persists in Mórrope.

Colonial Mórrope was established quickly. Its location was strategic. The town was on one end of the route by which goods, information, and people traversed the desert between Lambayeque and Piura (Peralta 1998). The

Chapel of San Pedro de Mórrope was established in June 1536 and abandoned sometime between 1720 and 1751(Modesto Rubiños y Andrade 1936 [1782]).

The first phase of a planned two-decade study of colonial Lambayeque spanned 10 months (2004–2006) of large-scale excavation and laboratory data collection in Mórrope. A total of 322 burials were documented in the chapel and represented the remains of at least 867 individuals who spanned an Early/Middle and Middle/Late Colonial sequence from the 1530s to the 1750s.

The investigation in Mórrope sought to define the effects of contact and colonization on Muchik health, physical activity, genetic diversity, and mortuary rituals; results are reported in detail elsewhere (Klaus 2008, 2012, 2014a, 2014b, 2014c; Klaus and Ortner 2014; Klaus and Tam 2009a, 2009b, 2010; Klaus et al. 2009, 2010). Key findings included a range of statistically significant differences between Mórrope and regional late pre-Hispanic Lambayeque Valley Complex health patterns. Rates of nonspecific periosteal infection skyrocketed in Mórrope, while evidence of childhood anemia increased. Subadult growth stunting was detected, and female fertility declined in Mórrope. Enamel hypoplasia prevalence declined, but instead of reflecting better health, this may have been produced by a shift toward new forms of acute childhood stress driving elevated childhood mortality. Prevalence of degenerative joint disease (DJD) was elevated in multiple joint systems in Mórrope and is consistent with the ethnohistoric descriptions of intense physical labor extraction. Poorer oral health in Mórrope appears to have involved a dietary shift toward greater reliance on starchy cultigens.

Biologically, the situation in Mórrope appears as a near-stereotypical example of declining native health following conquest. Mórrope might equally be expected to be a setting of ethnocide, where European culture overwhelmed and erased indigenous society, ideas, and ritual life. Instead, mortuary patterns in Mórrope revealed a complex array of hybrid funerary activities, blending elements of Muchik and European traditions. Millennia-old Muchik rituals were particularly persistent in a range of post-depositional alterations and manipulations of skeletons, and reproduced (in form, if not also elements of meaning) highly conserved pre-Hispanic living-dead interactions. Syncretism in Mórrope could have reflected the dynamic, negotiated compromises that emerged from the dialectical tensions between the Europeans and the Muchik. Also, Mórrope periodically lacked a priest, and the Muchik may have independently developed hybrid rituals in the absence of direct doctrinal presence. They could have also represented encoded cultural resistance, especially as they reproduced distinctly non-Catholic forms of interaction with the dead.

RESEARCH HYPOTHESES

Following the work in Mórrope, we came to question if these particular patterns of health and cultural responses to conquest reflected a broader, shared experience of the colonial order in coastal Peru. Subsequent excavation of the ruins of the colonial town of Eten could begin to test a range of hypotheses about regional postcontact patterns. Indeed, the Lambayeque valley and its surroundings were subject to the same general edicts, policies, and forms of direct Spanish rule. Ostensibly, the nearby towns were subject to the same overarching agenda for religious conversion and resulted in similar compromises and syncretism. Both *reducciones* were characterized by unprecedented population nucleation and living conditions promoting the formation of an ideal "disease reactor" (Klaus and Tam 2009b:Figure 7). Expectations of relatively uniform biocultural outcomes in the Lambayeque might seem predictable. Thus, we hypothesize that (1) the negative health outcomes in Mórrope were also experienced by the people of Eten, and that (2) hybrid Euro-Andean mortuary rituals as seen in Mórrope and even further afield in Magdalena de Cao (Ortiz et al., this volume) also arose in Eten.

Materials and Methods

COLONIAL ETEN

Eten is located in the southwest corner of the Lambayeque region by the mouth of the Reque river. Its immediate environs contain a five-thousand-year cultural sequence spanning Preceramic to Chimú occupations (Alva 1985; Elera 1986). Eten also sits on a unique ecotone, straddling resource-rich marine, coastal, riverine, and lagoon microenvironments. The primary source of information about colonial Eten comes from local oral history and lore, though brief tangential references exist in local written sources that are not well detailed. German ethnologist Hans Heinrich Brüning worked in Eten to rescue the final remnants of the Muchik language in the early twentieth century (Salas 2004; Schaedel 1988).

Local oral traditions state that, in 1533, a lone Franciscan missionary encountered a Muchik community called Ätim (Salas 2004), which was

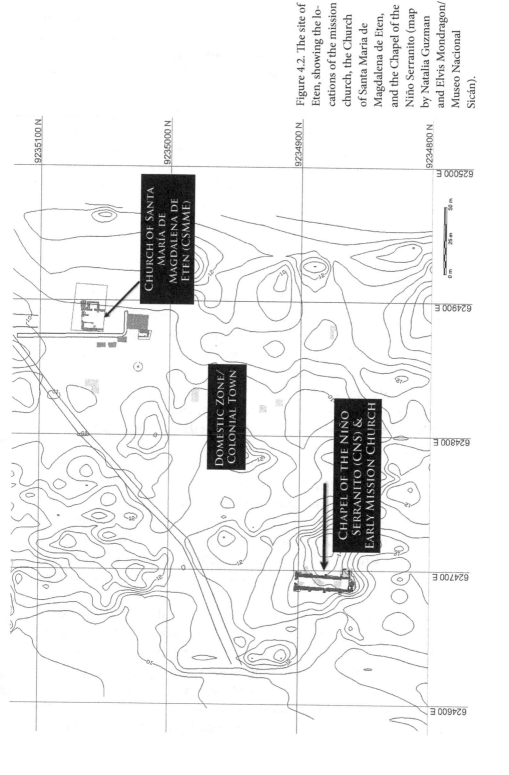

Figure 4.2. The site of Eten, showing the locations of the mission church, the Church of Santa María de Magdalena de Eten, and the Chapel of the Niño Serranito (map by Natalia Guzman and Elvis Mondragon/Museo Nacional Sicán).

likely an occupationally specialized fishing village. The priest soon began to construct a *ramada*, or mission church. Ätim was renamed Santa Maria de Magdalena de Eten. The town's late-sixteenth-century population of nearly one thousand appears to have been one of the more demographically and economically stable communities of the Lambayeque region (Cook 1981; Ramírez 1996). At some point in the early 1600s, Eten had outgrown its mission church, and a second church, larger and more elaborate, the Church of Santa Maria de Magdalena de Eten (CSMME) (Figure 4.2), was constructed sometime between 1620 and 1640. In 1649 a trio of mystical apparitions of the Christ Child, or *Divino niño*, at the CSMME was confirmed by church officials from Chiclayo (Modesto Rubiños y Andrade 1936 [1782]). This bestowed widespread notoriety, and Eten became a pilgrimage site, which it remains to this day.

Eten was abandoned sometime between 1740 and 1760. While local folklore invokes the role of a devastating tsunami, we found no physical evidence of an inundation. More likely, unstoppable northward encroachment of sand dunes drove the abandonment. During this event, the population fissioned. Economically specialized fishers established Puerto Eten 1 km to the south, while people with a more agricultural economic foci settled the inland location of Ciudad de Eten, 1.5 km to the northeast. The colonial town appears to have been moved—literally, brick-by-brick. Excavations revealed a range of domestic structures that were pristine inside. Even adobe walls were disassembled to their foundations and evidently rebuilt elsewhere.

After the town had been abandoned, another apparition purportedly occurred in 1776 that involved the Christ Child saving a stricken vessel just off the beach. The ship's captain, the Spaniard Miguel Castillo, built a new chapel to commemorate the event. This new structure was christened as the Chapel of the Niño Serranito (CNS) (Figure 4.3). The CNS was never apparently an active or consecrated church in the eyes of the Catholic authorities, but served as a kind of local spiritual monument until abandonment around 1900.

Accordingly, excavations at the CNS aimed to document a Late Colonial/Republican era mortuary sample. It was to our complete surprise that buried underneath the CNS were the ruins of a smaller and Early Colonial church. Multiple and independent lines of stratigraphic, architectural, temporally linked stylistic variation of grave goods and other evidence indicate that this was the first mission church of Eten, built sometime in the 1530s. It represents the Early/Middle Colonial occupation of Eten. In other

Figure 4.3. The ruins of the abandoned Chapel of the Niño Serranito. Underneath—and inside—this eighteenth-century structure, a definitively Early/Middle Colonial chapel and mortuary population were encountered (photo by Haagen D. Klaus).

words, Captain Castillo, in the 1770s, had constructed the CNS atop the ruined mission church that had been abandoned more than a century before. Thus, three different occupations were archaeologically documented in Eten, and accord independently with local oral history. At the CNS, a distinct Early/Middle Colonial phase (ca. A.D. 1530s–1620) was followed directly by the activities and burials at the CSMME, which reflects the community during its Middle/Late Colonial occupation (ca. A.D. 1620–1750). Finally, a handful of shallow intrusive burials at the CNS correspond to limited, post-abandonment, Terminal Colonial and Republican era use of the CNS as a burial ground (ca. 1776–1900).

Study of the CNS, the CSMME, and the buried town spanned 12 months of excavation and lab work from 2009 to 2012. In both church ruins, large and dense subfloor cemeteries were documented. At the CNS, the Early/Middle Colonial burial sample consisted of 253 burials. However, this sample contained a total of at least 450 individuals as isolated bones, disturbed contexts, and small, commingled assemblages that contained the remains of at least an additional 197 people. At the CSMME, a Middle/Late Colonial sample of 256 funerary contexts was documented. Secondary burials, commingled remains, and disturbed contexts, again reflecting the reuse of cemetery space, corresponded to an additional 52 people, resulting in a Middle/Late Colonial assemblage pertaining to the remains of at least 308 people. Importantly, no pre-Hispanic burials were found anywhere in Eten, as the colonial cemeteries appear to have been placed on previously unoccupied ground.

BIOARCHAEOLOGICAL VARIABLES

The characterization of life, death, and society in Eten involved study of multiple skeletal biological characteristics and pathological conditions that represent independent but complementary forms of evidence to characterize health, well-being, diet, and physical activity across life history and at different points therein. Due to space limitations, quantitative techniques and differential diagnoses used in this study are summarized below and discussed in extensive detail elsewhere (see Klaus 2008; Klaus and Tam 2009a, 2010; Klaus et al. 2009).

First, subadult systemic biological stress was measured via patterning of (a) linear enamel hypoplasias, or bands of decreased enamel thickness on teeth, and result from acute childhood stress such as infection, inadequate nutrition, and weaning diarrhea (Goodman and Rose 1991); and (b) porotic hyperostosis lesions of the cranial vault indicative of chronic childhood anemia (Walker et al. 2009). Second, adult systemic biological stress was characterized by (a) nonspecific periostitis, or chronic, nonfatal bilateral infection of the tibiae, and provides a baseline of immune status and community health (Larsen 2015); and (b) female fertility, a paleodemographic function related to female health and energetic status. The D_{30+}/D_{5+} ratio estimates fertility as the relative proportion of skeletal individuals older than 30 years over the number of individuals older than 5 years (Buikstra et al. 1986). Third, inferences about physical activity among adults were derived from the prevalence of DJD in the principal load-bearing joint systems (Klaus et al. 2009:Table 2), which shed light on habitual movements and motions of bodies (Hemphill 1999; Liverse et al. 2007). Fourth, documentation of traumatic injury included all forms of perimortem and antemortem bone fractures, sharp force, and projectile-related injury. Fifth, a basic characterization of oral biology as related to diet was assessed (Klaus and Tam 2010) via dental caries and antemortem tooth loss prevalence (Hillson 2008), the prevalence of which are tethered to the proportional consumption of dietary carbohydrates.

Age was estimated using the summary age procedure (Lovejoy et al. 1985) in a custom program in SAS 9.1 (SAS Institute, Inc. 2002–2003). Skeletons were assigned into one of six standardized age classes or cohorts, from perinatal to 45 years and above (Klaus 2008). Sex was estimated using the standard morphological variation of the *os coxa* and skull (Buikstra and Ubelaker 1994). Age class-structured prevalence comparisons based on the prevalence or absence of enamel hypoplasias, porotic hyperostosis, periostosis, DJD, and trauma were calculated in SAS 9.1 between the Eten and Mórrope samples using odds ratios. Waldron (2007) and Klaus (2014d) demonstrate that odds ratios avoid the potential pitfalls of crude prevalence comparisons where age structures within a data set can shape crude prevalence more than the actual patterns of a disease itself. Odds ratios are not without a few shortcomings. They lead to some data reduction as information must be transformed into dichotomized data points (usually presence/absence) and are not easily adapted to qualitative data. Oral health data were best suited for comparisons using G-tests between individual age cohorts in Eten and Mórrope. This statistic is also known as the maximum-likelihood chi-square test (Sokal and Rohlf 1995).

MORTUARY PATTERNS

Documentation of funerary contexts involved detailed standardized data-collection protocols that documented three-dimensional provenience, matrix characteristics, horizontal and vertical stratigraphy, use of grave goods, coffin construction and decoration, cardinal orientation, and positioning of every bone. The latter reflects application of an archaeothanatological approach that considers the natural and cultural processes that affect the body before and after burial, differential preservation of skeletal elements, how a body transitions from corpse to skeleton, and the dynamic interaction of that process within a grave environment (Duday 2009; also Klaus and Tam 2015). Archaeothanatological perspectives allow for detailed and secure identification and interpretation of primary burials, delayed primary burial, secondary inhumations, large-scale deposits including mass graves, and charnel houses. In Eten, archaeothanatological observations focused especially on missing or disarticulated skeletal elements and entomological activity aimed to reconstruct Colonial period funerary programs vis-à-vis the interactions between the living and the dead.

Table 4.1. Odds ratio comparison of skeletal pathological conditions between Mórrope and Eten

Pathological condition	Mórrope $N_{affected}$/N_{total} (% affected)	Eten $N_{affected}$/N_{total} (% affected)	OR[a]	χ^2_1	Interpretation
Enamel hypoplasias	37/155 (23.9%)	95/363 (26.2%)	1.13	0.20	1.13 times more common in Mórrope; no significant difference
Porotic hyperostosis	165/309 (53.4%)	65/379 (17.2%)	5.69	85.22	**5.69 times more common in Mórrope; significantly different****
Nonspecific periostitis	28/60 (46.7%)	17/106 (16.0%)	5.75	20.35	**5.75 times more common in Mórrope; significantly different****
DJD–shoulder	95/139 (68.3%)	39/107 (36.4%)	3.80	22.05	**3.8 times more common in Mórrope; significantly different****
DJD–elbow	80/115 (69.6%)	61/121 (50.4%)	2.17	7.49	**2.17 times more common in Mórrope; significantly different****
DJD–wrist	23/53 (43.4%)	17/98 (17.3%)	4.02	12.45	**4.02 times more common in Mórrope; significantly different****
DJD–hand	12/52 (23.1%)	13/96 (13.5%)	1.97	2.16	1.97 times more common in Mórrope; no significant difference
DJD–C-spine	20/56 (35.7%)	29/100 (29.0%)	1.62	1.47	1.62 times more common in Mórrope; no significant difference
DJD–T-spine	27/53 (50.9%)	44/101 (43.6%)	1.71	1.65	1.71 times more common in Mórrope; no significant difference
DJD–L-spine	34/55 (61.8 %)	46/100 (46.0%)	2.68	5.93	**2.68 times more common in Mórrope; significantly different***
Schmorl's depressions	7/55 (12.7%)	5/100 (5.0%)	3.0	3.32	3.0 times more common in Mórrope; no significant difference
DJD–hip	9/58 (15.5%)	16/98 (16.3%)	1.07	0.02	1.07 times more common in Mórrope; no significant difference
DJD–knee	76/123 (61.8%)	34/98 (34.7%)	3.73	15.86	**3.73 times more common in Mórrope; significantly different****
DJD–ankle	16/49 (32.7%)	12/86 (14.0%)	1.49	0.74	1.49 times more common in Mórrope; no significant difference
DJD–foot	8/49 (16.3%)	19/84 (22.6%)	0.62	0.88	1.61 times more common in Eten; no significant difference

[a]OR, or common odds ratio value, for each pathological condition. This summary statistic measures overall prevalence differences between the two samples and is derived from prevalence measurements of each of the six standardized age categories contained within (Age Class 1 = 0–4.9; Age Class 2 = 5.0–14.9; Age Class 3 = 15.0–24.9; Age Class 4 = 25.0–34.9; Age Class 5 = 35.0–44.9; Age Class 6 = 45-plus).

*Significant at the 0.05 level

**Significant at the 0.01 level

RESULTS

SKELETAL BIOLOGY

The Eten skeletal sample appears to be a relatively representative death assemblage of a living population (e.g., Coale and Demeney 1966) in terms of its age-at-death distribution and sex ratios between males and females. Odds-ratio comparisons between Eten and Mórrope reveal a consistent pattern: the prevalence of nearly every pathological condition is *lower* in Eten (Table 4.1). Many of these patterns are statistically significant. The prevalence of enamel hypoplasias (Figure 4.4a) is virtually identical between the

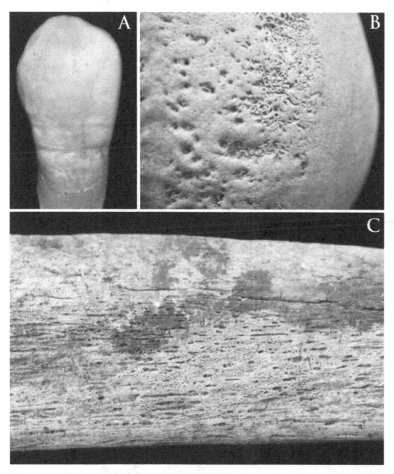

Figure 4.4. Skeletal pathological conditions reflecting various forms of biological stress. A: linear enamel hypoplasias, Burial CNS U3-44; B: healed porotic hyperostosis lesions of the posterior cranium, Burial CNS U2-52; C: periosteal inflammation of the left tibial diaphysis of Burial CNS U4-15 (photos by Haagen D. Klaus).

Table 4.2. G-test comparison of dental caries and antemortem tooth loss between Eten and Mórrope

Anterior dental caries: Age class	Mórrope N carious teeth/N teeth obs (% carious)	Eten N carious teeth/N teeth obs (% carious)	G	p	Interpretation	Posterior dental caries: Age class	Mórrope N carious teeth/N teeth obs (%carious)	Eten N carious teeth/N teeth obs (% carious)	G	p	Interpretation
0–4.9 years	36/748 (4.8%)	34/1498 (2.3%)	9.4	0.002	Mórrope +	0–4.9 years	26/498 (5.2%)	43/1129 (3.8%)	1.5	0.22	No difference
5.0–14.9 years	8/61 (13.1%)	42/506 (8.3%)	1.15	0.28	No difference	5.0–14.9 years	10/101 (9.9%)	78/659 (11.8%)	0.26	0.61	No difference
15.0–24.9 years	12/85 (14.1%)	4/234 (1.7%)	15.3	<0.001	Mórrope +	15.0–24.9 years	40/175 (22.9%)	74/391 (18.9%)	0.75	0.39	No difference
25.0–34.9 years	2/149 (1.3%)	37/296 (12.5%)	17.6	<0.001	Eten +	25.0–34.9 years	64/261 (24.5%)	83/465 (17.8%)	2.96	0.09	No difference
35.0–44.9 years	6/50 (12.0%)	22/208 (10.6%)	0.07	0.8	No difference	35.0–44.9 years	23/112 (20.5%)	56/317 (17.7%)	0.3	0.58	No difference
45 years+	6/80 (7.5%)	8/184 (4.3%)	0.93	0.34	No difference	45 years+	20/147 (13.6%)	46/311 (14.8%)	0.1	0.77	No difference
0–4.9 years	0/840 (0%)	0/1594 (0%)	0	-	No difference	0–4.9 years	1/720 (0.13)	0/1208 (0%)	1.97	0.76	No difference
5.0–14.9 years	1/90 (1.1%)	9/596 (1.5%)	0.9	0.76	No difference	5.0–14.9 years	0/148 (0%)	1/625 (0.2%)	0.42	0.51	No difference
15.0–24.9 years	26/240 (10.8%)	0/278 (0%)	38.6	<0.001	Mórrope +	15.0–24.9 years	26/339 (10.9%)	1/423 (0.23)	43.7	<0.001	Mórrope +
25.0–34.9 years	4/182 (2.2%)	8/346 (2.3%)	0.01	0.93	No difference	25.0–34.9 years	29/315 (9.2)	50/571 (8.8%)	0.04	0.84	No difference
35.0–44.9 years	31/108 (28.7%)	10/221 (4.5%)	27.8	<0.001	Mórrope +	35.0–44.9 years	57/184 (31.0%)	25/346 (7.2%)	36.8	<0.001	Mórrope +
45 years+	6/80 (7.5%)	8/184 (4.3%)	0.93	0.34	No	45 years+	136/320 (42.5%)	66/382 (17.3%)	30.18	<0.001	Mórrope +

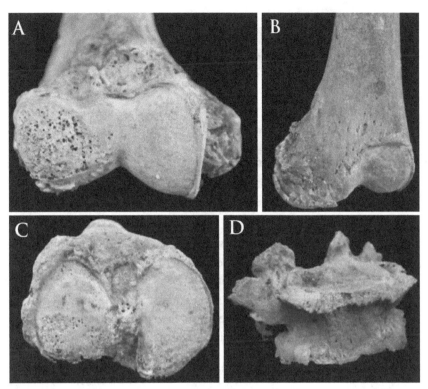

Figure 4.5. Various examples of degenerative joint disease lesions from various individuals documented at the Chapel of the Niño Serranito in Eten. Lesions include osteophytosis, subchrondral bone porosity, and eburnation of (A) a distal humerus, (B) distal femur, (C) proximal tibia, and (D) a lumbar vertebral body (photos by Haagen D. Klaus).

two sites, though evidence of chronic anemia is 5.69 times more common in Mórrope (Figure 4.4b). Nonspecific periostosis is 5.75 times more common among Mórrope adults (Figure 4.4c). Female fertility was markedly lower in Mórrope ($D_{30+}/D_{5+} = 0.6028$) than in Eten ($D_{30+}/D_{5+} = 0.4030$), and a z-ratio test shows the difference between these two proportions to be statistically significant ($z = 2.9$; $p = 0.018$).

Prevalence of DJD is greater in virtually all observed adult joint systems in the Mórrope sample, and differences in the shoulder, elbow, wrist, lumbar spine, and knee all demonstrate a strong difference due to Eten's lower prevalence (Figure 4.5). Odds-ratio values comparing traumatic injury rates do vary between Mórrope and Eten, though in Eten, more than half of the 28 individuals with broken bones possessed healed or healing rib fractures (Figure 4.6). This pattern was absent in Mórrope. Evidence of interpersonal violence is rare in both samples, though a child in Eten appears

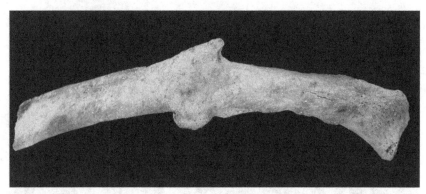

Figure 4.6. A well-healed rib fracture, Burial CNS U4-4 (photo by Haagen D. Klaus).

to have suffered a combination of sharp-force and blunt-force injuries to the frontal bone, consistent with being struck by a bladed metal weapon such as a sword (Figure 4.7).

Baseline oral-health data (Table 4.2) demonstrate little meaningful difference between the people of Mórrope and Eten in dental caries prevalence involving either the anterior dentition (incisors and canines) or posterior dentition (premolars and molars) (Figure 4.8). However, systematically

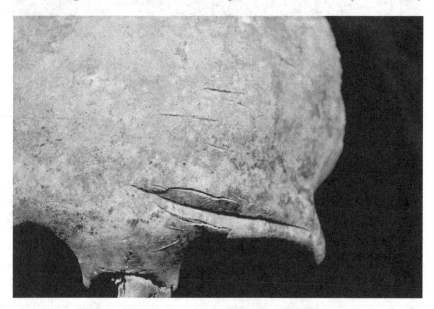

Figure 4.7. The frontal bone of Burial CSMME U5 E37. This child appears to have suffered a combination of sharp-force and blunt-force injuries to the frontal bone, consistent with being struck by a bladed metal weapon such as a sword (photo by Haagen D. Klaus).

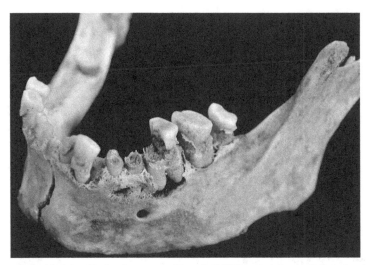

Figure 4.8. Mandibular dentition of Burial CNS U3-50. Advanced dental caries, alveolar inflammation, apical abscesses, and calculus formation are all visible in this view (photo by Haagen D. Klaus).

higher prevalence of antemortem tooth loss is evident in several Mórrope age classes. In Eten, several individuals exhibited an unusual pattern of anterior antemortem tooth losses, typically maxillary incisors. Yet other individuals in Eten demonstrated unique extramasticatory buccal wear to their anterior dentitions, suggestive of habitual use of the teeth as some kind of tool or processing device.

BURIAL PATTERNS

Of the 253 funerary contexts recorded at the CNS (Early/Middle Colonial Period) and the 256 burials documented at the CSMME (Middle/Late Colonial Period), almost all were primary burials interred in a highly repetitive and relatively invariant mortuary pattern (Figure 4.9). In Eten, shroud-wrapped corpses were placed in an extended position with either the hands clasped on the chest or waist in a praying position. In Mórrope, over 100 coffin burials were found. In Eten, only 20 coffin burials were documented. In Eten, bone positioning and other taphonomic variables revealed 315 contexts (58 percent) were intact and undisturbed primary interments. Prolonged primary burial appears not to have been practiced in Eten until entomological evidence of this practice emerges among intrusive nineteenth-century burials at the CNS.

A total of 169 (31 percent) burial contexts in Eten were missing bones and had been reduced at some point. Unlike Mórrope, where 58 interments

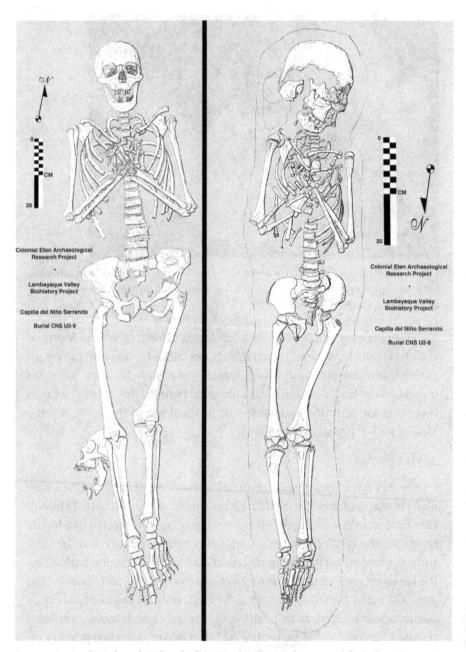

Figure 4.9. Two burials at the Chapel of the Niño Serranito that exemplify the burial patterns shared at both that location and the later Church of Santa Maria de Magdalena de Eten cemeteries. Both Burials U3-9 (old adult female, 45-plus years) and U2-8 (subadult, 5–7 years) were positioned as to have their hands in a folded, praying position in accordance with sixteenth-century Catholic rites (drawings by Haagen D. Klaus).

possessed characteristics of staged exhumation following pre-Hispanic ritual style, every one of the 169 altered burial contexts in Eten is associated with disruption from a subsequent inhumation. These do not appear to be ritualized disruption, and are most certainly a function of cemetery crowding.

Secondary burial was a very infrequent practice in Eten. The three largest secondary burials at the CNS were all closest to the altar. Each consisted of the completely disarticulated remains of between 5 and 17 individuals. These secondary burials were dispersed, unlike the organized ossuaries in Mórrope. Three secondary burials were in fact not coeval with the CNS cemetery but were produced when intrusive nineteenth-century burials were placed and indiscriminately disrupted the uppermost strata of the Early/Middle Colonial cemetery.

Secondary burial of isolated skeletal elements was observed at the CNS in Eten but was on a completely different scale. Many of the isolated bones at the CNS were single ribs, teeth, long bones (majority of subadults), and only occasionally cranial elements. Secondary burial of isolated remains at the later CSMME was not observed.

Discussion: Contrasting Colonial Experiences

SKELETAL BIOLOGY

The Muchik people of Eten appear to have been skeletally healthier throughout their lives than their neighbors in Mórrope just to the north, leading us to reject our first hypothesis. The Eten population endured measurably less childhood and adult stress, higher birthrates and higher female fertility, and less arduous forms of physical activity. Qualitative patterns of traumatic injury suggest that at least some of the people of Eten engaged in more physically hazardous behaviors. Though antemortem tooth loss is a multifactorial pathological condition, it is often linked to advanced dental caries (Klaus and Tam 2010), and these patterns suggest that the average diet in Eten was not dominated by the same degree of starchy carbohydrates or abrasive foods.

In many ways, these results, when combined with archaeological contexts and other lines of data (see below), serve as a strong case study that demonstrates how differing social realities and lived experiences can be quite literally "embodied" or otherwise incorporated in skeletal tissues (e.g., Gravlee 2009; Krieger 2004, 2005). Indeed, various factors may have been at play in the emergence of differential health outcomes in these two contemporaneous Muchik communities. Life for the Muchik in Mórrope appears to have been particularly challenging in both ethnohistoric and archaeological perspectives. Mórrope, located in a *monte* microenvironment, is characterized by saline and nutrient-poor soils and periodic water shortages, including drinking water. Ethnohistoric accounts depict Mórrope as a neglected, rural locale that experienced multiple and unsuccessful conflicts with neighboring communities over water and property rights, severe droughts, and heavy Spanish labor demands (Modesto Rubiños y Andrade 1936 [1782]). Ceramic production (Cleland and Shimada 1998), pastoralism and herding of goats and donkeys (Peralta 1998), and the mining of salt, gypsum, and phosphorus appear to have been the foundation of the local economy. Overall, the embodied bioarchaeological reflections of lived experiences in Mórrope reveal the lived experiences of sociopolitical political marginalization throughout the life histories.

Eten's situation appears to have involved a markedly different set of circumstances and realities. Two fundamental and linked variables may have been at play: microenvironmental variation and economy. Eten sits on an ecotone between desert, ocean, riverine, and lagoon ecologies. All but the desert is relatively resource-rich and biotically diverse. Unlike Mórrope, there was likely year-round access to drinking water, and varied nutritional resources surrounded the people of Eten.

Macro- and micro-paleobotanical evidence from Eten demonstrates a notable range of comestible foodstuffs, spanning maize, beans, various chenopods, peppers, oranges, bananas, gourds, squashes, nightshades (potatoes, tomatoes, eggplants), guanabana, and algarrobo (Castillo 2011). Inferentially, much of this food was locally grown, as the areas immediately to the north of colonial Eten have long been irrigated fields. Similarly, a variety of faunal remains were documented in Eten, including an abundance of sheep, goats, cuy, dogs, rabbits, duck, pigs, cows, and seabirds (Del Alcazar 2011). Other food remains included substantial proportions of marine resources, such as *Donax* sp., crabs, and a diversity of fish (Del Alcazar 2011; Puse 2012). Accessing such sources of food, especially marine resources, involved a walk of less than 400 m to the beach. The Muchik of Eten probably accessed these resources rather independently, and could have been done independently of the demands of the Spanish political economy. The elevated prevalence of rib fractures of Eten men may plausibly reflect hazards associated with the use of small traditional watercraft (*cabellito de torota*).

Eten's fishing grounds are known for their heavy surf, steep cliffs, riptides, and rocky coastlines replete with shallow submerged boulders.

If the subsistence economy of Eten appears robust, so do other areas of the town's economy. Analysis of a diverse corpus of ceramic wares point to significant use of paddle-and-anvil-impressed *paleteada* ceramics. This late pre-Hispanic ceramic production technology was portable, household-focused, and generally exempt from state control (Cleland and Shimada 1998). The colonial *paleteada* encountered in Eten shows simplified decorative diversity (Torres 2012), but abundance of nearby clay deposits suitable for potting leads us to strongly suspect there were *paleteada* workshops in Eten, and the town could have been a center of domestic ceramic production. However, the people of Eten were also connected to broader trade networks that went far beyond the boundaries of Peru. In Eten we documented a very wide variety of Panamanian *majolica,* wares produced in England, and even sherds from Ming dynasty China (Torres 2012). Eten's economic standing was also reflected in the high-quality materials and significant investment of labor and craftsmanship that went into its public and religious architecture such as the CSMME and nearby structures. For the Tipu Maya of Belize (Harvey et al., this volume), it may have been Tipu's relative isolation that spared its indigenous inhabitants from the more forms of human suffering produced by the Spanish colonial program. For Eten, the opposite seems to have held true. Eten's fortuitous economic engagement with the colonial world may have promoted a similar "escape" from the more destructive potential outcomes of conquest and colonialism.

In sum, key factors underlying these differences in biological status appear to involve a dynamic confluence of a resource-rich microenvironment and relatively vibrant economy. Also, outcomes involving biological stress are strongly concordant with archaeological and historical contexts within and between these two communities. It would be difficult to argue for interpretations that might think that the "osteological paradox" broadly applies to either Mórrope or Eten. However, the regional postcontact decrease in enamel defect prevalence does present a more complex problem, likely linked to the pathogenesis of linear enamel hypoplasias and a shifting epidemiological environment. It will also be important in future work to assess the potential underlying frailty of individuals who may have died from epidemic disease in Eten (*sensu* DeWitte and Wood 2008).

In terms of depopulation, Cook (1981:132) noted that areas in Lambayeque that were ecologically and economically sound experienced minimal population losses in the Early/Middle Colonial Period. This pattern may also extend to aspects of quality of life and well-being. The people of Eten appear to have worked out strategies to buffer against some of the more negative potential outcomes of the postcontact world. The range of diverse nutritional resources in Eten's multiple surrounding microenvironments no doubt provided some of the "raw materials" for the foundations of such buffering strategies and biological outcomes. This finding reinforces the notion that the postcontact adaptive transition, even between nearby towns, appears fundamentally variable.

BURIAL PATTERNS

The burial patterns in Eten are similar, on some levels, to those in Mórrope. Both are oriented north-south (instead of the standard east-west doctrinal Catholic configuration). The north-south axis orientation was an alignment reflecting some kind of pre-Hispanic *axis mundi* shared between both civic-ceremonial structures and human burials since the Formative and Cupisnique periods (2500–600 B.C.) (Klaus 2008). Yet, the more intense expressions of conserved pre-Hispanic funerary activities in Mórrope involved protracted and complex interactions between the living and the dead involving delayed primary burials, staged exhumations, and ritualized manipulations of many skulls and long bones. Similar mortuary behaviors are markedly absent in Eten.

It is possible that missionization in Eten may have been quite successful from the Spanish point of view. The Muchik people of Eten seemingly converted into practicing Catholics and adhered closely to the new belief system, at least as what can be read from the physical remnants of their burial practices. There also may have also been a more constant ecclesiastical presence and doctrinal enforcement in Eten. Especially after the 1649 apparitions of the Christ Child, attention toward Eten would have shone upon them like a proverbial spotlight. Mórrope was more far isolated. Periodic absence of their priest imaginably provided opportunities for the Muchik townspeople to interact with their dead in traditional ways. Similar hybridity and syncretism may have been varyingly suppressed in Eten.

Hybridity in Mórrope has been looked at in terms of a form of symbolic resistance and intense dialectical tension (Klaus 2013; Klaus and Tam 2009b). While there are many complexities and caveats surround the archaeology of resistance (see chapters in Liebmann and Murphy 2011), the particular forms of interaction with the dead in Mórrope might have indeed been forged in contexts of cultural conflict, economic marginalization, and physical suffering. Might the evidence of a stronger economy and less bio-logical distress in Eten reflect a setting where there was "less to resist," and that missionization could be more effective? Do these burial patterns reflect different colonial Muchik identities—one in Mórrope that involved resis-tance, and one in Eten where there was participation in Catholic praxis? Did Eten's people represent an assimilated Catholic Muchik subculture in colonial Lambayeque?

It is also important to consider the role of multiple waves of epidemic diseases that ravaged Peru's north coast in the late sixteenth and seven-teenth centuries (Cook 1981). Zooarchaeological evidence shows what might be a reflection of a significant rat population (or infestation) in Eten (Del Alcazar 2011). This no doubt posed a problem for the people in terms of providing abundant vectors for zoonotic diseases to infect humans. Sev-eral of the first mid-sixteenth-century burials in Eten (as well as various subsequent interments) were simultaneous, multiple burials that appear to be mass graves (for the taphonomic identification criteria of a mass grave used here, see Duday 2009) (Figure 4.10). The largest (and also one of the very first) mass grave at the CNS contained the piled bodies of 22 people. Several others were double interments (again, suggestive of multiple, si-multaneous deaths). At the later CSMME, there are additional potential mass graves and double burials. There was no evidence of cause of death in any of these skeletons, and given this setting, epidemic disease is clearly a possible reason for such large, synchronous interments. In Mórrope, mul-tiple burials are completely absent. Perhaps one of the consequences of greater economic integration in Eten was elevated exposure to epidemic disease, while Mórrope's greater isolation acted as a buffer. The rats in Eten no doubt made matters worse. Perhaps an interest in preventing commu-nity health crises drove the rapid disposal of the bodies of those who died of smallpox, typhus, or scarlet fever. In this manner, links between the liv-ing and the dead may have been permanently severed in Early Colonial Eten, and a pattern was set for the rest of the colonial era.

Conclusions

The conquest and colonization of the Western Hemisphere by European powers was one of the most consequential historical processes of the sec-ond millennium A.D. It produced a remarkably complex spectrum of con-sequences that continue to resonate throughout the world. At least on the north coast of Peru, the indigenous responses to conquest and colonization

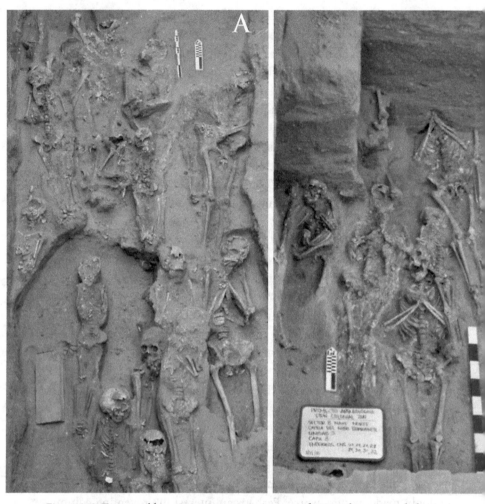

Figure 4.10. Two possible mass interments. A: A group of 22 simultaneous and physically entwined skeletons in the deepest (earliest) strata of Unit 4 in the mission church
cemetery at the Chapel of the Niño Serranito from the Early Colonial period. B: Multiple
interments involving directly superimposed bodies in CNS Unit 3 (photos by Haagen D.
Klaus).

do not appear particularly universal or monolithic. In this comparative
case study, data from human remains and burial patterns in colonial Eten
and Mórrope effectively challenge a uniformitarian vision of contact consequences even on small, local scales to further demonstrate the variable
nature of biological and cultural engagements within the colonial world.
In the case of Eten, this community seems to have escaped some of the
negative consequences of contact as they developed relatively buffering

mechanisms against various negative changes that came to the Andean world in the sixteenth century.

This work also leads to new questions. How many other communities were like Eten, shielded against negative potential outcomes of conquest? What was the broader impact of epidemic diseases? How effective were other early missionization efforts? What additional variations existed in the timing and configuration of hybrid or syncretic responses in the colonial entanglement? As we move forward to explore these questions, we hope to have underscored that empirical and interpretative reconstructions of contact can benefit from an explicit integration of skeletal, funerary, ecological, zooarchaeological, paleobotanical, and material culture data. Context-embedded approaches can advance the bioarchaeology of contact, conquest, and colonialism and recursively inform anthropological reconstructions of the lives of the people whose skeletal remains are the focus of this work.

Acknowledgments

Grants from the National Science Foundation (Grant BCS 1026169) and the Wenner-Gren Foundation for Anthropological Research (Grants 7302, 8009, 8132) and funds from Utah Valley University's College of Humanities and Social Sciences, The Center for Engaged Learning, SCOP program, Presidential Scholar Award, Department of Behavioral Science, and the International Center funded this work from 2004 to 2012. We are grateful to the Peruvian, Canadian, and American members of the Lambayeque Valley Biohistory Project whose tireless effort in the field and lab made this work possible, especially the people of Ciudad and Puerto Eten, crew chief Raul Saavedra, and at the Museo Brüning, Carlos Wester and Marco Fernández. The co-director of the 2009 field season was Jorge Centurión. We thank Melissa Murphy, Clark Larsen, Kate Teel, and the anonymous reviewers for their thoughtful and constructive comments on this chapter.

References Cited

Alva, W.
1985   Pampa de Eten. In *Presencia historica de Lambayeque. Chiclayo: Sociedad de investigación de la ciencia, cultura y arte norteño*, edited by E. Mendoza, p. 52. Sociedad de Investigación de la Ciencia, Cultura, y Arte Norteño, Chiclayo.
Alva, W., and C. B. Donnan
1993   *Royal Tombs of Sipán*. Fowler Museum of Cultural History, University of California, Los Angeles.

Alva Meneses, I.
2012   *Ventarrón y Collud: Origin y Augue de la civilización en la costa norte del Perú.* Ministerio de Cultura, Lima.

Baker, B. J.
1994   Pilgrim's Progress and Praying Indians: The Biocultural Consequences of Contact in Southern New England. In *In the Wake of Contact: Biological Responses to Conquest,* edited by C. S. Larsen and G. R. Milner, pp. 34–45. Wiley-Liss, New York.

Benavides, O. H.
2001   Returning to the Source: Social Archaeology as Latin American Philosophy. *Latin American Antiquity* 12:355–370.

Brezine, C.
2013   A Change of Dress on the Coast of Peru: Technological and Material Hybridity in Colonial Peruvian Textiles. In *The Archaeology of Hybrid Material Culture,* edited by J. Card, 239–259. Southern Illinois University Press, Carbondale.

Buikstra, J. E.
1977   Biocultural Dimensions of Archeological Study: A Regional Perspective. In *Biocultural Adaptation in Prehistoric America,* edited by R. L. Blakey, pp. 67–84. Southern Anthropological Society Proceedings No. 11. University of Georgia Press, Athens.

Buikstra, J. E., L. W. Konigsberg, and J. Bullington
1986   Fertility and the Development of Agriculture in the Prehistoric Midwest. *American Antiquity* 51:528–546.

Buikstra, J. E., and D. H. Ubelaker (editors)
1994   *Standards for Data Collection from Human Skeletal Remains.* Arkansas Archaeological Survey Research Series No. 44, Fayetteville.

Castillo, H.
2011   *Informe de análisis macro- y microbotantica, Proyecto Arqueológico Eten Colonial.* Technical report on file with the authors.

Chatfield, M.
2013   Worshipping with Hybrid Objects: Assessing Culture Contact through Use Contexts. In *The Archaeology of Hybrid Material Culture,* edited by J. Card, pp. 131–164. Center for Archaeological Investigation Occasional Paper No. 39.Southern Illinois University Press, Carbondale.

Cleland, K. M., and I. Shimada
1998   Paleteada Potters: Technology, Production Sphere, and Sub-culture in Ancient Peru. In *Andean Ceramics: Technology, Organization, and Approaches,* edited by I. Shimada, pp. 111–150. Museum Applied Science Center for Archaeology and University of Pennsylvania Museum of Archaeology and Anthropology, Philadelphia.

Coale, A., and P. Demeney
1966   *Regional Model Life Tables and Stable Populations.* Princeton University Press, Princeton.

Cohen, M. N., K. O'Connor, M. Danforth, K. Jacobi, and C. Armstrong
1994   Health and Death at Tipu. In *In the Wake of Contact: Biological Responses to Conquest*, edited by C. S. Larsen and G. R. Milner, pp. 121–133. Wiley-Liss, New York.
1997   Archaeology and Osteology of the Tipu Site. In *Bones of the Maya: Studies of Ancient Skeletons*, edited by S. L. Whittington and D. M. Reed, pp. 78–86. Smithsonian Institution Press, Washington, D.C.

Cook, N. D.
1981   Demographic Collapse: Indian Peru, 1520–1620. Cambridge University Press, Cambridge.

Cummins, T.
2002   Forms of Andean Colonial Towns, Free Will, and Marriage. In *The Archaeology of Colonialism*, edited by C. L. Lyons and J. K. Papadopoulous, pp. 199–240. Getty Research Foundation, Los Angeles.

Del Alcazar, O. M.
2011   *Informe de análisis zooarqueológico del Proyecto Arqueológico Eten Colonial.* Museo de Historia Natural—UNMSM, Lima.

DeWitte, S. N., and J. W. Wood
2008   Selectivity of Black Death Mortality with Respect to Pre-existing Health. *Proceedings of the National Academy of Sciences of the United States of America* 105:1436–1441.

Duday, H.
2009   *The Archaeology of the Dead: Lectures in Archaeothantology.* Translated by A. M. Cipriani and J. Pearce. Oxbow, Oxford.

Elera, C.
1986   *Investigaciones sobre patrones funerarios en el sitio formativo del Morro de Eten, valle de Lambayeque, costa norte del Peru.* Memoira de Bachiller, Pontificia Universidad Católica del Perú, Lima.

Fitzsimmons, J. L., and I. Shimada (editors)
2011   *Living with the Dead: Mortuary Ritual in Mesoamerica.* University of Arizona Press, Tucson.

Goldstein, L.
2006   Mortuary Analysis and Bioarchaeology. In *Bioarchaeology: The Contextual Analysis of Human Remains*, edited by J. E. Buikstra and L. Beck, pp. 375–387. Academic Press, Amsterdam.

Goodman, A. H., and J. C. Rose
1991   Dental Enamel Hypoplasias as Indicators of Nutritional Status. In *Advances in Dental Anthropology*, edited by M. Kelley and C. S. Larsen, pp. 279–293. Wiley-Liss, New York.

Gowland, R., and C. Knüsel
2006   Introduction. In *Social Archaeology of Funerary Remains*, edited by R. Gowland and C. Knüsel, pp. ix–xiv. Oxbow, Oxford.

Gravlee, C.
2009   How Race Becomes Biology: Embodiment of Social Inequality. *American Journal of Physical Anthropology* 139:47–57.

Hemphill, B.
1999   Wear and Tear: Osteoarthritis as an Indicator of Mobility among Great Basin
            Hunter-Gatherers. In *Prehistoric Lifeways in the Great Basin Wetlands: Bio-
            archaeological Reconstruction and Interpretation,* edited by B. Hemphill and
            C. S. Larsen, pp. 241–289. University of Utah Press, Salt Lake City.

Heyerdahl, T., D. Sandwiess, and A. Narvaéz
1995   Pyramids of Túcume: The Quest for Peru's Forgotten City. Thames and Hud-
            son, London.

Hillson, S.
2008   The Current State of Dental Decay. In *Technique and Application in Dental
            Anthropology,* edited by J. D. Irish and G. C. Nelson, pp. 111–135. Cambridge
            University Press, Cambridge.

Jacobi, K. P.
2000   *Last Rights for the Tipu Maya: Genetic Structuring in a Colonial Cemetery.*
            University of Alabama Press, Tuscaloosa.

Klaus, H. D.
2008   *Out of Light Came Darkness: Bioarchaeology of Mortuary Ritual, Health, and
            Ethnogenesis in the Lambayeque Valley Complex, North Coast Peru, A.D.
            900–1750.* Ph.D. dissertation. Department of Anthropology, Ohio State Uni-
            versity, Columbus.

2012   The Bioarchaeology of Structural Violence: Theoretical Model and Case
            Study. In *The Bioarchaeology of Violence,* edited by D. L. Martin, R. P. Har-
            rod, and V. R. Pérez, pp. 29–62. University Press of Florida, Gainesville.

2013   Hybrid Cultures . . . and Hybrid Peoples: Bioarchaeology of Genetic Change,
            Religious Architecture, and Burial Ritual in the Colonial Andes. In *Hybrid
            Material Culture: The Archaeology of Syncretism and Ethnogenesis,* edited by
            J. Card, pp. 207–238. Center for Archaeological Investigations, Southern Il-
            linois University, Carbondale.

2014a   La población Muchik de la cultura Sicán Medio: Una primera aproximación
            a un sustrato cultural prehispánico tardío del valle de Lambayeque. *Cultura
            Sicán: Esplendor preincaico de la costa norte,* edited by I. Shimada, pp. 239–
            261. Fondo Editorial del Congreso del Perú, Lima.

2014b   A History of Violence in the Lambayeque Valley: Conflict and Death from
            the Late pre-Hispanic Apogee to the Era of European Colonization of Peru
            (A.D. 900–1750). In *The Bioarchaeology of Human Conflict: "Traumatized
            bodies" from Early Prehistory to the Present,* edited by M. J. Smith and C. J.
            Knüsel, pp. 389–414. Routledge, London.

2014c   Scurvy in Andean South America: Evidence of Vitamin C Deficiency in
            the Late pre-Hispanic and Colonial Lambayeque Valley, Peru. *International
            Journal of Paleopathology* 5:34–45.

2014d   Frontiers in the Bioarchaeology of Stress and Disease: Cross-Disciplinary
            Perspectives from Pathophysiology, Human Biology, and Epidemiology.
            American Journal of Physical Anthropology 155:294–308.

Klaus, H. D., C. S. Larsen, and M. E. Tam
2009   Economic Intensification and Degenerative Joint Disease: Life and Labor on
            the Postcontact North Coast of Peru. *American Journal of Physical Anthro-
            pology* 139:204–221.
Klaus, H. D., and D. J. Ortner
2014   Treponemal Infection in Peru's Early Colonial Period: A Case of Complex
            Lesion Patterning and Unusual Funerary Treatment. *International Journal of
            Paleopathology* 4:25–36.
Klaus, H. D., and M. E. Tam
2009a   Surviving Contact: Biological Transformation, Burial, and Ethnogenesis in
            the Colonial Lambayeque Valley, North Coast of Peru. In *Bioarchaeology
            and Identity in the Americas*, edited by K. Knudson and C. Stojanowski, pp.
            136–154. University Press of Florida, Gainesville.
2009b   Contact in the Andes: Bioarchaeology of Systemic Stress in Colonial Mór-
            rope, Peru. *American Journal of Physical Anthropology* 138:356–368.
2010   Oral Health and the Postcontact Adaptive Transition: A Contextual Recon-
            struction of Diet in Mórrope, Peru. *American Journal of Physical Anthropol-
            ogy* 141:594–609.
2015   Requiem Aeternam? Archaeothanatology of Mortuary Ritual in Colonial
            Mórrope, North Coast of Peru. In *Between the Living and the Dead: Cross-
            Disciplinary and Diachronic Perspectives, Volume 1: Andes*, edited by I. Shi-
            mada and J. Fitzsimmons, pp. 267–303. University of Arizona Press, Tucson.
Klaus, H. D., A. Wilbur, D. H. Temple, J. E. Buikstra, A. Stone, M. Fernández, C. Wester,
            and M. E. Tam
2010   Tuberculosis on the North Coast of Peru: Skeletal and Molecular Paleopa-
            thology of Pre-Hispanic and Postcontact Mycobacterium Disease. *Journal of
            Archaeological Science* 37:2587–2597.
Knüsel, C. J.
2010   Bioarchaeology: A Synthetic Approach. *Les Bulletins et Mémoires de la So-
            ciété d'Anthropologie de Paris* 22:62–73.
Kosok, P.
1965   *Life, Land and Water in Ancient Peru*. Long Island University Press, New
            York.
Krieger, N.
2004   *Embodying Inequality: Epidemiological Perspectives*. Baywood, Amityville,
            N.Y.
2005   Embodiment: A Conceptual Glossary for Epidemiology. *Journal of Epidemi-
            ology and Community Health* 59:350–355.
Larsen, C. S.
2015   *Bioarchaeology: Interpreting Behavior from the Human Skeleton*. Cambridge
            University Press, Cambridge.
Larsen, C. S., and D. H. Thomas
1982   *The Anthropology of St. Catherines Island 4. The St. Catherines Period Mortu-
            ary Complex*. Anthropological Papers Vol. 57, Pt. 4. American Museum of
            Natural History, New York.

Liebmann, M., and M. S. Murphy (editors)
2011   *Enduring Conquests: Rethinking the Archaeology of Resistance to Spanish Co-lonialism in the Americas.* School for Advanced Research Press, Santa Fe.

Liverse, A. R., A. W. Weber, V. I. Bazaliiskiy, O. I. Goriunova, and N. A. Savel'ev
2007   Osteoarthritis in Siberia's Cis-Baikal: Skeletal Indicators of Hunter-Gatherer Adaptation and Cultural Change. *American Journal of Physical Anthropology* 132:1–16.

Lovejoy, C. O., R. S. Meindl, R. P. Mensforth, and T. J. Barton
1985   Multifactorial Determination of Skeletal Age at Death: A Method and Blind Tests of Its Accuracy. *American Journal of Physical Anthropology* 68:1–14.

Mendoza, E.
1985   Conquista. In *Presencia historica de Lambayeque*, edited by E. Mendoza, pp. 178–179. Sociedad de Investigación de la Ciencia, Cultura y Arte Norteño, Chiclayo.

Millaire, J.-F., and M. Morlion (editors)
2009   *Gallinazo: An Early Cultural Tradition on the Peruvian North Coast.* Cotsen Institute of Archaeology Press, Los Angeles.

Modesto Rubiños y Andrade, D. J.
1936 [1782] Noticia previa por el Liz. D. Justo Modesto Rubiños, y Andrade, Cura de Mórrope Año de 1782. *Revista Historica* 10:291–363.

Murphy, M. S., E. Goycohea, and G. Cock
2011   Resistance, Persistence, and Accommodation at Puruchuco-Huaquerones, Peru. In *Enduring Conquests: Rethinking the Archaeology of Resistance to Spanish Colonialism in the Americas*, edited by M. Liebmann and M. S. Murphy, pp. 57–76. School for Advanced Research Press, Santa Fe.

Palkovich, A. M.
1996   Historic Depopulation in the American Southwest: Issues of Interpretation and Context-Embedded Analyses. In *Bioarchaeology of Native American Adaptation in the Spanish Borderlands,* edited by B. J. Baker and L. Kealhofer, pp. 179–197. University Press of Florida, Gainesville.

Peralta, V.
1998   Caminantes de desierto: Arrieros y comerciantes indígenas en Lambayeque, siglo XVIII. In *El norte en la historia regional, siglos XVIII–XIX*, edited by S. O'Phelan Godoy and Y. Saint-Geours, pp. 143–167. Instituto Francés de Estudios Andinos, Lima.

Pillsbury, J. (editor)
2008   *Guide to Documentary Sources for Andean Studies, 1530–1900.* 3 vols. University of Texas Press, Austin.

Puse, E. E.
2012   *Informe de análisis malacológico, Proyecto Arqueológico Eten Colonial.* Technical report on file with the authors.

Quilter, J.
2007   El Brujo a inicios de la colonia/El Brujo at the beginning of the colonial period. In *El Brujo: Huaca Cao, centro ceremonial Moche en el valle de Chicama/*

El Brujo: Huaca Cao, a Moche Ceremonial Center in the Chicama Valley, edited by E. Mujica, pp. 287–303. Fundación Wiese, Lima.

2011   Cultural Encounters at Magdalena de Cao Viejo in the Early Colonial Period. In *Enduring Conquests: Rethinking the Archaeology of Resistance to Spanish Colonialism in the Americas*, edited by M. Liebmann and M. S. Murphy, pp. 103–125. School for Advanced Research Press, Santa Fe.

Ramírez, S. E.

1996   *The World Upside Down: Cross-Cultural Contact and Conflict in Sixteenth-Century Peru*. Stanford University Press, Stanford.

Ramos, G.

2010   *Death and Conversion in the Andes: Lima and Cuzco, 1532–1670*. University of Norte Dame Press, Notre Dame.

Salas, J. A.

2004   *Mochica Wörterbuch/Diccionario Mochica: Mochica-Castellano/Castellano-Mochica*. Universidad San Martin de Porres, Lima.

SAS Institute, Inc.

2002–2003   SAS version 9.1. SAS Institute Inc., Cary.

Schaedel, R. P.

1988   *La etnografia Muchik en las fotografias de H. Brüning, 1886–1925*. Ediciones COFIDE, Lima.

1992   The Archaeology of the Spanish Colonial Experience in South America. *Antiquity* 66:214–242.

Shimada, I.

1990   Cultural Continuities and Discontinuities on the Northern North Coast of Peru, Middle-Late Horizons. In *The Northern Dynasties: Kingship and Statecraft in Chimor*, edited by M. Moseley and A. Cordy-Collins, pp. 297–392. Dumbarton Oaks, Washington, D.C.

1994   *Pampa Grande and the Mochica Culture*. University of Texas Press, Austin.

1995   *Cultura Sicán: Dios, riqueza y poder en la costa norte del Peru*. Edubanco, Lima.

2000   The Late Prehispanic Coastal societies. In *The Inca World: The Development of Pre-Columbian Peru, AD 1000–1534*, edited by L. Laurencich Minelli, pp. 49–110. University of Oklahoma Press, Norman.

Shimada, I. (editor)

2014   *Cultura Sicán: Esplendor preincaico de la costa norte*. Fondo Editorial del Congreso del Perú, Lima.

Shimada, I., and R. Vega-Centeno

2011   Peruvian Archaeology: Its Growth, Characteristics, Practice, and Challenge. In *Comparative Archaeologies: A Sociological View of the Science of the Past*, edited by L. R. Lonzy, pp. 569–612. Springer, New York.

Sokal, R. R., and F. J. Rohlf

1995   *Biometry: The Principles and Practice of Statistics in Biological Research*. W. H. Freeman, New York.

Stojanowski, C. M.
2010   *Bioarchaeology of Ethnogenesis in the Colonial Southeast.* University Press of
            Florida, Gainesville.
2013   *Mission Cemeteries, Mission Peoples: Historical and Evolutionary Dimen-
            sions of Intracemetery Bioarchaeoloyg in Spanish Florida.* University Press of
            Florida, Gainesville.

Tiesler, V., and P. Zabala
2010   Dying in the Colonies: Death, Burial, and Mortuary Patterning in Campeche's
            Main Plaza. In *Natives, Europeans, and Africans in Colonial Campeche: Histo-
            ry and Archaeology,* edited by V. Tiesler, P. Zabala, and A. Cucina, pp. 70–94.
            University Press of Florida, Gainesville.

Tiesler, V., P. Zabala, and A. Cucina (editors)
2010   *Natives, Europeans, and Africans in Colonial Campeche: History and Archae-
            ology.* University Press of Florida, Gainesville.

Torres, R.
2012   *Análisis del material ceramico, Proyecto Arqueológico Eten Colonial.* Techni-
            cal report on file with the authors.

Ubelaker, D. H.
1994   The Biological Impact of European Contact in Ecuador. In *In the Wake of
            Contact: Biological Responses to Conquest,* edited by C. S. Larsen and G. R.
            Milner, pp. 147–160. Wiley-Liss, New York.

Ubelaker, D. H., and L. A. Newson
2002   Patterns of Health and Nutrition in Prehistoric and Historic Ecuador. In
            The Backbone of History: Health and Nutrition in the Western Hemisphere,
            edited by R. Steckel, and J. Rose, pp. 343–375. Cambridge University Press,
            Cambridge.

Ubelaker, D. H., and C. E. Ripley
1999   *The Ossuary of San Francisco Church, Quito, Ecuador: Human Skeletal Biol-
            ogy.* Smithsonian Contributions to Anthropology No. 42. Smithsonian Insti-
            tution Press, Washington, D.C.

Waldron, T.
2007   *Paleoepidemiology: The Measure of Disease in the Human Past.* Left Coast
            Press, Walnut Grove, California.

Walker, P. L., R. R. Bathhurst, R. Richman, R. Gjerdrum, and V. A. Andrushko
2009   The Causes of Porotic Hyperostosis and Cribra Orbitalia: A Reappraisal of
            the Iron Deficiency Anemia Hypothesis. *American Journal of Physical An-
            thropology* 139:109–125.

Wernke, S. A.
2011   Convergences: Producing Early Colonial Jybridity at a Doctrina in Jighland
            Peru. In *Enduring Conquests: Rethinking the Archaeology of Resistance to
            Spanish Colonialism in the Americas,* edited by M. Liebmann and M. S. Mur-
            phy, pp. 77–101. School for Advanced Research Press, Santa Fe.
2013   *Negotiated Settlements: Andean Communities and Landscapes under Inka and
            Spanish Colonialism.* University Press of Florida, Gainesville.

5

The Social Structuring of Biological Stress in Contact-Era Spanish Florida

A Bioarchaeological Case Study from Santa Catalina de Guale, St. Catherines Island, Georgia

LAUREN A. WINKLER, CLARK SPENCER LARSEN, VICTOR D. THOMPSON,
PAUL W. SCIULLI, DALE L. HUTCHINSON, DAVID HURST THOMAS,
ELLIOT H. BLAIR, AND MATTHEW C. SANGER

In virtually every setting in the world today, social inequality leads to an unequal distribution of resources (Elo 2009; Macintyre 1998; Marmot 2001; Palloni et al. 2008; Sapolsky 2004; Strickland and Shetty 1998). In many circumstances, those at the higher end of the social spectrum have better nutrition and experience less stress than those at the lower end (Bennike et al. 2005; Bielicke and Welon 1982; Haviland 1967; Porčić and Stefanović 2009; Robb et al. 2001; White et al. 1993). This kind of inequality is well documented in living populations today and has begun to be identified in ancient societies (Goodman and Martin 2002; Robb et al. 2001). Human remains from archaeological contexts are an excellent source for identifying stress variation in past societies (Larsen 2015; Steckel et al. 2002). Bioarchaeological analyses can reveal social variability through the analysis of stress indicators: individuals on the higher end of the social spectrum have enhanced access to quality nutrition and should show fewer signs of physiological stress relative to individuals with reduced access to nutrition-rich resources. Previous studies show clear positive associations between social status and health indicators, with higher status individuals being, in general, more positive, indicating better nutrition and general well-being

(Angel 1984; Cohen 1989; Goodman 1998; Larsen 2015; Mayes and Barber 2008; Schoeninger 1979).

The purpose of the study presented in this chapter is to develop a more informed understanding of the link between stress, access to resources, and social status in Spanish Florida, specifically in a community of Guale, a chiefdom inhabiting the northern Georgia coast both before and during the colonial era. This community, Santa Catalina de Guale, located on St. Catherines Island, Georgia, provides a considerable bioarchaeological record that can be articulated within the context of a rich archaeological setting. Specifically, human remains from Santa Catalina de Guale provide an opportunity to document and interpret patterning in stress as it is linked to social inequality and the distribution of food and other resources. This bioarchaeological work provides a record of population structure and contributes to existing knowledge of colonial encounters in Spanish Florida. Much of the record of Spanish colonial Florida is understood from historical sources. While extremely valuable, these sources sometimes carry an inherent Spanish bias and perspective. By documenting variation among the Guale through archaeological and bioarchaeological research, this study mitigates this bias, in part, by addressing issues of population structure directly, especially as it relates to society, rank, and access to key resources.

Although manifestations of stress and social status are difficult to determine from skeletal remains alone, several key variables are used in this chapter to represent each. In this investigation, stress is documented via the analysis of four indicators—dental caries, linear enamel hypoplasias, tooth size, and long bone length. Social status in Guale society was determined by presence, quantity, and quality of burial artifacts, the location of interments, and the location of burial relative to the ritual nucleus of the church, the altar (Larsen 1990; Thomas 1988). These biological and social variables are statistically compared to identify associations between stress indicators and social status within the cemetery population of Santa Catalina de Guale.

We test the hypothesis that individuals having indicators of lower social status (fewer associated mortuary artifacts and interred relatively farther from the altar) are expected to have a higher prevalence of dental caries and hypoplasias, smaller teeth, and shorter femur length, indicating higher levels of stress than others associated with higher social status (Larsen 2015; Mayes and Barber 2008; Robb et al. 2001; White et al. 1993). That is, we predict that stress and quality of life generally are linked to access to resources, especially food and nutrition, and that these health outcomes will show a clear spatial pattern of distribution in the Santa Catalina cemetery as per location of graves and their relative position in Guale society.

BIOCULTURAL CONTEXT OF MORTUARY BEHAVIOR IN LA FLORIDA

Most knowledge of the Guale social structure comes from Spanish historical sources and archaeological documentation (Bushnell 1994; Thomas 1987, 2008, 2012, 2014; Worth 2001, 2002, 2007). During the prehistoric Deptford and Wilmington phases (ca. 350 B.C.–A.D. 800), the indigenous people of the Georgia coast were organized into primarily egalitarian societies (Thomas 2009). However, mortuary evidence suggests that after A.D. 800 or so, leadership and social status developed into a ranked inherited system of wealth (Thomas 2008; Thompson 2009; Thompson and Worth 2011). Chiefly status was often reflected in the mortuary record through the number and quality of associated burial artifacts. Prehistoric burials representing elites were associated with mound interment, while mortuary rituals for commoners were often not as materially elaborate (Larson 1978). Remains interred in burial mounds and other elite ritual contexts along the Georgia coast were sometimes associated with shell gorgets, stone and copper ceremonial celts, clay pipes, and pottery vessels (Caldwell and McCann 1941; Thomas 2008; Thompson 2009).

The lifestyle and social structure of the late prehistoric Guale inevitably changed with the arrival of the Spanish and subsequent missionization in the sixteenth century (Worth 2002). The mission period (1566–1706) involved intensive interactions between Europeans and indigenous populations and between native communities living along the Georgia coast (Hann 1996; Thomas 2012; Worth 2007). Despite having considerable political and economic influence on native societies, the Spanish authorities did not abolish important elements of Guale social structure, including its social hierarchy involving control of resources by elites. Moreover, Spaniards and Indians had what can be best characterized as a relationship of mutual dependency, with each depending on the other for access to wealth and resources and political and economic functions (Thomas 2012, 2014).

Historical accounts mention specific Guale chiefs throughout the Spanish mission era, indicating the maintenance of some form of ranking system having its roots well prior to European contact and colonization (Hann 1996; Saunders 2000; Thomas 2012; Thompson 2009; Worth 2007). In particular, the Mississippian social hierarchy continued into the colonial period: native communities continued economic control and political authority characteristic of late prehistoric societies, but they were subordinate to the Spanish Crown (Thomas 2012, 2014; Worth 2002). As the archaeological and historical records show, social status and ranking clearly continued during the colonial era, including those living in mission settings throughout Spanish Florida (Thomas 2012). Individuals in the higher end of the hierarchy essentially "continued their Mississippian heritage of using ostentatious displays of wealth and status items to reinforce their hereditary status" (Thomas 2012:119).

What would have motivated the elite—especially chiefly authorities—to adopt an entirely new life involving European political and economic ties, a new religion, and dramatic changes in mortuary practices? Some chiefs adopted much of what went with evangelization, including a wholly new belief system (Christianity) and altered economic structure (labor exploitation, especially for food production), but they would have done so to what was perceived as beneficial to them. Ties with the Spanish would have given native elites and their communities access to a powerful military alliance and protection, exotic goods for ostentatious displays, and a means of enhancing local control (Thomas 2012; Worth 2002). Thus, in certain contexts, there were benefits to specific individuals (i.e., chiefs and other elites). Such relationships with the Spanish would have allowed the indigenous system of political hierarchy to flourish, at least for time.

Because the Guale were able to preserve their social hierarchy in some key ways, it seems highly likely that such differentiation would be visible in their mortuary record. Indeed, the extraordinary material record from the mission cemetery at Santa Catalina—far more than any other mission in Spanish Florida—suggests a clear pattern of unequal distribution of material culture, indicating clear social distinctions. Excavations of the Santa Catalina cemetery revealed nearly seventy thousand beads and an extraordinary range of other, predominantly European produced, grave inclusions, far more than any other location in La Florida (Blair 2009b; Blair et al. 2009; Thomas 1988). Prior to missionization, chiefly status was reflected in death through the types and quantities of burial artifacts and the prestige of a mound burial. In contrast, Christian burials normally would not include mortuary items with the remains of the deceased (Blair 2009b; Blair et al. 2009; Thomas 1988). Although the Spanish considered the inclusion of burial artifacts with the deceased as a traditional, non-Christian ritual of the Guale, the pattern is certainly consistent with the notion that native elites retained considerable autonomy (Thomas 2012, 2014). Other aspects of burial both at Santa Catalina and elsewhere in Spanish Florida, however, follow strict church guidelines, such as burial position and location beneath the floor of the church in blessed ground (Larsen 1993; McEwan 2001).

COMMUNITIES IN GUALE

By the mid-1600s, the province of Guale had six primary mission towns stretching north to the mouth of the Ogeechee River drainage and south to the mouth of the Altamaha River drainage. The capital of the province was Santa Catalina, located on St. Catherines Island (Worth 2007). Historical sources reveal that the original church at Santa Catalina de Guale, established by 1566, was destroyed by fire in September 1597 during a clash between rival chiefs in Guale (Francis and Kole 2011; Thomas 2012, 2014). After a period of abandonment, the community was resettled in 1604 and the church rebuilt by 1607 (Thomas 1988). The cemetery was used until 1680, when the mission was attacked by Westos and quickly abandoned (Jones 1978; Larsen 1990; Thomas 1988; Worth 2007). The Christian Guale from Santa Catalina relocated southward, eventually settling on Amelia Island, Florida, where a new Santa Catalina de Guale mission was established (Worth 2007).

The Santa Catalina cemetery on St. Catherines Island (Figure 5.1) is confined to the interior of the church and contained the remains of 432 individuals. The high degree of disturbance in the cemetery reflects its intensive use for burial over seven decades. Only 52.4 percent ($n = 226$) of individuals were found in primary, undisturbed contexts (Larsen 1990). Within the cemetery, there are no clear patterns of distribution by age or sex (Larsen 1990). Preservation of skeletal remains was generally poor, and many individuals are represented only by their dentitions. A considerable bioarchaeological record of stress and lifestyle for this and other mission Native American populations was analyzed, identifying key aspects of health and lifestyle for Spanish Florida generally (reviewed in Larsen et al. 2001; and see Stojanowski 2013 for fundamental aspects of population history and biodistance).

DOCUMENTING STRESS: BIOLOGICAL MARKERS OF HEALTH, WELL-BEING, AND STRESS

A stressor can be defined as any environmental factor that forces the individual or population out of equilibrium (Goodman et al. 1984; Larsen 2015; Martin et al. 1985). The bioarchaeological record of stress is generally

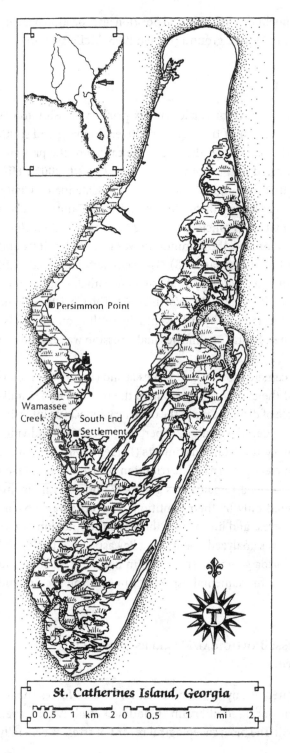

Persimmon Point

Wamassee
Creek

South End
Settlement

St. Catherines Island, Georgia

0 0.5   1   km   2 0   0.5   1   mi   2

Figure 5.1. Map and lo-
cation of Santa Catalina
de Guale (crucifix) on
St. Catherines Island, La
Florida (created by the
authors).

manifested as physiological disruptions in growth (Larsen 2015). This discussion focuses on nutritional and developmental stress—in particular, dental caries, linear enamel hypoplasias, tooth size, and long bone length (Larsen 2015).

DENTAL CARIES

Dental caries is a disease process characterized by the focal demineralization of dental hard tissues by lactic acid, a by-product of the bacterial fermentation of dietary carbohydrates (Alvarez and Navia 1989; Larsen 2015; Powell 1985). Dietary carbohydrates in this setting were largely maize, consumed at considerably high levels during the mission era by native populations at Santa Catalina (Larsen et al. 1991, 2001; Schoeninger et al. 1990). The implications for a diet highly focused on maize are primarily nutritional; that is, maize provides sufficient energy (calories), but owing to its deficiencies in key amino acids (lysine, isoleucine), it provides its consumers with a protein-poor diet, in addition to its cariogenic properties promoting dental caries.

Owing to the fragmentary and incomplete nature of many of the skeletal remains, age at death could not always be estimated for individuals (Larsen et al. 2001). The dental record, however, is quite comprehensive, allowing for seriation of most of the dentitions via occlusal surface wear and estimation of age at death (Russell et al. 1990). All available dentitions as defined by an individual having at least one tooth available for observation were used in this study ($n = 291$).

HYPOPLASIAS

Enamel hypoplasias result from disruptions in the process of enamel formation due to metabolic stress, such as that caused by poor nutrition, disease, or a combination of poor nutrition and disease occurring during the time when the dentition is developing (Goodman and Rose 1991; Larsen 2015). Because enamel is formed during the years of growth and development, hypoplasias do not reflect the individual's current stress for the period after the dentition has formed fully following adolescence (Goodman et al. 1984; Goodman and Rose 1991; Larsen 2015; Steckel et al. 2002). For deciduous teeth, the developmental window commences in the fifth fetal month and terminates in the twelfth postnatal month. Adult or permanent dental formation begins at birth and ends at about 14 years with the completion of third molar crowns (Smith 1991).

LONG BONE LENGTH AND HEIGHT

Stature or terminal height, represented here by long bone length, is a poly-genic trait that can be partially explained by environmental constraints in genetically related populations. Terminal height is a product of factors such as nutritional intake and disease history; individuals with high-quality diets are more likely to achieve their genetic potential for height than those with malnutrition (Larsen 2015; Steckel 1995; Steckel et al. 2002). Thus, long bone length as a proxy for stature can be used to analyze social hierarchy within a genetically related population and to analyze how nutrition may have been differentially distributed (Robb et al. 2001; Vercellotti et al. 2011).

TOOTH SIZE

Like long bone length, tooth size can also be used to indicate developmental stress, although teeth have a stronger genetic component than other skeletal elements. Approximately 10–20 percent of tooth size can be attributed to environmental factors (Kieser 1990; Larsen 2015; Townsend et al. 2009). This environmental component is influenced by developmental stress: variation in tooth size represents deviation from a genetic potential and has been used in numerous studies as a measure of stress (Garn et al. 1979; Larsen 1983; Simpson et al. 1990; Stojanowski et al. 2007). Simply, individuals with smaller tooth size may have experienced greater developmental stress than other individuals (and see Simpson et al. 1990; Stojanowski et al. 2007).

Documenting Social Status: Mortuary Materiality in Guale

At its most basic form, social inequality is the exertion of control by one individual over another (Brown 1971; Parker Pearson 2000; Tainter 1978). Inequality can occur in a number of different social dimensions, such as political, economic, or ideological (Brown 1971; Flannery and Marcus 2012; Parker Pearson 2000; Price and Feinman 1995). Most complex societies display varying levels of inequality along dimensions of sex, age, and ability. Status indicates the relative access to and control of resources or other individuals that a person holds in society, either through achievement or heredity (Parker Pearson 2000). Thus, access to resources is often revealed in societies via the associations between the material record and the deceased in the archaeological record. This chapter discusses social status for each individual. The word "stratification" will be avoided and the term "ranked" employed instead, allowing differences through either achieved or ascribed status.

SANTA CATALINA MORTUARY ARTIFACTS

For purposes of this discussion, we document the presence, quantity, and quality of mortuary artifacts in the Santa Catalina cemetery as a record of social position within Guale society. This approach is based on the assumption that status as displayed in death represents status in life. This record can also provide an important perspective on whether status in a society is either achieved or ascribed. In a society where status is achieved, mortuary artifacts should follow a continuous distribution along sex and age lines. Because achieved status accrues during a lifetime, younger children in an achieved-rank society should have fewer mortuary artifacts than adults (Parker Pearson 2000; Rothschild 1979). In hierarchical societies, status is ascribed in early childhood, reflecting the social standing of the parents; mortuary artifacts are associated with individuals or groups that defy age and sex lines (Carr 2005; Tainter 1978). However, for the purpose of this study, mortuary artifacts are included as a means to identify status, regardless of whether it was achieved or ascribed. The historical record for Guale is more consistent with the latter than the former (Worth 2002).

BURIAL LOCATION

The location of interments has been shown to be particularly useful when identifying clusters of high-status individuals within a cemetery (Mainfort 1985; Mayes and Barber 2008; Pechenkina and Delgado 2006). Although most baptized Guale were likely interred within the confines of the mission church, burial location within the church likely continued to reflect their ideas regarding social structure, with the elite being interred closer to the altar than non-elite. There appear to be distinct linear concentrations of interments in the cemetery that may be related to social boundaries. In particular, the cemetery is divided into three linear clusters of burials (see Figure 5.2, sections A, B, and C). These clusters may reflect a status hierarchy among the Guale, with those in the group in the altar cluster (A) among the most elite and those farthest from the altar (C) among the least elite (Blair 2009b). Burials located near the altar were less disturbed than burials elsewhere in the cemetery, perhaps indicating the importance of these individuals in Guale society.

Data Analysis

Stress Markers and Mortuary Artifacts

All individuals are treated collectively as a single temporal unit spanning the occupation of the post-revolt mission (ca. A.D. 1607–1680). This is roughly equivalent to the length of three to four generations. This is a relatively short time for significant changes in social structure, so we assume that the same basic social statuses were maintained for all members of the community over the use of the cemetery.

Dental caries and hypoplasias were analyzed by their presence or absence. The number of carious lesions, the size of carious lesions (ranging from small pits not penetrating the enamel to large lesions extending to the pulp chamber), and their location within the cemetery were recorded for each permanent molar. Hypoplasias were recorded on the left permanent maxillary and mandibular central incisors and canines. These teeth were chosen because the highest frequency of hypoplasias is usually found on the maxillary central incisor, followed by the maxillary canine (Cucina and Işcan 1997; Goodman and Armelagos 1985; Larsen 2015). Hypoplasias were recorded for presence or absence and the number of hypoplasias per tooth under 10x magnification.

Occlusal surface tooth wear was recorded for the left maxillary and mandibular permanent first, second, and third molars, central incisor, and canine. Wear degree was recorded on a scale of 1–8, ranging from unworn (value of 1, or no wear) to severe loss of crown height (value of 8, or full dentin exposure and substantial crown reduction), following methods developed by Smith (1984) and adopted for this series (Russell et al. 1990). For this study, these data were then grouped in relation to three categories by tooth wear degree—wear stages 1–2, 3–4, and 5–8—and used as an indicator of relative age in the analysis of stress indicators.

Hypoplasias were analyzed first with respect to those individuals having all four teeth (maxillary left upper and lower I1, C). Due to the small number of individuals in the 5–7 wear category, this category was excluded from the study. This also eliminates the possible complication arising from loss of hypoplasias owing to severe tooth wear and significant reduction of crown height. We also assessed the incomplete presence of teeth—in some instances, posterior teeth may have been preserved, but not anterior teeth—and elimination of highly worn teeth. Due to these factors, the sample size of the series was considerably reduced. Therefore, in order to

Table 5.1. Mortuary artifacts categories analyzed by sex and age

Artifacts code		1	2	3	4
	N	8	28	45	351
Sex:	Male	0	5	4	25
	Female	1	3	10	30
	Indeterminate	7	20	31	296
Age range:	0–10	3	3	4	63
	11–20	3	6	8	60
	21–30	2	4	14	82
	31–40	0	6	10	59
	41+	0	1	1	4
	Adult	0	5	1	22
	Indeterminate	0	3	7	61

increase the sample size and statistical power, we combined the maxillary teeth (I1 and C) into a unit and mandibular teeth (I1 and C) into a unit. Individuals were divided into three categories: hypoplasias present on both teeth (++), hypoplasias on one tooth but not the other (+-), and hypoplasias absent from both teeth (- -). Dental caries was first analyzed using every individual who had at least one molar. To account for missing teeth, all the molars were also analyzed individually.

For femur length and tooth size, individuals were grouped into categories of "small," "average," and "large" based on the average size. Individuals who fell more than one standard deviation below the mean femur length or tooth size were classified as short or small, respectively. Those who were more than one standard deviation above the mean femur length or tooth size were considered tall or large, respectively. All other individuals who were within plus or minus one standard deviation from the mean were placed in the average category. Maximum lengths were measured for all available adult femora, and buccal-lingual diameters were measured for all first molars. In addition to analysis of tooth size for the population as a unit, individuals were distributed according to their occlusal wear categories. The G-test was used to determine the statistical significance of associations between the three wear categories and the presence/absence of mortuary artifacts.

Mortuary artifacts were analyzed with regard to both quality and quantity. Using Blair's (2009a) report, a list of artifacts associated with each burial was compiled. Individuals were then divided into four categories (Table 5.1). Category 1 refers to individuals associated with the highest quality of burial artifacts, including presence of majolica plates, a rattlesnake gorget, medallions, coffin burial, mirrors, finger rings, and other elaborate material objects. Category 2 pertains to individuals with more than 100 beads or beads clearly from a necklace or rosary. Category 3 refers to individuals with fewer than 100 beads. This number was chosen as a dividing point between categories, because very few individuals approached 100 beads: there were many individuals with a small number of beads (ca. 1–50) and many individuals who had significantly more than 100 beads, ranging into the thousands. For this reason, 100 seemed a reasonable division. Category 4 are those with no associated burial artifacts.

STRESS MARKERS AND BURIAL LOCATION

A one-way ANOVA test was used to determine the significance of the average distance from the altar for each stress marker. The test determined whether individuals with stress indicators present were (on average) closer or farther from the altar than individuals lacking those stress indicators. The proximity of burial location to the altar was measured from site maps within a geographic information system (GIS). The GIS was developed by coauthors Matthew C. Sanger and Elliot H. Blair for the study of the mission cemetery using field records and maps of artifact and burial locations developed by coauthor Clark Spencer Larsen. The altar was located in excavation unit S102, and each burial was measured to a fixed point in the center of this excavation unit. Fully extended individuals were measured from the center of the burial, while individuals represented by fragmentary skeletal remains were measured from the central location of those fragments. Some remains were so fragmentary that they were not plotted on the map but located within an excavation square. In these instances, the individual was assigned a measurement from the center of that excavation unit. Because each excavation square is only 2 m × 2 m, there is a relatively small margin of error.

Long bone length and tooth size were both analyzed within the three respective categories as described above. Hypoplasias were analyzed in several ways in order to account for different biases relating to tooth preservation. The data set was analyzed with respect to any individual having at least one tooth present (maxillary I1, C, mandibular I1, C). However, missing teeth could be problematic in this test. Individuals with only one of the four teeth present might show no sign of hypoplasias, while their three missing teeth may have shown evidence of considerably higher levels of stress. For this reason, the ANOVA test was also completed using only individuals with all four teeth present. Lastly, hypoplasias were also analyzed using only individuals with either both their maxillary or mandibular I1 and canine present.

Dental caries and distance were analyzed in the same fashion as hypoplasias. Individuals were divided into "present" and "absent" groups for dental caries to include individuals having at least one molar present. To further characterize the relationship between burial location and dental caries, individuals were divided into present and absent caries groups for each individual molar.

To deal with issues of missing teeth, the analysis was refined to include individuals having four or more molars available for study. The total number of carious lesions on all molars was divided by the total number of molars present for each individual. This product as a number was compared to the distance from the altar for determining association between caries experience and location (see Table 5.5). This test was repeated for individuals with 8 or more molars and with 10 or more molars.

In order to identify the statistical significance of a non-random distribution of individuals having dental caries among and between the different sections (A1, A2, B, C), a χ^2 test was performed (Figure 5.2). In order to simplify the analysis, altar sections A1 and A2 were combined and compared to sections B and C to identify variation in caries prevalence in relation to distance from the altar.

Results

STRESS MARKERS AND MORTUARY ARTIFACTS

Statistical treatment of hypoplasia prevalence was performed by χ^2 test, and tooth size and long bone length by the G-test (Tables 5.2 and 5.3). This analysis revealed that none of the statistical tests of hypoplasias, tooth size, or long bone length showed a significant association with mortuary artifacts ($p > 0.05$). That is, having hypoplasias does not predict status as it relates to presence of artifacts.

Similarly, dental caries indicated no association with mortuary artifacts. To account for missing teeth, all molars were analyzed by tooth type. This analysis revealed that only one tooth type (mandibular right first molar) showed a statistically significant association with mortuary artifact presence/absence ($p < 0.05$). In addition, two other tooth type approach significance: maxillary left second molar and mandibular right first molar (Table 5.3). However, these values are not unexpected, as chance should account

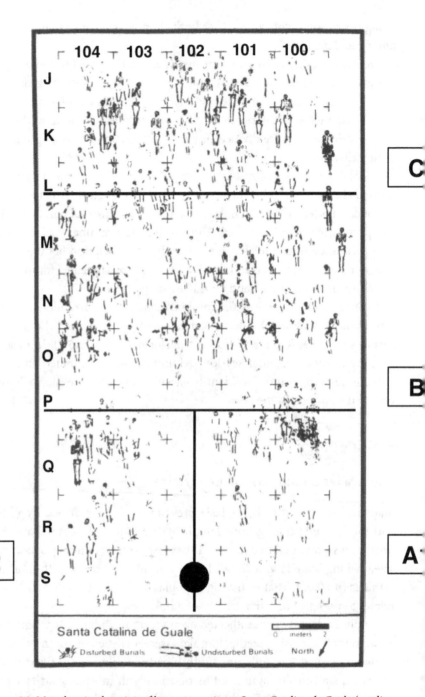

Figure 5.2. Map showing location of human remains at Santa Catalina de Guale (modified from Larsen 1990). Circle represents likely location of altar. Lines separate distinct segments seen in burial pattern (created by the authors).

Table 5.2. Adjusted χ^2 values comparing stress indicators and mortuary artifacts

Stress marker	Sample size (N)	χ^2 value	Adjusted χ^2 value	p
Combined hypoplasias present	111	0.557	0.552	0.46
Combined hypoplasia absent	16	1.039	0.974	0.32
Lower left hypoplasias: ++	18	0.18	0.17	0.68
Lower left hypoplasias: +-	35	0.47	0.46	0.50
Lower left hypoplasias: --	14	0.42	0.39	0.53
Upper left hypoplasias: ++	25	2.93	2.81	0.09*
Upper left hypoplasias: +-	17	0.018	0.017	0.97
Upper left hypoplasias: --	9	0.00	0.001	0.97

Note: H_0: hypoplasias and mortuary artifacts are distributed independently in the cemetery. *$p > 0.05$, the null hypothesis is not rejected; see p. 139 for explanation (++, +-, --).

for one or two significant values. The relatively small number of p-values approaching significance does not change the overall result that dental caries has a poor association with burial artifacts.

STRESS MARKERS AND DISTANCE FROM THE ALTAR

The ANOVA test identified the statistical significance of the distances from the altar for individuals with and without stress indicators (Table 5.4). Statistical comparison of the spatial distribution of the three femur length categories (short, average, and tall) showed no statistical difference for females in regard to distance from the altar (ANOVA; Table 5.4). However, the F value for males approached significance ($F = 2.89$, $p \sim 0.08$). Average distance from the altar was calculated for each of the femur categories. Individuals with short femur lengths were an average of 3.2 m closer to the altar than individuals with tall or average femora.

Mortuary artifact categories were analyzed for location within the cemetery. A one-way ANOVA test compared the presence or absence of mortuary artifacts to analyze mean distance from the altar (Table 5.4). Comparison of basic mortuary artifact categories showed no association with distance. However, when analyzed in relation to the quantity/quality categories (1–4), the F value approaches statistical significance ($F = 2.5$, $p \sim 0.06$). In particular, individuals in mortuary artifact category 1 (the most prestigious objects) were on average 5 m closer to the altar than individuals of categories 2, 3, and 4.

Both hypoplasias and tooth size showed poor association with distance from the altar. One of the hypoplasia tests had a value that approached significance (hypoplasias for individuals with left maxillary dentition; $p =$

Table 5.3. G-test comparing stress indicators and mortuary artifacts

Stress marker	Sample size (N)	G-value (likelihood ratio)	Probability
FEMUR LENGTH			
Female femur length	22	0.50	0.78
Male femur length	22	2.13	0.35
DENTAL CARIES			
Compiled caries +	82	2.92	0.24
Compiled caries -	122	3.10	0.21
LLM1 caries +	35	2.15	0.34
LLM1 caries -	78	1.09	0.57
LLM2 caries +	23	5.83	0.54
LLM2 caries -	95	2.73	0.26
LLM3 caries +	19	2.28	0.32
LLM3 caries -	75	0.21	0.90
ULM1 caries +	14	1.20	0.55
ULM1 caries -	90	3.91	0.14
ULM2 caries +	10	1.27	0.26
ULM2 caries -	111	5.25	0.07*
ULM3 caries +	14	1.05	0.59
ULM3 caries -	70	1.04	0.59
LRM1 caries +	16	6.22	0.05**
LRM1 caries -	88	7.97	0.02**
LRM2 caries +	18	0.01	0.91
LRM2 caries -	105	0.56	0.76
LRM3 caries +	24	0.02	0.90
LRM3 caries -	68	3.97	0.14
URM1 caries +	9	3.51	0.17
URM1 caries -	119	1.85	0.40
URM2 caries +	15	1.23	0.54
URM2 caries -	99	2.02	0.36
URM3 caries +	16	1.65	0.44
URM3 caries -	68	3.31	0.19
TOOTH SIZE			
LLM1	119	0.02	0.99
LRM1	116	0.40	0.82
ULM1	113	0.09	0.96
URM1	128	1.34	0.51
WEAR 3–4 TOOTH SIZE			
Maxillary	63	0.51	0.78
Mandibular	57	4.38	0.11
WEAR 5–7 TOOTH SIZE			
Maxillary	26	1.28	0.53
Mandibular	20	0.24	0.54

*This value approaches significance; + = caries present, - = caries absent.

**These values are significant; + = caries present, - = caries absent.

Table 5.4. ANOVA values for stress markers and distance correlation

Marker	Sample size	DF	SSQ	MSQ	F value	Pr >F
FEMUR LENGTH						
Male femur length	22	2	100.71	50.35	2.89	0.08*
Female femur length	22	2	32.65	16.32	0.53	0.60
HYPOPLASIAS						
Compiled hypoplasias	178	1	92.54	92.54	3.50	0.06
Compiled hypoplasias—all teeth	43	1	3.48	3.48	0.14	0.71
Lower left hypoplasias	75	2	12.96	6.48	0.26	0.77
Upper left hypoplasias	55	2	90.10	45.05	2.00	0.15
DENTAL CARIES						
Compiled caries	290	1	180.83	180.83	6.92	0.009**
Compiled caries—>20 years	131	1	85.92	85.92	3.57	0.06*
Compiled caries, tooth wear 1–2	46	1	129.66	129.66	5.58	0.023**
Compiled caries, tooth wear 3–4	87	1	1.01	1.01	0.04	0.84
Compiled caries, tooth wear 5–7	18	1	0.356	0.356	0.01	0.91
URM1 caries	127	1	14.83	14.83	0.61	0.44
URM2 caries	114	1	8.96	8.96	0.34	0.56
URM3 caries	88	1	48.57	48.57	1.79	0.18
LRM1 caries	118	1	86.52	86.52	3.08	0.08*
LRM2 caries	221	1	37.28	37.28	1.45	0.23
LRM3 caries	91	1	2.94	2.94	0.10	0.75
ULM1 caries	102	1	41.22	41.22	1.59	0.21
ULM2 caries	119	1	7.12	7.12	0.26	0.61
ULM3 caries	85	1	68.04	68.04	2.32	0.13
LLM1 caries	129	1	29.19	29.19	1.11	0.29
LLM2 caries	117	1	40.08	40.08	1.70	0.20
LLM3 caries	92	1	88.98	88.98	3.41	0.07*
MORTUARY ARTIFACTS						
Mortuary artifacts categories	420	3	190.91	63.64	2.50	0.06*
Mortuary artifacts presence/absence	420	1	27.77	27.77	1.08	0.30
TOOTH WEAR						
Categories 1–8	149	6	360.89	60.15	2.48	0.03**
TOOTH SIZE						
URM1	128	2	10.77	5.38	0.21	0.81
ULM1	113	2	39.99	19.99	0.76	0.47
LRM1	115	2	119.14	59.57	2.09	0.13
LLM1	117	2	50.65	25.32	0.97	0.38
MAXILLARY TOOTH SIZE WITH WEAR						
1–4	63	2	10.06	5.03	0.27	0.77
5–7	26	2	72.84	36.42	1.29	0.30
MANDIBULAR TOOTH SIZE WITH WEAR						
1–4	57	2	5.38	2.69	0.12	0.89
5–7	20	2	34.50	17.25	0.59	0.57

*These values approach significance.
**These values are significant.

Table 5.5. Correlation between number of dental caries and distance from altar

Number of teeth	Sample size	Correlation	SE
4+	156	0.15	0.068*
8+	63	0.25	0.053**
10+	30	0.32	0.082*

*These values approach significance.
**This value is significant.

0.09). However, subsequent ANOVA tests with individuals who had all or most teeth present were not significant ($p < 0.05$). This test demonstrates that the original significance resulted from missing teeth and that the association between these variables is poor.

Distribution of dental caries in the cemetery is clearly associated with burial location. That is, ANOVA tests showed a statistical significance to distance from the altar for individuals with dental caries versus without dental caries. Owing to complications resulting from missing teeth, statistical treatment of the data set was restricted to individuals with four or more molars (Table 5.5). This value approaches significance ($p = 0.06$) and is still noteworthy as it demonstrates a clear trend in the data, albeit not statistically significant. Similarly, the 8+ molars test had a significant value ($p < 0.05$), and the 10+ molar test had a value approaching significance ($p < 0.08$), indicating that individuals having relatively few carious lesions were positioned closer to the altar than individuals having relatively more carious lesions.

To mitigate age bias with dental caries, individuals were divided into tooth wear groups 1–2, 3–4, and 5–7. Wear group 1–2 had an F value that was statistically significant ($F = 5.58$, $p = 0.023$), thus rejecting the null hypothesis that dental caries is equally distributed throughout the cemetery (Table 5.4). Tooth wear categories 3–4 and 5–7 were not significant. However, heavy wear on teeth potentially obscured identification of dental caries, which could explain the lack of association in the higher wear categories.

All molars were analyzed individually to further identify the relationship between burial location and dental caries (Table 5.4). Two of twelve molars (mandibular right first molar and mandibular left third molar) have an F value approaching statistical significance ($F = 3.08$, $p = 0.08$, and $F = 3.41$, $p = 0.07$, respectively). For both molar types, average distance from the altar is less than for individuals without dental caries. The significance

Table 5.6. Chi-square analysis: Presence/absence of dental caries among cemetery sections

Cemetery sections	Sample size (N)	χ^2 value	Likelihood ratio χ^2
A1, A2, B, C	291	0.08	0.07*
A1 vs. A2	112	0.28	0.27
A, B, C	194	0.05	0.05**
A vs. B	195	0.05	0.05**
A vs. C	210	0.025	0.025**
B vs. C	179	0.85	0.85

*This value approaches significance.
**These values are significant.

of mandibular right first molar and mandibular left third molar contributes to a trend seen in the test of compiled teeth, even though most individual molars show no difference between location and presence of dental caries. Individuals without dental caries are consistently closer to the altar than individuals with dental caries.

Statistical treatment (χ^2) of the number of individuals with or without dental caries among different sections of the cemetery reveals a similar pattern of location variation (Table 5.6). Dental caries prevalence showed no difference between sections A1 and A2 (the left and right sides of the altar) (χ^2; $p > 0.05$). However, a statistical comparison of sections A, B, and C indicated that the area closer to the altar had a smaller percentage of individuals with dental caries (25 percent) than the area farther from the altar (39 percent). Sections B and C showed no significant difference from each other, but section A was significantly different from both sections B and C (χ^2; $p < 0.05$).

STRESS AND STATUS AT SANTA CATALINA DE GUALE

Results indicate a generally poor association between stress indicators and burial artifacts. However, when focusing just on the stress variable and its relation to the altar, there are clear associations and patterns of spatial variation consistent with a pattern of social status within this Guale community. Namely, distance from the altar is associated with dental caries and male femur length (Table 5.7), which implies a relationship between stress and social status in this Guale community.

Table 5.7. Average size range for long bone length and tooth size

Variable	Average range (mm)
LONG BONE LENGTH	
Male femur length	422.97–466.21
Female femur length	393.46–449.54
TOOTH SIZE	
LLM1	10.66–11.73
LRM1	10.72–11.83
ULM1	11.51–12.70
URM1	11.59–12.69
Maxillary	11.64–12.74
Mandibular	10.67–11.79

DENTAL CARIES

In Spanish Florida, dental caries has been noted as an indicator of a maize-rich diet that is low in animal protein (Hutchinson and Norr 2006; Larsen et al. 2001; Organ et al. 2005). The routine consumption of maize promotes elevated levels of bacterial fermentation and increased focal demineralization of dental hard tissues, thus resulting in more cavities (Alvarez and Navia 1989; Larsen 2015; Powell 1985). Everywhere maize is adopted as a significant part of diet, we see elevated caries prevalence (for Spanish Florida, see Hutchinson and Norr 2006; Larsen 1995; Larsen et al. 2001; Stojanowski 2013). While maize is clearly cariogenic, protein has cariostatic properties that slow or prevent bacterial fermentation and tooth decay (Larsen et al. 2001; Organ et al. 2005; Rowe 1982).

The record from Spanish Florida reveals that individuals without dental caries were interred closer to the altar than individuals with dental caries, suggesting dietary differences among sections of the cemetery that may demarcate status distinctions. We suggest that individuals interred farther from the altar consumed in life a diet of primarily maize and that individuals closer to the altar likely had greater access to animal sources of protein. Similar results have been documented in other investigations in which individuals of higher status have diet differentiation resulting in greater access to higher-quality protein (Haller et al. 2006; Le Huray and Schutkowski 2005; Vercellotti et al. 2011; White et al. 1993), including other mission settings in Spanish Florida (Stojanowski 2013). If burial location within the cemetery reflects social status, then higher-status individuals were placed in the area closest to the altar. The remaining two-thirds of the cemetery represent lower-status individuals.

MALE FEMUR LENGTH

Male femur length showed the opposite trend between social status and stress than expected. Past studies have shown a relationship between increased stature estimates and higher social status, assuming that diet increases in quality with a higher social position (Haviland 1967; Zakrzewski 2003). In the Santa Catalina de Guale population, the position within the cemetery associated with higher social status contains individuals with shorter femora. Vercellotti et al. (2011) document a similar association between social status and long bone length. Their investigation reveals that elite males had increased stature but exhibited decreased lower limb length. Stressors during growth periods can cause disruption in development regardless of social status (Bogin et al. 2002; Goodman and Martin 2002; Larsen 2015). Catch-up growth can sometimes overcome the disruptive circumstances in earlier life and allow the individual to attain normal stature in later childhood and adolescence (Cameron et al. 2005; Martorell et al. 1994). Timing of growth disruption can affect body proportions of the individual (Vercellotti et al. 2011). Increased stature and decreased lower limb length in elite males represents a stressor during growth that affected limb length in earlier life but was overcome in later growth and development to attain tall stature.

The record of stature at Santa Catalina indeed shows that the population was likely taller than their ancestors living during the time prior to Spanish contact (Ruff and Larsen 2001). This is likely attributed to having sufficient dietary energy (calories) for reaching their growth potential. Thus, shorter femora do not necessarily indicate reduced access to resources; they may be associated with just the opposite. If individuals of higher social status had greater access to resources, then it may have allowed them to survive through episodes of stress (Vercellotti et al. 2011; Wood et al. 1992).

An important mitigating factor in this analysis is skeletal preservation. Individuals closest to the altar had the least-well-preserved skeletons (Larsen 1990). Estimation of long bone length from this area may have been underestimated when compared to the better-preserved femora farther from the altar, resulting in the observed association between femur length and distance from the altar. However, given the similar trend seen in Vercellotti et al. (2011; and see Ruff and Larsen 2001), it seems more likely a significant difference and not an underestimation of femur length.

TOOTH SIZE AND HYPOPLASIAS

The lack of association between tooth size and indicators of the material record of social status was not entirely surprising to us, as tooth size is under tighter genetic control than femur size (Kieser 1990; Larsen 2015). Therefore, variation in tooth size is expected to be smaller than variation in femur size in a genetically related population such as in the Santa Catalina community. The lack of association with hypoplasias could be explained by their high frequency in the Santa Catalina population. The number of individuals without any hypoplasias ($n = 36$) is considerably less than the number of those with hypoplasias present ($n = 142$). Linear enamel hypoplasias are associated with nutritional stress relating to an agricultural-based diet low in protein. In this regard, like the Santa Catalina series, Goodman et al. (1984), Cucina and Işcan (1997), and Mayes and Barber (2008) reveal that regardless of status, members of the populations they studied had hypoplastic teeth. If hypoplasias are equally common throughout the population, as is suggested by this study, then they may not necessarily show an association with social rank.

MORTUARY ARTIFACTS

The most interesting result from this study was the lack of direct association between stress and mortuary artifacts. We offer three explanations for the lack of association between mortuary artifacts and stress indicators. First, the mortuary artifacts *do* represent different social statuses, but there are no tangible differences in stress. Second, mortuary artifacts are distributed by some pattern other than social status. Third, the lack of association may simply be due to the highly fragmentary and incomplete nature of many of the skeletons, especially in the regions either near to or directly associated with the altar. The fact that burial location varies with stress indicators rules out the first option. There are tangible differences in stress levels between the social statuses; these differences are just not associated with mortuary artifacts. With regard to the second option, mortuary artifacts are not necessarily a direct representation of the deceased's status but rather show an intermixing of the funeral organizer's intentions (Carr 2005). They should not be thought of as simple reflections on the individual buried, but instead are the culmination of actions by mourners to express their grief and honor the deceased (Parker Pearson 2000). It is possible that burial artifacts associated with children (which are traditionally assumed to be a symbol of inherited status within a population) (Tainter 1978) could simply represent mourner's overcompensation for a life ended early (Blair 2009b; Parker Pearson 2000). In the most elaborate burial artifact category, 75 percent ($n = 6$) of the individuals were under the age of 20 years. However, stress indicators were only analyzed for adults (20+ years of age), which effectively excluded all children and juveniles from the sample. Thus, the problem may not be a lack of association between mortuary artifacts and stress indicators, but simply that these individuals were excluded from the sample due to their young age. Lastly, another potential cause may simply be temporal. That is, perhaps interment occurred in a sequential fashion, with the earlier burials being placed close to the altar and successive burials located further and further from the altar. If that is the case, then the relative distribution of more elaborate grave accompaniments may reflect individuals buried earlier in the seventeenth century.

Be that as it may, we suggest the strong likelihood of the third explanation. In this regard, owing to the poorer record of preservation in the altar region especially, the relatively poor preservation of teeth and skeletal elements may prohibit the exposure of a statistical association between the actual individuals and artifacts in identification of the stress experience. For example, some of the most elaborate mortuary artifacts had no skeletal remains or very poorly preserved remains in association owing to disturbance from later interments as well as very poor preservation. The non-random distribution of mortuary artifacts and the non-random record of dental caries and femoral lengths strongly suggest the presence of a social hierarchy having unequal distribution of nutrition, a pattern that is fully consistent with the descriptions of Guale society in the historical record and the expectation of health outcomes in such a context.

SPANISH COLONIAL ENCOUNTERS

It is impossible to understand the population structure of the Guale in La Florida without addressing issues relating to processes of population change and colonialism. Colonial encounters were a dominant form of social interaction between the Spanish and Guale in this area (Bushnell 1994; Jones 1978; Rothschild 2003; Thomas 2008, 2012; Worth 2002). Spanish documents supply a story of Spanish domination and exploitation, resulting from their expansion into Guale territory (Worth 2002, 2007). However, colonial encounters were not one-sided—although the Spanish were a considerably more powerful entity, the Guale were not passive in this experience, and they maintained a relative degree of political and economic independence (Francis and Kole 2011; Thomas 2012, 2014; Thompson et al. 2013).

Bioarchaeology provides a means for studying the effects of colonial encounters on the Guale directly, bypassing the inherent bias and limited detail of Spanish historical documents. Guale social statuses are mentioned through the period of Spanish missionization (Worth 2002), and it is likely that these differences were not in name only and that the Guale maintained tangible differences in their social ranking despite some drastic changes in lifestyle that occurred during missionization.

A critical change to Guale society was heavy depopulation owing to the composite impact of infectious disease, declining nutrition, and heavy labor exploitation (Larsen 1990; Larsen et al. 2001). These factors resulted in a loss of labor for food production, which led to a decrease in agricultural surplus and loss of power for Guale chiefs (Worth 2002). Indigenous towns were assimilated into Spanish missions, which used the Guale as a source of labor. The resource base that had once supported the chief's power was now under control of the Spanish (Worth 2002).

The association between male femur length, dental caries, and burial location in the cemetery suggests that some sort of variation existed in the Santa Catalina de Guale community and that some of the members of this community experienced more stress, especially nutritional, than other members. This variation suggests the retention of Guale social status during the mission period with unequal access to resources.

IMPLICATIONS FOR BIOARCHAEOLOGY

This study contributes to a growing record of bioarchaeological analysis of social inequality. By using a range of stress indicators we attempted to assess the lifestyle and risks faced by the Guale community at Santa Catalina. However, there is a major bias when studying stress in a skeletal population, as it requires an assessment from the skeletal remains viewed in the larger context of living circumstances. Assessing the overall stress of an individual is much more complex than simply identifying and measuring individual stressors (Larsen 2015; Steckel et al. 2002). Not all factors that contribute to the overall stress of an individual will leave a skeletal signature. For example, an individual's mental well-being, lifestyle, and environment will all play a role in determining that person's overall stress level (Macintyre 1998). The skeletal record emphasizes chronic over acute illnesses, and many acute conditions are unlikely to affect the skeleton (Goodman and Martin 2002;

Steckel et al. 2002). Similarly, problems such as reduced eyesight or hearing or a change in mental status will almost never be recorded and thus not factored into the idea of stress for a skeletal population (Steckel et al. 2002).

Although there are some potential biases when associating stress and social status, such comparisons are possible as long as the researchers articulate and address the assumptions they are making. No single skeletal or mortuary variable wholly indicates the stress or social status of a once-living individual. If only hypoplasias and mortuary artifacts had been used to represent biological and social variation in this study, no association would have been apparent. By including multiple indicators for both variables, the association between stress and social status was evident.

As this study demonstrates, different stress markers can differentiate status in a population, depending on the cultural context (Le Huray and Schutkowski 2005; Mayes and Barber 2008; Pechenkina and Delgado 2006; Porčić and Stefanović 2009; Robb et al. 2001; Stojanowski 2013). In this study, indicators of nutritional and developmental stress were used. Other studies have found social differences based on specific physical activity musculoskeletal markers (Porčić and Stefanović 2009), higher workload (Robb et al. 2001), and stable isotopes (Le Huray and Schutkowski 2005). A lack of association between nutritional stressors and social status indicators does not mean that different status levels did not exist at Santa Catalina de Guale or that these status levels were homogeneous in lifestyle. There is no "best" stress marker to compare social status within a population and between different regions. Rather, stressors that discern social statuses may vary based on the activities and patterns unique to each population.

Conclusions

This study examined the social structure at seventeenth-century Santa Catalina de Guale by analyzing stress indicators and marks of social status present on Guale skeletons from the mission cemetery. Stress was identified by dental caries, linear enamel hypoplasias, tooth size, and long bone length; mortuary artifacts (both quantity and quality) and burial location in the cemetery were used to determine social status. Although mortuary artifacts showed no association with stress indicators, individuals buried closer to the altar display fewer carious lesions and shorter femur length than individuals farther from the altar. We suggest that factors leading to alteration in oral health and growth were influenced by relative position in Guale society.

This research adds to the study of inequality in the Spanish colonial period by exploring the relationship between social status and stress in the Guale population of Santa Catalina de Guale. Multiple stress indicators elucidate a clear population structuring at Santa Catalina where varying social statuses have tangible differences in nutritional stress and access to resources. This result holds important implications when studying colonial encounters between the Guale and Spanish authorities. Historical sources from the region mention the Guale chiefdom throughout the mission period. This study confirms that such social statuses persevered in more than name only and that individuals of different social status in the Guale mission population likely had differential access to resources.

ACKNOWLEDGMENTS

Since 1974 the American Museum of Natural History, under the direction of David Hurst Thomas, has been exploring the archaeology of St. Catherines Island. From 1982 to 1986, Larsen (1990) directed the excavation and study of human remains from the mission church Santa Catalina de Guale. The bioarchaeology program was funded by the National Science Foundation and the St. Catherines Island Foundation. Dental caries, osteometric, and odontometric data were collected by Clark Spencer Larsen, enamel hypoplasia data by Dale L. Hutchinson, and GIS data by Lauren A. Winkler and Victor D. Thompson using base information provided by Matthew C. Sanger and Elliot G. Blair. We express our gratitude to Katherine Russell and Scott Simpson for their role in skeletal data collection. We thank Melissa Murphy and Haagen Klaus for their invitation to present these results in the symposium organized by them at the 2012 meetings of the American Association of Physical Anthropologists held in Portland, Oregon, and their invitation to contribute to this book.

REFERENCES CITED

Alvarez, J. O., and J. M. Navia
1989   Nutritional Status, Tooth Eruption, and Dental Caries: A Review. *American Journal of Clinical Nutrition* 49:417–426.
Angel, J. L.
1984   Health as a Crucial Factor in the Changes from Hunting to Developed Farming in the Eastern Mediterranean. In *Paleopathology at the Origins of Agriculture,* edited by M. Cohen and G. Armelagos, pp. 51–74. Academic Press, Orlando.

Bennike, P., M. E. Lewis, H. Schutkowski, and F. Valentin
2005   Comparison of Child Morbidity in Two Contrasting Medieval Cemeteries
            from Denmark. *American Journal of Physical Anthropology* 128:734–746.
Bielicke, T., and Z. Welon
1982   Growth Data as Indicators of Social Inequalities: The Case of Poland. *American Journal of Physical Anthropology* 25:153–167.
Blair, E. H.
2009a   The Distribution and Dating of Beads from St. Catherines Island. In *The Beads of St. Catherines Island*, edited by E. H. Blair, L. S. A. Pendleton, and P. J. Francis Jr., 125–166. Anthropological Papers Vol. 89. American Museum of Natural History, *New York*.
2009b   The Role of Beads on St. Catherines Island. In *The Beads of St. Catherines Island*, edited by E. H. Blair, L. S. A. Pendleton, and P. J. Francis Jr., 167–178. Anthropological Papers Vol. 89. American Museum of Natural History, New York.
Blair, E. H., L. S. A. Pendleton, and P. J. Francis Jr. (editors)
2009   *The Beads of St. Catherines Island*. Anthropological Papers Vol. 89. American Museum of Natural History, New York.
Bogin, B., P. Smith, A. Orden, M. Varela Silva, and J. Loucky
2002   Rapid Change in Height and Body Proportions of Maya American Children. *American Journal of Human Biology* 14:753–761.
Brown, J. A. (editor)
1971   *Approaches to the Social Dimensions of Mortuary Practices*. Memoirs of the Society for American Archaeology No. 25.
Bushnell, A. T.
1994   *Situado and Sabana: Spain's Support System for the Presidio and Mission Provinces of Florida*. Anthropological Papers Vol. 74. American Museum of Natural History, New York.
Caldwell, J. R., and C. McCann
1941   *Irene Mound Site, Chatham County, Georgia*. University of Georgia Press, Athens.
Cameron, N., M. A. Preece, and T. J. Cole
2005   Catch Up Growth or Regression at the Mean? Recovery from Stunting Revisited. *American Journal of Human Biology* 17:412–417.
Carr, C.
2005   The Question of Ranking in Havana Hopewellian Societies. In *Gathering Hopewell: Society, Ritual, and Ritual Interaction*, edited by C. Carr and D. T. Case, pp. 238–257. Kluwer Academic/Plenum, New York.
Cohen, M. N.
1989   *Health and the Rise of Civilization*. Yale University Press, New York.
Cucina, A., and M. Y. İşcan
1997   Assessment of Enamel Hypoplasia in a High Status Burial Site. *American Journal of Human Biology* 9:213–222.

Elo, I. T.
2009   Social Class Differentials in Health and Mortality: Patterns and Explanations
            in Comparative Perspective. *Annual Review in Sociology* 35:553–572.
Flannery, K., and J. Marcus
2012   *The Creation of Inequality: How Our Prehistoric Ancestors Set the Stage for
            Monarchy, Slavery, and Empire.* Harvard University Press, Cambridge.
Francis J. M., and K. M. Kole
2011   *Murder and Martyrdom in Spanish Florida: Don Juan and the Guale Uprising
            of 1597.* Anthropological Papers Vol. 95. American Museum of Natural His-
            tory, New York.
Garn, S. M., R. H. Osbone, and K. D. McCabe
1979   The Effect of Prenatal Factors on Crown Dimensions. *American Journal of
            Physical Anthropology* 51:665–678.
Goodman, A. H.
1998   The Biological Consequences of Inequality in Antiquity. In *Building a New
            Biocultural Synthesis: Political-Economic Perspectives on Human Biology,* ed-
            ited by A. H. Goodman and T. L. Leatherman, pp. 147–169. University of
            Michigan Press, Ann Arbor.
Goodman, A. H., and G. J. Armelagos
1985   Factors Affecting the Distribution of Enamel Hypoplasias within the Human
            Permanent Dentition. *American Journal of Physical Anthropology* 68:479–
            493.
Goodman, A. H., and D. L. Martin
2002   Reconstructing Health Profiles from Skeletal Remains. In *The Backbone of
            History: Health and Nutrition in the Western Hemisphere,* edited by R. H.
            Steckel and J. C. Rose, pp. 11–60. Cambridge University Press, Cambridge.
Goodman, A. H., D. L. Martin, and G. J. Armelagos
1984   Indications of Stress from Bone and Teeth. In *Paleopathology at the Origins
            of Agriculture,* edited by M. N. Cohen and G. J. Armelagos, pp. 51–74. Aca-
            demic Press, Orlando.
Goodman, A. H., and J. C. Rose
1991   Dental Enamel Hypoplasias as Indicators of Nutritional Status. In *Advances
            in Dental Anthropology,* edited by M. A. Kelley and C. S. Larsen, pp. 279–293.
            Wiley-Liss, New York.
Haller, M. J., G. M. Feinman, and L. M. Nicholas
2006   Socioeconomic Inequality and Differential Access to Faunal Resources at El
            Palmillo, Oaxaca, Mexico. *Ancient Mesoamerica* 17:39–56.
Hann, J. H.
1996   The Missions of Spanish Florida. In *The New History of Florida,* edited by M.
            Gannon, pp. 78–99. University Press of Florida, Gainesville.
Haviland, W. A.
1967   Stature at Tikal, Guatemala: Implications for Ancient Maya Demography
            and Social Organization. *American Antiquity* 32:316–325.

Hutchinson, D. L., and L. Norr

2006   Nutrition and Health at Contact in Late Prehistoric Central Gulf Coast Florida. *American Journal of Physical Anthropology* 129:375–386.

Jones, G. D.

1978   The Ethnohistory of the Guale Coast through 1684. In *The Anthropology of St. Catherines Island: 1. Natural and Cultural History*, edited by D. H. Thomas, G. D. Jones, R. S. Durham, and C. S. Larsen, pp. 178–210. Anthropological Papers of the American Museum of Natural History 55.

Kieser, J. A.

1990   *Human Adult Odontometrics: The Study of Variation in Adult Tooth Size.* Cambridge University Press, Cambridge.

Larsen, C. S.

1983   Deciduous Tooth Size and Subsistence Change in Prehistoric Georgia Coast Populations. *Current Anthropology* 24:225–226.

1990   Biological Interpretation and the Context for Change. In *The Archaeology of Mission Santa Catalina de Guale: Biocultural Interpretations of a Population in Transition,* edited by C. S. Larsen, pp. 11–25. Anthropological Papers Vol. 68. American Museum of Natural History, New York.

1993   On the Frontier of Contact: Mission Bioarchaeology in La Florida. In *The Spanish Missions of La Florida,* edited by B. McEwan, pp. 322–356. University Press of Florida, Gainesville.

1995   Biological Changes in Human Populations with Agriculture. *Annual Reviews in Anthropology* 24:185–213.

2015   *Bioarchaeology: Interpreting Behavior from the Human Skeleton.* 2nd ed. Cambridge University Press, Cambridge.

Larsen, C. S., M. C. Griffin, D. L. Hutchinson, V. E. Noble, L. Norr, R. F. Pastor, C. B. Ruff, K. F. Russell, M. J. Schoeninger, M. Schultz, S. W. Simpson, and M. F. Teaford

2001   Frontiers of Contact: Bioarchaeology of Spanish Florida. *Journal of World Prehistory* 15:69–123.

Larsen, C. S., R. Shavit, and M. C. Griffin

1991   Dental Caries Evidence for Dietary Change: An Archaeological Context. In *Advances in Dental Anthropology,* edited by M. A. Kelley and C. S. Larsen, pp. 179–202. Wiley-Liss, New York.

Larson, L. H.

1978   Historic Guale Indians of the Georgia Coast and the Impact Spanish Missions Effort. In *Tacachale: Essays of the Indians of Florida and Southeastern Georgia during the Historic Period,* edited by J. Milanich and S. Proctor, pp. 120–140. University Press of Florida, Gainesville.

Le Huray, J. D., and H. Schutkowski

2005   Diet and Social Status during the La Tenè Period in Bohemia: Carbon and Nitrogen Stable Isotope Analysis of Bone Collagen from Kutná Hora-Karlov and Radovesice. *Journal of Anthropological Archaeology* 24:135–147.

Macintyre, S.

1998   Social Inequalities and Health in the Contemporary World: Comparative Overview. In *Human Biology and Social Inequality,* edited by S. S. Strickland and P. S. Shetty, pp. 20–35. Cambridge University Press, Cambridge.

Mainfort, R. C.
1985   Wealth, Space, and Status in a Historic Indian Cemetery. *American Antiquity*
            50:555–579.
Marmot, M.
2001   Inequalities in Health. *New England Journal of Medicine* 345:134–136.
Martin, D. L., A. H. Goodman, and G. Armelagos
1985   Skeletal Pathologies as Indicators of Quality and Quantity of Diet. In *The
            Analysis of Prehistoric Diets,* edited by R. I. Gilbert and H. Mielke, pp. 227–
            279. Academic Press, Orlando.
Martorell, R., L. K. Khan, and D. G. Schroeder
1994   Reversibility of Stunting: Epidemiological Findings in Children from Devel-
            oping Countries. *European Journal of Clinical Nutrition* 48:S45–S57.
Mayes, A. T., and S. B. Barber
2008   Osteobiography of a High-Status Burial from the Lower Río Verde Valley of
            Oaxaca, Mexico. *International Journal of Osteoarchaeology* 18:573–588.
McEwan, B. G.
2001   The Spiritual Conquest of La Florida. *American Anthropologist* 103:633–644.
Organ, J. M., M. F. Teaford, and C. S. Larsen
2005   Dietary Inferences from Dental Occlusal Microwear at Mission San Luis de
            Apalachee. *American Journal of Physical Anthropology* 128:801–811.
Palloni, A., C. Milesi, R. G. White, and A. Turner
2008   Triggering Inequality and Health Gradients: Do Health Selection Effects
            Matter? In *Demographic Challenges for the 21st Century: A State of the Art in
            Demography,* edited by J. Surkyn, J. van Bavel, and P. Deboosere, pp. 175–209.
            Liber Amicorum for Ron Lesthaeghe. Vrije Universiteit Press, Brussels.
Parker Pearson, M. P.
2000   *The Archaeology of Death and Burial.* Texas A&M University Press, College
            Station.
Pechenkina, E., and M. Delgado
2006   Dimensions of Health and Social Structure in the Early Intermediate Period
            Cemetery at Villa El Salvador, Peru. *American Journal of Physical Anthropol-
            ogy* 131:218–235.
Porčić, M., and S. Stefanović
2009   Physical Activity and Social Status in Early Bronze Age Society: The Mokrin
            Necropolis. *Journal of Anthropological Archaeology* 28:259–273.
Powell, M. L.
1985   The Analysis of Dental Wear and Caries for Dietary Reconstruction. In *The
            Analysis of Prehistoric Diets,* edited by R. I. Gilbert and J. H. Mielke, pp.
            307–338. Academic Press, Orlando.
Price, T. D., and G. M. Feinman
1995   Foundation of Prehistoric Social Inequality. In *Foundations of Social Inequal-
            ity,* edited by T. D. Price and G. M. Feinman, pp. 3–14. Plenum Press, New
            York.
Robb, J., R. Bigazzi, L. Lazzarini, S. Scarsini, and F. Sonego
2001   Social "Status" and Biological "Status": A Comparison of Burial Artifacts and

Skeletal Indicators from Pontecagnano. *American Journal of Physical Anthropology* 115:213–222.

Rothschild, N. A.

1979   Mortuary Behavior and Social Organization at Indian Knoll and Dickson Mounds. *American Antiquity* 44:658–675.

2003   *Colonial Encounters in a Native American Landscape: The Spanish and Dutch in North America.* Smithsonian Institution Press, Washington, D.C.

Rowe, N.

1982   Dental Caries. In *Dimensions of Dental Hygiene,* edited by P. F. Steele, pp. 209–237. 3rd ed. Lea and Febiger, Philadelphia.

Ruff, C. B., and C. S. Larsen

2001   Reconstructing Behavior in Spanish Florida: The Biomechanical Evidence. In *Bioarchaeology of Spanish Florida: The Impact of Colonialism,* edited by C. S. Larsen, pp. 113–145. University Press of Florida, Gainesville.

Russell, K. F., I. Choi, and C. S. Larsen

1990   The Paleodemography of Santa Catalina de Guale. In *The Archaeology of Mission Santa Catalina de Guale: Biocultural Interpretations of a Population in Transition,* edited by C. S. Larsen, pp. 36–49. Anthropological Papers Vol. 68. American Museum of Natural History, New York.

Sapolsky, R. M.

2004   Social Status and Health in Humans and Other Animals. *Annual Reviews in Anthropology* 33:393–418.

Saunders, R.

2000   The Guale Indians of the Lower Atlantic Coast: Change and Continuity. In *Indians of the Greater Southeast: Historical Archaeology and Ethnohistory,* edited by B. G. Ewan, pp. 57–84. University Press of Florida, Gainesville.

Schoeninger, M.

1979   Diet and Status at Chalcatzingo: Some Empirical and Technical Aspects of Strontium Analysis. *American Journal of Physical Anthropology* 51:295–310.

Schoeninger, M. J., N. J. van der Merwe, K. Moore, J. Lee-Thorp, and C. S. Larsen

1990   Decrease in Diet Quality between the Prehistoric and Contact Periods. *The Archaeology of Mission Santa Catalina de Guale: 2. Biocultural Interpretations of a Population in Transition,* edited by C. S. Larsen, pp. 78–93. Anthropological Papers Vol. 68. American Museum of Natural History, New York.

Simpson, S. W., D. L. Hutchinson, and C. S. Larsen

1990   Coping with Stress: Tooth Size, Dental Defects, and Age-at-Death. In *The Archaeology of Mission Santa Catalina de Guale: 2. Biocultural Interpretations of a Population in Transition,* edited by C. S. Larsen, pp. 66–77. Anthropological Papers Vol. 68. American Museum of Natural History, New York.

Smith, B. D.

1984   Patterns of Molar Wear in Hunter-Gatherers and Agriculturalists. *American Journal of Physical Anthropology* 63:39–56.

Smith, B. H.

1991   Standards of Human Tooth Formation and Dental Age Assessment. In *Advances in Dental Anthropology,* edited by M. A. Kelley and C. S. Larsen, pp. 143–168. Wiley-Liss, New York.

Steckel, R. H.
1995   Stature and the Standard of Living. *Journal of Economic Literature* 33:1903–
            1940.
Steckel, R. H., P. W. Sciulli, and J. C. Rose
2002   A Health Index from Skeletal Remains. In *The Backbone of History: Health
            and Nutrition in the Western Hemisphere*, edited by R. H. Steckel and J. C.
            Rose, pp. 61–92. Cambridge University Press, New York.
Stojanowski, C. M.
2013   *Mission Cemeteries, Mission Peoples: Historical and Evolutionary Dimen-
            sions of Intracemetery Bioarchaeology in Spanish Florida*. University Press of
            Florida, Gainesville.
Stojanowski, C. M., C. S. Larsen, T. A. Tung, and B. G. McEwan
2007   Biological Structure and Health Implications From Tooth Size at Mission
            San Luis de Apalachee. *American Journal of Physical Anthropology* 132:207–
            222.
Strickland, S. S., and P. Shetty
1998   Human Biology and Social Inequality. In *Human Biology and Social Inequal-
            ity*, S. S. Strickland and P. S. Shetty editors, pp. 1–20. Cambridge University
            Press, Cambridge.
Tainter, J. A.
1978   Mortuary Practices and the Study of Prehistoric Social Systems. In *Advances
            in Archaeological Method and Theory*, vol 1., edited by M. B. Schiffer, pp.
            105–141. Academic Press, New York.
Thomas, D. H.
1987   *The Archaeology of Mission Santa Catalina de Guale: 1. Search and Discovery*.
            Anthropological Papers Vol. 63, Pt. 2. American Museum of Natural History,
            New York.
1988   Saints and Soldiers at Santa Catalina de Guale. In *The Recovery of Meaning:
            Historical Archaeology in the Eastern United States*, edited by M. P. Leone and
            P. B. Potter Jr., pp. 73–140. Smithsonian Institution Press, Washington, D.C.
2008   Synthesis: The Aboriginal Landscape of St. Catherines Island. In *Native
            American Landscapes of St. Catherines Island, Georgia III*, edited by D. H.
            Thomas, pp. 990–1042. Anthropological Papers Vol. 88. American Museum
            of Natural History, New York.
2009   Native American Landscapes of St. Catherines Island. In *The Beads of St.
            Catherines Island*, edited by E. H. Blair, L. S. A. Pendleton, and P. J. Francis
            Jr., pp. 15–34. Anthropological Papers Vol. 89. American Museum of Natural
            History, New York.
2012   War and Peace on the Franciscan Frontier. In *From La Florida to La Cali-
            fornia: Franciscan Evangelization in the Spanish Borderlands*, edited by T.
            J. Johnson and G. Melville, pp. 105–130. Academy of Franciscan History,
            Berkeley.
2014   Materiality Matters: Colonial Transformations Spanning the Southwestern
            and Southeastern Borderlands. In *Transformations during the Colonial Era:*

Divergent Histories in the American Southwest, edited by J. G. Gouglass and W. M. Graves. University of Colorado Press, Boulder. In press.

Thompson, V. D.
2009 The Mississippian Production of Space through Earthen Pyramids and Public Buildings on the Georgia Coast, USA. *World Archaeology* 41:445–470.

Thompson, V. D, J. A. Turck, A. D. R. Thompson, and C. B. DePratter
2013 Entangling Events: The Guale Landscape before and after the Arrival of the Spanish Missions. In *Life among the Tides: Recent Archaeology on the Georgia Bight*, edited by V. D. Thompson and D. H. Thomas, pp. 423–440. Anthropological Papers Vol. 98. American Museum of Natural History, New York.

Thompson, V. D., and J. E. Worth
2011 Dwellers by the Sea: Native American Adaptations along the Southern Coasts of Eastern North America. *Journal of Archaeological Research* 19:51–101.

Townsend, G., T. Hughes, M. Luciano, M. Bockmann, and A. Brook
2009 Genetic and Environmental Influences on Human Dental variation: A Critical Evaluation of Studies Involving Twins. *Archives of Oral Biology* 54S:S45–S51.

Vercellotti, G., S. D. Stout, R. Boano, and P. W. Sciulli
2011 Intrapopulation Variation in Stature and Body Proportions: Social Status and Sex Differences in an Italian Medieval Population (Trino Vercellese, VC). *American Journal of Physical Anthropology* 145:203–214.

White, C. D, P. F. Healy, and H. P. Schwarcz
1993 Intensive Agriculture, Social Status, and Maya Diet at Pacbitun, Belize. *Journal of Anthropological Research* 49:347–375.

Wood, J. W., G. R. Milner, H. C. Harpending, and K. M. Weiss
1992 The Osteological Paradox: Problems of Inferring Prehistoric Health from Skeletal Samples. *Current Anthropology* 33:343–370.

Worth, J. E.
2001 The Ethnohistorical Context of Bioarchaeology in Spanish Florida. In *Bioarchaeology of Spanish Florida: The Impact of Colonialism*, edited by C. S. Larsen, pp. 1–21. University Press of Florida, Gainesville.

2002 Spanish Missions and the Persistence of Chiefly Power. In *The Transformation of the Southeastern Indians, 1540–1760*, edited by R. Ethridge and C. Hudson, pp. 39–64. University Press of Mississippi, Jackson.

2007 *The Struggle for the Georgia Coast*. Rev. ed. University of Alabama Press, Tuscaloosa.

Zakrzewski, S. R.
2003 Variation in Ancient Egyptian Stature and Body Proportions. *American Journal of Physical Anthropology* 121:219–229.

II

FRONTIERS, COLONIAL ENTANGLEMENTS, AND DIVERSITY

6

Living on the Edge

Maya Identity and Skeletal Biology on the Spanish Frontier

AMANDA R. HARVEY, MARIE ELAINE DANFORTH, AND MARK N. COHEN

Sustained contact between distinct cultures, whether or not it is the result of a colonial process, often promotes resoundingly transformative processes. This is especially true for the Maya of the Yucatán and lowland regions of Central America beginning in the sixteenth century A.D. Those Maya residing on the northern Yucatán coast, which was critical to facilitate travel and trade with the Valley of Mexico, had the earliest and most intense exposure to the colonial Spanish world and the greatest degree of negative transformations of precontact lifeways. The effects of colonialism on this area have been relatively well documented in historical records, especially compared to those of the southern portions of the Yucatán Peninsula (de Landa 1978; Vogt 1976). The Maya living further inland managed to escape this rapid acculturation to a large degree, but less is known about their experiences and engagement with the postcontact world (Jones 1989). However, we would expect that more ephemeral contact with Europeans would have resulted in different responses to contact compared to their counterparts on the coast. It is thus reasonable to postulate that the alternate unfolding of historical interactions in the inland regions of the Maya lowlands created different cultural milieus, indigenous identities, and biological outcomes than in other various regions of more direct Spanish control.

In this chapter, we first present evidence that appears to demonstrate the creation of a local hybrid Maya/Spanish identity in the colonial town of Tipu of west-central Belize. As in other colonial Spanish settings (including several that are discussed in other chapters in this book), we hypothesize that mortuary patterns and material culture will reflect the maintenance of certain Maya traditions balanced with syncretisms drawn from Spanish religion and other aspects of life. Second, the negative biological impacts of contact, as documented among other colonial Maya sites or forcibly conquered peoples in general (again, as seen in various chapters in this book), appear to be absent among the Maya residents at Tipu. We argue that the unique location of this community on the Spanish frontier permitted them to better negotiate their social, political, economic, and biological relationships within the new colonial reality.

THE BIOARCHAEOLOGY OF IDENTITY AND "THIRD SPACES" IN POSTCONTACT BORDERLAND COMMUNITIES

Over the last few decades, interpretive approaches in archaeology and bioarchaeology have burgeoned to study dimensions of individual, social, and ethnic identity (e.g., Agarwal and Glencross 2011; Jones 1997; Knudson and Stojanowski 2009; Knüsel et al. 2010; Stojanowski 2013). Broadly speaking, identity is a multi-component, multidimensional concept that includes self-defined expressions of ethnicity, gender, sexuality, kinship, politics, religion, and age (Barth 1969; Buikstra and Scott 2009). The inclusion of skeletal remains as an extension or embodiment of material culture, lived experiences, and the realm of social ideas (Sofaer 2006) glimpses the crossroads between social behavior cultural identity at both individual and population levels. Klaus and Tam (2009) and Reycraft (2005) advocate for an approach to ethnicity as the mechanism by which individuals who share a common social identity *use* culture to symbolize and enact solidarity, solve problems, and create a more stable social order in times of rapid cultural change. The latter phenomenon may be seen as expressive of ethnogenesis: the process and a tool many Native Americans deployed in postcontact settings involving radical change and discontinuity that embodied various social and political struggles (e.g., Klaus 2013). Further, Jones extends Bourdieu's (1977) classic concept of habitus to the archaeology of identity to conceive that "the construction of ethnicity, and the objectification of cultural differences that this entails, is a product of the intersection between people's habitual dispositions with concrete social conditions characterizing any given social situation" (1997:120). In other words, identity is not necessarily only the construction of who people were or where they came from, but it represents peoples' attempt to define *who they thought they were* (Knudson and Stojanowski 2009:5). Identity in this way relates to the larger social phenomena that characterize a group's existence within their overarching cultural sphere on both conscious and unconscious levels.

Within colonial encounters of any era or place, hybrid blends of cultures in contact tend to arise. This phenomenon might be tethered to the inherent liminality and cultural "mixing" of colonial situations (Bhabha 1994). Van Dommelen (2005) and Klaus (2013) also see how hybridity may be a more active, fluid, transformative, and manipulated process involving the interaction and negotiations between peoples of differing origins, agendas, and traditions. Further, one useful theoretical construct to help understand the nature of postcontact cultural change can be the concept of a "third space." Postcolonial theory (Naum 2010:101; Ribot et al., this volume) envisions third spaces as frontier zones and ambiguous landscapes upon which new, dynamic identities emerge (Bhabha 1996; Bolatagici 2004). Third spaces are realms of negotiation, translation, and remaking that can subvert the authority of the dominant discourse (Bhabha 1996; Naum 2010; Wernke 2010). These fluid zones of interaction are also socially, culturally, ideological, and politically charged, allowing for the construction, negotiation, and manipulation of the identities of those who reside in these areas.

Along these lines, the inland Maya communities of the Yucatán Peninsula of what is today Mexico and Belize probably represented an array of complex third-space settings. This series of colonial-era mission sites, administered by the Spanish capital of Salamanca de Bacalar, extended from the northern border of Belize to the eastern portion of the Guatemalan Petén near Lake Petén Itzá (Figure 6.1). Although 15 *visita* missions were established, only 2 have been located: Lamanai and Tipu. Tipu, as the southernmost *visita*, was on the borderlands of Spanish-controlled territory (Graham et al. 1989; Jones 1989; Jones et al. 1986). In this way, the bioarchaeological study of Tipu is ideally situated to further elucidate Maya biocultural and historic processes of postcontact transformation. It is also well suited to explore the interconnections between social practices, biological stress, and the formation of new identities in postcontact settings.

HISTORICAL BACKGROUND OF TIPU

Tipu was located in a dynamic no-man's-land between areas of direct Spanish control in Yucatán and parts of the Petén controlled by Itzá Maya of Tayasal (Figure 6.1). Tipu was both a center for Yucatecán Maya refugees fleeing more direct Spanish control to the north and a hub of the cacao trade

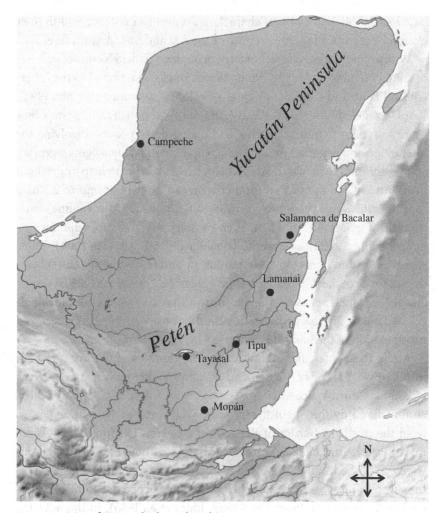

Figure 6.1. Map of Tipu and other colonial Maya sites.

for much of the Petén. The cohabitation of many smaller and previously independent Maya groups likely promoted material culture innovation and extended trade contacts, aiding in the creation of new group norms and likely shaping identities for the population at Tipu (Naum 2010).

The Spanish had a significant impact on the Tipu community even before first direct contact. Spanish soldiers from Cuba introduced epidemic diseases to Yucatán as early as 1517. It has been estimated that the population of Yucatán had been reduced from 800,000 to as a few as 250,000 when Spaniards first contacted Tipu in 1544 (Graham et al. 1989:1256). The Yucatán region was then visited repeatedly by epidemics during the sixteenth and seventeenth centuries. Typhus struck in 1566, 1569–1570, 1575–1576, and 1609. A yellow fever/smallpox epidemic spanned 1648–1650, and either measles or smallpox struck in 1659, 1692–1693, and 1699 (Farriss 1984:61). Famines were almost equally common, occurring in 1535–1541, 1564, 1571–1572, 1575–1576, 1604, 1618, 1627–1631, 1650–1653, 1692–1693, and 1700 (Farriss 1984:61). Similar sequences of events are reported from areas of Guatemala for the same periods (Lovell 1982; Veblen 1982).

Spanish influence at Tipu began in 1544 following a "violent and vicious" rebellion by the Tipuan inhabitants (Jones 1989:22), evidently resisting European encroachment. However, this initial contact does not seem to have resulted in significant reorganization of the Tipu community (Graham et al. 1989). In 1567 and 1568 the Spanish used Tipu as a military base in their efforts at pacifying the surrounding lowland countryside, and their direct presence in the community was more significant at that time. Spanish administrators imposed the *reducción* system to the newly conquered Maya lowland. The forced migration from this system likely caused the splitting of some kin groups and social networks along with remodeling of the existing sociopolitical structure. The *reducción* also brought many smaller Maya groups with broadly similar cultural backgrounds together at Tipu. As with most other large-scale social changes, the degree of impact and identity transformation probably varied by community and region (Klaus and Alvarez-Calderón, this volume). For example, Tipu remained comparably independent and autonomous, and as such it fared somewhat better than communities experiencing the *reducción*, such as the forcibly relocated population of the neighboring and partly contemporary colonial-era people at Lamanai, located 100 km north of Tipu (Graham et al. 1989).

In 1638 the Tipu Maya overthrew the Spanish, and for the next half century they remained largely independent. In the 1690s the population at Tipu chose to reestablish contact with the Spanish at Mérida, initiating a period of peace and the reestablishment of Christianity in the region. However, after the Spanish conquest of the Itzá in 1697, Tipu apparently declined in importance. Occupation of the town finally ended in 1707 when Tipu's inhabitants were forcibly removed to the Petén region.

Historical documents suggest that Tipu's population was exclusively Maya. This fact leads us to think that certain indigenous cultural traditions (e.g., kinship patterns, social stratification, economic ties) were far more likely to be preserved. Because it was a *visita* mission, a Spanish priest, assisted by local converts, would have visited the town only occasionally. According to the 1618 census, the community consisted of about 350 people.

However, if the colonial documents are accurate, the population fluctuated dramatically. By 1622 it may have dropped to as few as 30 people, but in the 1640s it rebounded to 1,000 or more. By 1680 the population dipped to 700, and by 1697 it had fallen to 400 (Jones 1989:116).

The Archaeology of Tipu

Archaeological investigations at Tipu indicate a history of long-term settlement that began during the Maya Late Preclassic period (ca. 300 B.C.) and persisted into the Spanish colonial period (a period of time roughly spanning A.D. 1542 to 1798) with architectural features and material culture reflecting both Postclassic and Colonial occupations. Cemetery excavations at the *visita* mission uncovered the remains of nearly 600 individuals, of which 588 date to the colonial period. Of these, 253 were intact primary burials and 106 were partly disturbed primary burials. The remaining funerary contexts were seriously disturbed by subsequent inhumations. Burials were present in multiple areas, including near the altar, densely packed commingled remains in the nave of the church, and extending some 10 to 12 m outside the church on the northern, southern, and western sides of the nave.

Tipu was a community of considerable size and importance at the time of initial Spanish contact in 1544. Spanish goods in early colonial Tipu confirm contact through trade during the period of initial mission activity. More importantly, the presence of such goods associated with typically Postclassic architectural features of indigenous, rather than Christian, style suggests that a non-Christian population—or at least non-Christian activities—extended into the period of Spanish trade, allowing for an extension of the precontact Maya cultural ideas and identity.

Trade goods and ceramic styles also suggest that Tipu was part of the Itzá economic sphere. Graham et al. (1989) note that the Spanish had relatively little impact on Maya material culture at Tipu other than some relatively privileged access to European goods. Only a veneer of trade items was superimposed on the structure of local Maya economy, unlike the economic disruptions brought about by demands for tribute at other sites. Maize and squash served as major crops, and the community continued to exploit a wide range of fauna similar to Postclassic subsistence strategies (Emery 1999; Thornton 2011). An important advantage of Tipu was the production of cacao. Control over this prestige item would have warranted individual and communal power, possibly influencing social status (*sensu* Marx 1978; Weber 1958) and aiding in shaping identities.

MORTUARY ARCHAEOLOGY AND IDENTITY AT TIPU

The ruins of one Christian church, the *visita* mission, have been found at Tipu (Figure 6.2). Utilization of the church for the deposition of human remains is loosely bounded in historical records by the dates of 1544 and 1707, which mark the founding and abandonment of the colonial town, but its use may have been of even shorter duration. Based on the limited nature of Maya mortuary characteristics, it appears that the church does not represent the very earliest period of Spanish influence on the site. However, Tipu was considered a "spiritual garrison" that was used to help convert many Maya to Christianity, with accounts of around six hundred conversions there during one short period of time in the 1560s (Jones 1989:138). Graham et al. (1989) believe that the church cemetery probably came into use in 1567–1568 and that the church was desecrated and abandoned during the historically documented rebellion of 1638.

Even though the duration of its use may be somewhat limited, the mortuary patterns could suggest the unique individual identities of some of its interments. These include a few flexed burials, one prone burial, one

Figure 6.2. The foundations of the Tipu *visita* mission during excavation in the 1980s (photo by Mark N. Cohen).

limestone crypt, and two women buried holding hands. In all other cases, Spanish Christian mortuary practices were strictly followed at the cemetery of Tipu (in some ways not unlike the Eten cemetery in Peru; see Klaus and Alvarez-Calderón, this volume). Most individuals were buried extended in a supine position, with their heads to the west and their hands placed over their abdomen or chest. The cramped position of the feet and the occasional presence of bone or metal pins on the body suggest that individuals were normally interred in shrouds. Few other goods were found in the graves (Cohen et al. 1997; Jacobi 1996).

Some discrete patterns of sex, age, and body position emerge within the burial population. Those at the front of the church were exclusively primary burials of older persons with distinctly individual placement. One such individual, an adult male of relatively advanced age, was buried in a coffin (as indicated by the patterning of oxidized iron nails surrounding the skeleton) in the area of the nave directly in front of the altar. Additionally, the placement of an unfired clay model of a Spanish censer with one individual from the front probably implies her special place within the community compared to the rest of the population, though scholars have yet to study this unique object extensively (Jones 1989). In comparison, skeletal remains of people buried in the back and outside of the church walls were more commonly disturbed by later single inhumations, formations of secondary burials, and the placement of multiple burials (Jacobi 2000) suggestive of extensive reuse by lower-status individuals. Simultaneously, anthropomorphic effigies in caches of buildings and refuse deposits indicate that precontact Maya religious practices were not completely eradicated (Cohen et al. 1997; Graham et al. 1989).

At Tipu there are no mass burials of the type that might occur during or after epidemics. Most bodies clearly have been interred with care during single events. The apparently arbitrary vertical alignment of groups of burials suggests repeated reuse of the space in the nave and the presence of "family plots" outside of the church walls. Several unusual discrete dental traits cluster together within the cemetery strengthening the kinship hypothesis (Jacobi 1996, 2000). These traits include labial grooves on central incisors, the deflecting wrinkle on lower molars, sixth and seventh cusps on lower molars, enamel pearls, three-rooted lower molars, odontomes, palatal canines, and peg-shaped teeth. Discrete dental trait analysis also suggests that there was little if any Spanish admixture in the population, and that no Spaniards were interred at Tipu (Jacobi 1996, 2000).

It still remains impossible to evaluate with certainty if interments were still carried out after 1638. Graham's excavations have revealed one struc-ture built over a collapsed section of the church wall, and contains intrusive Christian-style burials. The implication is that at least some Christian-style burials continued after the desecration of the church and expulsion of Span-ish administration. Moreover, other bodies in the surrounding churchyard seem to have been interred but misaligned with the majority of those in the cemetery. These individuals might represent continued burial in still-hallowed ground by people who no longer had a standing church to orient them. Furthermore, burials outside the church to the west and north that on the basis of discrete dental traits appear to be separate from the main cemetery (Jacobi 2000) further supporting the idea that the church was invested in creating a colonial Maya identity at Tipu.

A recent thesis examined levels of fluorine in order to explore tempo-ral patterns of interment in the church and cemetery. Musselwhite (2015) used rib samples from 140 adults following the analytical methods outlined in Schurr (1989), and divided the fluorine values into five groups. Results show no strong differences in spatial and demographic distributions over time, but there are some observations that are intriguing. The great major-ity of the earliest burials are inside the church. This pattern continues into the next period of burials as well, although to a lesser degree, but they are more equally distributed spatially in later time periods. Demographically, the most recent burial group is unusual in that it is nearly entirely com-posed of young adults (23 of 24 aged individuals between 18 and 30 years old) and are predominantly males. This particular subsample could repre-sent historically known refugees from elsewhere in the Maya world, and would suggest that immigrants arrived late in the lifetime of the town, and further supports the symbolic nature of the church in the colonial Maya identity.

Archaeologically, reflections of identity of those people buried at Tipu is multifaceted. On one hand, there are still traditional Maya elements such as effigy caches, Postclassic architectures, the continued subsistence pat-terns (Emery 1999) and ritual circuit animal trade (Thornton 2011), Maya-style ceramics (Aimers 2004), and use of 'exotic' trade goods (Aimers et al. 2015) suggesting a persistence of precontact Maya culture. Muddled in the middle, Tipu metallurgists were mixing old and new techniques by draw-ing on methods from preexisting networks in the Yucatán and recycling and mixing metals left behind by Spanish friars (Cockrell et al. 2013). On the opposite side, mortuary patterns, Spanish architecture, Christian ma-terial culture, and the possible continued use of the church graveyard for burials after Tipu's abandonment imply the incorporation of new cultural customs. It is likely that archaeology of the site points to the emergence of some kind of hybrid identity of the Tipuans, something blending various Spanish and Maya elements, that represented a unique configuration of cultural elements in the postcontact Americas.

BIOARCHAEOLOGY OF TIPU

Between 1983 and 1988, bioarchaeological investigations by Mark Cohen (with the assistance of undergraduate and graduate students from State University of New York, Plattsburgh) recovered a sample of approximately six hundred individuals from within the nave of the Tipu church and the surrounding cemetery. Laboratory study of the human remains has resulted in multiple doctoral dissertations, master's theses, and undergraduate research papers (Ballinger 1999; Danforth 1989; Jacobi 1996; O'Connor 1995) Work on the sample has continued from 1983 to the present, utilizing historical, osteological, and archaeological data to assess the impact of Spanish influence on postcontact Maya life.

The Maya lowlands are a notoriously hot and humid tropical area. Rapid bone degradation typically occurs in the acidic soils of the Yucatán Peninsula. Thus, the quality of skeletal preservation at most Maya sites (with the general exception of those buried in protective coffins or tombs [Webster 1997]) is uneven, but often is characterized as poor. Although the condition of the Tipu remains is excellent by comparison with other Maya samples, some skeletons were too fragmented for study. Consequently, sample sizes differ among the various analyses presented. In the following we describe the demographic characteristics of the Tipu sample, followed by multiple measures of childhood biological stress, adult health and infectious disease, and trauma. The conceptual aim that underlies the use of multiple but independent lines of evidence is not only to reconstruct the health of the colonial Tipu Maya (which is an intrinsically valuable goal) but also to understand how the biology of the people reflected the social experiences of living in the unique third space of that Tipu evidently represented.

DEMOGRAPHY

For the colonial period, 173 males, 119 females, 47 adults of unknown sex, and 249 children were identified (Figure 6.3). Of these 588 individuals, 492 were sufficiently well preserved to be aged by one or more techniques (see Cohen et al. 1994). This distribution indicates fewer individuals at the

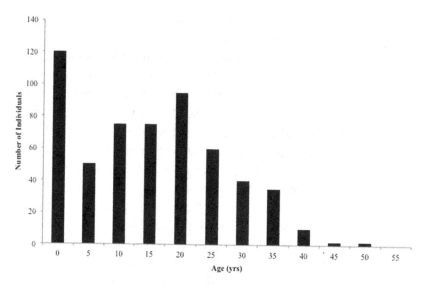

Figure 6.3. Age distribution of the Tipu population.

youngest and oldest ends of the life span than would be expected. Although it is not easily noted in Figure 6.3, infants (0–2 years) are underrepresented at Tipu. This presumably reflects the common archaeological pattern of poor preservation and recovery of the very young. It may also result from the *visita* nature of the Tipu mission, because if unbaptized individuals were denied access to the cemetery, per Spanish Christian traditions of that era, it is likely that many perinatal individuals would have been disposed of elsewhere.

Under-enumeration of individuals in the oldest age categories is also indicated for this sample. The Tipu age-at-death distribution is an exaggerated example of the disproportionately high numbers of young and mid-adult skeletons and the relatively low numbers of older adults. This is often observed in skeletal samples (Acsadi and Nemeskeri 1970; Bennett 1973; Howell 1982; Lovejoy et al. 1977; Walker et al. 1988; Weiss 1973). Only two individuals 50 years of age or older were identified, representing only 0.4 percent of the sample.

Four explanations for the apparent deficit of older adults and a disproportionately high representation of the early and mid-adults (Buikstra and Konigsberg 1985) are considered. First, it is possible that there were socially selective forces at work preventing the burial of elderly individuals who were religiously conservative in a newly established Christian cemetery (Thwaites 1959, cited in Devens 1986:465). However, this possibility only makes sense if the cemetery was of short duration—not the 70 to 160 years during which the cemetery was used.

Second, documented patterns of frontier immigration, which are likely to have involved disproportionately high percentages of young adults, may have biased the cemetery sample. But we would have to assume that the great majority of newcomers also died shortly after their arrival. Otherwise, they too would grow old and add their numbers to the upper end of the age distribution. Still, the rapid changes in population size at Tipu documented in the ethnohistorical record might work against this argument.

Third, age estimates may be skewed because of the research methods used or by the researchers applying these methods. However, the techniques used for Tipu were applied by the same investigators to skeletal samples from precontact Maya samples at Copán, Barton Ramie, Seibal, and Tikal. Older adults tended to be more common in those samples, suggesting that methodological issues alone cannot account for the apparent absence of older individuals at Tipu. In addition, Wright (1989) used tooth root cementum annulation to estimate the ages of 38 individuals previously aged by macroscopic methods. The mean age-at-death estimate for the sample was comparable to that derived for the same individuals by the macroscopic techniques.

Fourth, it is possible that people died in their prime from epidemic diseases that left no direct mark on the skeleton. However, there is no evidence of hasty or mass burials that might be expected to occur under epidemic conditions. Still, successive waves of different high-mortality diseases might have contributed to the low frequency of older adults. If the younger age cohorts of the population were previously unexposed to each high-mortality disease, and epidemics occurred at relatively short intervals (i.e., shorter than a generation), then individuals who survived an epidemic of one disease might demonstrate elevated frailty and heightened risk of mortality (*sensu* DeWitte and Wood 2008) when subsequently exposed to additional high-mortality diseases in their remaining lifetimes. The end result would be a cemetery sample with proportionally fewer individuals who attained old age. Although no adequate historical data exist to investigate this possibility for the Tipu population, sources do indicate that in some Maya areas, epidemics of different diseases occurred approximately every 10 to 20 years, such as seen in highland Guatemala (Lovell 1982:114; Veblen 1982:97) and in colonial Yucatán (Farriss 1984:61).

In addition to the epidemic diseases, other high-mortality diseases, such as malaria or dengue fever, are believed to have been endemic in the frontier lowland areas and may have been an important cause of early adult death (Jones 1989). Based on her analysis of enamel defects in the historic Lamanai series, Wright (1990) concluded that the disease was present at that site. Endemic malaria, successive exposure to different high-mortality epidemic diseases, and frequent famines (sometimes the consequence of socioeconomic disruptions following epidemics) (e.g., Jones 1989:334) may have together presented health stresses so burdensome that few individuals could survive them all and, hence, live to old age. However, as discussed below, there are few signs of "burdensome" stresses during the lives of the Tipu individuals.

PALEOPATHOLOGICAL INVESTIGATIONS

Cohen and other investigators have conducted extensive paleopathological analysis on the Tipu skeletal sample. They reported on subadult health patterns (Danforth et al. 2009; Herndon 1994), dental enamel defects (Danforth 1989; Harvey 2011, 2012), stature (Danforth 1991), cortical thickness as related to nutritional status (Cohen et al. 1997; Danforth 1991; Danforth et al. 1985), and long bone pathology and trauma (Armstrong 1989).

Childhood Health and Biological Stress

Long Bone Growth

Danforth et al. (2009) undertook the analysis of long bone growth patterns among the Tipu subadults (0–18 years). Using complete or nearly complete humeri, femora, and tibiae from 96 individuals under age 12, mean diaphyseal lengths were determined by half-year age intervals with ages based on dental development. As seen in Figure 6.4, the Maya at Tipu followed typical childhood growth curves, demonstrating accelerated growth during the first few years of life and then again after age 7 (Bogin and Smith 1996). When compared to curves of attained growth curves from other populations, the Tipu children were the very shortest group, with only a Late Woodland North American sample possessing smaller diaphyseal lengths during mid-childhood only. This finding supports the observation that the Maya long have been characterized by the lowest stature values among populations around the world (Márquez Morfín et al. 2002). This research also produced regression formulas that can be used for age estimation in subadults in other Maya populations.

Danforth et al. (1985) also found that cortical bone area and femoral diaphyseal length increased regularly with age in their small sample of

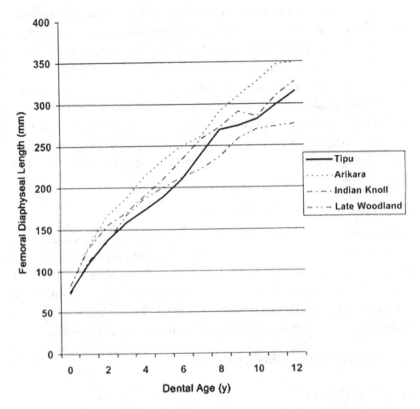

Figure 6.4. Comparison of Tipu femoral growth curve with those seen in other North American populations (Danforth et al. 2009:9).

subadult individuals. This was later confirmed by an analysis of 96 sub-adult skeletons from the entire population showing steady gains in bone thickness through childhood, suggesting that severe protein-calorie mal-nutrition was absent (Bennett and Casey in Cohen et al. 1989; cf. Garn et al. 1966; Huss-Ashmore et al. 1982) and that bone development at Tipu proceeded along relatively normal ontogenetic pathways.

Stature

Mean adult stature at Tipu is typical for Maya populations. Comparison with data available from other precontact Maya skeletal samples indicates that growth was not compromised by significant economic deprivation. From the measurement of maximum femur length, the 149 adult male individuals in the Tipu sample averaged 160.3 cm tall, and the average of stature

Table 6.1. Mean adult stature by sex at selected southern lowland Maya sites

Time period and site	N	Adult male mean (cm)	N	Adult female mean (cm)
Late Classic				
Altar de Sacrificios	2	162.3	2	153.0
Barton Ramie	10	156.6	6	145.7
Copán	10	158.0	16	147.2
Palenque	3	158.8	1	148.0
Seibal	18	159.1	4	145.7
Tikal	21	157.4	11	148.7
Postclassic				
Sarteneja	3	163.0	1	146.7
Colonial				
Tipu	149	160.3	106	148.3
Modern	128	155.5	94	142.8

Note: Adapted from Danforth 1994.

of 106 adult females was 148.3 cm (regression formulas from Genovés 1967). The values for Tipu are well within the ranges of earlier sites in the region, providing further support that there was no local decline in terminal adult stature since the Late Classic period (A.D. 600–900) (Danforth 1999). Drawing upon the work of Floyd and Littleton (2006), these results also suggest that whatever chronic biological stress the children of Tipu endured, it was probably concentrated after the closing of the critical period for skeletal growth (0–2 years), during which incurred growth deficits are generally unrecoverable (Table 6.1).

Dental Enamel Defects

The dentition provides one of the most reliable sources of information of health during childhood (Goodman and Rose 1990), and it has been analyzed in a number of studies of the Tipu series. Harvey's (2011) analysis of linear enamel defects examined stress episode patterns and associated age-at-defect formation (Harvey 2012). The presence of all hypoplasias were visually identified and tactilely verified by running a fingernail over the crown surface creating a low threshold for identification. The position of each defect was then determined by measuring the distance from its center to the cementoenamel junction and using scoring methods suggested by Buikstra and Ubelaker (1994). Chi-square tests were performed to determine significance.

Of the 325 individuals in the dental sample, only 237 (73 percent) had observable canines and 241 (74 percent) had scorable central incisors. Overall,

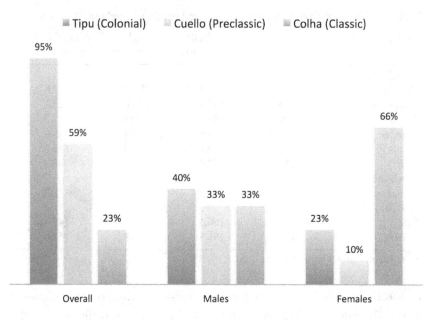

Figure 6.5. Percent of individuals displaying hypoplasia during precontact periods in comparison to Tipu (Harvey 2011:82).

207 of 237 (87 percent) canines displayed at least one defect. Similarly, 191 of 241 (79 percent) central incisors possessed defects. The younger adult (18–35 years old) subgroup had a significantly ($\chi^2 = 8.03$, $df = 1$, $p = 0.01$) higher percentage of affected canines, with 108 of 120 (90 percent) teeth affected, than did the older adults of the sample, with the lowest rate at 17 of 25 (68 percent) displaying lesions. Subadults had the highest mean number of hypoplasias and a higher frequency of moderate and severe hypoplasias. Within the entire sample, there is an average of 1.28 hypoplasias per tooth, and canines predictably averaged more episodes of enamel formation disruption than incisors, while maxillary teeth were more often affected than mandibular teeth. Females displayed approximately 0.33 more lesions per tooth than did males, and those dying as subadults had only slightly more episodes than those surviving to adulthood. Over 90 percent of the defects recorded were of mild severity, while 8.33 percent were moderate and only 0.31 percent were severe. No differences in patterns of severity by sex were found, though males more commonly displayed more than one defect than females on both the central incisor and canine (Harvey 2011). In comparisons to the precontact Maya site of Cuello and Colha, the Tipu inhabitants had a notably higher overall frequency of enamel defects (Figure

Table 6.2. Tipu and Campeche comparative hypoplasia frequencies

Site	Mean incisor	Percentage of incisors affected (n)	Mean canine	Percentage of canines affected (n)
Tipu	1.93	79.3 (241)	1.41	87.3 (237)
Campeche	2.52	90.9 (21)	2.94	90.0 (17)

Note: Data from Harvey 2011:83.

Table 6.3. Comparisons of hypoplasia severity levels at Tipu and Lamanai—percentage of episodes scored

Site	Mild/Shallow	Moderate/Mild	Severe/Acute
Tipu	91%	8%	0.35%
Lamanai	87%	8%	6%

Note: Data from Harvey 2011:84.

6.5). While differences between the sexes varied, males had less variation in overall percentages than females (Harvey 2011).

Yet, in contrast to the rates of enamel hypoplasia formation documented at the postcontact sites of Campeche and Lamanai, the Tipu sample is characterized by less childhood biological stress. Overall, the residents of Campeche had a higher mean number of defects and therefore seem to have experienced more episodes of nonspecific physiological stress than did the inhabitants of Tipu (Table 6.2). The most comparable data reported are from Lamanai (Wright 1990), where the number of macroscopic hypoplasias were classified into three categories of defect expression (Table 6.3). Even though the sample from Lamanai had a slightly lower percentage of mild/shallow defects, that group also had almost 15 times greater a rate of severe/acute defects than did the Tipuans. This may be indicative of greater levels of chronic childhood stress for those individuals at Lamanai (Harvey 2011).

The findings concerning hypoplasia formation were compared with macroscopic lesions observed in a series of Late Classic Maya samples from Tikal ($n = 28$), Barton Ramie ($n = 37$), and Seibal ($n = 27$) (Danforth 1989). Danforth found that both the Late Classic and Historic Maya samples displayed relatively few disruptions in tooth development through the first two years of life. Evidence for prenatal stress was very rare, suggesting that these people did not suffer chronic maternal nutritional insufficiency (Cohen et al. 1989; Danforth 1989; see also Blakey and Armelagos 1985). At Tipu there was some increase in the frequency of stress during the perinatal period, but early childhood appears to be relatively stress-free: only 26 percent of deciduous canines in the Tipu sample were affected by macroscopic enamel hypoplasias, and most were morphologically shallow and short. Observations of permanent canines also suggest that stress was rare for individuals under two years of age, but the samples show an increase in enamel defects related to the probable age of weaning between three and five years. Dentitions from neither the Colonial nor the Classic period commonly display signs of recurrent stress events (Danforth 1989).

Using a large sample of anterior dentition (n = 144 for maxillary central incisors; n = 206 for mandibular canines) from colonial Tipu, Harvey (2011) determined peak age at occurrence using three different macroscopic methods developed by Goodman et al. (1980), Goodman and Rose (1990), and Lewis and Roberts (1997). Martin et al. (2008) have argued that if differences in peak ages are small, with roughly a six-month difference, then it is not biologically meaningful, since the period of stress was not long enough to create distinctive enamel defects.

After eliminating unlikely age ranges based on tooth eruption rates and normal wear patterns, there are similar peak ages for the central incisor and canine. Even though the peak age approximation of 2.5 years using Goodman et al. (1980) is close to the end of incisor formation time, it is probably the most likely peak time of occurrence compared with the other two methods. Yet, this age is similar to other reported (using the same method) prehistoric populations' peak age of defect formation (Danforth and Cook 1994), possibly hinting at a bias. The peak ages of occurrence in the canine were more consistent among the various age standards than the central incisor. Lewis and Roberts's (1997) method most commonly derived the canine's peak age interval at 2.0–2.5 years. This is an entire year younger than the peak age estimated from Goodman et al.'s (1980) technique at 3.5 years. Therefore, this could represent two distinct periods of childhood stress, but assessing which is most accurate is not possible.

Two microdefects in enamel formation, striae of Retzius and Wilson bands, were also examined by Danforth (1989) in these same samples. These defects represent different forms of interruption to dental development (Hillson 1986:107–150). The relatively high frequency of striae seen in most human teeth suggests that they result from mild sources of stress. Wilson bands, which are striae with a disruption in prism orientation, also appear to be associated with shorter-term acute stress, whereas enamel hypoplasias are usually associated with longer-term, chronic health disruption (Rose et al. 1985). Defects were observed by viewing longitudinal sections of deciduous canines, permanent canines, and third molars under magnification (40–400X).

Danforth (1989) concluded that the postcontact Tipu sample did not display patterns of enamel defects suggestive of high levels of biological stress associated with epidemic or zoonotic infections or with severe nutritional deprivation. Instead, the pattern of dental defects is consistent with the interpretation of a generally healthy, even privileged, population. Moreover, the Tipu sample displayed fewer dental defects than the Late Classic samples. While the Tipu sample had high frequencies of striae of Retzius suggesting relatively frequent mild biological stress, the Late Classic samples displayed a higher frequency and greater severity of the more severe defects (Wilson bands and severe enamel hypoplasia). Both groups average six striae per canine, but the Late Classic populations had significantly more Wilson bands. Similarly, the earlier Maya averaged 3.75 enamel hypoplasias per canine as compared to 2.75 in the colonial period sample. Hypoplastic defects in the Late Classic group were more than twice as likely to be classified as severe. Finally, all three defects occurred together most often in the Late Classic groups.

Co-occurrence of Childhood Stress Markers

In a more comprehensive study of subadult biological stress at Tipu, Herndon (1994) assessed differences in patterns of several disease markers in male and female children, with sex estimated by discriminant function analyses based on sexual dimorphism of tooth size among the adult population as documented by Jacobi (1996). Her findings are concordant with those of Danforth (1989) that the subadult years at Tipu were relatively a healthy period of life. Out of the 249 identified subadults at Tipu, only 36 (18 males and 18 females) were analyzed because of the sporadic availability of the canine needed for sex estimation. Herndon inferred that male children experienced slightly more privileged lives than females. Differences in health between the sexes were demonstrated by the lower frequency of enamel hypoplasias and anemia in males, and cortical bone thickness was within the natural range of variation for both sexes. Herndon's (1994) study concurs with the other paleopathological investigations on childhood health, suggesting this period of life as relatively healthy and not stressful, especially compared with other prehistoric and colonial Maya populations.

Patterns of Health during Adulthood

Periosteal Reactions

Bilateral periosteal reactions of long bones, usually linked to nonspecific infection, were also infrequent at Tipu, although they were somewhat more common than traumatic injuries. These lesions occurred most commonly on the tibia, followed in order by the fibula, femur, radius, ulna, and humerus (Armstrong 1989), and further follow a general global pattern of lesion distribution (Larsen 2015). Even though it is slightly higher than the frequency of trauma, periostosis affects less than 0.1 percent of observable bones, with the tibia (8.4 percent, 59/704) and humerus (5.5 percent, 33/601) showing the most periosteal new bone formation. Between the sexes, males displayed higher frequencies, with 36 of 159 males, (22.6 percent) showing lesions as compared to females with only 16 of 116 (13.8 percent) exhibiting periosteal reactions. As with trauma, subadults exhibited few infectious reactions, with only 4 of the 182 bones scored displaying some form of periostitis. Among complete individuals, 36 of 159 males (22.6 percent) display a pathological involvement of at least one bone; 16 of 116 females (13.8 percent) were similarly afflicted. Overall, only 19 of the 457 individuals (4.2 percent) scored showed evidence that could be attributed to systemic infection (reactions on more than one bones). Most changes are relatively minor and mild, although two individuals demonstrated severe periosteal reactions.

Also, the absence of additional patterns of lesions on other bones such as the cranium or the sabre-shin-type defect suggests that treponemal disease was not present in the Tipu population. No signs of the dental stigmata associated with congenital treponematosis were observed. Additionally, although the preserved sample of axial skeletal elements is much smaller compared to those in other parts of the skeleton, the absence of periosteal inflammation of vertebrae, the absence of Pott's disease–associated vertebral collapse, and the absence of periosteal lesions on ribs suggest that skeletal tuberculosis or tuberculosis-like infections did not occur at Tipu. The proportion of skeletons with bony lesions (primarily periostitis) is low by comparison with most prehistoric populations (see Cohen 1989; Cohen and Armelagos 1984; Cohen and Crane-Kramer 2007; Lambert 2000). In contrast to other populations (see Perry, this volume, and Killgrove, this volume), periosteal reaction rates do not suggest the presence of widespread chronic stress as related to infectious disease processes and again tend to resemble the case of Eten on the north coast of Peru (Klaus and Alvarez-Calderón, this volume).

Skeletal Trauma

A total of 457 skeletons were examined for trauma (Armstrong 1989; Cohen et al. 1989). Trauma is rare, occurring in less than 2 percent of individuals, and is most commonly seen on the tibia. For adult bones, 1.8 percent (13/710) of tibiae and 1.1 percent (7/610) of fibulae show signs of fracture-related injury, while only 0.2 percent (1/649) of humeri displays trauma. Among subadult bones, only 0.4 percent (1/236) of tibiae examined display trauma; no other subadult long bones display trauma. Among complete skeletons, 8.7 percent of adults (24/275) display some form of traumatic injury. This includes 10.4 percent of adult males (16/154) and 6.9 percent (8/116) of adult females. In addition, one adult has a crushed left zygomatic arch (with signs of healing) that may reflect a blow to the face. One cranium has a probable partially healed sword cut on the frontal bone, and one tibia displays some kind of entry wound that appears to have healed extensively prior to death. Besides these possible exceptions, no other evidence suggests Spanish weapons inflicted any skeletal injuries at Tipu. The low occurrence of skeletal trauma implies that those buried in the cemetery at Tipu did not experience the ongoing warfare or large-scale violent conflict associated with the tumultuous social changes that happened elsewhere in the region. Overall, the Tipu pattern of trauma suggests occasional interpersonal violence, not endemic political strife (Armstrong 1989; Cohen et al. 1994, 1997). Just as other osteological phenomenon demonstrate, the low frequency of trauma is further evidence of a unique lifestyle at Tipu.

Cortical Bone Maintenance

Cortical bone thickness is partially representative of a population's protein-calorie nutritional intake. Danforth et al. (1985) sectioned femora to investigate cortical involution in a sample of 127 adult individuals and 37 children (0–12 years). Each femur was sectioned immediately distal to mid-shaft, and the cortical area was measured. In addition, the thickness of the cortex was measured at 12 points around its circumference. Mean cortical thickness was expressed as a function of femur length, and Nordin's index (Nordin 1962) and percent cortical area were calculated. Osteoporosis was found in only 3 percent of adult individuals after adjusting Nordin's radiographic standard for dry bone. This quality of bone maintenance may be related to good calcium/phosphorous ratios in the diet resulting from maize preparation methods or grit from limestone *metates* (Coe 1980:599–600; Cotron 1989; Katz et al. 1974). However, it should be noted that the sample is composed primarily of young adults, which makes finding osteoporosis unlikely. There was a lack of sexual dimorphism in Nordin's index resulting from a low absolute level of cortical bone in men, perhaps suggestive of some malnutrition.

Another study related to bone maintenance and biomechanics was conducted by Ballinger (1999), who investigated cortical bone geometry in the bones of the shoulder girdle and arm from Late Classic samples of Altar de Sacrificios and Copán along with postcontact Tipu. In all groups, she found a consistent pattern of sexual dimorphism in which males were some 10 percent larger than females. Overall, the bones of the Late Classic individuals were judged to be stronger than those in Tipu. Ballinger found no significant difference in activity patterns among females, but she did observe that Tipu males had greater robusticity of the clavicle and proximal ulna; the muscles associated with these regions are involved in a wide variety of motions. There also was no difference in bilateral asymmetry among any of the populations, leading Ballinger to conclude that the residents of Tipu participated in the same sort of general subsistence activities that characterized their ancestors.

Discussion

Reconstructing of the consequences of European contact on the biology and culture of Native American populations is complicated by the various methodological and analytical problems associated with osteological data and archaeological contexts. In particular, the frequencies and age patterns of both mortality and morbidity extrapolated from skeletons can be influenced by non-representative samples (skewed from sampling, cultural selection, or taphonomic factors), competing causes of death, and problems associated with age-at-death estimation methods (Buikstra and Konigsberg 1985; Moore et al. 1975; Wood et al. 1992). Therefore, inferences about past health based on such data remain tentative. However, multiple lines of independent evidence, such as ethnohistorical documents, material culture, and the osteological picture of biological stress, can help tease out the various factors contributing to identity, social experiences, and health.

The archaeological evidence of Spanish political influence at Tipu is limited, yet ethnohistorical documents support the notion of change in local political systems to draw attention to the forced immigration of many people to Tipu. The low frequency of cranial and dental modification along with the mortuary program implies that native bodies were part of the Christian universe during life as well as at death. This adoption of at least some Spanish practices is further supported by other observations, such as use of Spanish first names among the Tipu Maya, as indicated in the ethnohistorical records. The adoption of certain Christian symbols, such as the inclusion of the censer with in one person's burial, also speaks to this interpretation.

Though the burial program was nominally Christian, the presence of anthropomorphic effigy caches, Postclassic architecture, continued subsistence patterns, the presence of flexed burials, and cacao production and control support the notion that the Tipu Maya fashioned a unique biocultural environment in their community that influenced both their social status and their identity. It can be suggested that their uninterrupted kinship and social structures, continued trade with the Itzá, and general "acceptance" of Spanish ideology allowed for a relatively smooth transition to a some kind of a new colonial hybrid Maya identity composed of traditional Maya cultural behaviors and new Spanish influences.

Drawing upon Meskell (1998), a population within an inferred third space such as Tipu often demonstrates a collective embodiment, or a communal experience of the complex interplay between two contrasting traditions—in this case, both Maya and Spanish social, cultural, natural, and cognitive phenomena. This fostered a place-specific, hybrid ethnic identity of the colonial Tipuan, not unlike many settings in the pre- and postcontact Mesoamerican and South American regions (Bawden 2005; Buikstra and Scott 2009; Klaus and Tam 2009; Luke and Luke 1999; Reycraft 2005). A "hybrid" identity is one that is without a single origin but which maintains a situational sense of difference and tension between two cultures (Bolatagici 2004). Since identity is place-bound both geographically and abstractly (Luke and Luke 1999), borderland settings are places where social identities are reshaped and personhoods invented and reinvented. This creates a communal hybrid ethnicity with a unique mixing of cultural entities in which origin and home are vaguely defined.

The human body is also a locus where social and political negotiations are played out (Fowler 2004; White et al. 2009:156; Yates 1993). Though the colonial period was a time of change, Tipuans young and old were able to maintain the aspects of Maya practice that benefited their health, as well as incorporate Spanish cultural norms in adaptive ways. Paleopathological evidence is indicative of a low prevalence of trauma, biological stress, and infectious disease. Biomechanical analyses, cortical bone thickness data, and terminal adult stature also indicate that Tipuans maintained traditional subsistence strategies as limited *encomienda* demands helped them maintain an adequate nutritional intake. Even childhood at Tipu was a time of relatively limited biological stress. Individuals who died during childhood representing the subadult portion of the population are characterized by overall low frequencies of stress and disease, indicating a relatively healthy time of life in terms of stressors that affect skeletal tissue. Overall, the picture drawn from skeletal biology at Tipu seems to represent a unique colonial lifestyle at Tipu again almost certainly part of a unique identity held among the people who lived and died in this colonial town.

Conclusions

The frontier nature of Tipu introduces a unique factor to the possible interpretation of Maya identities in the colonial world. As a space of hybridity, this borderland town functioned as a "third space" (Bhabha 1996; Bolatagici 2004) or an area with a degree of inbetween-ness, as it is characterized by social and cultural transformation and change, along with constant dialogue and remaking. Living in this liminal zone between the different political spheres allowed for Tipuans to create a distinct identity (Naum 2010:126) that was a mixture of Maya and Spanish cultural norms. It would appear that the Tipu Maya were able to successfully negotiate a coexistence with the Spanish. The relative lack of widespread biological stress, morbidity, and disruption were important factors that helped foster a setting where Tipu's residents could balance integration with Spanish religious norms (as seen by the mortuary program) with the maintenance of traditional Maya economic activities and subsistence practices (as reflected in their low prevalence of biological stress). During a time of expected change and cultural decimation, Tipuans adapted to an ever-changing world by creating a new, hybrid identity for themselves. Frontier realities like Tipu illustrate that the relationship between artifacts and identities is ambiguous, and that culture is not an abstract entity but a dynamic creation (Naum 2010:127). Hybrid identities are a construction of something new out of difference (Luke and Luke 1999:231), and at Tipu there seems to have been a smooth creation of a new hybrid, colonial Maya identity composed situated somewhere between traditional Maya culture and limited Spanish influences.

ACKNOWLEDGMENTS AND NOTES

Parts of this chapter were adapted from Cohen et al. (1994) with additional references to later works. The excavation and analysis of Tipu have been supported by National Science Foundation grants BNS 83-03693 and BNS 85-06785. The Tipu skeletal collection is open for study but has been moved to the University of Southern Mississippi and is now curated by Marie Danforth. We thank Haagen Klaus and Melissa Murphy for their comments on previous drafts of this chapter.

REFERENCES CITED

Acsadi, G., and J. Nemeskeri
1970   History of Human Life Span and Mortality. Akadémiai Kiadó, Budapest.
Agarwal, S. C., and B. A. Glencross
2011   Building a Social Bioarchaeology. In Social Bioarchaeology, edited by S. C. Agarwal and B. A. Glencross, pp. 1–11. Wiley-Blackwell, Malden.
Aimers, J. J.
2004   Cultural Change on a Temporal and Spatial Frontier: Ceramics of the Terminal Classic to Early Postclassic Transition in the Upper Belize River Valley. British Archaeological Reports International Series No. 1325. British Archaeological Reports, Oxford.
Aimers, J. J., E. Haussner, D. Farthing, and T. Guderjan
2015   The Ugly Duckling: Insights into Ancient Maya Commerce and Industry from Pottery Petrography. Research Reports in Belizean Archaeology 12.
Armstrong, C.
1989   Pathological Analysis of Long Bones within the Tipu Population. Unpublished M.A. thesis, Liberal Studies, State University of New York at Plattsburgh.
Ballinger, D.
1999   Sexual Dimorphism in Cortical Bone Geometry in Two Maya Populations. Ph.D. dissertation, Department of Anthropology, Indiana University, Bloomington. University Microfilms, Ann Arbor.
Barth, F.
1969   Introduction. In Ethnic Groups and Boundaries: The Social Organization of Culture Different, edited by F. Barth, pp. 9–38. Little, Brown, Boston.
Bawden, G.
2005   Ethnogenesis at Galindo, Peru. In Us and Them: Archaeology and Ethnicity in the Andes, edited by R. Reycraft, pp. 285–305. Costen Institute of Archaeology, University of California, Los Angeles.
Bennett, K. A.
1973   On the Estimation of Some Demographic Characteristics of a Prehistoric Population from the American Southwest. American Journal of Physical Anthropology 39:223–232.

Bhabha, H. M.
1994   *The Location of Culture*. Routledge, London.
1996   The Other Question: Difference, Discrimination, and the Discourse of Co-
            lonialism. In *Black British Cultural Studies: A Reader*, edited by H. A. Baker,
            M. Diawara, and R. H. Lindeborg, pp. 87–106. University of Chicago Press,
            Chicago.
Blakey, M., and G. J. Armelagos
1985   Deciduous Enamel Defects in Prehistoric Americans from Dickson Mounds.
            American Journal of Physical Anthropology 66:371–380.
Bogin, B., and B. H. Smith
1996   Evolution of the Human Life Cycle. *American Journal of Human Biology*
            8:703–716.
Bolatagici, T.
2004   Claiming the (N)either/(N)or of "Third Space": (Re)presenting Hybrid
            Identity and the Embodiment of Mixed Race. *Journal of Intercultural Studies*
            25:76–85.Bourdieu, P.
1977   *Outline of a Theory of Practice*. Cambridge University Press, Cambridge.
Buikstra, J. E., and L. W. Konigsberg
1985   Paleodemography: Critiques and Controversies. *American Anthropologist*
            87:316–333.
Buikstra, J. E., and R. E. Scott
2009   Key Concepts of Identity. In *Bioarchaeology and Identity in the Americas*,
            edited by K. J. Knudson and C. M. Stojanowski, 24–55. University Press of
            Florida, Gainesville.
Buikstra, J. E., and D. H. Ubelaker
1994   *Standards for Data Collection from Human Skeletal Remains*. Arkansas Ar-
            chaeology Research Series No. 44. Arkansas Archaeological Survey, Fayette-
            ville.
Cockrell, B., M. Martinón-Torre, and E. A. Graham
2013   Negotiating a Colonial Maya Identity: Metal Ornaments from Tipu, Belize.
            Open Journal of Archaeometry 1(24):115–121.
Coe, W. R.
1980   Artifacts of the Maya Lowlands. In *Archaeology of Southern Mesoamerica,
            Part II, Handbook of Middle American Indians*, vol. 3., edited by G. R. Willey,
            pp. 594–602. University of Texas Press, Austin.
Cohen, M. N.
1989   *Health and the Rise of Civilization*. Yale University Press, New Haven.
Cohen, M. N., and G. J. Armelagos (editors)
1984   *Paleopathology at the Origins of Agriculture*. Academic Press, Orlando.
Cohen, M. N., S. Bennett, and C. W. Armstrong
1989   *Health and Genetic Relationships in a Colonial Maya Population*. Final re-
            port on grant BNS-85-06785 submitted to the National Science Foundation,
            Washington, D.C.

Cohen, M. N., and G. M. M. Crane-Kramer (editors)
2007   *Ancient Health: Skeletal Indicators of Agricultural and Economic Intensifica-*
            tion. University Press of Florida, Gainesville.
Cohen, M. N., K. A. O'Connor, M. E. Danforth, K. P. Jacobi, and C. W. Armstrong
1994   Health and Death at Tipu. In *In the Wake of Contact*, edited by C. S. Larsen
            and G. R. Milner, pp. 121–133. Wiley-Liss, New York.
1997   Archaeology and Osteology of the Tipu Site. In *Bones of the Maya: Studies*
            of Ancient Skeletons, edited by S. L. Whittington and D. M. Reed, pp. 78–86.
            Smithsonian Institution Press, Washington, D.C.
Cotron, R. S., V. Kumar, and S. L. Robbins
1989   *Robbins' Pathological Basis of Disease.* 4th ed. Saunders, Philadelphia.
Danforth, M. E.
1989   Comparison of Health Patterns in Late Classic and Colonial Maya Popula-
            tions Using Enamel Microdefects. Unpublished Ph.D. dissertation, Depart-
            ment of Anthropology, Indiana University, Bloomington.
1991   Childhood Health Patterns at Tipu: Evidence from Harris Lines. Poster pre-
            sented at the annual meeting of the American Association of Physical An-
            thropologist, Milwaukee.
1999   Coming Up Short: Stature and Nutrition among the Ancient Maya of the
            Southern Lowlands. In *Reconstructing Ancient Maya Diet*, edited by C.
            White, pp. 103–118. University of Utah Press, Salt Lake City.
Danforth, M. E., S. Bennett, M. N. Cohen, and H. Melkunas
1985   Femoral Cortical Involution in a Colonial Maya Population. Paper presented
            at the 54th meetings of the American Association of Physical Anthropolo-
            gists, Knoxville.
Danforth, M. E., and D. C. Cook
1994   The Human Remains from Carter Ranch Pueblo, Arizona: Health in Isola-
            tion. *American Antiquity* 59:88–101.
Danforth, M. E., G. D. Wrobel, C. W. Armstrong, and D. Swanson
2009   Juvenile Age Estimation Using Diaphyseal Long Bone Lengths among An-
            cient Maya Populations. *Latin American Antiquity* 20:3–13.
de Landa, D.
1978   *Yucatan before and after Conquest.* New York, Dover.
Devens, C.
1986   Separate Confrontations: Gender as a Factor in Indian Adaptation to Euro-
            pean Colonization in New France. *American Quarterly* 88:461–480.
DeWitte, S. N., and J. W. Wood
2008   Selectivity of Black Death Mortality with Respect to Pre-Existing Health.
            Proceedings of the National Academy of Sciences of the United States of Amer-
            ica 105:1436–1441.
Emery, K. F.
1999   Continuity and Variability in Postclassic and Colonial Animal Use at La-
            manai and Tipu, Belize. In *Reconstructing Ancient Maya Diet*, edited by C.
            White, pp. 61–81. University of Utah Press, Salt Lake City.

Farriss, N.
1984   *Maya Society under Colonial Rule.* Princeton University Press, Princeton.
Floyd, B., and J. Littleton
2006   Linear Enamel Hypoplasia and Growth in an Australian Aboriginal Com-
            munity: Not So Small, But Not So Healthy Either. *Annals of Human Biology*
            33:424–443.
Fowler, C.
2004   *The Archaeology of Personhood: An Anthropological Approach.* Routledge,
            London.
Garn, S. M., C. G. Rohmann, and M. A. Guzman
1966   Malnutrition and Skeletal Development in Preschool Children. In *Preschool
            Child Malnutrition,* pp. 43–62. National Academy of Sciences National Re-
            search Council, Washington, D.C.
Genovés, S.
1967   Proportionality of Long Bones and Their Relation to Stature among Meso-
            americans. *American Journal of Physical Anthropology* 26:67–77.
Goodman, A. H., G. J. Armelagos, and J. Rose
1980   Enamel Hypoplasia as an Indicator of Stress in Three Prehistoric Populations
            from Illinois. *Human Biology* 52:515–518.
Goodman, A. H., and J. C. Rose
1990   Assessment of Systemic Physiological Perturbations from Dental Enamel
            Hypoplasias and Associated Histological Structures. *Yearbook of Physical
            Anthropology* 33:59–110.
Graham, E., D. M. Pendergast, and G. D. Jones
1989   On the Fringes of Conquest: Maya-Spanish Contact in Colonial Belize. *Sci-
            ence* 246:1254–1259.
Harvey, A. R.
2011   Consequences of Contact: Evaluation of Health Patterns Using Enamel Hy-
            poplasias among the Colonial Maya of Tipu. Unpublished M.A. thesis, De-
            partment of Anthropology, University of Southern Mississippi, Hattiesburg.
2012   Dog Days of Stress: A Comparison of Methods for Determining Age at Oc-
            currence of Enamel Hypoplasias. Paper presented at the 81st meeting of the
            American Association of Physical Anthropologists, Portland.
Herndon, K. S.
1994   The Children of Tipu. Unpublished M.A. thesis, Department of Anthropol-
            ogy and Sociology, University of Southern Mississippi, Hattiesburg.
Hillson, S.
1986   *Teeth.* Cambridge University Press, Cambridge.
Hooton, E.
1940   Skeleton from the Cenote of Sacrifice at Chichen Itza. In *The Maya and Their
            Neighbors,* edited by C. L. Hay, pp. 270–280. Dover, New York.
Howell, N.
1982   Village Composition Implied by a Paleodemographic Life Table: The Libben
            Site, Ohio. *American Journal of Physical Anthropology* 59:63–270.

Huss-Ashmore, R., A. H. Goodman, and G. J. Armelagos
1982   Nutritional Inference from Paleopathology. In *Advances in Archaeological Method and Theory*, vol. 5, edited by M. J. Schiffer, pp. 395–474. Academic Press, New York.

Jacobi, K. P.
1996   An Analysis of Genetic Structuring in a Colonial Maya Cemetery, Tipu, Belize, Using Dental Morphology and Metrics. Unpublished Ph.D. dissertation, Department of Anthropology, Indiana University, Bloomington.
2000   *Last Rites for the Tipu Maya*. University of Alabama Press, Tuscaloosa.

Jones, G.
1989   *Maya Resistance to Spanish Rule*. University of New Mexico Press, Albuquerque.

Jones, G., R. Kautz, and E. Graham
1986   Tipu: A Maya Town on the Spanish Colonial Frontier. *Archaeology* 39:40–47.

Jones, S.
1997   *The Archaeology of Ethnicity: Constructing Identities in the Past and Present*. Routledge, London.

Katz, S. H., M. I. Hediger, and L. A. Valleroy
1974   Traditional Maize Processing Techniques in the New World. *Science* 184:765–768.

Klaus, H. D.
2013   Hybrid Cultures . . . and Hybrid Peoples: Bioarchaeology of Genetic Change, Religious Architecture, and Burial Ritual in the Colonial Andes. In *The Archaeology of Hybrid Material Culture*, edited by J. Card, pp. 207–238. Center for Archaeological Investigations, Occasional Papers 39, Carbondale.

Klaus, H. D., and M. E. Tam
2009   Surviving Contact: Biological Transformation, Burial, and Ethnogensis in Peru. In *Bioarchaeology and Identity in the Americas*, edited by K. J. Knudson and C. Stojanowski, pp. 126–152. University Press of Florida, Gainesville.

Knudson, K. J., and C. M. Stojanowski
2009   The Bioarchaeology of Identity. In *Bioarchaeology and Identity in the Americas*, edited by K. J. Knudson and C. M. Stojanowski, pp. 1–23. University Press of Florida, Gainesville.

Knüsel, C. J., C. M. Batt, G. Cook, J. Montgomery, G. Müldner, A. R. Ogden, C. Palmer, B. Stern, J. Todd, and A. S. Wilson
2010   The Identity of the St Bees Lady, Cumbria: An Osteobiographical Approach. *Medieval Archaeology* 54(1):271–311.

Lambert, P. M. (editor)
2000   *Bioarchaeological Studies of Life in the Age of Agriculture: A View from the Southeast*. University of Alabama Press, Tuscaloosa.

Larsen, C. S.
2015   *Bioarchaeology: Interpreting Behavior from the Human Skeleton*. 2nd ed. Cambridge University Press, Cambridge.

Lewis, M., and C. Roberts
1997   Growing Pains: The Interpretation of Stress Indicators. *International Journal of Osteoarchaeology* 7:581–586.
Lovejoy, C. O., R. S. Meindl, T. R. Pryzbeck, T. J. Barton, K. G. Heiple, and D. Knotting
1977   Paleodemography of the Libben Site, Ottawa County, Ohio. *Science* 198:291–293.
Lovell, W. G.
1982   Collapse and Recovery: A Demographic Profile of the Cuchumatan Highlands of Guatemala 1520–1821. In *The Historical Demography of Highland Guatemala*, edited by R. M. Carmack, J. Early, and C. Lutz, pp. 103–120. Institute for Mesoamerican Studies, Publication No. 6. State University of New York at Albany, Albany.
Luke, C., and A. Luke
1999   Theorizing Interracial Families and Hybrid Identity: An Australian Perspective. *Education Theory* 49:223–249.
Márquez Morfín, L., R. McCaa, R. Storey, and A. Del Angel
2002   Health and Nutrition in Pre-Hispanic Mesoamerica. In *The Backbone of History: Health and Nutrition in the Western Hemisphere*, edited by R. H. Steckel and J. C. Rose, pp. 307–340. Cambridge University Press, Cambridge.
Martin, S. A., D. Guatelli-Steinberg, P. W. Sciulli, and P. L. Walker
2008   Brief Communication: Comparison of Methods for Estimating Chronological Age at Linear Enamel Formation on Anterior Dentition. *American Journal of Physical Anthropology* 135:362–365.
Marx, K.
1978   The German Ideology: Part 1. In *The Marx-Engels Reader*, edited by R. C. Tucker, pp. 148–200. 2nd ed. Norton, New York.
Meskell, L.
1998   The Irresistible Body and the Seduction of Archaeology. In *Changing Bodies, Changing Meanings: Studies on the Human Body in Antiquity*, edited by D. Montserrat, pp. 139–161. Routledge, London.
Moore, J. A., A. C. Swedlund, and G. J. Armelagos
1975   The Use of Life Tables in Paleodemography. *American Antiquity* 40:57–70.
Musselwhite, N. M.
2015   An Analysis of Fluorine Levels to Determine Burial Sequence at the Maya Colonial *Visita* Mission of Tipu, Belize. Thesis in progress, Department of Anthropology and Sociology, University of Southern Mississippi, Hattiesburg.
Naum, M.
2010   Re-emerging Frontiers: Postcolonial Theory and Historical Archaeology of the Borderlands. *Journal of Archaeological Method and Theory* 17:101–131.
Nordin, B. E. C.
1962   The Problem of Osteoporosis. *Gerontology Clinic* 4:19–32.
O'Connor, K. A.
1995   The Age Pattern of Mortality: A Micro-analysis of Tipu and a Meta-analysis

of Twenty-Nine Paleodemographic Samples. Unpublished Ph.D. dissertation, Department of Anthropology, State University of New York, Albany.

Reycraft, R. M. (editor)

2005   *Us and Them: Archaeology and Ethnicity in the Andes.* Costen Institute of Archaeology, University of California, Los Angeles.

Rose, J. C., K. W. Condon, and A. H. Goodman

1985   Diet and Dentition: Developmental Disturbances. In *The Analysis of the Prehistoric Diet,* edited by R. I. Gilbert and J. H. Mielke, pp. 281–305. Academic Press, New York.

Saul, F. P.

1972   *The Human Skeletal Remains of Altar de Sacrificios.* Papers of the Peabody Museum of Archaeology and Ethnology Vol. 63. Harvard University, Cambridge.

1975   Human Remains. In *Excavations at Seibal, Department of Petén, Guatemala,* edited by A. L. Smith, G. R. Willey, and J. A. Sabloff. Peabody Museum of Archaeology and Ethnography. Harvard University, Cambridge.

1982   Appendix II. The Human Skeletal Remains from Tancah, Mexico. In *On the Edge of the Sea: Mural Painting at Tancah-Tulum, Quintana Roo, Mexico,* edited by A. Miller, pp. 115–128. Dumbarton Oaks, Washington, D.C.

Schurr, M. R.

1989   Fluoride Dating of Prehistoric Bones by Ion Selective Electrode. *Journal of Archaeological Science* 16:265–270.

Sofaer, J.

2006   *The Body as Material Culture: A Theoretical Osteoarchaeology.* Cambridge University Press, Cambridge.

Steggerda, M.

1941   *Maya Indians of Yucatan.* Carnegie Institution, Washington, D.C.

Stojanowski, C. M

2013   Uncovering Identity in Mortuary Analysis: Community-Sensitive Methods for Identifying Group Affiliation in Historical Cemeteries. *Journal of Interdisciplinary History* 44(1):138–139.

Thornton, E. K.

2011   Reconstructing Ancient Maya Animal Trade through Strontium Isotopes ($^{87}Sr/^{86}Sr$) Analysis. *Journal of Archaeological Science* 38:3254–3263.

Thwaites, R. G.

1959   *The Jesuit Relations and Allied Documents.* 73 vols. Burrows Brothers, Cleveland.

Van Dommelen, P.

2005   Colonial Interactions and Hybrid Practices: Phoenician and Carthaginian Settlement in the Ancient Mediterranean. In *The Archaeology of Colonial Encounters,* edited by G. Stein, pp. 109–144. School of American Research Press, Santa Fe.

Veblen, T. T.

1982   Native Population Decline in Totonicapan, Guatemala. In *The Historical Demography of Highland Guatemala,* edited by R. M. Carmack, J. Early, and C.

Lutz, pp. 81–102. Institute for Mesoamerican Studies, Publication No. 6. State University of New York, Albany.

Vogt, E. Z.

1976   *Tortillas for the Gods: A Symbolic Analysis of Zinacanteco Rituals.* University of Oklahoma Press, Normal.

Walker, P. L., J. R. Johnson, and P. M. Lambert

1988   Age and Sex Biases in the Preservation of Human Skeletal Remains. *American Journal of Physical Anthropology* 76:183–188.

Weber, M.

1958   Class, Status, Party. In *From Max Weber: Essays in Sociology*, translated and edited by H. H. Gerth and C. W. Mills, pp. 180–195. Oxford University Press, New York.

Webster, D.

1997   Studying Maya Burials. In *Bones of the Maya: Studies of Ancient Skeletons*, edited by S. L. Whittington and D. M. Reed, pp. 3–12. Smithsonian Institution Press, Washington, D.C.

Weiss, K.

1973   *Demographic Models for Anthropology.* Memoirs of the Society for American Antiquity No. 27. Society for American Antiquity, Washington, D.C.

Wernke, S. A.

2010   Convergences: Producing Early Colonial Hybridity at a Doctrina in Highland Peru. In *Enduring Conquests: Rethinking the Archaeology of Resistance to Spanish Colonialism in the Americas*, edited by M. Liebmann and M. S. Murphy, pp. 77–101. School for Advanced Research Press, Santa Fe.

White, C. D.

1986   Paleodiet and Nutrition of the Ancient Maya at Lamanai, Belize: A Study of Trace Elements, Stable Isotopes, Nutrition and Dental Pathology. Unpublished M.A. thesis, Department of Anthropology, Trent University, Peterborough.

White, C. D., F. J. Longstaffe, D. M. Pendergast, and J. Maxwell

2009   Cultural Embodiment and the Enigmactic Identity of the Lovers. In *Bioarchaeology and Identity in the Americas*, edited by K. J. Knudson and C. M. Stojanowksi, pp. 155–176. University Press of Florida, Gainesville.

Wood, J. W., G. R. Milner, H. C. Harpending, and K. M. Weiss

1992   The Osteological Paradox: Problems of Inferring Prehistoric Health from Skeletal Samples. *Current Anthropology* 33:343–370.

Wright, L. E.

1989   Cemental Annulation: A Test of Its Application to the Colonial Maya of Tipu, Belize. Unpublished M.A. thesis, Department of Anthropology, University of Chicago, Chicago.

1990   Stresses of Conquest: A Study of Wilson Bands and Enamel Hypoplasias in the Maya of Lamanai, Belize. *American Journal of Human Biology* 2:25–35.

Yates, T.

1993   Frameworks for the Archaeology of the Body. In *Interpretive Archaeology*, edited by C. Tilley, pp. 31–72. Berg, Oxford.

7

Double Coloniality in Tierra del Fuego, Argentina

A Bioarchaeological and Historiographical Approach to Selk'nam
Demographics and Health (La Candelaria Mission,
Late Nineteenth and Early Twentieth Centuries)

RICARDO A. GUICHÓN, ROMINA CASALI, PAMELA GARCÍA LABORDE,
MELISA A. SALERNO, AND ROCIO GUICHÓN

At the southernmost reaches of South America, Tierra del Fuego was one of the last places on Earth to be populated by humans and was one of the last settings of colonization by Europeans. As a result, a thoroughly unique colonial situation unfolded here. Human settlement in Tierra del Fuego dates back about twelve thousand years, and when Westerners arrived in the region they identified four different cultural groups. The Selk'nams (Onas) lived in the interior of the island and depended on hunting and gathering for survival. The Yamanas (Yaganes) occupied the area surrounding the Beagle Channel, while the Kaweskars (Alacalufes) occupied the channels located in western Patagonia, and both subsisted on maritime resources. Haush people lived on Mitre Peninsula and relied chiefly on pinnipeds for food (Figure 7.1).

The permanent occupation of Tierra del Fuego by Westerners did not begin until the end of the nineteenth century. In this chapter we will discuss the particular features of the unique colonial relationships in this region. Along these lines, we will examine the health and demographic changes experienced by the Selk'nam community through a bioarchaeological case study of the Salesian mission of Nuestra Señora de La Candelaria (Río Grande, Argentina). First, we will consider the particular features that underscored and structured cultural interactions in Tierra del Fuego, suggesting that colonialism in the region could be understood in terms of

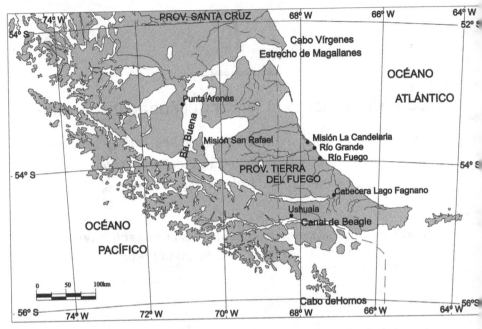

Figure 7.1. Map showing the location of important towns, estancias, and religious missions in Tierra del Fuego (prepared by the authors).

a "double coloniality." Second, we will present the results of the analysis of living conditions at the mission, considering the hypothesis that sanitary changes had a negative impact on the demographic dynamics of the Selk'nam community (for references on the impact of imperial interests on health and quality of life, see Perry, this volume).

Any approach to a colonial encounter needs to simultaneously explore different scales of analysis. On the one hand, it is relevant to discuss the role of broad historical processes that encouraged the relationships among different groups. On the other, it is worth considering the circumstances that surrounded colonial situations in a specific context, as well as the impact of broad historical processes on regional or local levels (and vice versa). Here, it is possible to ask questions about the timing of interaction, the nature of cultural relationships, and the dimensions of change, among other issues. In this chapter we will consider the colonial context brought about by the emergence of the Atlantic trade system—in other words, the emergence of the Western Hemisphere in its most recent political and economic form. As a cause and effect of modernity, these circumstances were closely related to colonialism, Eurocentrism, and capitalism (Orser 1996).

COLONIALITY AND CULTURAL ENCOUNTERS

From the sixteenth century onward, it is no longer possible to think of modernity without considering "coloniality." In this work we intentionally use the term "coloniality" in lieu of "colonialism" to conceptualize what was (and still is) "the dark side" of modernity. It was "constitutive" but not "derivative" of modernity (Mignolo 2003). Both coloniality and modernity were associated with capitalism, which is frequently defined as a "world-system" (Wallerstein 1979). In this framework, some regions became centralized, while others assumed a peripheral status. Eurocentrism made a clear distinction between a superior "us" (heir to Western modernity) and an inferior "them" (heir to tradition). Some researchers understand this relationship in dialectical terms, as if all parts making up the whole were the result of reciprocal conditioning. In the Western Hemisphere, the American continent appeared as the "inner outside" shaping the self-definition of Europe (Mignolo 2003).

Coloniality found different expressions at a smaller scale. At one end, it is possible to refer to the short-term encounters that described the first moments of interaction. Scholars frequently call these situations "contact" (Silliman 2005). Impact and power inequalities existed but were not overwhelming. At the other end of the spectrum were the continual and long-lasting "entanglements" that described later moments of interaction (Thomas 1991). Researchers usually connect these circumstances to "colonialism" and "power issues," respectively (Gosden 2004). We adopt a conception of coloniality that allows discussing colonialism and the coloniality of power—in other words, the dynamics of planned or exercised coercion and the responses given from a "colonial difference" (Mignolo 2003; Quijano 2000). This conception makes it possible to understand the world-system not only from its own perspective but also from the standpoint that is shaped by the colonial "other."

Coloniality involved two issues. First, although colonial relationships were asymmetrical, power had a dynamic and multi-directional nature (Foucault 1975) that allowed people to resist (Silliman 2005). Second, coloniality transformed all parties involved, as it was part of a new context of interaction and negotiation. Coloniality was connected to destruction, but also to creativity and creation (Gosden 2004). Colonial cultures were no better than or absolutely different from previous cultures, but were the products of complex cultural intersections and shared stories (Thomas 1991). All of this confers upon coloniality a complex and contingent reality.

Beyond global processes, the strength of the "local," contingency, and the power of the colonized gave way to the multiple trajectories defining coloniality (Andrade Lima 1999, 2001; Funari et al. 1999; Funari and Zarankin 2004; Senatore and Zarankin 2002).

Tierra del Fuego provides a unique context in which to study coloniality. Unlike many other regions of the Americas, and even though initial encounters date back to the sixteenth century, it was not until the late nineteenth and early twentieth centuries that the relationships between Western and indigenous peoples became everyday realities. Tierra del Fuego was part of the ultra-periphery of Europe and a marginal region of the nation-states of Argentina and Chile (for other perspectives on frontier colonial contexts, see Harvey et al., this volume). Here, coloniality had opportunities to display different features from those described by dominant research models created to understand other regions of the world. Tierra del Fuego is an island, and cultural interaction was affected by this fact of geography as well.

CONTACT AND COLONIALISM IN TIERRA DEL FUEGO

The modern history of Tierra del Fuego involved cultural contact and colonialism. Between the discovery of the strait by Ferdinand Magellan in 1520 and the last third of the nineteenth century, European powers undertook several voyages to the region. These voyages were exploratory and strategic in character, as sailing conditions were tough both in the Strait of Magellan and around Cape Horn. However, these circumstances did not prevent Europeans from sealing and whaling around Tierra del Fuego. Indirect cultural contact was often initiated as shipwrecks and material remains reached the shores (Borrero 1992). Meanwhile, direct cultural contact was sporadic and involved small groups of people (Fugassa and Guichón 2004).

Direct contact situations had serious implications for the health of the indigenous population and resulted in the spread of measles, rubella, smallpox, leprosy, and venereal diseases in the area surrounding the Beagle Channel (Belza 1974; Bridges 2008; Bridges 1891, 1893; Canclini 1986; Gusinde 1951). The 1869 establishment of an Anglican mission in present-day Ushuaia was a major event in the history of Tierra del Fuego, both for representing the beginning of actual colonization, and for its consequences on the Yamana community. The English presence on the channel became economic and strategic in nature. By 1880, nation-states managed to gain strength in the region, and in 1884 Argentina established the subprefecture of Ushuaia.

It could be said that Tierra del Fuego did not have a colonial era like that of other regions of the Americas, since the conquest and economic exploitation of the territory only started in the late nineteenth century (in striking contrast to all of the other New World settings described in this volume). Nevertheless, and given the historical characteristics of the southern region of South America, it is still possible to define its own colonial reality. The absence of a "typical" colonial era associated with the political control of a European metropolis, and the subsequent lack of a transition to an era dependent on internal colonialism, did not prevent the development of a historical reality with both forms of colonialism acting together. From 1880 onward, Tierra del Fuego was colonized by the nation-states of Argentina and Chile through the presence of European agents, including capitalist enterprises and religious communities such as the Anglican and Salesian missions.

In the case of Tierra del Fuego, it is possible to think of European coloniality as initiatory, without ignoring precedents set in other colonial settings or suggesting that the local historical contingencies at play involved the conquest of some pristine indigenous reality. As we mentioned earlier, initial encounters between Western and indigenous people were short-term and sporadic. Indigenous groups were "primordial" in the sense of not having experienced the maximum expression of colonial power. The territory was not dramatically changed until the development of Western-style productive activities, specifically, gold mining and sheep farming. In the last quarter of the nineteenth century, Tierra del Fuego could no longer be equated with biodiversity and a natural ecosystem, but with natural resources extraction and the dominance of technical interventions. The region was part of the equation capital = natural resources, and it became the venue for savage predation and violence against indigenous people and the territory (a characteristic of that period of capitalism). The Selk'nam community suffered the consequences of enclosure and "the brutal separation from their means of self-provision known as primitive accumulation" (Galafassi 2012:7, our translation).

Another distinguishing feature of the European presence in Tierra del Fuego was the weakness of government agencies. Southern Patagonia (including Tierra del Fuego, southern Santa Cruz, and the Magellan region of Chile) was "an example of autarchic integration and self-generated development" (Martinic 2001:477, our translation). It could be described as a territorial unity with a dynamic of its own (Luiz and Schillat 1997), and the city of Punta Arenas was the articulating axis. Argentinean governors complained to the national state about the lack of resources (everything was channeled through the Chilean city of Punta Arenas) (Belza 1974:118). In 1910, economic transactions at Estancia San Pablo were registered in British pounds.[1] In 1912 the salaries of civil servants in Ushuaia were paid by the Bank of Punta Arenas,[2] and in 1920 the diaries of the Salesian mission Nuestra Señora de La Candelaria mentioned the celebration of a Chilean national holiday, the commemoration of the First National Government Council.[3] It was in this setting that national matters faded away (Bandieri 2005). This was the cause and effect of the double coloniality.

The development of an enclave economy, with little involvement of national authorities, illustrates well this particular form of coloniality. Mining activities started in 1881. The Romanian engineer Julius Popper became notorious for his despotism, crimes against indigenous peoples, and the constant challenges to the Argentinean government (he even issued his own coins and stamps to symbolize his power) (Bandieri 2005). In 1890, Popper successfully challenged the authority of Governor Cornero, who was suspended in 1893 for the conflict that followed. At that time, Argentina considered the possibility of closing down the government of Tierra del Fuego and annexing it to Santa Cruz.

If such political instability was one dimension of local coloniality, a second component was the enclave economy, which was heavily dependent on sheep production. Some people were granted large tracts of land (*latifundios*). While this process was not exclusive to Tierra del Fuego, we should agree that it is not so common to talk of an island with a small number of landowners. Sheep farmers acted as businessmen and acquired lands throughout Tierra del Fuego and Patagonia (Barbería 1995). They operated freely on both sides of the international border. In 1883, Chile started making land grants, and by 1890 the national government had given up 482,000 hectares (96 percent of the lands suitable for sheep farming) under four different licenses. Three of the latter belonged to the Sociedad Explotadora de Tierra del Fuego (SETF). Between 1897 and 1899 this company acquired the best lands for sheep farming on the Argentinean side of the island.

Sheep production was enhanced by technological and industrial development, a result of British investments and capital concentration. From the very beginning, most of the companies followed an expansionist policy, creating slaughterhouses and processing establishments, cold stores, and fat-rendering plants. The facilities were modern, and the establishments were true models of production. Late-nineteenth and early-twentieth-century sheep breeding in Tierra del Fuego implemented so many technological innovations that contemporary practices in the region have not changed significantly since then (Martinic 1992).

The action of sheep-herding entrepreneurs frequently eliminated the role of the state. These businessmen were the local representatives of authority and the main suppliers of state agencies. They controlled lands, food, horses, forage, road maintenance, telegraph and telephone communications, and other elements of the infrastructure.[4] The Argentinean settlements (Ushuaia and La Candelaria) depended on the supply of provisions from Punta Arenas. The steamboats transporting the goods were the property of the SETF. Police officers acted as guardians of the interests of the companies, and in many cases, everyday conflicts were resolved with only the intervention of landowners.[5]

The enclave economy also benefited from the strategic location of the Strait of Magellan and the declaration of Punta Arenas as a free port in 1867 (Belza 1975). However, between 1914 and 1922 the southernmost region of South America lost importance as a result of several factors. These included the opening of the Panama Canal, the crisis caused by the falling price of wool, the drop in demand, workers' strikes, the drought of 1921–1922, and the collection of rising customs duties (Barbería 1995). The region was gradually nationalized. Santa Cruz and the Argentinean side of Tierra del Fuego stopped being an area dependent from Punta Arenas and became a peripheral region of Argentina (Barbería 1995).

This economic coloniality brought with it another distinctive (though not exclusive) feature of earlier forms of coloniality: the burden of race. Without ignoring the diversity of social actors, "race and racial identity were established as instruments for basic social classification . . . as a way of granting legitimacy to the relations of domination imposed by the conquest" (Quijano 2000:534). In Tierra del Fuego, the idea of race had an impact on social events, relations, and articulations. The new racial identities were closely related to a specific division of labor. The overlapping of the double coloniality brought the logic of race close to the logic of class.

The coloniality we are here referring to did not prevent the development of a national or internal coloniality. Marginal participation in the labor market went hand in hand with people's marginal participation as citizens. The national coloniality that facilitated both forms of subordination also facilitated the application of sovereign and disciplinary power devices—previously executed by viceroyalties (Boccara 1996). Military expeditions to Tierra del Fuego were simultaneous with the establishment of Salesian and Anglican missions. National coloniality was associated with political domination and held certain legal and administrative consequences. It was crucial for the process of exclusion, subordination, and invisibility that characterized sovereign expansion. National coloniality was enabled not only by the integration of people living in conditions of marginality, poverty, and illegality into the labor market (Nacach 2011) but also by their subordinated participation in society. Nation-states created a new internal "other," or the subjugated, impoverished indigenous people, who were assimilated as defeated groups and thus differentially integrated into the national identity. Scientific institutions were used to support the process that transformed indigenous communities into exotic people much more related to the past than to the present (Nacach 2011).

We believe that the absence of a transition between the two forms of coloniality could not lead to a period of negotiation between these indigenous communities and their conquerors. Analysis of ethnographic and ethnohistorical sources shows that capitalism and the power devices operating in Tierra del Fuego (persecutions, killings, deportations, religious missions) left the members of the Selk'nam community with few strategies to cope with the consequences of conquest. In the medium term, they had no chance to create a counterhegemonic political project (Casali 2008, 2013; see also Stojanowski 2013). This fact had an enormous impact on indigenous people and their health (for other Latin American transition scenarios, see, in this volume, Harvey et al., Klaus and Alvarez-Calderón, and Murphy et al.).

The health of any human population needs to be understood beyond strictly biological terms. It is relevant to consider the etiology of disease, its biological substratum, and its natural history from a holistic perspective (Almeida Filho and Rouquayrol 2011). Epidemiology, the changes in morbidity and mortality, is part of the world of health, that is, relational to the social, economic, demographic, cultural, political, scientific, and ecological aspects of life (Bernabeu Mestre and Robles González 2000; Bernabeu Mestre 1994) that allow discussing the how and why of disease causation, or the "multiple causes of catastrophe" (Livi Bacci 2003). The social character of disease includes health care, the existence of a sanitary infrastructure, public politics, and medicalization of disease consistent with each historical context. In this case study we will provide some references on the experience of disease in a particular case study dominated by inter-ethnic contact and missionalization.

Case Study: La Candelaria Mission

Our ongoing research project conducted at the Salesian mission Nuestra Señora de La Candelaria has been especially interested in skeletal pathology as a window on coloniality in Tierra de Fuego, but it also considers related issues such as demography, diet, housing, mobility, and labor conditions. The complex and synergistic nature of health demands an interdisciplinary approach. La Candelaria offers an opportunity to study both an intact cemetery and documentary sources that promote a rich dialogue between archaeology, history, and biology.

La Candelaria was established in 1893. However, the definitive building (Figure 7.2) was erected in 1897 when the first structure was destroyed in a fire. La Candelaria came into existence long before the present-day city of Río Grande. It was a reference point for the northern area of Tierra del Fuego, providing not only shelter to visitors but also a setting for interaction between landowners and state authorities. However, the main actors in the mission setting were the Salesian Fathers, the Daughters of Mary Help of Christians, and the members of the Selk'nam community. In the context of double coloniality, the Fathers and the Daughters sought to rescue the Selk'nams from the threat of extinction by means of resettlement,

Figure 7.2. Mission La Candelaria, viewed from behind (Museo del Fin del Mundo, Ushuaia, photographic archive).

evangelization, and civilization. In spite of this purpose, the mission acted as a powerful means of shaping the living conditions of the indigenous community (for other references on the action of religious institutions, see, in this volume, Harvey et al., Klaus and Alvarez-Calderón, Murphy et al., and Tiesler and Zabala). La Candelaria served as a mission until 1930, even though the indigenous presence had reached its peak at the beginning of the twentieth century. In the 1940s the few women still living at the mission were transferred to the city, and La Candelaria started functioning as an agro-technical school. The old cemetery remained in use until 1947.

EVIDENCE AND METHODS

The historiographic approach considered ecclesiastical sources, such as the Book of Deaths II, the Chronicles of the Daughters of Mary Help of Christians, the Chronicles of the Salesian Fathers, the Chronicles of Father Zenone, and a series of official documents such as letters and reports by police officers, governors, and other officials. We generated data, hypotheses, and expectations on the living conditions of indigenous people at the mission and tested them with the information obtained from the bioarchaeological record.

Archaeological excavations focused on the southern area of the cemetery (Figure 7.3). We were able to find the remains of 33 people in a surface of 84 square meters. In this chapter we present the results obtained for 20 of these individuals. In the case of adults, sex estimation depended on methods for the identification of morphological variation of the skull and the pelvis (Buikstra and Ubelaker 1994). In the case of subadults we employed the sex estimation method proposed by Schutkowski (1993) and supplemented it with osteometric assessment of long bones (Loth and Henneberg 2001; Scheuer and Black 2000).

Age was estimated by the methods of Todd and Suchey-Brooks for the analysis of pubic symphysis and the fusion of epiphyses (Buikstra and Ubelaker 1994). Furthermore, we considered dental eruption and the patterns of epiphyseal closure as an indicator of age for subadults (Ubelaker 1989). The estimation of age in perinatal individuals was estimated by the measure of long bones and the skull (Fazekas and Kosa 1978; Krogman and Iscan 1986; Schaefer et al. 2009; Scheuer and Black 2000). For paleopathological analysis we used a detailed descriptive and differential diagnostic approach, observing the anomalies in texture, shape, and bone dimensions. The works of Ortner (2003), Aufderheide and Rodríguez Martin (1998), and Campillo (2001), among others, helped to define normal anatomical

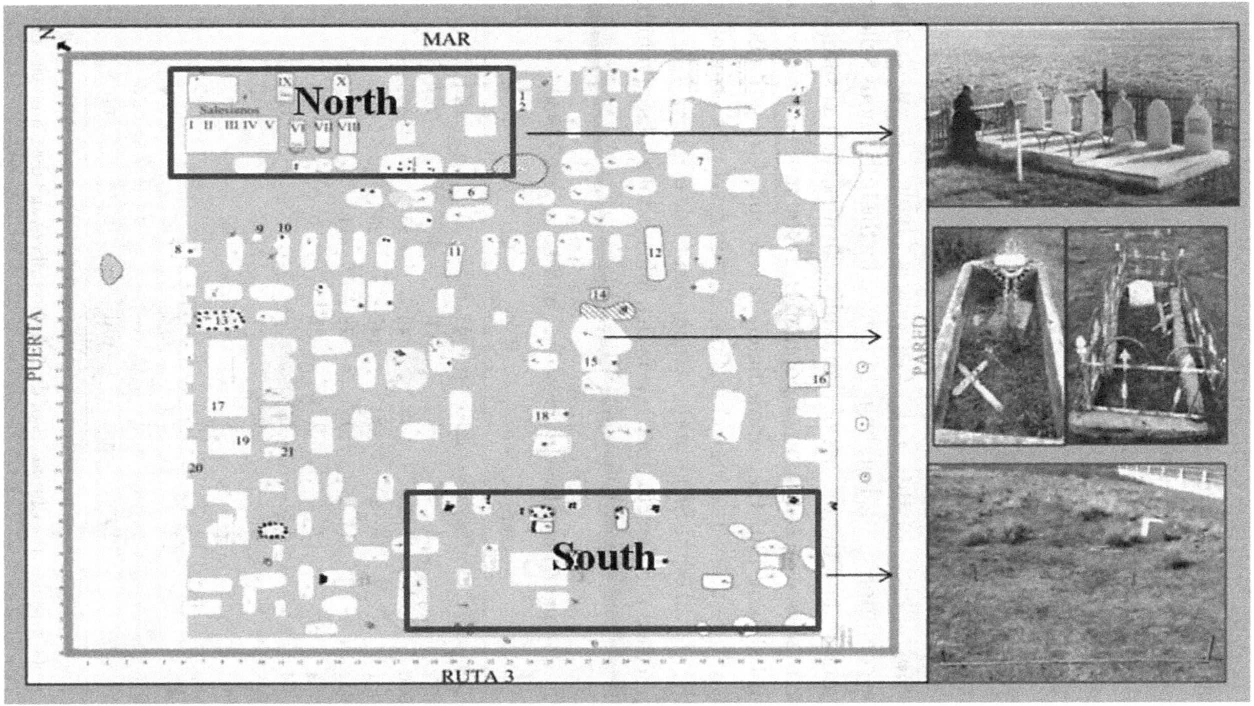

Figure 7.3. General plot of the old cemetery, showing some funerary structures in its northern, middle, and southern areas (prepared by the authors).

variation and the differential diagnosis of skeletal pathology. Emphasis was placed on abnormal bone formation and destruction, as well as the possible association of one or more etiological syndromes (co-morbidity) (Buikstra and Cook 1980; Miller et al. 1996). Through this approach, the study evaluated indicators of systemic processes connected with nutritional and metabolic pathologies (porotic hyperostosis, cribra orbitalia, dental enamel hypoplasia, tooth decay, dental wear) and infectious diseases (periosteal reactions on the long bones and ribs). The results obtained for the mission were compared with those obtained for 52 hunter-gatherers who lived in the area who date to both before and after the establishment of La Candelaria (Guichón 1994).

Results and Implications

The demographic structure at La Candelaria (Table 7.1) was connected with the condition of the buildings inhabited by the indigenous Selk'nams, their mobility, and the impact of economic activities such as sheep farming. The highest concentration of population at the mission was recorded between 1899 and 1902 (i.e., immediately before and during the outbreak of epidemic disease). The indigenous population reached a peak of 168 in 1900. The arrival of the SETF at the Argentinean side of Tierra del Fuego in 1897 increased the persecution, saw police officers take a large number of

Table 7.1. Demographic information for La Candelaria, 1897–1930

Date	Women	Men	Boys	Girls	Total
January 1897	n/d	n/d	42	39	n/d
05/19/1899	n/d	n/d	n/d	n/d	163
06/05/1900	90		43	35	168
02/05/1901	36	30	47	20	133
03/03/1902	21	19	25	11	76
01/01/1904	12	12	5	6	35
05/06/1904	n/d	n/d	3	3	n/d
02/25/1905	6	5	2	2	15
07/18/1905	7	5	3	2	17
04/01/1906	12	10	5	0	27
11/11/1909	12	n/d	n/d	n/d	n/d
12/31/1916	5	n/d	4	4	n/d
1930	11	n/d	n/d	6	n/d

Note: Prepared by the authors, based on information in the Chronicles of the Daughters of Mary Help of Christians, the Chronicles of the Salesian Fathers, and the Chronicles of Father Zenone; n/d = no data.

Figure 7.4. Area of the "small houses" built for the Selk'nams (Mission La Candelaria, Father Juan Ticó's personal archive).

natives to the mission, and gave the Selk'nams no option but to seek help at the mission. Up to that moment the Selk'nams had stayed at the mission for only a few days, mostly in the tents they set up in the vicinity. They still were highly mobile, usually in groups of more than 100 people. At first, very few Selk'nams lived at the mission (e.g., "two girls"). In 1897, immediately after the fire destroyed the structure, the indigenous residents were accommodated in a warehouse. In 1899 they started to live in the central building of the mission, and to a lesser extent in small houses that the clergy had built for the married couples (Figure 7.4). In subsequent years, the groups visiting La Candelaria were smaller. A negative demographic trend that started in 1902 could not be reversed.

In 1907, besides the activities conducted at La Candelaria, mobile missions started visiting the areas frequented by the Selk'nams, including Fagnano Lake and the estancia of the Bridges family in Río Fuego (Figure 7.1). This situation was clearly documented by written sources: while 284 baptisms were performed at La Candelaria, 46 were performed in nearby areas (including the police station and the estancia of the Menéndez family) and 253 in remote locations. It is relevant to distinguish between different estancias: the SETF only accepted single men and married couples as part of the workforce, while the Bridges family tolerated the development of a communal lifestyle. Intermarriage was much more common in the establishments of the SETF than in the lands of the Bridges. This demographic trend was accompanied by changes in mobility and territoriality connected with sheep farming. The use of space and resources went from being "predatory" to "logistic," and both La Candelaria and the estancia of the Bridges family played a significant role in the process (see Casali 2013 for more details).

Figure 7.5. Selk'nam women weaving at the entrance of the workshop (Museo del Fin del Mundo, Ushuaia, photographic archive).

The settlement pattern was associated with the intensity of work, people's nutrition, and the epidemiological profile of the community. Men took care of the herd and maintained the mission during the whole year. They also participated in sheep bathing and shearing during the summer. Meanwhile, the women were involved in yarn spinning and weaving. Work was especially intense between 1900 and 1905. In the following years, the

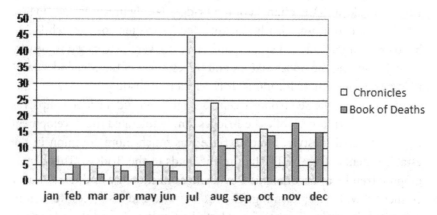

Figure 7.6. Deaths and seasonality, 1897–1931 (prepared by the authors, based on the Chronicles of the Daughters of Mary Help of Christians, the Chronicles of the Salesian Fathers, and the Chronicles of Father Zenone).

number of non-indigenous workers increased as a result of a decline in the indigenous population. Child labor, including the participation of boys and girls, was significant. Women were victims of particular health problems. They worked all year long, holding strenuous body positions and postures while doing almost no physical exercise (Figure 7.5). One of the most important factors affecting women was confinement. According to documentary sources (and the material conditions of the still existing workshop), all rooms at the mission were small, with low ceilings, and were poorly ventilated. Women also received religious and pedagogic instructions in these rooms (an activity particularly extended during the winter). This setting could have reactivated the outbreaks of tuberculosis in adults and of primary infections in children, young men, and young women. It is worthwhile considering the seasonality of the deaths: mortality rates usually increased from August to November and decreased during the summer, reaching their peak in autumn (Figure 7.6).

The analysis of documentary sources indicated that at least 251 indigenous people died and were buried at the mission between 1897 and 1931. When the cause of death was explicitly mentioned, 69 percent of the cases were related to tuberculosis. However, the epidemiological profile of some other cases also could have corresponded to tuberculosis. Fifty-five percent of the individuals affected by tuberculosis were women, mostly between 5 and 12 years of age. Almost half of the deaths (48.2 percent) took place between 1900 and 1902 (Figure 7.7), during what could have been an epidemiological event. The impact of tuberculosis on children was associated with the demographic structure of the mission (where women and children were numerous), but it could have also been connected with the behavior of the disease. Even though children are not the group most susceptible to tuberculosis (Benenson 1992), several studies conducted on indigenous populations showed a higher incidence of the disease among people under 15 years of age (Canadian Tuberculosis Committee 2002; Haldane 2000; Kunimoto et al. 2004). While men could be more susceptible to tuberculosis, women could die in greater numbers—especially at the beginning of an epidemic. This tendency could later reverse for women over 30 years of age (Daniel 1981; Haldane 2000; Johnston 1995). This could be precisely the case of La Candelaria. Based on our interdisciplinary approach, the bioarchaeological analysis was aimed to investigate these possibilities further.

Thirty-five percent of the bodies excavated at the cemetery were male; 45 percent corresponded to female individuals, and in 20 percent of the cases it was not possible to determine sex (Table 7.2). Ten individuals were adults

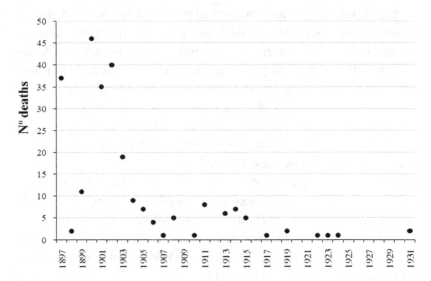

Figure 7.7. Total number of deaths per year, 1897–1931 (prepared by the authors, based on the Chronicles of the Daughters of Mary Help of Christians, the Chronicles of the Salesian Fathers, and the Chronicles of Father Zenone).

between 18 and 60 years of age; while the remaining 10 individuals were subadults under age 18. Mitochondrial DNA analysis conducted on 13 individuals showed their Native American maternal ancestry (Guichón et al. 2013). Adult skeletons were generally better preserved and more complete (more than 50 percent) when compared to subadult remains (much less than 50 percent) (Table 7.2). Following the same trend, the preservation of the remains was good or very good in the case of adults, and average to poor in the case of subadults. Even though the sample is small, females and individuals ages 4–12 and 20–35 were prominent in the sample (and is in accordance with documentary sources).

Paleopathological analysis (Table 7.3) focused on infectious diseases showed the presence of periosteal reaction in the long bones of 70 percent of the adults.[6] It is worth considering that in the rest of the adults (30 percent), lesions could not be scored given the condition of the bones. Therefore, taphonomic processes could have masked evidence of disease. In 50 percent of the adults it was possible to identify periosteal reaction on the ribs[7] (Figure 7.8). These are considered as one of the most frequent lesions resulting from infectious/inflammatory diseases affecting the lungs, such as tuberculosis (Roberts and Buikstra 2003; Santos and Roberts 2006).

Table 7.2. Sex-age structure of the bioarchaeological sample

Individual	Sex	Age category	Age	Completeness	Conservation
15–16	F	Old adult (>35)	45–60 years	50–75%	Good
15–16	F	Old adult (>35)	35–49 years	75–100%	Moderate
12–13	M	Old adult (>35)	35–45 years	75–100%	Very Good
15–16 (2bis)	M	Mid-adult (25–35)	30–40 years	75–100%	Good
15	M	Mid-adult (25–35)	25–39 years	50–75%	Good
13	F	Mid-adult (25–35)	25–35 years	50–75%	Good
7–8	M	Young adult (18–24)	24–26 years	75–100%	Very Good
16 (Bis)	F	Young adult (18–24)	21–45 years	75–100%	Very Good
14 (2)	F	Young adult (18–24)	19–20 years	75–100%	Good
14	M	Young adult (18–24)	18–20 years	50–75%	Good
14 (1)	M	Old subadult (12–17)	12–15 years	25–50%	Moderate
–E 14	M	Mid-subadult (5–11)	10–14 years	0–25%	Poor
15–16 (1)	F	Mid-subadult (5–11)	6–11 years	0–25%	Poor
–E 13	F	Mid-subadult (5–11)	6–10 years	0–25%	Good
14–15 (1)	I	Mid-subadult (5–11)	4–6 years	0–25%	Poor
14–15 (2)	F	Mid-subadult (5–11)	2–6 years	0–25%	Poor
16	I	Perinatal (< 1)	7 months of gestation to 2 months	0–25%	Poor
11	F	Perinatal (< 1)	6 months of gestation to 6 months	0–25%	Moderate
15–16 (2)	I	Perinatal (< 1)	4 months of gestation to 2 months	0–25%	Poor
11–12	I	Perinatal (< 1)	4–9 months of gestation	0–25%	Moderate

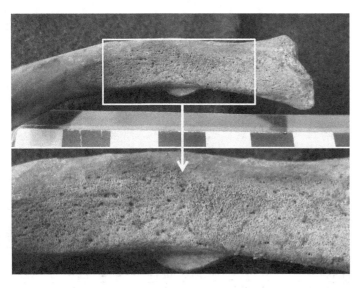

Figure 7.8. Example of periosteal reaction on the ribs. Individual C 14 (2) (photo by Richard Guichón).

Table 7.3. Presence of paleopathological conditions on the individuals of the sample, with comparison of frequencies inside and outside the mission

Individual	Cribra orbitalia	Porotic hyperostosis	Periosteal reaction— long bones	Periosteal reaction—ribs	Dental enamel hypoplasia	Tooth decay	Dental wear
C 15–16	NO	NO	*	NO	NO	YES	Moderate
D 15–16	NO	NO	*	NO	NO	YES	Mild
E 12–13	NO	YES	*	NO	YES	YES	Mild
E 15–16 (2bis)	NO	YES	YES	YES	YES	NO	Mild
C 15	NO	YES	YES	YES	YES	YES	Moderate
C 13	*	YES	YES	NO	NO	NO	Moderate
C 7–8	YES	YES	YES	YES	YES	YES	Mild
D 16 (Bis)	NO	YES	YES	NO	YES	NO	Moderate
C 14 (2)	YES	YES	YES	YES	YES	NO	Mild
D 14	NO	YES	YES	YES	NO	YES	Absent
C 14 (1)	*	NO	*	YES	YES	NO	Absent
D–E 14	NO	YES	*	YES	YES	NO	Absent
E 15–16 (1)	*	*	YES	NO	YES	NO	Absent
D–E 13	*	*	YES	YES	*	*	*
E 14–15 (1)	YES	*	*	*	YES	NO	Absent
E 14–15 (2)	NO	NO	*	*	YES	NO	Absent
D 16	*	*	*	*	*	*	*
E 11	*	*	*	NO	*	*	*
E 15–16 (2)	*	*	*	*	*	*	*
C 11–12	*	*	*	NO	*	*	*
Frequency of adults at the mission	25% (n = 12)	69% (n = 13)	100% (n = 9)	50% (n = 16)	73% (n = 15)	40% (n = 15)	Mild to moderate
Frequency of adults in Tierra del Fuego (outside the mission)	29% (n = 38)	15% (n = 46)	*	*	42% (n = 21)	40% (n = 52)	Moderate to severe

Note: Data from Guichón 1994; * = observation could not be made as a result of the absence of the skeletal element or the action of taphonomic processes. n = number

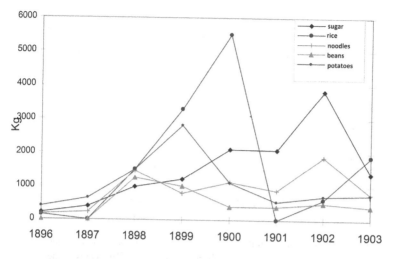

Figure 7.9. Relationship between products bought by the mission and the number of Selk'nams living there (prepared by the authors, based on the Chronicles of the Salesian Fathers).

Nutrition was also connected with settlement conditions. Between 1894 and 1897, when the Selk'nams lived in the tents that they set up in the vicinity of the mission, the relationship between these people and the members of the religious community was established by means of "cookies." Baked cookies were explicitly requested by the indigenous residents, and they represented a useful tool for the missionaries. Cookies were not necessarily supplied on a daily basis, and they frequently were used as a means of exchange or reward. The distribution of cookies was sporadic, and it was more closely related to the strategies of contact than to nutrition. In 1899 the members of the Salesian Order started to supply food on a daily basis for those living in the central building of the mission and the small houses. Documentary sources indicated a correlation between the demographic dynamic of the Selk'nams and the amounts of flour, sugar, rice, noodles, beans, and potatoes contained in different vessels. The trend started between 1897 and 1899, with a peak in 1900, a slight oscillation between 1900 and 1902, and a significant drop after 1902 (Figures 7.9 and 7.10). It was only in 1903, and especially after 1906, that there was an increase in meat consumption per individual on a regular basis.

Sheep farming reduced the number of camelids (guanacos) on the island. It is worth noting that although the number of guanacos started decreasing with sheep farming, the critical period began in 1900 when pressure

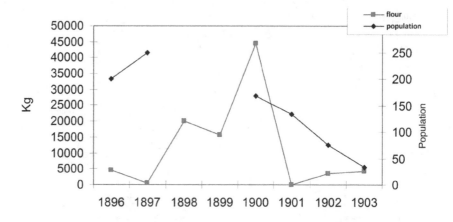

Figure 7.10. Relationship between flour bought by the mission and the number of Selk'nams living there (prepared by the authors, based on the Chronicles of the Salesian Fathers).

on native resources coincided with the nutritional changes experienced by the Selk'nam community at the mission. Sheep production had a profound impact on the environment, as sheep ended up competing with native species. Our analysis of the situation shows that the population of guanacos was displaced from the steppe between 1903 and 1906, forced into the ecotone and the woods (an environment traditionally marginal for camelids), resulting in extreme ecological pressure for the camelids (Casali 2013).

Regarding diet, dental analysis (Figure 7.11; Table 7.3) showed a notable presence of dental caries (60 percent), which coincides with a documented increase in sugar and carbohydrate intake. Dental wear was minimal, as it was connected with further food processing. We observed dental enamel hypoplasias in 73 percent of the individuals, reflecting periods of relatively acute metabolic stress in childhood. Other stress indicators involved porotic hyperostosis in 80 percent of the adults, and cribra orbitalia in 23 percent of individuals. The presence of these lesions could be related to anemia. Even though anemia can be caused by several factors, in this case it could have been associated with a decrease in meat consumption, echoing the impact of disease and nutrition in other historical contexts (see Perry, this volume; Killgrove, this volume). Compared to the information for hunter-gatherers living in the region before and after the establishment of the mission (Table 7.3) (Guichón 1994), increase in tooth decay, porotic hyperostosis, and cribra orbitalia was observed, while tooth wear decreased.

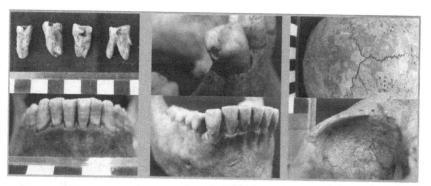

Figure 7.11. Detail of tooth decay (*top left*), dental enamel hypoplasia (*bottom left*), porotic hyperostosis (*top right*), and cribra orbitalia (*bottom right*) (prepared by the authors).

Especially with regard to possible lesions produced by tuberculosis, the immunological-dietary model realized by Wilbur et al. (2008) is useful as a model that underscores the results of the paleopathological and historiographical analysis. This model evaluates the influence of two nutrients (protein and iron) on the immune response to tuberculosis, presenting five categories to describe the interaction among nutrition, immune function, and infectious diseases. The model argues that severe and chronic malnutrition produces a quick and high mortality from tuberculosis, even before the disease manifests on the bones. However, in some cases it is possible to identify the growth of new bone on the visceral surface of the ribs. Iron deficiency can limit the intracellular growth of the bacteria, forcing the infection to remain dormant until iron supplements could favor the reactivation of the infections. Considering the model for the relationship between tuberculosis and diet, the above-mentioned expectations could result from a deficit in protein but not in iron consumption. Therefore, the La Candelaria mission could fall into the model's Category 3, where the immune response to tuberculosis would be fatal in the short term and not produce extensive lesions in affected individuals (García Laborde et al. 2012).

The bioarchaeological analysis of the individuals found at the cemetery could be better understood when compared to the analysis of the individuals found at non-missionary contexts of the region. Ethnographic works (Cooper 1967; Gusinde 1982, 1989) and stable isotope analyses (conducted on human remains with secure chronological dates [Borrero et al. 2001]) pointed out the range of potential of dietary variability in pre- and post-contact times. The frequency of tooth decay before and after contact shows disparate tendencies. Castro and Aspillaga (1991) described an increase in tooth decay after contact. This was also suggested by Guichón (1995) in terms of expectations, without having access to chronologically ordered samples. At the same time, Schinder and Guichón (2003) analyzed a series of well-dated samples and could not identify evidence of an increase in tooth decay in pre- or postcontact times, but they did identify an increase in dental wear in postcontact times.[8] Dental enamel hypoplasia and porotic hyperostosis also failed to show changes in pre- and postcontact samples (Schinder and Guichón 2003). Even though it would be useful to increase the numbers of bioarchaeological samples of non-missionary pre- and postcontact peoples to better compare with La Candelaria, the current observations are fully consistent with documentary evidence which shows that the Selk'nams living at the mission experienced an increase in carbohydrate intake.

FINAL WORDS

Tierra del Fuego was one of the last places on Earth to be populated by humans. High southern latitudes and insularity provided the biogeographical framework for the colonial encounter. The arrival of Europeans in the sixteenth century was fleeting, but their permanent settlement in the late nineteenth and the early twentieth centuries led to accelerated and negative changes in the living conditions and health of the native peoples. Approaching Tierra del Fuego in terms of double coloniality allows for an emphasis on power relationships, without ignoring the tremendous impact on indigenous communities. It allows rethinking the background from previous studies that, despite considering the action of nation-states and in some cases of European actors, did not associate these processes with coloniality. As an interpretive framework, coloniality gives access to the multidirectionality of power relationships.

The Salesian mission Nuestra Señora de La Candelaria served the interests of the double coloniality. As a power device, it affected the members of the Selk'nam community. On an epidemiological level, the presence of tuberculosis was relevant. At the beginning of the nineteenth century the disease was indeed spreading on a global level (Farga 1992), but there were no certainties about its treatment. The health-care structure of the island was inadequate (Casali 2014), and the missionaries naturalized the death of the indigenous, being mostly interested in their religious instruction and their "edifying death" (Casali 2013). But the "inevitability" of the disease was not incompatible with the fact that living conditions at La Candelaria facilitated its spread through several factors that had an impact on the immune system, particularly the kind of sedentism that emerged there (*sensu* Wilbur et al. 2008). So, nutritional changes were important, but overcrowding was probably a lynchpin factor shaping these particular outcomes (especially in the case of women). The work done by men was different from that performed at other missions on the continent, where indigenous peoples were subjected to extreme working conditions and even slavery, for instance, in colonial mines or plantations. Here, working conditions were instead influenced by the educative, civilizing, paternalist, and familiar project of the Salesian Order. For this particular case, we propose a high initial prevalence of tuberculosis, considering the immunological history of the Selk'nams (see model by Wilbur and Buikstra 2006), and a high subsequent prevalence of the disease encouraged by the social conditions of coloniality.

Coloniality also had an impact on the local demographic dynamic. The resulting crisis was associated with several factors, including the role played by religious missions. In the case of San Rafael, another Salesian mission in Tierra del Fuego (Dawson Island, Chile), the arrival of deported Selk'nams was connected with the establishment of the SETF, and between 1894 and 1898 it affected 626 people. San Rafael was larger than La Candelaria: in 1898 it provided shelter for 550 indigenous individuals (Aliaga Rojas 1984), while La Candelaria reached a peak of only 168. As mentioned above, documentary sources recorded 251 deaths at La Candelaria between 1897 and 1931, while in San Rafael the number of dead was about 800 (Aliaga Rojas 1984). Researchers frequently refer to a population of 1,500 or 4,000 indigenous people prior to colonization, but this figure corresponds to a particular demographic model (García Moro 1992). Considering this model, as well as Chilean censuses and ethnographic sources, it is possible to estimate that the Selk'nam population reached 2,400–2,700. The demographic decline at the mission was not balanced or neutralized by migratory flows. The combination of these factors prevented any increase of fertility. The events taking place at La Candelaria reproduced to some extent the events taking place at the island, where the demographic decline was irreversible.

These results can be read in terms of a crisis, but they do not imply an idea of "passive extinction." Setting aside the impact of double coloniality between 1890 and 1920, the Selk'nams expressed their resistance in both subtle and explicit ways. At the mission and more generally on the island, indigenous people intended to survive, strategically adopting some practices and transforming some others. They re-signified the use of space, mobility, and resource provisioning and were part of a biological and cultural "mestizaje." At present we are working side by side with those who recognize themselves as Selk'nams to reconstruct their history, as the bioarchaeological record of the unique colonial encounter in Tierra de Fuego holds insights to inform future paths of the Selk'nam descendants as well.

NOTES

1. Posting journal, 1910. Documentary archive of Estancia San Pablo.

2. Punta Arenas branch manager to the president of the National Bank of Argentina, 03-02-1912, AMFM, "Governors" box, file no. 4582.

3. Chronicles of the Salesian Fathers, 09-18-1920.

4. In 1986, Argentina rented three plots from Mauricio Braun with an aim of establishing Río Grande police station.

5. J. V. González to the Minister of Internal Affairs, 08-09-1902, file no. 4903, Archivo General de la Nación.

6. In the case of subadults, even though we took note of the lesions, we decided not to include them in the calculation of percentages. The presence of new tissue over cortical tissue could be considered normal in growing children and not necessarily pathological.

7. Ongoing molecular analyses conducted by Stone and Buikstra at Arizona State University will be useful to discuss the diagnosis of tuberculosis.

8. On the one hand, the presence of high dental wear in pre- and postcontact times could be the result of similar dietary practices. On the other, it is possible that some abrasive agents (e.g., the sand transported by the wind, which is so typical of the region) could be acting independently from dietary practices.

REFERENCES CITED

Aliaga Rojas, R. F.
1984   La misión en la Isla Dawson (1889–1911). *Anales de la Facultad de Teología (Annales of the School of Theology)* 32(2). Universidad Católica, Santiago.
Almeida, Filho N., and M. Z. Rouquayrol
2011   *Introducción a la epidemiología.* Lugar Editorial, Buenos Aires.
Andrade Lima, T.
1999   El huevo de la serpiente: Una arqueología del capitalismo embrionario en el Río de Janeiro del siglo XIX. In *Sed non satiata: Teoría social en la arqueología latinoamericana contemporánea,* edited by A. Zarankin and F. Acuto, pp. 189–238. Del Tridente, Buenos Aires.
2001   Marcos teóricos da arqueología histórica, suas possibilidades e límites. In *Arqueología uruguaya: Hacia el fin del milenio,* edited by Asociación Uruguaya de Arqueología, vol. 1, pp. 11–29. MEC, Montevideo.
Aufderheide, A. C., and C. Rodriguez Martin
1998   *The Cambridge Encyclopedia of Human Paleopathology.* Cambridge University Press, Cambridge.

Bandieri, S.
2005   *Historia de la Patagonia.* Sudamericana, Buenos Aires.
Barbería, E.
1995   *Los dueños de la tierra en la Patagonia austral, 1880–1920.* Universidad Federal de la Patagonia Argentina, Santa Cruz.
Belza, J. E.
1974   *En la isla del fuego: Encuentros.* Instituto de Investigaciones Históricas de Tierra del Fuego, Buenos Aires.
1975   *En la isla del fuego: Colonización.* Instituto de Investigaciones Históricas de Tierra del Fuego, Buenos Aires.
Benenson, A. S.
1992   *El control de las enfermedades transmisibles en el hombre.* Organización Panamericana de la Salud, Washington, D.C.
Bernabeu Mestre, J.
1994   Enfermedad y población: Introducción a los problemas y métodos de la epidemiología histórica. *Seminari d'Estudis sobre la Ciència* (Monografías, 5). Valencia.
Bernabeu Mestre, J., and E. Robles González
2000   Demografía y problemas de salud: Unas reflexiones críticas sobre los conceptos de transición demográfica y sanitaria. *Política y Sociedad* 35:45–54.
Boccara, G.
1996   Notas acerca de los dispositivos de poder en la sociedad colonial-fronteriza, la resistencia y la transculturación de los Reche-Mapuche del Centrosur de Chile (XVI–VIII). *Revista de Indias* 56:659–695.
Borrero, L. A.
1992   El registro arqueológico del contacto: Enfermedad y discontinuidad poblacional. *Simposio encuentro de dos culturas.* Centro Cultural General San Martín, Buenos Aires.
Borrero, L. A., R. Guichón, R. Tykot, R. Kelly, A. Prieto, and P. Cárdenas
2001   Dieta a partir de isótopos estables en restos óseos humanos de Patagonia austral: Estado actual y perspectivas. *Anales Instituto Patagonia* 29:119–127.
Bridges, L.
2008   *El último confín de la tierra.* Marymar, Buenos Aires.
Bridges, T.
1891   Datos sobre Tierra del Fuego comunicados por el reverendo Thomas Bridges. *Revista del Museo de la Plata* 3:19–25.
1893   La Tierra del Fuego y sus habitantes. *Boletín del Instituto Geográfico Argentino* 14:221–241.
Buikstra, J. E., and D. C. Cook
1980   Paleopathology: An American Account. *Annual Review of Anthropology* 9:433–470.
Buikstra, J. E., and D. H. Ubelaker (editors)
1994   *Standards for Data Collection from Human Skeletal Remains.* Series No. 44. Arkansas Archaeological Survey Research, Fayetteville.

Campillo, D.
2001   Introducción a la paleopatología. Bellaterra Arqueología, Madrid.
Canadian Tuberculosis Committee
2002   Tuberculosis in Canadian-Born Aboriginal Peoples. Public Health Agency of
            Canada. http://www.phac-aspc.gc.ca/tbpc-latb/pubs/tbcan12pre/index-eng.
            php, accessed November 29, 2015.
Canclini, A.
1986   Tierra del Fuego, su historia en historias. Galerna, Buenos Aires.
Casali, R.
2008   Contacto interétnico en el norte de Tierra de Fuego: Primera aproximación
            a las estrategias de resistencia Selk'nam. Magallania 36(2):45–61.
2013   Movilidad y uso del espacio: Análisis demográfico de la trayectoria selk'nam
            ante la colonización. Tierra del Fuego, Argentina, 1890–1930. Anuario del
            Instituto de Historia Argentina No 13. La Plata: Instituto de investigaciones
            en humanidades y ciencias sociales (IdIHCS-UNLP-CONICET). Centro de
            Historia Argentina y Americana, in press.
2014   Salud en los extremos: Escenario epidemiológico y sanitario en Tierra del
            Fuego, 1890–1930. Ciencias de la Salud: Sección Estudios Sociales de la Salud
            12:271–288.
Castro, M. M., and E. A. Aspillaga
1991   Fueguian Paleopathology. Antropología Biológica 1:1–13.
Cooper, J. M.
1967   Analytical and Critical Bibliography of the Tribes of Tierra del Fuego and Ad-
            jacent Territory. Johnson Reprint Corporation, Washington, D.C.
Daniel, T. M.
1981   An Inmunochemist's View of the Epidemiology of Tuberculosis. In Prehis-
            toric Tuberculosis in the Americas, edited by J. E. Buikstra. Northeastern Uni-
            versity Archaeological Program, Chicago.
Farga, V.
1992   Tuberculosis. Mediterráneo, Santiago.
Fazekas, I., and K. Kosa
1978   Forensic Fetal Osteology. Hungary Akademiai Kiado, Budapest.
Foucault, M.
1975   Discipline and Punish: The Birth of the Prison. Random House, New York.
Fugassa, M., and R. Guichón
2004   Transición epidemiológica en Tierra del Fuego: El contacto indirecto y las
            enfermedades infecciosas entre 1520 y 1850. Magallania 32:99–113.
Funari, P., S. Jones, and M. Hall
1999   Introduction: Archaeology in History. In Historical Archaeology, edited by P.
            Funari, S. Jones, and M. Hall, pp. 1–20. Routledge, London.
Funari, P., and A. Zarankin
2004   Arqueología histórica en América del Sur: Los desafíos del siglo XXI. In
            Arqueología histórica en América del Sur: Los desafíos del siglo XXI, edited by
            P. Funari and A. Zarankin, pp. 5–10. Ediciones Uniandes, Bogota.

Galafassi, G.

2012   Renovadas versiones de un proceso histórico en marcha: La predación del territorio y la naturaleza como acumulación. *Theomai* 25:1–14.

García Laborde, P., R. A. Guichón, and L. O. Valenzuela

2012   Interaction between Infectious Diseases and Stress in the Salesian Mission La Candelaria Rio Grande, Tierra del Fuego, Argentina. Paper presented at the 39th Annual Meeting of the Paleopathology Association, Portland, Oregon.

García Moro, C.

1992   Reconstrucción del proceso de extinción de los Selk'nam a través de los libros misionales. *Anales del Instituto de la Patagonia* 21:33–46.

Gosden, C.

2004   *Archaeology and Colonialism: Cultural Contact from 5000 BC to the Present.* Cambridge University Press, Cambridge.

Guichón, R. A.

1994   Antropología física de Tierra del Fuego: Caracterización biológica de las poblaciones prehispánicas. Unpublished Ph.D. dissertation, School of Arts and Sciences, University of Buenos Aires, Buenos Aires.

1995   Vías de análisis, problemas y discusiones den antropología biológica de Tierra del Fuego. *Relaciones de la Sociedad Argentina de Antropología* 20:239–256.

Guichón, R. A., J. E. Buikstra, A. C. Stone, K. M. Harkins, L. Valenzuela, P. Garcia Laborde, R. Casali, M. Salerno, and R. Guichón

2013   Análisis moleculares para tuberculosis e isótopos estables en el Cementerio de la Misión Salesiana Nuestra de la Candelaria, Tierra del Fuego. Paper presented at the Paleopathology Association Meeting in South America, Santa Marta, Colombia.

Gusinde, M.

1951   *Hombres primitivos en la Tierra del Fuego (de investigador a compañero de tribu).* Escuela de Estudios Hispano-Americanos, Sevilla.

1982   *Los indios de Tierra del Fuego.* Centro Argentino de Etnología Americana, CONICET, Buenos Aires.

1989   *Los indios de Tierra del Fuego: Antropología física.* Tomo IV. Vols. 1 and 2. Centro Argentino de Etnología Americana, CONICET, Buenos Aires.

Haldane, D.

2000   Bacteriologic Aspects of Tuberculosis and Mycobacterial Infection. In *Canadian Tuberculosis Standards*, 5th ed., Canadian Lung Association. www.migrantclinician.org/mcn_service_dl/service_dl?fid=263, accessed November 29, 2015.

Johnston, D.

1995   Tuberculosis. In *The Cambridge World History of Human Disease*, edited by K. Kiple, pp. 1059–1068. Cambridge University Press, Cambridge.

Krogman, W., and M. Iscan

1986   *The Human Skeleton in Forensic Medicine.* Charles C. Thomas, Springfield, Illinois.

Kunimoto, D., K. Sutherland, A. Wooldrager, A. Fanning, L. Chui, J. Manfreda and R. Long
2004   Transmission Characteristics of Tuberculosis in the Foreign-Born and the Canadian-Born Populations of Alberta, Canada. *International Journal of Tuberculosis and Lung Disease* 8(10):1213–1220.

Livi Bacci, M.
2003   Las múltiples causas de la catástrofe: Consideraciones teóricas y empíricas. *Revista de Indias* 63:31–48.

Loth, S. R., and M. Henneberg
2001   Sexually Dimorphic Mandibular Morphology in the First Few Years of Life. *American Journal of Physical Anthropology* 115(2):179–186.

Luiz, M. T., and M. Schillat
1997   *La frontera austral: Tierra del Fuego, 1520–1920.* Servicio de publicaciones de la Universidad de Cádiz, Cádiz.

Martinic, M.
1992   *Historia de la región Magallánica.* Vol. 2. Universidad de Magallanes, Santiago.
2001   Patagonia Austral, 1885–1925: Un caso singular y temprano de integración regional autárquica. In *Cruzando la cordillera . . . la frontera argentino-chilena como espacio social,* edited by S. Bandieri, pp. 450–486. Neuquén CEHIR, Universidad Nacional del Comahue, Neuquén.

Mignolo, M.
2003   La colonialidad a lo largo y a lo ancho: El hemisferio occidental en el horizonte colonial de la modernidad. In *La colonialidad del saber: Eurocentrismo y ciencias sociales. Perspectivas latinoamericanas,* edited by E. Lander, pp. 57–85. CLACSO, Buenos Aires.

Miller, E., B. Ragsdale, and D. Ortner
1996   Accuracy in Dry Bone Diagnosis: A Comment on Paleopathological Methods. *International Journal of Osteoarchaeology* 6:221–229.

Nacach, G.
2011   La deriva de la alteridad entre las lógicas de raza y clase en la Patagonia: El censo de 1895 en el contexto del proceso de incorporación diferenciada de los indígenas. Unpublished Ph.D. dissertation, School of Arts and Sciences, University of Buenos Aires, Buenos Aires.

Orser, C.
1996   *A Historical Archaeology of the Modern World.* Plenum, New York.

Ortner, D. J.
2003   *Identification of Pathological Conditions in Human Skeletal Remains.* Elsevier Science/Academic Press, New York.

Quijano, A.
2000   Colonialidad del poder, eurocentrismo y América Latina. In *La colonialidad del saber: Eurocentrismo y ciencias sociales. Perspectivas latinoamericanas,* edited by E. Lander, pp. 216–264. CLACSO, Buenos Aires.

Roberts, C., and J. E. Buikstra
2003   *The Bioarchaeology of Tuberculosis: A Global View on a Reemerging Disease.*
          University Press of Florida, Gainesville.
Santos, A. L., and C. Roberts
2006   Anatomy of a Serial Killer: Differential Diagnosis of Tuberculosis Based on
          Rib Lesions of Adult Individuals from the Coimbra Identified Skeletal Col-
          lection, Portugal. *American Journal of Physical Anthropology* 130:38–49.
Schaefer, M., S. Black, and L. Scheuer
2009   *Juvenile Osteology.* Elsevier, New York.
Scheuer, L., and S. Black.
2000   *Developmental Juvenile Osteology.* Academic Press, London.
Schinder, G., and R. A. Guichón
2003   Isótopos estables y estilo de vida en muestras óseas humanas de Tierra del
          Fuego. *Magallania* 31:33–44.
Schutkowski, H.
1993   Sex Determination of Infant and Juvenile Skeletons: I. Morphognostic Fea-
          tures. *American Journal of Physical Anthropology* 90:199–205.
Senatore, M. X., and A. Zarankin
2002   Leituras da sociedade moderna em Latinoamerica: Cultura material, discur-
          sos e praticas. In *Arqueología da sociedade moderna na America do Sul: Cul-
          tura material, discursos e praticas,* edited by A. Zarankin and M. X. Senatore,
          pp. 5–18. Ediciones del Tridente, Buenos Aires.
Silliman, S.
2005   Culture Contact or Colonialism? Challenges in the Archaeology of Native
          North America. *American Antiquity* 70:55–74.
Stojanowski, C. M.
2013   *Mission Cemeteries, Mission Peoples: Historical and Evolutionary Dimen-
          sions of Intracemetery Bioarchaeology in Spanish Florida.* University Press of
          Florida, Gainesville.
Thomas, N.
1991   *Entangled Objects: Exchange, Material Culture, and Colonialism in the Pacific.*
          Harvard University Press, Cambridge.
Ubelaker, D. H.
1989   *Human Skeletal Remains: Excavation, Analysis and Interpretation.* 2nd ed.
          Taraxacum Press, Washington, D.C.
Wallerstein, I.
1979   *The Modern World-System.* 3 vols. Academic Press, New York.
Wilbur, A. K., and J. E. Buikstra
2006   Patterns of Tuberculosis in the Americas: How Can Modern Biomedicine
          Inform the Ancient Past? *Memorias do Instituto Oswaldo Cruz* 101(Supp.
          3):59–66.
Wilbur, A. K., A. W. Farnbach, K. Knudson, and J. E. Buikstra
2008   Diet, Tuberculosis, and the Paleopathological Record. *Current Anthropology*
          49:963–991.

8

Impacts of Imperial Interests on Health and Economy in the Byzantine Near East

MEGAN A. PERRY

Traditionally, historical archaeology has involved documenting the effects of post-1492 A.D. colonial expansion, exploration, and the establishment of modern world-systems. Perhaps most notable are the archaeological and bioarchaeological studies of the impact of European contact in the Americas. Some scholars, such as Andrén (1998) and Funari (1999), argue that historical archaeology, as a discipline, should include all researchers wrestling with similar issues incorporating written documentation with the material remains of an ancient community. Post-1500 historical archaeology and the primarily pre-1500 historical archaeology of the Old World have countless similar research agendas, such as the consequences of population aggregation, outcomes of trade and social networks, ideas of ethnicity and identity, and, as discussed in this volume, the effects of contact between different populations and impact of colonial or imperial rule on local communities. Indeed, both Old and New World historical archaeologies would not have existed without colonial expansions.

In this chapter I take a different perspective on colonialism and imperialism, examining the imperial activities of the decidedly pre-1500 early Byzantine Empire (fourth–seventh centuries A.D.) in the Near East through assessing the impact of imperial interest on health and quality of life in different communities. This investigation demonstrates that, along with the other chapters in this volume, researchers grappling with texts and material and biological data should bridge the New versus Old World and pre- versus post-1500 divisions that exist within the discipline. In addition, as pointed out in Buzon and Smith's chapter (this volume), New World models of colonialism may not necessarily apply to *longue durée* Old World colonial interactions.

As noted above, the investigation of Old World, pre-1500 A.D. literate societies, as exemplified in Classical or Near Eastern archaeology, and post-1500 communities is existentially or historically intertwined with the products and histories of European colonial activities, primarily in Africa and Asia. Many scholars have exploited or perverted archaeology and history to provide justification of their country's imperial and colonial activities (see Andrén 1998:27; Bernal 1994:121; Hingley 1999:138; Webster 1996:4). The search for the past in the Near East, for instance, was seen as a patriotic aspiration in Europe, and "the Bible and Greek and Roman literature . . . were seen as the spiritual inheritance of the people of Europe" (Silberman 1989:3; see also Trigger 1990:160–161). The success of Roman imperialism supported the perception of European superiority over other nations and cultures, mirroring the triumph of European colonialism in Rome's acquisition of parts of Asia, Africa, and Europe (Dondin-Payre 1991; Freeman 1996; Hingley 1999; Mattingly 1996; van Dommelen 1997). Some European nations founded their colonial idealism on ancient textual evidence that frequently extolled the success of Greek and Roman imperial domination (Lyons and Papadopoulos 2002:11).

The Classical Near East (332 B.C.–A.D. 634) seems to provide, at first glance, an archetypical case study concerning the influence of a foreign colonial power over indigenous populations. From the fourth century B.C. through the first century A.D., the Nabataeans controlled the region of the Israeli Negev desert and nearly all of modern-day Jordan. Rome then annexed the Nabataean kingdom in A.D. 106 to create Provincia Arabia, later reorganized by the Constantinople-based Byzantine Empire into Palaestina Tertia. The direct takeover by Rome did not stimulate drastic political or social change for the Nabataeans despite the relatively foreign cultural influence of Europeans. Not only had the Nabataeans actively modeled administration, military, and architecture on Greco-Roman ideals, but after annexation, the emperors in Rome served only as distant facilitators of imperial control mediated through regional centers. Rather than locals experiencing the colonizing event(s) as a defining moment, it rather emerged as just a new stage in a continuous indigenous history (see Buzon and Smith, this volume, and Murphy et al., this volume). Thus, Roman and Byzantine colonialism in Provincia Arabia and Palaestina Tertia did not represent a fundamental or drastic break from previous local cultural and political structures. Such a context demonstrates the need to reconsider the traditional colonizer/colonized and center/periphery dichotomies when considering the effects of rule based in Rome or Constantinople.

Understanding the realities of Byzantine notions of colonialism can allow understanding of Palaestina Tertia not as a Byzantine province but as social and political construct that indigenous populations resisted against or generally ignored. Bioarchaeological study of such a setting can instead focus on the fluid and diverse interactions between different communities residing in the area of Provincia Arabia and Palaestina Tertia. In this case, evidence of health and quality of life using bioanthropological methods is useful to reflect these communities' access to material resources and the biological effects of colonial control exhibited on the eastern frontier of the Byzantine Empire.

BYZANTINE RULE IN JORDAN

The beginning of the Byzantine era in Jordan generally is marked by the late third century A.D. administrative and military reforms of the emperor Diocletian along with Constantine I's conversion to Christianity and foundation of a new imperial capital at Constantinople in the early fourth century. The relative proximity of the new capital, in addition to the region's new role as the imperial Holy Land, elevated the administrative, military, and economic importance of the eastern sector of the former Roman Empire. Scholars do not agree how this specifically is related to a documented increase in settlement in the Near East, but clearly, during the fourth and fifth centuries the area was relatively free from external and internal skirmishes, and this allowed trade, food production, and extraction of resources to continue unabated (Watson 2008:447). This situation became disrupted in the late fifth through the seventh centuries, when the empire became embroiled in repeated skirmishes with Persia and the imperial leadership recruited tribes external to the empire to fill provincial military and administrative roles. During this period, many agricultural villages began to face the multiple burdens of providing for their own defense while having to cover often-exorbitant taxes. Agricultural villages relying on dry farming and irrigation, which was the case for most of Palaestina Tertia, generally had low yields, and surplus resources necessary to cover their taxes frequently fell short (Nevo 1991:98; Pollard 2000:102–103). Internal threats starting in the fifth century primarily from nomadic groups led villages to take local defense into their own hands (Isaac 1998). Defense of many villages was left to a locally-raised military (*limitanei*), and eventually in the

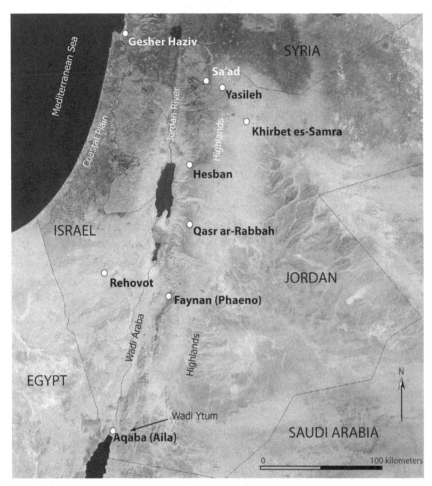

Figure 8.1. Map of sites used in this study (adapted from Perry et al. 2011)

sixth century, the emperor Justinian ceased payment to these troops that further limited imperial oversight (see Parker 2000a:382). Archaeological and historical evidence thus demonstrates an overall decline in imperial interests and investment into manufacturing, industry, agriculture, and the military from the fifth century until the seventh-century Muslim conquest.

The two sites at the center of this study, Faynan and Aila, both served as important contributors to the imperial and local economies (Figure 8.1). Byzantine Faynan (Phaeno) was a highly organized imperial system that included extensive mining operations and agricultural field systems (Barker 2002:499–500; Mattingly et al. 2007). It also purportedly served as a prison camp for individuals *damnatio ad metallum* (damned to the mines). Eusebius of Caesarea, writing in the early fourth century A.D., describes the horrors that Christian martyrs faced when sent to the Phaeno mines during this period (*Ecclesiastical History* VIII.8, 10; *Martyrs of Palestine* 7.4, 8.1, 13.1–3). Later fourth-century writers, often influenced by Eusebius's descriptions (Gustafson 1994), also focus on Christian heretics from Alexandria and elsewhere condemned to *metallum* and sent to Phaeno, "where even a condemned murderer is scarcely able to live a few days" (Athanasius, *Historia Arianorum* 60; also see Theodoret, *Historia Ecclesiastica* 4.22.26, 4.22.28; Epiphanius, *Panarion Haer* 68.3.6). Eusebius similarly mentions that Phaeno contained prisoners from Egypt and other Palaestina provinces, supporting the inference that the Roman and Byzantine Empires often transported criminals over long distances to serve their sentences (Millar 1984:139).

Palynological and geochemical studies of the landscape have discovered that mining operations ceased in the late sixth to early seventh centuries, likely due to a combination of overextraction of copper ore and pollution of the environment that decreased agricultural yields, essentially poisoning the local population (Barker 2002; Hunt et al. 2007). The severely denuded environment of Byzantine Phaeno mirrors numerous environmental disasters seen around the globe today that result from an imbalance in the needs of a state versus the well-being and sustenance of people or the environment.

Aila served as a major manufacturing center (including of copper goods from Phaeno ores) and maritime port on the Red Sea. In addition, during the late third century the Legio X Fretensis, a Roman legionary garrison, was transferred from Jerusalem to Aila (*Notitia Dignatatum Orientis* 34.30), making it an important military post in addition to a trade center. Unlike Phaeno, the saline soil made agriculture within the city's environs difficult (Parker 2002). The city's climate reflects the surrounding desert and craggy Precambrian granite mountains, with rainfall averaging 34.84 mm per annum (Jordan Water Authority 1980) and summer temperatures regularly exceeding 40°C. However, paleobotanical evidence has identified the presence of cotton, dates, and barley growing at the site (Ramsay n.d.). Sheep, goats, and other herd animals were brought in "on the hoof" for consumption of meat and their by-products. A majority of grain for the city residents was likely imported from Egypt in the plentiful Egyptian amphorae recovered from the site (Parker 2002).

These two cities, both characterized by a strong imperial presence and economic significance, imaginably could have either suffered or benefited from their role and importance in the imperial scheme of things. In this chapter I assess how these imperial settings shaped health and disease patterns as observed in skeletal remains, in addition to biogeochemical evidence of the geographic origin of food and water consumed during childhood as reflected in strontium isotopes in dental enamel; these data may serve as a proxy for population movement and economic integration. Data from these two sites are compared to combined information from agricultural villages in the region, which, as noted above, experienced diminished imperial influence or interaction over time. The nature of resource extraction and ancient textual evidence of mining at Faynan, including the potential presence of prisoners, would imply poorer health and disease levels at Faynan than at the agricultural villages, with a population that, unless they emigrated from elsewhere, consumed primarily a local diet. Aila's diverse economy and long-term economic prosperity would likely result in better health than the agricultural villages and a mix of local and non-local dietary sources (making it difficult to identify non-locals within the population). The results of this study demonstrate the multifaceted nature of imperial interaction with and impact on local, indigenous populations in Palaestina Tertia.

INVESTIGATING ANCIENT HEALTH AND CHILDHOOD DIETARY SOURCES

The human skeleton is a palimpsest of life experiences and history, not only of metabolic status, diet, trauma, and regions of residence but also body modification and ideas of physical beauty (Sofaer 2006). Health and nutrition generally are assessed through observing evidence of growth perturbations, infectious disease, and other pathologies in the skeleton. In this study, dental enamel hypoplasias (DEHs), periostitis, and porotic hyperostosis/cribra orbitalia provided evidence for quality of life. DEHs represent cessation and resumption in dental enamel calcification during childhood growth as a result of physiological or metabolic stress (Cuttress and Suckling 1982; Goodman and Armelagos 1985; Sarnat and Schour 1941). Since dental enamel does not remodel after formation, non-specific DEHs are retained through adulthood unless dental wear, tooth loss, or death during the stressful event makes them unobservable. Infections of bone periosteum (periostitis) or the bone itself (osteitis) result from either generalized infection or from specific infectious diseases, and periostitis especially can reflect various baselines of chronic but non-fatal disease burden within a population (Ortner 2003). Finally, cribra orbitalia and porotic hyperostosis can indicate acquired anemia (in areas where congenital anemias are not endemic) due to diets that are poor in vitamins B_9 and B_{12} and, to some degree, possibly iron (Oxenham and Cavil 2011; Walker et al. 2009), weaning diarrhea, and intestinal parasites (El-Najjar et al. 1976; Stuart-Macadam 1992; Sullivan 2005). Other metabolic pathological conditions were evaluated in the skeletal remains, such as the presence of rickets due to vitamin D deficiency (Ortner 2003) and pathological lesion patterns indicative of vitamin C deficiency (scurvy) (Crandall and Klaus 2014; Ortner et al. 2001).

The Faynan (Phaeno) sample comes from the third–sixth century A.D. Southern Cemetery excavated by the former British Institute in Amman for Archaeology and History (now the Council for British Research in the Levant) and Yarmouk University in 1996 (Findlater et al. 1998; Mattingly et al. 2007). Extensive looting in the Southern Cemetery had effectively destroyed over 700 of the estimated 1,200 graves in the cemetery, although 45 undisturbed primary burials were excavated during the 1996 season. The excavated funerary contexts display a uniform internment style, with an oblong pit cut oriented east-west, the bottom of which was a covered with sandstone slabs. The bodies were placed on their backs in an extended position with their heads to the west and hands resting in the pelvic area. Preservation varied across the site, but in many cases the bodies were found enclosed within textile shrouds or tunics and wearing leather sandals. Funerary stelae marked most of the graves, some inscribed with Christian crosses. Other than personal clothing, very few material objects or grave goods were recovered from the graves.

The 46 burials recovered from Aila were excavated from two cemeteries, Areas A and M, under the auspices of North Carolina State University's Roman Aqaba Project from 1994–2000 (Parker 1996, 1998, 2000a, 2000b; Perry 2002, 2016). In most cases, single primary interments were buried within mudbrick cist tombs, and some were covered with mudbrick capstones. Those without tomb architecture were buried in a simple pit. No primary artifacts were discovered with the burials, with the exception of a few beads, and artifacts placed within the burial fill and the overlying strata date no later than the late fourth to early fifth century A.D. The burials appear to have been wrapped in textile shrouds, the only evidence of which comes from textile imprints on the bones and organic stains resembling "shadows" surrounding the bodies.

Demographic and pathological data collection for the Aila and Faynan samples followed the protocol of Buikstra and Ubelaker (1994). Frequencies of pathological conditions at Aila and Faynan were compared to other contemporary Roman and Byzantine sites in Israel and Jordan in order to place these results into context. Agricultural communities with supposed minimal imperial influence, such as Tell Hesban ($MNI = 191$), Qasr ar-Rabbah ($MNI = 15$), Gesher Haziv ($N = 24$), Yasileh ($MNI = 47$), Sa'ad ($MNI = 338$), Rehovot ($N = 96$), and Khirbet es-Samra ($N = 128$), were hypothesized to have more evidence of disease and poorer nutrition that the trading port of Aila, where less disease burden and better nutrition would be observed than at the mining community at Faynan.

To complement these data, previously published information from Faynan and preliminary data from Aila were applied to investigate the origin of childhood diets, which can identify not only where food sources derived but also whether or not individuals buried at the sites grew up in a different region and migrated to that area. The ratio of strontium-87 to strontium-86 ($^{87}Sr/^{86}Sr$) varies across the landscape based on the geological age of the underlying bedrock and other geological features (Faure and Powell 1972). Strontium isotope signatures enter the food chain through water and plant uptake, and then through consumption of these plant and water resources. Humans absorb strontium by ingesting these resources, each of which reflects the respective geological regions from where is originated. Dental enamel, which forms and calcifies during childhood dental development, will present a permanent record of the sources of childhood diet. Local signature of a region tends to be defined by a range of values derived from local fauna (Bentley 2006; Price et al. 2002).

Previous strontium isotope studies in Jordan (Perry et al. 2008, 2009, 2011) have demonstrated the difficulty in pinning down a "local" signature to compare with human values. Local fauna tend to provide a much more limited range than humans, partially due to the extensive geological variation in western Jordan and also the wide range of food sources during the Byzantine period. Therefore, it is more prudent to envision $^{87}Sr/^{86}Sr$ values as reflecting the sources of foods consumed at a site rather than as the site's specific geological signature, with the assumption that individuals in a community would generally rely on similar food sources during childhood (see Montgomery 2010). Local human values would therefore fall within a normal range of variation, with statistical outliers representing individuals with arguably different childhood food sources, perhaps reflecting a different community or region of origin.

Dental enamel from 45 individuals at Faynan in addition to 1 archaeological rodent dental enamel sample and 8 archaeological land snail shells from the site's environs were processed for strontium isotope analysis. In addition, dental enamel from 23 individuals buried at Aila, along with 2 archaeological rodent dental enamel and 13 geological samples from the region, were selected for strontium isotope analysis. The dental enamel, faunal enamel, and geological samples were prepared for analysis in the Bioarchaeology and Geology Laboratories at East Carolina University, and all isotopic analysis was completed at the Geosciences Laboratory at UNC Chapel Hill. The dental enamel in each tooth was sectioned using a Dremel saw, and a small piece at least 10 mg was cleaned using a carbide burr to remove any soil and dental dentine. The human dental enamel samples were subjected to chemical cleaning through repeated washing with distilled water and cleaning with glacial acetic acid at approximately 80°C for 10 hours. After cleaning, the tooth enamel was dissolved in 500 μL of twice-distilled 7N HNO_3 and then evaporated and redissolved in 250 μL of 3.5N HNO_3. Solid geological samples were reduced to centimeter-sized chips using standard rock-crushing equipment, and 50–100 mg were placed into beakers for dissolution. All samples were spiked with concentrated [84]Sr. Solid geological samples were dissolved in a sealed beaker on a hotplate in HF/HNO_3 and then dried and redissolved in HCl.

All samples were dried a final time and dissolved in 3.5M HNO_3 in preparation for column chromatography. Isolation of strontium was accomplished using a resin bed of approximately 35 μL of EiChrom Sr-Spec™ resin. Following collection of strontium, all samples had 1μL of concentrated H_3PO_4 added and were dried prior to loading. Samples were loaded on single rhenium filaments with $TaCl_5$ and analyzed in triple-dynamic multicollector mode with [88]Sr-3V ($10^{-11}\Omega$ resistor) on the VG Sector-54 housed in the Department of Geological Sciences at the University of North Carolina. All ratios are reported relative to a value of 0.710270 ±0.000014 (2σ) for the NBS 987 standard. Internal precision for strontium runs is typically ±0.000012 to 0.000018 percent (2σ) standard error based on 100 dynamic cycles of data collection.

RESULTS: ANCIENT HEALTH, DIET, AND IMPERIAL INTERESTS

The health and disease levels of individuals at Aila and Faynan were compared with those at a number of agricultural settlements from the region (Table 8.1). As noted above, throughout the fifth and sixth centuries Byzantine imperial interest in these villages waned with the exception of tax collection, leaving them more or less autonomous in terms of day-to-day life but struggling to cover their tax burden. Aggregating data in this manner can mask any intra-site variation that may exist in these villages, but in this case their health profiles did not vary significantly with the exception of the reported 0 percent frequency of DEHs from the rather large ($N = 128$) Khirbet es-Samra sample (Nabulsi 1998). The lack of DEHs at Samra could be due to methodological issues in data collection.

Only three types of pathological conditions were observed in the samples used in this study: DEHs, periosteal infections, and porotic hyperostosis/cribra orbitalia. The original observers of Faynan (Abu-Karaki 2000; El-Najjar and Al-Shiyab 1998) did not record periostitis frequencies. No evidence of other metabolic stress, such as vitamin C or D deficiencies, or specific infections conditions existed. Similar to Killgrove's investigation of the cemeteries of Rome (this volume), these two provincial sites with economies and resources overseen by the empire clearly have very divergent health and nutrition patterns. The port city and military garrison of Aila had lower frequencies of porotic hyperostosis/cribra orbitalia and a higher frequency of periostitis than the agricultural villages. Aila also possessed lower porotic hyperostosis/cribra orbitalia and DEHs frequencies than the mining site of Faynan. Faynan demonstrated higher DEH frequency than the agricultural villages as well, but similar levels of porotic hyperostosis.

Table 8.1. Frequencies of specific pathological conditions at Aila, Faynan, and contemporaneous agricultural village sites from Jordan and Israel

Pathology	Aila		Faynan		Agricultural villages	
	%	N/MNI	%	N/MNI	%	N/MNI
DEHs[a]	48	21	83	18	37	415
Periostitis	15	46	n/r	n/r	5	741
Porotic hyperostosis/ cribra orbitalia[b]	9	33	33	52	42	268

Note: n/r = not reported.

[a]Percentages based on number of individuals with observable central maxillary incisors or mandibular canines

[b]Percentages based on number of individuals with observable parietals and/or frontal bones

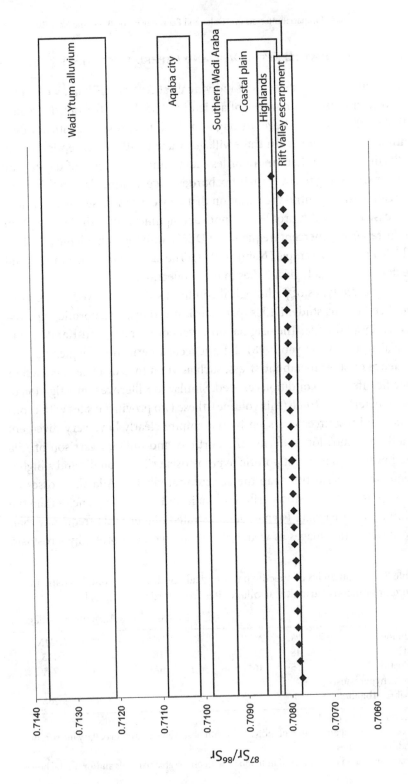

Figure 8.2. $^{87}Sr/^{86}Sr$ results from Faynan compared with local ranges.

All differences were determined through a χ^2 test with the Bonferroni correction for multiple comparisons, and those noted above were significantly different at the $p \leq 0.05$ level.

Strontium isotope data from Faynan indicate that the inhabitants consumed a homogeneous diet during childhood (Figure 8.2; see Perry et al. 2009, 2011). The local faunal signature only represents one part of the biologically available strontium represented by the human values. Most individuals relied on food sources from the rift valley escarpment (the geological locale of Faynan) and parts of Wadi Araba, with perhaps a small component from the more fertile highlands. In general, it appears that these individuals, with one exception having higher strontium isotope values than the others, relied on a relatively local diet with few differences among this population.

The data from Aila, on the other hand, display surprising variation in dietary sources during childhood (Figure 8.3). Aila is surrounded by mountains of Precambrian granite, some of the oldest formations in Jordan, with $^{87}Sr/^{86}Sr$ values exceeding 0.7120, and related alluvium with similarly high values. However, contributions from these sources to human strontium would be very low, as determined by their lower ppm (parts per mil) values. All other environmental sources tested at Aila fall between $^{87}Sr/^{86}Sr$ = 0.7076142–0.708643 (Perry et al. 2016). Therefore, most of the individuals buried at Aila had strontium isotope signatures much higher than is biologically or geologically possible in the region. The closest tested regions with values above 0.7100 include parts of Europe, inland North Africa, and surrounding the Indus Valley stem. Therefore, while their exact origin cannot be determined, the individuals at Aila clearly originated far from the site, likely drawn there through trade or commercial networks (Perry et al. 2016).

Discussion: Does Imperial Investment Impact Health in Palaestina Tertia?

Clearly, factors beyond imperial interest affect disease within the Byzantine Empire's Palaestina Tertia. The nature of the imperial denudation of the landscape at Faynan likely had a profound impact on disease and nutrition of the population, many of whom probably originated from the lower socioeconomic levels of society (see Perry et al. 2009). The high level of DEHs within this sample attests to a childhood exposed to fairly acute stressors, although these individuals were not so frail as to perish from these stresses,

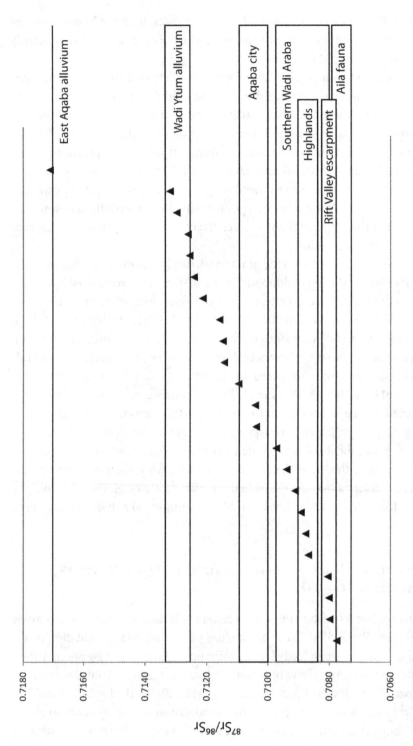

Figure 8.3. $^{87}Sr/^{86}Sr$ results from Aila compared with local ranges.

and most of them lived into adulthood. Widespread extraction and processing of copper ore in the vicinity of Faynan resulted in substantial industrial pollution that was not ameliorated by environmental processes such as rainfall, leaching, or geomorphic and geologic cycling (Grattan et al. 2005). The by-products of ancient mining and smelting operations in fact continue to cycle through the modern environment (Pyatt et al. 1999, 2000, 2002, 2005). Ancient soils at the site as a result display extremely high copper and lead concentrations (Grattan et al. 2003, 2004; Pyatt and Grattan 2002; Pyatt et al. 2000, 2005) that would be considered an environmental disaster in some parts of the world today (Grattan et al. 2005). The levels of heavy metal concentrations vary across the site and appear to be localized around or immediately downwind from metallurgical activities (Grattan et al. 2007). The high level of heavy metals in the bones of some Faynan residents (see Grattan et al. 2005; Perry et al. 2011) indicates the impact of the polluted environment in which the ancient inhabitants lived, worked, and died. Unfortunately, the porotic hyperostosis/cribra orbitalia data collected by Abu-Karaki are not presented by individual, making it difficult to determine if a relationship exists between lead concentration levels and overall skeletal pathological status similar to Killgrove's study in this volume. The $^{87}Sr/^{86}Sr$ analysis of foods consumed during childhood identifies a relatively homogeneous diet primarily originating from the wadis and mountains systems along the rift valley escarpment and from Wadi Araba. These data indicate that, at least in childhood, these individuals subsisted on a relatively local diet, probably from animals herded by pastoral nomads near the site and from agricultural products grown nearby. Many of these items would have had decreased yield and high toxicity due to the polluted environment, which could have had an impact on health throughout an individual's life.

Aila also served an important role in the imperial administration of Palaestina Tertia, in the form of a maritime port and home for a legionary garrison. At least for the individuals within this study sample, this imperial presence was not very detrimental to their health, with the exception of the children. The periosteal reactions seen at Aila were active, systemic reactions in subadults that co-occurred with active porotic lesions (Perry 2002). While data on the type of periosteal lesions and the age breakdown of their occurrence are not available for most of the agricultural village samples, it may be that the children at Aila were under stress but that these relatively "frail" individuals died and were removed from the population, leaving a relatively healthy assemblage of adult skeletons. The $^{87}Sr/^{86}Sr$ data demonstrate that those buried in the Area A and M cemeteries at Aila derived from different locales far from the city. This cemetery has no indication that it served as a military, as opposed to a civilian place of burial. Aila's role as a maritime port serves as the most logical explanation for the presence of so many individuals hailing from long distances. It is not clear if they resided at Aila, or the cemeteries served as a catchment for individuals perishing on a trade mission, but their presence attests to the city's role in long-distance trade during the Byzantine period.

The role of the city as an economic center, and its relatively hostile environment for large-scale agricultural production, would have meant that a variety of foods would have been transported in not only for the military legion but also for the local population. Seafood likely provided a regular supplement to the local diet, which in other cases has provided the nutrients necessary to maintain health even when other sources of subsistence are limited (e.g., Hutchinson et al. 2007). However, the crowded habitat at Aila may have led to poor sanitation and high levels of infant morbidity and mortality, particularly from causes that lead to iron-deficiency anemia.

Therefore, Byzantine imperial rule in the southern Levant probably had an indirect, but not predictable, impact on the health and dietary sources of local communities. Similar to Killgrove's study, it is difficult to identify the exact causes for poor health at Faynan or childhood stress at Aila. Environmental pollution that affected local crop yields and, likely, community health at Faynan, and very probably the imperial needs for extraction of valuable resources, sped up or heightened the process of site toxicity. The economic needs of the legionary garrison and the role of the city as a seaport likely benefited the population of Aila. However, crowding and, perhaps, disease pathogens brought in with traders from numerous locales did not improve the lives of Ailaean children. Therefore, similar to the impact of Egypt's interest in raw resources in Nubia on the health of local populations reported on by Buzon and Smith, or the health of individuals in ancient Rome presented by Killgrove, Byzantine involvement in the province of Palaestina Tertia had minimal impact on health and disease experiences among indigenous client populations. Similar to colonial Peru (Klaus and Alvarez-Calderón, this volume; Murphy et al., this volume), uniformitarian responses of local populations to imperial or colonial rule are not supported by bioarchaeological data in the Near East. Clearly, despite their diverse histories, scholarship of colonized groups in the Old and New Worlds can provide comparative perspectives for researchers working in many parts of the world.

ACKNOWLEDGMENTS

I would like to thank the editors for their invitation to contribute to this volume and their helpful comments along the way. In addition, I appreciate the observations of the anonymous peer reviewers. I am also grateful to George Findlater and Abdel Halim al-Shiyab for access to the Faynan skeletons, currently held at Yarmouk University in Irbid, Jordan. In addition, S. Thomas Parker, director of the Roman Aqaba Project, made the Aila Byzantine cemetery a research priority, which is much appreciated. Drew Coleman of the Department of Geological Sciences at University of North Carolina at Chapel Hill was responsible for the ^{87}Sr/^{86}Sr analysis with the assistance of Cammie Jennings. As always, this research could not have been possible without the support and cooperation of the Department of Antiquities of Jordan and the American Center of Oriental Research in Amman, who provided the author a Council of American Overseas Research Centers Senior Research Fellowship to collect data used in this study.

REFERENCES CITED

Abu-Karaki, L.
2000   Skeletal Biology of the People of Wadi Faynan: A Bioarchaeological Study. Unpublished Master's thesis, Yarmouk University, Irbid, Jordan.
Andrén, A.
1998   *Between Artifacts and Texts: Historical Archaeology in Global Perspective.* Plenum Press, New York.
Athanasius
1993   *History of the Arians (Historia Arianorum).* Eastern Orthodox Books, Willits, California.
Barker, G.
2002   A Tale of Two Deserts: Contrasting Desertification Histories on Rome's Desert Frontiers. *World Archaeology* 33:488–507.
Bentley, R. A.
2006   Strontium Isotopes from the Earth to the Skeleton: A Review. *Journal of Archaeological Method and Theory* 13:135–187.
Bernal, M.
1994   The Image of Ancient Greece as a Tool for Colonialism and European Hegemony. In *Social Construction of the Past: Representations as Power,* edited by G. C. Bond and A. Gilliam, pp. 117–128. Routledge, London.
Buikstra, J. E., and D. H. Ubelaker
1994   *Standards for Data Collection from Human Skeletal Remains.* Arkansas Archaeology Research Series No. 44. Arkansas Archaeological Survey, Fayetteville.

Crandall, J. J., and H. D. Klaus
2014   Advancements, Challenges, and Prospects in the Paleopathology of Scurvy: Current Perspectives on Vitamin C Deficiency in Human Skeletal Remains. In *Advances in the Paleopathology of Scurvy: Papers in Honor of Donald J. Ortner* (Special Issue of the International Journal of Paleopathology), edited by J. J. Crandall and H. D. Klaus. *International Journal of Paleopathology* 5:1–8.

Cuttress, T. W., and G. W. Suckling
1982   The Assessment of Non-Carious Defects of Enamel. *International Dental Journal* 32:117–122.

Dondin-Payre, M.
1991   *L'exercitus* Africae inspiratrice de l'armée française d'Afrique: *Ense et Aratro. Antiquités Africaines* 27:141–149.

El-Najjar, M., and A. H. Al-Shiyab
1998   Skeletal Biology and Pathology of the People of Wadi Faynan in Southern Jordan. *Mu'tah Lil-Buhuth wad-Dirasat* 13:9–39.

El-Najjar, M. Y., D. J. Ryan, C. G. Turner II, and B. Lozoff
1976   The Etiology of Porotic Hyperostosis among the Prehistoric and Historic Anasazi Indians of Southwestern United States. *American Journal of Physical Anthropology* 44:477–488.

Epiphanius
1994   *The Panarion of Epiphanius of Salamis.* Brill, Leiden.

Eusebius of Caesarea
1927   *Ecclesiastical History and the Martyrs of Palestine.* Macmillan, New York.

Faure, G., and J. L. Powell
1972   *Strontium Isotope Geology.* Springer-Verlag, New York.

Findlater, M., M. El-Najjar, A. H. Al-Shiyab, M. O'Hea, and E. Easthaugh
1998   The Wadi Faynan Project: The South Cemetery Excavation, Jordan 1996: A Preliminary Report. *Levant* 30:69–83.

Freeman, P.
1996   British Imperialism and the Roman Empire. In *Roman Imperialism: Post-Colonial Perspectives,* edited by J. Webster and N. Cooper, pp. 19–34. School of Archaeological Studies, University of Leicester, Leicester.

Funari, P. P. A.
1999   Historical Archaeology from a World Perspective. In *Historical Archaeology: Back from the Edge,* edited by P. P. A. Funari, M. Hall, and S. Jones, pp. 37–66. Routledge, London.

Goodman, A. H., and G. J. Armelagos
1985   Factors Affecting the Distribution of Enamel Hypoplasias within the Human Permanent Dentition. *American Journal of Physical Anthropology* 68:479–493.

Grattan, J. P., L. Abu-Karaki, D. Hine, H. Toland, D. D. Gilbertson, Z. Al Saad, and B. Pyatt
2005   Analyses of Patterns of Copper and Lead Mineralization in Human Skeletons Excavated from an Ancient Mining and Smelting Centre in the Jordanian Desert: A Reconnaissance Study. *Mineraological Magazine* 69:653–666.

Grattan, J. P., D. D. Gilbertson, and C. O. Hunt
2007   The Local and Global Dimensions of Metalliferous Pollution Derived from
            a Reconstruction of an Eight Thousand Year Record of Copper Smelting
            and Mining at a Desert-Mountain Frontier in Southern Jordan. *Journal of
            Archaeological Science* 34:83–110.
Grattan, J. P., G. K. Gillmore, D. D. Gilbertson, F. B. Pyatt, C. O. Hunt, S. J. McLaren, P. S.
            Phillips, and A. Denman
2004   Radon and "King Solomon's Miners": Faynan Orefield, Jordanian Desert.
            Science of the Total Environment 319:99–113.
Grattan, J. P., S. I. Huxley, and F. B. Pyatt
2003   Modern Bedouin Exposures to Copper Contamination: An Imperial Lega-
            cy? *Ecotoxicology and Environmental Safety* 55:108–115.
Gustafson, M.
1994   Condemnation to the Mines in the Later Roman Empire. *Harvard Theologi-
            cal Review* 87:421–433.
Hingley, R.
1999   The Imperial Context of Romano-British Studies and Proposals for a New
            Understanding of Social Change. In *Historical Archaeology: Back from the
            Edge*, edited by P. P. A. Funari, M. Hall, and S. Jones, pp. 137–150. Routledge,
            London.
Hunt, C. O., D. D. Gilbertson, and H. A. El-Rishi
2007   An 8000-Year History of Landscape, Climate, and Copper Exploitation in
            the Middle East: The Wadi Faynan and the Wadi Dana National Reserve in
            Southern Jordan. *Journal of Archaeological Science* 34:1306–1338.
Hutchinson, D. L., L. Norr, and M. F. Teaford
2007   Outer Coast Foragers and Inner Coast Farmers in Late Prehistoric North
            Carolina. In *Ancient Health: Skeletal Indicators of Agricultural and Economic
            Intensification*, edited by M. N. Cohen and G. M. M. Crane-Kramer, pp.
            52–64. University Press of Florida, Gainesville.
Isaac, B.
1998   *The Near East under Roman Rule: Selected Papers*. Leiden: Brill.
Jordan Water Authority
1980   Rainfall in Jordan for the Water Years 1976–1980. Amman: Jordan Water
            Authority, Water Resources Department, Surface Water Division Technical
            Paper No. 50.
Lyons, C. L., and J. K. Papadopoulos (editors)
2002   *The Archaeology of Colonialism*. Getty Research Foundation, Los Angeles.
Mattingly, D.
1996   From One Colonialism to Another: Imperialism and the Maghreb. In *Roman
            Imperialism: Post-Colonial Perspectives*, edited by J. Webster and N. Cooper,
            pp. 46–69. School of Archaeological Studies, University of Leicester, Leices-
            ter.
Mattingly, D., P. Newson, O. Creighton, R. Tomber, J. P. Grattan, C. O. Hunt, D. D. Gilb-
            ertson, H. el-Rishi, and B. Pyatt.
2007   A Landscape of Imperial Power: Roman and Byzantine *Phaino*. In *Archaeol-*

ogy and Desertification: The Wadi Faynan Landscape Survey, Southern Jordan, edited by G. Barker, D. D. Gilbertson, and D. Mattingly, pp. 305–348. Oxbow Books, Oxford, U.K.

Millar, F.
1984 Condemnation to Hard Labour in the Roman Empire, from the Julio-Claudians to Constantine. *Papers of the British School at Rome* 52:124–147.

Montgomery, J.
2010 Passports from the Past: Investigating Human Dispersals Using Strontium Isotope Analysis of Tooth Enamel. *Annals of Human Biology* 37:325–346.

Nabulsi, A.
1998 The Byzantine Cemetery in Samra. In *Fouilles de Khirbet es-Samra en Jordanie*, edited by J.-B. Humbert and A. Desreumaux, pp. 271–279. Brepols, Turnhout.

Nevo, Y. D.
1991 *Pagans and Herders: A Re-examination of the Negev Runoff Cultivation Systems in the Byzantine and Early Arab Periods.* IPS Ltd., Negev.

Ortner, D. J.
2003 *Identification of Pathological Conditions in Human Skeletal Remains.* Academic Press, Amsterdam.

Ortner, D. J., W. Butler, J. Cafarella, and L. Milligan
2001 Evidence of Probable Scurvy in Subadults from Archeological Sites in North America. *American Journal of Physical Anthropology* 114:343–351.

Oxenham, M. F., and I. Cavill
2011 Porotic Hyperostosis and Cribra Orbitalia: The Erythropoietic Response to Iron Deficiency Anaemia. *Anthropological Science* 118:199–200.

Parker, S. T.
1996 The Roman Aqaba Project: The 1994 Campaign. *Annual of the Department of Antiquities of Jordan* 40:231–257.
1998 The Roman Aqaba Project: The 1996 Campaign. *Annual of the Department of Antiquities of Jordan* 42:375–394.
2000a The Defense of Palestine and Transjordan from Diocletian to Heraclius. In *The Archaeology of Jordan and Beyond: Essays in Honor of James A Sauer*, edited by L. E. Stager, J. A. Greene, and M. D. Coogan, pp. 367–388. Eisenbrauns, Winona Lake, Indiana.
2000b The Roman Aqaba Project: The 1997 and 1998 Campaigns. *Annual of the Department of Antiquities of Jordan* 44:373–394.
2002 The Roman Aqaba Project: The 2000 Campaign. *Annual of the Department of Antiquities of Jordan* 46:409–428.

Perry, M. A.
2002 Health, Labor, and Political Economy: A Bioarchaeological Analysis of Three Communities in *Provincia Arabia*. Unpublished Ph.D. dissertation, Department of Anthropology, University of New Mexico, Albuquerque.
2016 Chapter IV: Area A. In *The Roman Aqaba Project Final Report. Volume II: Excavation Reports and Material Culture*, edited by S. T. Parker. Eisenbrauns, Winona Lake, Indiana.

Perry, M. A, D. Coleman, and N. Delhopital
2008   Mobility and Exile at 2nd Century A.D. Khirbet edh-Dharih: Strontium Isotope Analysis of Human Migration in Western Jordan. *Geoarchaeology* 23:528–549.

Perry, M. A., S. Coleman, D. L. Dettman, J. P. Grattan, and A. H. al-Shiyab
2011   Condemned to *Metallum*: The Origin and Role of 4th–6th Century A.D. *Phaeno* Mining Camp Residents Using Multiple Chemical Techniques. *Journal of Archaeological Science* 38:558–569.

Perry, M. A., D. Coleman, D. L. Dettman, and A. H. Hal-Shiyab
2009   An Isotopic Perspective on the Transport of Byzantine Mining Camp Laborers into Southwestern Jordan. *American Journal of Physical Anthropology* 140:429–441.

Perry, M., Jennings, C., and D. S. Coleman
2016   Strontium isotope evidence for long-distance immigration into the Byzantine port city of Aila, modern Aqaba, Jordan. *Anthropological and Archaeological Sciences*. doi:10.1007/s12520-016-0314-3.

Pollard, N.
2000   *Soldiers, Cities, and Civilians in Roman Syria*. University of Michigan Press, Ann Arbor.

Price, T., J. H. Burton, and R. A. Bentley
2002   The Characterization of Biologically Available Strontium Isotope Ratios for the Study of Prehistoric Migration. *Archaeometry* 44:117–136.

Pyatt, A. J., G. W. Barker, P. Birch, D. D. Gilbertson, J. P. Grattan, and D. J. Mattingly
1999   King Solomon's Miners—Starvation and Bioaccumulation? *Ecotoxicology and Environmental Safety* 43:305–308.

Pyatt, F. B., D. Amos, J. P. Grattan, A. J. Pyatt, and C. Terrell-Nield
2002   Invertebrates of Ancient Heavy Metal Spoil and Smelting Tip Sites in Southern Jordan: Their Distribution and Use as Bio Indicators of Metalliferous Pollution Derived from Ancient Sources. *Journal of Arid Environments* 52:53–62.

Pyatt, F. B., G. Gilmore, J. P. Grattan, C. O. Hunt, and S. J. McLaren
2000   An Imperial Legacy? An Exploration of the Environmental Impact of Ancient Metal Mining and Smelting in Southern Jordan. *Journal of Archaeological Science* 27:771–778.

Pyatt, F. B., and J. P. Grattan
2002   A Public Health Problem? Aspects and implications of the Ingestion of Copper and Lead Contaminated Food by Bedouin. *Environmental Management and Health* 13:467–470.

Pyatt, F. B., A. J. Pyatt, C. Walker, T. Sheen, and J. P. Grattan
2005   The Heavy Metal Content of Skeletons from an Ancient Metalliferous Polluted Area in Southern Jordan with Particular Reference to Bioaccumulation and Human Health. *Ecotoxicology and Environmental Safety* 60:295–300.

Ramsay, J.
n.d.   Manuscript. In *The Roman Aqaba Project Final Report. Volume II: Excavation Reports and Material Culture*, edited by S. T. Parker. Eisenbrauns Winona Lake, Indiana.

Sarnat, B. G., and I. Schour
1941   Enamel Hypoplasia (Chronologic Enamel Aplasia) in Relation to Systemic Disease: A Chronologic, Morphologic, and Etiologic Classification. *Journal of the American Dental Association* 28:1989–2000.

Seeck, O. (editor)
1876   *Notitia Dignitatum in Partibus Orientis Occidentus*. G. Lange, Berlin.

Silberman, N. A.
1989   *Between Past and Present: Archaeology, Ideology, and Nationalism in the Modern Middle East*. Henry Holt, New York.

Sofaer, J. R.
2006   *The Body as Material Culture: A Theoretical Osteoarchaeology*. Cambridge University Press, Cambridge.

Stuart-Macadam, P.
1992   Porotic Hyperostosis: A New Perspective. *American Journal of Physical Anthropology* 87:39–47.

Sullivan, A.
2005   Prevalence and Etiology of Acquired Anemia in Medieval York, England. *American Journal of Physical Anthropology* 128:252–272.

Theodoret
1843   *A History of the Church, in Five Books from A.D. 322 to the Death of Theodore of Mopsuestia, A.D. 427*. S. Bagster, London.

Trigger, B. G.
1990   *A History of Archaeological Thought*. Cambridge University Press, Cambridge.

van Dommelen, P.
1997   Colonial Constructs: Colonialism and Archaeology in the Mediterranean. *World Archaeology* 28:305–323.

Walker, P. L., R. R. Bathhurst, R. Richman, T. Gjerdrum, and V. A. Andrushko
2009   The Causes of Porotic Hyperostosis and Cribra Orbitalia: A Reappraisal of the Iron-Deficiency-Anemia Hypothesis. *American Journal of Physical Anthropology* 139:109–125.

Watson, P.
2008   The Byzantine Period. In *Jordan: An Archaeological Reader*, edited by R. B. Adams, pp. 443–482. Equinox Press, London.

Webster, J.
1996   Roman Imperialism and the "Post Imperial Age." In *Roman Imperialism: Post-Colonial Perspectives*, edited by J. Webster and N. Cooper, pp. 1–17. School of Archaeological Studies, University of Leicester, Leicester.

9

Imperialism and Physiological Stress in Rome, First to Third Centuries A.D.

Rome during the Imperial period (27 B.C.–A.D. 476) is easily identifiable as an urban center in the archaeological and historical records. By virtue of Rome's central geographical position in the empire and because it served as the home of the emperors, it was long viewed as the imperial core, with the provinces seen as the periphery. For over a century, abundant scholarship on "romanization" was based on a modern, Western, colonialist perspective through which archaeologists, historians, and other scholars sought to understand how Rome civilized the "barbarians" in the provinces. More recently, the core/periphery and civilized/barbarian dichotomies have been jettisoned in favor of reframing the phenomenon of population interaction as a bidirectional negotiation among groups that shared significant culture and history (e.g., Terrenato and Keay 2001; Webster 2001). Imperialism in the Roman world was not merely a function of population or geographic magnitude; it represented a cultural undertaking by a variety of people, a multidimensional idea that involved environmental, social, and economic stressors. These dimensions can be empirically measured in modern populations and are known to be causally related to one another (Schwirian et al. 1995). Previous approaches to understanding the results of the urbanization of Rome and its imperial domination focus on demography but tend to sideline topics such as migration, diet, and disease in the absence of strong skeletal data sets (e.g., Lo Cascio 2006; Paine and Storey 2006). This chapter therefore contributes a bioarchaeological perspective to the character of urban Rome in the middle of the Imperial period (first–third centuries A.D.).

The extended reach of Rome began during the Republic, and by the late first century B.C. the Roman world stretched from France to North Africa and from Spain to Syria (Keppie 1998). At the end of the third century A.D. the imperial territory was interconnected by a massive road network that facilitated transportation of goods, movement of people, and exchange of ideas between Rome and the Empire (Laurence 1999). Towns, cities, and peoples could choose to distance themselves from Rome culturally, often in opposition to their common perceptions of the city and its culture, but the extension of Roman citizenship to every person in the Empire became the primary means by which people organized and conceived of themselves as Roman (Laurence and Berry 1998). The population of Italy in the third century A.D. was no longer more politically influential than that of the provinces, save the Emperor, and the people of the Empire became more geographically dispersed.

The sheer breadth and depth of interaction among people of the Roman Empire require a nuanced approach to imperialism. Raising questions of "entanglements" between various groups is preferable to imagining uni-directional acculturation. Anthropological approaches to colonialism and imperialism used in this volume illustrate the complications inherent in understanding these important relationships. Buzon and Smith, for example, point to a familiarity between Egypt and Nubia that does not match with the traditional colonialist model of European invasion of the New World, and Perry questions the utility of the colonizer/colonized dichotomy in Byzantine Jordan. In both of these Old World cases, a history of interaction belies a clear difference between colonizing population and colonized population, in spite of an apparent power differential. Similarly, Murphy and her colleagues find that the traditional ways of conceiving of Spanish-Inca interaction as either active resistance or passive acceptance elide the potential "in-betweenness" in indigenous responses to colonialism.

It is no longer tenable to conceive of Rome as the "core" and the provinces as the monolithic "periphery," so a similar shift needs to be made in approaching the prevailing dichotomy that governs the understanding of health in Imperial Rome. On the one hand, public health concerns were paramount, and the Roman government created considerable infrastructure and laws to ensure access to basic resources. The aqueducts, which channeled 115 million gallons of water per day into Rome from springs in the rural outskirts, fed flushable toilets, city fountains for drinking water, and large bath complexes (Taylor 2000). Roman medicine and dentistry were quite advanced for the time. The Roman doctor's toolkit included a variety of instruments, like a modern-looking speculum and metal catheters, and there are historical accounts of intricate cataract surgeries (Cruse

2004). Bioarchaeological evidence shows skillful extraction of teeth by a dentist practicing in the Roman Forum along with palliative care for carious lesions (Becker 2014; Fejerskov et al. 2012). The link between dead bodies and disease was sufficiently understood that burial within the city was forbidden (Hope and Marshall 2000;Toynbee 1971). Finally, the food dole—first of wheat and later of bread, pork, olive oil, and wine—was a by-product of Rome's ability to extract resources from provinces like Egypt and was made available for free or at a heavily subsidized cost to Roman male heads of households (Garnsey 1988, 1999; Garnsey and Rathbone 1985; White 1976). Viewed in this way, Rome was the wealthy center of the Empire, replete with natural and cultural resources that provided a good way of life for those fortunate enough to live and work in the greater Rome area.

On the other hand, Rome has also been viewed as a "pathopolis," an urban jungle teeming with disease and poor living conditions (e.g., Mumford 1961; Scobie 1986). At the height of the Empire in the first century A.D., Rome had a population density higher than modern-day Manhattan or Mumbai, with around one million people living in fourteen square kilometers (Hopkins 1978; Scheidel 2001; Storey 1997b; Wiseman 1969). The *suburbium* outside the walls was also densely settled, with close to half a million people living among marginal businesses—slaughterhouses, brick-making facilities, quarry pits, landfills, and cemeteries—excluded from the city for religious or public safety reasons (Carafa et al. 2005; Champlin 1982; Morley 1996; Witcher 2005). Rome and its *suburbium* existed in a web of interdependent urban and suburban development, and many accounts call life in the city crowded, unsanitary, violent, and impoverished (Champlin 1982; Morley 2005; Parkin 1992; Scheidel 2003; Scobie 1986), particularly for the lower classes—urban commoners (*plebs urbana*), rural peasants (*plebs rustica*), and slaves (*servi*). In an often-cited article on sanitation in the Roman world, Scobie (1986) concluded from a textual and archaeological assessment of lower-class Roman living conditions that high frequencies of diseases such as cholera, typhoid, dysentery, gastroenteritis, leptospirosis, and infectious hepatitis could be attributed to food and water contamination by fecal material, open latrines in the kitchen, and defecation and urination in the streets. There is also ample historical evidence from such ancient authors as Celsus and Pliny the Younger attesting to the presence of diseases like malaria, leprosy, and tuberculosis in the population (Grmek 1989; Meinecke 1927; Patrick 1967).

These two opposing views of health in an imperial capital developed without inclusion of bioarchaeological data because, until about thirty years ago, there was great inconsistency in the practice of saving and analyzing human skeletal remains from Rome. The scant skeletal record has provided some evidence of infectious disease in ancient Italy:[1] malaria is assumed to have been endemic (Angel 1966; Sallares 2002); leprosy is found as early as the fourth century B.C. (Mariotti et al. 2005); and tuberculosis is known from a handful of sites (Canci et al. 2005; Ricci et al. 1997; Roberts and Buikstra 2003). Within the greater suburban area of Imperial Rome (roughly a 12 km radius from the walls), though, there is a limited amount of bioarchaeological data available. Three cemeteries from the *suburbium* have been relatively well published in terms of osteological demographics, methods, and results. Basiliano/Collatina represents a cemetery with over 2,200 individuals, but 142 have been studied (Buccellato et al. 2003; Buccellato, Caldarini, et al. 2008). Vallerano has just 26 individuals but has produced high-quality data (Cucina et al. 2006; Ricci et al. 1997). Finally, Osteria del Curato II contained 71 individuals (Catalano 2001; Catalano and Di Bernardini 2001; Egidi et al. 2003). In total, just 239 individuals from three cemeteries in Rome have been thoroughly investigated. Very limited osteological data from additional cemetery samples can be found in the aggregate (Catalano 2001; Catalano and Di Bernadini 2001; Catalano et al. 2012; Ottini et al. 2001). Further from Rome (25 km or more), data can be found from the Imperial-era cemetery of Isola Sacra associated with urban Portus Romae (Manzi et al. 1991; Prowse 2001; Prowse et al. 2004, 2005, 2007) and the rural sites of San Vittorino (Catalano et al. 2001; Ottini et al. 2001) and Lucus Feroniae (Manzi et al. 1999; Salvadei et al. 2001; Sperduti 1997).

Many of these archaeological samples from Rome have been investigated with the hypothesis that "ancient empires with high population density and highly developed trading systems were ideal for the cultivation of such diseases and the ravages of epidemics" (Acsádi and Nemeskéri 1970:217). It is equally important, though, to test and refine this hypothesis with new data. This chapter presents demographic and skeletal pathology data drawn from two Imperial-era cemeteries—Casal Bertone and Castellaccio Europarco—in order to broaden our understanding of physiological stress among the lower classes buried in the Roman *suburbium*. Where possible, inter-site and inter-sex variation in disease frequency is assessed, and comparisons are made between the study sites and other published Imperial Roman cemeteries. Some of the previously published data sets, however, do not present enough information for statistical comparisons to be made, so these data and interpretations are used with caution. Finally, in order to set a new precedent in pathological analyses of Imperial Rome, all data used in this chapter are available in a full online relational database, as are photographs of all porotic hyperostosis lesions, at https://github. com/killgrove/RomanOsteology. The picture that results from investigating multiple cemeteries in ancient Latium is complex and belies sweeping conclusions often made about health and disease in Imperial Rome.

EVALUATING THE HEALTH STATUS OF IMPERIAL ROMANS

The two most commonly recorded pathological conditions on Imperial Roman skeletons are porotic hyperostosis (PH) and dental enamel hypoplasia (DEH). J. L. Angel (1966) first used the term *porotic hyperostosis* to refer both to lesions of the orbital roof (also known as cribra orbitalia, or CO) and to lesions on the skull vault (also known as cribra cranii, or CC). There is considerable debate as to whether these two conditions have the same etiology (Lewis 2007; Rothschild et al. 2004; Stuart-Macadam 1989), but the changes to the orbital and vault bones are similar: a cycle of loss and overproduction of red blood cells in the bone marrow causes expansion of the inner, diploic tissue of the skull and thinning of the outer, compact bone matrix (Angel 1966). Porotic hyperostosis appears macroscopically (Figure 9.1) as abnormal holes or networks of furrows and is easily recorded using a variety of grading systems (Buikstra and Ubelaker 1994; Hengen 1971; Nathan and Haas 1966). Whereas palaeopathologists used to contend that the most common cause of PH was diet-related iron deficiency, recent literature cautions against this interpretation (Waldron 2009; Walker et al. 2010), and researchers suggest a variety of mechanisms that could cause these lesions, most notably hemolytic forms of anemia (e.g., thalassemia, G6PD deficiency, lead poisoning) and megaloblastic forms of anemia (e.g., dietary insufficiency of iron, vitamin C, or vitamin B12; parasites; infection) (Crandall and Martin 2012; Oxenham and Cavill 2010). Since there are numerous possible etiologies to PH, it is used as a nonspecific indicator of overall health status within a population that generally reflects childhood metabolic health in the form of some kind of chronic anemic stress (Goodman and Martin 2002). Dental enamel hypoplasia results from a disturbance in normal enamel production (amelogenesis) and is macroscopically evident as lines or pits on the adult dentition. The pause in dental enamel formation during childhood is likely related to a prolonged episode of health stress—such as weaning, malnutrition, or illness—so DEH is also

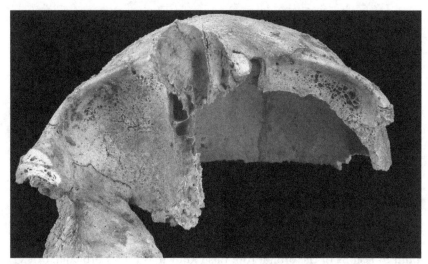

Figure 9.1. Cribra orbitalia bilaterally in Individual T70 from Casal Bertone (photo by Kristina Killgrove).

generally considered a nonspecific health indicator (Goodman and Rose 1990; King et al. 2005) and provides complementary information to PH (Goodman and Martin 2002).

Scholars of the ancient world have attempted to identify and interpret the frequencies of PH and DEH seen in individual skeletal samples in the Imperial Roman *suburbium* (Buccellato et al. 2003; Catalano et al. 2001; Cucina et al. 2006; Facchini et al. 2004; Manzi et al. 1999; Ricci et al. 1997; Salvadei et al. 2001), but syntheses of these data have only been published since 2010. Interestingly, the most recent attempts at synthesis of the skeletal evidence of PH, DEH, and stature as avenues to investigate systemic health stress have been accomplished by Roman historians interested in ancient demography (e.g., Pilkington 2013; Scheidel 2014), pointing to the growing need for Roman bioarchaeologists to present and interpret data in a way that aids interdisciplinary research in the Roman world. The most thorough treatment of the skeletal evidence and the multifactorial causes of systemic health stress in Rome, however, is Gowland and Garnsey's (2010) synthesis of the PH and DEH data published up to that point. Surveying many of the same populations employed in this analysis, Gowland and Garnsey note the very high prevalence of CO and DEH within the cemeteries from Imperial Rome and suggest that "the clinical and bioarchaeological evidence strongly points to the significance of malaria in terms of the presence of a high prevalence of cribra orbitalia" (2010:149). Nevertheless, they note that "it is quite likely—indeed, to be expected—that a more complex pattern will emerge than is suggested by the evidence that is currently available," particularly considering the difficulties they encountered in using published Imperial Roman studies that lack detailed methods and data (2010:131; Gowland and Redfern 2010). The data presented in this chapter contribute to the more complex pattern that Gowland and Garnsey (2010) foresaw. Imperial Rome was composed of a huge variety of people who differed in their geographic origins (Killgrove and Montgomery 2016), in their diet (Killgrove and Tykot 2013), in their exposure to toxins (Montgomery et al. 2010), and in the location of their residence. All of these differences could have affected their susceptibility to disease and their health outcomes. While we cannot yet identify from skeletal data where in the *urbs* or *suburbium* a person lived, previously published biochemical data from the two cemeteries presented here can be examined as complementary data sets to help explicate the PH frequencies, and possible causes for the heterogeneity of health status in Imperial Rome will be detailed in the Discussion section below.

MATERIALS AND METHODS

Roman cemeteries were almost always placed outside the city walls for both religious and hygienic reasons. Located less than 2 km east of the walls along the ancient Via Praenestina, the cemetery of Casal Bertone was closely associated with Rome (Figure 9.2). Excavations by the Soprintendenza Archeologica di Roma took place between 1989 and 2007 and were largely salvage in nature (Calci and Messineo 1989; Musco et al. 2008; Nanni and Maffei 2004). Skeletons were recovered from the cemetery between 2000 and 2003, and in 2007 a residential villa and a large industrial complex were found nearby. The cemetery was in use from the second to the third century A.D., based on pottery and coins found with the burials (Musco et al. 2008). In total, 139 skeletons were available for osteological analysis from Casal Bertone. Castellaccio Europarco, located 11.5 km south of Rome along the ancient Via Laurentina, was excavated by the Soprintendenza Archeologica di Roma between 2003 and 2007 (Buccellato 2007; Buccellato, Catalano, and Pantano 2008). Although archaeologists found architectural remains in the area, it is unclear if they are directly associated with the Imperial-era burial context, which yielded 47 inhumations dated by grave goods to A.D. 50–175 (Buccellato, Catalano, and Pantano 2008). In total, the sample analyzed includes 186 Imperial-period skeletons, most

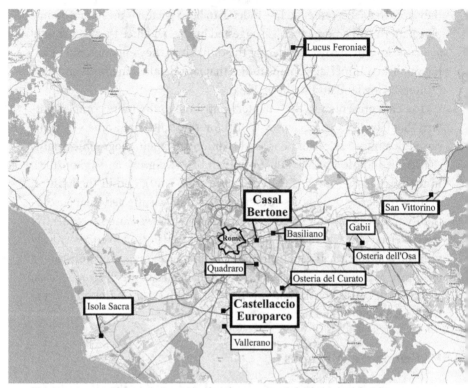

Figure 9.2. Locations of cemetery sites mentioned (base map tiles © OpenStreetMap.org contributors, available for use under the Open Database License [CC BY-SA 2.0]).

of which were from simple inhumations—pit, amphorae, or *a cappuccina* styles (Toynbee 1971). Not every individual could be assessed for PH and DEH, so the total number of individuals, teeth, or bony elements examined is reported in the pertinent tables.

Demographic data were collected from the skeletons based on the guidelines established by Buikstra and Ubelaker (1994). Pubic symphysis morphology (Brooks and Suchey 1990; Todd 1921a, 1921b), auricular surface changes (Lovejoy et al. 1985), and cranial suture closure (Meindl and Lovejoy 1985) were used to assess age at death of adults, who were placed in categories as per Buikstra and Ubelaker (1994): Young Adult (YA: 20 to 35 years), Middle Adult (MA: 35 to 50), and Older Adult (OA: 50 and older). Subadult age at death was estimated using tooth formation and eruption (Anderson et al. 1976; Gustafson and Koch 1974; Moorrees et al. 1963a, 1963b) as well as epiphyseal union and long bone length (Baker et al. 2005; Johnston 1962). Subadults were placed in age-at-death categories as follows per Baker et al. (2005): Infant (0–12 months), Young Child (YC: 1–6 years), Older Child (OC: 7–12), and Adolescent (Adol: 12–20). Sex of adults and older adolescents (16–20 years) was estimated based on pelvic morphology (Buikstra and Ubelaker 1994; Phenice 1969), cranial features (Acsádi and Nemeskéri 1970), and long bone measurements (Ousley and Jantz 1996) where appropriate.

Macroscopic identification of pathological conditions on the skeletons was made based primarily on Ortner (2003). Porotic hyperostosis of the orbit (CO) and the vault (CC) was scored based on severity criteria in Hengen (1971) and is reported as crude prevalence rates—CPR%, or the number of individuals exhibiting the condition (n) divided by the number of individuals examined (N) × 100. Cribra orbitalia is further reported as the number of eye orbits exhibiting the condition (n) divided by the number of orbits examined (N) × 100. Macroscopic identification of DEH on the permanent dentition was made based on *Standards for Data Collection from Human Skeletal Remains* (Buikstra and Ubelaker 1994). Frequency data for DEH are reported here as crude prevalence rates—CPR%, or the number of teeth exhibiting the condition (n) divided by the number of teeth examined (N) × 100—to facilitate comparison with other Imperial Roman cemetery samples.

RESULTS

DEMOGRAPHICS

The age-at-death profile for the two sites can be seen in Figure 9.3. The high number of subadult deaths and peak in adult death in the Middle Adult age range is consistent with the work of historical demographers of Rome (Acsádi and Nemeskéri 1970; Frier 2001; MacDonnell 1913; Parkin 1992; Scheidel 2001; Storey 1997a, 1997b), with the exception of the high number of deaths in the Adolescent age category. Individuals of this age were generally at a lower risk of mortality than were infants (Parkin 1992), but life-stage transitions—young Roman women could marry and become pregnant, and young men would start new occupations or apprenticeships—are possible explanations for the rise in death in this age category. Both sites, however, suffer from a statistically significant underrepresentation of females (Casal Bertone—χ^2 = 11.538, $p < .001$; Castellaccio Europarco—χ^2 = 9.323, $p < .01$), making sex-based comparisons in pathology frequencies difficult.

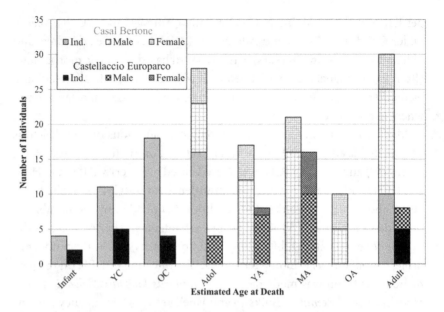

Figure 9.3. Demographics for Casal Bertone and Castellaccio Europarco.

POROTIC HYPEROSTOSIS

Table 9.1 presents all the raw PH data for individuals, and the CO data are broken down by age and sex in Table 9.2. Hengen's (1971) PH scoring system was employed to facilitate comparisons with other published studies from Imperial Rome. Photographs of all scored lesions from Casal Bertone and Castellaccio Europarco can be found in the online repository, labeled with individual burial number (e.g., ET31 for Castellaccio Europarco Tomb 31).

Two-tailed Fisher's exact tests were used to compare frequencies of CO and CC between the two samples, between subadults and adults in both populations, and between males and females from Casal Bertone. Significant differences in pair-wise comparisons include the frequency of CC in the two populations (p = 0.006), with Castellaccio Europarco having 15.6 percent and Casal Bertone just 1.2 percent, and the frequency of CO between subadults and adults of the combined samples (p = 0.018), with 44.4 percent of examined subadults affected by CO and 9.3 percent of adults affected. This latter result is unsurprising, however, given the etiology of PH. No significant differences were found in the other comparisons of CO frequency (CB-CE p = 1.0; CB subadult-CB adult p = 0.054; CE subadult-CE adult p = 0.227; CB male-CB female p = 0.557) nor in comparing CC

Table 9.1. Porotic hyperostosis data for Casal Bertone and Castellaccio Europarco by individual

Individual	Age	Sex	Condition	Hengen (1971) Score	Active/Healing
T31	YC (3–4 yrs. old)		CC	2	H
T45	Adol		CC/CO	3/2	H/H
T63	OC (7–9 yrs. old)		CC/CO	2/4	H/H
T67	OC (c. 12 yrs. old)		CC/CO	1/3	H/H
T69	YA	M	CC	2	H
10B	OC (c. 7 yrs. old)		CO	5	A
11C	OC (c. 12 yrs. old)		CO	4	A
13A	OC (c. 7 yrs. old)		CO	1	H
1D	Adol (16–18 yrs. old)	M	CO	3	H
5A	YA	M	CO	3	H
7B	Adult	M	CC	2	H
22	YA	M	CO	4	H
23	YA	M	CO	4	H
32	Adol		CO	1	A
36	Adol (14–16 yrs. old)		CO	4	A
70	OC (c. 7 yrs. old)		CO	4	A

Note: ET = Castellaccio Europarco; F = Casal Bertone; T = Casal Bertone.

frequency between males and females from Casal Bertone (*p* = 1.00). The samples from Casal Bertone and Castellaccio Europarco were, on the whole, affected by PH in similar ways.

In order to situate the Casal Bertone and Castellaccio Europarco samples within the context of the Roman *suburbium*, skeletal pathology frequencies from published cemeteries in the area dating to the Imperial period are listed in Table 9.3 along with distance from Rome. Information on both

Table 9.2. Cribra orbitalia frequencies from two Imperial Roman cemeteries (calculated as number affected/number examined)

	Casal Bertone		Castellaccio Europarco	
	Orbits	Individuals	Orbits	Individuals
Male	6/60 (10%)	4/33 (12.1%)	2/21 (9.5%)	1/12 (8.3%)
Female	0/17 (0%)	0/11 (0%)	0/6 (0%)	0/3 (0%)
Subadult	10/33 (30.3%)	6/19 (31.6%)	4/12 (33.3%)	2/7 (28.6%)
Total	16/110 (14.5%)	10/63 (15.9%)	6/39 (15.4%)	3/22 (13.6%)

Table 9.3. Individuals affected and crude prevalence rates (CPR) of porotic hyperostosis among comparative Imperial populations

	Distance from Rome (km)	Cribra orbitalia		Cribra cranii	
		CPR	(n/N)	CPR	(n/N)
Casal Bertone	2	15.9%	(10/63)	1.2%	(1/83)
Basiliano/Collatina[a]	4	c. 65%	—	50%	—
Quadraro[b]	4	8%	—	—	—
Osteria del Curato II[c]	11	79.2%	—	53.6%	—
Castellaccio Europarco	12	13.6%	(3/22)	15.6%	(5/32)
Vallerano[d]	12	69.2%	(18/26)	26.8%	—
Lucus Feroniae[e]	30	49.5%	(46/93)	10.7%	(14/131)
San Vittorino[b]	30	0%	—	—	—

[a]Data from Buccellato et al. 2003.
[b]Data from Ottini et al. 2001.
[c]Data from Egidi et al. 2003.
[d]Data from Ricci et al. 1997, Cucina et al. 2006.
[e]Data from Salvadei et al. 2001.

data-collection methods and number of individuals examined is available only for the larger populations of Vallerano and Lucus Feroniae, however.

Two-tailed Fisher's exact tests were used to compare the frequencies of CO among cemeteries near Rome, and the results are presented in Table 9.4. Clearly, Vallerano and Lucus Feroniae have high CO frequencies compared to Casal Bertone and Castellaccio Europarco, but the two sites with high PH frequencies are not significantly different from one another. In addition, a statistical difference was found between frequencies of CC at Casal Bertone and Lucus Feroniae ($p = 0.0108$) but not between the frequencies of this condition at Castellaccio Europarco and Lucus Feroniae. Whereas two Roman cemeteries—one suburban and one rural—have high PH frequencies, two others—one periurban and one suburban—have comparatively low PH frequencies.

Table 9.4. Comparative Imperial Roman populations—Fisher's exact test of cribra orbitalia frequencies (two-tailed p values)

	Casal Bertone	Castellaccio Europarco	Vallerano	Lucus Feroniae
Casal Bertone	—	1.00	< 0.0001	< 0.0001
Castellaccio Europarco		—	0.0001	0.0033
Vallerano			—	0.0806
Lucus Feroniae				—

DENTAL ENAMEL HYPOPLASIA

Every permanent tooth was assessed for evidence of DEH of the linear or pit variety. In all, 2,525 permanent teeth were examined from the two samples, with a total of 109 individuals at Casal Bertone and 34 individuals at Castellaccio Europarco. Crude prevalence rates of DEH are presented in Table 9.5. Differences in DEH frequencies in the Casal Bertone and Castellaccio Europarco samples were investigated using Fisher's exact test, but no statistically significant differences ($p = 1.00$) were found between the two samples. Two-tailed Fisher's exact tests between every other pairing of Casal Bertone, Castellaccio Europarco, Vallerano, and Isola Sacra, however, were significant, all with p values less than 0.0001. Imperial Roman samples appear to vary significantly in the TPR of DEH, but the Casal Bertone and Castellaccio Europarco samples are unique in having significantly lower frequencies than the other three groups for which CPR is reported.

REPUBLICAN PHASES AT CASTELLACCIO EUROPARCO

At the present time, examining diachronic change in osteological data from Rome is nearly impossible because of the paucity of immediately pre- and post-Imperial data sets.[2] During the Republican era that preceded the Empire, roughly 510–27 B.C., the dominant burial rite was cremation (Toynbee 1971). As Roman art collectors over the past several centuries have prized intact examples of ceramic vessels, marble sarcophagi, and statues, a vast number of cremated remains have certainly been discarded and destroyed. Cremations and inhumations have been found side-by-side at sites like Osteria del Curato (Egidi et al. 2003) and Castellaccio Europarco (Buccellato

Table 9.5. Dental enamel hypoplasia frequencies in comparative Imperial Roman samples

Site	Number affected (n)/ Number examined (N)	Crude prevalence rate (n/N %)
Casal Bertone	52/1962	2.2%
Basiliano/Collatina[a]	—	42.0%
Castellaccio Europarco	14/563	2.5%
Vallerano[b]	502/790	63.5%
Isola Sacra[c]	281/791	35.5%

[a]Data from Buccellato et al. 2003 report a (possibly rounded) CPR but not sample size.
[b]Data from Cucina et al. 2006, Ricci et al. 1997.
[c]Data from Manzi et al. 1999.

2007; Buccellato, Catalano, and Pantano 2008), but there have been no large-scale studies of cremations from Rome to date.

The Castellaccio Europarco necropolis, however, has two earlier phases of burial: fourth–third centuries B.C. (Phase 1, inhumation MNI = 17) and second–first centuries B.C. (Phase 2, inhumation MNI = 11) (Buccellato 2007; Buccellato, Catalano, and Pantano 2008). These are very small sample sizes, made even smaller when only individuals who could be scored for pathological lesions are considered, so statistical analysis is not possible. The PH and DEH data from Republican Castellaccio Europarco are presented here in the hopes that as more data from these time periods become available,[3] a diachronic examination of health at the Republic-to-Imperial transition can be made.

Of the 17 inhumed individuals who date to Phase 1 of Castellaccio Europarco, 10 could be scored for CO and 10 could be scored for CC. No instances of either condition were found, however. In Phase 2, 1 out of the 6 scorable individuals displayed CC, and 1 out of the 4 scorable individuals displayed CO. Calculating the CPRs for CO for the various phases gives 0 percent in Phase 1, 25 percent in Phase 2, and 13.6 percent in Phase 3. CPR for CC is 0 percent in Phase 1, 16.6 percent in Phase 2, and 15.6 percent in Phase 3. It is possible that a decline in health is occurring between the middle Republic (Phase 1) and the late Republic/beginning of the Empire (Phase 2), but the sample sizes are too small to say anything definitive.

Of the 17 Phase 1 burials at Castellaccio Europarco, 7 individuals presented a total of 135 adult teeth for assessment of DEH. No hypoplastic lesions were found in these individuals, however. Of the 11 Phase 2 burials, 4 individuals presented a total of 68 adult teeth for assessment. No hypoplastic lesions were found in these individuals either. The TPRs for the various phases are therefore 0 percent (Phase 1), 0 percent (Phase 2), and 2.5 percent (Phase 3). The trend in DEH frequency through time at Castellaccio Europarco, then, appears to increase in the Imperial period.

Discussion

GENERAL HEALTH IN IMPERIAL ROME

The demographic and pathological data collected from the periurban Casal Bertone sample and the suburban Castellaccio Europarco sample suggest that lifestyle, health, diet, and disease ecology at these sites were similar in the Imperial period. Nevertheless, the age distribution and the composition of these cemetery samples were both certainly affected by a number of variables in antiquity, including epidemic diseases, migration, and living conditions (Wood et al. 1992). Although Casal Bertone and Castellaccio Europarco are similar in terms of health stress, comparing PH and DEH frequencies with other published sites from the Roman *suburbium* paints a significantly more complicated picture of population heterogeneity and defies easy interpretation.

Both Casal Bertone and Castellaccio Europarco have significantly lower frequencies of PH than do the populations from Basiliano/Collatina, Osteria del Curato II, Vallerano, and Lucus Feroniae; they are comparable, however, to the lower frequencies of PH in the small samples at Gabii,[4] Quadraro, and San Vittorino (Catalano et al. 2001; Ottini et al. 2001). In all the studies that refer to Hengen (1971) grades, the vast majority of the individuals with PH have lesions between grades 1–4 (Buccellato et al. 2003:347; Ottini et al. 2001:365; Ricci et al. 1997:119), with only a few individual mentions of the more severe PH grades 5 and 6.

The number of individuals examined for PH in these reported cemetery samples is quite small, generally numbering fewer than 25 individuals, and this could be biasing the data. The two larger samples—Casal Bertone with 63 individuals and Lucus Feroniae with 93 individuals—have significantly different frequencies of PH. They are also, however, located in very different parts of Imperial Rome. The few statistical tests that could be performed suggest that the populations buried at suburban Vallerano and rural Lucus Feroniae were under greater disease loads and therefore had worse overall health than the populations buried at periurban Casal Bertone and suburban Castellaccio Europarco.

Without additional information about the context of the cemetery samples, however, we can simply say that PH frequencies vary widely, from none seen in a small sample from rural Latium to over three-quarters of the population affected in a sample from the Roman *suburbium*. Different areas of the greater Rome area likely had different population attributes, different disease ecology, and different access to a wide variety of resources, like food, water, medicine, and flush toilets, any combination of which could explain variation in PH frequencies.

As with PH frequencies, the frequencies of DEH at Casal Bertone and Castellaccio Europarco were significantly lower than at any other reported site, each with under 3 percent of teeth exhibiting a hypoplastic lesion, an order of magnitude lower than frequencies reported at periurban Basiliano/ Collatina, suburban Vallerano, and urban Isola Sacra. Differences in DEH frequencies point to variation in physiological stress during childhood for these populations.

The population of Vallerano deserves additional consideration because of its high frequencies of PH and DEH and because of its proximity to Castellaccio Europarco (see Figure 9.2), which had low frequencies of these pathological lesions. Vallerano is also the sample most easily compared to the study sites, because Cucina et al. (2006) describe in detail their methods of data collection and report both the number of individuals or teeth examined and the total sample examined for pathological lesions. It is clear that the population buried at Vallerano, associated with a villa in the Roman *suburbium*, was systemically stressed, both in childhood (DEH) and as adults (PH). Considering the close proximity of Vallerano and Castellaccio Europarco, the vast difference in CO and DEH frequencies suggests that factors other than geographic location affected health. Although it is roughly contemporaneous with Castellaccio Europarco, Vallerano dates to the second–third century A.D., while archaeologists report dates of A.D. 50–175 for Castellaccio Europarco (Buccellato, Catalano, et al. 2008). Changes in the population of the Roman *suburbium* between the times of these two sites could have affected health, as could have changes in the infrastructure of Rome. Ricci et al. (1997:126), in attempting to explain the PH and DEH frequencies and life expectancy at Vallerano, point to the so-called Imperial Crisis of the third century A.D., which devastated Rome's transportation infrastructure and thereby the ability to move crops and other foodstuffs around. The population buried at Casal Bertone, however, also dates to the second–third centuries but has far lower frequencies of PH and DEH. It is possible the people buried at Casal Bertone were socioeconomically insulated from the crisis, but it would be useful to have more specific dates (i.e., radiocarbon dates) for cemeteries around Imperial Rome in order to combine the historical and palaeopathological records.

Finally, in spite of an attempt to control in this study for similar data-collection methods, it is possible that differences in inter-observer identification or recording practices contributed to the disparities in frequencies. It is additionally possible that factors intrinsic to the population samples, such as nutrition, water sources, and disease ecology, differentially affected the health of individuals buried in these cemeteries. Until more data are published, we need to use alternative methods to investigate the possible factors involved in systematic health stress within the Imperial Roman population.

POSSIBLE FACTORS AFFECTING ROMAN HEALTH

As illustrated in other contributions to this volume, the consequences of colonialism and imperialism are diverse. Specific to the Old World, Perry finds that Byzantine involvement in Jordan had little impact on local health, but Buzon and Smith find that the high frequency of active cribra orbitalia in colonial-era Tombos suggests significant stress on children's health. Clearly, variables like geographic location, diet, population change, environmental conditions, and socioeconomic buffering are instrumental in affecting people's health, and these variables need to be teased out of bioarchaeological data sets as best as possible.

The sheer amount of biochemical data produced from Casal Bertone and Castellaccio Europarco is currently unparalleled in Rome (Killgrove 2010), and these data can be combined in numerous ways to investigate questions of diet, migration, and disease. Relevant to the etiology of PH are carbon and nitrogen isotopes to look for potential dietary causes (Killgrove and Tykot 2013); strontium and oxygen isotopes to investigate PH in people who immigrated to Rome (Killgrove and Montgomery 2016); and lead concentration data to see if they correlate with presence of PH (Montgomery et al. 2010). These preliminary investigations, detailed below, cannot confirm an etiology of PH but do show the potential of biochemical data to inform palaeopathological analysis of a complex population.

Diet

As noted above, an early assumption of PH etiology was dietary insufficiency of iron. More recent studies, though, have suggested that vitamin B12 deficiency resulting from lack of meat in the diet is a possible cause of PH (Domínguez-Rodrigo et al. 2012; Walker et al. 2010). Forty-eight individuals from Casal Bertone and Castellaccio Europarco were previously tested for carbon and nitrogen isotopes (Killgrove and Tykot 2013), and seven of those individuals had evidence of PH (see Table 9.6). As nitrogen isotopes give a general idea of the proportion of meat that made up the ancient diet (Katzenberg 2008), individuals with PH lesions and low $\delta^{15}N$ values may be suffering from a dietary insufficiency. Of the individuals in Table 9.6, however, only ET69 had a $\delta^{15}N$ value more than one standard deviation lower than the mean for the site (9.8 ‰; SD 1.5). At least in this small sample, a low-meat diet does not sufficiently explain the distribution of PH in these two samples.

Table 9.6. Paleodietary data from individuals with porotic hyperostosis

Individual	PH	δ^{13}C ‰ VPDB	δ^{15}N ‰ AIR
ET31	CC	-18.3	11.8
ET69	CC	-19.5	7.8
F5A	CO	-17.5	9.3
F7B	CC	-17.7	10.8
T23	CO	-18.1	11.6
T36	CO	-18.1	10.8
T70	CO	-18.5	10.2

Note: Data from Killgrove and Tykot 2013.

Migration

The Roman population was also very heterogeneous in its origins, with millions of slaves and other immigrants flooding into Rome every year (Noy 2000; Scheidel 2005). Researchers such as Hengen (1971:66) have noted an association between PH frequency and geographic latitude, with populations living closer to the equator having higher PH frequencies than those living closer to the poles. Figure 9.4 shows immigrants to Rome (based on both oxygen and strontium isotopes), with a box indicating the local limits expected for both carbon and oxygen (see Killgrove and Montgomery 2016 for full explanation of the data). Individuals with higher δ^{18}O values are likely from areas hotter and drier than Rome.

None of the individuals with suggested geographic origins similar to Rome (within the box) and from areas cooler and wetter than Rome (lower δ^{18}O values) were found to have evidence of PH. Several individuals, however, with oxygen isotope values that place their origin in warmer, drier parts of the Roman world do have PH. Although these small sample sizes cannot lend definitive explanations to the cause of PH, these data suggest that further investigation into the relationship between migration and parasitic infection, malaria, and other diseases present in the southern parts of the Roman Empire is warranted.

Disease

Figure 9.4 has a bit more to tell, however. The Roman Empire is notorious for its abundant use of lead in weaponry, jewelry and makeup, aqueduct pipes, pottery glazes, and even food seasonings (*sapa* or *defrutum* was grape must boiled in lead or pewter pots until it absorbed some of the lead sugar). The Romans themselves knew of the ill effects of lead (e.g., Vitruvius 8.6.1–11), and scholars have wondered whether lead caused large-scale

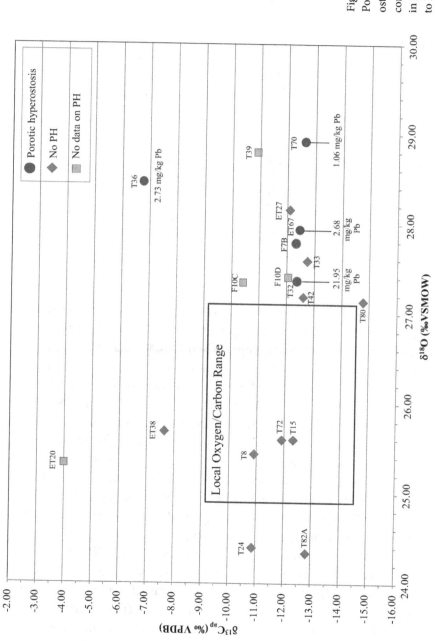

Figure 9.4. Porotic hyperostosis and lead concentration in immigrants to Rome.

Table 9.7. Lead concentrations and porotic hyperostosis from Castellaccio
Europarco and Casal Bertone

Individual	Pb mg/kg	PH
ET58	0.24	None
ET27	0.32	None
ET72	2.52	None
ET67	2.68	CO
ET42	3.61	Unobservable
ET31	6.97	CC
ET69	9.50	CC
T70	1.06	CO
T18	1.68	None
T36	2.73	CO
T23	3.11	CO
T30	5.17	None
F12A	5.64	None
F11A	8.85	None
T33	13.0	None
T32	21.9	CO

Note: Data from Montgomery et al. 2010.

health issues in the Empire (e.g., Nriagu 1983; Waldron 1973). Lead poisoning can cause hemolytic anemia, which can in turn result in PH lesions on
skeletons. Using data from Montgomery et al.'s (2010:206) study of 7 individuals from Castellaccio Europarco and 10 individuals from Casal Bertone, it is possible to correlate lead concentration with presence of PH (see
Table 9.7). Considering a safe limit for lead in the blood is about 0.5 mg/kg
(Montgomery et al. 2010:207), Figure 9.4 shows that 4 of the 5 individuals
with PH were likely exposed to high levels of lead as children, possibly in
addition to a different pathogen load in their home environment. Further,
all 7 individuals who had PH and who were tested for lead concentration
(ET67, ET31, ET69, T70, T36, T23, and T32) had unsafe levels of lead in
their teeth, ranging from 1.06 mg/kg to 21.9 mg/kg, suggesting that hemolytic anemia caused by lead poisoning could have resulted in PH lesions.
However, there is an equal split between individuals with high (greater than
1 mg/kg) lead concentrations: 7 of those individuals have PH, while 7 others
(ET72, T18, T30, F12A, F1A, F11A, and T33) had no evidence of PH. While
lead poisoning is likely a factor in development of PH in the population
of Imperial Rome, it is not the only etiology. Perry (this volume) similarly
found that colonialism in early Byzantine Faynan and Aila in Jordan cannot
be the only explanation for health outcomes, but that other factors such as

environmental pollution from mining activities likely contributed to childhood stress and poor health.

Stress and the *Suburbium*

It is likely that the disease ecology of the seven hills of Rome and the *suburbium* was strikingly varied. Poorer inhabitants tended to live and work in the marshier, lower-lying areas of Rome without as good access to clean water (Sallares 2002). These individuals would have been at high risk of contracting malaria or another parasitic infection, and many may have suffered from nutritional deficiencies owing to inconsistent access to food (Garnsey 1991). Immigrants to the Imperial capital introduce another level of complexity to the question of overall health. An additional factor in the development of anemia and therefore PH is the metabolic imbalance and consequential hemolytic anemia caused by ingesting too much lead.

Many of the individuals buried in the Roman *suburbium* were obviously systemically stressed. Consistently, the previous interpretation of indicators of physiological stress in Imperial Rome has been malaria and poor diet (Buccellato et al. 2003; Catalano et al. 2001; Cucina et al. 2006; Facchini et al. 2004; Gowland and Garnsey 2010; Gowland and Redfern 2010; Salvadei et al. 2001), but it is clear that significant diversity exists within the bioarchaeological remains of the Roman *suburbium* and that discerning the interrelated causes of that diversity will be challenging. Compared to contemporary health outcomes, it is possible to conclude that life in Rome was nasty, brutal, and short, but the reality is much more complex, and additional bioarchaeological analyses of PH and DEH, as well as other pathological indicators, are necessary to better understand health in Imperial Rome.

CONCLUSIONS

With its high population density and lack of proper hygiene, Rome during Imperial times has long been considered a *pathopolis*, a city of mortal suffering in which the *plebs urbana* was disproportionately affected (Mumford 1961). This palaeopathological and demographic assessment of individuals buried at periurban Casal Bertone and at suburban Castellaccio Europarco, however, has shown that some people did live short lives, some suffered significant health stress, but some lived beyond their fifties and others had seemingly good health until their death. This heterogeneity in health outcomes means that the common perception of life in urban Rome as one full of violence, stress, and disease is simply not the only story given the osteological evidence. Understanding the variation in health and the disease load of the population of this massive preindustrial urban center is complicated by geography, disease ecology, diet, and genetic variation, as well as by inconsistent reporting of osteological data in the bioarchaeological literature.

The lives of the lower classes were complex, and people living in Rome and its suburbs had wide-ranging, heterogeneous experiences in the urban center. To the extent that these experiences are written on their bodies, we can start to explore questions of differential exposure to pathogens, levels of physiological stress, and health outcomes through the palaeopathological record of Rome. Future studies of both Republican and Imperial cemetery samples would therefore benefit from more complete palaeopathological analyses and reporting of the indicators of stress found in human skeletons from the *suburbium* of Rome. Additionally, further information on lead usage and its effects on Roman bodies, the distribution of fresh water via aqueducts, the topography and disease ecology of Rome, and the genetic background of the Roman population may contribute to a better understanding of the quality of life of all residents of this important Imperial capital.

ACKNOWLEDGMENTS

Data collection at Casal Bertone and Castellaccio Europarco (2007) was funded by an NSF Doctoral Dissertation Improvement Grant (BCS-0622452). Permission to study the materials from these two sites was granted by Paola Catalano of the Servizio di Antropologia of the Soprintendenza Speciale per i Beni Archeologici di Roma. For helpful comments on this project, I thank Dale Hutchinson and Nicola Terrenato, as well as the participants in the Crossing Boundaries conference (Cambridge, 2012), where I spoke about many of the issues discussed in this chapter. I have also greatly appreciated feedback from anonymous and peer reviewers at all stages of this project, as well as the invitation of Melissa Murphy and Haagen Klaus to contribute to this volume. Any errors, of course, remain my own.

NOTES

1. Ongoing research into large amounts of feces found in sewers at Pompeii and Herculaneum (e.g., Sullivan 2010), however, may soon generate a new line of information about pathogens and diseases that were present in Imperial Italy.

2. See, however, examples from around Italy such as Salvadei et al. 2001, Macchiarelli and Salvadei 1994, and Fornaciari et al. 1989.

3. See Killgrove 2013 for strontium and oxygen isotope results from the Republican phases of burial.

4. New research is forthcoming from the recently excavated Imperial cemetery in the city center of Gabii, which similarly has a low frequency of pathological conditions (Killgrove 2012).

REFERENCES CITED

Acsádi, G., and J. Nemeskéri
1970   History of Human Lifespan and Mortality. Akadémiai Kiadó, Budapest.
Anderson, D. L., G. W. Thompson, and F. Popovich
1976   Age of Attainment of Mineralization Stages of the Permanent Dentition. Journal of Forensic Sciences 21:191–200.
Angel, J. L.
1966   Porotic Hyperostosis, Anemias, Malarias, and Marshes in the Prehistoric Eastern Mediterranean. Science 153:760–763.
Baker, B. J., T. L. Dupras, and M. W. Tocheri
2005   The Osteology of Infants and Children. Texas A&M University Press, College Station.
Becker, M.
2014   Dentistry in Ancient Rome: Direct Evidence for Extractions Based on the Teeth from Excavations at the Temple of Castor and Pollux in the Roman Forum. International Journal of Anthropology 29:209–226.
Brooks, S. T., and J. Suchey
1990   Skeletal Age Determination Based on the Os Pubis: A Comparison of the Acsádi-Nemeskéri and Suchey-Brooks Methods. Human Evolution 5:227–238.
Buccellato, A.
2007   L'antica via Laurentina: L'arteria e le infrastrutture. FASTI Online 88.
Buccellato, A., C. Caldarini, P. Catalano, S. Musco, W. Pantano, C. Torri, and F. Zabotti
2008   La nécropole de Collatina. Les Dossiers d'Archéologie 330:22–31.
Buccellato, A., P. Catalano, B. Arrighetti, C. Caldarini, G. Colonnelli, M. Di Bernardini, S. Minozzi, W. Pantano, and E. Santandrea
2003   Il comprensorio della necropoli di via Basiliano (Roma): In'indagine multidisciplinare. Mélanges de l'École Française de Rome: Antiquité 115:311–376.
Buccellato, A., P. Catalano, and W. Pantano
2008   La site et la nécropole de Castellaccio. Les Dossiers d'Archéologie 330:14–19.

Buikstra, J. E., and D. H. Ubelaker (editors)

1994   *Standards for Data Collection from Human Skeletal Remains: Proceedings of a Seminar at the Field Museum of Natural History.* Arkansas Archeological Survey, Fayetteville.

Calci, C., and G. Messineo

1989   Casal Bertone (circ. V). *Bullettino della Commissione Archeologica Comunale di Roma* 93:133–4.

Canci, A., L. Nencioni, S. Minozzi, P. Catalano, D. Caramella, and G. Fornaciari

2005   A Case of Healing Spinal Infection from Classical Rome. *International Journal of Osteoarchaeology* 15:77–83.

Carafa, P., A. Carandini, and M. C. Capanna

2005   Origin and Development of the Roman Landscape: The *Suburbium* Experiment. In *Roman Villas around the Urbs, Projects and Seminars,* edited by B. S. Frizell and A. Klynne. Swedish Institute in Rome. Available at http://www.isvroma.it/public/villa/print/carafacarandinicapanna.pdf.

Catalano, P.

2001   Bioarcheologia: Archivio antropologico. In *Archeologia e Giubileo: Gli interventi a Roma e nel Lazio nel Piano del Grande Giubileo del 2000,* edited by F. Filippi, pp. 123. Ministero per i Beni e le Attività Culturali, Ufficio Centrale per i Beni Archeologici, Architettonici, Artistici e Storici, Napoli.

Catalano, P., B. Arrighetti, L. Benedettini, C. Caldarini, G. Colonnelli, M. Di Bernardini, S. Di Giannantonio, D. Galani, L. Maffei, L. Nencioni, W. Pantano, and S. Minozzi

2001   Vivere e morire a Roma tra il primo ed il terzo secolo. *Mitteilungen des Deutschen Archäologischen Instituts, Römische Abteilung* 108:355–363.

Catalano, P., and M. Di Bernardini

2001   Nota antropologica sull'intervento nell'area sub divo delle Catacombe di San Zotico. In *Archeologia e Giubileo: Gli interventi a Roma e nel Lazio nel Piano del Grande Giubileo del 2000,* edited by F. Filippi, p. 269. Ministero per i Beni e le Attività Culturali, Uffcio Centrale per i Beni Archeologici, Architettonici, Artistici e Storici, Napoli.

Catalano, P., W. Pantano, C. Caldarini, F. de Angelis, A. Battistini, and I. Iorio

2012   The Contribution of the Anthropological Study to the Analysis of Ancient Cemeteries: The Demographic Profile of Six Roman Imperial Age Necropolis. *Journal of Biological Research-Bollettino della Società Italiana di Biologia Sperimentale* 85:224–226.

Champlin, E. J.

1982   The Suburbium of Rome. *American Journal of Ancient History* 7:97–117.

Crandall, J. J., and D. L. Martin

2012   On Porotic Hyperostosis and the Interpretation of Hominin Diets. Comment on Manuel Domínguez-Rodrigo et al. 2012. Earliest Porotic Hyperostosis on a 1.5-Million-Year-Old Hominin, Olduvai Gorge, Tanzania. *PLoS ONE* 7(10):e46414.

Cruse, A.

2004   *Roman Medicine.* Tempus, Stroud, U.K.

Cucina, A., R. Vargiu, D. Mancinelli, R. Ricci, E. Santandrea, P. Catalano, and A. Coppa
2006   The Necropolis of Vallerano (Rome, 2nd–3rd Century AD): An Anthropological Perspective on the Ancient Romans in the Suburbium. *International Journal of Osteoarchaeology* 16:104–117.

Domínguez-Rodrigo, M., T. R. Pickering, F. Diez-Martín, A. Mabulla, C. Musiba, G. Trancho, E. Baquedano, H. T. Bunn, D. Barboni, M. Santonja, D. Uribelarrea, G. M. Ashley, M. Martínez-Avila, R. Barba, A. Gidna, J. Yravedra, and C. Arriaza
2012   Earliest Porotic Hyperostosis on a 1.5-Million-Year-Old Hominin, Olduvai Gorge, Tanzania. *PLoS ONE* 7:e46414.

Egidi, R., P. Catalano, and D. Spadoni (editors)
2003   *Aspetti di vita quotidiana dalle necropoli della via Latina, località Osteria del Curato.* Ministero per i Beni e le Attività Culturali, Soprintendenza Archeologica di Roma, Rome.

Facchini, F., E. Rastelli, and P. Brasili
2004   Cribra Orbitalia and Cribra Cranii in Roman Skeletal Remains from the Ravenna Area and Rimini (I–IV Century AD). *International Journal of Osteoarchaeology* 14:126–136.

Fejerskov, O., P. G. Bilde, M. Bizzarro, J. N. Connelly, J. Skovhus Thomsen, and B. Nyvad
2012   Dental Caries in Rome, 50–100 AD. *Caries Research* 46:467–473.

Fornaciari, G., M. G. Mezzetti, and C. Cuni
1989   Iperostosi porotica nella Campania costiera antica: Malnutrizione o anemie emolitiche congenite? I risultati delle indagini paleonutrizionale a Pontecagnano, Salerno (VII–IV secolo a.C.). *Rivista di Antropologia* 67:149–160.

Frier, B. W.
2001   More Is Worse: Some Observations on the Population of the Roman Empire. In *Debating Roman Demography*, edited by W. Scheidel, pp. 139–160. Brill, Boston.

Garnsey, P.
1988   *Famine and Food Supply in the Graeco-Roman World.* Cambridge University Press, Cambridge.
1991   Mass Diet and Nutrition in the City of Rome. In *Nourrir la plèbe: Actes du colloque tenu a Genève les 28 et 29 IX 1989 en hommage a Denis van Berchem*, edited by A. Giovannini, pp. 67–101. Friedrich Reinhardt Verlag Basel, Kassel.
1999   *Food and Society in Classical Antiquity.* Cambridge University Press: Cambridge.

Garnsey, P., and D. Rathbone
1985   The Background to the Grain Law of Gaius Gracchus. *Journal of Roman Studies* 75:20–25.

Goodman, A. H., and D. L. Martin
2002   Reconstructing Health Profiles from Skeletal Remains. In *The Backbone of History: Health and Nutrition in the Western Hemisphere*, edited by R. H. Steckel and J. C. Rose, pp. 11–60. Cambridge University Press, Cambridge.

Goodman, A. H., and J. C. Rose
1990   Assessment of Systemic Physiological Perturbations from Dental Enamel Hypoplasias and Associated Histological Structures. *Yearbook of Physical Anthropology* 33:59–110.

Gowland, R. L., and P. Garnsey
2010   Skeletal Evidence for Health, Nutritional Status, and Malaria in Rome and the Empire and Implications for Mobility. In *Roman Diasporas: Archaeological Approaches to Mobility and Diversity in the Roman Empire*, edited by H. Eckardt, pp. 131–156. *Journal of Roman Archaeology*, Supplement 78, Portsmouth, Rhode Island.

Gowland, R. L., and R. C. Redfern
2010   Childhood Health in the Roman World: Perspectives from the Centre and Margin of the Empire. *Childhood in the Past* 3:15–42.

Grmek, Mirko D.
1989   *Diseases in the Ancient Greek World.* Johns Hopkins University Press, Baltimore.

Gustafson, G., and G. Koch
1974   Age Estimation up to 16 Years of Age Based on Dental Development. *Odontologisk Revy* 25:297–306.

Hengen, O. P.
1971   Cribra Orbitalia: Pathogenesis and Probable Etiology. *Homo* 22:57–75.

Hope, V. M., and E. Marshall (editors)
2000   *Death and Disease in the Ancient City.* Routledge, New York.

Hopkins, M. K.
1978   *Conquerors and Slaves.* Cambridge University Press, Cambridge.

Johnston, F. E.
1962   Growth of the Long Bones of Infants and Young Children at Indian Knoll. *American Journal of Physical Anthropology* 20:249–254.

Katzenberg, M. A.
2008   Stable Isotope Analysis: A Tool for Studying Past Diet, Demography, and Life History. In *Biological Anthropology of the Human Skeleton*, edited by M. A. Katzenberg and S. R. Saunders, pp. 413–442. Wiley-Liss, New York.

Keppie, L.
1998   *The Making of the Roman Army: From Republic to Empire.* University of Oklahoma Press, Norman.

Killgrove, K.
2010   Migration and Mobility in Imperial Rome. Unpublished Ph.D. dissertation, Department of Anthropology, University of North Carolina, Chapel Hill.

2012   Palaeopathology and Urban Decline at Imperial Gabii (Italy) [abstract]. *American Journal of Physical Anthropology* Supplement 147:180.

2013   Biohistory of the Roman Republic: The Potential of Isotope Analysis of Human Skeletal Remains. *Post-Classical Archaeologies* 3:41–62.

Killgrove, K., and J. Montgomery
2016   All Roads Lead to Rome: Exploring Human Migration to the Eternal City

through Biochemistry of Skeletons from Two Imperial-Era Cemeteries (1st–3rd c. AD). *PLoS ONE* 11(2):e0147585.

Killgrove, K., and R. H. Tykot

2013   Food for Rome: a Stable Isotope Investigation of Diet in the Imperial Period (1st–3rd Centuries AD). *Journal of Anthropological Archaeology* 32:28–38.

King, T., L. T. Humphrey, and S. Hillson

2005   Linear Enamel Hypoplasias as Indicators of Systemic Physiological Stress: Evidence from Two Known Age-at-Death and Sex Populations from Post-medieval London. *American Journal of Physical Anthropology* 128:547–559.

Laurence, R.

1999   *The Roads of Roman Italy: Mobility and Cultural Change.* Routledge, New York.

Laurence, R., and J. Berry (editors)

1998   *Cultural Identity in the Roman Empire.* Routledge, New York.

Lewis, M. E.

2007   *The Bioarchaeology of Children.* Cambridge University Press, Cambridge.

Lo Cascio, E.

2006   Did the Population of Rome Reproduce Itself? In *Urbanism in the Preindustrial World: Cross-Cultural Approaches,* edited by G. Storey, pp. 52–68. University of Alabama Press, Tuscaloosa.

Lovejoy, C. O., R. S. Meindl, T. R. Pryzbeck, and R. P. Mensforth

1985   Chronological Metamorphosis of the Auricular Surface of the Ilium: A New Method for the Determination of Adult Skeletal Age at Death. *American Journal of Physical Anthropology* 68:15–28.

Macchiarelli, R., and L. Salvadei

1994   Paleodemography and Selective Practices at Latium Vetus, Middle-Tyrrhenian Italy. *Anthropologischer Anzeiger* 68:37–52.

MacDonnell, W. R.

1913   On the Expectation of Life in Ancient Rome, and in the Provinces of Hispania and Lusitania, and Africa. *Biometrika* 9:366–380.

Manzi, G., L. Salvadei, A. Vienna, and P. Passarello

1999   Discontinuity of Life Conditions at the Transition from the Roman Imperial Age to the Early Middle Ages: Example from Central Italy Evaluated by Pathological Dento-alveolar Lesions. *American Journal of Human Biology* 11:327–341.

Manzi, G., A. Sperduti, and P. Passarello

1991   Behavior-induced Auditory Exostoses in Imperial Roman Society: Evidence from Coeval Urban and Rural Communities near Rome. *American Journal of Physical Anthropology* 85:253–260.

Mariotti, V., O. Dutour, M. G. Belcastro, F. Facchini, and P. Brasili

2005   Probable Early Presence of Leprosy in Europe in a Celtic Skeleton of the 4th–3rd Century BC (Casalecchio di Reno, Bologna, Italy). *International Journal of Osteoarchaeology* 15:311–325.

Meindl, R. S., and C. O. Lovejoy

1985   Ectocranial Suture Closure: A Revised Method for the Determination of

Skeletal Age at Death Based on the Lateral-Anterior Sutures. *American Journal of Physical Anthropology* 68:57–66.

Meinecke, B.

1927   Consumption in Classical Antiquity. *Annals of Medical History* 9:379–402.

Montgomery, J., J. A. Evans, S. Chenery, V. Pashley, and K. Killgrove

2010   "Gleaming, White and Deadly": Lead Exposure and Geographic Origins in the Roman Period. In *Roman Diasporas: Archaeological Approaches to Mobility and Diversity in the Roman Empire*, edited by H. Eckardt, pp. 199–226. *Journal of Roman Archaeology*, Supplement 78, Portsmouth, Rhode Island.

Moorrees, C. F. A., E. A. Fanning, and E. E. Hunt Jr.

1963a   Age Formation by Stages for Ten Permanent Teeth. *Journal of Dental Research* 42:1490–1502.

1963b   Formation and Resorption of Three Deciduous Teeth in Children. *American Journal of Physical Anthropology* 21:205–213.

Morley, N.

1996   *Metropolis and Hinterland: The City of Rome and the Italian Economy, 200 B.C.–A.D. 200.* Cambridge University Press, Cambridge.

2005   The Salubriousness of the Roman City. In *Health in Antiquity*, edited by H. King, pp. 192–204. Routledge, New York.

Mumford, L.

1961   *The City in History: Its Origins, Its Transformation, and Its Prospects.* Harcourt, Brace & World, New York.

Musco, S., P. Catalano, A. Caspio, W. Pantano, and K. Killgrove

2008   Le complexe archéologique de Casal Bertone. *Les Dossiers d'Archéologie* 330:32–39.

Nanni, A., and L. Maffei

2004   Nodo di Roma: Penetrazione urbana A V—linea FM2. Italferr/TAV. Relazione antropologica. Area AI (E). Casal Bertone. Necropoli e Mausoleo. Soprintendenza Archeologica di Roma, Servizio di Antropologia.

Nathan, H., and N. Haas

1966   On the Presence of Cribra Orbitalia in Apes and Monkeys. *American Journal of Physical Anthropology* 24:351–359.

Noy, D.

2000   *Foreigners at Rome: Citizens and Strangers.* Duckworth, London.

Nriagu, J. O.

1983   Saturnine Gout among Roman Aristocrats: Did Lead Poisoning Contribute to the Fall of the Empire? *New England Journal of Medicine* 308:662.

Ortner, D. J.

2003   *Identification of Pathological Conditions in Human Skeletal Remains.* Academic Press, New York.

Ottini, L., F. Ricci, L. R. Angeletti, R. Mariani-Costantini, and P. Catalano

2001   Le condizioni di vita nella popolazione di età imperiale. *Mitteilungen des Deutschen Archäologischen Instituts, Römische Abteilung* 108:364–366.

Ousley, S. D., and R. L. Jantz
1996   FORDISC 2.0: Personal Computer Forensic Discriminant Functions. Forensic
            Anthropology Center, University of Tennessee, Knoxville.
Oxenham, M. F., and I. Cavill
2010   Porotic Hyperostosis and Cribra Orbitalia: The Erythropoietic Response to
            Iron-Deficiency Anaemia. Anthropological Science 118:199–200.
Paine, R. R., and G. R. Storey
2006   Epidemics, Age at Death, and Mortality in Ancient Rome. In Urbanism in
            the Preindustrial World: Cross-Cultural Approaches, edited by Glenn Storey,
            pp. 69–85. University of Alabama Press, Tuscaloosa.
Parkin, T. G.
1992   Demography and Roman Society. Johns Hopkins University Press, Baltimore.
Patrick, A.
1967   Disease in Antiquity: Greece and Rome. In Diseases in Antiquity: a Survey of
            the Diseases, Injuries, and Surgery of Early Populations, edited by D. Broth-
            well and A. T. Sandison, pp. 238–248. Charles C. Thomas, Springfield, Il-
            linois.
Phenice, T. W.
1969   A Newly Developed Visual Method of Sexing in the Os Pubis. American
            Journal of Physical Anthropology 30:297–301.
Pilkington, D.
2013   Growing Up Roman: Infant Mortality and Reproductive Development. Jour-
            nal of Interdisciplinary History 44:1–36.
Prowse, T. L.
2001   Isotopic and Dental Evidence for Diet from the Necropolis of Isola Sacra
            (1st–3rd Centuries AD), Italy. Unpublished Ph.D. dissertation, McMaster
            University.
Prowse, T. L., H. P. Schwarcz, P. Garnsey, M. Knyf, R. Macchiarelli, and L. Bondioli
2007   Isotopic Evidence for Age-Related Immigration to Imperial Rome. American
            Journal of Physical Anthropology 132:510–519.
Prowse, T. L., H. P. Schwarcz, S. R. Saunders, R. Macchiarelli, and L. Bondioli
2004   Isotopic Paleodiet Studies of Skeletons from the Imperial Roman–Age Cem-
            etery of Isola Sacra, Rome, Italy. Journal of Archaeological Science 31:259–272.
2005   Isotopic Evidence for Age-Related Variation in Diet from Isola Sacra, Italy.
            American Journal of Physical Anthropology 128:2–13.
Ricci, R., D. Mancinelli, R. Vargiu, A. Cucina, E. Santandrea, A. Capelli, and P. Catalano
1997   Pattern of Porotic Hyperostosis and Quality of Life in a II Century A.D. Farm
            near Rome. Rivista di Antropologia 75:117–128.
Roberts, C. A., and J. E. Buikstra
2003   The Bioarchaeology of Tuberculosis: A Global View on Reemerging Disease.
            University Press of Florida, Gainesville.
Rothschild, B. M., F. J. Rühli, J. I. Sebes, V. L. Naples, and M. Billard
2004   The Relationship between Porotic Hyperostosis and Cribra Orbitalia. Paleo-
            bios 13:4–7.

Sallares, R.
2002   *Malaria and Rome: A History of Malaria in Ancient Italy.* Oxford University Press, Oxford.

Salvadei, L., F. Ricci, and G. Manzi
2001   Porotic Hyperostosis as a Marker of Health and Nutritional Conditions during Childhood: Studies at the Transition between Imperial Rome and the Early Middle Ages. *American Journal of Human Biology* 13:709–717.

Scheidel, W.
2001   Progress and Problems in Roman Demography. In *Debating Roman Demography*, edited by W. Scheidel, pp. 1–82. Brill, Boston.
2003   Germs for Rome. In *Rome the Cosmopolis*, edited by C. Edwards and G. Woolf, pp. 158–176. Cambridge University Press, Cambridge.
2005   Human Mobility in Roman Italy, II: The Slave Population. *Journal of Roman Studies* 95:64–79.
2014   "Germs for Rome" Ten Years After. In *Les affaires de Monsieur Andreau: Économie et société du monde romain*, edited by C. Apicella, M.-L. Haaco, and F. Lerouxel, pp. 311–315. Ausonius, Paris.

Schwirian, K. P., A. L. Nelson, and P. M. Schwirian
1995   Modeling Urbanism: Economic, Social and Environmental Stress in Cities. *Social Indicators Research* 35:201–223.

Scobie, A.
1986   Slums, Sanitation, and Mortality in the Roman World. *Klio* 68:399–433.

Sperduti, A.
1997   Life Conditions of a Roman Imperial Age Population: Occupational Stress Markers and Working Activities in Lucus Feroniae (Rome, 1st–2nd Cent. AD). *Human Evolution* 12:253–267.

Storey, G. R.
1997a   Estimating the Population of Ancient Roman Cities. In *Integrating Archaeological Demography: Multidisciplinary Approaches to Prehistoric Population*, edited by R. R. Paine, pp. 101–130. Center for Archaeological Investigations, Southern Illinois University at Carbondale.
1997b   The Population of Ancient Rome. *Antiquity* 71:966–978.

Stuart-Macadam, P.
1989   Porotic Hyperostosis: Relationship between Orbital and Vault Lesions. *American Journal of Physical Anthropology* 80:187–193.

Sullivan, R.
2010   Pompeii Poop. *Discovery Channel Magazine* June/July:91–97.

Taylor, R. M.
2000   *Public Needs and Private Pleasures: Water Distribution, the Tiber River, and the Urban Development of Ancient Rome.* L'Erma di Bretschneider, Rome.

Terrenato, N., and S. Keay (editors)
2001   *Italy and the West: Comparative Issues in Romanization.* Oxbow, Oxford.

Todd, T. W.
1921a   Age Changes in the Pubic Bone I: The Male White Pubis. *American Journal of Physical Anthropology* 3:285–334.

1921b Age Changes in the Pubic Bone III: The Pubis of the White Female. *American Journal of Physical Anthropology* 4:1–70.

Toynbee, J.

1971 *Death and Burial in the Roman World.* Cornell University Press, Ithaca, New York.

Waldron, H. A.

1973 Lead Poisoning in the Ancient World. *Medical History* 17:391–399.

Waldron, T.

2009 *Palaeopathology.* Cambridge University Press, Cambridge.

Walker, P. L., R. R. Bathurst, R. Richman, T. Gjerdrum, and V. A. Andrushko

2010 The Causes of Porotic Hyperostosis and Cribra Orbitalia: A Reappraisal of the Iron-Deficiency-Anemia Hypothesis. *American Journal of Physical Anthropology* 139:109–125.

Webster, J.

2001 Creolizing the Roman Provinces. *American Journal of Archaeology* 105:209–225.

White, K. D.

1976 Food Requirement and Food Supplies in Classical Times. *Progress in Food and Nutrition Science* 2:143–191.

Wiseman, T. P.

1969 The Census in the First Century B.C. *Journal of Roman Studies* 59:59–75.

Witcher, R. E.

2005 The Extended Metropolis: Urbs, Suburbium, and Population. *Journal of Roman Archaeology* 18:120–138.

Wood, J. W., G. R. Milner, H. C. Harpending, and K. M. Weiss

1992 The Osteological Paradox: Problems of Inferring Prehistoric Health from Skeletal Samples. *Current Anthropology* 33:343–370.

III

THE BODY AND IDENTITY UNDER COLONIALISM

10

Survival and Abandonment of Indigenous Head-Shaping Practices in Iberian America after European Contact

VERA TIESLER AND PILAR ZABALA

The guiding theme of this volume is the embodiment of contact and colonialism by the societies affected by often monumental cultural change. This process was neither static nor uniform, as has been underlined already in the introduction and voiced repeatedly among the pages of this book. The complexity involved in the dynamics of colonization and their diverse outcomes has to do with the fact that each colonial setting was unique, depending on the interplay of a host of factors related to the colonizing power, colonization strategies, and transformations, on one side, and on the other side, aspects that characterize the colonized, their interaction, reactions, and change (Stein 2005).

This chapter addresses this complexity through the lens of native infant head modeling in Iberian America, a highly visible form of native physical embodiment that we wish to examine before and after contact in the light of colonization strategies, cultural rupture versus resilience, and social crisis versus assimilation and transformation. Grounded in a systematic survey of historical testimonies from the Ibero-American continental sphere and tangible evidence from the human skeletal record (Tiesler 2014; Zabala 2014), we will treat this topic on a continental level in order to highlight broad historical trends that transcended the local dynamics of colonization. These are to be discussed in the light of some key attributes of infant head shaping. Some were enacted in the hidden, private, domestic spheres pertaining to females, while others were displayed in the open, signaling identity, ethnicity, and social status, thus being exposed and easily subjected to the pressure from the new dominant social sectors. We expect that the contextualized discussion of these aspects of head shaping and its conservative quality should provide fertile points of departure to understand the postcontact shifts in native physical embodiment and identity.

But first a definition: artificial head shaping, also known as cranial vault modification, is a visible body modification performed on the infant head that has been employed cross-culturally to express identity, ethnicity, status, and gender (Dingwall 1931). Technically speaking, cranial modifications are conducted by constricting or compressing the still flexible infant cranium as it grows. After this procedure, which can last for a few weeks after birth into the first years of life, the skull tissue progressively reaches its final shape and rigidity and the changes become permanent. The individual will then carry the culturally produced head morphology for the remainder of his or her life. To effect the changes in the infant's cranial vault, the mostly female practitioners employed a wide range of methods, ranging from massages, tight hats that were fitted on the baby's head, wraps, head splints, and compression cradles.[1]

Upon close examination, infant head shaping acquires many shades, dimensions, and cultural undertones that surpass the visible outcome. Some qualities are purely behavioral; some are quotidian, private, doxic, and spurious; others relate directly to the altered head morphology, which is permanent and often intended to be played out in the public sphere. Because the individual and collective enactment of this practice involves different age groups (concretely, second- and third-generation adult practitioners and their infants who would display the resulting morphology for the remainder of their lives), head shaping is generation-bridging to signalize enduring social identities, physical embodiment, and long-standing ideas on the body and child rearing (Duncan and Hofling 2011; Tiesler 2014). This essentially conservative quality of cranial modification raises its cultural role above that of more ephemeral body fashions and turns it into an enormously useful point of departure for examining the evolution of collective cultural dynamics of social integration and embodied group identity, long-term expressions of ethnicity, and group ancestry, either real or pretended. These fall into the realm of *long durée* mentalities, or those elements in the social fabric that are more enduring than other, less embedded aspects of social experience, such as economic or political networks (Braudel 1974:68).

In the last century, research into cultural cranial modifications has evolved into an established subject of interest in anthropology with a major portion of attention directed toward the Americas, specifically, the pre-Columbian Andes and Mesoamerica. In both cultural spheres, head-shaping practices were simultaneously long-standing and diversified traditions, embedded at the hard core (*núcleo duro*) of sophisticated cosmologies and cultural expressions, a term coined by López Austin (2001) for the Mesoamerican sphere to designate the essences or intimate elements of an ideological framework. Beyond the Mesoandean territories, artificial cranial modification was a nearly ubiquitous tradition in most parts of the Americas before the European contact, looking back on several millennia of practice (Dembo and Imbelloni 1938; Lozada and Buikstra 2002; Romano Pacheco 1972; Weiss 1961). The notoriety of pre-Columbian cranial modifications in the Americas led scholars of the nineteenth century to speak of the New World as the "headquarters" of cultural head modifications (Flower 1881; see also Dembo and Imbelloni 1938; Dingwall 1931; Imbelloni 1932; Weiss 1961).

Pre-Hispanic cranial modification practices have been the research domain of physical anthropologists and, more recently, bioarchaeologists as well. Bioarchaeological approaches, which combine the information retrieved from skeletons with that of the archaeological record and—depending on the cultural setting—a wide range of additional sources of cultural information, are best suited to grant insights that transcend the morphological description of the cranial vault toward the cultural meanings these changes once held in terms of beauty norms, gender and its ritual enactment, and as expression of identity, distinction, and ethnicity (Blom et al. 1998; Duncan 2009; Duncan and Hofling 2011; Lozada 2011; Tiesler 2011, 2012a, 2012b; Torres-Rouff 2009).

Apart from the cranial record, the written statements of those who still witnessed indigenous head shaping as a living practice are highly valuable sources of information. Most of the historical references on infant head modifications date to the sixteenth century. Especially in the territories of New Spain, colonists took interest in the native cultural repertoires (Tiesler and Zabala 2011; Zabala 2014). Yet it was the Spanish Empire itself that soon opposed and actively suppressed head shaping and other indigenous customs. The Lima and Quito councils forbade native Peruvian head modifications under punishment by law (Archivo General de Indias, Sevilla [AGI], Patronato 189, R. 40; Toledo 1929 [1573]; Figure 10.1). These eradication efforts by the Spanish Crown can be understood as part of a broader colonization strategy of forced assimilation of all non-European sectors. Subsequently, native head modeling was either abandoned altogether by

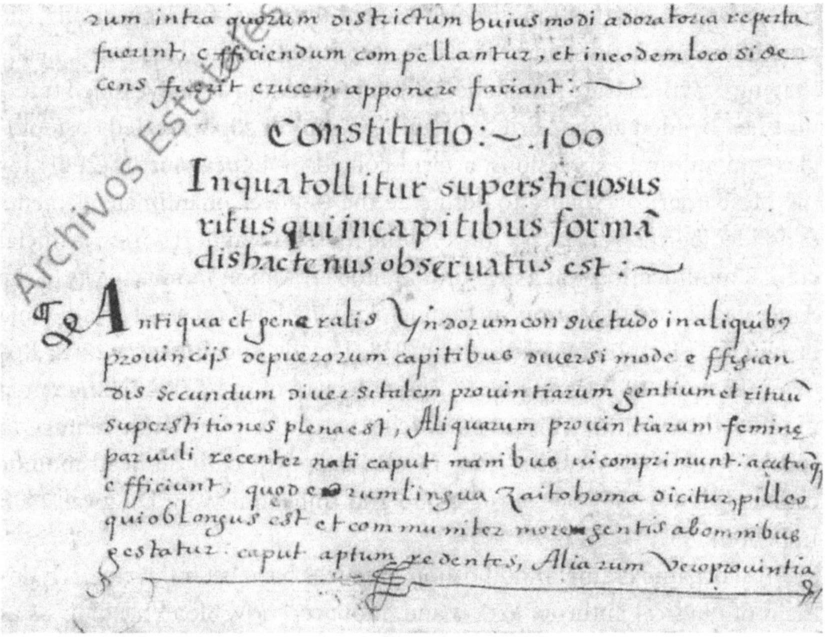
rum intra quorum districtum huiusmodi adoratoria reperta
fuerint, efficiendum compellantur, et in eodem loco si de-
cens fuerit crucem apponere faciant:~

Constitutio:~.100

In qua tollitur superstitiosus
ritus qui in capitibus formā
dis hactenus obseruatus est:~

Antiqua et generalis Indorum consuetudo in aliquibus
prouincijs de puerorum capitibus diuersi mode effigian-
dis secundum diuersitatem prouintiarum gentium et rituu
superstitiones plena est, Aliquarum prouintiarum femine
paruuli recenter nati caput manibus comprimunt: acutum
efficiunt, quod eorum lingua Caitohoma dicitur, pilleo
qui oblongus est et communiter more gentis ab omnibus
gestatur. caput aptum redentes, Aliarum vero prouintia

Figure 10.1. Prohibition constitution 100 (AGI Patronato, 189-R. 40).

the natives or was gradually replaced by alternative practices. Cognizant of the generalized Iberian refusal of native head-shaping practices, we were surprised to learn during our review of Ibero-American historical testimonies of the many twists that these practices took in postcontact Latin America. This was a welcome point of departure for this study to understand the underlying dynamics and reasons for keeping or abandoning it. These delineate decidedly human facets of colonial history, as the changing motivations underscoring head shaping inform broader reflections on cultural resilience, adaptation, and change in times of crisis and exodus.

For this study, we have combined historical and craniological data sets. We will specifically refer to both pre- and postcontact skeletal series from Mesoamerica and beyond. We have also assembled over a hundred colonial statements and more recent travel accounts and ethnographies from Iberian America, which are transcribed in full in other recently published work (Tiesler 2014; Zabala 2014). Most colonial documents come from the Archivo Histórico Nacional in Madrid and the Archivo General de las Indias in Seville.[2] The majority of transcriptions on head shaping that date to postcolonial times derive from the admirable recompilation of historical sources by E. J. Dingwall (1931). Care was taken to examine each historical transcription critically within its particular historical context to avoid over-simplification and interpretive biases. Our combination of data sets and our social attributions of head-shaping practices ground this synthesis of body traditions and a discussion of those processes and circumstances that reflected important social shifts after European contact. For this purpose, we first confront the Mesoamerican and Andean autochthonous motives for modifying the heads of newborns with the colonizers' strategy of forced religious and cultural assimilation of all non-European sectors. From there we discuss different native cultural reactions during and after the Colonial period.

PRE-COLUMBIAN HEAD-SHAPING PRACTICES IN IBERIAN AMERICA

Before European contact, artificial cranial modification was a deeply rooted tradition in most parts of the pre-Columbian world, specifically in Meso-america and the Andes, as one can see in the continental geography of cranial modifications first delineated by Imbelloni (1932; Figure 10.2), then

Figure 10.2. Distribution of pre-Columbian head shaping in the territories of Iberian America: tabular oblique (TO), tabular erect (TE) and annular (AN) (adapted from Dembo and Imbelloni 1938:320–321).

by Weiss (1961) and Romano Pacheco (1974). Despite the early progress, to-day's scholarship awaits a systematic continental synthesis on head imple-ments and shapes. There are still no maps that refer to the artificial head forms and shaping techniques of a given time, area, or cultural sphere. This absence is most probably due to the lack of supra-regional archaeological coverage and certainly also of academic initiative. Most noticeably in the Peruvian setting, contextual glitches limit the possibilities of nuanced sur-veys of most of the earlier cranial collections, such as those accrued from the many devastated, looted cemeteries in the Ancón, Chancay, Pachac-amac, Paracas, Santa, and Chicama regions (Klaus 2008:269; Lozada and Buikstra 2002).

Quite differently from the varied late Andean head forms, coeval Meso-americans staged uniformly broad and short (tabular erect) cranial shapes from widespread cradleboard use (Dávalos Hurtado 1951; Romano Pacheco 1974; Tiesler 2014). The morphological homogeneity is most noticeable in those areas that still before the Postclassic period showed diversity in head-wear, such as the Western Central Highlands, southern Veracruz, or the Lowland Maya (Tiesler 2014). At the verge of European contact, over 90 percent of the diverse Maya peoples exhibited a broad-headed "unilook" that must have vaguely denoted a pan-Mesoamerican notion of identity and personhood (Tiesler and Zabala 2011). This cultural identification is perhaps more apparent in the Mesoamerican borderlands than in its in-terior. A historical source from the western fringes of Mesoamerica high-lights, for example, that the local natives from the Lake Pascua area rejected the naturally "round heads" of (non-Mesoamerican) Tarascans for not car-rying the credentials of courage and bravery of (Mesoamerican) men who had their heads "compressed and flattened as a cake" (Anonymous 1977 [1541]:145; see also Pereira 1999:166–168) (Figure 10.3).

Given the homogeneity in Mesoamerican head morphology at the time of European contact, it follows that its cultural significance should not have been tied so much to any emblematic forms of embodiment. But if it was not for its visibility, as we believe, what could have been a suitable mo-tivation for enacting head compression in Mesoamerican infants? As we have concluded in other work (Tiesler 2011, 2012a; Tiesler and Zabala 2011; see also Duncan and Hofling 2011), we think that late Mesoamerican head compression was generally conceived less as a shaping process and more as a protective measure that would guide the baby through the initial lim-inal stages of life by retaining its animical balance in preparation for later upbringing and evolving personhood. Mesoamericans sought specifically

Figure 10.3. Colonial rendering of Tlazolteotl priest; the head is shown with a reclined forehead and a flattened occiput (adapted and redrawn by the authors from Trejo 2007:21).

to reduce the rear portion of the infant's head, as occipital bulging was thought to have a negative impact on the harmonious functioning of a person's living essences and therefore was deemed potentially harmful to health and animical integrity (Chávez 2014; Guiteras Holmes 1986; López Austin 1989; Tiesler 2012b). Francisco López de Gómara confirms this notion in his *Historia de la conquista de México,* writing that "the midwives manipulate the babies so they have no occiput, and mothers lay them in compression cribs so that they do not grow them because they consider them beautiful without them" (1987 [1552]:246). Contact Yucatecans used the term *up' k'abtah* to describe the act of straightening out the head of the baby and to mend or to adapt it (Barrera-Vásquez 1938:901; see also Chávez 2014 for examples from other parts of Mesoamerica).

Further south and across the Isthmus of Panama lies the other hub of New World native head-shaping practices under study. We may assume that in the Andean hemisphere were additional ritual dimensions of head shaping essential to child rearing, as the recurrent testimonies of crib rituals hint at. Among the Inca, who celebrated the "presentation of the crib to the divinity" (*huahua, quirau*), a carefully selected male relative of the

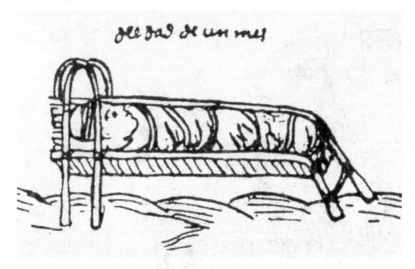

Figure 10.4. A depiction of an Inca compression cradle (adapted and redrawn by the authors from the cover of Purizaga 1991).

mother was responsible for fabricating the child's compression crib while invoking the *huaca* (totem) of the family in order to shelter the baby and protect it against harm (Latcham 1929:542; Purizaga Vega 1991:43–45). Contrary to Postclassic-period Mesoamericans, Andean peoples appear to have adapted their compression devices in a predetermined way in order to reproduce the specific group "emblem" in infant heads (Lozada and Buikstra 2002; Weiss 1958, 1961; Yepez Vásquez 2006, 2009). For this effect, the Aymara used the so-called *llautu*, a cushioned head harness that gave their infants' heads an elongated, tubular, and sometimes inclined appearance. Other areas used headboards as splints, while compression cradles, called *quirau* in Quechua, were the standard device along the Pacific coast and in some of the Highland areas dominated by the Inca at the times of European contact (Figure 10.4). These cradleboards led to characteristically short and broad head morphologies.

Unsurprisingly, the pre-Hispanic diversity in head expressions has left its traces in the skeletal record of the second millennium, characterized by formal diversity among and even within each cultural territory (Hoshower et al. 1995; Lozada and Buikstra 2002; Weiss 1961). It is telling that Andean taxonomies name specific head morphologies after the ethnic groups and archaeological spheres that once performed them (Weiss 1961; Yepez Vásquez 2006). Within Tiwanaku culture, for example, modified head shapes appear to have been linked to sociocultural boundaries separating distinct populations (Blom 2005a, 2005b; Buikstra 1995). Recent Andean scholarship has provided additional feedback on the meanings by supplementing more nuanced reasons for Andean cultural head shaping. These range from visibly signaling *ayllu* (family) membership to emulating venerated natural features, such as the Collagua volcanic mountain or other totemic emblems and mythical ancestors, which sometimes would be portrayed on the infant's cradle itself (Blom et al. 1998; Latcham 1929; Lozada 2011; Lozada and Buikstra 2002; Purizaga Vega 1991:56; Ullúa y Mogollón 1965 [1586]).

Both the European newcomers and the Andean natives voiced more mundane motives for cranial vault modification in their writings, including the use of specific head forms in signaling conferred privilege, lineage, and even warrior status. The Inca went to the extremes of actually overseeing the visible outcome of the custom and instructed the different peoples within their empire to flatten the heads of their children in specific ways so that their group membership would be displayed and their obedience to the Inca be manifest, as Lloque Yupanqui is said to have commanded his vassals (Casas 1967:594; Santa Cruz Pachacuti 1879 [1613]). From the above it is clear that the visible outcome of head-shaping procedures was indeed crucial for most Andean peoples. Different from the vague phenomenological and behavioral components of precontact Mesoamerican head-shaping procedures, Andean manipulation of head form was to signal ethnicity, cultural identity, and distinction in their human carriers.

Our knowledge of head-shaping practices to the north and the east of the Andes—namely, the tropical forests of the Amazon lowlands—is much less eloquent than the written and skeletal records from postcontact Mesoamerica and Peru (Zabala 2014). Colonial witnesses are few, as the Amazon basin was not colonized until centuries after the initial Andean conquest. The lack of information in this research domain is probably also attributable to the poor skeletal preservation in the tropics and the lack of bioarchaeological research east of the Andes.

EUROPEAN ENCOUNTERS AND ATTITUDES TOWARD
NATIVE BODY PRACTICES

Colonial Iberian America may be charted roughly into four spheres according to the divides in European colonial powers, strategies, and timing: the Antilles, Portuguese Brazil, Mesoamerica, and Peru. We will center our attention in this chapter on the latter two, where jurisdictions were characterized by an absolutist claim to streamline culture and transform the social fabric to conform with the needs of the Spanish Crown (which included the forced assimilation of culture, and more so, religion and belief systems). Conversely, the heavily forested areas east of the Peruvian highlands remained for the most part isolated and unexplored for decades and centuries to come. From the Atlantic side of the continent, Brazilian establishments were mainly restricted to economic exploitation and limited to the coastal areas. Deeper incursions into the Amazon basin did not occur until the seventeenth and eighteenth centuries (Fournier García 1999; Lucena 2005:102). Much more severely affected by contact were Caribbean settings. In the Lesser and Greater Antilles, autochthonous head traditions either faced extinction along with their human carriers or persisted only on the more isolated islands.

Regarding the colonization centers of Iberian America in the years following discovery and conquest, the Spanish Crown remained acutely observant to native beliefs and ways of life. This awareness was neither purely genuine nor scholarly, but was destined also to learn of and better control the dominated indigenous sectors of Iberian society. Specifically, the Spanish aimed to ban those native customs that they considered to be a health hazard, barbarous, superstitious, or sacrilegious to Catholic thought. Apart from these aspects, our combined source analysis of the mostly synodal and ecclesiastic accounts on cranial modification also reflects upon more general notions of the European mentality of the moment and specifically on Catholic attitudes toward the body (Figure 10.5). According to church doctrine, natural head form "has been created by God to mirror his own image" (Cieza de León, 1984:227), and so its "arbitrary" modification was judged an aberration and a sacrilege to faith. As head modification operated in opposition to the God-given physical order of nature (namely, the physiological head morphology granted to humans by divine resolve), it was recurrently considered by the Iberians as immoral and corrupt.

The extensive European references on various head morphologies and their social underpinnings are noteworthy for the Andean sphere. Further north, the chroniclers' focus of the Mesoamerican native traditions is not the head morphology itself, which is described bluntly as short and broad, and is treated almost as a given native physical attribute (Sahagún 1989). Nor do New Spain's detailed accounts on Mesoamerica's rich and diversified folklore of everyday and festive adornments leave much room to pronounce on the visibly modified head shapes of the majority of natives, as is evident from the cranial record of the contact period (Dávalos Hurtado

Figure 10.5. Shaded countries with early colonial references to head-shaping practices from database (Zabala 2014).

1951; Tiesler 2012a). Instead, it is the daily compression routine and the active manipulation of the baby's occipital bulge, with its implied health risks, that raised the scorn and preoccupation of the Spaniards. Friar Diego de Landa (in Tozzer 1941:125) takes a position on Maya collective health, stating that "the poor children's inconvenience and hazard was so great, that some were at risk [of losing their lives] . . . and when they had finished with the torture of flattening forehead and [back of the head], they took them to the priest to know the future and the craft [of their child] and to give it the name that it would have for the time of its childhood."

Other European sources do allude to a host of native motivations for enacting cradle compression in infants, namely, the reduction of the back of the head, beauty, prestige, braveness, and better disposition to support the heavy weights of tumplines later in life (Bobadilla in D'Olwer 1963:352; Hernández 2001:111; López de Gómara 1987 [1552]:246; see also Dingwall 1931; Tiesler and Zabala 2011; and Tiesler 2014 for an extensive examination of Ibero-American sources). We cannot judge the credibility of each source, as there were probably other, deeper motivations related to the Mesoamerican cosmos and to identity and personhood in native thought, as we have argued above. Apparently, these dimensions of head-shaping practices were not understood by the Iberian newcomers, as can be inferred from the written testimonies that have survived.

Further south, the abundant written accounts on Andean head-shaping practices in the viceroyalty of Peru contrast starkly with the vague notions given to Mesoamerican cradleboard use. Here, Spanish sources do emphasize specific head shapes as related to aristocratic distinction, class, ancestral emulation, and ethnicity (Casas 1967:179; Cieza de Léon 1984:227; Torquemada 1723). Apart from visible emblematic identifications, the Spaniards cite other meanings of the custom. For example, Pedro Cieza de Léon (1984:145) states the benefits of flattening in carrying the heavy burdens of their occupations. We think that these interpretations, although indirectly, might refer to a status assignment, such as in this case, of the commoner or underprivileged social strata that were the laborers and producers within these societies.

Most of the early colonial testimonies are permeated by derogatory ethnocentric rhetoric. The references appear increasingly hostile to the resilience of the native practice, which in the case of Peru was still conducted by the local population after almost a century of colonial oppression. It is here that repression was put into a legal framework already present in the first ecclesiastical councils that convened in Lima and Quito in the mid-sixteenth century (Figure 10.1).

Explicit prohibitions still appear published by the Spanish authorities in 1614, when Archbishop Gerónimo de Loayza of the Lima Council states that "the superstition of flattening the head must disappear completely" (Pardal 1938:69). He also calls for sanctions of those who still modeled the head of their offspring:

In antiquity and in a generalized fashion did the Indians of those provinces engage in the custom of modifying the heads of their children in different manners by flattening it from the back as part of a superstitious rite of the lineages of the different provinces. . . . In some provinces, women compressed the heads of their newborns in a pointed fashion with their hands, a custom that in the Zaitahoma language is called "pilleo" when it led to an elongated form, generally this horrid custom implied binding the head. . . . However, in other provinces, the head without its posterior portion is custom [and accomplished] by flattening the occiput, which in the native language is called "paltahoma," when different devices are put on the soft head of the children and compressed with a band until they break it. This custom must not be continued, and consciousness must be raised of the evil nature and other terrible madnesses that can result when the natural order of the human kind is changed. One has to put an end to the tradition of such an undesirable custom of some lineages. . . . The Christian religion . . . detests these ceremonies and sacrilegious rites that put such harm to the care of the diligent priests of the Indians. (AGI, Patronato 189, R. 40; translated from Latin by Pilar Zabala)

This transcription blatantly reveals the Crown's harsh judgment of head-shaping traditions and at the same time allows insights on the continuity and resilience of native ways.

Trajectories of Head-Shaping Practices during the Colonial Period

Despite the assimilation pressure exerted by the Spanish Crown, natives did not abandon their ancient traditions readily. What strategies did they employ to hide the practice? And when change did occur, what were the transformations, and how did they reconcile with other elements of autochthonous ideology? What influenced native attitudes toward abandonment or permanence? What kind of circumstances or strategies of suppression triggered the abandonment of this ancestral tradition? Did it undergo similar transformations in the Iberian urban settlements as in the rural backwaters of colonization? Instead of replying to these and other questions in a categorical and ad hoc manner, it is wise to approach the subject of native cultural adjustments by recalling some key features of native head-shaping practices:

First, we have to keep in mind that female caretakers, and prominently mothers, were in charge of the daily handling of their infants (Tiesler 2011). From this perspective, it is clear that the routine of daily head compression was embedded in a female domain, a more secluded domestic environ. Due to the intense colonial constructions of gender distinctions in the Andes or Mesoamerica, head shaping could, in all likelihood, be easily concealed from the male-dominated spheres of European colonizers. Certainly, this female component must have come in handy in the natives' efforts to continue their head-compression practices in the relative privacy of domestic spaces. For Colonial Peru, Latcham proclaims, "the Indians were very secretive in all these things [ritual ceremonies] and hid them from the Spaniards, not allowing anyone [to assist them] except for the family members of their blood line" (1929:544; translated by the authors).

Yet, paradoxically, there is also a public element involved in head compression that relates to the visible head morphology the carrier would exhibit for the rest of his or her life, given the permanent nature of cultural head modifications. In principle, the outcome of head flattening or elongation should have been much more visible to the reproaching eyes of Iberians than other, less outwardly expressed body traditions and therefore more easily subjected to abandonment. This fact leads to a second observation that we think is key to evaluate the colonial impact on native head compression in different settings. This involves the original importance and motives for practicing head shaping in the first place and, naturally, the intended visibility and distinctiveness of the morphological results. The colonial onlooker would surely grasp such facets by perceiving the affluence of people with artificially shaped heads in a given location or region and by recognizing the diversity of the natives' head forms.

Put in context, the divergent roles that head-shaping practices held among Mesoamerican and Andean practitioners explain the information communicated by the chroniclers during the sixteenth century and ultimately, the different evolution of these practices in New Spain and Peru. Even after seventy years of colonial oppression in South America, native central Andeans were still observed with artificially shaped skulls to the point that sanctions against those who still modeled the heads of their offspring were called into action. The difficulty in eradicating the deeply rooted body tradition is evident here (Flower 1881:12). In addition to permanent changes in head form, the chroniclers prominently mention distinctive native hat forms and other highly visible headgear (Lozada 2011). In the context of oppression, it remains unclear if these head fashions were designed either to hide the forbidden head forms beneath or, quite to the opposite, were to carry on the meanings of altered cranial morphology simply by other means. This is what Lozada (2011) argues for the Collaguas' tall white hats with a peaked top. She holds that this emblematic form was to supplement the originally modeled head forms of the area's native settlers, thus keeping with its original message. This cultural association (between head shape and headwear) still awaits systematic examination for Andean cultures, particularly in view of the lack of studies of skull shapes in Colonial-period cemeteries from the Andes (see also Klaus 2008; Tiffiny Tung and Haagen Klaus, personal communication, 2011).

Less detailed than the Peruvian colonial accounts on native reactions are those from New Spain, where cradleboarding falls silently into disuse and is no longer mentioned in the colonial records after 1570. A dozen post-contact skeletal collections from the Maya territories help to compensate for this lack of written information (Tiesler 2012a; Tiesler and Zabala 2011; Table 10.1). Our research indicates that the frequency of artificial modeling drops from 93 percent during the Late Postclassic period ($N = 127$ examined cranial vaults) to only 31 percent ($N = 77$ examined cranial vaults) among native skeletal populations dated to Colonial times, with evidence hinting at the continued role of cradleboarding in both rural and urban settings at least during the sixteenth century. This reflects the results described for a series from the early colonial cemetery of Tipu, Belize, where the low frequency of cranial modification suggests that bodies were increasingly treated according to Christian norms (see Harvey et al., this volume).

The presence of modified head shapes among individuals buried at an early colonial cemetery from the town of Campeche is especially telling if we take into consideration the direct interaction of natives with other sectors within the social and living spaces of this Hispanic port town, and the sense of rejection and repudiation that it must have caused in their Spanish counterparts (Table 10.1). Especially in the multicultural urban settings, the meaning of pertinence and cultural identity that cranial modification once must have externalized in their native carriers should have been destined to undergo a dialectic transformation to denote not inclusion but exclusion and otherness in the town's new multi-racial and multicultural fabric.

This idea introduces a third element involved in native head-shaping practices, one that must have played a strong role in the process of acculturation: the sense of exodus and cultural failure that surely dominated the minds of many Native Americans during the first two centuries of colonization, doomed by forced resettlement and a progression of deadly diseases,

Table 10.1. Postcontact skeletal samples from the Maya territories that supplement the missing written record in these settings

Archeological site, location, and time frame	Urban/rural settings	Number of artificially modified crania (number of examined individuals)	Type of modification
Central plaza of the town of Campeche, Campeche, Mexico (16th–17th centuries)	urban	7 (45)	Tabular erect
Atrium of the San Francisco Monastery of the town of Campeche, Campeche, Mexico (16th–17th centuries)	urban	4 (6)	Tabular erect
Cathedral of Mérida, Yucatán, Mexico (16th–18th centuries)	urban	0 (6)	No modification
General Cemetery of Mérida, Yucatán, Mexico (recovered 1927)	urban	4 (100)	Irregular frontal flattening (tumpline use) and sagittal grooving
Skull of Caste War leader Bernadino Cen, Xuxub, Quintana Roo, Mexico (19th century)	rural	0 (1)	No modification
Church of Maxcanú, Yucatán, Mexico, (19th century)	rural	0 (1)	No modification
Sihó, Yucatán, Mexico (16th–18th centuries)	rural	1 (1)	Tabular erect
Osumacinta, Chiapas, Mexico (16th–18th centuries)	rural	0 (3)	No modification
Lacandon rock-shelter sanctuaries, Mensabak, Chiapas, Mexico (16th–20th centuries)	rural	21 (21)	Tabular erect

Note: Data from Tiesler 2012a; Tiesler and Zabala 2011.

malnutrition, catastrophic demographic decline, and direct assaults upon their cultures (Chuchiak 2006; see also Harvey et al., this volume). This lowered cultural self-esteem surely worked in favor of the Spanish assimilation efforts, at least in the urban strongholds of the now Iberian-controlled social tapestry (see Chuchiak 2006). If the visible marks of physical embodiment had signaled native social identities and group cohesion before contact, now the flattened cranial vaults were to undergo a dramatic transformation in the bearers' minds, denoting marginalization and otherness (*sensu* the notion of "coloniality" as explored by Guichon et al. in this volume), especially in the urban tapestry of New Spain under the watch of the European newcomers (Tiesler and Oliva 2010:149–150).

The reduced proportion of modeled skulls during this period demonstrates that the popularity of this custom was in decline in Yucatán (Tiesler 2012a). A cemetery sample similar to that of Campeche but a century later in time was documented in the colonial atrium of the Cathedral of Mérida excavated by a team from the Instituto Nacional de Anthropologia e Historia (Tiesler et al. 2003). The approximately twenty burials recovered from the atrium did not show clear signs of head modification, despite the indigenous ancestry that the majority of the skeletons indicate through their dental morphology.

Even though the results cannot be generalized to the rest of the region for lack of more precise chronological information and a sufficient sample size, the urban populations appear to stand out against the native backwaters of colonization, where research does emphasize the continued practice of cranial modification (Fernández Souza et al. 2010; Havill et al. 1997; Saul 1980; Tiesler and Zabala 2011). It will be certainly necessary to expand the framework of these studies in order to assess more specific cultural and social trends, in particular between rural and urbanized Maya populations and of Mesoamerican and Andean populations in general.

RESILIENCE AND SURVIVAL OF NATIVE HEAD-SHAPING PRACTICES AFTER THE COLONIAL PERIOD

Up to this point we have discussed the transformations of native head-shaping practices during colonial times by examining their autochthonous meanings and some other key elements in their enactment. We have examined these facets of head shaping with an eye toward the attitudes and assimilation interests of the Iberian colonizers. We think that among the native neighborhoods of the colonial jurisdictions, such as Mexico, Campeche, and Mérida, head shaping should have been eliminated within one or two generations at the most, and thereafter would be spotted only sporadically on incoming rural folk. This scenario is also confirmed by the information conveyed by a historical skeletal series from the General Cemetery of Mérida, Yucatán (Table 10.1). Its adult population reflects the

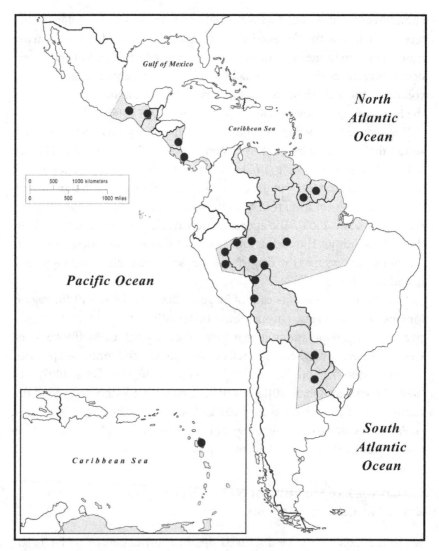

Figure 10.6. Shaded countries with early colonial references on head-shaping practices, and dots indicate places of historical reference in the database (Zabala 2014).

second half of the nineteenth century, a period dominated in Yucatán by the so-called Caste War, a lengthy quarrel between independence-seeking Maya and local Yucatecans of European decent. Among the 100 cranial remains, 3 individuals showed weak signs of frontal flattening, more attributable to tumpline use than to proper cradleboard use. One additional individual exhibited a strong sagittal groove from superior head straps.

So, what about the indigenous dwellers of the vast selvatic stretches that would remain isolated and out of reach of Iberian control well into and beyond the Colonial period? As we have learned from the skeletal record of the rural backwaters of New Spain, here the abandonment of the practice occurred much later than their disappearance from the European centers (Tiesler 2012a) (Figure 10.6). We think that in colonial townships such as Mexico and Campeche, head shaping should have been eliminated within two or three generations at the most.

It appears that head massages and cradleboarding were maintained in native rural areas for centuries after European contact, only gradually to be abandoned or supplanted by other measures of child care. Within the Mesoamerican sphere, continued strongholds of the practice are found in the rural jungle hinterlands of southern Mexico and Guatemala. Namely, the Lago Peten Itzá Maya persisted as an independent native state until being conquered in 1697. Here, skeletal analysis has confirmed the continued use of head shortening that had been so popular in earlier times (Duncan 2009).

Other natives, such as the nomadic Lacandon Maya, maintained a nearly independent lifestyle of isolated hamlets deep in the tropical forest, which were too inaccessible to control. At the turn of the twentieth century, sources still mention Lacandon cradleboard use and relate it to the receding foreheads still observed among the elderly: "the extremely sloping forehead [of elder Lacandon males] was not quite so noticeable in the younger men, and it may be that the custom of binding back the forehead in infancy, which undoubtedly obtained amongst the ancients, is being now abandoned" (Maudslay and Maudslay 1899:236). Further north, in the Maya hinterlands of Santa Elena, eyewitnesses still recall the use of head-compression tablets among Maya families in the Puuc mountains of Yucatán during the second half of the nineteenth century (Omar Antonio Sosa Guillén, personal communication, 2013). Further west, natives from Coatlán in the Mexican state of Oaxaca are portrayed around the same time with a similarly receding forehead and flattened occiput (Shattuck 1933:29; Trias de Bes et al. 1928:84; Figure 10.7).

Unsurprisingly, the changes and final substitution of Mesoamerican infant head compression did not relate so much to its visible outcome, which had not been the prime motive still before the contact, as we have argued above. Instead, the transformations in head-shaping practices responded likely to the needs of animate protection and strengthening of living energies within the baby. Other measures, deemed suitable to supplant the

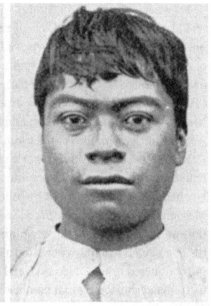

Figure 10.7. View of head of Mixe from Coatlán, Oaxaca, showing inclined forehead and occiput (Trias de Bes et al. 1928:84).

protective role that cradleboard practices had always held, were now called upon. Waddling rituals, baths, wraps, covers, and massages of the newborn's body were equally deemed apt to stabilize its health and guarantee the harmonious transformation into the person it was to be. Many of these measures are still part of today's Mesoamerican indigenous heritage and are enacted by mothers and female kin on a daily basis (Duncan 2009:187–188; Guiteras Holmes 1986:102; León Pasquel 2005:128–136; Tiesler 2011, 2014:252–253).

Except for some remote highland valleys in Bolivia, we could not find any historical reference of continued practice from the second half of the seventeenth century to the present within the Andean cultural domain. We infer from this that the prohibitions by the colonial authorities must have taken their toll rapidly. This is also the scenario projected by a recently documented cranial series from the colonial period Lambayeque Valley on the Peruvian north coast (Klaus 2008:497, 557). The skulls that are dated to the Early and Middle Colonial period attest the lack of cultural flatting, which suggests an abrupt and complete extermination of an infant cradle practice that in this area had been continually practiced for at least two thousand years.

Only in the Bolivian Andes was head shaping still officially suppressed voiced past independence. Head shaping continued to be described in 1912 in isolated parts of the Bolivian highlands and among some native inhabitants around the shores of Lake Titicaca (Dingwall 1931:214). The Bolivian national government prohibited its practice still at the turn of the twentieth century (Forbes 1870; Topinard [1886] in Dingwall 1931:25–26), a clear sign that for centuries, head-compression techniques had continued to be in place on the fringes of Iberian society. The resilience of this native tradition underlines once more its importance in native life and demonstrates the failure of colonial pressures.

Recent head-shaping practices have been documented also east of the Andes, namely, among several native Amazonian groups, such as the Shipibo Conibo and the Omagua (Figure 10.8). Also, other remote settings further south and north, such as the Panamenian Cuna or the Carribean Ulwas of Karawala in Costa Rica, head-compression devices were still used

Figure 10.8. Ucayali Indian mother and child, Peru. The child is wearing a device used to intentionally deform the head, causing a flattening of the cranium (photo by F. W. Chaffey).

Figure 10.9. Wood engraving of Omagua group showing mitre-shaped head morphologies, Condamine Amazonian Brasil tour to the Omagua Indians during 1774 (adapted by the authors from Édouard Riou 1875). *Inset*: Omagua couple in costume with blowgun, near Marquor River, Amazonia, Peru (National Anthropological Archives, Smithsonian Museum Support Center, Suitland, Maryland, photograph collection from ca. 1860s to 1960s).

until the nineteenth and twentieth centuries. Such was also the case among surviving natives in the Caribbean, where Leblond (1813) witnessed infants wearing head boards during his travels to the Antilles. The French missionary Father Borde (1886) mentions the custom around that same time in Surinam, Guayana Británica, and Stedman (2010 [1790]) describes it as identity consignment and status dependent among some isolated Dutch Guyana communities, whereas more-exposed native groups ceased the practice by the eighteenth and early nineteenth centuries.

As in the Andes, Amazonian compression procedures appear to have been substituted by other suitable means of showing head form, including Omagua hats and specific headwear that emulated the morphological results of infant binding (Figure 10.9). We may wonder if this substitution, purposeful or not, was a way to perpetuate the original meanings attached to the custom, to conserve cultural coherence, or to confer identity and ethnic pertinence.

A change in European judgment is also worth considering when comparing sources. If the early colonial sources still had underscored the "aberrant" and heretical qualities of the practice, its witnesses of the eighteenth and nineteenth centuries would highlight its physiognomic results with racist undertones. Less importance is given to the head procedures or its cultural embedded meanings, as Alcedo Herrera's mention from 1883 on the Misquito of Honduras and Nicaragua shows (Conzemius 1932; see also Román Solano 2012): "These flatheaded monsters have the custom of splinting babies upon birth and when they grow up they are missing a forehead, without any space between the hairs of the head to the hairs in the eyebrows, which makes them unimaginably horrible" (in Conzemius 1932:28; translated by Maria Fernanda Boza).

Finally, into the twentieth century, these undertones gave way to more culturally sensitive ethnographic approaches, which consent to emic perspectives when assigning the roles of these traditions within broader cultural frames. These efforts are recognized in many of the recent anthropological surveys. These accounts of vanishing head-shaping practices allow rare last glimpses, evoking more or less nuanced native notions of totem emulation, ethnic identity, and beauty among the Omagua, the Conibo, and the Shipibo of eastern Peru (Comas 1958; Illius 1987; Tessmann 1930; Veigl 1798).

Conclusions

We have learned in the course of this work that the diversity in meanings and outcomes of head transformations reflect upon a host of aspects, some of them autochthonous (enactment and visible qualities of head shaping), while others related to the attitudes toward and active suppression of native head modeling by the European colonizers and indigenous resilience strategies. It is clear from this survey that the native reactions to European suppression efforts, whether in the form of continuing and hiding, substituting, transforming, or abandoning altogether infant head modeling, were active and diverse and did not progress uniformly within the broader sphere of Iberian America. We conclude that the changes occurred, quite unsurprisingly, more rapidly in the Iberian strongholds of Iberian America. This is especially true in the southern and central Andean world, most of whose inhabitants carried strong and distinctive cranial vault modifications, which—at least before contact—openly signaled the ethnic identity and social distinction of their human carriers. In the new colonial order, they were subsequently subject to cultural and legal alienation, finally to be substituted by other, equally visible forms of headwear.

In Mesoamerica, where practically only a single type of culturally produced head shape persisted at the time of contact, the Spaniards targeted cradleboarding itself, which vanished first among the natives residing in the Iberian-dominated urban centers and much later in more remote native peripheries of colonial power. Here and in other parts of Latin America, the shifts in acting out resilient, embedded native cultural elements were expressed by transformation and substitution, as the head-compression instruments were supplanted gradually by other infant head-shaping practices. These were deemed similarly effective by their native practitioners to protect and prepare, to imbue with vital energies, and to balance the life of the growing child. Unsurprisingly, those peoples that were too remote or simply unapproachable to the Iberian colonizers continued to reproduce ancestral head-shaping practices for centuries to come.

In closing, this chapter has explored the direct and indirect impact of European colonization on indigenous head-shaping traditions in Iberian America, specifically on Mesoamerican cultures and the Andean world. The combination of multi-scaled analyses (from the continental to the local scale) of discursive historical media and bioarchaeological information (although admittedly incomplete) provides invaluable points of departure to not only examine the original roles that these long-standing body modification practices held in their communities but also to understand the underlying social and cultural dynamics involved in the diverse native experiences and outcomes of the entanglements past the European contact. Taken together, the different native trajectories of head-shaping practices provide fascinating glimpses on the colonial and postcolonial interactions between non-native and native peoples and ideas and illustrate different forms of assimilation, substitution, and resistance, which were sadly not captured in most historical or documentary sources. The active notion of native resilience in the light of unprecedented change and crisis has been one of the discoveries of this work.

ACKNOWLEDGMENTS

We are grateful to Haagen Klaus and Jorge Gómez Valdés for their useful advice and help. We also wish to credit and thank the following projects and institutions for providing access to the skeletal series illustrated or mentioned in this chapter: the Proyecto Arqueológico Parque Principal de Campeche; Proyecto Arqueológico Atrio del Templo de San Francisco, Campeche (Centro INAH Campeche); Proyecto Arqueológico T'ho, Catedral de Mérida (Centro INAH Yucatán); Dirección de Antropología Física/INAH: Archaeological Site of Osumacinta, Chiapas; Museo Na Bolom, San Cristóbal de las Casas, Chiapas: Frans Blom Archaeological Collections; Proyecto Arqueológico Mensabak, Chiapas (University of Illinois at Chicago; Proyecto Xanvil, Chiapas); and the Peabody Museum at Harvard University (Cementerio General de Mérida). Lastly, we are indebted to Antonio Sosa Guillén for sharing with us his family testimonies from the times of the Caste War at Santa Elena, Yucatán.

NOTES

1. In this chapter we use the terms "head shaping," "cranial vault modification," "cranial modeling," and "molding" synonymously to refer to the artificial compression or constriction of the infant's head during the first months and years of life. Many authors distinguish "intentional" modifications from "unintentional cradleboarding." While we do not deny that some cranial vault changes could have been unintentional by-products of infant-carrying devices, we will avoid this term here. We think that the distinction oversimplifies the multi-layered meanings of most native head-compression practices, some of which were clearly unrelated to the visible head morphology (Tiesler, 2011, 2012b, 2014). Therefore, we will refer to it as "cranial vault modification" or "head shaping."

2. Colonial documents were examined from the Archivo General de Indias (Seville) (AGI), Patronato 189, R. 40, and the Archivo Histórico Nacional (Madrid) (AHN), Diversos-Colecciones, 31 N.96.

References Cited

Anonymous
1977 [1541]   *Relación de Michoacán*. Translated by J. Tudela. Balsas Editores Morelia.
Barrera-Vásquez, A.
1938   Introducción. In *Relación de las cosas de Yucatán*. E. G. Triay e Hijos, Mérida.
Blom, D. E.
2005a   Embodying Borders: Human Body Modification and Diversity in Tiwanaku
              Society. *Journal of Anthropological Archaeology* 24:1–24.
2005b   A Bioarchaeological Approach to Tiwanaku Group Dynamics. In *Us and
              Them: Archaeology and Ethnicity in the Andes*, edited by R. M. Reycraft, pp.
              153–182. Monograph 53, Costen Institute of Archaeology at University of
              California, Los Angeles.
Blom, D. E., B. Hallgrimsson, L. Keng, M. C. Lozada, and J. E. Buikstra
1998   Tiwanaku "Colonization": Bioarchaeological Implications for Migration in
              Moquegua Valley, Peru. *World Archaeology* 30:238–261.
Borde, P. de la
1886   History of the Origin, Religion, Wars and Travels of the Caribs. Translation
              by G. J. Bosch-Reitz. *Timehri* 5:224–254.
Braudel, F.
1974   *La historia y las ciencias sociales*. Alianza Editorial, Madrid.
Buikstra, J. E.
1995   Tombs for the Living . . . or . . . for the Dead: The Osmore Ancestors. In
              Tombs for the Living: Andean Mortuary Practices, edited by T. D. Dillehay,
              pp. 229–280. Dumbarton Oaks, Washington, D.C.
Casas, B. de las
1967   *Apologética historia sumaria*. Vols. 1 and 2, edited by E. O'Gorman. Univer-
              sidad Nacional Autónoma de México, Mexico City.
Chávez, M.
2016   Modificaciones craneales como posibles medidas de cuidado y potencial-
              ización de las energías anímicas en el análisis de textos coloniales en maya
              yucateco. In *Modificaciones cefálicas culturales en Mesoamérica: Una perspec-
              tiva continental*, edited by V. Tiesler and C. Serrano. Universidad Nacional
              Autónoma de México, Mexico City, in press.
Chuchiak, J. F., IV
2006   Yaab Uih Yetal Maya Cimil: Colonial Plagues, Famines, Catastrophes and
              their Impact on Changing Yucatec Maya Concepts of Death & Dying, 1570–
              1794." In *Jaws of the Underworld: Life, Death, and Rebirth among the Ancient
              Maya*, edited by P. Colas, G. LeFort, and B. L. Tersson, pp. 3–18. Acta Meso-
              americana 16. Markt Schwaben, Anton Saurwein, Munich.
Cieza de León, P.
1984   *La crónica del Perú*. Manuel Ballesteros, Madrid.
Comas, J.
1958   La deformación cefálica intencional en la región del Ucayali, Perú. *Miscel-*

lánea Paul Rivet Octogenario Dicata, II. Universidad Nacional Autónoma de México, Mexico City.

Conzemius, E.
1932   Ethnographical Survey of the Miskito and Sumo Indians of Honduras and Nicaragua. Bulletin 106. Smithsonian Institution, Washington, D.C.

Dávalos Hurtado, E.
1951   La deformación craneana entre los tlatelolca. Tesis de licenciatura y maestría en Antropología Física, Escuela Nacional de Antropología e Historia. Instituto Nacional de Antropología e Historia, Mexico City.

Dembo, A., and J. Imbelloni
1938   Deformaciones intencionales del cuerpo humano de carácter étnico. Biblioteca Humanior, Buenos Aires.

Dingwall, E. J.
1931   Artificial Cranial Deformation: A Contribution to the Study of Ethnic Mutilations. Bale & Sons & Danielsson, London.

D'Olwer, L. N.
1963   Cronistas de las culturas precolombinas. Serie de Cronistas de Indias, Fondo de Cultura Económica, Mexico City.

Duncan, W. N.
2009   Cranial Modification among the Maya: Absence of Evidence or Evidence of Absence? In Bioarchaeology and Identity in the Americas, edited by K. J. Knudson and C. M. Stojanowski, pp. 177–193. University Press of Florida, Gainesville.

Duncan, W. N., and C. A Hofling.
2011   Why the Head? Cranial Modification as Protection and Ensoulment among the Maya. Ancient Mesoamerica 22:199–210.

Fernández Souza, L., R. Cobos Palma, S. Jiménez Álvarez, C. Götz, and V. Tiesler
2010   Morir al fijo del tiempo: Un entierro infantil colonial en urna en Sihó, Yucatán. Mexicon 32:82–87.

Flower, W. H.
1881   Fashion in Deformity. Humboldt, New York.

Forbes, D.
1870   On the Aymara Indians of Bolivia and Peru. Journal of the Ethnological Society of London 2:193–305.

Fournier García, P.
1999   La arqueología del colonialismo en Iberoamérica: Balance y perspectivas. Boletín de Antropología Americana 34:75–87.

Guiteras Holmes, C.
1986   Los peligros del alma: Versión del mundo tzotzil. 2nd ed. Fondo de Cultura Económica, Mexico City.

Havill, L. M., D. M. Warren, K. P. Jacobi, K. D. Gettelman, D. C. Cook, and K. A. Pyburn
1997   Late Postclassic Tooth Filing at Chau Hiix and Tipu, Belize. In Bones of the Maya: Studies of Ancient Skeletons, edited by S. L. Whittington and D. M. Reed, pp. 89–104. Smithsonian Institution Press, Washington, D.C.

Hernández, F.
2001   Antigüedades de la Nueva España. Dastin, Madrid.

Hoshower, L. M., J. E. Buikstra, P. Goldstein, and A. Webster
1995   Artificial Cranial Deformation at the OMO M10 Site: A Tiwanaku Complex from the Moquegua Valley, Peru. Latin American Antiquity 6:145–164.

Illius, B.
1987   Ani Shinan: Schamanismus bei den Shipibo-Conibo (Ost-Peru). Ethnologische Studien 12, S&F Tübingen, Münster.

Imbelloni, J.
1932   América, cuartel general de las deformaciones craneanas. Memorias del XXV Congreso Internacional de Americanistas, 1:59–68. Universidad Nacional de La Plata, Buenos Aires.

Klaus, H. D.
2008   Out of Light Came Darkness: Bioarchaeology of Mortuary Ritual, Health, and Ethnogenesis in the Lambayeque Valley Complex, North Coast of Peru (A.D. 900–1750). Unpublished Ph.D. dissertation, Department of Anthropology, Ohio State University, Columbus.

Latcham, R. E.
1929   Las creencias religiosas de los antiguos Peruanos. Balcells, Santiago de Chile.

Leblond, J.-B.
1813   Voyage aux Antilles. Paris.

León Pasquel, M. de Lourdes
2005   La llegada del alma, lenguaje, infancia y socialización entre los mayas de Zinacantán. Instituto Nacional de Antropología e Historia, Mexico City.

López Austin, A.
1989   Cuerpo humano e ideología (las concepciones de los antiguos Nahuas). Universidad Nacional Autónoma de México, Mexico City.
2001   El núcleo duro, las cosmovisión y la tradición Mesoamericana. In, Cosmovisión, Ritual e Identitdad de los Pueblos Indígenas de México, edited by J. Broda and F. Baez-Jorge, pp. 47–65. CONACULTA, Fondo de Cultura Económica, Mexico City.

López de Gómara, F.
1987 [1552] La historia de la conquista de México. Collección Crónica de America, Historia 16, Madrid.

Lozada, M. C.
2011   Marking Ethnicity through Premortem Cranial Modification among the Pre-Inca Chiribaya, Perú. In The Bioarchaeology of the Human Head: Decapitation, Decoration, and Deformation, edited by M. Bonogofsky, pp. 228–240. University Press of Florida, Gainesville.

Lozada, M. C., and J. E. Buikstra
2002   El Señorío de Chiribaya en la costa sur del Perú. Instituto de Estudios Peruanos, Lima.

Lucena, M.
2005   Atlas histórico de Latinoamérica desde la prehistoria hasta el siglo XXI. Editorial Síntesis, Madrid.

Maudslay, A. C., and A. P. Maudslay
1899   *Glimpse of Guatemala.* John Murray, London.
Pardal, R.
1938   La deformación intencional del cráneo por los indios de América. *Actas Ciba* 3:67–81.
Pereira, G.
1999   *Potrero de Guadalupe: Anthropologie funéraire d'une communauté pré-Tarasque du Nord du Michoacán, Mexique.* British Archaeological Research International Series No. 816. Archaeopress, Oxford.
Purizaga Vega, M.
1991   *El rito del nacimiento entre los Inca.* Universidad de San Martín de Porres, Lima.
Romano Pacheco, A.
1972   Un cráneo precerámico con deformación intencional. *Boletín del INAH, 2a época* 1:35–36. Instituto Nacional de Antropología e Historia, Mexico City.
1974   Deformación cefálica intencional. In *Antropología física, época prehispánica*, edited by J. Comas, pp. 197–227. Instituto Nacional de Antropología e Historia, Mexico City.
Román Solano, D.
2012   A forma e as aparências: Historia e vida social dos Ulwas de Karawala, Caribe Nicaragüense. Unpublished Ph.D. dissertation, Universidad do Brasil, Brasilia.
Sahagún, B.
1989   *Historia general de las cosas de Nueva España.* Porrúa, Mexcio City.
Santa Cruz Pachacuti ,Y. S. J.
1879 [1613]   *Relación de antigüedades desde Reyno de Perú: Tres relaciones de ant. Perú, etc.* Madrid.
Saul, F. P.
1980   Appendix II: The Human Skeletal Remains from Tankah, Mexico. In *On the Edge of the Sea: Mural Painting at Tancah and Tulum*, by A. G. Miller, pp. 115–128. Dumbarton Oaks, Washington, D.C.
Shattuck, G. C.
1933   *The Peninsula of Yucatan: Medical, Biological, Meteorological and Sociological Studies.* Carnegie Institute of Washington, Washington, D.C.
Stedman, J. G.
2010 [1790]   *Narrative of a Five Years Expedition against the Revolted Negroes of Surinam.* Price and Price, New York.
Stein, G. J.
2005   Introduction: The Comparative Archaeology of Colonial Encounters. In *The Archaeology of Colonial Encounters: Comparative Perspectives*, edited by G. J. Stein, pp. 3–31. School of American Research Press, Santa Fe, New Mexico.
Tessmann, G.
1930   *Die Indianer Nordosten Perus.* Friederichsen, De Gruyter, Hamburg.

Tiesler, V.

2011   Becoming Maya: Infancy and Upbringing through the Lens of Pre-Hispanic Head Shaping. *Childhood in the Past* 4:117–132.

2012a   *Transformarse en Maya: El modelado cefálico entre los Mayas prehispánicos y coloniales.* Universidad Autónoma de Yucatán, Universidad Nacional Autónoma de México, Mexico City.

2012b   Studying Cranial Vault Modifications in Ancient Mesoamerica. *Journal of Anthropological Sciences* 90:1–26.

2014   *The Bioarchaeology of Artificial Cranial Modifications: New Approaches to Head Shaping and Its Meanings in Pre-Columbian Mesoamerica and Beyond.* Springer Press, New York.

Tiesler, V., and I. Oliva

2010   Identity, Alienation, and Integration: Body Modifications in the Early Colonial Population from Campeche. In *Natives, Europeans, and Africans in Colonial Campeche: History and Archaeology*, edited by V. Tiesler, P. Zabala, and A. Cucina, pp. 130–151. University Press of Florida, Gainesville.

Tiesler, V., and P. Zabala

2011   El modelado artificial de la cabeza durante la colonia: Una tradición maya en el espejo de las fuentes históricas. *Estudios de Cultura Maya* 38:75–96.

Tiesler, V., P. Zabala, and A. Peña Castillo

2003   Vida y muerte en Mérida durante los siglos XVI y XVII: Rescate de las osamentas del atrio de la catedral. In *Mérida-Miradas múltiples: Investigaciones de antropología social, arqueología e historia*, edited by F. F. Repetto and J. H. Fuentes Gómez, pp. 41–55. Cámara de Diputados, Mérida.

Toledo, F. de

1929 [1573] *Ordenanzas de Don Francisco de Toledo, Virrey del Perú 1569–1581.* Edited by R. Levillier. Imprenta de Juan Pueyo Madrid.

Torquemada, J. de.

1723   *Parte de los veynte y un libros rituales y Onarquia Indiana.* Madrid.

Torres-Rouff, C.

2009   The Bodily Expression of Ethnic Identity: Head Shaping in the Chilean Atacama. In *Bioarchaeology and Identity in the Americas*, edited by K. J. Knudson and C. M. Stojanowski, pp. 212–227. University Press of Florida, Gainesville.

Tozzer, A. M.

1941   Landa's *Relación de las Cosas de Yucatán.* Peabody Museum, Harvard University, Cambridge.

Trejo, S.

2007   Xochiquétzal y Tlazoltéotl: Diosas mexicas del amor y la sexualidad. *Arqueología Mexicana* 15:18–25.

Trias de Bes, L., P. Bosch Gimpera, J. C. Serra-Ràfols, D. J. Batista y Roca, and D. A. del Castillo Yurrita

1928   *Las razas humanas: Su vida, sus costumbres, su arte.* Vol. 2. Instituto Gallach, Barcelona.

Ullúa y Mogollón, J. de
1965 [1586]   Relación de la Provincia de los Collaguas. In *Relaciones geográficas de Indias*, edited by M. Jiménez de la Espada, Vol. 2, pp. 326–333. Biblioteca de Autores Españoles Vol. 183, Madrid.

Veigl, F. X.
1798   *Gründliche Nachrichten üher die Verfassung Landschaft von Maynas in Süd-Amerika bis zum Jahre*. Bey Johann Eberhard Zeh, Nürnberg.

Weiss, P.
1958   *Osteología cultural: Prácticas cefálicas*. 1a parte: *Cabezas trofeos, trepanaciones, cauterizaciones*. Universidad Nacional de San Marcos, Lima.
1961   *Osteología cultural: Prácticas cefálicas*. 2a parte. *Tipología de la deformaciones cefálicos y de algunas enfermedades seas*. Universidad Nacional de San Marcos, Lima.

Yepez Vásquez, Z. L.
2006   La práctica cultural de modelar la cabeza en dos culturas andinas del antiguo Perú: Paracas y Chancay. Un estudio de los procesos de significación de la cabeza modelada intencionalmente. Ph.D. dissertation, Facultad de Filosofía y Letras/Instituto de Investigaciones Antropológicas, Universidad Nacional Autónoma de México, Mexico City.
2009   El simbolismo de la modificación cultural de la cabeza en la ultura andina de paracas del antiguo Perú. In *Estudios de antropología biológica, Vol. XIV, Tomo II*, pp. 526–543. Universidad Nacional Autónoma de México, Instituto Nacional de Antropología e Historia, Asociación Mexicana de Antropología Biológica, Mexico City.

Zabala, P.
2014   Appendix: Source Compilation on Head-Shaping Practices in Hispanic America. In *The Bioarchaeology of Artificial Cranial Modifications: New Approaches to Head Shaping and Its Meanings in Pre-Columbian and Colonial Mesoamerica*, edited by V. Tiesler, pp. 99–127. Springer, New York.

11

A Glimpse of the Ancien Régime in the French Colonies?

A Consideration of Ancestry and Health at the Moran Site (22HR511), Biloxi, Mississippi

MARIE ELAINE DANFORTH, DANIELLE N. COOK, J. LYNN FUNKHOUSER,
BARBARA T. HESTER, AND HEATHER GUZIK

The New World territories of France stretched from modern-day Canada to the Gulf Coast and also included parts of the Caribbean and northern coast of South America. Although great cultural diversity existed among the various regions (Pritchard 2007), one tenet that guided much of the organization of the French colonies, at least at an idealistic level, was the opportunity they represented to establish a revived version of the ancien régime, the strict hierarchical system that had dominated French social and economic life since the Middle Ages. As Allain (1988:70) has noted, "the colonies should be extensions of the mother country . . . very much like old France, but improved," with all the inhabitants "blend[ing] into a harmonious, orderly whole, white settlers, converted Indians, and in the case of Louisiana, contented black laborers." European Catholics were regarded as the foundation of this new society, serving to edify the non-European and non-Catholic segments of the population (Spear 2009). However, the ancien régime required social and often spatial separation of the various ethnic, gender, religious, and economic contingencies, the imposition of which was ultimately enshrined in the establishment of the *Code noir* in Louisiana in 1724 (Spear 2009).

The establishment of the European foundation was challenging, however. France sought to economically exploit the colonies to replenish her coffers that had been depleted from decades of warfare (Giraud 1966). Strict administrative policies were set in place that overregulated immigration and stifled individual economic success (Briggs 1985:22–25, 31). In 1750, New France had but seventy thousand European residents, as compared to more than one million in the English territories, which controlled less than half the amount of land. In the more northern areas of New France, where the fur trade was especially lucrative, representatives of the Crown sought to compensate for the small population through the creation and maintenance of political and economic alliances with local Native American communities (White 1991), alliances that often were based on marriage ties that produced children.

In Louisiana, however, another strategy was employed. The Crown turned over financial proprietorship of the struggling colony to private financiers, first Antoine Crozat in 1712, then Scotsman John Law in 1717 (Giraud 1966). As part of his contract, Law agreed to bring thirty-five hundred Africans and five thousand Europeans to Louisiana to work the concessions along the Mississippi River and Gulf Coast. The Africans would be organized as part of the slave trade, but in order to provide the promised number of Europeans, efforts involving enticement through propaganda were undertaken. When they failed, officials resorted to forced roundups of social undesirables in Europe, particularly in urban centers of France, in order to obtain immigrants.

New Biloxi, located on modern-day Mississippi Gulf Coast, was the capital of the Louisiana colony from 1719 to 1722 during the height of the power of Law and the Company of the Indies. It also served as a staging area for one of the largest efforts to bring immigrants to the region (Giraud 1966), with local Native Americans being an essential part of the community as well. However, little information exists concerning the extent of interaction of these groups, specifically, whether the rules of the ancien régime were being successfully enforced, or, as was seen at the slightly later St. Peter Street Cemetery (Owsley and Orser 1984; Owsley et al. 1987), the rules seem to have been disregarded in the frontier community.

In 2009, Hurricane Katrina exposed a cemetery that dates to this often overlooked period in the history of the French colonial efforts in the New World, and evaluation of the human remains present has the potential to lend data to answer this question. In this chapter we examine demographic patterns, especially ancestry, seen among the 32 burials recovered, based on a variety of skeletal indicators. Because health and social standing are integrally connected, findings will also be discussed in the light of a number of stress markers that were also assessed as the lives of the individuals in this unusual colonial setting are explored. Although comparatively little is noted in the historical records about those who were interred at New Biloxi, fortunately, as Stojanowski has observed (2010:3), the human body offers "a more enduring and impartial record of experience."

THE BIOARCHAEOLOGY OF NEW FRANCE

Compared to the number of colonial Spanish and even British sites that have yielded human remains, relatively few French sites from the era been the focus of cemetery excavations. Not surprisingly, several cemeteries from the seventeenth and eighteenth centuries have been investigated in eastern Canada, especially Montreal and Quebec City (e.g., Gagné 1995; Larocque 1995; Larocque and Gagné 1981), where the large majority of the French population in the New World resided. Other remains have been identified at French sites in the Caribbean region, specifically, Sainte-Marguerite in Guadeloupe (Courtaud and Romon 2004) and in French Guiana (Bain et al. 2011). However, only six sites yielding skeletal material have been found in the United States. The oldest dates to the early seventeenth century, with a cemetery containing the burials of 25 sailors who died of scurvy on St. Croix Island, Maine, as they waited out the winter (Crist n.d.; Hadlock 1950; Harrington and Hadlock 1951; also Crist and Sorg 2014). Three other sites at which human remains have been excavated—Fort Michilimackinac (20EM51) in Michigan (Stone 1974), Fort Ouiatenon in Indiana (Noble 1977; Sauer et al. 1988), and Fort Rosalie (22AD999) in Mississippi (Manhein et al. 2003)—were outposts established along the waterways around 1715, operating after Queen Anne's War in order to facilitate the valuable fur trade, which had become the backbone of New France, and to protect it from English and Spanish incursion. The final two cemeteries—St. Peter Street (16OR92) in New Orleans (Listi and Manhein 2012; Owsley and Orser 1984; Owsley et al. 1987) and Moran (22HR511) in Biloxi (Danforth et al. 2013)—were recovered at sites with functions quite different from the others.' Both New Orleans and Biloxi served at various times as the capital of the Louisiana colony and thus were arguably under more direct administrative control concerning French colonial policy.

St. Peter Street Cemetery was first revealed in the mid-1980s during construction of a condominium complex. It was excavated by Owsley et al. (Owsley and Orser 1984; Owsley et al. 1987), and the remains of some 29 individuals were recovered. In 2012 an additional 15 individuals were found during further construction activity in the area (Listi and Manhein

2012). The site was identified as the first cemetery in New Orleans based on historical records, and was in use from about 1725 until 1788, when it was closed after being designated a public health hazard. Bioarchaeological analysis showed most individuals to be of African ancestry, and thus it was most likely a slave cemetery. However, Owsley et al. (1987) identified three individuals, all adult males, of likely European ancestry based on cranial and facial morphology. Additionally, three individuals of possible admixed ancestry were noted, including a young adult male and a young adult female who exhibited morphological traits suggestive of both European and African ancestry, and a child who was thought to be of European and Native American parentage as evidenced by presence of shovel-shaped incisors.

Although presumably the *Code noir* had become an essential part of Louisiana society by the time most of the burials in St. Peter Street Cemetery took place, the findings of Owsley et al. (1987) challenge the success of its segregationist policies, especially as they applied in the most intimate aspects of life. Written records from the time, including census categories such as Creole, acknowledge the presence of individuals of mixed ancestry. Dawdy (2008) has argued that the bioarchaeological data also show that the rules of the *Code noir* were not adhered to in death, since individuals of European and African ancestry were found interred next to each other (Owsley and Orser 1984; Owsley et al. 1987). Furthermore, the individuals thought to be of admixed ancestry also were buried in close proximity possibly indicative of family plots, supporting the existence of consensual *métissage*, which had always been presumed to exist by historians despite the strict social regulations.

Dawdy believes this flaunting of the rules was tied to the nature of the New Orleans community itself, noting that "the mobility, clutter and noise of a town facilitated escape from social containment. Sailors, runaways, and vagabonds were inspired to jump the bounds of their worlds . . . as *les petits* mixed and corrupted one another" (2008:141). This description aptly illustrates the ideas of Horowitz (1975:131), who suggests that when faced with "objectification from above or beyond," individual ethnic differences within a populace are minimized and factors they share in common are enhanced.

Given these findings, the concepts of segregation and mixing in French colonial society were investigated at a roughly contemporaneous cemetery located on the shores of the Mississippi Sound in Biloxi. Those interred at the cemetery at the Moran site are believed to be part of Scottish financier

John Law's efforts to settle the Louisiana colony in a failed scheme that became known as the Mississippi Bubble. His Company of the West, which was given financial proprietorship of the colony by the French Crown in 1717, initially attempted to recruit immigrants from Europe, especially France, Germany, and Switzerland, using propaganda presenting Biloxi as an almost idyllic setting. When word got back concerning the dismal conditions at the site, the number of volunteer immigrants evaporated. Instead, the city streets of France were reportedly swept to collect up convicts, prostitutes, salt smugglers, indigents, blasphemous youth, and other undesirables; even asylums were emptied at times to fill the boats coming to the Gulf Coast (Allain 1988; Conrad 1970; Giraud 1966). In fact, many administrators believed that bringing them to Louisiana might help to rehabilitate some of these social outcasts. Ultimately, up to twenty-five hundred Europeans made the trip to New Biloxi between 1717 and 1723, mostly without their consent.

Other ethnicities were represented at New Biloxi as well. Historical documents note the arrival of several shiploads of Africans during the early seventeenth century (Hall 1992), and a 1722 map records an African Habitation Area on the north side of the Biloxi peninsula, a few miles from the proposed Fort Louis (Figure 11.1). Interestingly, this site was found near the main source of clay in the region, and a brick works is also demarcated in the area on the map. It is possible that the slaves were used in part for brick production. Giraud (1966) states that the slaves frequently had skills that were prized in the community and that European immigrants were often sent to conduct more dangerous activities so as to protect the more highly valued commodity. Unfortunately, no archaeological evidence for Giraud's conjecture has been found for the habitation area. That region of the Biloxi peninsula has endured much erosion as well as development, which together may have destroyed any remnants of the site (Hester 2008). One other possibility is that the habitation area was never built. Other features noted on the period map, such as Fort Louis, existed only as plans on paper, which is not surprising given the short time span in which French colonial New Biloxi was in operation.

At New Biloxi there was also extensive contact with local Native American populations, primarily through trade interactions. The local Pascagoula and Biloxi tribes often supplied food to the New Biloxi community, especially hominy, meat, and sagamity, and during times of provisioning shortage, administrators sent some of the Europeans to live with the indigenous groups (Usner 1990:36). They also likely provided goods such as

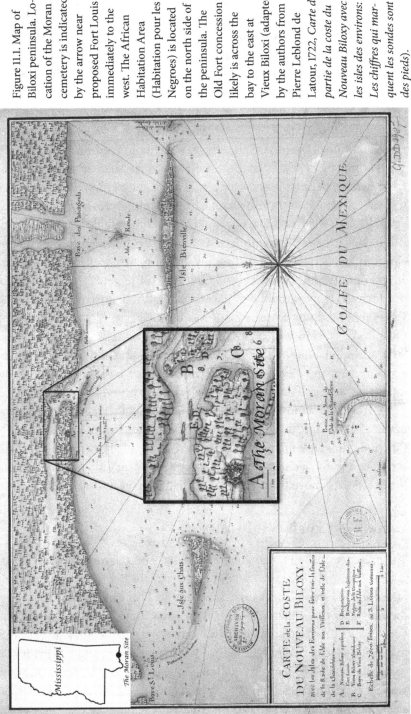

Figure 11.1. Map of Biloxi peninsula. Location of the Moran cemetery is indicated by the arrow near proposed Fort Louis immediately to the west. The African Habitation Area (Habitation pour les Negroes) is located on the north side of the peninsula. The Old Fort concession likely is across the bay to the east at Vieux Biloxi (adapted by the authors from Pierre Leblond de Latour, 1722, *Carte de partie de la coste du Nouveau Biloxy avec les isles des environs: Les chiffres qui marquent les sondes sont des pieds*).

baskets and ceramics and may have performed some paid labor, such as rowing pirogues (small boats used in shallow waters) (Usner 1990:60–61). Some of the Native Americans in the region were enslaved (Giraud 1966; Usner 1990:56–59), and occasionally the women became the wives of European men (Duval 2008) in the Louisiana colony, but the extent of either practice at New Biloxi is not known.

When the various immigrants, both African and European, arrived in New Biloxi, instead finding a New World utopia, they were met with horrific conditions (DuPratz 1947). Too few flat-bottomed boats were available to carry them inland, so the immigrants languished for months on the coast, where, because stays were meant to be temporary, there had been limited investment in infrastructure. The promised provisioning also was sporadic, and when it did arrive, food was often inedible from decomposition. Nevertheless, the immigrants reportedly preferred to wait for the wheat to arrive rather than eat locally grown maize, which they regarded as appropriate only for animals (Giraud 1966). The sandy soil also was not conducive to crops, should they have tried to plant them. DuPratz (1947:29) writes that food was so scarce that rats on the beaches resorted to eating the gunstocks. Under such circumstances, infectious disease, such as malaria, was rampant as it was compounded by widespread malnutrition. In a sad irony, many died from eating contaminated oysters, one of the few foods that were available. Many of the unfortunate immigrants—estimates range from five hundred to nine hundred—ultimately perished from the devastating circumstances (Conrad 1970; DuPratz 1947; Giraud 1966). At this same time, the financial scheme that Law had created to support his activities at New Biloxi imploded. This perfect storm ultimately resulted in the decision to move the capital of Louisiana to New Orleans in 1722.

The Moran Cemetery (22HR511)

The presence of the French colonial cemetery on the Moran family property was first identified in 1969 during repair to the foundation of their house and art studio after Hurricane Camille. Local archaeologists located the remains of 12 individuals. Based on a few grave goods recovered, the burials were presumed to date to the early eighteenth century. The skeletal material was then covered in shellac so as to preserve it, and was left *in situ* under the house (Greenwell 2008). In 2003, faculty and students from the University of Southern Mississippi were allowed to go under the art studio and reexamine the burials. The limited analysis suggested that most of the

8 individuals present (4 individuals appear to have been lost during subsequent construction to the property) exhibited European features, and a carbon-14 test of a bone sample confirmed the early colonial date (Carter et al. 2004).

In 2005, Hurricane Katrina destroyed the house and art studio and in turn commingled the previously exposed 8 individuals. Subsequent salvage excavations resulted in the recovery of an additional 20 individuals, providing a total of 32 for the site (Cook 2011; Cook et al. 2010; Danforth 2011; Danforth et al. 2013; Funkhouser 2014). As seen in Figure 11.2, most of the interments were oriented either north or south, but the cemetery in general displays little regularity in burial spacing or depth. Only two individuals were in coffins, one of whom was placed over the remains of two other individuals. Because of he sand midden and proximity of the cemetery to the shore, there is no stratigraphic evidence that would demarcate the grave shafts and determine whether it occurred as a single event. The rest of the interred appear to have been buried naked in shrouds, since no signs of clothing, other than a few isolated buttons, were found. The only grave goods recovered were a few shroud pins and a crucifix, which, interestingly, was identical to one recovered at Fort Michilimackinac (Rinehart et al. 1990:134) and to another found at a protohistoric Native American site in Louisiana (Brain 1979:173), demonstrating the role of the Catholic Church in linking the various regions of New France.

The original size of the Moran cemetery remains uncertain. Although recent systematic excavation to the north, east, and west of the extant burials identified the edges of the cemetery (Danforth et al. 2013), the property to the south could not be investigated. However, early newspaper articles (*Biloxi Sun-Herald* 1914) and more recent reports from residents tell of stories of skeletal remains, at times in large numbers, being exposed when the southern area was developed into a major road and gas station (Greenwell 2008). Therefore it is possible that the 32 individuals recovered may have been only a small portion of the original cemetery.

Although there are no known historical notations for this particular cemetery, records do exist for 171 individuals who died from 1720 to 1723 in an area called Old Biloxi, likely located a few miles away on the eastern side of Biloxi Bay (Delahaye 1727 in Maduell 1972) (Figure 11.1). The information provided includes name, sex, date of death, and at times age at death, occupation, and country of origin. As may be seen in Table 11.1, there is a strong male bias among those who died, and only five children were noted. All individuals appear to have been European colonists, and

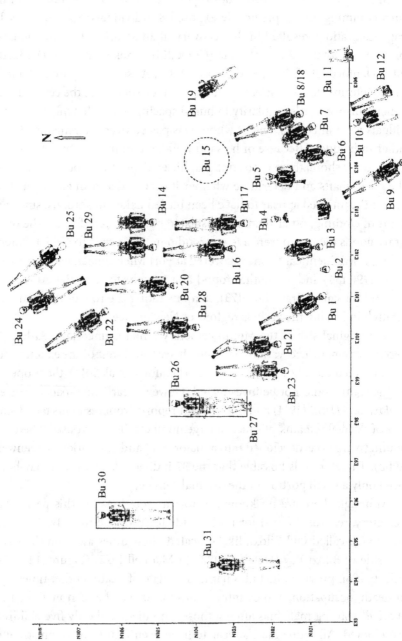

Figure 11.2. Map of burials from cemetery at Moran site (Danforth et al. 2013:121).

Table 11.1. Age and sex distribution of European individuals interred in the Old Fort concession, Biloxi, Mississippi

	Infant	Juvenile	18–34y	35–50y	50+y	Adult	Unknown	Total
Male	0	3	8	5	0	48	66	130
Female	0	2	5	3	0	12	19	41

Note: Compiled from Delahaye 1727 in Maduell 1972.

the most common occupations were convict, soldier, and those involved in construction trades, although silk merchant and nun are also listed. Overall, these data fit expectations concerning the characteristics of the New Biloxi.

FINDINGS

DEMOGRAPHIC ANALYSIS OF THE MORAN SKELETAL SERIES

Standard criteria for age and sex estimation (Buikstra and Ubelaker 1994) were applied in analysis of the human remains. Results show that the great majority of those interred at Moran were between 15 and 40 years old, and the sex ratio was overwhelmingly skewed toward males (Table 11.2). The only juvenile remains encountered were several teeth from an 18-month-old scattered in a small area of the eastern side (see Figure 11.2). Since no other skeletal elements from a child were recovered, this burial has subsequently been removed from the total number of interments.

Ancestry was evaluated in the Moran skeletal population using a variety of indicators. As Stojanowski (2010:55) has noted, "phenotypic variation is reflective of the choices one makes within social constraints within the field of reproduction." Standard metric and anthroposcopic observations of the cranium and teeth commonly used in forensic assessments were employed (Gill and Rhine 1990; Turner et al. 1991). Data were then compared with mean values for dimensions seen in several other, more homogeneous populations, including (1) a sixteenth-century population from Wamba, Spain

Table 11.2. Age and sex distribution of human remains recovered at Moran

	Infant	Subadult	18–34y	35–50y	50+y	Adult	Total
Male	0	0	12	5	0	5	22
Female	0	0	1	1	0	0	2
Unknown	1	0	0	0	0	7	8
Total	1	0	13	6	0	13	32

(Ann Ross, personal communication, 2003); (2) the seventeenth-century French colonial population from St. Croix, Maine (Crist n.d.); (3) an Arikara population from the Upper Plains (Howells 1973); and (4) a Dogon population from Mali (Howells 1973).

Unfortunately, preservation conditions at Moran reduced the number of individuals who could be evaluated for many of the traits under consideration, but the findings seen would seem to suggest a somewhat heterogeneous population. A medium to broad skull has been traditionally associated with Native American ancestry (Gill 1998), and the great majority of those at Moran displayed cranial indices with values exceeding 0.80. Interestingly, however, the mean values for both males and females in the Arikara population were below this value. Several crania at the site also exhibit unusually broad noses, exceeding a mean index of 0.53, a trait more frequently associated with African ancestry. In comparison, the roughly contemporaneous Spanish population from Wamba had a mean index of about 0.50 and the Dogon an index of about 0.60. The French population from St. Croix, however, had an average mean index of 0.58. Furthermore, those with broad noses at Moran possessed other midfacial metrics—namely, maximum bizygomatic breadth and maxillary alveolar breadth—that were generally narrow in expression. Among the non-metric cranial observations made, three cases of shoveled incisors, two slight and one moderate, were observed (Figure 11.3), and other dental morphology traits were documented, such as Bushman's premolar, which are not usually found in Europeans (Scott and Turner 1987).

Based on these mixed findings from skeletal morphology, often within the same individual, Cook (2011) concluded that approximately one-third of those interred at Moran could be confidently classified as European and that nearly one-half had traits that leaned toward European but were ambiguous. However, she concluded that two individuals in particular were possibly admixed. Burial 20 was a female aged 17 to 20 years at death with a broad nose, rectangular palate, and slight prognathism. The individual also had slight shoveling of the incisors and a Y-cusp pattern of M2. Burial 14, a young adult male, displayed prominent shoveling of the incisors. As will be discussed later, both these individuals were eventually found to have European mtDNA haplogroups, but Cook (2011) notes that these haplogroups have been observed in some African populations.

Stable isotope values assessing diet were also used to investigate ethnicity at Moran. Both bone collagen and bone apatite were evaluated for levels of carbon to determine whether individuals had subsisted on C_3

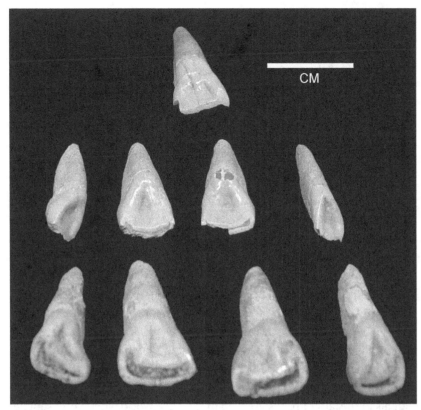

CM

Figure 11.3. Incisor shoveling present in maxillary incisors in the Moran series: Burial 14 (*top*); Burial 20 (*middle*), and Burial 23 (*bottom*) (Danforth et al. 2013:145).

(temperate grasses) plants, which would most likely suggest an individual of Old World origin, or C_4 (tropical grasses) plants, which would most likely suggest New World origin (Katzenberg 2000; Page 2007). Bone samples from all 32 burials, as well as a number of isolated surface samples of bones disturbed by Hurricane Katrina, underwent isotopic analysis (Danforth et al. 2013; Page 2007). Only one sample, an isolated femur fragment recovered in a disturbed context on the surface, had carbon isotope values indicative of a C_4 diet. All the other bone samples tested, including all of the identified burials, were indicative of a C_3 (likely wheat) diet.

The mtDNA of a subsample of individuals at Moran was also sequenced. Eight individuals from the cemetery were tested, all selected either because of unusual mortuary contexts or because of indication of possible non-European ancestry based on skeletal morphology. Teeth were used for all but two burials, for whom cortical bone from the femur was substituted, and all possible precautions concerning contamination were taken, since it was of particular concern in this excavation given that most excavators at the site were of European ancestry. Polymerase chain reaction was conducted by PaleoDNA Laboratories in Lakehead, Ontario. The results showed that mtDNA haplogroups represented were H, J, and U (Cook et al. 2011), all traditionally associated with Europeans (Kaestle and Horsburgh 2002). Thus, all of the markers tested suggest the Moran population was relatively homogeneous in its ancestral composition.

HEALTH PATTERNS AT MORAN

Given the lower-status socioeconomic circumstances in which most of the immigrants at Moran are supposed to have originated, the human remains were analyzed for childhood growth and nutritional indicators. Stature is especially valuable in this regard, in that although a genetic component is present, most researchers emphasize the role of protein and other nutrients in determining adult height (Bogin 1999). Using the Trotter-Gleser (1958) formulae for whites, stature was estimated for 14 males and 2 females. Mean male height was 164.8 cm, while females averaged 152.3 cm. As may be seen in Figure 11.4, these values are fairly short compared to stature values seen for the colonial United States (Angel 1976) and Fort Michilimackinac (Danforth et al. 2013). However, this is not unexpected, since most individuals in the latter groups grew up in the New World where food supplies and living conditions were likely more favorable. The mean stature estimation for males at Moran, however, is very similar to those seen in French, Irish, and British soldiers of the time (Kolmos and Cinnirella 2005). This is not entirely unexpected, since the soldiers likely also came from the lower social echelons, and furthermore, a number of individuals at Moran may have been soldiers. However, the values also resemble those seen in several bioarchaeological studies of northern European populations from the time period (Steckel 2001:38), suggesting the conditions in which the people grew up may not have been unusually severe for Europe during the early eighteenth century. In contrast, the females at Moran were short regardless to whom they are compared (Figure 11.4).

Hypoplastic defects of tooth enamel were observed on the dentition in 10 of the 12 individuals who could be evaluated, with 6 of those exhibiting multiple defects. As may be seen in Figure 11.5, many of the episodes could be quite pronounced. When frequencies from the various sites are compared, the frequency of episodes very high compared to rates seen at Fort Michilimackinac (5/11, 45.5 percent) (Danforth et al. 2013) and St. Croix

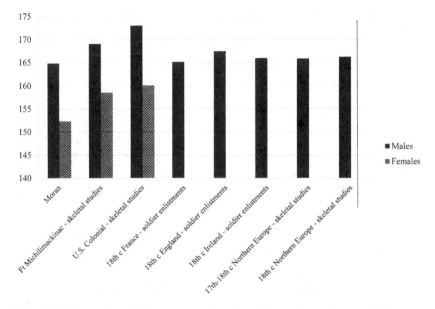

Figure 11.4. Comparison of mean statures of various eighteenth-century populations (adapted from Danforth et al. 2013:143).

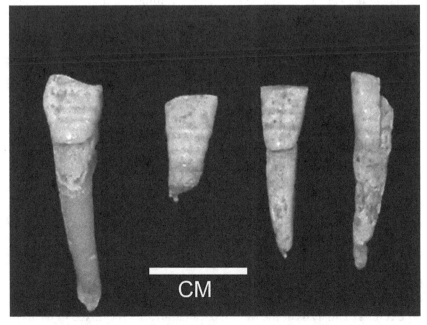

Figure 11.5. Example of enamel hypoplasia formation in the Moran series (Burial 23) (adapted from Danforth et al. 2013:145).

(7/21, 33.3 percent) (Crist n.d.). Furthermore, the episodes seen in both populations were all very slight in terms of severity. The apparently good childhood health enjoyed by those at St. Croix has been attributed to the fact that a number of those interred were "gentlemen" and of higher social status (Crist n.d.).

In contrast, other metabolic disturbances were relatively rare at Moran. No convincing cases of porotic hyperostosis or cribra orbitalia were seen. In contrast, some 25 percent (2 of 8) of those who could be evaluated at St. Peter Street Cemetery exhibited signs of porotic hyperostosis. As discussed before, scurvy was rampant in the sailors from St. Croix (Crist and Sorg 2014), but no cases could be observed in either Moran or St. Peter Street (Owsley and Orser 1984).

The Moran series did have one case of healed rickets. Burial 17, a young adult male, exhibited medial bowing of both tibiae. Although neither femur showed any lateral bowing, some anterior bowing unrelated to normal anterior-posterior curvature that often is present was evident. The greater trochanter area was not present in order to allow determination of whether flattening of the neck and head occurred (Natasha Vang, personal communication, 2013). With only one instance observed, however, rickets condition does not appear to have been especially common in the Moran population, and the condition was not reported at any of the comparative sites.

The human remains at Moran were also considered for any health differences related to social status. The primary indication of status distinctions involved the presence of two coffin burials, both belonging to young adult males. Funkhouser (2014) examined both individuals for any evidence of health advantages that might be associated with a presumed more privileged existence, but none were seen. In fact, the individuals interred were immensely typical of the rest of the Moran sample.

In summary, the Moran population does show signs of childhood stress in its high rates of hypoplasia, thereby reflecting the effects of the low socioeconomic status in which most were supposed to have grown up. Frequencies of most other health indicators, however, appear to be fairly typical of other European groups of the era.

Discussion

The results of analysis of the Moran population are very mixed in terms of correlation with expectations for composition of the cemetery based on historical information. It must be remembered that it is a very small sample and may not be representative of the New Biloxi community at large. When the demographic findings are compared with those seen in records from a concession cemetery in the immediate area (Delahaye 1727 in Maduell 1972), the preponderance of young males at Moran is striking. Temporal patterns in the demographics of those interred at the Old Fort concession showed it to be primarily composed of soldiers and convicts in 1720–1721, whereas proportionately greater numbers of women and children were entered in the records during 1722–1723 (Delahaye 1727 in Maduell 1972). It is possible that the Moran cemetery might date to that slightly earlier period as well, giving an indication of the occupational background of those interred. The relatively young age of most of those in the population would also be consistent with this interpretation. Unfortunately, there is no other evidence that can be used in support of this notion. Temporally associated grave goods would be one possibility, but they were almost nonexistent at the site.

In the Moran cemetery, both the mtDNA and stable isotope results are consistent with an essentially homogeneous European population. Although mitochondrial DNA reveals only maternal line ancestry, certain likelihoods concerning biological ancestry can still be drawn based on social mores of the time. A person with non-European maternal ancestry could have been either entirely African, Native American, or of mixed ancestry. However, an individual with a European haplogroup most likely was of European ancestry on the father's side as well, since it would have been highly unlikely for a European woman to have had a child sired by a non-European; European women in the early days of the Louisiana colony were especially rare, and thus any who did immigrate to the colony, even those of dubious reputation, easily found husbands (Spear 2009). When interpreting ancestry at the Moran site, it must also be taken into consideration that the African and European immigrants brought to New Biloxi were known to have originated in the Old World, increasing the likelihood, although not completely eliminating the possibility, that they were not of admixed ancestral heritage.

The isotope results were similarly consistent. The one sample suggestive of a C_4 diet is somewhat surprising. It theoretically may have belonged to an individual from West Africa or southern Europe where maize cultivation had been adopted by the 1700s (McCann 2007), but the more parsimonious explanation is that it came from a person of Native American ancestry. After the excavation of the Moran cemetery after Hurricane Camille in 1969, it became a local urban legend of sorts that Native American females had been identified by a visiting anthropologist, but such information is not mentioned in the site report from that investigation, and the archaeologist in charge at the time confirmed the fact as well (Greenwell 2008). Furthermore, the one female and possible female identified during the more recent reevaluation of the 1969 remains, which had been disturbed by Hurricane Katrina, both yielded C_3 chemistry. Thus, at this point no clear explanation can be offered concerning the origin of the sample. It is possible that local Native Americans adopted Catholicism and therefore chose to be buried in sacred ground, as was seen at both St. Catherines Island (Winkler et al., this volume) and Tipu (Harvey et al., this volume). This, however, seems highly unlikely given the short duration of New Biloxi. It seems more likely that any Native American deceased would have been returned to his or her family for interment in a burial ground used by the kin group.

The interpretations concerning ancestry at Moran might have been different, however, if DNA testing had not been available, and indeed with many studies it is not permitted and/or is cost-prohibitive. Without DNA analysis, bioarchaeologists wishing to explore ancestry, which is a frequent issue of concern in many colonial settings, have little alternative other than to work with morphological traits, necessarily employing at least a somewhat typological approach in interpreting data. Moran, however, can serve as evidence concerning the challenges associated with this approach, especially in terms of dealing with the wide range of expression of most morphological traits within populations. For example, defined incisor shoveling (Figure 11.5) is a trait that typically would be interpreted to indicate Native American genetic contributions. Yet, the three individuals in the cemetery who exhibited shoveling all had European haplogroups. Cybulski (1988) also noted that 35 percent of the English prisoners recovered buried in the walls of eighteenth-century Old Quebec displayed shovel-shaped incisors, but the rest of the skeletal morphology for that population exhibited was consistently European. Shoveling also appears to be the trait used to identify admixture in the child of presumed European–Native American ancestry at St. Peter Street, which may call into question as to whether mixed ancestry was actually present in that individual, especially in the light of the lack of further evidence.

The generally high frequency of brachycephaly, which also might have been taken to suggest non-European ancestry, might actually reflect poor health status of those interred at Moran. Recent studies have found that skulls have generally become higher and narrower over the past 100 years (Jantz 2001; Jantz and Meadows Jantz 2000; Wescott and Jantz 2005).

Previously, Angel (1982) had suggested that the decreased skull height seen in many earlier populations was caused by basiocranial flattening. Weakened by the effects of poor nutrition, the cranial base was thought to have flattened under the weight of the brain. More recent interpretations, however, suggest that the increased skull height is instead the result of increased growth of the brain over the last century (Wescott and Jantz 2005), again credited to improved nutrition.

This interpretation would be consistent with expectations for childhood health patterns at the site. Given that the cemetery was indeed primarily European, it would be anticipated that most of the individuals would display signs of growth arrest associated with the impoverished childhood they likely endured in their homelands. Owning land was the primary source of wealth in Europe at the time, but it was available to only a limited few. This situation was reinforced by the policies of the ancien régime. It was not until the latter part of the eighteenth century that incipient industrialization with the advantages in farming, transportation, and manufacturing broke this pattern (Braudel 1982). For those living in the urban centers of France, life would have involved a continual challenge to survive the rampant crowding and poor sanitation, factors that traditionally have affected large cities throughout history, including ancient Rome (Killgrove, this volume). Food shortages would have been frequent, and diseases from smallpox to tuberculosis and syphilis would have been rampant. Although perhaps a bit overdramatically, one observer of the time described Paris as "this filthy den of every vice and evil, where people are all crammed together in air poisoned by a thousand putrid vapours, amid cemeteries, hospitals, slaughter-houses, drains . . . where the heavy, fetid air is so thick you can see and feel the atmosphere more than three leagues away in every direction" (Mercier 1783 quoted in Roche 1987:50). Such conditions inevitably must have had a decidedly negative impact on the lives of those without sufficient power or opportunity to escape the station they were given in life.

However, the indications of poor health in the individuals at Moran did not manifest nearly to the degree anticipated. The only marker that attested to frequent childhood biological stress was enamel hypoplasia. The members of the population were also short compared to stature values seen in New World populations of the eighteenth century, most of whom enjoyed relatively good nutrition and lived in settlements with lower population densities; indeed, the well-documented fertility of women in New France was attributed to these very conditions (Landry 1993). However, when the mean stature values at Moran are considered in the light of those found in European populations, they were not atypical. Again, the stature values used were taken from soldiers, who also likely came from lower socioeconomic conditions, so this interpretation of this marker remains somewhat inconclusive.

Neither porotic hyperostosis nor cribra orbitalia was observed at Moran, although both were seen in notable segments of the population from St. Peter Street (Owsley and Orser 1984). This was especially surprising since the condition is most often associated with a deficiency of vitamin B12, which is usually gained from meat sources (Walker et al. 2009), something that would seem to have been in short supply in urban centers of Europe. Rickets and scurvy were also in very low frequency at Moran. Although they too would seem to proliferate in the circumstances associated with eighteenth-century life, the conditions were also infrequent in the comparative populations as well as in modern Europe (1500–1950) in general (Mays 2014). Thus it appears that the unhealthy conditions in which most urban residents lived did not manifest themselves in childhood health markers seen in these particular skeletons.

Although there are many possible explanations for this suite of findings, one is that the cemetery may not have been for New Biloxi but was associated with a specific concession. The concession workers may not have been representative sample of the community at large, particularly if the African slaves were participating in brickmaking on the northern side of the peninsula. Funkhouser (2014) has also that noted although the cemetery is located near the proposed Fort Louis near the heart of New Biloxi according to a period map (Lablond de Latour 1722), it is also situated on the property assigned to Claude LeBlanc, who was serving as minister of war in France at the time. Funkhouser argues that the size of the cemetery, even allowing for the fact that it likely extended further to the south, is much smaller than what would be anticipated for a community of the size of New Biloxi. It is also suggested that those buried in coffins may have been some sort of officers associated with management of the concession.

Regardless of the origins of the individuals, the harshness of their existence in New Biloxi is clear according to historical records of the time. Hester (2012:234) has cogently argued that the prevailing attitude concerning the administration of New Biloxi was not one of a social experiment concerning imposition of the ancien régime, but rather one of "commodification of all forces—persons, places, things." Under these circumstances, those interred at the Moran site would have arguably comprised a community based on shared interest rather than one based on shared culture using the categorizations of Cornell (1996). Although all were European Catholics, this most likely did not provide the strongest type of bond uniting them. Instead, it may be argued that they more closely conform to being a community of interest in that all were theoretically invested pursuing a common interest or goal, particularly one involving material gain of some sort and having external forces encouraging the group's internal alliance.

If there ever even were a common interest of a better life in the New World for this group compared to what they had known before, it likely quickly degenerated into the desire for basic survival. Most of the immigrants had not chosen to come to the Louisiana colony, and most of them assuredly did not want to stay given the conditions they were forced to endure. Their treatment by John Law and the Company of the West showed little regard for their quality of their existence. The immigrants at New Biloxi coped as well as their conditions would allow them, as the apparent sharing of the belongings of the dead with those who still remained alive would attest. For those interred in the Moran cemetery, survival was a goal that eluded them despite these efforts.

Conclusions

New Biloxi served as the capital of Louisiana from 1719 to 1722 and also was a staging community for European and African arrivals destined to work on the inland concessions. It was theoretically operating under the rules of the ancien régime, but as was seen in St. Peter Street Cemetery, the social segregation outlined by these rules often appears to have been rejected in the colonial outposts such as New Orleans in the early eighteenth century. However, genetic, isotope, and skeletal morphological evidence indicates that the Moran cemetery was used exclusively for interment of Europeans, which would superficially suggest that the more rigid social norms instigated by administrators in metropolitan areas were indeed being heeded (Giraud 1966). Another explanation for the findings, however, is that the cemetery may represent a setting used only for one concession rather than for the community at large, which unfortunately would limit the ability to test for the degree of social segregation in practice at New Biloxi. The health markers, however, failed to suggest a particularly stressed population as was anticipated given the undesirables that comprised the majority of immigrants brought to the area as part of the contract that financier John Law arranged with the French Crown in 1717.

The relatively quick death from malnutrition and infectious diseases such as malaria that most are reported to have experienced is unlikely to be recorded in their bones, but the mere presence of their remains reminds us of the variety of circumstances and settings in which those inhabiting the French colonies both lived and died.

ACKNOWLEDGMENTS

We would like to thank a number of individuals and organizations who helped in excavation and analysis of the Moran site. First and foremost among these is the Moran family, who generously gave permission for excavation and provided valuable background information about the property. Edmond Boudreaux provided extensive assistance concerning the history of the Gulf Coast, and Gregory Waselkov and Bonnie Gums assisted with our understanding of the local French colonial presence. The contributions of the students who worked the site are also greatly appreciated. Funding for the project was generously provided by the National Endowment for the Humanities, Mississippi Department of Marine Resources, Mississippi Department of Archives and History, and the University of Southern Mississippi. We also appreciate the suggestions provided by Melissa Murphy and Haagen Klaus.

REFERENCES CITED

Allain, M.
1988   *Not Worth a Straw: French Colonial Policy and the Early Years of Louisiana.* University of Southwestern Louisiana Press, Lafayette.
Angel, J. L.
1976   Colonial to Modern Skeletal Change in the USA. *American Journal of Physical Anthropology* 45:723–736.
1982   A New Measure of Growth Efficiency: Skull Base Height. *American Journal of Physical Anthropology* 58:297–305.
Bain, A., R. Auger, and Y. LeRoux
2011   Archaeological Research at Habitation Loyola, French Guiana. In *French Colonial Archaeology in the Southeast and Caribbean*, edited by K. G. Kelly and M. D. Hardy, pp. 206–224. University Press of Florida, Gainesville.
Biloxi Sun-Herald
1914   Indian Skull Is Found in Biloxi in Grading Yard. 1 May:1.
Bogin, B.
1999   *Patterns of Growth.* 2nd ed. Cambridge University Press, Cambridge.

Brain, J.
1979   *Tunica Treasure.* Peabody Museum of Archaeology and Ethnology Papers
            No. 71. Harvard University Press, Cambridge.
Braudel, F.
1982   *Civilization and Capitalism, 15th–18th Century.* Vol. 2, *The Wheels of Com-
            merce.* University of California Press, Berkeley.
Briggs, W.
1985   The Forgotten Colony: *Le Pays des Illinois.* Unpublished Ph.D. dissertation,
            Department of History, University of Chicago.
Buikstra, J. E., and D. H. Ubelaker (editors)
1994   *Standards for Data Collection from Human Skeletal Remains.* Research Series
            No. 44.Arkansas Archaeological Survey, Fayetteville.
Carter, C. P., A. Seidell, D. P. Craig, E. A. Boudreaux, K. L. Burleigh, J. A. Gardner, S. A.
            Young, and M. E. Danforth.
2004   A Bioarchaeological Analysis of the French Colonial Burials at the Moran
            Gallery, Biloxi, MS. *Mississippi Archaeology* 39:39–69.
Conrad, G. R.
1970   *Immigrants and War: Louisiana, 1718–1721, from the Memoir of Charles LeG-
            ac.* University of Southwestern Louisiana Press, Lafayette.
Cook, D. N.
2011   Ancestral Analysis of the French Colonial Moran Cemetery, Biloxi, Missis-
            sippi. Unpublished Master's thesis, Department of Anthropology and Sociol-
            ogy, University of Southern Mississippi, Hattiesburg.
Cook, D. N., B. T. Hester, M. Stephens, T. D. Hensley, and M. E. Danforth
2010   Determination of Ancestry in a French Colonial Cemetery in Biloxi, MS,
            Using mtDNA and Isotope Analyses. *Mississippi Archaeology* 42:45–66.
Cornell, S.
1996   The Variable Ties That Bind: Content and Circumstances in Ethnic Process-
            es. *Ethnic and Racial Studies* 19:265–289.
Courtaud, P., and T. Romon
2004   Le site d'Anse Sainte-Marguerite (Guadeloupe, Grande Terre): Presentation
            d'un cimetiere d'epoque coloniale. *Journal of Caribbean Archaeology*, Special
            Publication No. 1, pp. 58–67.
Crist, T. A.
n.d.   Physical Anthropology section. In *St. Croix Island Archaeological Project.* St.
            Croix, Maine, National Park Service.
Crist, T. A., and M. H. Sorg
2014   Adult Scurvy in New France: Samuel de Champlain's "Mal de la Terre" at
            Saint Croix Island, 1604–1605. *International Journal of Paleopathology* 5:95–
            105.
Cybulski, J. S.
1988   Skeletons in the Walls of Old Quebec. *Northeastern Historical Archaeology*
            17:61–84.
Danforth, M. E.
2011   An Early Eighteenth Century French Colonial Cemetery in Nouveau Biloxi,

Mississippi. In *French Colonial Archaeology in the Southeast and Caribbean*, edited by K. G. Kelly and M. D. Hardy, pp. 64–80. University Press of Florida, Gainesville.

Danforth, M. E., D. N. Cook, M. Greer, A. R. Harvey, J. L. Funkhouser, B. T. Hester, H. W. Webster, R. Wise, and H. Guzik

2013   Archaeological and Bioarchaeological Investigations of the French Colonial Cemetery at the Moran Site (22HR511), Harrison County, Mississippi. Submitted to The Mississippi Department of Marine Resources, Biloxi.

Dawdy, S. L.

2008   *Building the Devil's Empire: French Colonial New Orleans*. University of Chicago Press, Chicago.

Delahaye

1727   Archives des Colonies. Series GI, volume 412, folio 1. Archives Nationales, Paris.

DuPratz, A.

1947   *The History of Louisiana*. Reprint of 1774 edition. Pelican Press, New Orleans.

Duval, K.

2008   Indian Intermarriage and *Metissage* in Colonial Louisiana. *William and Mary Quarterly* 65:267–304.

Funkhouser, J. L.

2014   The Paleopathology of the Moran Site (22HR511), Biloxi, MS. Unpublished Master's thesis, Department of Anthropology and Sociology, University of Southern Mississippi, Hattiesburg.

Gagné, G.

1995   La reduction de Sillery: Examen osteoarcheologique d'un cimetiere autochtone du XVIIth siècle. *Paleo-Quebec* 23:103–121.

Gill, G. W.

1998   Craniofacial Criteria in the Skeletal Attribution of Race. In *Forensic Osteology*, edited by K. J. Reichs, pp. 293–315. Charles C. Thomas, Springfield, Illinois.

Gill, G. W., and S. Rhine (editors)

1990   *Skeletal Attribution of Race*. Anthropological Papers No. 4, Maxwell Museum of Anthropology. University of New Mexico Press, Albuquerque.

Giraud, M.

1966   *Histoire de la Louisiane francaise, Tome III: L'epoque de John Law (1717–1720)*. Presses Universitaires de France, Paris.

Greenwell, D.

2008   *Moran Burial Site (22HR511): Archaeological Project of 1969 (Post-Hurricane Camille)*. D'Iberville Historical Society, D'Iberville, Mississippi.

Hadlock, W. S.

1950   *Preliminary Archaeological Exploration at St. Croix Island, ME*. Manuscript on file. National Park Service North Atlantic Regional Office, Boston.

Hall, G. M.

1992   *Africans in Colonial Louisiana: The Development of Afro-Creole Culture in the Eighteenth Century*. Louisiana State University Press, Baton Rouge.

Harrington, J. C., and W. S. Hadlock

1951   Preliminary Archaeological Explorations on St. Croix Island, ME, St. Croix Island National Monument (Project). Manuscript on file. National Park Service North Atlantic Regional Office, Boston.

Hester, B. T.

2008   Searching for Evidence of the Second French Colonial Presence in Biloxi, Mississippi (1719–1723). Paper presented at the annual meetings of the Southeastern Archaeological Conference, Charlotte.

2012   Commoditization of Persons, Places and Things during Biloxi's Second Tenure as Capital of French Colonial Louisiana. In *French Colonial Archaeology in the Southeast and Caribbean*, edited by K. G. Kelly and M. D. Hardy, pp. 47–63. University Press of Florida, Gainesville.

Horowitz, D. L.

1975   Ethnic Identity. In *Ethnicity: Theory and Experience*, edited by N. Glazer and D. P. Moynihan, pp. 111–140. Harvard University Press, Cambridge.

Howells, W. W.

1973   *Cranial Variation in Man: A Study by Multivariate Analysis of Patterns of Differences among Recent Human Populations.* Papers of the Peabody Museum of Archaeology and Ethnology, Vol. 67. Peabody Museum, Harvard University, Cambridge.

Jantz, R. L.

2001   Cranial Change in Americans: 1850–1975. *Journal of Forensic Science* 46:784–787.

Jantz, R. L., and L. Meadows Jantz

2000   Secular Change in Craniofacial Morphology. *American Journal of Human Biology* 12:327–338.

Kaestle, F. A., and K. A. Horsburgh

2002   Ancient DNA in Anthropology: Methods, Applications, and Ethics. *American Journal of Physical Anthropology* 119:92–130.

Katzenberg, M. A.

2000   Stable Isotope Analysis: A Tool for Studying Past Diet, Demography, and Life History. In *Biological Anthropology of the Human Skeleton*, edited M. A. Katzenberg and S. R. Saunders, pp. 329–350. Wiley-Liss, New York.

Kolmos, J., and F. Cinnirella

2005   European Heights in the Early Eighteenth Century. Discussion Paper 2005-05, Department of Economics, University of Munich. Electronic document, http:/Epub.ub.uni-muenchen.de/muenchen.de/572/1/european_heights_in_the_early_eighteenth_century.pdf, accessed March 25, 2008.

Landry, Y.

1993   Fertility in France and New France: The Distinguishing Characteristics of Canadian Behavior in the 17th and 18th Centuries. *Social Science and History* 17:577–592.

Larocque, R.

1995   La redecouverte d'un cimetiere du Vieux-Quebec: Les restes humains du Cimetiere Sainte-Anne (CeEt-36). *Paleo-Quebec* 23:123–144.

Larocque, R., and G. Gagné
1981   Analyse de la Sepulture 1-H d'eglise Notre Dame de Foy. In *Église Notre Dame de Foy: Fouilles archeologiques 1981*. Report submitted to the Ministère des Affaires Cuturelles de Quebec, Quebec City.

Listi, G. A., and M. H. Manhein
2012   Bioarchaeological Analysis of Burials Recently Excavated from New Orleans' Oldest Cemetery. Paper presented at the meetings of the Southeastern Archaeological Conference, Baton Rouge.

Maduell, C. R.
1972   *The Census Tables for the French Colony from Louisiana from 1699 through 1732*. Genealogical Publishing, Baltimore.

Manhein, M. H., E. R. Salter-Pedersen, K. M. Gordon, J. Suskewicz, H. B. Bassett, T. Van Winkle, G. A. Listi, and N. E. Barrow
2003   Analysis of Human Remains from 22AD599, Natchez Bluffs, Bicentennial Gardens [Fort Rosalie]. Forensic Anthropology and Computer Enhancement Services Laboratory, Louisiana State University. Report submitted to Coastal Environments, Inc., Baton Rouge.

Mays, S.
2014   The Paleopathology of Scurvy in Europe. *International Journal of Paleopathology* 5:55–62.

McCann, J. C.
2007   *Maize and Grace: Africa's Encounter with a New World Crop, 1500–2000*. Harvard University Press, Cambridge.

Mercier, L. S.
1783   *Tableau de Paris*. Vol. 1, pp. 6–7. Amsterdam.

Noble, V. E.
1977   Excavations at Fort Ouiatenon, 1977 Field Season: Preliminary Report. Michigan State University, East Lansing.

Owsley, D. W., and C. E. Orser
1984   *An Archaeological and Physical Anthropological Study of the First Cemetery in New Orleans, LA*. Department of Geography and Anthropology, Louisiana State University, Baton Rouge.

Owsley, D. W., C. E. Orser, R. W. Mann, P. H. Moore-Jansen, and R. L. Montgomery
1987   Demography and Pathology of an Urban Slave Population from New Orleans. *American Journal of Physical Anthropology* 74:185–197.

Page, M. D.
2007   Dietary Reconstruction through Stable Isotope Analysis at the Moran French Colonial Cemetery on the Mississippi Gulf Coast. Unpublished Master's thesis, Department of Anthropology and Sociology, University of Southern Mississippi, Hattiesburg.

Pritchard, J.
2007   *In Search of Empire: The French in the Americas, 1670–1730*. Cambridge University Press, Cambridge.

Rinehart, C. J., D. C. Crass, and S. D. Smith
1990   *Crucifixes and Medallions: Their Role at Fort Michilimackinac*. South Caroli-
        na Institute of Archaeology and Anthropology. University of South Carolina,
        Columbia.

Roche, D.
1987   *The People of Paris: An Essay in Popular Culture in the 18th Century*. Univer-
        sity of California Press, Berkeley.

Sauer, N. J., S. S. Dunlap, and L. R. Simson.
1988   Medicolegal Investigation of an Eighteenth Century Homicide. *American
        Journal of Forensic Medicine and Pathology* 9:66–73.

Scott, G. R., and C. G. Turner
1987   *Geographic Variation in Tooth Crown and Root Morphology: Dental Morphol-
        ogy and Its Variation in Recent Human Populations*. Cambridge University
        Press, Cambridge.

Spear, J. M.
2009   *Race, Sex and Social Order in Early New Orleans*. Johns Hopkins University
        Press, Baltimore.

Steckel, R. H.
2001   *Health and Nutrition in the Preindustrial Era: Insights from a Millennium
        of Average Heights in Northern Europe*. Working Paper No. 8542. National
        Bureau of Economic Research, Washington, D.C.

Stojanowski, C. M.
2010   *Bioarchaeology of Ethnogenesis in the Colonial Southeast*. University Press of
        Florida, Gainesville.

Stone, L. M.
1974   *Fort Michilimackinac, 1715–1781: An Archaeological Perspective on the Revo-
        lutionary Frontier*. Anthropology Museum, Michigan State University, East
        Lansing.

Trotter, M., and G. Gleser
1958   A Re-evaluation of Stature Based on Measurements Taken during Life and
        of Long Bones after Death. *American Journal of Physical Anthropology* 16:79–
        123.

Turner, C. G., C. R. Nichol, and G. R. Scott
1991   Scoring Procedures for Key Morphological Traits of the Permanent Denti-
        tion: Arizona State University Dental Anthropology System. In *Advances in
        Dental Anthropology*, edited by M. A. Kelley and C. S. Larsen, 13–31. Wiley-
        Liss, New York.

Usner, D. H.
1990   *Indians, Settlers and Slaves in a Frontier Economy: The Lower Mississippi Val-
        ley before 1783*. University of North Carolina Press, Chapel Hill.

Walker, P. L., R. R. Bathurst, R. Richman, T. Gjerdrum, and V. A. Andrushko
2009   The Causes of Porotic Hyperostosis and Cribra Orbitalia: A Reappraisal of
        the Iron-Deficiency Anemia Hypothesis. *American Journal of Physical An-
        thropology* 139:109–125.

Wescott, D. J., and R. Jantz
2005   Assessing Craniofacial Secular Change in American Blacks and Whites Using Geometric Morphometry. In *Modern Morphometrics in Physical Anthropology, Part 2*, edited by D. E. Slice, pp. 231–245. Kluwer Academic/Plenum, New York.

White, R.
1991   *The Middle Ground: Indians, Empires, and Republics in the Great Lakes Region, 1650–1815.* Cambridge University Press, Cambridge.

12

Effects of Colonialism from the Perspective of Craniofacial Variation

Comparing Case Studies Involving African Populations

ISABELLE RIBOT, ALAN G. MORRIS, AND EMILY S. RENSCHLER

This chapter will focus on the global increase of gene flow among populations forced into the diaspora during the slave trade. As in Chapter 11 of
the present book, phenotypic data and craniofacial variation in particular
are used as a source of complementary information to the historical and
archaeological record. As with genetics, phenotypic expressions can provide valuable information on fluctuating gene flow within past populations
(Klaus 2008; Ossenberg et al. 2006; Relethford 1994; Stojanowski 2004;
Stojanowski and Schillaci 2006). By focusing on diaspora skeletal samples
from two different regions, the Cape Colony and Cuba, we aim here to un-
derline the diverse effects of colonialism that occurred globally. Although
these two case studies have different historical contexts, both examples are
believed to be related to the African diaspora and to represent people of
heterogeneous origins.

As a consequence of colonialism, population composition and structure
around the world have been reshaped dramatically, especially in areas affected by the slave trade. In eighteenth-century Cape Colony and Cuba,
gene flow occurred between enslaved people, who were mainly African,
and other groups, including local populations and European settlers. A
phenotypic exploration of hybridization processes that occurred within
various African diaspora populations is rare in bioarchaeology (Jackson et
al. 2004). Most of this research focused mainly on aspects of health and demography (Angel et al. 1987; Corruccini et al. 1985; Martin et al. 1987; Owsley et al. 1987; Rankin-Hill 1997; Rankin-Hill et al. 2000; Rathbun 1985).

Postcolonial theory encourages numerous disciplines to critically analyze the cultural legacies of colonialism and imperialism (Bayly 2004; Biccum 2002; Orser 2010, 2012; Said 1993; Spivak 1987). What happens to the colonized person in terms of identity and social relations within a colonial society and later through the decolonization processes? This central question is of major interest, especially when exploring the slave trade and proto-capitalist societies through time (Haviser and MacDonald 2006). How did forced labor appear, and how did slaves resist the culture of the colonizer (Gosden 2012)? It is important to acknowledge the effects of the slave trade on various levels, including economy, demography, culture, and biology (Lovejoy 1989; Morgan 2008; Nunn 2008; Tishkoff et al. 2009; Wescott and Jantz 2005). Postcolonial theory also gives the opportunity to a wide range of neglected communities—indigenous, hybrid, or Creole—to explore their complex and rich history in both the political and the intellectual sense (Cohen 2007; Rotimi 2003).

Africans forced into slavery and diaspora were exposed to dramatic biocultural changes (Blakey 2001). In the short term, living standards and health decreased dramatically as a result of new environments and the extreme hardships often involved with plantation labor. In the long term, a variety of new identities emerged in both the New World and the Old World as a process of ethnogenesis (Klaus 2008; Murphy et al. 2011; Patterson and Kelley 2000). Diverse cultural contacts and gene-flow patterns contributed to the transformation of the original people into something ethnically new. In the context of both contact and colonial sites, the issue of identity is very complex. This is true especially for our present case studies involving African diaspora populations, and eventually the formation of hybrid and new identities. A slave cemetery is by its nature cosmopolitan because of the arrival of different ethnic groups and the transformation of the local demographic composition through cultural and biological exchange. Thus, bioarchaeologists ask questions related not only to health but also to life histories and geographical localizations. Are they locals, first-generation, or second-generation descendants who emerged from forced migrations? Where did they grow up? And were they either enslaved or free?

These questions lead to the notion of identity of the enslaved populations and how identity changed chronologically either in colonial Cuba or the Cape Colony. This issue also needs to be placed into its broader historical context and recent bioarchaeological research (Mitchell 2004; Mrozowski 2006; Palus et al. 2006). The African diaspora is considered one of the largest forced migrations of people between continents before contemporary globalization (Thomas 1997). It coincides with mercantile sociopolitical transformations between the sixteenth and mid-nineteenth centuries where profits from the slave trade paralleled intensification of food production, increasing urbanization, nationalism, and later, industrialization. This phenomenon was not uniform (Patterson and Kelley 2000). A comparison of the slave trade in different regions and colonies is dependent on contextual, environmental, and historical factors (Knight 1997; Lange et al. 2006). The Spanish tended to introduce enslaved Africans into the New World in large numbers to work on plantations. Cuba presents some similarities with the Cape Colony. In both cases, precolonial societies were small and were decimated by social disruption and disease at the time of European contact. As in the Cape Colony, Cuban slaves originated from across Africa and from the Indian Ocean. The South African case differs somewhat because fewer slaves were imported from broader geographical regions (sub-Saharan Africa to southwest Asia) (Eltis 1982; Shell 1994; Singleton 2005).

Research on enslaved African cemeteries in colonial sites is based on a multidisciplinary approach derived from postcolonial theory and historical work. Biohistories have been reconstructed for a few seventeenth- and eighteenth-century slave cemeteries in both urban and rural areas (Handler and Lange 1978; Schroeder et al. 2009). For the New York African Burial Ground, phenotypic and paleogenetic data did not establish precise ethnic origins for each individual, but rather broad macro-ethnic affiliations from various African regions (Jackson et al. 2004). However, isotope analyses further supported the African origins in terms of residence and diet (Goodman et al. 2004). Other studies have combined isotopes with paleogenetics to better understand the demographic composition of slave cemeteries (Cox et al. 2001; Jackson et al. 2004; Lee et al. 2009; Nystrom et al. 2011; Price et al. 2006; Salas et al. 2004).

Despite these new methods, studies using highly heritable morphological traits remain a paleogenetic proxy to help to understand human variation through time (Franklin et al. 2010; Howells 1995, 1996; Humphries et al. 2013; Irish and Konigsberg 2007; Ousley et al. 2009; Pietrusewsky 2008; Ross et al. 2002). However, recent biodistance analyses that add model-bound quantitative genetics are able to measure the effects of gene flow (and drift) in shaping past population structure (Klaus 2008; Relethford 1994; Relethford and Blanguero 1990; Stojanowski 2004; Stojanowski and Schillaci 2006). This approach focusing on a region and community is appropriate, especially when reconstructing the history of multi-ethnic groups exposed to various migrations and interactions.

Thus, this chapter aims to understand how morphological variation within each case study can reflect historical processes through different patterns of gene flow. Our hypothesis is that the slaves of the urban Cape Colony (Cobern: Case Study 1) will show less morphological variability than those who lived on a rural Cuban plantation (Morton Collection: Case Study 2). These expectations are supported by sources reporting a slave trade history that was much longer and more intense for Cuba than for the Cape Colony. Although the slave trade in the Cape brought a diversity of people not only from Africa but also from Asia, its scale (number of slaves, duration of phenomenon) never reached the levels observed in Cuba (Elphick and Giliomee 1990; Knight 1997; Shell 1994).

An issue is the hybridization/creolization in Cuba and the Cape. In both colonies there was a growing admixed population born locally (Creoles, Cape Coloured) and also immigrants already highly admixed, especially from southeast Africa (Madagascar) (Elphick and Giliomee 1990; Knight 1997). The genetics of the living South African Cape Coloured (de Wit et al. 2010) and Cubans (Mendizabal et al. 2008) have already demonstrated the outcome of this process, and it will be tested here by using phenotypic data from two historic case studies.

BACKGROUND AND OBJECTIVES

CASE STUDY 1: THE INFORMAL GRAVEYARD OF COBERN STREET, CAPE TOWN (SOUTH AFRICA)

This first case study is well documented archaeologically, as the human remains were discovered during a rescue excavation (Morris 1997, 1999, 2011). Several bioarchaeological analyses have been undertaken on this past population, examining burial patterns, cultural remains (Apollonio 1998; Graf 1996), health and activity (Friedling 2007; Ledger et al. 2000; Manyaapelo 2007), and diet and life histories (Cox 1999; Cox et al. 2001).

In 1994, during construction work on Cape Town's Cobern Street, a burial ground was partly uncovered with 63 intact graves containing the skeletal remains of 121 individuals in total (Morris 1997, 1999, 2011). This appeared to be an unofficial cemetery for the lower socioeconomic classes, and was uncharted. Actively used in the second half of the eighteenth century, it was no longer in use by 1827. Associated grave goods confirmed this dating sequence, and archives indicate that the land was sold in 1827 (Apollonio 1998; Graf 1996).

The deceased interred there can be tied to a specific transitional period in the history of Cape Town (under Dutch and British rules). In the Cape, slavery was present until abolition in 1834 (Elphick and Shell 1990). Archives mention that 63,000 slaves were imported to the Cape from 1652 to 1808 (Shell 1994). In 1827, 6,222 slaves were living in Cape Town out of a total population of 18,781 (Banks 1991:236). The Dutch East India Company created a diverse cultural and biological population in the Cape with African and Asian mixes. The company first drew slaves from West and Central Africa (Dahomey, Angola), and later from elsewhere in Africa and Asia (East Africa, 26 percent; India, 26 percent; Sri Lanka, 23 percent; Madagascar, 25 percent) (Shell 1994). By 1760, locally born slaves outnumbered imported slaves, and men outnumbered women. Admixture with indigenous nomadic pastoralists (Khoekhoen), free Africans, free Europeans (Dutch traders and English colonial settlers), Chinese convicts, political prisoners, and exiles from East Indies had begun (Shell 1994), but only after 1795 did the boundaries between these groups begin to significantly erode (Elphick and Shell 1990). Conversions (Christianity or Islam), incorporation of Khoekhoe as wage laborers, manumission, and intermarriage slowly encouraged intergroup gene flow, especially among the poor people of the city. High levels of genetic diversity observed in contemporary Cape Town's population support these long-term processes of population admixture (Cohen 2007), which is linked to the complex history of the city, and which led to the establishment of the unique admixed "Coloured" population known in South Africa today (de Wit et al. 2010; Patterson et al. 2009; Quintana-Murci et al. 2010; Tishkoff et al. 2009).

The informal Cobern Street graveyard represents a late-eighteenth-century "snapshot" of the hybridization process. Skeletal identities in the cemetery have already been inferred from burial patterns (Apollonio 1998). Clear differences were suggested in relation to the position of the dead between precolonial (body seated, or Type A graves) and colonial phases (body lying with extended lower limbs, or Types B and C graves). Type B is the most common burial style (45 of 63 graves), with the body lying prone in a coffin, often with grave goods. This is consistent with Christian practices. Although Type C was relatively rare (5 of 63 graves), it clearly suggested Muslim practices with the body lying dextrally (neither within a coffin nor having grave goods) and oriented toward Signal Hill, the Muslim area of Cape Town (Apollonio 1998). Grave styles hint to some degree the dynamic population origin of the people buried there.

Lastly, dietary information from stable isotope analysis on bone and teeth (Cox and Sealy 1997; Cox et al. 2001; Sealy et al. 1993, 1995) has revealed the presence of locally and foreign-born individuals within the Cobern Street cemetery. Clusters of burial types matched groups that did or did not undergo specific dietary changes due to migration (carbon and nitrogen isotopic ratios). For example, a C_4-based diet in childhood was observed for several individuals buried in a Type B style, suggesting the presence of African immigrants or slaves originating from tropical regions rich in C_4 plants. This is in contrast to temperate regions such as Cape Town (dominated by C_3 plants and sea foods). These findings were corroborated by the observation of dental modifications characteristic of East African (Mozambique) origin. Other Type B individuals showed no dietary shift, suggesting that they were second-generation Cape inhabitants. However, one young woman (Individual Accession Number UCT 535) presented dental modifications but no dietary change (C_4 in childhood and adulthood). Cox et al. (2001) therefore inferred that she was likely to have recently arrived at the Cape and had not yet time for her bone composition to reflect a new diet. The presence of first-generation immigrants was suggested not only from within Africa but also from the Indian Ocean, as Madagascar was also a major source of slaves (Elphick and Giliomee 1990; Worden et al. 1999). Four out of the five Type C graves examined by Cox et al. (2001) showed a childhood C_3-based diet (low in proteins and small quantities of C_4 plants), followed by an adult diet richer in seafood. Cox et al. (2001) have argued that this dietary change in combination with the Muslim-style graves indicates emigration from the East.

Since Cox et al.'s (2001) study, which explored the identity of this mixed population, no other work has been published on the ancestry of the Cobern Street population. As a result, two specific questions are addressed: (1) Do levels of morphological diversity within the Cobern Street sample support a multi-regional origin hypothesis as suggested by previous work? (2) Do they differ between presumed subgroups of first- and second-generation immigrants as they possibly experienced different levels of gene flow?

CASE STUDY 2: AFRICAN CRANIA FROM MORTON'S SKELETAL COLLECTION

The second case study focuses on a series of human crania that are part of the Samuel G. Morton Collection, housed at the University of Pennsylvania's

Museum of Archaeology and Anthropology (Mann 2009). There is no archaeological information relating to this sample, as the human remains were collected more than 150 years ago as part of a personal skeletal collection (Morton 1849). Morton amassed human crania from various world populations for a collection, to become the largest of its kind at that time (Brace 2005; Mann 2009; Stanton 1960). Renschler (2007) found information in Morton's publications and letters indicating that the many of the so-called African crania included in his study were from enslaved Africans who died shortly after their arrival in Cuba. These remains were sent in two shipments to Morton in 1840 from Cuba (Morton 1849). In a letter to Morton dated July 27, 1840, Dr. Cisneros of Havana describes how and where these crania, pure rare Africans, were found. They came from the sandy soils of the Vedado farm/plantation where more *negros bozales* were buried (Morton Papers, American Philosophical Society, Philadelphia). Cisneros's use of the Cuban term *bozales* indicated that the individuals were enslaved native Africans (Turnbull 1840), who were most likely used as plantation labor. The Vedado farm, which was located on the agricultural outskirts of Havana, might have been used as one of those outlying places to which Africans, after their arrival in Spanish ports, were often sent in order to restore their health and be prepared for sale (Sheridan 1985).

Since Morton's time (1849) it has been therefore assumed that this collection represented native Africans. This assumption was based on information from Morton's contact in Cuba. A few studies have mentioned this collection (Lewis et al. 2011; Michael 1988; Renschler 2007; Renschler and Monge 2008, 2013). However, Renschler's (2007, 2008) study was the only investigation that focused specifically upon the crania of native Africans and revisited the geographical origins. Her skeletal analysis identified two features suggestive of African ancestry (Renschler 2007). First, preliminary craniometrical analyses based on Howells's database (1996) showed morphological affinities with various West and Central Africans. Second, skeletal modifications were observed, suggesting direct ancestral links with Africa, where these practices were found (Friedling and Morris 2005; Goose 1963; Gould et al. 1984; Van Rippen 1918). For example, anterioposterior cranial deformation observed by Renschler (2007) suggested a Central African origin for one individual. In the Congo, such a practice was noticed especially among the Mangbetu (Lagercrantz 1941). Dental modifications were also observed on the upper teeth of five individuals. One person had a filed canine and four others demonstrated ablation of first and/or second maxillary incisor. Filing and removal of anterior dentition is well documented both ethnographically and archaeologically among various historical African and African-descendant populations (Cox et al. 2001; Handler et al. 1982). Although tooth modification varies geographically, it is difficult to identify a single ethnic group in particular. In the Caribbean and North America, this African custom apparently disappeared among second-generation slaves, according to ethnohistorical and bioarchaeological data (Handler 1994). As in South Africa, the presence of such cultural features is often used to identify African-born individuals. However, the present case could be an exception to the rule. In fact, dental modifications in Cuba, such as point filing, which was associated with initiation rites, were still practiced in the twentieth century among descendants of African slaves (Handler 1994; Ortiz 1929; Rivero de La Calle 1973). Furthermore, as various Africans were already present from the late eighteenth century (Singleton 2005), these dental modifications cannot be necessarily associated with one ethnic group but possibly with various (i.e., Nigeria, Congo) (Handler 1994).

The various data mentioned above suggest that the individuals represented by this cranial collection died during the peak period of the Cuban slave trade (1790–1860). If this assumption is accurate, we may first hypothesize that this group represents Africans of diverse cultures from West and Central Africa, from both coastal and inland areas (Bergad et al. 1995; Fraginals et al. 1983). Eltis (1982) estimates that around 325,000 slaves entered Cuba during the period from 1790 to 1820 alone. Ethnolinguistic groups, or *naciones*, were, for example, the Yoruba, the Ibo (Nigeria, Benin), the Mande (Senegal, Mali), the Kongo (D.R.C., Angola), and the Makwas (Mozambique) (Singleton 2005). Cuba, the leading producer of sugar in the world at the time, was one of the largest slave importers in Spanish colonial America, and in the nineteenth century it became the core of the Caribbean transatlantic slave trade. When the West African slave trade declined, slaves came particularly from southeastern Africa, an area extending from the Cape of Good Hope to Cape Delgado, including Madagascar (Knight 1997; Thomas 1997). In 1817 the British exported between three thousand and four thousand Madagascan slaves to various regions in the Indian Ocean (Mauritius) as well as the Americas, especially Cuba. As a consequence of this intense trade, the workforce on Cuban plantations was mainly composed of African-born slaves. Demographic estimates for the whole island (Cuba) show that, in 1830, the population was very diverse and was composed of slaves (41 percent), whites (44 percent), and free persons of color (15 percent) (Knight 1997:52). The latter might have included

Caribbean-born or Creole individuals as well as indigenous Amerindians as suggested by genetics of present-day Cubans (Colombo and Martínez 1985; Mendizabal et al. 2008). By the 1840s the slave trade had become illegal around the world, but it continued in Cuba until the 1880s, as population diversity increased with the arrival of various non-African groups. For example, Chinese were imported as a labor force, while Spanish settlers were encouraged to migrate to Cuba in order to whiten the population in the fear of slave rebellions (Hu-Dehart 1993; Singleton 2005).

In the light of this questionable historical context, two questions arise: (1) Is this sample composed of individuals of African ancestry only, as described in Morton's records referring to a period before 1840? (2) Is morphological variation more consistent with a multi-regional origin of these individuals, reflecting the presence of various admixed populations born locally and/or from elsewhere?

MATERIALS AND METHODS

CASE STUDY 1

Twenty-three adult individuals from the Cobern Street burial assemblage were used for craniometrical analysis. The skulls were chosen for their skeletal completeness, but they also represented a group that cross-cut the various burial patterns (Types A, B, and C), dietary diversity (C_4- and C_3-based diet), and dental modifications (presence/absence) (Table 12.1). Ten females and 13 males reflect the broad range of cultural diversity: there are 12 individuals of possibly non-Muslim origin (Type B burial), 5 Muslims (Type C burial), 2 precolonial (Khoekhoen pastoralists, Type A burial), and 2 unidentified individuals (Type D, disturbed burial). Five of the 12 Type B specimens present dental modification typical of the Congo and Gold Coast Region (Manyaapelo 2007). Sex and age were determined from diagnostic skeletal features (Buikstra and Ubelaker 1994; Friedling 2007; Maat et al. 2002).

Eight craniometric traits were recorded (Howells 1995, 1996; Morris 1992; Pietrusewsky 2008; Ribot 2003, 2004, 2011): three variables for the vault (glabella-opisthocranion length, or GOL; maximum cranial length, or XCB; basion-bregma height, or BBH) and five for the face (basion-nasion length, or BNL; basion-prosthion length, or BPL; bizygomatic breadth, or ZYB; nasion-prosthion height, or NPH; nasal breadth, or NLB). Sliding and spreading calipers were used to take these measurements (to the nearest mm) on both sides. The measurements were selected to maximize the number of Cobern Street crania in the analysis as well as the comparative set. The latter originated from personal and compiled data whose authors are listed with population codes in Table 12.2. Four broad regions are included here, in order to cover the possible origins of the Cobern Street sample: Africa ($N = 300$), Indian Ocean ($N = 94$), Asia ($N = 204$) and Europe ($N = 98$). Forty-three percent of this set is African and represents regions related to the site's history and the slave trade (Southern Africa, $N = 200$; Central Africa, $N = 100$). The other 43 percent originates from the Indian Ocean and Asia, where the Dutch traded slaves, and the remainder is represented by Europeans.

After pre-data procedures (normality tests), two types of multivariate statistics were performed: population structure analysis (model-bound quantitative genetics) and multiple discriminant analysis (MDA). Analyses were run separately for females and males, in order to evaluate differences and similarities in variation and gene-flow patterns. To explore population structure, R-matrix analysis was performed using RMET 5.0 (Relethford 2004). This method generates three population genetic parameters of interest (Relethford 1994, 2002; Relethford and Blangero 1990). First, matrices of intergroup distances assess isolation by distance among groups. Second, F_{ST} values, defined as the ratio of the among-group variation to total variation, compare levels of phenotypic diversity between groups. Third, the residual variance analysis based on patterns of observed and expected within-group variation can evaluate extra-local gene flow (outside Africa). Genetic distances were calculated for the whole sample. In order to also compare levels of diversity, F_{ST} values were calculated for the whole sample, the four-sample subsets (Cobern and three African groups only), and the two-sample subsets (Cobern with one of the seven comparative groups separately). The third parameter to evaluate extra-local gene flow was calculated for the four-sample subsets, as the latter represented local populations only. Following Relethford (1994, 2002), heritability was set at 0.55. As effective population sizes could not be reliably estimated, the value 1.0 was entered for each group (Relethford and Blangero 1990). Estimated F_{ST} values were corrected for sampling bias following Relethford (2004).

MDA helps to explore further patterns of morphological variation within and between samples. Described extensively in the literature, it weights and combines, in a linear matter, two or more discriminating variables in such a way that the intercorrelations of the variables are considered and the ratio of between group-variance to the within-group (total) variance is

Table 12.1. Cobern Street sample and various additional information

Burial type	Female	Male	Diet later in life			Mesial or distal filing on incisors
			C_3	C_3/C_4	C_4	
A (precolonial)	1	1	2	0	0	0
B (non-Muslim)	5	7	0	6	1	5 (2 females, 3 males)
C (Muslim)	2	3	3	5	0	0
D (bone scatter)	2	2	—	—	—	—

Note: Data from Cox et al. 2001; Friedling 2007; Manyaapelo 2007.

maximized (Pietrusewsky 2008). MDA was conducted in SPSS 20.0 with stepwise and jacknife analyses (with Mahalanobis distance, or D^2). Group classifications with cross-validation were calculated, as well as the first two posterior probabilities (PP) of belonging to a group for each unknown individual (Cobern Street).

CASE STUDY 2

Thirty-four complete adult crania were used here. Crania clearly showing intentional vault deformations were purposely excluded. As no postcranial bones were available, Renschler (2007) attempted sex identification on the crania only according to Buikstra and Ubelaker (1994). Three individuals appeared to be female, 13 male, and 18 of indeterminate sex.

Variables and multivariate statistics were similar to Case Study 1. South Africans and Asians were not included, but the comparative sample

Table 12.2. Comparative sample used for the craniometrical analysis of the Cobern Street individuals

Broad region	Population information	Population code	Source	Females (N)	Males (N)
Southern Africa	Zulu, R.S.A.	ZUL	Howells 1996	49	51
	Khoesan	KHOES	Howells 1996	49	51
Central Africa	Basuku, D.R.C.	BAS	Ribot 2003, 2004, 2011	49	51
Indian Ocean	Sakalave & Bets-ileo, Madagascar	MADA	This work	46	48
Asia	Burma	BUR	Tildesley 1921	50	50
	Andaman Islands	AND	Van Bonin and Med 1931	49	55
Europe	Zalavar, Hungary	HUN	Howells 1996	45	53

Table 12.3. Comparative sample used for the craniometrical analysis of S. G. Morton's Afri‹ collection

Broad region	Population information	Population code	Source	Females (N)	Mal‹ (N‹
West Africa	Ashanti (Ghana)	ASH	Shrubsall 1899; Ribot 2003, 2004, 2011	56	5.
Central Africa	Basuku, D.R.C.	BAS	Ribot 2003, 2004, 2011	49	5]
East Africa	Teita, Kenya	TEIT	Howells 1996	50	3:
Indian Ocean	Sakalave & Betsileo, Madagascar	MADA	This work	46	4٤
South America	Natives, Peru	PER	Howells 1996	55	5٥
Europe	Zalavar, Hungary	HUN	Howells 1996	45	5:

included a broad range of global groups (N = 599), compiled from various sources (Table 12.3). It covers regions targeted by the Cuban slave trade that were located in Africa (49 percent) and the Indian Ocean (16 percent). Another 35 percent of the sample is non-African (n = 208), corresponding to other groups (Native American, European) that may have contributed to the genetic makeup of present-day Cubans, as suggested by population admixture (Knight 1997; Mendizabal et al. 2008). In the absence of data on Cuban Native Americans (Tainos and Ciboneys), South America was selected as a comparative region, as archaeological and genetic evidence indicates a South American origin for precolonial Cubans (Dacal-Moure and Rivero de La Calle 1986; Lalueza-Fox et al. 2003).

Finally, because most of the individuals of Morton's skeletal sample remained unsexed (18 of 34), it was more appropriate to group females and males together for the analysis. Each half of Morton's unsexed sample was randomly grouped into both sexes, and a Z-score standardization within each sex was then calculated for the whole sample (Relethford 1994, 2002). Residual variance analysis was not performed here, as the present case study cannot be compared to available skeletal samples drawn directly from local populations (precolonial Cubans).

RESULTS

CASE STUDY 1

Genetic distances show that, for both sexes, Cobern is closest in decreasing order to ZUL and MADA (Figure 12.1; see Tables 12.2 and 12.3 for

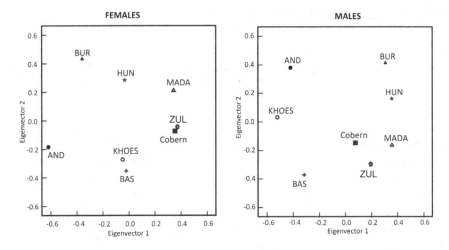

Figure 12.1. Genetic distance ordinations for Case Study 1 (see Table 12.2 for population codes).

population codes). A pattern of clinal variation is apparent, reflecting isolation by distance between Cobern and Asian groups at each of the extremes. However, differences are noted between the two sexes, possibly in relation to different gene-flow patterns: males from Cobern are slightly closer to the Burmese than the females, but slightly more distant from the Khoesan.

Levels of phenotypic diversity systematically decrease when the analysis is confined to a four-sample subset (Cobern and Africans only) (Table 12.4). The range of the values (bias-corrected F_{ST}: 0.2472–0.1278) appears comparable to previous African data (Relethford 2002 reported F_{ST} values between 0.2125 and 0.1136). When analyzing all samples and the four-sample subset, unbiased F_{ST} values are slightly higher for the males than the females, possibly reflecting some differential gene-flow pattern. When analyzing seven two-sample subsets (Cobern with each comparative group), they tend to decrease, as Cobern's genetic distances with other groups decrease (Table 12.4). Females showed lowest values for Cobern and MADA (0.0211) and the highest for Cobern and AND (0.2634). Males showed lowest values for Cobern and ZUL (0.0285) and the highest for Cobern and KHOES (0.1572).

Residual variance analysis performed on the four-sample subset shows high positive residuals for Cobern females (0.131), indicating substantial extra-local gene flow (Table 12.5). For other groups (apart from Khoesan males: 0.157), residuals are close to zero or even negative, with a low value

Table 12.4. F_{ST} values with standard errors (SE) for Case Study 1

Sample	F_{ST}		Unbiased F_{ST}		SE	
	Females	Males	Females	Males	Females	Males
All samples	0.2537	0.2605	0.2383	0.2472	0.0096	0.0084
Cobern and African samples	0.1480	0.1819	0.1278	0.1649	0.0146	0.0131
Cobern and ZUL	0.0793	0.0526	0.0491	0.0285	0.0216	0.0164
Cobern and KHOES	0.1241	0.1813	0.0931	0.1572	0.0251	0.0245
Cobern and BAS	0.1025	0.1178	0.0724	0.0936	0.0236	0.0221
Cobern and MADA	0.0515	0.0737	0.0211	0.0492	0.0183	0.0189
Cobern and BUR	0.1394	0.1127	0.1094	0.0885	0.0258	0.0218
Cobern and AND	0.2935	0.2501	0.2634	0.2263	0.0279	0.0250
Cobern and HUN	0.1819	0.1309	0.1514	0.1069	0.0276	0.0227

Note: See Table 12.2 for comparative population codes.

for Cobern males (-0.062), suggesting less-than-average external biological interaction. Therefore, Cobern females clearly show more gene flow than Cobern males, possibly from outside Africa. Although gene-flow patterns seem to differ not only between sexes but also between groups, interpretations remain cautious. Few variables have been analyzed, and the nature of the Khoesan sample is probably heterogeneous (Howells 1996).

The MDAs provide a total group classification rate (after cross-validation) of 65.6 percent for the females and of 63.0 percent for the males. Pairwise group comparisons between comparative samples support that differences are at the highest level of significance. For each group, the correct

Table 12.5. Residual variance analysis for Case Study 1 (Cobern Street and other African samples)

Groups	r_{ii} [a]		$\tilde{V}_i$ [b]		$E_{(\tilde{v}i)}$ [c]		$\tilde{V}_i - E_{(\tilde{v}i)}$ [d]	
	Females	Males	Females	Males	Females	Males	Females	Males
Cobern	0.074	0.061	0.977	0.757	0.846	0.819	0.131	-0.062
ZUL	0.126	0.159	0.701	0.723	0.799	0.735	-0.098	-0.011
KHOES	0.177	0.311	0.699	0.758	0.753	0.601	-0.053	0.157
BAS	0.136	0.128	0.810	0.678	0.790	0.761	0.020	-0.083

Note: See Table 12.2 for population codes.
[a] Regional phenotypic distances to centroid.
[b] Observed mean variance.
[c] Expected mean variance.
[d] Residual variance.

Table 12.6. Classification summary for the comparative groups obtained from the female MDA (Case Study 1)

	ZUL % (n)	KHOES % (n)	BAS % (n)	MADA % (n)	BUR % (n)	AND % (n)	HUN % (n)
ZUL	**57.1 (28)**	10.2 (5)	6.1 (3)	20.4 (10)	4.1 (2)	0	2.0 (1)
KHOES	6.1 (3)	**59.2 (29)**	12.2 (6)	0	2.0 (1)	8.2 (4)	12.2 (6)
BAS	8.2 (4)	12.2 (6)	**65.3 (32)**	4.1 (2)	4.1 (2)	2.0 (1)	4.1 (2)
MADA	21.7 (10)	0	10.9 (5)	**50.0 (23)**	4.3 (2)	4.3 (2)	8.7 (4)
BUR	2.0 (1)	2.0 (1)	2.0 (1)	8.0 (4)	**74.0 (37)**	0	12.0 (6)
AND	2.0 (1)	8.2 (4)	6.1 (3)	0	4.1 (2)	**79.6 (39)**	0
HUN	2.2 (1)	2.2 (1)	2.2 (1)	13.3 (6)	4.4 (2)	2.2 (1)	**73.3 (33)**

Note: See Table 12.2 for comparative population codes.

classification rate is often above 50 percent for females (Table 12.6) and for males (Table 12.7). Three groups (AND, BUR, HUN), especially those from Asia, are well differentiated from the others, with a correct classification rate above 70 percent. African groups (ZUL, BAS, KHOES) are differentiated from each other in a variable manner (correct classification rates: 41.2–70.6 percent). The latter present the lowest correct classification rate (females, 50.0 percent; males, 41.7 percent), as it is misclassified into a wide range of groups for females (Table 12.6) and males (Table 12.7).

Cobern's intra-sample variation is very high, as shown with the probabilistic affinities. According to first PPs, individuals are classified into four or five groups, three of which are non-African: for the females, KHOES 30.0%, BAS 30.0%, MADA 30.0%, and BUR 10.0% (Table 12.8); and for the males, ZUL 30.8%, BAS 30.8%, BUR 15.4%, HUN 15.4%, and MADA 7.7% (Table 12.9).

Table 12.7. Classification summary for the comparative groups obtained from the male MDA (Case Study 1)

	ZUL % (n)	KHOES % (n)	BAS % (n)	MADA % (n)	BUR % (n)	AND % (n)	HUN % (n)
ZUL	**41.2 (21)**	3.9 (2)	17.6 (9)	25.5 (13)	0	2.0 (1)	9.8 (5)
KHOES	7.8 (4)	**70.6 (36)**	9.8 (5)	0	0	5.9 (3)	5.9 (3)
BAS	11.8 (6)	3.9 (2)	**62.7 (32)**	7.8 (4)	2.0 (1)	9.8 (5)	2.0 (1)
MADA	14.6 (7)	2.1 (1)	10.4 (5)	**41.7 (20)**	10.4 (5)	4.2 (2)	16.7 (8)
BUR	10.0 (5)	2.0 (1)	2.0 (1)	2.0 (1)	**70.0 (35)**	8.0 (4)	6.0 (3)
AND	0	10.9 (6)	3.6 (2)	3.6 (2)	1.8 (1)	**78.2 (43)**	1.8 (1)
HUN	1.9 (1)	5.7 (3)	0	13.2 (7)	3.8 (2)	1.9 (1)	**73.6 (39)**

Note: See Table 12.2 for comparative population codes.

Table 12.8. First and second posterior probabilities (PP) of belonging to a group referenc obtained from the MDA for 10 Cobern Street females

Grave number	Accession number	1st PP in % (closest group)	2nd PP in % (closest group)	Burial type	Diet in childhood	Diet later in life	Mesia tal fil inci
37a	UCT 531	65.3 (KHOES)	32.6 (HUN)	A	C_3	C_3	
20b	UCT 511	55.0 (MADA)	43.2 (ZUL)	B	C_4	C_3	Ye
60	UCT 558	54.6 (MADA)	33.2 (ZUL)	B	C_4	C_3	Ye
40	UCT 535	40.7 (BAS)	34.4 (ZUL)	B	C_4	C_4	Ye
21	UCT 514	89.1 (BUR)	3.7 (MADA)	B	C_4	C_3	
58	UCT 556	63.7 (MADA)	28.4 (ZUL)	B	C_4	C_3	
57	UCT 555	39.7 (KHOES)	16.3 (ZUL)	C	Low C_3	C_3/C_4	
65	UCT 563	56.0 (BAS)	24.5 (MADA)	C	Low C_3	C_3/C_4	
S95/3	UCT 475	48.4 (BAS)	35.5 (MADA)	D	-	-	
Scatter O	UCT 491	35.2 (KHOES)	26.0 (HUN)	D	-	-	

Note: See Table 12.2 for comparative population codes. Funerary, dietary, and dental data from Cox et a Friedling 2007; Manyaapelo 2007.

Table 12.9. First and second posterior probabilities (PP) of belonging to a group referenc obtained from the MDA for 13 Cobern Street males

Grave number	Accession number	1st PP in % (closest group)	2nd PP in % (closest group)	Burial type	Diet in childhood	Diet later in life	Mesial/d tal filing incisor
42a	UCT 539	66.1 (HUN)	11.3 (ZUL)	A	C_3	C_3	
20a	UCT 510	33.4 (ZUL)	19.2 (BAS)	B	C_4	C_3	yes
49	UCT 547	43.6 (BAS)	33.5 (ZUL)	B	C_4	C_3	yes
54	UCT 552	68.5 (ZUL)	26.5 (BAS)	B	C_3	C_3	
12	UCT 500	47.2 (MADA)	26.7 (BUR)	B	C_3	C_3	
47	UCT 545	78.1 (BAS)	16.7 (ZUL)	B	C_3	C_3	
51	UCT 549	38.9 (ZUL)	30.4 (KHOES)	B	-	C_3	
56	UCT 554	66.2 (BAS)	14.8 (AND)	B	-	C_3	
32	UCT 526	31.8 (BAS)	25.9 (MADA)	C	Low C_3	C_3/C_4	
59	UCT 557	71.3 (BUR)	10.8 (BAS)	C	Low C_3	C_3/C_4	
64	UCT 562	97.6 (BUR)	1.2 (MADA)	C	Low C_3	C_3/C_4	
S95/4	UCT 476	45.1 (ZUL)	37.9 (MADA)	D	-	-	
41 (b)	UCT 537	62.8 (HUN)	16.9 (MADA)	D	-	-	

Note: Funerary, dietary, and dental data from Cox et al. 2001; Friedling 2007; Manyaapelo 2007.

CASE STUDY 2

According to genetic distances (Figure 12.2), Morton's sample is slightly more distant from its comparative groups than the Coburn Street sample. It remains relatively close to Madagascans and, in decreasing order, to four other groups mainly from Africa (HUN, ASH, BAS, TEIT). Morton's sample is very distant from the Peruvians, who are at the other end of the clinal variation.

Levels of phenotypic diversity were calculated for the whole sample as well as for sample subsets in order to explore its variation (Table 12.10). When analyzing all samples or Morton's sample with Africans only, unbiased F_{ST} values are broadly similar to Case Study 1 and previous data (Relethford 2002). When analyzing each two-sample subset (Morton and one comparative group), unbiased F_{ST} values tend to decrease as the Morton sample's genetic distance from comparative groups decreases, showing lowest levels with Madagascans (0.0992) and highest with Peruvians (0.2730) (Table 12.10). Morton's sample appears closest to Madagascans just as the Cobern data (Case Study 1). However, when the latter is also analyzed with Madagascans, unbiased F_{ST} values are even lower than for Morton's sample (Table 12.4: females: 0.0211; males: 0.0492). This fact indirectly supports the interpretation that Morton's sample is more heterogeneous than the Cobern Street sample, although this might be due here to the procedure of pooling sexes.

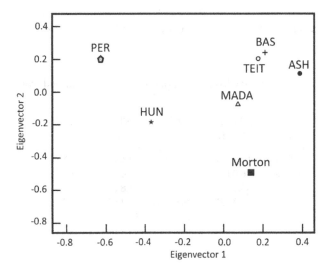

Figure 12.2. Genetic distance ordinations for Case Study 2 (see Table 12.3 for population codes).

Table 12.10. F_{ST} values with standard errors (SE) for Case Study 2

Sample	F_{ST}	Unbiased F_{ST}	SE
All samples	0.2391	0.2327	0.0072
Morton and African samples	0.1690	0.1614	0.0078
Morton and MADA	0.1092	0.0992	0.0139
Morton and HUN	0.1432	0.1333	0.0149
Morton and ASH	0.1535	0.1438	0.0150
Morton and TEIT	0.1861	0.1757	0.0161
Morton and BAS	0.1513	0.1415	0.0151
Morton and PER	0.2826	0.2730	0.0158

Note: See Table 12.3 for comparative population codes.

The MDA provides a total group classification (after cross-validation) of 60.8 percent, slightly lower than in Case Study 1, but still showing inter-group differences at the highest level of significance (pairwise group comparisons). Four comparative groups show correct classification rates well above 50 percent; these are, in decreasing order, PER, HUN, TEIT, and BAS (Table 12.11). West Africans (43.1 percent) and Madagascans (46.8 percent) are less well differentiated than the others, as they are often misclassified. Probabilistic affinities show that Morton's intra-sample variation is also very high (Table 12.12). According to first PPs, individuals are classified mainly into four comparative groups, two of which are non-African (32% HUN, 29% MADA) and two African (24% BAS, 12% ASH). Only 1 percent of the sample is classified with East Africans (TEIT), and individuals are never classified with Native Americans (PER). Two clusters are observed, possibly reflecting different levels of admixture: 47 percent of the sample ($n = 16$) is clearly classified with one main group (first PP above 60 percent),

Table 12.11. Classification summary for the comparative groups obtained from the MDA (Case Study 2)

	ASH % (n)	BAS % (n)	TEIT % (n)	MADA % (n)	PER % (n)	HUN % (n)
ASH	**43.1 (47)**	24.8 (27)	10.1 (11)	17.4 (19)	2.8 (3)	1.8 (2)
BAS	20.0 (20)	**61.0 (61)**	8.0 (8)	5.0 (5)	5.0 (5)	1.0 (1)
TEIT	13.3 (11)	9.6 (8)	**63.9 (53)**	8.4 (7)	4.8 (4)	0
MADA	17.0 (16)	8.5 (8)	5.3 (5)	**46.8 (44)**	6.4 (6)	16.0 (15)
PER	0	2.7 (3)	3.6 (4)	3.6 (4)	**81.8 (90)**	8.2 (9)
HUN	2.0 (2)	2.0 (2)	2.0 (2)	11.2 (11)	15.3 (15)	**67.3 (66)**

Note: See Table 12.3 for comparative population codes.

Table 12.12. First and second posterior probabilities (PP) of belonging to a group, obtained from the MDA for 34 individuals from the S. G. Morton African collection

Accession number	Sex	1st PP in % (closest group)	2nd PP in % (closest group)	Antemortem tooth loss	Filed tooth
68, NBIA	Female	90.8 (MADA)	6.1 (ASH)		
64, NBIA	Unknown	89.0 (HUN)	5.9 (MADA)	Maxillary RI1, Maxillary RI2, Maxillary LI2	
08, NBIA	Unknown	89.2 (HUN)	10.0 (MADA)		Maxillary RC
23, NBIA	Male	87.1 (HUN)	5.9 (MADA)		
62, NBIA	Unknown	80.7 (BAS)	8.0 (ASH)		
24, NBIA	Male	79.7 (BAS)	11.9 (TEIT)		
76, NBIA	Male	73.1 (BAS)	24.5 (ASH)		
21, NBIA	Unknown	65.9 (HUN)	16.3 (BAS)		
18, NBIA	Unknown	69.5 (HUN)	11.7 (TEIT)	Maxillary RC	
03, NBIA	Unknown	68.6 (MADA)	27.4 (HUN)		
15, NBIA	Male	68.1 (MADA)	18.3 (ASH)		
27, NBIA	Male	66.6 (HUN)	15.6 (MADA)		
65, NBIA	Male	66.5 (ASH)	28.7 (BAS)		
58, NBIA	Unknown	66.1 (MADA)	31.4 (HUN)		
01, NBIA	Unknown	64.2 (TEIT)	12.8 (MADA)	Maxillary LI2	
71, NBIA	Female	62 (MADA)	33.7 (HUN)		
19, NBIA	Unknown	59.5 (HUN)	38.0 (MADA)		
26, NBIA	Unknown	57 (BAS)	26.5 (HUN)		
17, NBIA	Unknown	56.9 (ASH)	23.4 (TEIT)		
66, NBIA	Male	56.7 (BAS)	21.0 (ASH)		
20, NBIA	Unknown	56.2 (MADA)	19.1 (TEIT)		
12, NBIA	Unknown	55.4 (MADA)	35.6 (HUN)		
13, NBIA	Unknown	52.4 (ASH)	38.1 (MADA)		
62, NBIA	Unknown	51.5 (MADA)	18.1 (BAS)		
11, NBIA	Unknown	50.7 (BAS)	23.6 (HUN)		
09, NBIA	Unknown	49.9 (HUN)	38 (MADA)		
63, NBIA	Female	49.2 (ASH)	31.2 (MADA)		
75, NBIA	Male	48.6 (HUN)	26.5 (MADA)		
05, NBIA	Male	48.4 (BAS)	21.3 (ASH)		
75, NBIA	Male	45.0 (HUN)	30.3 (MADA)		
02, NBIA	Male	45.0 (BAS)	31.5 (ASH)		
04, NBIA	Male	43.0 (HUN)	34.2 (PER)		
25, NBIA	Unknown	42.9 (MADA)	41.7 (TEIT)		
07, crosse	Male	41.8 (MADA)	33.9 (HUN)		

Note: See Table 12.3 for comparative population codes. Dental modification data from Emily S. Renschler, personal communication, 2013.

and the remainder ($n = 18$) appears very heterogeneous, as they present relatively low first PP (below 60 percent) and often nearly as high second PP.

INTERPRETATIONS

CASE STUDY 1

Both population structure analysis and MDAs show that Cobern sample is very heterogeneous, with a fair degree of defined population structure, and that it does not correspond to a single homogeneous population or a hybrid biological aggregate. Therefore, this evidence tends to support a multi-origin hypothesis proposed by historical data. Genetic distances and MDA classifications show that Cobern is close to not only various Southern and Central African groups (Zulu, Basuku) but also Madagascans. This fact supports historical data about Madagascans used as slaves at the Cape (Elphick and Giliomee 1990).

Interestingly, results also differ between sexes. When large samples (Cobern compared with all samples or just Africans only) are analyzed, F_{ST} values reflect higher group differentiation for males than for females. Asymmetrical gene flow due to predominant mating patterns (patrilocality) could partly explain this fact, as it has been observed for sub-Saharan Africans with genetics (Destro-Bisol et al. 2004). When focusing on Cobern only, all results show that females are closer to Khoesan than are males.

These phenotypic data also support genetic observations about a greater maternal contribution than paternal of the Khoesan peoples to the South African Coloured populations of the Cape (Quintana-Murci et al. 2010). However, in contrast to modern genetics, which explores human variation of postslavery periods, bioarchaeological studies have the advantage of providing information on earlier periods. In this respect, the data show that gene flow from Khoesan females in the urban Cape population probably started before slavery ended. Furthermore, residual variance analysis and MDA classifications indicate that Cobern females have a stronger Madagascan component than Cobern males, who in turn are closer to local Africans and non-Africans (Europeans, Asians).

This result suggests that enslaved Madagascans might have been predominantly females during the Cobern Street era, which is supported historically. According to Sleigh and Westra (2013), Dutch slavers sent to Madagascar often returned with more women than men, as women and children were easier to capture. However, according to Campbell et al. (2005), a greater proportion of women imported to the Cape can also be explained by the fact that they were highly valued, not only on farms but also in domestic labor, which was an important component in non-plantation systems of slavery.

In order to explore whether there is increased morphological variation through presumed first- and second-generation immigrants, probabilistic affinities are examined, and compared to previous data (Tables 12.8 and 12.9). It was assumed that the cemetery contained at least three groups who died there contemporaneously or not (local people, first- and second-generation immigrants from Africa and elsewhere).

First, as broadly expected, the two precontact individuals (Type A burial, C_3-based diet) (female UCT 531, male UCT 539) appear close to three groups (KHOES, HUN, ZUL), with one first PP above 60 percent for the Khoesan (UCT 531). Similarities with Europeans are explained here by the small number of variables analyzed and poor intergroup discrimination.

Second, the seven presumed first-generation immigrants from (sub) tropical regions (Type B burial, shift from a C_4- to a C_3-based diet except for UCT 535, who possessed dental modifications) are close to a wider range of groups for the females (MADA, BUR, ZUL) (Table 12.8) than for the males (ZUL, BAS) (Table 12.9). For the females in particular, relatively high first PPs (above 50 percent) are obtained: UCT 514 is closest to BUR, and UCT 511, UCT 558, and UCT 556 are closest to MADA. This group reflects a significant non-local contribution (Indian Ocean, Asia) and a local one (Africa). It supports the hypothesis that they are first-generation immigrants, but possibly from already admixed populations such as the Madagascans, but differences between sexes remain difficult to interpret due to small sample size (5 females, 2 males).

Third, the five presumed second-generation immigrants from (sub)tropical regions in Africa or elsewhere (Type B burial, a C_3-based diet throughout life, no dental modifications) show affinities with Africans (BAS, ZUL, KHOES) and non-Africans (MADA, BUR) (Table 12.9). Only three individuals have relatively high first PPs: UCT 545 and UCT 554 (both closest to BAS) and UCT 552 (closest to ZUL). This third group, composed of males only, is also rather heterogeneous, but in comparison to the previous sample, composed mainly of females (second group), it reflects gene flow predominantly with local people (Africans). Due to absence of both dietary change and dental modification, they are initially considered as second-generation immigrants. As they seem less diverse than the first-generation immigrants, their genetic signature (with initial non-local contribution) could have faded with time due to continuous internal gene flow with Africans from the Cape or other regions. This could indicate the emergence of a growing group that resulted from mixed marriages. According to historical sources, unions were allowed in the early Cape society, not only between slaves and indigenous Khoekhoe but also between European men and various groups (slaves, Khoekhoe, females of mixed parentage) (Keegan 1996; Mountain 2003).

Fourth, the five presumed first-generation immigrants from Asia and elsewhere (Type C burials, depleted C_3-based diet suggesting rice consumption and little sea food) show relatively close affinity to various groups (BUR, BAS, KHOES, MADA, ZUL) (Table 12.9). Two males, UCT 562 and UCT 557, are consistent with a non-African birth and genetic origin: their first PPs are highest (above 70 percent) and are morphologically closest to the Burmese. However, as affinities of one male (UCT 526) and two females are very diverse, they suggest that they originated from very mixed groups (possibly via Madagascar) or were non-Asian converts to Islam.

The remaining four individuals of unknown historic context (Type D burial) have affinities with a wide range of groups (HUN, ZUL, BAS, KHOES, MADA). Only one individual has a relatively high first PP (UCT 537 close to HUN) (Tables 12.8 and 12.9).

In conclusion, although the Cobern Street sample is far from sufficiently representative of the early Cape urban poor society, it provides a snapshot of the morphological diversity that is ancestral to the present Cape Coloured people. Intragroup variation in the Cobern sample shows subtle differences between first- and second-generation immigrants. As people admixed increasingly (and increased genetic homogeneity) through later generations, levels of morphological diversity predictably appear to decrease, as observed with the third group (males predominantly African with Type B burial and C_3-based diet). This case study illustrates a scenario of hybridization that could have occurred in the Cape since the seventeenth century. Various groups from Africa and elsewhere arrived in the region: they were phenotypically quite diverse, and some (i.e., Madagascans) had experienced already high levels of external gene flow in their population history. Thereafter, they tended to be united by internal gene flow through mixed marriages with local and non-local people, finally giving birth to a new hybrid or Cape Coloured population.

CASE STUDY 2

All multivariate analyses showed that Morton's sample is morphologically very diverse, showing similarities not solely with Africans but also with various non-Africans (Madagascans and Europeans). This supports the presence of enslaved Africans within the sample, the latter corresponding possibly to nearly half of the sample. However, as reported by historical sources (Knight 1997; Singleton 2005), high levels of heterogeneity within the sample could also be the result of the presence of already highly ad-mixed people, as, for example, the Cuban-born people resulting from vari-ous intergroup unions between Africans and non-Africans, which probably occurred from the beginning of the slave trade and with the later arrival of Madagascans in Cuba.

The local component (Native Americans) seems to have contributed little, or not at all, to the diversity observed within Morton's sample. This fact could support historians' description of the small number of local Am-erindians as a result of colonial decimation (Eltis 1982; Shell 1994). Still, it remains difficult to interpret, as the South American sample selected to represent Native Americans (Tainos and Ciboneys) may have been not entirely appropriate. However, in contrast to our phenotypic data, genetic data show that the precolonial people contributed to some extent to mod-ern Cuban diversity (Mendizabal et al. 2008).

As mentioned above, second-generation diaspora individuals could not be identified here, as cultural features (dental modifications) were not considered a reliable tool to identify first-generation descendants (Handler 1994; Ortiz 1929; Rivero de La Calle 1973). Although the historical con-text remains questionable, our analysis shows that highly admixed people (Caribbean-born people or Madagascans) were possibly in greater num-bers than Africans. So far it is not possible to verify this with previous demographic estimates, as they are based on limited archival information. Knight (1997) provides data on various general categories (slaves, whites, free persons of color) that were present in Cuban populations, but he can-not specify the place of birth within the slaves group.

Nevertheless, if Morton's sample originates from a nineteenth-century Cuban cemetery, it well illustrates a process of biological hybridization on the island as an indirect consequence of colonialism. It reflects mainly non-local components (Africa, Indian Ocean, Europe) that admixed to some extent. High levels of phenotypic diversity, genetic distances, and MDAs support that the precolonial Cuban population composition has been significantly reshaped by extra-local gene flow over a long period (Singleton 2005). Nevertheless, a final scenario could not be excluded: if certain crania of Morton's collection were labeled incorrectly as native Africans, they could be from another continent and may not have been slaves. Unfortunately, the current interpretation cannot go any further, as more contextual information is required.

REFLECTIONS ON THE TWO CASES STUDIES AND CONCLUSIONS

Each case study analyzed provided information on the nature of the skeletal sample and highlighted issues relating to biohistory. According to the first PPs of the MDAs suggesting group affinities, both show an African component for more than half of the cases for Cobern Street (61 percent) (Tables 12.8 and 12.9), and less than half for the Morton collection (38 percent) (Table 12.12). Madagascans also constitute possibly an important component within both samples and more significantly for the Cuban case study (Morton: 29 percent; Cobern: 17 percent). Furthermore, when first PPs of MDAs are below 60 percent, more than half of the sample often shows affinities with more than one group (Cobern, 57 percent; Morton, 53 percent). These facts suggest that neither case reflects a single homogeneous biological population, and in a sense this fits very well with the historical context of the slave trade and its effects on populations (i.e., biological hybridization). The high levels of morphological heterogeneity observed within both samples support a multi-origin hypothesis for colonial populations, as well as the presence of population admixture. We know from contextual data and genetics (Cox et al. 2001; de Wit et al. 2010; Elphick and Giliomee 1990) that the Cobern Street sample was drawn from different geographical regions and continents, and this is confirmed here. For Morton's sample this information is even more valuable, as complementary data were lacking and can only be hypothetically inferred (Knight 1997; Mendizabal et al. 2008).

If we look back at our initial hypothesis, which predicted less morphological diversity within the sample from the Cape Colony (Case Study 1: Cobern Street) than from Cuba (Case Study 2: the Morton collection), our results are indeed consistent with this notion. For example, as indicated by population structure analysis, levels of phenotypic diversity appeared to be higher in Morton's sample (Table 12.10) than in the Cobern sample (Table 12.4). Although in both settings the crania were morphologically closest to highly admixed populations such as the Madagascans, Morton's sample appeared to be more distant from its comparative groups (Figure 12.2) than was the Cobern sample (Figure 12.1). These facts support that, in comparison to Cobern, Morton's collection is more heterogeneous and more distant from its possible parent populations. This, in turn, could indirectly reflect extra-local gene flow occurring on a longer time span for Cuba than for the Cape Colony, as suggested by historical sources (Elphick and Giliomee 1990; Knight 1997; Singleton 2005). Hybridization processes might have been therefore extremely intense, especially during the nineteenth century with the arrival in Cuba of various Africans and Madagascans during the transatlantic slave trade and later from other parts of the world (China, Mesoamerica, Europe). The local component also appeared to be more significant in the Cape Colony (Khoesan, sub-Saharan Africans) than in Cuba (Native Americans), with particularly interesting results for Cobern Street about asymmetrical gene-flow patterns already suggested by geneticists (Quintana-Murci et al. 2010).

However, it is important to remind ourselves that our interpretations are preliminary, as they are based on two case studies that are difficult to compare for several reasons. First, they used slightly different comparative groups representing different parent populations in relation to a specific historical context. The results could be therefore affected by the nature of the comparative groups, which were probably less appropriate for Morton's sample than for the Cobern sample. Second, the geographical origin of the parent population in terms of population affiliation still remains poorly understood, especially in Morton's sample. It is quite possible that these individuals came from various ethnic backgrounds not represented by the comparative samples. The Ashanti used here for example, were probably not the only West Africans present in Cuba (Singleton 2005), and a more exhaustive study could provide more detailed and nuanced results. Third, museum ethnic collections probably do not truly reflect the craniofacial population variation they purport to represent: they are a small sample subset and reflect population admixture due to culture contacts prior to European contact. This is an especially important factor given the fact that there is far greater craniometric variation within than between skeletal samples (Relethford 2002). The same observation has been made in molecular genetic studies of the Khoesan in particular (de Wit et al. 2010; Tishkoff et al. 2009). In a similar case study, Jackson et al. (2004) were able to use craniometrics to support African ancestry for most of the individuals excavated from the New York African Burial Ground, but similarly, they were not able to specify ethnic affiliation accurately.

These two case studies represent two extreme situations. One is a well-documented archaeological sample, and the other is a museum collection for which information is sparse. They are very different from each other, due to the nature of their discovery, the contextual information available, as well as skeletal preservation. And this, of course, will affect the accuracy of any interpretations made from craniometry. Case Study 1 resulted in a more nuanced morphometrical interpretation, as documentary information was available about the known historical site of Cobern Street. Here, data related to burial patterns, diet, dental modification, and sex helped considerably in proposing precise hypotheses, as we saw in Chapter 11 of the present book. Cape Town–born individuals (possibly second-generation slaves) appeared easily distinguishable from recently arrived immigrants (African and/or Asian), and they could already reflect a process of population admixture. Instead, in Case Study 2, much less is known about the mortuary contexts, the identity of the individuals, and the demographic composition of the sample. It was not yet possible to support or reject the presence of first- and second-generation immigrants, in contrast to Case Study 1, which used isotopic data as a complementary tool for biodistance studies. Morton's collection needs to be explored further.

In conclusion, each cemetery excavation or museum skeletal collection is unique in terms of its chronological and historical context. To better understand factors influencing human population dynamics such as the African diaspora and subsequent gene-flow patterns, further research is needed on additional well-documented cemetery sites around the world post-1600 A.D. The Cobern Street sample, and especially the Morton sample, could benefit from further isotope research, looking at diet (carbon, nitrogen), mobility (oxygen, strontium), and ancient DNA. Lastly, in order to better match past human diversity, the establishment of comparative databases from archaeological samples (in relation to eighteenth- and nineteenth-century Africans, Asians, Mesoamericans, Dutch, British, and Spanish) has the potential to improve the comparative analysis of craniofacial variation. We believe that bioarchaeology can be enriched by comparing different case studies that involve populations from the African diaspora on different continents and regions. Despite various limitations mainly related to the nature of the sample analyzed, the Cobern Street and Morton collections suggested phenotypically a biohistory that could easily match historical data. In Cuba and the Cape, the effects of the colonialism are similar in some ways, as the local population composition was reshaped with the arrival of diasporic groups (Africans, Madagascans, Asians, and/or Europeans) and later with varying degrees of population admixture. Nevertheless, they still remained different because of the scale of the slave trade phenomenon, which was more intense in the Caribbean than in southern Africa.

ACKNOWLEDGMENTS

This research was in part funded by the University of Montreal (SSHRC small grant and sabbatical research funds). We would like to thank master's student Caroline Deswarte for collecting and sharing the Madagascan data from the Musée de l'Homme, and Alain Froment for facilitating access to these skeletal samples. Thanks to John Relethford for providing access to the RMET 5.0 program and advice on the R-matrix analyses. All statistical errors remain the responsibility of the authors. Finally, thanks also to all the reviewers and editors for their preliminary comments, which significantly helped to improve the chapter.

REFERENCES CITED

Angel, J. L., J. O Kelley, M. Parrington, and S. Pinter
1987   Life Stresses of the Free Black Community as Represented by the First Af-
            rican Baptist Church, Philadelphia, 1823–1841. *American Journal of Physical
            Anthropology* 74:213–229.
Apollonio, H.
1998   Identifying the Dead: Eighteenth Century Mortuary Practices at Cobern
            Street, Cape Town. Unpublished Master's thesis, Department of Archaeol-
            ogy, University of Cape Town.
Banks, A.
1991   The Decline of Urban Slavery at the Cape, 1806 to 1843. The Centre for Afri-
            can Studies *Communications*, No. 22, University of Cape Town, Cape Town.
Bayly, C. A.
2004   *The Birth of the Modern World, 1780–1914.* Blackwell, Oxford.
Bergad, L. W., L. W. Garcia, and M. D. C. Barcia
1995   *The Cuban Slave Market, 1790–1880.* Cambridge University Press, Cam-
            bridge.
Biccum, A. R.
2002   Interrupting the Discourse of Development: On a Collision Course with
            Postcolonial Theory. *Culture, Theory and Critique* 43:33–50.
Blakey, M. L.
2001   Bioarchaeology of the African Diaspora in the Americas: Its Origins and
            Scope. *Annual Review of Anthropology* 30:387–422.
Brace, C. L.
2005   *Race Is a Four-Letter Word.* Oxford University Press, Oxford.

Buikstra, J. E., and D. H. Ubelaker (editors)
1994   *Standards for Data Collection from Human Skeletal Remains.* Arkansas Archaeological Survey Research Series, Fayetteville.

Campbell, G., S. Miers, and J. C. Miller
2005   Women in Western Systems of Slavery. *Slavery and Abolition: A Journal of Slave and Post-Slave Studies* 26:161–179.

Cohen, R.
2007   Creolization and Cultural Globalization: The Soft Sounds of Fugitive Power. *Globalizations* 4:369–384.

Colombo, B., and G. Martínez
1985   Hemoglobin Variants in Cuba. *Hemoglobin* 9:415–422.

Corruccini, R. S., K. P. Jacobi, and J. S. Handler
1985   Distribution of Enamel Hypoplasias in an Early Caribbean Slave Population. *American Journal of Physical Anthropology* 66:158.

Cox, G.
1999   Cobern Street Burial Ground: Investigating the Identity and Life Histories of the Underclass of Eighteenth Century Cape Town. Unpublished Master's thesis, Department of Archaeology, University of Cape Town.

Cox, G., and J. Sealy
1997   Investigating Identity and Life Histories: Isotopic Analysis and Historical Documentation of Slave Skeletons found on the Cape Town Foreshore, South Africa. *International Journal of Historical Archaeology* 1:207–224.

Cox G., J. Sealy, C. Schrire, and A. G. Morris
2001   Stable Carbon and Nitrogen Isotopic Analyses of the Underclass at the Colonial Cape of Good Hope in the Eighteenth and Nineteenth Centuries. *World Archaeology* 33:73–97.

Dacal-Moure, R., and M. Rivero de la Calle
1986   *Arqueología aborigen de Cuba.* Editorial gente nueva, Havana.

Destro-Bisol, G., F. Donati, V. Coia, I. Boschi, F. Verginelli, A. Caglia, S. Tofanelli, G. Spedini, and C. Capelli
2004   Variation of Female and Male Lineages in Sub-Saharan Populations: The Importance of Sociocultural Factors. *Molecular Biology and Evolution* 21:1673–1682.

de Wit, E., W. Delport, C. H. Rugamika, A. Meintjes, M. Möller, P. D. van Helden, C. Seoighe, and E. G. Hoal
2010   Genome-wide Analysis of the Structure of the South African Coloured Population in the Western Cape. *Human Genetics* 128:145–153.

Elphick, R., and H. Giliomee (editors)
1990   *The Shaping of South African Society, 1652–1840.* 2nd ed. Maskew Miller Longman, Cape Town.

Elphick, R., and R. Shell
1990   Intergroup Relations: Khoikhoi, Settlers, Slaves and Free Blacks, 1652–1795. In *The Shaping of South African Society, 1652–1840*, edited by R. Elphick and H. Giliomee, pp.184–239. 2nd ed. Maskew Miller Longman, Cape Town.

Eltis, D
1982   Nutritional Trends in Africa and the Americas: Height of Africans, 1819–
          1839. *Journal of Interdisciplinary History* 12:453–475.
Fraginals, M. M., H. S. Klein, and S. L. Engerman
1983   The Level and Structure of Slave Prices on Cuban Plantations in the Mid-
          Nineteenth Century: Some Comparative Perspectives. *American Historical
          Review* 88:1201–1218.
Franklin, D., A. Cardini, and C. E. Oxnard
2010   A Geometric Morphometric Approach to the Quantification of Population
          Variation in Sub-Saharan African Crania. *American Journal of Human Biol-
          ogy* 22:23–35.
Friedling, L. J.
2007   Grave Tales: An Osteological Assessment of Health and Lifestyle from 18th
          and 19th Century Burial Sites around Cape Town. Unpublished Ph.D. thesis,
          Department of Human Biology, University of Cape Town.
Friedling, L. J., and A. G. Morris
2005   The Frequency of Culturally Derived Dental Modification Practices on the
          Cape Flats in the Western Cape. *Journal of the South African Dental Associa-
          tion* 60:97–102.
Goodman, A. H., J. Jones, J. Reid, M. Mack, M. L. Blakey, D. Amarasiriwardena, P. Burton,
          and D. Coleman
2004   Isotopic and Elemental Chemistry of Teeth: Implications for Places of Birth,
          Forced Migration Patterns, Nutritional Status, and Pollution. In *The New
          York African Burial Ground Skeletal Biology Final Report*, edited by M. L.
          Blakey and L. M. Rankin-Hill, pp. 216–265. Howard University Press, Wash-
          ington, D.C.
Goose, D.
1963   Tooth Mutilation in West Africans. *Man* 65:91–93.
Gosden, C.
2012   Postcolonial Archaeology: Issues of Culture, Identity and Knowledge. In
          Archaeological Theory Today, edited by I. Hodder, pp. 241–261. Polity Press,
          Cambridge, U.K.
Gould, A., A. Forman, and D. Corbitt
1984   Mutilations of the Dentition in Africa: A Review with Personal Observa-
          tions. *Quintessenz International* 75:89–94.
Graf, O. H. T.
1996   Cobern Street: A Truly Unique Site in Cape Town, South Africa. *Society for
          Clay Pipe Research Newsletter* 50:25–35.
Handler, J. S.
1994   Determining African Birth from Skeletal Remains: A Note on Tooth Mutila-
          tion. *Historical Archaeology* 28:113–119.
Handler, J. S., R. S. Corruccini, and R. J. Mutaw
1982   Tooth Mutilation in the Caribbean: Evidence from a Slave Burial Population
          in Barbados. *Journal of Human Evolution* 11:297–313.

Handler, J. S., and F. W. Lange
1978   *Plantation Slavery in Barbados: An Archeological and Historical Investigation.* Harvard University Press, London.

Haviser, J. B., and K. C. MacDonald
2006   *African Re-Genesis: Confronting Social Issues in the Diaspora.* University College Press, London.

Howells, W. W.
1995   *Who's Who in Skulls: Ethnic Identification of Crania from Measurements.* Papers of the Peabody Museum of Archaeology and Ethnology, Vol. 82. Harvard University Press, Cambridge.
1996   Howells' Craniometric Data on the Internet. *American Journal of Physical Anthropology* 101:441–442.

Hu-Dehart, E.
1993   Chinese Coolie Labour in Cuba in the Nineteenth Century: Free Labour or Neo-Slavery? *Slavery and Abolition: A Journal of Slave and Post-Slave Studies* 14:67–86.

Humphries, A. L., A. B. Maxwell, A. H. Ross, and D. H. Ubelaker
2013   A Geometric Morphometric Study of Regional Craniofacial Variation in Mexico. *International Journal of Osteoarchaeology* DOI: 10.1002/oa.2345.

Irish, J. D., and L. Konigsberg
2007   The Ancient Inhabitants of Jebel Moya Redux: Measures of Population Affinity Based on Dental Morphology. *International Journal of Osteoarchaeology* 17:138–156.

Jackson, F., A. Mayes, M. Mack, A. Froment, S. Keita, R. Kittles, M. George, K. Shujaa, M. L. Blakey, and L. M. Rankin-Hill
2004   Origins of the New York African Burial Ground Population: Biological Evidence of Geographical and Macroethnic Affiliations: Using Craniometrics, Dental Morphology, and Preliminary Genetic Analysis. In *The New York African Burial Ground Skeletal Biology Final Report*, edited by M. L. Blakey and L. M. Rankin-Hill, pp. 150–215. Howard University Press, Washington, D.C.

Keegan, T.
1996   *Colonial South Africa and the Origins of the Racial Order.* David Philips, Cape Town.

Klaus, H. D.
2008   Out of Light Came Darkness: Bioarchaeology of Mortuary Ritual, Health, and Ethnogenesis in the Lambayeque Valley Complex, North Coast Peru, A.D. 900–1750. Unpublished Ph.D. dissertation, Department of Anthropology, Ohio State University, Columbus.

Knight, F. W.
1997   *General History of the Caribbean.* Vol. 3, *The Slave Societies of the Caribbean.* UNESCO, London.

Lagercrantz, S.
1941   Schadeldeformationen und ihre Verbreiterung in Afrika. *Ethnos* 3–4:135–173.

Lalueza-Fox, C., M. T. Gilbert, A. J. Martínez-Fuentes, F. Calafell, and J. Bertranpetit
2003   Mitochondrial DNA from Pre-Columbian Ciboneys from Cuba and the Pre-historic Colonization of the Caribbean. *American Journal of Physical Anthropology* 121:97–108.

Lange, M., J. Mahoney, and M. vom Hau
2006   Colonialism and Development: A Comparative Analysis of Spanish and British Colonies. *American Journal of Sociology* 111:1412–1462.

Ledger, M., L-.M. Holtzhausen, D. Constant, and A. G. Morris
2000   Biomechanical Beam Analysis of Long Bones from a Late 18th Century Slave Cemetery in Cape Town, South Africa. *American Journal of Physical Anthropology* 112:207–216.

Lee, E. J., L. M. Anderson, V. Dale, and A. Merriwether
2009   MtDNA Origins of an Enslaved Labor Force from the 18th Century Schuyler Flatts Burial Ground in Colonial Albany, NY: Africans, Native Americans, and Malagasy? *Journal of Archaeological Science* 36:2805–2810.

Lewis, J. E., D. DeGusta, M. R. Meyer, J. M. Monge, A. E. Mann, and R. L. Holloway
2011   The Mismeasure of Science: Stephen Jay Gould versus Samuel George Morton on Skulls and Bias. *PLoS Biology* 9:1–6.

Lovejoy, P. E.
1989   The Impact of the Atlantic Slave Trade on Africa: A Review of the Literature. *Journal of African History* 30:365–394.

Maat, G. J. R., R. G. A. M. Panhuysen, and R. W. Mastwijk
2002   *Manual for the Physical Anthropology Report.* Barge's Anthropologica No. 6. Leiden.

Mann, A.
2009   The Origins of American Physical Anthropology in Philadelphia. *Yearbook of Physical Anthropology* 52:155–163.

Manyaapelo, T.
2007   An Odontological Analysis of 18th and 19th Century Burial Sites from in and around Cape Town. Unpublished M.Sc. thesis, Department of Human Biology, University of Cape Town.

Martin, D. L., A. L. Magennis, and J. C. Rose.
1987   Cortical Bone Maintenance in an Historic Afro-American Cemetery Sample from Cedar Grove, Arkansas. *American Journal of Physical Anthropology* 74:255–264.

Mendizabal, I., K. Sandoval, G. Berniell-Lee, F. Calafell, A. Salas, A. Martínez-Fuentes, and D. Comas
2008   Genetic Origin, Admixture, and Asymmetry in Maternal and Paternal Human Lineages in Cuba. *BMC Evolutionary Biology* 8:213–223.

Michael, J. S.
1988   A New Look at Morton's Craniological Research. *Current Anthropology* 29:349–354.

Mitchell, P.
2004   *African Connections: Archaeological Perspectives on Africa and the Wider World.* AltaMira, Walnut Creek, California.

Morgan, P. D.
2008   The Cultural Implications of the Atlantic Slave Trade: African Regional Origins, American Destinations, and New World Developments. *Slavery and Abolition: A Journal of Slave and Post-Slave Studies* 18:122–145.
Morris, A. G.
1992   *The Skeletons of Contact: Protohistoric Burials from the Lower Orange River Valley*. Witwatersrand University Press, Johannesburg.
1997   History of the Cobern Street Site. Abstract of paper presented at the 27th Annual Congress of the Anatomical Society of Southern African, Cape Town, South Africa.
1999   The Cobern Street Cemetery: Using Cranial Variation to Reconstruct the Biological Diversity of the Common People of 18th century Cape Town. Abstract of paper presented at the Fourth World Archaeological Congress, University of Cape Town.
2011   *Missing and Murdered: A Personal Adventure in Forensic Anthropology*. Zebra Press, Cape Town.
Morton, S. G.
1849   *Catalogue of Skulls of Man and Inferior Animals*. Merrihew and Thompson, Philadelphia.
Mountain, A.
2003   *The First People of the Cape*. David Philip, Cape Town.
Mrozowski, S. A.
2006   Environments of History: Biological Dimensions of Historical Archaeology. In *Historical Archaeology*, edited by M. Hall and S. W. Silliman, pp. 23–41. Blackwell, Oxford.
Murphy, M. S., E. Goycochea, and G. Cock
2011   Resistance, Persistence, and Accommodation at Puruchuco-Huaquerones, Peru. In *Enduring Conquests: Rethinking the Archaeology of Resistance to Spanish Colonialism in the Americas*, edited by M. Liebmann and M. S. Murphy, pp. 57–76. School for Advanced Research Press, Santa Fe.
Nunn, N.
2008   The Long-Term Effects of Africa's Slave Trades. *Quarterly Journal of Economics* 121:139–175.
Nystrom, K. C., L. A. Amato, and L. A. Jankowitz
2011   Strontium Isotopic Reconstruction of the Composition of an Urban Free Black Population from the 19th Century United States. *Journal of Archaeological Science* 38:3505–3517.
Orser, C. E.
2010   Twenty-First-Century Historical Archaeology. *Journal of Archaeological Research* 18:111–150.
2012   An Archaeology of Eurocentrism. *American Antiquity* 77:737–755.
Ortiz, F.
1929   Los Afrocubanos dientimellados. *Archivos del Folklore Cubano* 4:16–29.

Ossenberg, N. S., Y. Dodo, T. Maeda, and Y. Kawakubo
2006   Ethnogenesis and Craniofacial Change in Japan from the Perspective of Nonmetric Traits. *Anthropological Science* 114:99–115.

Ousley, S., R. Jantz, and D. Freid
2009   Understanding Race and Human Variation: Why Forensic Anthropologists are Good at Identifying Race. *American Journal of Physical Anthropology* 139:68–76.

Owsley, D. W., C. E. Orser, R. W. Mann, P. H. Moore-Jansen, and R. L. Montgomery
1987   Demography and Pathology of an Urban Slave Population from New Orleans. *American Journal of Physical Anthropology* 74:185–97.

Palus, M. M., M. P. Leone, and M. D. Cochran
2006   Critical Archaeology: Politics Past and Present. In *Historical Archaeology*, edited by M. Hall and S. W. Silliman, pp. 84–104. Blackwell, Oxford.

Patterson, N., D. C. Petersen, R. E. van der Ross, H. Sudoyo, R. H. Glashoff, S. Marzuki, D. Reich, and V. M. Hayes
2009   Genetic Structure of a Unique Admixed Population: Implications for Medical Research. *Human Molecular Genetics* 19:411–419.

Patterson, T. R., and R. D. G. Kelley
2000   Unfinished Migrations: Reflections on the African Diaspora and the Making of the Modern World. *African Studies Review* 43:11–45.

Pietrusewsky, M.
2008   Metric Analysis of Skeletal Remains: Methods and Applications. In *Biological Anthropology of the Human Skeleton*, edited by M. A. Katzenberg and S. R. Saunders, pp. 487–532. 2nd ed. Wiley-Liss, New York.

Price, T. D., V. Tiesler, and J. H. Burton
2006   Early African Diaspora in Colonial Campeche, Mexico: Strontium Isotopic Evidence. *American Journal of Physical Anthropology* 130:485–490.

Quintana-Murci, L., C. Harmant, H. Quach, O. Balanovsky, V. Zaporozhchenko, P. D. Bormans van Helden, E. G. Hoal, and D. M. Behar
2010   Strong Maternal Khoisan Contribution to the South African Coloured Population: A Case of Gender-Biased Admixture. *American Journal of Human Genetics* 86:611–620.

Rankin-Hill, L. M.
1997   *A Biohistory of 19th Century Afro-Americans: The Burial Remains of a Philadelphia Cemetery*. Bergin and Garvey, Westport, Connecticut.

Rankin-Hill, L. M., M. L. Blakey, S. H. H. Carrington, and J. E. Howson
2000   Political Economy of Fertility and Population Growth among Enslaved Africans in Colonial New York. *American Journal of Physical Anthropology Supplement* 30:259.

Rathbun, T. A.
1985   Health and Disease at a South Carolina Plantation: 1840–1870. *American Journal of Physical Anthropology* 66:217.

Relethford, J. H.
1994   Craniometric Variation among Modern Human Populations. *American Journal of Physical Anthropology* 95:53–62.

2002   Apportionment of Global Human Genetic Diversity Based on Craniometrics and Skin Color. *American Journal of Physical Anthropology* 118:393–398.

2004   RMET 5.0. State University of New York, Oneonta. http://employees.oneonta.edu/relethjh/programs.

Relethford, J. H., and J. Blangero

1990   Detection of Differential Gene Flow from Patterns of Quantitative Variation. *Human Biology* 62:5–25.

Renschler, E. S.

2007   An Osteobiography of an African Diasporic Skeletal Sample: Integrating Skeletal and Historical Information. Unpublished Ph.D. Dissertation, University of Pennsylvania, Philadelphia.

2008   A Historical Osteobiography of the African Crania in the Morton Collection. *Expedition* 50:33.

Renschler, E. S., and J. M. Monge

2008   The Samuel George Morton Cranial Collection: Historical Significance and New Research. *Expedition* 50:30–38.

2013   The Crania of African Origin in the Samuel G. Morton Cranial Collection. *South African Archaeological Society Goodwin Series* 11:35–38.

Ribot, I.

2003   Craniometrical Analysis of Central and East Africans in Relation to History: A Case Study Based on Unique Collections of Known Ethnic Affiliation. *Bulletin de la Société Royale Belge d'Anthropologie et Préhistoire* 114:25–50.

2004   Differentiation of Modern Sub-Saharan African Populations: Morphology, Geography and History. *Bulletins et Mémoires de la Société d'Anthropologie de Paris* 16:143–165.

2011   *A Study through Skull Morphology on the Diversity of Holocene African Populations in a Historical Perspective.* British Archaeological Report International Series 2215. Archaeopress, Oxford.

Rivero de La Calle, M.

1973   La mutilación dentaria en la población negroide de Cuba. *Ciencias Biologicas* 6:1–21.

Ross, A. H., D. E. Slice, D. H. Ubelaker, and A. B. Falsetti

2002   Population Affinities of 19th Century Cuban Crania: Implications for Identification Criteria in South Florida Cuban Americans. *Journal of Forensic Sciences* 49:1–6.

Rotimi, C. N.

2003   Genetic Ancestry Tracing and the African Identity: A Double-Edged Sword? *Developing World Bioethics* 3:151–158.

Said, E. W.

1993   *Culture and Imperialism.* Knopf, New York.

Salas, A., M. Richards, M.-V. Lareu, R. Scozzari, A. Coppa, A. Torroni, V. Macaulay, and A. Carracedo

2004   The African Diaspora: Mitochondrial DNA and the Atlantic Slave Trade. *American Journal of Human Genetics* 74:454–465.

Schroeder, H., T. C. O'Connell, J. A. Evans, K. A. Shuler, and R. E. M. Hedges
2009   Trans-Atlantic Slavery: Isotopic Evidence for Forced Migration to Barbados. *American Journal of Physical Anthropology* 139:547–557.

Sealy, J. C., R. Armstrong, and C. Schrire
1995   Beyond Lifetime Averages: Tracing Life Histories through Isotopic Analysis of Different Calcified Tissues from Archaeological Human Skeletons. *Antiquity* 69:290–300.

Sealy, J. C., A. G. Morris, R. Armstrong, A. Markell, and C. Schrire
1993   An Historic Skeleton from the Slave Lodge at Vergelegen. *South African Archaeological Society Goodwin Series* 7:84–91.

Shell, R. C. H.
1994   *Children of Bondage: A Social History of the Slave Society at the Cape of Good Hope, 1652–1838.* Wesleyan University Press, Hanover, New Hampshire.

Sheridan, R. B.
1985   *Doctors and Slaves: A Medical and Demographic History of Slavery in the British West Indies, 1680–1834.* Cambridge University Press, Cambridge.

Shrubsall, F.
1899   Notes on Ashanti Skulls and Crania. *Journal of the Royal Anthropological Institute (of Great Britain and Ireland)* 28:95–103.

Singleton, T. A.
2005   Slavery at a Cuban Coffee Plantation. In *Dialogues in Cuban Archaeology,* edited by L. A. Curet, S. L. Dawdy, and G. L. R. Corzo, pp. 181–199. University of Alabama Press, Tuscaloosa.

Sleigh, D., and P. Westra
2013   *The Taking of the Slaver Meermin, 1766.* Africana Publishers, Cape Town.

Spivak, G.
1987   *In Other Worlds: Essays in Cultural Politics.* Routledge, London.

Stanton, W.
1960   *The Leopard's Spots: Scientific Attitudes toward Race in America, 1815–59.* University of Chicago Press, Chicago.

Stojanowski, C. M.
2004   Population History of Native Groups in Pre- and Postcontact Spanish Florida: Aggregation, Gene Flow, and Genetic Drift on the Southeastern U.S. Atlantic Coast. *American Journal of Physical Anthropology* 123:316–322.

Stojanowski, C. M., and M. A. Schillaci
2006   Phenotypic Approaches for Understanding Patterns of Intracemetery Biological Variation. *Yearbook of Physical Anthropology* 49:49–88.

Thomas, H.
1997   *The Slave Trade: The History of the Atlantic Slave Trade, 1440–1870.* Papermac, London.

Tildesley, M. L.
1921   A First Study of the Burmese Skull. *Biometrika* 13:176–262.

Tishkoff, S. A., F. A. Reed, F. R. Friedlaender, C. Ehret, A. Ranciaro, A. Froment, J. B. Hirbo, A. A. Awomoyi, J.-M. Bodo, O. Doumbo, M. Ibrahim, A. T. Juma, M. J. Kotze, G. Lema, J. H. Moore, H. Mortensen, T. B. Nyambo, S. A Omar, K. Powell, G. S. Pretorius, M. W. Smith, M. A. Thera, C. Wambebe, J. L. Weber, and S. M. Williams
2009   The Genetic Structure and History of Africans and African Americans. *Science* 324:1035–1044.

Turnbull, D.
1840   *Travels in the West: Cuba with Notices of Porto Rico and the Slave Trade.* Longman, Orme, Brown, Green and Longmans, London.

Van Rippen, B.
1918   Practices and Customs of the African Natives Involving Dental Procedures. *Journal of the Allied Dental Societies* 13:1–22.

Von Bonin, V. O. N. G., and D. R. Med
1931   Beitrag Zur Kraniologie von Ost-Asien. *Biometrika* 23:52–113.

Wescott, D. J., and R. L. Jantz
2005   Assessing Craniofacial Secular Change in American Blacks and Whites Using Geometric Morphometry. In *Modern Morphometrics in Physical Anthropology*, edited by D. E. Slice, pp. 231–245. Kluwer Academic/Plenum, New York.

Worden, N., E. Van Heyningen, and V. Bickford-Smith
1999   *Cape Town: The Making of a City.* David Philip, Cape Town.

13

Hybridity? Change? Continuity? Survival?

Biodistance and the Identity of Colonial Burials from Magdalena de Cao Viejo, Chicama Valley, Peru

ALEJANDRA ORTIZ, MELISSA S. MURPHY, JASON TOOHEY,
AND CATHERINE GAITHER

No one today is purely one thing. Labels like Indian, or woman, or Muslim, or American are not more than starting-points, which if followed into actual experience for only a moment are quickly left behind. Imperialism consolidated the mixture of cultures and identities on a global scale. But its worst and most paradoxical gift was to allow people to believe that they were only, mainly, exclusively, white, or Black, or Western, or Oriental. Yet just as human beings make their own history, they also make their cultures and ethnic identities.

Edward Said, *Culture and Imperialism* (1993:336)

Identity studies have gained considerable traction in the archaeology of colonial encounters and colonialism because of the different ways identities were imposed, negotiated, and transformed under colonial regimes (Klaus 2013; Klaus and Alvarez-Calderón, this volume; Lightfoot 1995; Lightfoot and Martinez 1995; Loren 2008; Naum 2010; Silliman 2005; Voss 2005). The colonizer-colonized dichotomy acts as a point of departure in these studies, because they have demonstrated the multiplicity and complexity of identities within colonial situations. These scholars have revealed that what were once considered monolithic groups are, for example, composed of many different Native American groups or tribes, of enslaved and free Africans and their descendants, of different European groups (e.g., English, Spanish, Russian), and of the many offspring between these different groups (e.g., *mestizo, criollo, ladino, sambo,* etc.), as well as comprising the different dimensions of gender, sexuality, status, and class (Deagan 2003, 2004). These works have also demonstrated the instability and fluidity of identity, such as how a person of mixed heritage was considered *mestizo/mestiza* (a man or woman of Spanish and indigenous descent) in one context but was classified as "Indian" in other settings. They also show how over the course of a lifetime a person transformed his or her identity, for example, from *bozal* (African man or a woman recently sold from the transatlantic slave trade and a person who could not speak or understand Spanish or may not have been baptized) to *criollo* (a man or woman of African descent born in the Americas) (Graubart 2007; O'Toole 2012a, 2012b). These approaches also emphasize individual agency in the creation of identities, at least in the aspects of one's identity that one could control or manipulate.

Bioarchaeologists regularly investigate identity, but usually only in terms related to biological sex, age, population affinity, or genetic affiliation. Only more recently have bioarchaeologists grappled with a multidimensional approach to identity (after Diaz-Andreu and Lucy 2005; Insoll 2007; Meskell 2007) and tackled the integration of religion, status, ethnicity, gender, age, and disability into identity studies (Klaus 2013; Knudson and Stojanowski, eds. 2009 and chapters therein; Scott 2011; Sofaer 2006). Knudson and Stojanowski (2009:5) define identity as how people "thought they were, how they advertised this identity to others, how others perceived it, and the resulting repercussions of this matrix of interpersonal and intersocietal relationships." In this chapter we will attempt to operationalize this definition for our study of identity of the people from the *reducción* (forced settlement) of Magdalena de Cao Viejo on the north coast of Peru, integrating skeletal and dental data with archaeological data. We will attempt to access the identities of the *reducción*'s residents, Magdaleneros, to learn how they may have identified themselves and how they may have negotiated these identities.

Magdalena de Cao Viejo was established in the Chicama Valley, first at the mouth of the Chicama River and later several meters inland atop the remains of a major pre-Hispanic temple complex (A.D. 100–700) at the larger El Brujo Archaeological Complex (Figure 13.1). Jeffrey Quilter (as a member of the Proyecto Arqueológico El Brujo, directed by Regulo Franco and colleagues) led the recent excavations and laboratory analyses of the church and town at its second location from 2004 to 2010. Quilter estimates the dates of occupation as 1578 to circa 1780 (during the early to middle Colonial Period), when the town was abandoned for unknown reasons (Quilter 2010, 2017; Quilter et al. 2010). Twenty-eight human burials were recovered underneath the floor of the church and in the cemetery to the west of the nave of the church (Figure 13.1). An earthquake hit the coast at some point during the seventeenth century (ca. 1650–1690), and the church collapsed

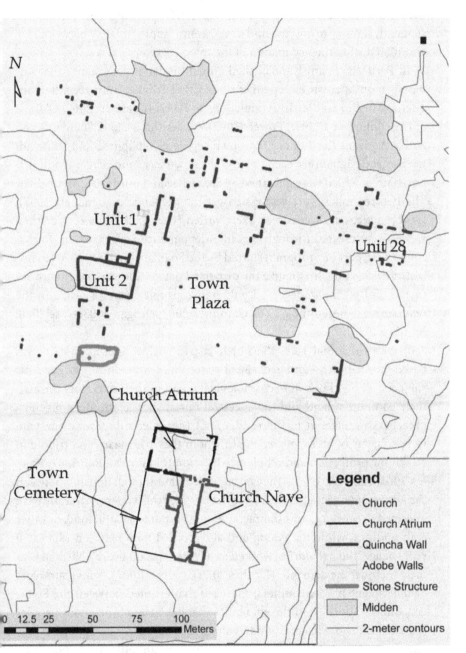

Figure 13.1. Location of Magdalena de Cao Viejo, Chicama Valley, Peru (map by Jeffrey Quilter).

and was abandoned. Horizontal stratigraphy and wall collapse indicate that the burials date to before the earthquake, likely sometime between the late sixteenth century to and the mid-seventeenth, approximately between 1578 and 1650 during the occupation of the town (Quilter 2017).

In Peru, the Spanish established a dual model of governance that was based upon Spanish experiences of exacting tribute from recently conquered Muslim and Jewish populations in Iberia (Graubart 2007; O'Toole 2012a; Phillips et al. 1991; Powers 2005). Under this system, Spaniards and native Andeans lived under their own separate "republics," and while not territorial designations, each possessed its own legal and religious authorities, both of which were governed by Spanish leaders and indigenous elites. The two republics were segregated yet interdependent (Graubart 2007); local practices and outcomes likely varied (Gasco 2005), and interstitial spaces were created through this interdependence and variation. *Reducciones* were part of a program started by the Spaniards in 1569–1570 to control, civilize, and Christianize the dispersed native Andean descent groups (*ayllus* and *parcialidades*), and only native peoples were to reside in the *reducciones* (Abercrombie 1998; Cummins 2002; Deagan 2003; Gose 2008; Ramírez 1996).

Prior to colonial rule, the north coast's socioeconomic system was based on reciprocity and exchange between a *cacique* (local lord) and his subjects, all of whom were cosmologically tied to their ancestors through their communal land and the ancestral burial sites. Dominican brother-preachers ministered to the residents of Magdalena de Cao Viejo, who were subjects of an *encomendero*, to whom they paid taxes and tribute in return for protection and religious education (Graubart 2000, 2007; Powers 2005; Ramírez 1996). The *caciques* mediated the relationship between the *encomendero* and his native subjects. Under this system, Andeans were expected to produce, for example, a certain amount of cloth, food, or other commodities, while the young and able-bodied men between 18 and 50 years of age, the *tributarios*, worked as day laborers on nearby haciendas to meet their tribute demands (Delibes 2017; Graubart 2007). Native survivors of the violent first encounters, the wars that erupted between the Spanish conquistadores, and the epidemics that decimated indigenous peoples (particularly those in communities along the coast and near Spanish cities) were gathered into these *reducciones*. These "Indian settlements" bore little resemblance to the pre-Hispanic socioeconomic geography. Many people were displaced and relocated under the colonial regime, and many native Andeans fled their assigned *reducciones* to seek out better circumstances under different *encomenderos* and local *caciques*. People may have been aggregated at Magdalena de Cao Viejo from within the Chicama Valley, from other north coast valleys, or from more distant regions of Spanish Peru. This chapter explores the population composition and community identity of a subsample of the burials from Magdalena de Cao Viejo through a series of biodistance analyses. Ethnohistorical documents indicate that Andeans preferred to be buried near their parents or relatives in the church or cemetery (Ramos 2010), so in order to "ground-truth" the written record, we tested whether or not the burials were interred and patterned according to kin relationships. Next, we ask whether or not these burials show any population continuity with pre-Hispanic samples from the El Brujo Archaeological Complex. Then, we investigate whether or not there is evidence for migration or gene flow between local native peoples, non-local native peoples, and their Spanish rulers. We conclude by integrating these biometric and morphological data with archaeological lines of evidence, namely, mortuary practices, food remains, and dress, in order to understand how the members of this community defined and negotiated the different components of their identities.

BIOMETRIC AND MORPHOLOGICAL METHODS

From the human remains at Magdalena de Cao Viejo (MCV) we collected three different data sets: craniometric, odontometric, and dental morphological data. Cranial measurements were collected following the nomenclature and standards established by Howells (1973, 1989). Maximum mesiodistal (MD) and buccolingual (BL) crown dimensions were recorded for both upper (U) and lower (L) permanent teeth—incisors (I), canines (C), premolars (P), and molars (M)—using the standard measurement protocol of Buikstra and Ubelaker (1994). Only the best-preserved side was scored, and all measurements were collected using a Mitutoyo sliding caliper calibrated to 0.01 mm. Morphological data for the MCV permanent dentitions were gathered using Turner et al.'s (1991) Arizona State University Dental Anthropology System (ASUDAS). All craniodental features examined in this study have been successfully used in previous investigations of inter- and intra-population biological variation (e.g., Corruccini et al. 2002; Hanihara 2008; Hanihara and Ishida 2005; Jantz and Owsley 2001; Nystrom 2006; Scott and Turner 1997; Stojanowski et al. 2007; Tiesler and Cucina 2008). Eleven crania or dentitions were recovered from MCV, but metric data were not collected from an 8-to-10-year-old subadult individual (specimen MIC-07-03). Of the 28 burials from MCV, the remaining 17 individuals were fetuses or neonates. Moreover, following a standard procedure in biodistance analyses, missing values for our metric data were imputed in SPSS via the expectation-maximization (EM) algorithm (Klaus 2008; Nystrom 2006; Stojanowski 2005; Stojanowski et al. 2007). With the exception of two cases (MIC-08-01 and MIC-08-02, also known as disturbed 1 and disturbed 2, respectively), no more than one measurement was estimated for any individual. Around 40 percent of the dental measurements were estimated for specimen MIC-08-01 and 60 percent for MIC-08-02 cranial data, and therefore their affinities with other individuals should be treated with caution, as specimens missing more than 20–25 percent of their data are generally not considered for analyses.

We first undertook an intra-cemetery analysis of biological variation in order to determine whether the distribution of individuals found in MCV was structured along the lines of kinship. Although a variety of different approaches and types of data have been proposed to address this issue (see Stojanowski and Schillaci 2006 for a review), we chose odontometrics in this study for practical and preservation reasons. The utility of tooth size for kinship analyses has been demonstrated by a long tradition of scholarship (Adachi et al. 2003; Bondioli et al. 1986; Hanihara et al. 1983; Stojanowski 2005; Stojanowski et al. 2007), and dental measurements have yielded results fairly consistent with mitochondrial DNA sequences (Adachi et al. 2003; see also Corruccini et al. 2002). Only measurements present in at least 90 percent of the study sample were considered for analysis. This includes the MD and BL dimensions of the UC, UP3, UP4, UM1, and UM2. Data were standardized in order to correct for age and sex differences (Williams-Blangero and Blangero 1989), and Euclidean distances were estimated between individuals for kinship reconstruction as suggested by Corruccini and Shimada (2002).

The estimation of biological distances between MCV and other populations was assessed using two different approaches. Selection of the type of data used was based on availability of comparative information. First, population continuity in the Chicama Valley was estimated from craniometric data derived from three temporarily different samples found at the El Brujo Archaeological Complex, including Moche (approximately A.D. 100–600), Classic Lambayeque (approximately A.D. 900/1000–1300), and MCV. Most individuals from these three samples present cranial deformation, and seven individuals from MCV (six adults and one subadult, who was excluded from these analyses) possessed culturally modified crania, specifically the type known as symmetrical fronto-occipital deformation. Therefore, in order to minimize the effects of cranial deformation, only nine measurements from the face were used in this analysis. This includes nasion-prosthion height (NPH), nasal height (NLH), nasal breadth (NLB), orbit height (OBH), orbit breadth (OBB), biorbital breadth (EKB), palate breadth (MAB), bifrontal breadth (FMB), and interorbital breadth (DKB). To determine group differences, discriminant function analyses (DFA) were performed on the raw measurements, rather than on the C-scores (Lalueza Fox et al. 1996; Pietrusewsky 1999; Pietrusewsky and Chang 2003; but see Howells 1989). Accuracy of the DFA was quantified by determining the percent of individuals correctly classified, with and without jackknifing. Female and male samples were considered separately. For the MCV sample, specimen MIC-08-01, categorized as "probable male," was treated as male in the DFA. Individuals from the Moche and Lambayeque comparative samples with missing values and/or uncertain sex attribution were removed from analysis.

The question of intra-valley population continuity throughout time was complemented by a second, more global analysis. Evidence for local gene flow and biological hybridity of the people from MCV were examined via dental morphological data. For that purpose, the MCV sample was compared with five spatially or temporarily different populations, including a pre-Ceramic sample from the Chicama Valley in the Peruvian northern coast (HP), two Late Intermediate Period/Late Horizon samples from the Rimac Valley and Cuzco region (CEN and CUZ, respectively), an Andean Colonial sample from San Pedro de Mórrope in the Lambayeque Valley Complex (SPM), and a group of Spanish individuals (SPA). Sample details are presented in Table 13.1, and all comparative data were scored using the ASUDAS. Thirteen dental traits were collected and used in the interpopulation analysis, except in the case of the SPM sample, where only 10 traits were available for comparative analyses. This analysis only includes variables collected on the key tooth type *sensu* Dahlberg (1945; see also Scott and Turner 1997) and with a minimum of three individuals in each group. Dental morphological traits show little to no sexual dimorphism (Hanihara 1992; Irish 1993, 1997; Scott and Turner 1997; Turner 1984), and thus males and females were combined for analysis. Trait frequencies were estimated using Turner and Scott's (1977) individual count method, which focuses on the antimere exhibiting the strongest degree of trait expression. Following Sjøvold (1977), trait expression was dichotomized into categories of presence or absence to facilitate the multivariate statistical analysis. All

Table 13.1. Comparative dental morphology samples used in this study

Sample	Dates	Geographic location
Magdalena de Cao Viejo (MCV)	A.D. 1571–1650	Chicama Valley, North Coast, Peru
Huaca Prieta (HP)	3500–1300 B.C.	Chicama Valley, North Coast, Peru
Cuzco—Inca (CUZ)	A.D. 1290–1532	Cuzco, Southern Highlands, Peru
Peru Central Coast (CEN)	A.D. 1450–1540	Rimac Valley, Central Coast, Peru
San Pedro de Mórrope (SPM)	A.D. 1536–1751	Lambayeque Valley, North Coast, Peru
SPAIN (SPA)		
Sant Pere	4th–13th centuries	Cataluña
Plaça Vela	16th–17th centuries	Cataluña
Molí de Can Fonoll[a]	10th–13th centuries	Ibiza
Pantà de Foix cave[b]	3000 B.C.	Cataluña

Note: Data from García Sívoli 2009; Haagen Klaus, personal communication; Klaus 2008; Ortiz 2013; Ortiz, unpublished data; Ortiz and Bailey 2008; Ortiz and Murphy, unpublished data; Pacelli and Márquez-Grant 2010; Subirà et al. 2014.
[a]Only used for UP3 root number.
[b]Only used for UM1 enamel extension.

traits were dichotomized at the standard breakpoints according to Scott and Turner (1997). As used extensively in previous population history studies (Bailey 2002; Haydenblit 1996; Irish 1993, 1997; Sutter 2000; Sutter and Verano 2007; Turner 1984), levels of differentiation among samples were calculated using the mean measure of divergence (MMD), and small sample sizes were corrected using the Freeman and Tukey angular transformation (see Irish 2010 for a detailed review of this method). The MMD provides a quantitative estimate of biological difference between two samples based on the degree of similarity of the entire data sets (Berry and Berry 1967; Harris and Sjøvold 2004; Irish 2010; Sjøvold 1977). Thus, a smaller value indicates greater affinity between samples. Divergence between two groups was considered significant at $p \leq 0.05$, when the MMD value is greater than twice its standard deviation (Sjøvold 1977). In addition to the MMD distance matrix, dental morphological variation among samples was assessed via principal component analyses (PCA) and cluster analyses using the unweighted pair-group average (UPGMA) algorithm based on the Euclidean distance. The latter method generated dendrograms depicting dental phenetic relationships among groups. Except for the MMD, all statistical analyses were performed in PAST (Hammer et al. 2001).

Results

Pre-Hispanic Andeans typically buried their dead in community burial zones, which were often organized by kin relationships. In the Colonial era, Christian burial arrangements as described in wills show that Andeans desired to occupy important areas inside churches and to be close to the interments of their parents and ancestors in these spaces (Ramos 2010). Therefore, this analysis aimed to determine the possible presence of familial clusters and whether biological relatedness based on odontometric data corresponds to the spatial pattern of interment found at MCV. Table 13.2 summarizes the means, standard deviations, and sample sizes for the MCV

Table 13.2. Descriptive statistics for Magdalena de Cao Viejo dental metric data

	Maxilla				Mandible		
	n	Mean	SD	Range	n	Mean	SD	Range
MD	7	7.86	1.19	5.38–9.01	5	4.54	0.76	3.70–5.68
BL	8	7.40	0.48	6.69–8.04	6	5.27	0.62	4.42–5.83
MD	6	6.60	1.17	4.49–7.45	7	5.67	1.06	3.48–6.68
BL	6	6.30	0.64	5.26–7.05	7	5.98	0.58	5.20–6.85
MD	9	7.94	0.39	7.33–8.58	7	7.08	0.47	6.41–7.82
BL	9	8.10	0.84	6.29–9.32	0	—	—	—
3MD	10	7.12	0.45	6.45–7.86	6	6.89	0.47	6.37–7.58
3BL	9	8.92	0.57	7.94–9.48	6	7.47	0.34	7.14–7.93
4MD	9	6.74	0.36	6.11–7.24	6	6.85	0.66	5.97–7.98
4BL	9	8.68	0.64	7.85–9.86	6	7.88	0.46	7.15–8.53
11MD	10	10.42	0.39	9.58–10.87	7	11.41	0.38	10.78–11.89
11BL	10	11.05	0.49	10.30–11.63	7	11.06	0.80	10.19–12
12MD	9	9.59	0.82	8.28–10.66	5	10.47	0.90	9.16–11.41
12BL	10	10.98	0.62	9.74–11.63	5	9.77	0.79	8.83–10.57
13MD	3	8.70	1.10	7.53–9.72	6	10.39	0.49	9.60–11.02
13BL	4	10.42	0.65	9.72–11.28	5	10.03	0.50	9.30–10.63

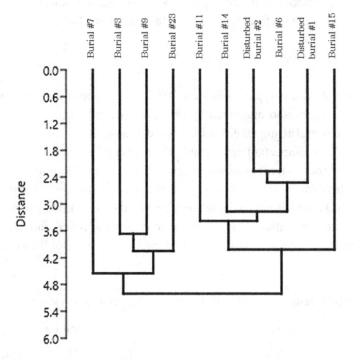

Figure 13.2. Cluster analysis (UPGMA) of the Magdalena de Cao Viejo individuals based on squared Euclidean distances using dental metrical data.

dental metric data. Dental metric similarity between individuals based on Euclidean distances is presented in Table 13.3. The dendrogram derived from Euclidean distances revealed two main clusters, possibly indicating the presence of two family groups (Figure 13.2). One cluster is formed by Burial 7 at the base, followed by Burial 23, and finally Burials 3 and 9. The second cluster comprises Burial 15 at the base, followed by Burials 11, 14, MIC-08-01, and then MIC-08-02 and Burial 6 showing the closest distance. No clear pattern regarding the spatial distribution of the burials is observed from these relationships. That is, archaeological work at MCV led by Jeffrey Quilter identified three areas where these burials were found: the cemetery adjacent to the church and two large units under the floor of the nave inside the church (located in the northeast and northwest corners of the nave and identified as NE and NW unit, respectively). Individual MIC-07-05 (Burial 3) was excavated from the cemetery adjacent to the church. Individuals MIC-07-03 (Burial 5), MIC-07-04 (Burial 6), MIC-07-06 (Burial 7), MIC-07-08 (Burial 9), MIC-07-10 (Burial 11), and MIC-07-12 (Burial 14) came

e 13.3. Euclidean distances between Magdalena de Cao Viejo individuals based on dental
ric data

	Dist. 1	Dist. 2	Burial 3	Burial 11	Burial 14	Burial 9	Burial 7	Burial 6	Burial 15	Burial 23
. 1	—									
. 2	2.597	—								
ial 3	4.902	5.857	—							
ial 11	3.096	3.699	4.541	—						
ial 14	2.625	3.599	6.299	3.451	—					
ial 9	4.250	4.729	3.667	4.033	5.594	—				
ial 7	3.744	5.216	4.674	3.770	4.592	4.253	—			
ial 6	2.444	2.269	5.518	3.275	3.283	4.076	5.133	—		
ial 15	3.566	3.543	5.851	3.880	4.952	5.451	5.884	4.141	—	
ial 23	4.381	5.622	3.879	4.803	5.503	4.223	4.730	4.349	6.066	—

from the NE unit and were distributed in a linear fashion within the unit.
The NW unit unearthed individuals MIC-08-06 (Burial 15) and MIC-08-
09 (Burial 23), located in the northeast and northwest corners of the NW
unit, respectively. Individuals MIC-08-01 and MIC-08-02 both correspond
to disturbed burials found in the nave inside the church, next to the new
northern nave. Archaeological and biodistance data, therefore, do not support the hypothesis of a kin-based burial pattern, as individuals exhibiting the greatest phenetic similarity were not necessarily interred in close
proximity to each other. Similarly, bioarchaeological work at the Colonial
sites of San Pedro de Mórrope (Klaus 2008) and Eten (Haagen Klaus, personal communication), also in the north coast of Peru, has found that inferred kin members were not necessarily buried in close proximity to each
other. We caution that further work is needed to say definitively whether
or not the burials at Magdalena de Cao Viejo are structured based on familial relationships, because a lack of phenetic similarity cannot rule out
genetic relatedness entirely (see Paul and Stojanowski 2015; Stojanowski,
this volume).

Descriptive statistics for the nine cranial measurements examined in our
MCV male and female groups, as well as those of our comparative Moche
and Classic Lambayeque samples, are presented in Table 13.4. As noted
above, DFAs were used to examine group differences and any evidence of
population continuity in the Chicama Valley. Figures 13.3 and 13.4 plot the

Table 13.4. Descriptive statistics for Magdalena de Cao Viejo, Lambayeque, and Moche craniometric data

Sample	Sex	n	NPH[a]		NLH[b]		NLB[c]		OBH[d]		OBB[e]		EKB[f]		MAB[g]		FMB[h]		DKB[i]	
			Mean	SD	Mean	SD	Mean	SD	Mean	SD	Mean	SD	Mean	SD	Mean	SD	Mean	SD
MCV	F	5	61.96	4.52	44.72	3.96	22.60	1.95	35.00	2.24	37.40	3.97	91.07	2.52	59.49	1.12	99.63	1.33	20.40	1.14
	M	5	66.17	3.73	49.94	4.15	24.46	1.06	37.71	4.11	37.80	1.30	97.18	3.87	63.43	1.16	103.00	4.30	19.07	3.52
Lambay-eque[j]	F	14	65.21	3.24	46.79	4.21	23.36	2.02	35.71	1.90	39.00	2.45	96.36	4.33	60.43	3.96	98.71	4.91	20.79	1.37
	M	27	67.15	3.66	50.93	2.62	23.70	2.05	35.37	1.92	39.48	2.49	98.44	4.00	64.44	4.00	101.19	4.08	21.59	2.59
Moche[j]	F	9	65.22	4.79	46.89	2.80	22.78	1.56	34.22	1.48	39.00	1.32	96.33	3.24	64.56	2.19	97.44	3.00	20.89	1.36
	M	4	62.50	5.80	49.00	1.41	24.25	3.40	35.50	1.00	39.75	1.26	98.50	2.52	63.75	3.77	101.00	4.97	22.25	4.11

[a]Nasion-prosthion height.
[b]Nasal height.
[c]Nasal breadth.
[d]Orbit height.
[e]Orbit breadth.
[f]Biorbital breadth.
[g]Palate breadth.
[h]Bifrontal breadth.
[i]Interorbital breadth.
[j]Gaither, unpublished data.

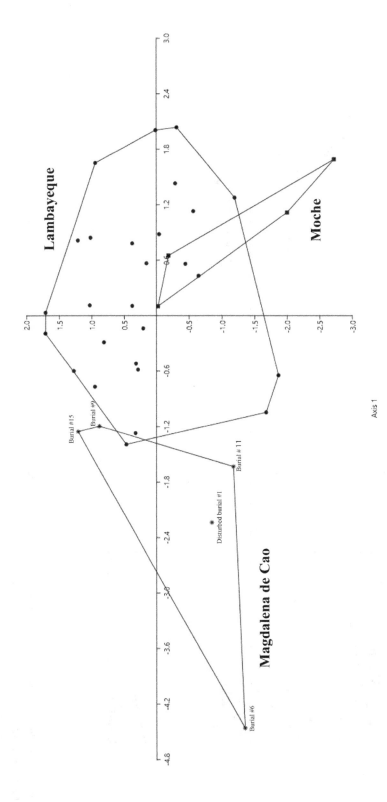

Figure 13.3. Plot of the first two discriminant functions of the three male samples using craniometric data. Magdalena de Cao Viejo (black stars), Lambayeque (black dots), and Moche (black squares).

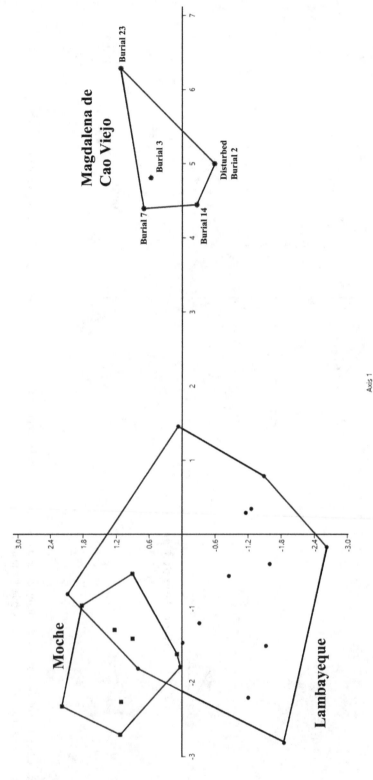

Figure 13.4. Plot of the first two discriminant functions of the three female samples using craniometric data. Magdalena de Cao Viejo (black stars), Lambayeque (black dots), and Moche (black squares).

first two discriminant functions for the male and female samples, respectively. For the male samples the first function accounts for 78.39 percent of the variance, with DKB, OBH, and FMB contributing the most to this axis. The second axis, on the other hand, encompasses 21.61 percent of the variance. Similar values were obtained for the female groups, as the first two functions are responsible for 89.25 percent and 10.75 percent of the variance. The variable contributing the most to the first axis in females is EKB, followed by MAB and NPH. Figure 13.3 demonstrates that the greatest degree of overlap among the male samples occurs between the Lambayeque and Moche males. MCV represents the most distinctive group, with little to no overlap with the other samples. As illustrated in Figure 13.4, results of the DFA using female craniometric data are slightly clearer with respect to group patterning, and although there is a moderate range of overlap between Lambayeque and Moche, MCV forms a well-differentiated group. The likelihood of individuals being accurately classified ranges between 66.67 percent (not jackknifed) and 50 percent (jackknifed) for males and between 89.29 percent (not jackknifed) and 67.86 percent (jackknifed) for females.

Biological affinities of the MCV population were also evaluated through dental morphological traits. The five comparative samples shown in Table 13.1 (HP, CUZ, CEN, SPM, and SPA) were used to characterize the morphology of the MCV dentitions. Frequencies of occurrence and total number of teeth scored per trait and sample are summarized in Table 13.5. The MCV sample is characterized by the relatively high frequency of LM2 four-cusped molar, as well as low frequencies of UI1 shoveling and double-shoveling, UP3 two-rooted premolar, UM1 Carabelli's trait, UM1 enamel extension, and LM1 cusp number. Interestingly, high frequencies of UI1 shoveling and double-shoveling, UM1 enamel extension, and LM1 cusp number are generally attributed to Sinodont populations, including those in the Americas and northeast Asia (Turner 1987, 1990). In our analyses we found the opposite pattern for the MCV group; that is, we found low frequencies of UI1 shoveling and double-shoveling, UM1 enamel extension, and LM1 cusp number. Furthermore, the relatively high frequencies of UP3 two-rooted premolar, UM1 Carabelli's trait, and LM2 four-cusped molars that we found in this study are patterns that generally occur in European populations (Scott and Turner 1997). These results, however, may be an artifact of our sample size.

Multivariate analyses were performed using both 13 and 10 variables, depending on whether or not the SPM comparative sample was excluded

Table 13.5. Frequency (%) and sample size (*n*) for dental morphology samples

Trait[a]	MCV		HP		CUZ		CEN		SPM		SPA	
	%	n	%	n	%	n	%	n	%	n	%	n
Winging UI1 (+ = ASUDAS 1)	33.3	9	0	16	10.5	19	0	16	—[b]	—[b]	8	25
Shoveling UI1 (+ = ASUDAS 2–6)	16.7	6	100	12	50	18	72.7	22	87	23	5.9	17
Double-shoveling UI1 (+ = ASUDAS 2–6)	0	6	63.6	11	18.2	11	10.5	19	66.7	27	3.3	30
Root number UP3 (+ = ASUDAS 2+)	12.5	8	25	12	20.5	39	25.8	31	—[b]	—[b]	57.3	171
Hypocone UM2 (+ = ASUDAS 2–5)	66.7	6	93.8	16	91.2	34	93.1	29	94.7	38	75.9	29
Cusp 5 UM1 (+ = ASUDAS 1–5)	25	4	8.3	12	3.4	29	4.8	42	2.9	34	7.7	13
Carabelli's trait UM1 (+ = ASUDAS 3–7)	0	9	62.5	8	3.7	27	6.5	31	14.7	34	21.1	19
Enamel extension UM1 (+ = ASUDAS 1–3)	11.1	9	72.7	11	51.6	31	60	30	26.5	34	25	12
Groove pattern LM2 (+ = ASUDAS Y)	0	4	7.7	13	2.9	35	14.3	28	—[b]	—[b]	13.9	36
Cusp number LM1 (+ = ASUDAS 6+)	0	6	53.8	13	36.1	36	12.9	31	9.7	31	0	39
Cusp number LM2 (+ = ASUDAS 4)	80	5	22.2	9	23.1	26	26.1	23	42.9	35	95	40
Protostylid LM1 (+ = ASUDAS 2–6)	20	5	0	13	0	30	0	25	0	31	0	38
Cusp 7 LM1 (+ = ASUDAS 1–4)	0	5	7.1	14	10.3	29	10.5	38	0	31	0	45

Note: See Table 13.1 for abbreviations for comparative samples.
[a]Scale of expression in parentheses
[b]Data not available for study

from examination. Pairwise comparisons based on a suite of 13 dental traits using the MMD statistical test are presented in Table 13.6. The MMD distance matrix based on 10 dental morphological characters is presented in Table 13.7. As shown in these tables, trait number does not alter suggested affinities between groups derived from the MMD analysis. MMD values range from 0 to 0.989 when 13 traits are considered and from 0 to 1.258 when 10 variables are used. With two exceptions, all pairwise comparisons show significantly high MMD values, indicating that most groups are morphologically distinct from each other. The exceptions to this statement are

Table 13.6. Mean measure of divergence (MMD) for 13 dental morphological traits

	MCV	HP	CUZ	CEN	SPA
MCV	—				
HP	**0.880**	—			
CUZ	**0.220**	**0.256**	—		
CEN	**0.295**	**0.216**	0.000	—	
SPA	0.070	**0.989**	**0.457**	**0.437**	—

Note: See Table 13.1 for abbreviations for comparative samples. Values in bold are significant at *p* < .05.

Table 13.7. Mean measure of divergence (MMD) for 10 dental morphological traits

	MCV	HP	CUZ	CEN	SPM	SPA
MCV	—					
HP	**1.095**	—				
CUZ	**0.308**	**0.334**	—			
CEN	**0.319**	**0.313**	0.000	—		
SPM	**0.516**	**0.228**	**0.204**	**0.174**	—	
SPA	0.013	**1.258**	**0.538**	**0.533**	**0.668**	—

Note: See Table 13.1 for abbreviations for comparative samples. Values in bold are significant at *p* < .05.

the low MMD values between contemporaneous CUZ and CEN (MMD = 0 based on both 13 and 10 traits) and, surprisingly, between MCV and SPA (MMD = 0.070 and 0.013 based on 13 and 10 variables, respectively). These two low MMD values are not statistically significant, which indicates that it is impossible to differentiate between samples based on the data set used. Interestingly, the second highest divergence (after HP vs. SPA) occurs between MCV and HP (MMD = 0.880 and 1.095 based on 13 and 10 variables, respectively). Although a large time span separates these two samples, both were recovered from sites in the El Brujo Archaeological Complex in the Chicama Valley.

Figures 13.5 and 13.6 plot MCV and the comparative samples along the first and second principal components using 13 and 10 dental morphological variables, respectively. When 13 traits are considered, the first component explains 75.7 percent of the variance, while the following two components account for 13.9 percent and 7.9 percent. Similar results were obtained for the 10-trait analysis, as the first and second components are responsible for 73.1 percent and 13.2 percent of the variance, respectively. In agreement with the MMD analysis, and regardless of trait number, the first axis places MCV closest to the Spanish sample. Finally, diagrams of the

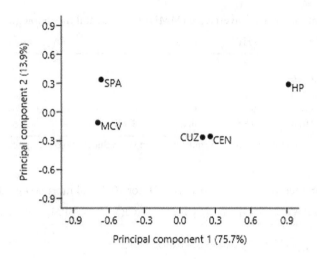

Figure 13.5. First and second principal components of Magdalena de Cao Viejo and comparative samples using 13 dental morphological variables. Magdalena de Cao Viejo (MCV), Huaca Prieta (HP), Cuzco (CUZ), Peru Central Coast (CEN), and Spain (SPA).

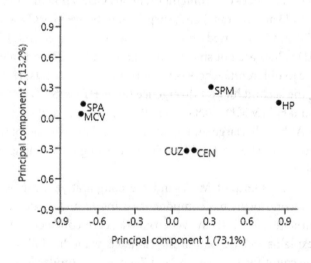

Figure 13.6. First and second principal components of Magdalena de Cao Viejo and comparative samples using 10 dental morphological variables. Magdalena de Cao Viejo (MCV), Huaca Prieta (HP), Cuzco (CUZ), Peru Central Coast (CEN), San Pedro de Mórrope (SPM), and Spain (SPA).

relationships based on UPGMA cluster analyses using the same data set of dental traits are presented in Figures 13.7 and 13.8. Two distinct clusters are evident in these dendrograms. The MCV and SPA samples form a single cluster, whereas the remaining groups represent a second cluster, with the shortest branch length occurring between CUZ and CEN.

While bearing in mind that the sample size is small and that not all of the burials are represented in these study samples, these results are consistent

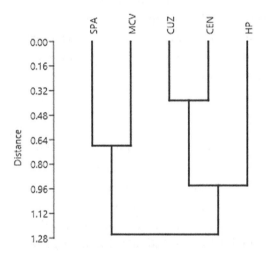

Figure 13.7. Cluster analysis (UPGMA) derived from the squared Euclidean distances depicting the relationships among Magdalena de Cao Viejo and four comparative samples. Dendrograms based on 13 dental morphological traits. Magdalena de Cao Viejo (MCV), Huaca Prieta (HP), Cuzco (CUZ), Peru Central Coast (CEN), and Spain (SPA).

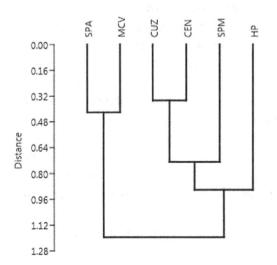

Figure 13.8. Cluster analysis (UPGMA) derived from the squared Euclidean distances depicting the relationships among Magdalena de Cao Viejo and five comparative samples. Dendrograms based on 10 dental morphological traits. Magdalena de Cao Viejo (MCV), Huaca Prieta (HP), Cuzco (CUZ), Peru Central Coast (CEN), San Pedro de Mórrope (SPM), and Spain (SPA).

with the possibility that either there was considerable gene flow between native residents and Spaniards or that Spanish individuals may have been interred in the cemetery, or both. There is little to no continuity of these burials from Magdalena de Cao Viejo with other pre-Hispanic peoples from the Chicama Valley, at least not in the comparative dental morphological samples from Huaca Prieta or from the craniometric data from the Moche or Lambayeque burials at the El Brujo Archaeological Complex. Moreover, judging from the comparative samples, there is no evidence that these Magdaleneros were brought to this *reducción* from the north coast town of San Pedro de Mórrope or from the more distant Cuzco or central coast regions. Finally, kin-group analysis detailed two possible kin groups, but it does not appear that the location of interment in the church or cemetery was organized by familial ties. However, we cannot rule out that interment location was based on marital ties.

Discussion

Archaeological lines of evidence show (1) the capitulation and restructuring of ancestral practices; (2) the continuation of some native Andean practices alongside foreign introductions; and (3) the creation of new material forms with Spanish-influenced innovations and styles with Andean components. The majority of the individuals recovered and analyzed were interred under the floor of church (*n* = 23), and only 5 individuals were recovered outside the church in the adjacent cemetery. Burials in Christian fashion and within the boundaries of consecrated ground appear to be the norm. Within the church, the remains were recovered from two areas under the nave at its northeast and northwest corners, respectively. The bodies in the northeast corner were arranged in a linear fashion from the northwest side to the northeast corner of the unit. The burials in the northwest corner of the nave were grouped in the northwest and the northeast sides and were stacked one on top the other, rather than positioned in the linear row arrangement observed in the northeast corner of the nave. Most of the individuals were supine and extended with arms crossed over the abdomen or chest and feet positioned toward the altar (Gaither and Murphy 2017; Gaither et al. 2012). These individuals were likely wrapped in textiles (see below), but few mortuary offerings or associations were recovered (Gaither and Murphy 2017; Gaither et al. 2012).

Five individuals were recovered in the adjacent cemetery and were also likely wrapped in textiles. Two of these individuals were arranged in a Christian position (extended, supine, arms crossed, etc.), as were the burials from the church, but three individuals, an adult female and two fetuses, were positioned and oriented differently. The adult female was in a semi-flexed, supine position with one of her arms folded across her abdomen (Gaither and Murphy 2017). She did not possess any paleopathological lesions or conditions that may help us interpret her non-Christian orientation or body position. The two fetuses were flexed and positioned on their sides. Both possessed abnormal periosteal reactions, but these were not the only subadults to have periosteal reactions, and other subadults were interred under the nave, including a fetus and three newborns, and some of them possessed periosteal reactions. So, the non-Christian position and orientation does not appear to be age-related or disease-related, at least not based on the available paleopathological data.

All burials were in consecrated ground, either in the cemetery or under the nave of the church; only three individuals were not arranged in Christian fashion, but only those baptized would have been interred in the cemetery or under the church (Eire 1995; Ramos 2010). It is possible that the adult female or her relatives rejected Christian convention in her burial orientation and position. Furthermore, some of the intact and articulated bodies within the church were missing skeletal elements that were removed prior to burial or prior to the superimposition of bodies in the next interment (Gaither and Murphy 2017; Gaither et al. 2012). Did the relatives of the deceased choose to ritually remove these body parts in resistance to and rejection of Christian burial rites? Or perhaps these cases are instances where Andean mortuary practices were restructured so as to allow the parallel practice of Christian and ancestral traditions, which the practitioners may not have deemed contradictory or sacrilegious. These phenomena and beliefs have been documented both ethnohistorically and archaeologically (Arriaga 1968 [1621]; Gose 2008; Klaus and Tam 2015).

Clothing and other superficial adornments to the body permit multiple ways to act under the colonial enterprise, including identification, appropriation, imitation, mockery, and resistance, and they rest at the interface between the body and society (Loren 2003; Rothschild 2008). Dress can be a form of unspoken communication of identity that has profound effects upon interpersonal interactions (Brezine 2011). In Colonial Peru, inappropriate dress was considered highly charged and dangerous, signaling a lack of civility, laziness, or worse. At Magdalena de Cao Viejo archaeologists recovered nearly four thousand textiles from the site, and a sample of these were analyzed in an investigation of colonial dress and adornment (Brezine 2011, 2013). Based on her findings, Brezine was able to reconstruct daily dress, as well as unusual and special garments, including possible funerary apparel. Brezine argues for several different forms of Spanish-indigenous hybridity in dress and textile technology of the Magdaleneros (Brezine 2011, 2013). She found a combination of local materials (cotton) with imported ones (i.e., wool and linen) in dress, the use of indigenous fibers with foreign fabric construction, and new styles of dress that she believes were influenced by Spanish ideas but was inhibited by the local material available (Brezine 2013:254). For example, knitted stockings woven from cotton demonstrate this material hybridity, since prior to colonial rule, native Andeans did not wear stockings, and Spanish stockings were typically made of silk or other materials, not from cotton (Brezine 2011, 2013). The incorporation of Spanish-style embroidering on Andean plain-weave garments and the inclusion of fasteners or buttons on fitted garments, both characteristics that were absent on traditional Andean garb, also evince this material hybridity (Brezine 2011, 2013). Several fragmentary funerary shrouds were recovered from the burials; although they were fashioned in indigenous style, they had European design and technological influences, which is consistent with the material hybridity of the dress and technology described above (Brezine 2017; Quilter 2017).

Comportment was a key component of Spanish religious conversion and "control," and one's habits of dress conveyed one's identity, all closely tied to efforts at homogenization and the process of civilizing (Boddy 2011; Loren 2003; Voss 2008), so those indigenous Magdaleneros who donned Spanish style of dress may be reflections of either successful assimilation or their knowledge of how to manipulate this intimate aspect of their identity to affiliate themselves with Spanish authorities or with indigenous lords or elites (Brezine 2013; O'Toole 2012a; Ramírez 1996). If Spaniards were the ones wearing some of these garments, which is certainly a possibility given the biodistance results described above, then Brezine's results show that the Spaniards made the most of the indigenous materials available in order to assert their Spanish identity in this colonial context (Brezine 2011, 2013).

Food is a form of "embodied material culture" that cannot be disentangled from identity or from the production and exchange of food under the colonial regime (Dietler 2007:222; Dietler 2010). Other chapters in this volume (Danforth et al.; Perry; Killgrove) found considerable variability in the diets of the colonial subjects in their samples. Zooarchaeological data from MCV suggest that the Magdaleneros subsisted on a similar diet to pre-Hispanic Andean coastal communities, and although the later residents of Magdalena de Cao Viejo (late seventeenth and early eighteenth centuries) probably transitioned to sheep and goat husbandry and consumption, the individuals from the church and cemetery lived predominantly as an agro-fishing community (Quilter 2017; Vásquez and Rosales 2008; Vásquez et al. 2017). Fish, shellfish, shore birds, peanuts, and avocados likely supplied most of the fat and protein macronutrients, but sheep and goat were also consumed, although the proportion of the diet composed of these animals cannot be ascertained (Vásquez et al. 2017). The Magdaleneros cultivated Old World plants that were Spanish introductions and likely consumed some of these new foods, such as different citrus fruits, watermelons, plantains, olives, castor beans, and wheat (Vásquez et al. 2017). Wheat, however, does not appear to have become the main carbohydrate or grain of choice (Vásquez and Rosales 2008; Vásquez et al. 2017). Archaeobotanical and zooarchaeological analyses indicate that the Magdaleneros relied upon traditional native starches and carbohydrates, such as manioc, potatoes, maize, squashes, and beans, and that they continued to cultivate and consume the traditional Andean product and seasoning ingredient, the *aji* pepper (Vásquez and Rosales 2008; Vásquez et al. 2017).

From the available data it is difficult to determine if some Magdaleneros rejected the cattle, goat, or sheep into their diets in favor of the traditional sources of protein (e.g., seafood, guinea pig, or alpaca and other South American camelids) as means of asserting their Andean identities, although a reliance upon South American camelids was an unlikely possibility given that most of them were exterminated during Colonial times. It could also be that these foods did not comprise a major component of the diet, as the establishment of Old World animal husbandry was a gradual one and had not yet become the dominant source of animal products. At some point, however, the people at Magdalena de Cao Viejo abandoned fishing (Delibes 2017), and while this moment has not been detected in the material record, perhaps it corresponds to the transition to complete dependence on the herding of sheep, goats, and cattle and the entrenchment of the Spanish colonial economy. Traditional fruits and vegetables remained dietary staples, but it appears that some Old World comestibles may have been cultivated and likely consumed alongside the Andean ones.

CONCLUSIONS: INTEGRATING THE DIFFERENT DIMENSIONS
OF IDENTITY

In this chapter we undertook a study of identity of colonial burials through the integration of biometric and morphological data with archaeological data, specifically mortuary data, textile data, and zooarchaeological and botanical data. Of the burials analyzed, biologically they appear to group more closely with the Spanish comparative sample, and they show no evident continuity with pre-Hispanic samples from the Chicama Valley. They also have a higher frequency of dental morphological traits typically observed in European samples and a lower frequency of dental morphological traits typically observed in Native American samples. Therefore, we believe that these individuals were either of mixed Spanish-Andean descent or were Spanish individuals interred in church and cemetery of an "Indian" town. Since Christian doctrine only permitted those individuals who were baptized to be interred in consecrated ground, and pagans were to be buried elsewhere, we interpret the interment of the latter as evidence for local entrenchment of the Christian faith or in some cases the conversion to Christianity. These interpretations, however, do not mean that some or all Andeans abandoned their ancestral beliefs, but rather that they found ways to reconstruct and resituate ancestral religion alongside Christianity (after Gose 2008:118–160).

Although the body's and the soul's rest were theoretically jeopardized with improper Christian mortuary treatment (Klaus and Tam 2015), it appears that some residents or relatives at Magdalena de Cao Viejo removed body parts from the deceased. Was this a means of continuing their ancestral beliefs alongside their Christian ones? Or does the evidence reflect a negotiation on the part of local priests to accommodate traditional beliefs? This phenomenon of accommodation on the part of the colonizers has been observed extensively throughout churches and missions in Spanish America, and here it is an interpretation that shows how colonialism was not unidirectional (from colonizer to colonized) (Deagan 2003; Larsen et al. 2001; Liebmann 2013, 2015; Milanich 1999; Thomas 1988).

Some Magdaleneros also maintained the practice of deliberate cranial modification, as six adults and one subadult possess symmetrically modified crania (Gaither and Murphy 2017). Tiesler and Zabala (this volume) assert that head shaping by native Andeans marked identity and was a permanent symbol of ethnicity, cultural identity, and distinction and that it continued for almost a century after Spanish invasion, which is consistent with our data. These authors also note that the practice was perpetuated by mothers or related female kin and, although permanent, could have been obscured in domestic areas and disguised by hats or headwear. As a dimension of identity, a modified head could be used to manipulate one's identity either through exposure or concealment, depending upon the context. The Spanish eventually forbade and suppressed the practice of head shaping in the seventeenth century; if discovered, it was a punishable offense (Tiesler 2014; Tiesler and Zabala, this volume; Zabala 2014). Cranial vault modification was an important marker of group identity in the pre-Hispanic Andes (Blom 2005; Tiesler and Zabala, this volume; Torres-Rouff 2009), and its continuation during the late sixteenth and early seventeenth centuries at Magdalena de Cao Viejo indicates the importance of this component of one's local native identity under colonial rule and despite the risk of punishment. The presence of this practice is difficult to reconcile with the other biometric and morphological results, unless these individuals were of mixed Spanish-Andean descent and if the mother was responsible for continuing the practice.

The evidence for material hybridity in the dress and funerary shrouds suggests that the residents of Magdalena de Cao Viejo dressed themselves as best they could in Spanish fashion, either because they were Spanish or because they emulated or mimicked Spanish fashions. For Spanish Andeans this was likely a form of survival as much as it was a means of identifying themselves as model citizens and Christians. Did Spanish dress or Spanish-influenced dress act as a form of camouflage (after Hodges 2005; Naum 2010)? The incorporation of some native embellishments and techniques may have been a subtle means of subversion or a form of resistance, or simply improvisations to make Spanish dress with the indigenous materials at hand. Further, these interpretations are not necessarily mutually exclusive.

Although we cannot say with precision what proportion of the diet some of these foods comprised, the local diet was predominantly based on traditional agro-maritime subsistence of the coastal Central Andes, and many of the highly prized coastal Andean staples are present. While there were foreign food introductions, wheat, cattle, sheep, and goats were not the primary means of subsistence, suggesting that the Magdaleneros were not yet tied into the global proto-capitalist economy and commercial food production. Unfortunately, it is beyond the scope of this chapter and our data to address whether these foods were prepared in Andean fashion or how they were seasoned or consumed and could reflect different dimensions of identity beyond just the consumption of the food items themselves. For example, while maize was cultivated and consumed, did the Magdaleneros transform and ferment it into the traditional alcoholic beverage (*chicha*) for binge drinking during festive occasions, despite the fact that such behaviors were discouraged and punishable under Spanish colonial rule, but at the same time, would blatantly practice one's indigenous identity?

But who were the Magdaleneros? Deagan (2013:268) questions "the extent to which genetic variability reflects cultural difference." Certainly the categories of "Native" or "Indian" or the numerous other formal racial categories were Spanish impositions on Andean peoples, who, prior to Spanish invasion, defined themselves by kinship membership and language groups. The Spaniards themselves were defined in a recently constructed ethnic category, fabricated from ethnic diversity and group conflict in Iberia (i.e., Castilian, Aragonese, and Basques) (Bryant et al. 2012:12). Here we attempted to engage with different facets of identity by integrating different lines of data. We found that our sample of Magdaleneros did not resemble the local pre-Hispanic groups from the Chicama region. On the one hand, we believe that the Magdaleneros were considered natives or of mixed Spanish-Andean descent by the Spaniards because they were interred in a *reducción*, which was exclusively a "pueblo de Indios." Andean women were forced into concubinage, and Spanish-Andean intermarriage was a necessity in the first decades of colonial rule due to the shortage of Spanish females and the need for legitimacy to land and labor on behalf of Spanish men (Deagan 2003; Graubart 2007; Silverblatt 1987), so the biometric and morphological results from this study should come as little surprise; rather, it would be a rarity to find a "local" who was not of "mixed" descent in the first hundred years after Spanish Conquest (Palmie 2013:467). Therefore, bioarchaeologists should expect to find evidence of ethnic and cultural pluralism in these colonial contexts, although this pluralism challenged life as dictated by the Spanish Church and Crown and as depicted in written religious and legal documents.

Life on the frontier or in rural areas of Spanish America was notably less affected by colonialism than life in the center or life in urban areas, where the importance and presence of the Spanish Church and Crown were particularly influential and strong (Deagan 2003). So perhaps these individuals were permitted to live and to be buried at Magdalena de Cao Viejo as an accommodation to life in this rural setting. Another interpretation, albeit unlikely, is that some of the individuals in our study were Spaniards whose bodies were unable to be transported and interred in the larger churches located in the cities, such as the Spanish cities of Trujillo or Lima, which is where most Spaniards desired to be buried (Gose 2008; Ramos 2010). It is possible that these individuals could not afford interment in one of the larger urban churches, a possibility that calls attention to class as a component of identity in this context (Deagan 2003). If these people were perceived as Spaniards living at Magdalena de Cao Viejo, were they there because they were of lower class or otherwise marginalized? Did they lack the financial means to live among the well-heeled Spaniards in Trujillo? Furthermore, since Magdalena de Cao Viejo was a fairly remote and rural setting, perhaps Spaniards were unable to find the means for rapid transport for interment of the deceased in the cities. In the chapter by Winkler et al. in this volume, the authors observed evidence for social inequality in their sample, whereby some of the indicators of poor health correlated with an individual's distance to the altar, so social inequality and class differences appear to be variably expressed across different regions under colonialism.

In this chapter we have contended with data that convey different but complementary dimensions of identity in order to explore the identities of the people from Magdalena de Cao Viejo. Some of these identities were forged from the colonial enterprise and our own scholarship (e.g., Indian, *mestizo*, mixed descent). Other data signify a different identity and contrast our biological data and archaeological snapshots we have of this community. We conclude that the Magdaleneros inhabited an ambiguous place where they were maneuvering and negotiating their complex relationships both within the community and with others, and where they had to inhabit multiple identities and selves. For example, while they may have donned Spanish style of dress, this may have camouflaged the ways in which they continued some pre-Hispanic practices (e.g., head modification) and reinvented themselves in this ever-changing landscape.

ACKNOWLEDGMENTS

The authors would like to thank Jeffrey Quilter and the entire crew from Magdalena de Cao Viejo, without whom this work would not have been possible. The Ministry of Culture of Peru and the Ministry of Culture of Trujillo are also to be acknowledged for graciously permitting the excavations and analyses. We would also like to thank the anonymous reviewers for their constructive criticism; of course, any mistakes and oversights rest with the authors.

References Cited

Abercrombie, T.
1998   *Pathways of Memory and Power: Ethnography and History among an Andean People.* University of Wisconsin Press, Madison.

Adachi, N., Y. Doyo, N. Ohshima, N. Doi, M. Yoneda, and H. Matsumara
2003   Morphologic and Genetic Evidence for the Kinship of Juvenile Skeletal Specimens from a 2,000-Year-Old Double Burial of the Usu-Moshiri Site, Hokkaido, Japan. *Anthropological Science* 111:347–363.

Arriaga, P. J. D.
1968 [1621]   *The Extirpation of Idolatry in Peru.* Translated and edited by L. C. Keating. University of Kentucky Press, Lexington.

Bailey, S. E.
2002   Neandertal Dental Morphology: Implications for Modern Human Origins. Unpublished Ph.D. dissertation. Arizona State University, Tempe.

Berry, A. C., and R. J. Berry
1967   Epigenetic Variation in the Human Cranium. *Journal of Anatomy* 101:361–379.

Blom, D. E.
2005   Embodying Borders: Human Body Modification and Diversity in Tiwanaku Society. *Journal of Anthropological Archaeology* 24:1–24.

Boddy, J.
2011   Colonialism: Bodies under Colonialism. In *A Companion to the Anthropology of the Body and Embodiment*, edited by F. E. Mascia-Lees, pp. 119–136. Wiley-Blackwell, Malden, Massachusetts.

Bondioli, L., R. S. Corruccini, and R. Macchiarelli
1986   Familial Segregation in the Iron Age Community of Alfedena, Abruzzo, Italy, Based on Osteodental Trait Analysis. *American Journal of Physical Anthropology* 71:393–400.

Brezine, C.
2011   Dress, Technology, and Identity in Colonial Peru. Unpublished Ph.D. dissertation, Department of Anthropology, Harvard University, Cambridge.
2013   A Change of Dress on the Coast of Peru: Technological and Material Hybridity in Colonial Peruvian Textiles. In *The Archaeology of Hybrid Material Culture*, edited by J. Card, pp. 239–259. Center for Archaeological Investigations, Southern Illinois University Press, Carbondale.
2017   Textiles and Clothing. In *Magdalena de Cao Viejo*, edited by J. Quilter. Peabody Museum Press, Harvard University, Cambridge, in press.

Bryant, S. K., B. Vinson III, and R. S. O'Toole.
2012   Introduction. In *Africans to Spanish America: Expanding the Diaspora*, edited by S. K. Bryant, B. Vinson III, and R. S. O'Toole, pp. 1–23. University of Illinois Press, Urbana-Champaign.

Buikstra, J. E., and D. H. Ubelaker (editors)
1994   *Standards for Data Collection from Human Skeletal Remains.* Arkansas Archaeological Survey Research Series No.44, Fayetteville.

Corruccini, R. S., and I. Shimada
2002   Dentally Determined Biological Kinship in Relation to Mortuary Patterning
            of Human Remains from Huaca Loro, Peru. *American Journal of Physical
            Anthropology* 117:113–121.
Corruccini, R. S., I. Shimada, and K.-I. Shinoda
2002   Dental and mtDNA Relatedness among Thousand-Year-Old Remains from
            Huaca Loro, Peru. *Dental Anthropology* 16:9–14.
Cummins, T.
2002   Forms of Andean Colonial Towns, Free Will, and Marriage. In *The Archae-
            ology of Colonialism,* edited by C. Lyons and J. Papadopoulos, pp. 199–240.
            Getty Research Institute, Los Angeles.
Dahlberg, A. A.
1945   The Changing Dentition of Man. *Journal of the American Dental Association*
            32:676–690.
Deagan, K.
2003   Colonial Origins and Colonial Transformations in Spanish America. *Histori-
            cal Archaeology* 27(4):3–13.
2004   Reconsidering Taíno Social Dynamics after Spanish Conquest: Gender and
            Class in Culture Contact Studies. *American Antiquity* 69(4):597–626.
2013   Hybridity, Identity, and Archaeological Practice. In *The Archaeology of Hy-
            brid Material Culture,* edited by J. Card, pp. 260–276. Center for Archaeo-
            logical Investigations, Southern Illinois University Press, Carbondale.
Delibes, R.
2017   The Town and Parish of Santa María Magdalena de Cao Viejo in the Histori-
            cal Administrative Records. In *Magdalena de Cao Viejo,* edited by J. Quilter.
            Peabody Museum Press, Harvard University, Cambridge, in press.
Diaz-Andreu, M., and S. Lucy (editors)
2005   *Archaeology of Identity.* Taylor and Francis, New York.
Dietler, M.
2007   Culinary Encounters: Food, Identity, and Colonialism. In *The Archaeology
            of Food and Identity,* edited by K. C. Twiss, pp. 218–242. Center for Archaeo-
            logical Investigations, Southern Illinois University Press, Carbondale.
2010   *Archaeologies of Colonialism: Consumption, Entanglement, and Violence in
            Ancient Mediterranean France.* University of California Press, Berkeley.
Eire, C.
1995   *From Madrid to Purgatory: The Art and Craft of Dying in Sixteenth-Century
            Spain.* Cambridge University Press, Cambridge.
Gaither, C., and M. S. Murphy
2017   Changing Times: A Bioarchaeological Glimpse of Life and Death in a *Re-
            ducción.* In *Magdalena de Cao Viejo,* edited by J. Quilter. Peabody Museum
            Press, Harvard University, Cambridge, in press.
Gaither, C., J. Quilter, M. S. Murphy, C. Lewis, and R. Franco
2012   The Impact of Colonization: Population Health in the Early Colonial *Reduc-
            ción* of Magdalena de Cao Viejo in Peru. Paper presented at the 111th meeting
            of American Anthropological Association, San Francisco.

García Sívoli, C.
2009   Estudio diacrónico de los Rasgos dentales en poblaciones del Mediterráneo Occidental: Mallorca y Cataluña. Unpublished Ph.D. dissertation. Universitat Autònoma de Barcelona.

Gasco, J.
2005   Spanish Colonialism and Processes of Social Change in Mesoamerica. In *The Archaeology of Colonial Encounters: Comparative Perspectives*, edited by G. Stein, pp. 69–108. School for Advanced Research Press, Santa Fe.

Gose, P.
2008   *Invaders as Ancestors: On the Intercultural Making and Unmaking of Spanish Colonialism in the Andes*. University of Toronto Press, Toronto.

Graubart, K. B.
2000   Weaving and the Construction of a Gender Division of Labor in Early Colonial Peru. *American Indian Quarterly* 24(4):537–561.
2007   *With Our Labor and Sweat: Indigenous Women and the Formation of Colonial Society in Peru, 1550–1700*. Stanford University Press, Stanford.

Hammer, Ø., D. A. T. Harper, and P. D. Ryan
2001   PAST: Paleontological Statistics Software Package for Education and Data Analysis. *Palaeontologia Electronica* 4:1–9.

Hanihara, K., A. Yamauchi, and Y. Mizoguchi
1983   Statistical Analysis on Kinship among Skeletal Remains Excavated from a Neolithic Site at Uwasato, Iwate Prefecture. *Journal of Anthropological Society of Nippon* 91:49–68.

Hanihara, T.
1992   Dental and Cranial Affinities among Populations of East Asia and the Pacific: The Basic Populations in East Asia, IV. *American Journal of Physical Anthropology* 88:163–182.
2008   Morphological Variation of Major Human Populations Based on Nonmetric Dental Traits. *American Journal of Physical Anthropology* 136:169–182.

Hanihara, T., and H. Ishida
2005   Metric Dental Variation of Major Human Populations. *American Journal of Physical Anthropology* 128:287–298.

Harris, E. F., and T. Sjøvold
2004   Calculation of Smith's Mean Measure of Divergence for Intergroup Comparisons Using Nonmetric Data. *Dental Anthropology* 17:83–93.

Haydenblit, R.
1996   Dental Variation among Four Pre-Hispanic Mexican Populations. *American Journal of Physical Anthropology* 100:225–246.

Hodges C.
2005   Faith and Practice at an Early-Eighteenth-Century Wampanoag Burial Ground: The Waldo Farm Site in Dartmouth, Massachusetts. *Historical Archaeology* 39:73–94.

Howells, W. W.
1973   *Cranial Variation in Man: A Study by Multivariate Analysis of Patterns of Dif-*

ference among Recent Human Populations. Papers of the Peabody Museum of Archaeology and Ethnology, vol. 67. Harvard University, Cambridge.

1989 *Skull Shapes and the Map: Craniometric Analyses in the Dispersion of Modern Homo.* Papers of the Peabody Museum of Archaeology and Ethnology, vol. 79. Harvard University, Cambridge.

Insoll, T. (editor)

2007 *The Archaeology of Identities: A Reader.* Routledge, New York.

Irish, J. D.

1993 *Biological Affinities of Late Pleistocene through Modern African Aboriginal Populations: The Dental Evidence.* Ph.D. dissertation. Arizona State University, Tempe.

1997 Characteristic High- and Low-Frequency Dental Traits in Sub-Saharan African Populations. *American Journal of Physical Anthropology* 102:455–467.

2010 The Mean Measure of Divergence: Its Utility in Model-Free and Model-Bound Analyses Relative to the Mahalanobis D^2 Distance for Nonmetric Traits. *American Journal of Human Biology* 22:378–395.

Jantz, R. L., and D. W. Owsley

2001 Variation among Early North American Crania. *American Journal of Physical Anthropology* 114:146–155.

Klaus, H. D.

2008 Out of Light Came Darkness: Bioarchaeology of Mortuary Ritual, Health, and Ethnogenesis in the Lambayeque Valley Complex, North Coast Peru, A.D. 900–1750. Unpublished Ph.D. dissertation. Ohio State University, Columbus.

2013 Hybrid Cultures . . . and Hybrid Peoples: Bioarchaeology of Genetic Change, Religious Architecture, and Burial Ritual in the Colonial Andes. In *The Archaeology of Hybrid Material Culture,* edited by J. Card, pp. 207–238. Center for Archaeological Investigations, Southern Illinois University Press, Carbondale.

Klaus, H. D., and M. E. Tam

2015 Requiem Aeternam? Archaeothanatology of Mortuary Ritual in Colonial Mórrope, North Coast of Peru. In *Living with the Dead in the Andes,* edited by I. Shimada and J. L. Fitzsimmons, pp. 267–303. University of Arizona Press, Tucson.

Knudson, K. J., and Stojanowski, C. M.

2009 The Bioarchaeology of Identity. In *Bioarchaeology and Identity in the Americas,* edited by K. J. Knudson and C. M. Stojanowski, pp. 1–23. University Press of Florida, Gainesville.

Knudson, K. J., and Stojanowski, C. M. (editors)

2009 *Bioarchaeology and Identity in the Americas.* University Press of Florida, Gainesville.

Lalueza Fox, C., A. Gonzalez Martin, and S. Vives Civit

1996 Cranial Variation in the Iberian Peninsula and the Balearic Islands: Inferences about the History of the Population. *American Journal of Physical Anthropology* 99:413–428.

Larsen, C. S., M. C. Griffin, D. L. Hutchinson, V. E. Noble, L. Norr, R. Pastor, C. B. Ruff, K. F. Russell, M. J. Schoeninger, M. Schultz, S. W. Simpson, and M. F. Teaford
2001   Frontiers of Contact: Bioarchaeology of Spanish Florida. *Journal of World Prehistory* 15:69–123.

Liebmann, M.
2013   Parsing Hybridity: Archaeologies of Amalgamation in Seventeenth-Century New Mexico. In *The Archaeology of Hybrid Material Culture*, edited by J. Card, pp. 25–49. Center for Archaeological Investigations, Southern Illinois University Press, Carbondale.
2015   The Mickey Mouse Kachina and Other "Double Objects": Hybridity in the Material Culture of Colonial Encounters. *Journal of Social Archaeology* 15:319–341.

Lightfoot, K.
1995   Culture Contact Studies: Redefining the Relationship between Prehistoric and Historical Archaeology. *American Antiquity* 60:199–217.

Lightfoot, K., and A. Martinez
1995   Frontiers and Boundaries in Archaeological Perspective. *Annual Reviews in Anthropology* 24:471–492.

Loren, D. D.
2003   Refashioning a Body Politic in Colonial Louisiana. *Cambridge Archaeological Journal* 13:231–237.
2008   *In Contact: Bodies and Spaces in the Sixteenth- and Seventeenth-Century Eastern Woodlands.* AltaMira, Lanham, Maryland.

Meskell, L. M.
2007   *Archaeologies of Identity.* In *The Archaeologies of Identity: A Reader*, edited by T. Insoll, pp. 23–43. Routledge, New York.

Milanich, J.
1999   *Laboring in the Fields of the Lord: Spanish Missions and Southeastern Indians.* Smithsonian Institution Press, Washington, D.C.

Naum, M.
2010   Re-emerging Frontiers: Postcolonial Theory and Historical Archaeology of the Borderlands. *Journal of Archaeological Method and Theory* 17:101–131.

Nystrom, K. C.
2006   Late Chachapoya Population Structure Prior to Inka Conquest. *American Journal of Physical Anthropology* 131:334–342.

Ortiz, A.
2013   Dental Morphological Variation among Six pre-Hispanic South American Populations with Implications for the Peopling of the New World. *Dental Anthropology Journal* 26:20–32.

Ortiz, A., and S. E. Bailey
2008   Intra- and Inter-regional Dental Morphological Variation in South American Populations. *American Journal of Physical Anthropology Supplement* 46:166–167.

O'Toole, R. S.
2012a   Bound Lives: Africans, Indians and the Making of Race in Colonial Peru. University of Pittsburgh Press, Pittsburgh.
2012b   To Be Free and Lucumí: Ana de la Calle and Making Diaspora Identities in Colonial Peru. In Africans to Spanish America. Expanding the Diaspora, edited by S. K. Bryant, R. S. O'Toole, and B. Vinson III, pp. 73–92. University of Illinois Press, Urbana-Champaign.

Pacelli, C. S., and N. Márquez-Grant
2010   Evaluation of Dental Non-Metric Traits in a Medieval Population from Ibiza (Spain). Bulletin of the International Association of Paleodontology 4:16–28.

Palmie, S.
2013   Mixed Blessings and Sorrowful Mysteries: Second Thoughts about "Hybridity." Current Anthropology 54:463–482.

Paul, K. S., and C. M. Stojanowski
2015   Performance Analysis of Deciduous Morphology for Detecting Biological Siblings. American Journal of Physical Anthropology 157:615–629.

Phillips, C., R. Phillips Jr., and D. William
1991   Spain in the Fifteenth Century. In Transatlantic Encounters: Europeans and Andeans in the Sixteenth Century, edited by K. J. Andrien and R. Adorno, pp. 11–39. University of California Press, Berkeley.

Pietrusewsky, M.
1999   Multivariate Craniometric Investigations of Japanese, Asians, and Pacific Islanders. In Interdisciplinary Perspectives on the Origins of the Japanese: International Symposium 1996, edited by K. Omoto, pp. 65–104. International Research Center for Japanese Studies, Kyoto.

Pietrusewsky, M., and C. Chang
2003   Taiwan Aboriginals and Peoples of the Pacific-Asia Region: Multivariate Craniometric Comparisons. Anthropological Science 111:293–332.

Powers, K. V.
2005   Women in the Crucible of Conquest: The Gendered Genesis of Spanish American Society, 1500–1600. University of New Mexico Press, Albuquerque.

Quilter, J.
2010   Cultural Encounters at Magdalena de Cao Viejo in the Early Colonial Period. In Enduring Conquests: Rethinking the Archaeology of Resistance to Spanish Colonialism in the Americas, edited by M. Liebmann and M. S. Murphy, pp. 103–125. School for Advanced Research Press, Santa Fe.

Quilter, J. (editor)
2017   Magdalena de Cao Viejo. Peabody Museum Press, Harvard University, Cambridge, in press.

Quilter, J., M. Zender, K. Spalding, R. Franco, C. Gálvez, and J. Castañeda
2010   Traces of a Lost Language and Number System Discovered on the North Coast of Peru. American Anthropologist 112:357–369.

Ramírez, S. E.
1996   The World Upside Down: Cross-Cultural Contact and Conflict in Sixteenth-Century Peru. Stanford University Press, Stanford.

Ramos, G.
2010   *Death and Conversion in the Andes, 1532–1670.* University of Notre Dame Press, South Bend, Indiana.

Rothschild, N. A.
2008   Colonised Bodies, Personal and Social. In *Past Bodies. Body-Centered Research in Archaeology,* edited by D. Borić and J. Robb, pp. 135–144. Oxbow Books, Oxford.

Said, E.
1993   *Culture and Imperialism.* Vintage Books, New York.

Scott, G. R., and C. G. Turner II
1997   *The Anthropology of Modern Human Teeth: Dental Morphology and Its Variation in Recent Human Populations.* Cambridge University Press, Cambridge.

Scott, R. E.
2011   Religious Identity and Mortuary Practice: The Significance of Christian Burial in Early Medieval Ireland. In *Breathing New Life into the Evidence of Death,* edited by A. Baadsgaard, A. Boutin, and J. E. Buikstra, pp. 55–77. School for Advanced Research Press, Santa Fe.

Silliman, S.
2005   Culture Contact or Colonialism? Challenges in the Archaeology of Native North America. *American Antiquity* 70:55–74.

Silverblatt, I. M.
1987   *Moon, Sun, and Witches. Gender Ideologies and Class in Inca and Colonial Peru.* Princeton University Press, Princeton.

Sjøvold, T.
1977   Non-Metrical Divergence between Skeletal Populations: The Theoretical Foundation and Biological Importance of C. A. B. Smith's Mean Measure of Divergence. *Ossa Supplement* 4:1–133.

Sofaer, J. R.
2006   *The Body as Material Culture: A Theoretical Osteoarchaeology.* Cambridge University Press, Cambridge.

Stojanowski, C. M.
2005   Spanish Colonial Effects on Native American Mating Structures and Genetic Variability in Northern and Central Florida: Evidence from Apalachee and Western Timucua. *American Journal of Physical Anthropology* 128:273–286.

Stojanowski, C. M., C. S. Larsen, T. A. Tung, and B. McEwan
2007   Biological Structure and Health Implications from Tooth Size at Mission San Luis de Apalachee. *American Journal of Physical Anthropology* 132:207–222.

Stojanowski, C. M., and M. A. Schillaci
2006   Phenotypic Approaches for Understanding Patterns of Intracemetery Biological Variation. *Yearbook of Physical Anthropology* 49:49–88.

Subirà, M. E., D. López-Onaindia, and R. Yll
2014   Cultural Changes in Funeral Rites during the Neolithic in the Northeast of the Iberian Peninsula? The Cave of Pantà de Foix (Barcelona). *International Journal of Osteoarchaeology* 1:104–113.

Sutter, R. C.

2000   Prehistoric Genetic and Culture Change: A Bioarchaeological Search for Pre-Inka Altiplano Colonies in the Coastal Valleys of Moquegua, Peru, and Azapa, Chile. *Latin American Antiquity* 11:43–70.

Sutter, R. C., and J. W. Verano

2007   Biodistance Analysis of the Moche Sacrificial Victims from Huaca de la Luna Plaza 3C: Matrix Method Test of their Origins. *American Journal of Physical Anthropology* 132:193–206.

Thomas, D. H.

1988   Saints and Soldiers at Santa Catalina: Hispanic Designs for Colonial America. In *The Recovery of Meaning*, edited by M. Leone and P. Potter, pp. 73–140. Smithsonian Institution Press, Washington, D.C.

Tiesler, V.

2014   *The Bioarchaeology of Artificial Cranial Modifications: New Approaches to Head Shaping and Its Meanings in Pre-Columbian Mesoamerica and Beyond.* Springer Press, New York.

Tiesler, V., and A. Cucina

2008   Afinidades biológicas y prácticas bioculturales del Sureste de Petén. In *XXI Simposio de Investigaciones Arqueológicas en Guatemala 2007*, edited by J. P. Laporte, B. Arroyo, and H. Mejía, pp.704–724. Museo Nacional de Arqueología y Etnología, Guatemala.

Torres-Rouff, C.

2009   The Bodily Expression of Ethnic Identity: Head Shaping in the Chilean Atacama. In *Bioarchaeology and Identity in the Americas*, edited by K. J. Knudson and C. M. Stojanowski, pp. 212–227. University Press of Florida, Gainesville.

Turner, C. G., II

1984   Advances in the Dental Search for Native American Origins. *Acta Anthropogenetica* 8:23–78.

1987   Late Pleistocene and Holocene Population History of East Asia Based on Dental Variation. *American Journal of Physical Anthropology* 73:305–321.

1990   Major Features of Sundadonty and Sinodonty, Including Some Suggestions about East Asian Microevolution, Population History, and Late Pleistocene Relationships with Australian Aboriginals. *American Journal of Physical Anthropology* 82:295–317.

Turner, C. G., II, C. R. Nichol, and G. R. Scott

1991   Scoring Procedures for Key Morphological Traits of the Permanent Dentition: The Arizona State University Dental Anthropology System. In *Advances in Dental Anthropology*, edited by M. A. Kelley and C. S. Larsen, pp. 13–31. Willey-Liss, New York.

Turner, C. G., II, and G. R. Scott

1977   Dentition of the Easter Islanders. In *Orofacial Growth and Development*, edited by A. A. Dahlberg and T. M. Graber, pp. 229–249. Mouton, The Hague.

Vásquez, V., and T. Rosales

2008   *Informe finale análisis de restos de fauna y vegetales de la iglesia y pueblo, Complejo Arqueologico El Brujo.* Ministry of Culture, Lima.

Vásquez, V., T. Rosales, and J. Quilter
2017   Plants and Animals. In *Magdalena de Cao Viejo*, edited by J. Quilter. Peabody Museum Press, Harvard University, Cambridge, in press.
Voss, B.
2005   From *Casta* to *Californio*: Social Identity and the Archaeology of Culture Contact. *American Anthropologist* 107:461–474.
2008   Poor People in Silk Shirts: Dress and Ethnogenesis in Spanish-Colonial San Francisco. *Journal of Social Archaeology* 8:404–432.
Williams-Blangero, S., and J. Blangero
1989   Anthropometric Variation and the Genetic Structure of the Jirels of Nepal. *Human Biology* 61:1–12.
Zabala, P.
2014   Source Compilation on Head-Shaping Practices in Hispanic America. In *The Bioarchaeology of Artificial Cranial Modifications: New Approaches to Head Shaping and Its Meanings in Pre-Columbian and Colonial Mesoamerica*, by Vera Tiesler, pp. 99–129. Springer, New York.

14

The Bioarchaeology of Colonialism

Past Perspectives and Future Prospects

CHRISTOPHER M. STOJANOWSKI

The year 2001 witnessed a defining moment in the bioarchaeological study of colonialism: the publication of Clark Larsen's edited volume *Bioarchaeology of Spanish Florida: The Impact of Colonialism*. The book summarized and synthesized several decades of work by Larsen and a series of collaborators on the indigenous mission populations of Florida and Georgia (e.g., Hutchinson and Larsen 1990; Hutchinson et al. 1998; Larsen and Ruff 1994; Larsen, Hutchinson, et al. 2001; for syntheses of this work, see also Larsen et al. 1990, 2002, 2007; and Larsen, Griffin, et al. 2001). Chapters included interpretations of several types of health data, dietary inferences, reconstruction of activity levels, and biological distance. Multiple sites were used from different regions with different ecologies and associated with distinct cultural groups known from the protohistoric record. Time periods were defined that emphasized the precontact–contact transition as well as ongoing changes that occurred throughout the seventeenth century. Historical documents and ethnohistoric data structured interpretations of spatiotemporal patterning of bioarchaeological data, which provided evidence of temporal declines in health, quality of life, dietary diversity, and increasing biomechanical stress—lifestyle transitions previously inferred from vague and incomplete historical descriptions and highly contested assessments of declining population size. In this sense, the project helped to humanize the mission period of La Florida while quantifying the extent of lifestyle changes they experienced. The project is an ideal example of a biocultural approach to the past that emphasizes health, demography, and lifestyle within a comparative perspective. Although, as noted by the editors in the introduction to this volume, La Florida was not the *only* place where mission bioarchaeology had taken place, I would argue that the La Florida Bioarchaeology Project is the most visible and has made the greatest impact on the way research continues to be structured and practiced today. Indeed, the above description of the research program should be very familiar to most readers and at this point seem normative. But it was not always this way, and it is easy to forget the overall impact this project has had on the business of bioarchaeology at the level of practice—site-based, spatially and temporally comparative, health-focused, indigenous, context-dependent. As the Winkler et al. chapter demonstrates (as does some of my own work), the bioarchaeological potential of the Florida missions is far from exhausted, and the story of these native lives has only partially been written.

As colonialism itself is a constant "work in progress," so too must be its study. Although osteological analyses of post-Columbian native or European skeletal remains are as ancient as anthropology itself, a "bioarchaeology of colonialism" only just emerged from the 1980s focus on diet, disease, and demography (e.g., Cohen and Armelagos 1984; Verano and Ubelaker 1994) in the lead-up to the Columbus Quincentenary (Baker and Kealhofer 1996; Larsen and Milner 1994; Thomas 1991a, 1991b, 1991c). As such, it is a relatively new field of study. As Murphy and Klaus (this volume) note, the first generation of bioarchaeologists defined the field, demonstrated its power for informing historical questions, and helped to dismantle the "monolithic response" paradigm that emerged from the intense gaze upon the undeniable tragedy of New World demographic collapse. These scholars qualified and verified long-held assumptions about demographic collapse, provided data on the health implications of the colonial period, and modified existing assumptions about the rate and homogeneity of population size changes in the post-Columbian era. While initial work was largely focused on New World (specifically North American) contexts, bioarchaeologists are now beginning to narrate the global experience of colonialism, including, for example, South and Central American, pan–North American, Greek, Roman, Near Eastern and Egyptian, and even Australian and Oceanic contexts. This geographic and temporal breadth reflects the fact that colonialism and contact are at once about capitalism and imperialism and are not just post-Columbian, premodern enterprises restricted to the "historical archaeology" of the New World. Although the La Florida project helped define a novel research area, a new generation of scholars (a second generation) will build the global comparative database to which this volume contributes a host of useful and novel data points. If definition and description is phase 1, and expansion and replication/qualification is phase 2, then the final phase is cross-regional synthesis within a social sciences research paradigm that answers ultimate questions of causation, perhaps offers predictions, and narrates humanistic assessments of the colonial legacy that we all still live (to varying degrees) to this very day.

In *Colonized Bodies, Worlds Transformed: Toward a Global Bioarchaeology of Contact and Colonialism*, the editors have compiled a series of chapters, most of them regional in focus, detailing aspects of colonialism or culture contact situations. This is a long-needed volume that will help solidify a base—where we have been since the year 2000—and thereby help propel the field in new and exciting research directions—where we are going. With one exception (the chapter by Tiesler and Zabala) the book is decidedly phase 2 in scope, as the editors themselves acknowledge.

In their introduction, Murphy and Klaus do much of the heavy lifting, defining numerous key research questions, summarizing the existing literature on the bioarchaeology of colonialism and culture contact, and providing summaries of the relevant sections and chapters. The global synthesis of prior work is, itself, a major contribution to the literature and should serve as an important starting point for future work on the topics of culture contact and colonialism. There are eleven substantive chapters presented here divided into three sections: (1) postcontact life, death, and mortuary practices; (2) colonial entanglements, frontiers, and diversity; and (3) identity and the body under colonialism. The first and second sections offer a global perspective on the effects of colonialism and culture contact on the health of variously defined "affected" communities: indigenous converts living in the frontier of colonial expansion, peripheral towns within an Old World empire, lower-class suburbanites within major urban centers, and even recent European immigrants to the New World. Importantly, the contributions move beyond the singular focus on indigenous New World communities. Notions of class, ethnicity, hybridity, and, perhaps most importantly, longevity of contact (*entanglement* being the preferred term here) provide important axes of variation and help flesh out the notion that colonialism was not a one-way process of cultural exchange, a monolithic process of health decline, a passive extirpation, or even necessarily a bad thing in some cases. The undercurrent of these chapters is one of resilience, with the bioarchaeological data providing evidence of dietary and health-related changes reflecting the various degrees to which different communities responded and adjusted to the colonial context.

As a testament to the endurance of the biocultural approach defined by

Larsen and his colleagues, enamel defects (macro and micro) are the most visible data offered in support of health-based inferences (9 of 12 chapters), followed by porotic hyperstosis (7 of 12 chapters), cribra orbitalia (6 of 12 chapters), and periosteal reactions (6 of 12 chapters). Dental health, trauma, demographic inferences, stature/long bone length, and isotopic analyses of diet and migration comprise a second tier of data (represented in between 25 percent and 33 percent of chapters), with a minority representation of enamel microdefects, tooth size as a reflection of diminished growth potential, inferences of osteoporosis, degenerative joint disease, and entheseal remodeling. These data, and the analyses used to understand them, should be familiar to most readers and are a testament to the non-methodological focus of this volume and the importance of generating data that are comparable across sites, regions, and time periods. Five of the health-focused chapters focus on indigenous New World populations, three on Old World empires, and one on European settlers in the post-Columbian Americas. Scales are either site-specific or regional in focus, and study designs varied from site-level description, to diachronic comparisons, to regional-spatial comparisons couched within ecological or social frameworks. It is easy to see the influence of the La Florida project throughout these chapters.

In combination, the health-focused chapters fulfill the primary goal of the volume—to expand our database of the colonial experience. Data, data presentation, analytical framework, and interpretive style are familiar. As with any edited volume, the coverage is spotty, as the editors acknowledge, and the lack of African or African American representation leaves plenty of room for expansion. There is no doubt that this will occur in the future, but some structuring may be needed such that higher-order inferences are "tiered" and compared in a stepwise fashion as the depth of bioarchaeological coverage increases regionally and globally. For example, although the inclusion of three Old World contexts is expected and needed (and commendable), at first glance I admit it is difficult to see the connections to New World contexts that are not only more recent in age but share the tradition of the Spanish mission experience (this alone is quite variable) and an immediacy derived from the clear connection between past peoples and their living descendants. As an intermediate step I could see focusing just on the Spanish missions of the New World, for which many confounding variables may be minimized and questions of interest more directly drawn from the data (cf. Baker and Kealhofer 1996; Graham 1994; Funari and Senatore 2015; Thomas 1991a, 1991b, 1991c; Van Buren 2010). There may be a danger in adopting an overly inclusive approach in which the value of specific topical paradigms diminishes as the boundaries of research themes blur. Colonialism is not colonization (lest we incorporate the peopling of the New World and Oceania, the repopulating of North Africa during the Green Sahara period, or even modern human emergence from Africa). In addition, "contact" clearly does not include the Levantine Neanderthal–modern human nexus circa 100–50 kya. The one unifying theme here, then, is that of the state, the imperialism of complex societies, and the effects that resource extraction and territorial expansion have on the colonizers and the colonized both in terms of health and social identity and identification. More than anything, the bioarchaeology of colonialism explores the consequences of power differentials; the health-centric chapters explore how and why life-course experience varied at multiple scales (within a single site/community, across towns within a river valley, or among urban neighborhoods), while the identity-centric chapters offer examples of how colonial power structures were resisted or repurposed.

The second major accomplishment of this volume is in some ways diametrically opposed to the first: to help define a bioarchaeology of colonialism that is *not* just focused on diet, disease, and demography. On this front the book is successful and makes a strong case for the value of a diversity of approaches that use body modification (Tiesler and Zabala), human skeletal morphology (Buzon and Smith; Danforth et al.; Ortiz et al.; Ribot et al.), and ancient DNA (Danforth et al.) to explore what I think is the most important contribution a bioarchaeology of colonialism can offer: the study of identity, hybridity, and ethnogenesis. Unlike vectors of disease, food imports, economic inequality, or many other imposed and imported systems of oppression and change, identity is an inherently internalized human product. Identity is blended by definition and removed from the rules of the natural world, including, most importantly, those of phylogeny and Darwinian selection (Moore 1994a, 1994b, 2001; Terrell 2001). This makes identities-based research decidedly humanistic, extremely challenging, and inherently historical, particularistic, relational, and not subject to prediction and laws. As such, the identities focus of the colonial bioarchaeology literature also runs counter to the somewhat nomothetic goals of the health-based focus. Although obviously related and intertwined, the two topics work in both complementary and contradictory ways. However, I would argue that it is the simple appreciation for the fact that human social identities *are* complex and mutable that has so much value. Parts endure or are discarded, elements are blended, biology may or may not matter, and culture (or cultural traits) may or may not persist (Hu 2013; Panich 2013;

Stojanowski 2010; Voss 2008; Weik 2014). Identity is non-linear, non-static, and inherently "gray," which makes its study all the more important in a world of increasingly black-and-white political and social discourse.

Elements of this complexity are interwoven throughout a number of the chapters, with the offerings by Tiesler and Zabala, Danforth et al., Ribot et al., and Ortiz et al. addressing identity most directly. Tiesler and Zabala adopt a strictly cultural definition of identity in their exploration of the meanings and changing practices associated with head-shaping behavior throughout the New World. In this case the meaning of identity is quite clear, because the confounding effects of genetics and inheritance are not relevant. However, the three other chapters in this section blur the lines a bit more. While it is easy to see all three as inherently about biological identity (i.e., ancestry in the strict evolutionary sense of the term), careful reflection on what is actually being proposed in each case shows a bit more subtlety is used by these authors. Danforth et al. consider the practical aspects of colonialist identity studies—identifying ancestry from the human skeleton and, more importantly, identifying admixed individuals. As the authors of that chapter note, this is a difficult and tenuous process steeped in Victorian notions of human variation and plagued by an uncertain relationship between population, genome, and phenome. Nevertheless, notions of purity wither as we approach the modern era, and bioarchaeological assessments of individuals of multiple ancestries could provide exciting new research directions that bridge the colonized-colonizer dichotomy. Ribot et al. carry this even further and consider the processes that "led to the establishment of the unique admixed 'Coloured' population known in South Africa today," thus linking the deeper colonialist past with modern societies. What is particularly interesting about the approach the authors use in this chapter is the allocation of individuals based on origin (so forensic allocation) as well as whether the individuals are first- or second-generation migrants. This approach has the potential to scale down the level of inference, allowing one to consider secular changes in health and lifestyle within a structure that is still in use today (first- vs. second-generation immigrants). This chapter demonstrates one potential outcome of colonialist bioarchaeology that has meaning to the modern world: the construction of collective biological histories, ones that cannot lie (although they can be misinterpreted), that come to us unfiltered through the lens of identity politics in the modern world and the written histories of the victors. Contrary to notions of nationalist purity and superiority, this is an important message to derive from work on cemeteries of the colonial period. And it is one that has clear global resonance and provides a strong reminder that the post-Columbian/post–Age of Discovery world is composed of many hybrid "peoples" whose history is complex and contested (Hill 1996).

With two major emphases (health and identity), the present volume offers important breadth and perspective to the bioarchaeology of colonialism literature. One thing I note is that even with the broader definition of colonialism used here (i.e., not just New World post-Columbian contexts) there is considerable overlap with various historical archaeologies. In the next section I explore how a bioarchaeology of colonialism articulates with historical archaeology, particular as practiced in the New World, to evaluate how well our research questions match with those of other areas of scholarship and to evaluate the impact the bioarchaeology of colonialism is having beyond our own specific disciplinary boundaries.

HISTORICAL BIOARCHAEOLOGY AS HISTORICAL ARCHAEOLOGY

Historical archaeology is a vibrant field. Numerous reflective, retrospective, and forward-thinking papers have been written that discuss the field's purpose, role, standing, and future in archaeology, anthropology, and history. The history of histories of historical archaeology is extensive indeed, beginning with Deagan's (1982) initial discussions and continuing up to the present day with works by Orser (2010) and emerging articulations with postcolonial scholars (Naum 2010; van Dommelen 2011). The intervening years witnessed a "who's who" of eminent figures in historical archaeology summarizing and reflecting on the current state of the field and its perennial challenges of self-definition and standing as a legitimate pursuit (for coverage of a variety of topics see, e.g., Deagan 1988; Funari et al. 1999; Gosden 2004; Lightfoot 1995; Little 1994; Orser 2001, 2010; Paynter 2000; Silliman 2005). There are also numerous book-length synthetic treatments of historical archaeology (Given 2004; Gosden 2004; Lyons and Papadopoulos 2002; Majewski and Gaimster 2009; Stein 2005) that are often global in scale and comparative in orientation, thus assuming a role similar to that of the current volume. Such reviews reflect a historical archaeology that is grappling with a number of difficult issues: the (artificial) divide between prehistoric and historic archaeology; definitional and "bounding" issues related to the use (and misuse) of historical texts; the distinct traditions of Old and New World archaeology and the attendant problems of defining "historic" periods; the importance of European imperialism, capitalism, and mercantilism in bounding the discipline's edges; the focus on global capitalism as an overarching research theme; temporal depth of research and its relation to the "modern world"; and semantic issues related to culture contact versus colonialism versus colonization versus entanglement, and so forth. It is not possible to review all of these issues here, nor as it turns out, would it necessarily even be relevant. This is not because concerns with semantics and topical branding are unimportant, but rather because the one thing barely visible in all of these treatments of historical archaeology, or the archaeology of colonialism, or modern world archaeology, or postcolonial archaeology, is bioarchaeology.

Although a lack of cross-subdisciplinary visibility is by no means unique to colonialist bioarchaeology, it should give us pause that our research assumes a limited place within discussions of the state of and future directions of historical archaeology, even in the New World (but see Van Buren 2010). Is this because previous bioarchaeological research is not asking archaeological questions in the way that historical archaeologists ask them, thereby relegating it to its own self-contained pursuit? Buoyed by its own success— as measured by the expansion of bioarchaeology academic positions and its increasing visibility at professional meetings and in professional journals—bioarchaeology may be suffering from deficiencies in translation and messaging (Stojanowski and Duncan 2015). Perhaps we are not upscaling our inferences sufficiently, remaining committed to the particularism that a contextual, bottom-up bioarchaeological approach requires. Rather than focusing on the historical aspects of our work (the text-based articulations with other arenas of scholarship), bioarchaeologists have tended to address more specific issues within the historical literature: colonialism and culture contact, diet and ecology, health and disease, and behavior and adaptation. In fact, the majority of the chapters here have a similar research orientation. Some of these topics align better with archaeological research questions than others, while some are clearly biological in nature and aligned with the natural sciences. Such is the legacy of the field's dual and blended emergence (see perspectives in Armelagos 2003; Buikstra 2006a; Cook 2006; Knüsel 2010; Larsen 2006; Martin et al. 2013; Rakita 2014), and it is clear that biology has not played a significant role in the work of many historians, despite its importance for understanding both short- and long-term trajectories of the human experience (see Brooke and Larsen 2014).

That the present volume emphasizes "colonialism" and "contact" to the exclusion of "historical" research agendas is meaningful. As the chapters in this volume indicate, the focus of colonial bioarchaeology has been the colonized, the indigenous, the periphery. With few exceptions (e.g., Anson

2004; Buzon 2008; Buzon and Richman 2007; Daverman 2011; Keenley-side et al. 2006; Killgrove 2005; Labidon 2012; McIlvaine 2012; Peck 2009), colonization and colonialism as research frameworks—conventions upon which we "hang" our data—remain largely embedded in the New World tradition of post-Columbian scholarship. Mostly this is an indigenous history, then, told using data often anathema to descendant communities. This is a history of health, disease, and hardship, some revitalization and resistance, but a history whose outcome is already known to descendant communities who live it every day of their lives—that is, if a descendant community still exists at all. That we give structure to this historical process is significant, and it is unlikely that the inferences about the past that bioarchaeology offers are replicated in other material forms, either written or disposed. As Perry (2007) notes, channeling decades of historical archaeologists before her (e.g., Deagan 1988), we must always be cognizant of inferred data purity, of scaled data hierarchies, of dilettante and hand-maiden status. We do not want to demonstrate that which is already known or simply fill the slivers of lacunae between the pages of historical texts. And, as a discipline, bioarchaeology has been quite adroit at avoiding both pitfalls in its forging of novel research questions.

The apparent uncoupling of historical archaeology and the bioarchaeology of colonialism has two possible explanations. The first is the social stigma of working with human remains, particularly with descendant community involvement and international trends toward repatriation as a means of formally acknowledging and addressing the most egregious acts of desecration of the colonial period (see Fine-Dare 2002; Kakaliou-ras 2008, 2012, 2014; Thomas 2000). This is a difficult topic that cannot be treated sufficiently here. But it is, nonetheless, an important one worthy of serious consideration given the temporal connections between past and present in colonialist frameworks. In the current political climate it is easy to discount the importance of bioarchaeology, but we must address ethical issues directly either through better messaging of the value of our work or by turning the bioarchaeological gaze upon ourselves. Here is where this volume makes important contributions by removing the singular focus on New World indigenous histories. For example, chapters by Killgrove and by Danforth et al. show us that research on European populations is certainly part of the colonialism paradigm, while chapters by Perry and by Buzon and Smith remind us that the "anthropological other" is not strictly defined by the color of one's skin or an individual's "indigenous" status. As such, these chapters are symbolic of a push within Americanist bioarchaeology to adapt the methods and questions that built the field to regions where our work is still permitted and (we hope) valued. Nonetheless, we have to consider whether the academic "normalization" of colonialist research detracts from or adds to the enduring narrative of hardship that pervades Americanist scholarship, and whether such a message is appreciated or not. The answer, of course, surely depends on one's particular views of body politics and the Western scientific tradition of evidence and expertise (see Crossland 2013; Curtis 2003; Goodnow 2006; Jones 2011).

The second possible explanation for the limited visibility of bioarchaeology may also reflect the field's development with a dual archaeological and physical anthropological tradition. The fact is that bioarchaeological research on colonialism is often under-theorized with respect to social theory, focusing on what happened and when, a descriptive enterprise that is comparative in structure but also hindered by basic issues of preservation, data comparability, and overdetermination. This suggests that bioarchaeological research on colonialism is geared toward specific goals not altogether in line with those derived from archaeological or historical scholarship—those of biology. Being data-driven, the work often focuses on *outcomes* of processes rather than the processes themselves. For example, we might generate inferences about the effects of imperial expansion on peripheral communities or the structure of power imbalances within a capitalist framework, but *not* produce general knowledge about the underlying "things" of contact—capitalism, colonialism, imperialism, race, power, identity, and heritage. This is not an inherent flaw of colonialist or historical bioarchaeology, but a symptom of a bottom-up, local-to-global, highly particularistic, and contextual approach that has also made the field the success that it is today. To this end it is worth asking whether we want to describe an *unfolded* historical process (a form of particularism), produce general theory about broadly defined phenomena, or even assume a position of advocacy through our work. The goal might be to do all three at once. Nevertheless, whether due to poor branding, difficult middle-range linkages between data and process, issues of scale, or poor data comparability, if bioarchaeology is to remain a vital approach for exploring the dynamics of colonialist, capitalist, and imperialist state-level histories, then we must establish better articulations with current research questions in these areas. I note again that this issue of unidirectional transfer (our work is couched within archaeology and history, but archaeologists and historians are not always incorporating our results into their metanarratives) is not a challenge of colonialist bioarchaeology alone but, in many cases, a challenge shared by the broader (bio)archaeological community. The current volume does offer a way forward, with several chapters in this volume engaging broader social theory either directly or indirectly. For example, chapters by Murphy et al., Perry, and Buzon and Smith provide strong evidence that a singular emphasis on "first contact" obscures some of the more interesting dynamics that result from pre-Columbian colonial encounters or instances of long-term colonial entanglements. The chapter by Murphy et al. reminds us that colonialism and imperialism in the Americas predates the Columbian Exchange, and the Andes in particular will be a vital source of comparative information on how Andean peoples responded to different periods of subjugation by a series of imperialist states. Such work is critical for moving beyond the intensely race-based patina of post-Columbian interaction and may provide important information on how the state itself, as a human political organization, creates or responds to those it incorporates. Likewise, Buzon and Smith show how long-term interactions between Egyptian and Nubian peoples reached an apparent equilibrium of exchange and hybridity in the absence of demographic collapse and the deleterious health effects so often seen in New World contexts. Similarly, Harvey et al.'s chapter on the Maya population at Tipu demonstrates that hybridity can also apparently buffer populations from deleterious health effects in the New World, interpreting their data with respect to the frontier status of the mission and social-theoretical concepts of contested or third spaces that align their research with postcolonial scholarship. Klaus and Alvarez-Calderón provide similar results for the inhabitants of colonial Eten. As such, this volume offers a number of new perspectives on colonialism that articulate with various social-theoretical perspectives that move beyond a singular focus on biocultural approaches.

I stress that identifying areas of articulation between bioarchaeology's strengths and historical archaeology's interests should *not* be difficult. For example, Orser's (2010) review of problem orientations in historical archaeology outlined four areas of emphasis that define cross-cutting research themes: (1) the importance of scale, (2) the historical archaeology of the capitalist project, (3) vectors of inequality, and (4) heritage and memory. Each of these themes is well aligned with bioarchaeological approaches. For example, bioarchaeologists have long been part of the study of capitalism's effects on indigenous communities but have simply not framed their research in such terms. A regionally comparative approach in which specific skeletal samples are overlaid with relevant facets of colonialism's manifestations could be productive. We see some evidence of that here in the chapters by Guichón et al., Harvey et al., and Klaus and Alvarez-Calderón. The latter two chapters provide important evidence for the variability of the colonial experience even within fairly localized regions, while the Guichón et al. chapter serves as a reminder that the capitalist project continues to this day (and see below on postcolonial bioarchaeology). Future work will commence in a similar bottom-up fashion, eventually reaching a point of data saturation allowing broad-scale hypothesis-driven research. This volume is surely a critical step toward realizing this potential.

Bioarchaeologists also have much to offer with respect to "vectors of inequality," here referencing the complex relational qualities of human social identities. As discussed above, the topic of identity was explored in this volume by Tiesler and Zabala, Danforth et al., Ribot et al., and Ortiz et al. most directly. However, identity and inequality manifest in almost every chapter within the volume in the form of dietary and health disparities. As recent literature attests (Agarwal and Glencross 2011; Baadsgaard et al. 2011; Gowland and Knüsel 2006; Knudson and Stojanowski 2008, 2009), bioarchaeology has much to offer identity studies in past populations—analyses of body modification and assessments of biological identity and diversity position bioarchaeology as integral to the exploration of colonial identities and their transformations, especially within an ethnogenetic research framework (e.g., Klaus 2008, 2013; Stojanowski 2005, 2009, 2010, 2011). Orser's (2010) discussion of heritage and memory outlines issues with cultural patrimony and historic preservation, topics that I align within a postcolonial bioarchaeological framework below. Here, I discuss Orser's (2010) first point most explicitly—that of multi-scalar perspectives—because this is an area where bioarchaeological data offer tremendous possibilities for both scientific and humanistic inferences.

SCALE AND BIOARCHAEOLOGY

One of the greatest challenges of "bioarchaeology as archaeology" is the need to work with local sites but interpret data within a larger theoretical framework. Linking the local to the global, working locally but interpreting globally, and understanding the flow of parameters and effects into and out of the specific region where you conduct your research is challenging given the depth and breadth of relevant literatures. While clearly this is an issue of scale, linking the local and global is, in my opinion, simple due diligence. It occurs almost by accident when attempting to frame interpretations of patterns in historical-period contexts, even if a topic was initially approached myopically. That is, linking the local and global is an inherent property of historical-period research, because the scale of interaction so sharply increased (it literally became global in this era) and the scale of population disruptions, migrations, and relocations was hemisphere wide, and in the case of the African slave trade broader still (see Lightfoot et al. 2013 on the linkage of European colonialism with the Anthropocene). There is simply no room for provincialism. But before research enters the phase of interpretation there is the reality of practice—what we actually do to generate data and how we frame research hypotheses. Here, Orser (2010:117) comments, "thinking about the local-global nexus is to envision the scale of archaeological research as a continuum that extends from the household to the various interlinked, intra- and transcontinental networks of interaction," further noting that "even world-systems theorists see the household as a primary unit of analysis. . . . [because] households constitute a basic unit of daily life." Orser continues developing this theme within the context of household archaeology, microhistory, and emerging sub-household-level perspectives on the small, quotidian, everyday "things" that have meaning in our lives. This reflects a clear shift toward a humanistic colonialist archaeology. However, the importance here is one of scalability, from object, to household, to community, to region, . . . to the world. A more complete understanding of colonialist and contact dynamics emerges when multiple scales of inference are combined. And there is nothing more scalable than a bioarchaeological approach. Archaeothanatology (Duday 2006, 2009) gives us moments, enamel cross-striations (Antoine et al. 2009)—days, osteobiography (Saul 1972; Saul and Saul 1989; Stodder and Palkovich 2012)—individual lives, kinship analysis (Alt and Vach 1998; Johnson and Paul 2016; Stojanowski and Schillaci 2006)—families, cemetery spatial analysis (Stojanowski 2013)—communities, fluorine analysis (Lyman et al. 2012; Reiche 2006)—generational contemporaries, and the archaeological record—entire breeding populations. Bioarchaeology's emphasis on the corporeality of the body, the vessel of biology imprinted with that individual's experience of the world through his or her life, can be contextualized to his or her contemporaries in an increasingly inclusive scale of relationships—my life, our family, the community, our people. The increasing ability to dissect the individual life through ever improving sampling techniques provides powerful evidence of the "archaeological moment" that resonates with how we experience our own lives. Yet at the same time, the development of bioarchaeology partially within the tradition of physical anthropology has instilled a distinct methodological emphasis. While this is sometimes criticized (Armelagos and Van Gerven 2003), and perhaps rightly so, it also means our data are much more comparable, systematized, and quantified than other data brought to bear on past human experience. This allows database building such as that presented by Tiesler and Zabala on head-shaping practices throughout the Iberian-controlled Americas, which can then be teased apart at the site level, and further to the scale of the individual (as done by Ribot et al. and Ortiz et al.). Although the authors note that scholarship on head shaping "still awaits a continental synthesis," this chapter compiles a tremendous amount of bioarchaeological data and makes the most use of existing historical records to suggest a macro-level understanding of the meaning of head-shaping practices through space and time, interpreted within the context of Spanish strategies for conversion and submission of indigenous populations. As noted above, the Tiesler and Zabala chapter is the only broad-scale synthetic chapter in the volume, and it provides an important model for how other researchers can engage large data sets at multiple scales of inference. The ability of Ribot et al. to evaluate biological hybridity in two vastly different contexts (the Cape Colony in South Africa and Morton's Africans from Cuba) is also reflective of the power of bioarchaeological data sets for multi-scalar, comparative inferences.

While most of the other chapters use the site as the unit of analysis, there are two chapters that adopt an intra-site orientation and attempt to identify and tease apart interactions and patterns at the intra-community level. Depending on the archaeological context, individuals can also be grouped into larger social units, for example, into specific households or larger kin groups defined more broadly than simply by residence (Alt and Vach 1998; Stojanowski and Schillaci 2006). The ability to place individuals within such meaningful units of social interaction implements a fine-grained analysis of intra-household biological variation, dietary variation, and health experience. In the absence of household-level data, which is not the norm, bioarchaeological data easily scales up to the level of the community, region, macro-region, continent, and world. But the ability to identify households, kin groups, or other segments of historic period populations below the level of the community provides a tremendous opportunity for bioarchaeologists to really bridge different scales of historical inference. If the community is the basic sphere of normal interaction and the household the basic sphere of daily interaction then our ability to group individuals into such meaningful segments of social networks is unique. Such an approach was implemented by Winkler et al.'s analysis of status and health-related co-variation at the Santa Catalina de Guale mission church. Status was indexed by burial position within the church and grave good richness and density. Data on health/stress and diet were compared against these variables to infer potential manifestations of class-based differences and inequalities among indigenous individuals living on St. Catherines Island during the seventeenth century. Although the results were mixed, the questions that were probed recall an important point about modern colonialist research. We must move beyond the European/non-European dichotomy, the colonized and the colonizer, and realize individual motivations may have superseded affiliations based on race, class, or ethnicity. Did Guale elites (individuals, families or lineages) act so differently from our own in their self-interest?

Similarly, the chapter by Ortiz et al. uses biological distance analyses to determine whether the church at Magdalena de Cao Viejo was structured according to family plots as suggested by both pre-Hispanic Andean and Spanish burial practices. Phenetic similarity did not correlate with spatial proximity within the church, which suggested to the authors that the cemetery was not kin-structured. Unfortunately, as the chapter by Danforth et al. indicates, phenotypic data are imperfect proxies for genetic relatedness. Such data are, in many cases, the only sources of data we have on biological relationships from archaeological sites, and more work is needed to evaluate the strengths and weaknesses of biodistance approaches at different scales of analysis (see Paul and Stojanowski 2015). Nonetheless, the site-specific analysis does succeed in inferring biological hybridization between Andean and Spanish populations, although the mixture of signatures (mortuary practices, head shaping in some individuals) complicates the interpretation considerably.

Here is a perfect example of the nested, multi-scalar potential of bioarchaeological data sets whose observations are embedded within the corporeal reality of the human body that can be combined, separated, recombined, and dissected. Although the limited resolution of morphology may be difficult to overcome, it would be fascinating to identify Spaniards, non-admixed Andeans, and admixed Andeans within the sample that could implement a whole host of dietary and health-related comparisons that tease apart the community dynamic at Magdalena de Cao Viejo.

Thus far I have highlighted two different potentials of bioarchaeological data sets to embrace the challenges and potentials of scale. Global analyses are both implemented by and limited by the comparability of our data sets. Such analyses are much rarer than regional, site-specific research and it is interesting to consider why. The answer, I suspect, is the particularistic, contextual framework that has defined bioarchaeology for the last three decades and there is no doubt this has been a net positive for the field. But big questions require big data to answer, and it will be interesting to see when other scholars adopt a similar approach to that offered by Tiesler and Zabala. On the other end of the scale are chapters that focus on site-level variation. Such work is clearly not possible for all sites and often requires strong temporal control and excellent contextual data (this shouldn't be a problem for most colonial era sites in the New World). However, despite offering considerable potential, these types of analyses are in the minority. Given my own interest in this scale (Stojanowski 2013) I clearly advocate for more work of a similar nature, and I have no explanation for why it is so rare in comparison to site-level comparative analyses (see also DeWitte and Stojanowski 2015 on the potential for intra-site analyses to inform the "osteological paradox" [Wood et al. 1992]).

Finally, the one truly remarkable quality of a multi-scalar bioarchaeological approach is that our basic unit of analysis is the corporeal, self-contained body of an individual. This body has the potential to tell a scientific and humanistic story that constitutes a microhistory of that person's life and death within a specific time and place, a type of analysis generally referred to as "osteobiography." Osteobiography has undergone revision in its scope since its introduction by Saul and Saul (Boutin 2012; Hawkey 1998; Robb 2002; Saul 1976; Saul and Saul 1989; Stodder and Palkovich 2012; Zvelebil and Weber 2013), from a more forensic approach to a more narrative and humanistic one that in some cases engages literary fictions. While a focus on the "colonial body" is a vibrant area of social-theoretical scholarship (e.g., Ballantyne and Burton 2005), the osteobiographical analysis of bodies from historic period sites is less visible in the literature, and by this I mean both the colonial bioarchaeology literature and the osteobiography literature (an exception is Larsen et al. 1996). This absence may have no real meaningful rationale. It may reflect a prior emphasis on comparative health research in the colonialism literature. Or, it may represent the pragmatics of identifying an individual whose life story can be told using osteobiographical analyses. That is, there usually must be something distinctive about a grave, its context, or the interred body for it to be identified as exceptional in some way—a unique quality in life *and* death carries forward. Ironically, elite graves often became undifferentiated during the colonial period (see, e.g., the Winkler et al. chapter) while the burials of non-elites received a fairly homogenous (but not absolutely identical—see, e.g., the Klaus and Alvarez-Calderón chapter) treatment within a Christian burial tradition that serves to anonymize the colonial individual in life and in death. However, osteobiographical approaches provide an important complement to the populational and broadly comparative analyses we see in the chapters included here because they narrate the colonial period within the scale of individual human experience. For example, Saartjie Baartman's story is so well known to us today specifically because of the treatment of her body (Moudileno 2009; White 2007). But other colonial individuals have equally compelling stories for which global colonialism intersected with human lives in ways that resulted in "exceptional" human bodies with considerable power as biographic microhistories (Glaubrecht et al. 2013; Kaeppler 2005; Mkhize 2009; Nienaber et al. 2008; Novak 2014; Pietrusewsky and Willacker 1997). The attachment of names, even through anthropological involvement, establishes individual personhood and can help critically center a bioarchaeology of colonialism within postcolonial scholarship, a topic I turn to next.

Postcolonial Bioarchaeology

It is difficult to define what a "postcolonial bioarchaeology" might look like or to determine whether it is a necessary or desirable future. As with many emerging theoretical positions, a clear and singular usage for "postcolonialism" has not coalesced (Faier and Rofel 2014; Gosden 2001; Lydon and Rizvi 2010; Naum 2010; van Dommelen 2006, 2011). Jordan (2009) outlines two differences of meaning: (1) the exploration of newly independent former colonies, or (2) an activist position that contests the legacies of colonialism and interrogates "notions of discourse and representation" (van Dommelen 2011:2; see also Faier and Rofel 2014). The two are not, of course, mutually exclusive. Given the latter definition, however, it is difficult to conceptualize what a postcolonial bioarchaeology might look like given the difficult history of how skeletal data sets came to be and the problematic relationships this creates with descendant indigenous communities (see Deloria 1989; Fine-Dare 2002; Riding In 2000; Thomas 2000). That is, in this sense a "colonial bioarchaeology" cannot evolve into a "postcolonial bioarchaeology" as long as biological remains continue to anchor the discipline's primary data source (see Kakaliouras 2008, 2012, 2014 for insightful commentary). To this point, much of what we see as colonial or historical bioarchaeology focuses on indigenous populations for which the existence of the samples to implement bioarchaeological research often is a manifestation of colonialism's legacy. In other words, the fact that these skeletal samples exist to be studied is itself a manifestation of colonial power relationships and worthy of postcolonial dissection. I doubt whether those of us who self-identify as bioarchaeologists are eager to draw the scalpel, and it is not possible to engage the topic fully without difficult discussions concerning the ethics of human remains research. Even a casual perusal of this literature indicates the difficulty of finding consensus (Fforde et al. 2002; Fluehr-Lobban 1998; Lambert 2012; Larsen and Walker 2005; Parker-Pearson 1995; Tarlow 2001; Wilkinson 2002; Zuckerman et al. 2014; see Deloria 1989 and Riding In 2000 for alternative viewpoints).

As one example we can consider the record from the southeastern United States. There are scanty details of bioarchaeological data sets that consist of Euro-American individuals, but analysis of these remains are largely tangential to the primary emphasis of North American historical bioarchaeology—early contact situations, mission environments, and the health effects of colonialism on indigenous populations. Part of this disparity may result from the simple realities of population size. In North America, there were many more Native Americans than Europeans in the fifteenth, sixteenth, and seventeenth centuries. Often the two groups were buried in distinct locations; Europeans in places that are archaeologically less visible/accessible today due to modern development. But one does have to ask if this is the sole reason for the comparative invisibility of historic period research on America's European colonial peoples. In Spanish Florida and Georgia there were over a dozen mission-period sites that were partially excavated that resulted in a distinct, named sample of Native American individuals (Larsen 1993). The Soledad cemetery in St. Augustine was also investigated archaeologically producing a sample of British and Spanish colonists (Koch 1983). The latter sample figures little in the narrative framework of the "bioarchaeology of La Florida," which has emphasized indigenous health and lifestyle changes through time and space (see Earle 2010, 2012 for a number of interesting perspectives on diet and health among Europeans in the New World). That the Soledad burials were all, ironically, reburied surely explains some of the differential scholarly interest, but this fact alone (reburial) may attract some of the harshest critiques from postcolonialist scholars (note that many of the indigenous samples have also been reburied). We must tread softly, indeed.

The chapter by Danforth et al. is an important contribution to the present volume in its emphasis on the French colonial population of Mississippi. These authors note the remarkable fact that only six sites in the United States have been found that contain individuals of French European ancestry, and this list grows little when expanded to the Caribbean and Canada. Again, within a postcolonial framework we might ask why this is so. However, Danforth et al.'s chapter conveys the important point that a bioarchaeology of colonialism is not just an indigenous enterprise. Colonialist bioarchaeologists are not just interested in the "other" but are legitimately concerned with understanding the lives and lifestyle transformations of all parties involved in the colonial enterprises of the Americas. What's even more interesting about this particular contribution is the finding that the health of these individuals was comparable to that of other contemporary European populations of the New World but that indicators of childhood stress were higher than average, thus reflecting the low social positions from which these individuals migrated. In other words, despite all of the other hardships, this particular group of French colonial individuals seems to have improved their lives as measured bioarchaeologically. As noted above, the inclusion in this volume of other non–New World chapters (Buzon and Smith; Perry; Killgrove) also helps define a bioarchaeological gaze that is not solely focused on the indigenous other.

However, it would be unwise to completely discount the relevance of bioarchaeological research to postcolonialist agendas. For example, when van Dommelen (2011:2) writes about "scrutinizing how colonizers represented themselves and, in particular, those whom they have conquered," one can't help but think of the potential contributions to be made by scholars focusing on "the body" and its materiality (see Borić and Robb 2008; Rebay-Salisbury et al. 2010; Sofaer 2006) as well as the burgeoning literature on social identity and its bioarchaeological signatures (see Agarwal and Glencross 2011; Baadsgaard et al. 2011; Gowland and Knüsel 2006; Knudson and Stojanowski 2008, 2009; and contributors therein). The key here, though, is the dual status of the archaeological body, literally the bones and dentition in the ground, as both a modifiable vehicle of representation and an immutable record of genetic conditioning. I have leveraged this advantage in my own work where dental phenotypes provided an indelible signature of human action in the field of reproduction (who one mates with) as compared with historical representations of native ethnonyms and migration patterns (Stojanowski 2005, 2009, 2010, 2011). That is, ethnonyms, language distributions (inferred from translator requests), and chiefdom boundaries may suggest certain patterns of population and identity stasis through time, whereas bioarchaeological data provide a less biased perspective on what people were actually doing on the ground—defining baseline conditions of community integration patterns and then inferring how those patterns changed through time. This is but one example, but it does illustrate the interrogative potential of bioarchaeological data sets within a postcolonial theoretical framework.

In addition, bioarchaeology could/should address Jordan's (2009) first definition of postcolonial scholarship—that of emerging, newly independent former colonies. If bioarchaeology is interested in the dynamics of human lives and experiences in the past, then "the past" can be liberally defined to include the mid- to late twentieth century—if we choose to engage this area of scholarship. This is, in part, why definitions of the field that invoke elements of archaeology—archaeological questions or archaeologically defined data sets—are somewhat limiting. If colonialist bioarchaeologists are interested in health and lifestyle changes at the onset of colonialism as well as culture contact and changes in health during an extended period of entanglement, then why should we ignore the offset of colonialism—the emergence of postcolonial nations? Doing so would add a human biology component to what we do, instill an element of social justice given the challenges the peoples of these nations often face, and help link present to past in a holistic theoretical framework. Engaging this kind of postcolonial bioarchaeology could actually help demonstrate the importance of applied knowledge to modern indigenous communities, showing the value of what we do and it why matters (see Baker et al. 2001; Buikstra 1983, 2006b; Hibbert 1998; Landau and Steele 1996; Ousley et al. 2005; Walker 2000).

The chapter by Guichón et al. provides a compelling example of how recent a colonial bioarchaeological project can be, and blurs the lines of what constitutes the archaeological record. Although in this case the use of cemetery remains clearly places the work within the purview of a bioarchaeological approach, the rich historical data brought to bear on the topic reflects, in part, the recentness of the colonial experience at the "ultra-periphery of Europe." The individuals studied may very well have direct living and known descendants. This, along with the recent date of the Candelaria mission's founding, 1893, reminds us that the colonial process is ongoing. This is not just an event of the past in which temporal distance defines an "otherness" of the materials and a certain quaintness to our perception of the colonial landscape. Indeed, there are many other examples of twentieth-century colonial entanglements that blur into the realm of forensics.

For example, at the same time that the Selk'nam of Tierra el Fuego were receiving the Salesian missionaries, the endgame of the pre-independence colonial era of Africa was playing out throughout the continent. Although a colonialist bioarchaeology of Africa could certainly target the development and spread of the Atlantic slave trade, a postcolonialist bioarchaeology could adopt identical methods and techniques for samples from the twentieth century (Lane 2011). Although the politics are delicate, projects on the postcolonial era overlap with forensic anthropology and human-rights research and could help rewrite the twentieth-century histories that, much like those from the post-Columbian Americas, are almost certainly biased representations of fact. For example, analyses of the victims of the 1994 Rwandan genocide could reveal ethnic health disparities or patterns of biological variation that could be richly interpreted with respect to the postcolonial history of that nation. But this is a difficult and gritty context without the emotional distance that the archaeological record affords. And this raises a final point about the reflexive potential of a postcolonial bioarchaeology—our role in unmasking, quantifying, and personifying what is a truly ugly period of human history while at the same time contextualizing this history with a deep time perspective.

I close with a final note about the reflexive potential of a postcolonial framework. It is impossible to talk about the colonial history of Africa without reference to the Congo Free State. Belgian King Leopold's exploits are now well known in fiction (Joseph Conrad's *Heart of Darkness*) and nonfiction (Adam Hochschild's *King Leopold's Ghost*), and more loosely in film (Coppola's *Apocalypse Now*). I approached Hochschild's best-seller (1998) as casual nonfiction reading until I turned to the image (shown here in Figure 14.1) titled "Nsala of Wala in the Nsongo District (ABIR Concession)." The photograph, attributed to Alice Seeley Harris and dated to 1904, depicts a man named Nsala staring at the severed hand and foot of his five-year-old daughter. Although the exact reason for and perpetrators of the act are debated, there is no doubt the act was a result of the Belgian colonial enterprise; the image, and others like it, helped bring exposure to atrocities committed against a people who have yet to recover. The image was reproduced in Mark Twain's satirical *King Leopold's Soliloquy* (Twain 1905:18) with this caption:

Foot and hand of child dismembered by soldiers, brought to missionaries by dazed father. From photograph taken at Baringa, Congo State, May 15, 1904.

There is no denying the power of the image, the sadness evident in the man's face and posture. And I include it here as a reminder of two things. First, it reminds us of the harsh brutality of colonialism, as defined throughout this volume, as a process inherently related to the (or a) state's "*monopoly of the legitimate use of physical force* within a given territory (Weber 1919:1; emphasis in source). The distance of time and the comparatively innocuous data we use in bioarchaeological research to quantify "misery" fail to fully convey what a single picture does so well. Second, within the postcolonialist framework, such imagery (that there are images at all) reminds us that European colonialism was not a time period but a temporal marker that can never be unwound or undone in human history. A bioarchaeology of colonialism would surely benefit from continued engagement with the recent past, as reflected in the Guichón et al. chapter included here, but this is no doubt an uncomfortable, community-based approach with great potential for affecting the lives of people today.

CONCLUSION

Although it targets a rather grim past, a concerted bioarchaeology of colonialism and culture contact has a bright future. We are just beginning to explore the repercussions of European expansionism throughout the world, and bioarchaeology is well positioned to address myriad issues that are both particularistic and generalizable; micro and macro in scale; and humanistic, social scientific, historical, or biological/evolutionary in orientation. While our field continues to forge its own path, define emerging research foci, and deal with its own peccadilloes of method and practice, we must also be aware of opportunities for broader articulation and broader impact. The one danger I see is a tendency toward self-containment, the doing of bioarchaeology by us and for us. Success and growth as a discipline can foster this, but it must not turn into complacency. There is no doubt that the topics that interest us as colonialist bioarchaeologists (health and adaptation) are important, but they are not the only kinds of inferences

Figure 14.1. "Nsala of Wala in the Nsongo District (ABIR Concession)." Photo by Alice Seeley Harris. The image dates to 1904 from the Belgian Congo and is widely reproduced as evidence of the cruelty and human cost of resource extraction in King Leopold's Congo (Wikimedia Commons).

we can offer. It would serve us all well to promote instances of broader articulation. As I have noted throughout this chapter, messaging and branding are important, particularly as the density of scholarship about any one topic expands beyond manageable levels. If bioarchaeology really is the pursuit of "archaeological questions" (Knüsel 2010:62) or the "reconstruction of human histories, with emphasis on anthropological problem solving and the integration of archaeological data" (Buikstra 2006c:xix), then self-containment through use of the "bioarchaeology of" literary device may be self-defeating in the long term. I, too, am guilty of this (Knudson and Stojanowski 2009; Stojanowski 2010, 2013), and at this point I can only highlight the issue and not suggest a viable solution.

This volume is the first to generate similar types of data from multiple colonial contexts and attempt to establish a more global footprint to such a database. Commonalities will emerge organically, whether these are regionally (Andean, southeastern United States) or temporally defined, or whether a broader perspective is adopted that focuses on comparative indigenous experiences within and among European colonial spheres of influence (Spanish vs. English, e.g.). I do think comparative research is crucial for a scientific handling of "big questions," overarching research themes, and the production of general knowledge—inferences of the few but with meaning for all. The global exploration of colonial-period sites will expand the basis for comparison until we reach a point where dedicated scholars can mine data, theorize, and synthesize. This carries forward the existing narrative structure of colonialist bioarchaeology in a way that addresses a broader scholarship. While the regional, comparative health framework is important, we would do well to adopt emerging bioarchaeological perspectives, address different scales of analysis, and focus on improving the temporal resolution of our data sets. The last decade has witnessed major theoretical expansion in comparison to the bioarchaeology of the 1980s and 1990s. Identity and theories of the body have become more visible; gender is a developing research theme; emphasis on children and the elderly is just beginning; and race, ethnicity and ethnogenesis remain perennially relevant topics that bioarchaeological data are well suited to address. Engaging the postcolonialist literature may also be fruitful; it would certainly be insightful. Regardless, continued interest in colonialist bioarchaeology should significantly change the field over the next decade. If successful, this chapter will seem dated by then. I can only hope that it does.

REFERENCES CITED

Agarwal, S. C., and B. A. Glencross (editors)
2011   Social Bioarchaeology. Blackwell, Malden, Massachusetts.
Alt, K. W., and W. Vach
1998   Kinship Studies in Skeletal Remains—Concepts and Examples. In Dental Anthropology: Fundamentals, Limits, and Prospects, edited by K. W. Alt, F. W. Rösing, M. Teschler, and M. Nicola, pp. 537–554. Springer, Wien.
Anson, T.
2004   The Bioarchaeology of the St. Mary's Free Ground Burials: Reconstruction of Colonial South Australian Lifeways. Unpublished Ph.D. dissertation, University of Adelaide, Adelaide.
Antoine, D., S. Hillson, and M. C. Dean
2009   The Developmental Clock of Dental Enamel: A Test for the Periodicity of Prism Cross-Striations in Modern Humans and an Evaluation of the Most Likely Sources of Error in Histological Studies of this Kind. Journal of Anatomy 214:45–55.
Armelagos, G. J.
2003   Bioarchaeology as Anthropology. Archeological Papers of the American Anthropological Association 13:27–40.
Armelagos, G. J., and D. P. Van Gerven
2003   A Century of Skeletal Biology and Paleopathology: Contrasts, Contradictions, and Conflicts. American Anthropologist 105:53–64.

Baadsgaard, A., A. T. Boutin, and J. E. Buikstra (editors)
2011   *Breathing New Life into the Evidence of Death: Contemporary Approaches to Bioarchaeology.* School for Advanced Research Press, Santa Fe.

Baker, B. J., and L. Kealhofer (editors)
1996   *Bioarchaeology of Native American Adaptation in the Spanish Borderlands.* University Press of Florida, Gainesville.

Baker, B. J., T. L. Varney, R. G. Wilkinson, L. M. Anderson, and M. A. Liston
2001   Repatriation and the Study of Human Remains. In *The Future of the Past: Archaeologists, Native Americans, and Repatriation,* edited by T. L. Bray, pp. 69–89. Garland, New York.

Ballantyne T., and A. Burton
2005   *Bodies in Contact: Rethinking Colonial Encounters in World History.* Duke University Press, Durham.

Borić, D., and J. Robb
2008   *Past Bodies: Body-Centred Research in Archaeology.* Oxbow Books, Oxford.

Boutin, A. T.
2012   Crafting a Bioarchaeology of Personhood: Osteobiographical Narratives from Alalakh. In *Breathing New Life into the Evidence of Death: Contemporary Approaches to Bioarchaeology,* edited by A. Baadsgaard, A. T. Boutin, and J. E. Buikstra, pp. 109–133. School for Advanced Research Press, Santa Fe.

Brooke, J. L., and C. S. Larsen
2014   The Nurture of Nature: Genetics, Epigenetics, and Environment in Human Biohistory. *American Historical Review* 119:1500–1513.

Buikstra, J. E.
1983   Reburial: How We All Lose. *Society for California Archaeology Newsletter* 17:2–5.

2006a   A Historical Introduction. In *Bioarchaeology: The Contextual Analysis of Human Remains,* edited by J. E. Buikstra and L. A. Beck, pp. 7–25. Academic Press, New York.

2006b   Repatriation and Bioarchaeology: Challenges and Opportunities. In *Bioarchaeology: The Contextual Analysis of Human Remains,* edited by J. E. Buikstra and L. A. Beck, pp. 389–415. Academic Press, New York.

2006c   Preface. In *Bioarchaeology: The Contextual Analysis of Human Remains,* edited by J. E. Buikstra and L. A. Beck, pp. xvii–xx. Academic Press, New York.

Buzon, M.
2008   A Bioarchaeological Perspective on Egyptian Colonialism in the New Kingdom. *Journal of Egyptian Archaeology* 94:165–181.

Buzon, M. R., and R. Richman
2007   Traumatic Injuries and Imperialism: The Effects of Egyptian Colonial Strategies at Tombos in Upper Nubia. *American Journal of Physical Anthropology* 133:783–791.

Cohen, M. N., and G. J. Armelagos (editors)
1984   *Paleopathology at the Origins of Agriculture.* Academic Press, Orlando.

Conrad, J.
1902   *Heart of Darkness*. William Blackwood and Sons, Edinburgh.
Cook, D. C.
2006   The Old Physical Anthropology and the New World: A Look at the Accomplishments of an Antiquated Paradigm. In *Bioarchaeology: The Contextual Analysis of Human Remains*, edited by J. E. Buikstra and L. A. Beck, pp. 27–71. Academic Press, New York.
Crossland, Z.
2013   Evidential Regimes of Forensic Archaeology. *Annual Review of Anthropology* 42:121–137.
Curtis, N. G. W.
2003   Human Remains: The Sacred, Museums and Archaeology. *Public Archaeology* 3:21–32.
Daverman, B. M.
2011   A Bioarchaeological Perspective on Diet and Health Consequences of Akkadian Imperial Consolidation at Kish, Iraq. Unpublished Master's thesis, Purdue University.
Deagan, K.
1982   Avenues of Inquiry in Historical Archaeology. In *Advances in Archaeological Method and Theory*, vol. 5, edited by M. B. Schiffer, pp. 151–177. Academic Press, New York.
1988   Neither History nor Prehistory: The Questions That Count in Historical Archaeology. *Historical Archaeology* 22:7–12.
Deloria, V., Jr.
1989   A Simple Question of Humanity: The Moral Dimensions of the Reburial Issue. *NARF Legal Review* 14:1–17.
DeWitte, S. N., and C. M. Stojanowski
2015   The Osteological Paradox 20 Years Later: Past Perspectives, Future Directions. *Journal of Archaeological Research* 23:397–450.
Duday, H.
2006   L'archéothanatologie ou l'archéologie de la mort (Archaeothanatology or the Archaeology of Death). In *Social Archaeology of Funerary Remains*, edited by R. Gowland and C. Knüsel, pp. 30–56. Oxbow Books, Oxford.
2009   *The Archaeology of the Dead: Lectures in Archaeothanatology*. Translated by A. M. Cipriani and J. Pearce. Oxbow Books, Oxford.
Earle, R.
2010   "If you eat their food . . .": Diets and Bodies in Early Colonial Spanish Florida. *American Historical Review* 115:688–713.
2012   *The Body of the Conquistador: Food, Race, and the Colonial Experience in Spanish America, 1492–1700*. Cambridge University Press, Cambridge.
Faier, L., and L. Rofel
2014   Ethnographies of Encounter. *Annual Review of Anthropology* 43:363–377.
Fforde, C., J. Hubert, and P. Turnbull (editors)
2002   *The Dead and Their Possessions: Repatriation in Principle, Policy and Practice*. Routledge, London.

Fine-Dare, K. S.
2002   *Grave Injustice: The American Indian Repatriation Movement and NAGPRA.* University of Nebraska Press, Lincoln.
Fluehr-Lobban, C.
1998   Ethics. In *Handbook of Methods in Cultural Anthropology,* edited by H. R. Bernard, pp. 173–202. AltaMira Press, Walnut Creek, California.
Funari, P. P. A., S. Jones, and M. Hall
1999   Introduction: Archaeology in History. In *Historical Archaeology: Back from the Edge,* edited by P. P. A. Funari, S. Jones, and M. Hall, pp. 1–20. Routledge, New York.
Funari, P. P. A., and M. X. Senatore (editors)
2015   *Archaeology of Culture Contact and Colonialism in Spanish and Portuguese America.* Springer, New York.
Given, M.
2004   *The Archaeology of the Colonized.* Routledge, London.
Glaubrecht, M., N. Seethaler, B. Teßmann, and K. Koel-Abt
2013   The Potential of Biohistory: Re-discovering Adelbert von Chamisso's Skull of an Aleut Collected during the *"Rurik"* Expedition 1815–1818 in Alaska. *Zoosystematics and Evolution* 89:317–336.
Goodnow, K.
2006   Why and When Do Human Remains Matter: Museum Dilemmas. In *Human Remains and Museum Practice,* edited by J. Lohman and K. Goodnow, pp. 16–20. Berghahn Books, New York.
Gosden, C.
2001   Postcolonial Archaeology: Issues of Culture, Identity, and Knowledge. In *Archaeological Theory Today,* edited by I. Hodder, pp. 241–261. Polity Press, Cambridge, U.K.
2004   *Archaeology and Colonialism: Cultural Contact from 5000 B.C. to the Present.* Cambridge University Press, Cambridge.
Gowland, R., and C. Knüsel (editors)
2006   *The Social Archaeology of Funerary Remains.* Oxbow Books, Oxford.
Graham, E.
1994   Mission Archaeology. *Annual Review of Anthropology* 27:25–62.
Hawkey, D. E.
1998   Disability, Compassion, and the Skeletal Record: Using Musculoskeletal Stress Markers (MSM) to Construct an Osteobiography from Early New Mexico. *International Journal of Osteoarchaeology* 8:326–340.
Hibbert, M.
1998   Galileos or Grave Robbers? Science, the Native American Graves Protection and Repatriation Act, and the First Amendment. *American Indian Law Review* 23:425–458.
Hill, J. D.
1996   Introduction: Ethnogenesis in the Americas, 1492–1992. In *History, Power, and Identity: Ethnogenesis in the Americas, 1492–1992,* edited by J. D. Hill, pp. 1–19. University of Iowa Press, Iowa City.

Hochschild, A.
1998   *King Leopold's Ghost: A Story of Greed, Terror, and Heroism in Colonial Africa*. Houghton Mifflin, New York.

Hu, D.
2013   Approaches to the Archaeology of Ethnogenesis: Past and Emergent Perspectives. *Journal of Archaeological Research* 21:371–402.

Hutchinson, D. L., and C. S. Larsen
1990   Stress and Lifeway Change: The Evidence from Enamel Hypoplasia. In *The Archaeology of Mission Santa Catalina de Guale No. 2: Biocultural Interpretations of a Population in Transition*, edited by C. S. Larsen, pp. 50–65. American Museum of Natural History, New York.

Hutchinson, D. L, C. S. Larsen, M. J. Schoeninger, and L. Norr
1998   Regional Variation in the Pattern of Maize Adoption and Use in Florida and Georgia. *American Antiquity* 63:397–416.

Johnson, K. M., and K. S. Paul
2016   Bioarchaeology and Kinship: Integrating Theory, Social Relatedness, and Biology in Ancient Family Research. *Journal of Archaeological Research* 24:75–123.

Jones, N. L.
2011   Embodied Ethics: From the Body as Specimen and Spectacle to the Body as Patient. In *A Companion to the Anthropology of the Body and Embodiment*, edited by F. E. Mascia-Lees, pp. 72–85. Wiley-Blackwell, Malden, Massachusetts.

Jordan, K. A.
2009   Colonies, Colonialism, and Cultural Entanglement: The Archaeology of Postcolumbian Intercultural Relations. In *International Handbook of Historical Archaeology*, edited by T. Majewsk and D. Gaimster, pp. 31–49. Springer, New York.

Kaeppler, A. L.
2005   Two Polynesian Repatriation Enigmas at the Smithsonian Institution. *Journal of Museum Ethnography* 17:152–162.

Kakaliouras, A. M.
2008   Leaving Few Bones Unturned: Recent Work in Repatriation by Osteologists. *American Anthropologist* 110:44–52.
2012   An Anthropology of Repatriation: Contemporary Physical Anthropological and Native American Ontologies of Practice. *Current Anthropology* 53:S210–S221.
2014   When Remains Are "Lost": Thoughts on Collections, Repatriation, and Research in American Physical Anthropology. *Curator: The Museum Journal* 57:213–223.

Keenleyside, A., H. Schwarcz, and K. Panayotova
2006   Stable Isotopic Evidence of Diet in a Greek Colonial Population from the Black Sea. *Journal of Archaeological Science* 33:1205–1215.

Killgrove, K.
2005   Bioarchaeology in the Roman World. Unpublished Master's thesis, University of North Carolina at Chapel Hill.

Klaus, H. D.
2008   Out of Light Came Darkness: Bioarchaeology of Mortuary Ritual, Health, and Ethnogenesis in the Lambayeque Valley Complex, North Coast Peru (A.D. 900–1750). Unpublished Ph.D.dissertation, Ohio State University, Columbus.
2013   Hybrid Cultures . . . and Hybrid Peoples: Bioarchaeology of Genetic Change, Religious Architecture, and Burial Ritual in the Colonial Andes. In *The Archaeology of Hybrid Material Culture*, edited by J. J. Card, pp. 207–238. Southern Illinois University Press, Carbondale.

Knudson, K. J., and C. M. Stojanowski
2008   New Directions in Bioarchaeology: Recent Contributions to the Study of Human Social Identities. *Journal of Archaeological Research* 16:397–432.

Knudson, K. J., and C. M. Stojanowski (editors)
2009   *Bioarchaeology and Identity in the Americas*. University Press of Florida, Gainesville.

Knüsel, C. J.
2010   Bioarchaeology: A Synthetic Approach. *Bulletins et Mémoires de la Société d'anthropologie de Paris* 22:62–73.

Koch, J.
1983   Mortuary Behavior Patterning and Physical Anthropology in Colonial St. Augustine. In *Spanish St. Augustine: The Archaeology of a Colonial Creole Community*, edited by K. A. Deagan, pp. 187–227. Academic Press, New York.

Labidon, S. L.
2012   Health in the Late Pre-Colonial and Early Colonial Period in the Philippines. Unpublished Master's thesis, University of Otago.

Lambert, P. M.
2012   Ethics and Issues in the Use of Human Skeletal Remains in Paleopathology. In *A Companion to Paleopathology*, edited by A. L. Grauer, pp. 17–33. Blackwell, New York.

Landau, P. M., and D. G. Steele
1996   Why Anthropologists Study Human Remains. *American Indian Quarterly* 20:209–228.

Lane, P.
2011   Possibilities for a Postcolonial Archaeology in Sub-Saharan Africa: Indigenous and Usable Pasts. *World Archaeology* 43:7–25.

Larsen, C. S.
1993   On the Frontier of Contact: Mission Bioarchaeology in La Florida. In *The Spanish Missions of La Florida*, edited by B. G. McEwan, pp. 322–356. University Press of Florida, Gainesville.
2006   The Changing Face of Bioarchaeology: An Interdisciplinary Science. In *Bioarchaeology: The Contextual Analysis of Human Remains*, edited by J. E. Buikstra and L. A. Beck, pp. p 359–374. Academic Press, New York.

Larsen, C. S. (editor)
2001   *Bioarchaeology of Spanish Florida: The Impact of Colonialism.* University
           Press of Florida, Gainesville.
Larsen, C. S., A. W. Crosby, M. C. Griffin, D. L. Hutchinson, C. B. Ruff, K. F. Russell, M.
           J. Schoeninger, L. E. Sering, S. W. Simpson, J. L Takács, and M. F. Teaford
2002   A Biohistory of Health and Behavior in the Georgia Bight: The Agricultural
           Transition and the Impact of European Contact. In *The Backbone of History:
           Health and Nutrition in the Western Hemisphere,* edited by R. H. Steckel and
           J. C. Rose, pp. 406–439. Cambridge University Press, Cambridge.
Larsen, C. S., M. C. Griffin, D. L. Hutchinson, V. E. Noble, L. Norr, R. F. Pastor, C. B. Ruff,
           K. F. Russell, M. J. Schoeninger, M. Schultz, S. W. Simpson, and M. F. Teaford
2001   Frontiers of Contact: Bioarchaeology of Spanish Florida. *Journal of World
           Prehistory* 15:69–123.
Larsen, C. S., D. L. Hutchinson, M. J. Schoeninger, and L. Norr
2001   Food and Stable Isotopes in La Florida: Diet and Nutrition before and after
           Contact. In *Bioarchaeology of Spanish Florida: The Impact of Colonialism,*
           edited by C. S. Larsen pp. 52–81. University Press of Florida, Gainesville.
Larsen, C. S., D. L. Hutchinson, C. M. Stojanowski, M. A. Williamson, M. C. Griffin, S. W.
           Simpson, C. B. Ruff, M. J. Schoeninger, L. Norr, M. F. Teaford, E. Monahan
           Driscoll, C. W. Schmidt, and T. A. Tung
2007   Health and Lifestyle in Georgia and Florida: Agricultural Origins and In-
           tensification in Regional Perspective. In *Ancient Health: Skeletal Indicators
           of Agricultural and Economic Intensification,* edited by M. N. Cohen and G.
           G. M. Crane-Kramer, pp. 20–34. University Press of Florida, Gainesville.
Larsen, C. S., H. P. Huynh, and B. G. McEwan
1996   Death by Gunshot: Biocultural Implications of Trauma at Mission San Luis.
           International Journal of Osteoarchaeology 6:42–50.
Larsen, C. S., and G. R. Milner (editors)
1994   *In the Wake of Contact: Biological Responses to Conquest.* Wiley-Liss, New
           York.
Larsen, C. S., and C. B. Ruff
1994   The Stresses of Conquest in Spanish Florida: Structural Adaptation and
           Change before and after Contact. In *In the Wake of Contact: Biological Re-
           sponses to Conquest,* edited by C. S. Larsen and G. R. Milner, pp. 21–34. Wi-
           ley-Liss, New York.
Larsen, C. S., M. J. Schoeninger, D. L. Hutchinson, K. F. Russell, and C. B. Ruff.
1990   Beyond Demographic Collapse: Biological Adaptation and Change in Native
           Populations of La Florida. In *Columbian Consequences, Volume 2: Archaeo-
           logical and Historical Perspectives on the Spanish Borderlands East,* edited
           by D. H. Thomas, pp. 409–428. Smithsonian Institution Press, Washington,
           D.C.
Larsen, C. S., and P. L. Walker
2005   The Ethics of Bioarchaeology. In *Biological Anthropology and Ethics: From
           Repatriation to Genetic Identity,* edited by T. R. Turner, pp. 111–119. State Uni-
           versity of New York Press, Albany.

Lightfoot, K. G.
1995   Culture Contact Studies: Redefining the Relationship between Prehistoric and Historical Archaeology. *American Antiquity* 60:199–217.
Lightfoot, K. G., L. M. Panich, T. D. Schneider, and S. L. Gonzalez
2013   European Colonialism and the Anthropocene: A View from the Pacific Coast of North America. *Anthropocene* 4:101–115.
Little, B. J.
1994   People with History: An Update on Historical Archaeology in the United States. *Journal of Archaeological Method and Theory* 1:5–40.
Lydon, J., and U. Z. Rizvi (editors)
2010   *Handbook of Postcolonial Archaeology*. Left Coast Press, Walnut Creek, California.
Lyman, R. L., C. N. Rosania, and M. T. Boulanger
2012   Comparison of Fluoride and Direct AMS Radiocarbon Dating of Black Bear Bone from Lawson Cave, Missouri. *Journal of Field Archaeology* 37:226–237.
Lyons, C. L., and J. K. Papadopoulos (editors)
2002   *The Archaeology of Colonialism*. Getty Research Institute, Los Angeles.
Majewski, T., and D. Gaimster (editors)
2009   *International Handbook of Historical Archaeology*. Springer, New York.
Martin, D. L., R. P. Harrod, and V. R. Pérez
2013   *Bioarchaeology: An Integrated Approach to Working with Human Remains.* Springer, New York.
McIlvaine, B. K.
2012   Greek Colonization of the Balkans: Bioarchaeological Reconstruction of Behavior and Lifestyle during Corinthian Expansion into Ancient Apollonia, Albania. Unpublished Ph.D. dissertation, Ohio State University, Columbus.
Mkhize, N.
2009   Nicholas Gcaleka and the Search for Hintsa's Skull. *Journal of Southern African Studies* 35:211–221.
Moore, J. H.
1994a   Ethnogenetic Theory. *National Geographic Research and Exploration* 10:10–23.
1994b   Putting Anthropology Back Together Again: The Ethnogenetic Critique of Cladistic Theory. *American Anthropologist* 96:925–948.
2001   Ethnogenetic Patterns in Native North America. In *Archaeology, Language, and History: Essays on Culture and Ethnicity*, edited by J. E. Terrell, pp. 31–56. Bergin and Harvey, Westport, Connecticut.
Moudileno, L.
2009   Returning Remains: Saartjie Baartman, or the "Hottentot Venus" as Transnational Postcolonial Icon. *Forum for Modern Language Studies* 45:200–212.
Naum, M.
2010   Re-emerging Frontiers: Postcolonial Theory and Historical Archaeology of the Borderlands. *Journal of Archaeological Method and Theory* 17:101–131.

Nienaber, W. C., M. Steyn, and L. Hutten
2008   The Grave of King Mgolombane Sandile Ngqika: Revisiting the Legend. *South African Archaeological Bulletin* 63:46–50.

Novak, S. A.
2014   How to Say Things with Bodies: Meaningful Violence on an American Frontier. In *The Routledge Handbook of the Bioarchaeology of Human Conflict*, edited by C. Knüsel and M. J. Smith, pp. 542–559. Routledge, Abingdon, U.K.

Orser, C. R., Jr.
2001   The Anthropology in American Historical Archaeology. *American Anthropologist* 103:621–632.

2010   Twenty-First-Century Historical Archaeology. *Journal of Archaeological Research* 18:111–150.

Ousley, S. D., W. T. Billeck, and R. E. Hollinger
2005   Federal Repatriation Legislation and the Role of Physical Anthropology in Repatriation. *Yearbook of Physical Anthropology* 48:2–32.

Panich, L. M.
2013   Archaeologies of Persistence: Reconsidering the Legacies of Colonialism in Native North America. *American Antiquity* 78:105–122.

Parker-Pearson, M.
1995   Ethics and the Dead in British Archaeology. *Field Archaeologist* 23:17–18.

Paul, K. S., and C. M. Stojanowski
2015   Performance Analysis of Deciduous Morphology for Detecting Biological Siblings. *American Journal of Physical Anthropology* 157:615–629.

Paynter, R.
2000   Historical Archaeology and the Post-Columbian World of North America. *Journal of Archeological Research* 8:169–217.

Peck, J. J.
2009   The Biological Impact of Culture Contact: A Bioarchaeological Study of Roman Colonialism in Britain. Unpublished Ph.D. dissertation, Ohio State University, Columbus.

Perry, M. A.
2007   Is Bioarchaeology a Handmaiden to History? Developing a Historical Bioarchaeology. *Journal of Anthropological Archaeology* 26:486–515.

Pietrusewsky, M., and L. M. Willacker
1997   The Search for Father Bachelot: First Catholic Missionary to the Hawaiian Islands (1827–1837). *Journal of Forensic Science* 42:208–212.

Rakita, G. F. M.
2014   Bioarchaeology as a Process: An Examination of Bioarchaeological Tribes in the USA. In *Archaeological Human Remains*, edited by B. O'Donnabhain and M. C. Lozada, pp. 213–234. Springer, New York.

Rebay-Salisbury, K., M. L. S. Sørensen, and J. Hughes (editors)
2010   *Body Parts, Bodies Whole*. Oxbow Books, Oxford.

Reiche, I.
2006   Fluorine and Its Relevance for Archaeological Studies. *Advances in Fluorine Science* 2:253–283.

Riding In, J.
2000   Repatriation: A Pawnee's Perspective. In *Repatriation Reader: Who Owns American Indian Remains?* edited by D. A. Mihesuah, pp. 106–120. University of Nebraska Press, Lincoln.

Robb, J.
2002   Time and Biography: Osteobiography of the Italian Neolithic Lifespan. In *Thinking through the Body: Archaeologies of Corporeality*, edited by Y. Hamilakis, M. Pluciennik, and S. Tarlow, pp. 153–171. Kluwer, New York.

Saul, F. P.
1972   *The Human Skeletal Remains of Altar de Sacrifícios: An Osteobiographic Analysis.* Papers of the Peabody Museum of Archaeology and Ethnology Vol. 62, No. 2. Peabody Museum, Harvard University, Cambridge.
1976   Osteobiography: Life History Recorded in Bone. In *The Measures of Man: Methodologies in Biological Anthropology*, edited by E. Giles and J. S. Friedlaender, pp. 372–382. Peabody Museum, Harvard University, Cambridge.

Saul, F., and J. M. Saul
1989   Osteobiography: A Maya Example. In *Reconstruction of Life from the Human Skeleton*, edited by M. Y. Işcan and K. A. R. Kennedy pp. 287–302. Alan R. Liss, New York.

Silliman, S. W.
2005   Culture Contact or Colonialism? Challenges in the Archaeology of Native North America. *American Antiquity* 70:55–74.

Sofaer, J. R.
2006   *The Body as Material Culture: A Theoretical Osteoarchaeology.* Cambridge University Press, Cambridge.

Stein, G. J. (editor)
2005   *The Archaeology of Colonial Encounters: Comparative Perspectives.* School of American Research Press, Santa Fe.

Stodder, A. L. W., and A. M. Palkovich (editors)
2012   *The Bioarchaeology of Individuals.* University Press of Florida, Gainesville.

Stojanowski, C. M.
2005   The Bioarchaeology of Identity in Spanish Colonial Florida: Social and Evolutionary Transformation before, during, and after Demographic Collapse. *American Anthropologist* 107:417–431.
2009   Bridging Histories: The Bioarchaeology of Identity in Postcontact Florida. In *Bioarchaeology and Identity in the Americas*, edited by K. J. Knudson and C. M. Stojanowski, pp. 59–81. University Press of Florida, Gainesville.
2010   *Bioarchaeology of Ethnogenesis in the Colonial Southeast.* University Press of Florida, Gainesville.
2011   Social Dimensions of Evolutionary Research: Discovering Native American History in Colonial Southeastern U.S. *Evolution: Education and Outreach* 4:223–231.
2013   *Mission Cemeteries, Mission Peoples: Historical and Evolutionary Dimensions of Intracemetery Bioarchaeology in Spanish Florida.* University Press of Florida, Gainesville.

Stojanowski, C. M, and W. N. Duncan

2015   Engaging Bodies in the Public Imagination: Bioarchaeology as Social Science, Science, and Humanities. *American Journal of Human Biology* 27:51–60.

Stojanowski, C. M., and M. A. Schillaci

2006   Phenotypic Approaches for Understanding Patterns of Intracemetery Biological Variation. *Yearbook of Physical Anthropology* 49:49–88.

Tarlow, S.

2001   Decoding Ethics. *Public Archaeology* 1:245–259.

Terrell, J. E. (editor)

2001   *Archaeology, Language, and History: Essays on Culture and Ethnicity*. Bergin and Harvey, Westport, Connecticut.

Thomas, D. H.

2000   *Skull Wars: Kennewick Man, Archaeology, and the Battle for Native American Identity*. Basic, New York.

Thomas, D. H. (editor)

1991a   *Columbian Consequences, Volume 1: Archaeological and Historical Perspectives on the Spanish Borderlands West*. Smithsonian Institution Press, Washington, D.C.

1991b   *Columbian Consequences, Volume 2: Archaeological and Historical Perspectives on the Spanish Borderlands East*. Smithsonian Institution Press, Washington, D.C.

1991c   *Columbian Consequences, Volume 3: The Spanish Borderlands in Pan-American Perspective*. Smithsonian Institution Press, Washington, D.C.

Twain, M.

1905   *King Leopold's Soliloquy: A Defense of His Congo Rule*. 2nd ed. The P. R. Warren C., Boston.

Van Buren, M.

2010   The Archaeological Study of Spanish Colonialism in the Americas. *Journal of Archaeological Research* 18:151–201.

van Dommelen, P.

2006   Colonial Matters: Material Culture and Postcolonial Theory in Colonial Situations. In *Handbook of Material Culture*, edited by C. Tilley, W. Keane, S. Küchler, M, Rowlands, and P. Spyer, pp. 104–124. Sage, London.

2011   Postcolonial Archaeologies between Discourse and Practice. *World Archaeology* 43:1–6.

Verano, J. W., and D. H. Ubelaker (editors)

1994   *Disease and Demography in the Americas*. Smithsonian Institution Press, Washington, D.C.

Voss, B.

2008   *The Archaeology of Ethnogenesis: Race and Sexuality in Colonial San Francisco*. University of California Press, Berkeley.

Walker, P. L.

2000   Bioarchaeological Ethics: A Historical Perspective on the Value of Human Remains. In *Biological Anthropology of the Human Skeleton*, edited by M. A. Katzenberg and S. R. Saunders, pp. 3–39. Wiley-Liss, New York.

Weber M.
1919   "Politics as a Vocation." Electronic document, http://anthropos-lab.net/wp/
            wp-content/uploads/2011/12/Weber-Politics-as-a-Vocation.pdf.
Weik, T. M.
2014   The Archaeology of Ethnogenesis. *Annual Review of Anthropology* 43:291–
            305.
White, L.
2007   The Traffic in Heads: Bodies, Borders and the Articulation of Regional His-
            tories. *Journal of South African Studies* 23:325–338.
Wilkinson, T. M.
2002   Last Rights: The Ethics of Research on the Dead. *Journal of Applied Philoso-
            phy* 19:31–41.
Wood, J. W., G. R. Milner, H. C. Harpending, and K. M. Weiss
1992   The Osteological Paradox: Problems of Inferring Prehistoric Health from
            Skeletal Samples. *Current Anthropology* 33:343–370.
Zuckerman, M. K., K. R. Kamnikar, and S. A. Mathena
2014   Recovering the "Body Politic": A Relational Ethics of Meaning for Bioar-
            chaeology. *Cambridge Archaeological Journal* 24:513–522.
Zvelebil, M., and A. W. Weber
2013   Human Bioarchaeology: Group Identity and Individual Life Histories—In-
            troduction. *Journal of Anthropological Archaeology* 32:275–279.

Contributors

Rosabella Alvarez-Calderón is lecturer at the Pontificia Universidad Católica de Péru.

Elliot H. Blair is assistant professor in the Department of Anthropology at the University of Alabama.

Maria Fernanda Boza is a PhD student in anthropology at Syracuse University.

Michele R. Buzon is associate professor in the Department of Anthropology at Purdue University.

Romina Casali is professor of history at the Núcleo de Estudios Interdisciplinarios de Poblaciones Humanas de Patagonia Austral, Laboratorio de Ecología Evolutiva Humana, Universidad Nacional del Centro de la Provincia de Buenos Aires, Quequén, Argentina.

Mark N. Cohen is Distinguished Professor of Anthropology at SUNY Plattsburgh.

Danielle N. Cook is a part-time faculty member in anthropology and archaeology at Columbus State University.

Marie Elaine Danforth is professor of anthropology in the Department of Anthropology and Sociology at the University of Southern Mississippi.

J. Lynn Funkhouser is a PhD student in anthropology at the University of Alabama.

Catherine Gaither is vice president of academics and research at the Osa Field Institute in Costa Rica.

Pamela García Laborde is an anthropologist with a specialization in archaeology at Núcleo de Estudios Interdisciplinarios de Poblaciones Humanas de Patagonia Austral, Laboratorio de Ecología Evolutiva Humana, Universidad Nacional del Centro de la Provincia de Buenos Aires, Quequén, Argentina.

Ricardo A. Guichón is professor of biological anthropology and archaeology at Núcleo de Estudios Interdisciplinarios de Poblaciones Humanas de Patagonia Austral, Laboratorio. de Ecología Evolutiva Humana, Universidad Nacional del Centro de la Provincia de Buenos Aires, Quequén, Argentina.

Rocio Guichón Fernández is a licenciatura student in archaeology at the Universidad Nacional del Centro de la Provincia de Buenos Aires, Provincia de Buenos Aires, Argentina.

Heather Guzik is an MA student at the University of Southern Mississippi.

Amanda R. Harvey is a PhD student in anthropology at the University of Nevada, Reno.

Barbara T. Hester is an MA student in history at the University of Southern Mississippi.

Dale L. Hutchinson is professor of anthropology at the University of North Carolina–Chapel Hill.

Kristina Killgrove is assistant professor in the Department of Anthropology at the University of West Florida.

Haagen D. Klaus is associate professor in the Department of Sociology and Anthropology at George Mason University.

Clark Spencer Larsen is Distinguished Professor of Social and Behavioral Sciences and chair of the Department of Anthropology at Ohio State University.

Alan G. Morris is professor emeritus in the Department of Human Biology at the University of Cape Town, South Africa.

Melissa S. Murphy is associate professor in the Department of Anthropology at the University of Wyoming.

Alejandra Ortiz is a postdoctoral scholar in the Institute for Human Origins in the School of Human Evolution and Social Change at Arizona State University.

Megan A. Perry is associate professor in the Department of Anthropology at East Carolina University.

Emily S. Renschler is adjunct lecturer in the Department of Sociology and Anthropology at Bowdoin College.

Isabelle Ribot is associate professor in the Département d'anthropologie at the Université de Montréal.

Melisa A. Salerno is professor of historical archaeology in the Department of Prehistory and Archaeology, El Instituto Multidisciplinario de Historia y Ciencias Humanas–CONICET, Buenos Aires, Argentina.

Matthew C. Sanger is assistant professor at Binghamton University.

Paul W. Sciulli is emeritus professor in the Department of Anthropology at Ohio State University.

Stuart Tyson Smith is professor of anthropology at the University of California, Santa Barbara.

Christopher M. Stojanowski is associate professor in the School of Human Evolution and Social Change, Center for Bioarchaeological Research at Arizona State University.

David Hurst Thomas is curator in the Division of Anthropology at the American Museum of Natural History.

Victor D. Thompson is associate professor in the Department of Anthropology at the University of Georgia.

Vera Tiesler is research professor and coordinator of the Laboratory of Bioarchaeology in the Facultad de Ciencias Antropológicas at the Universidad Autónoma de Yucatán.

Jason Toohey is assistant professor in the Department of Anthropology at the University of Wyoming.

Lauren A. Winkler is an independent scholar and marketing manager at W.W. Norton & Company.

Pilar Zabala is a research professor in the Facultad de Ciencias Antropológicas at the Universidad Autónoma de Yucatán.

Index

Massacres: Bioarchaeology and Forensic Anthropology Approaches, edited by Cheryl P. Anderson and Debra L. Martin (2019)

Mortuary and Bioarchaeological Perspectives on Bronze Age Arabia, edited by Kimberly D. Williams and Lesley A. Gregoricka (2019)

Bioarchaeology of Frontiers and Borderlands, edited by Cristina I. Tica and Debra L. Martin (2019)

The Odd, the Unusual, and the Strange: Bioarchaeological Explorations of Atypical Burials, edited by Tracy K. Betsinger, Amy B. Scott, and Anastasia Tsaliki (2020)

Bioarchaeology and Identity Revisited, edited by Kelly J. Knudson and Christopher M. Stojanowski (2020)

Leprosy: Past and Present, by Charlotte A. Roberts (2020)

Bioarchaeology of Care through Population-Level Analyses, edited by Alecia Schrenk and Lori A. Tremblay (2022)

CPSIA information can be obtained
at www.ICGtesting.com
Printed in the USA
LVHW081113310122
709853LV00009B/370